LABOR OF LOVE, LABOR OF SORROW

LABOR of LOVE, LABOR of SORROW

BLACK WOMEN, WORK, and the FAMILY,
from SLAVERY to the PRESENT

Jacqueline Jones

BASIC
BOOKS

A MEMBER OF THE PERSEUS BOOKS GROUP
New York

Books published by Basic Books are available at special discounts for bulk purchases
in the United States by corporations, institutions, and other organizations. For more
information, please contact the Special Markets Department at the Perseus Books
Group, 2300 Chestnut Street, Suite 200, Philadelphia, PA 19103, or call (800) 810-
4145, ext. 5000, or e-mail special.markets@perseusbooks.com.

Designed by Timm Bryson

Library of Congress Cataloging-in-Publication Data
Jones, Jacqueline, 1948-
  Labor of love, labor of sorrow : black women, work and the family, from slavery to
the present / Jacqueline Jones.
    p. cm.
  Rev. ed. of: Labor of love, labor of sorrow. 1985.
  Includes bibliographical references and index.
  ISBN 978-0-465-01881-9 (alk. paper)
  1. African American women—Employment—History. 2. African American
women—History. 3. African American families—History. I. Title.
  HD6057.5.U5J66 2009
  305.48'896073—dc22
                                    2009031903

LSC-C
10 9 8 7 6 5 4 3 2

For Jeffrey

How I got over, how did I make it over?
You know, my soul look back in wonder,
How did I make it over?
How I made it over,
Comin' on over, all these years.
You know, my soul look back in wonder,
How did I make it over?
Tell me how we got over, Lord;
Had a mighty hard time, comin' on over.
You know, my soul look back in wonder,
How did we make it over?
Tell me how we got over, Lord;
I've been falling and rising all these years.
But you know, my soul look back in wonder,
How did I make it over?

—FROM "How I Got Over," GOSPEL SONG

CONTENTS

vii

ACKNOWLEDGMENTS FOR THE 1985 EDITION

This project grew out of a course in women's history that I began teaching at Wellesley College in 1977. At the time, little in the way of published material on the history of black working women was available to undergraduates. Moreover, widely held among my (mostly white, middle-class) students was the conviction that work outside the home always amounted to a "liberating" experience for women regardless of their race, age, or marital status. Over the last few years, several classes of Wellesley students have become more familiar with the history of black working women, a topic of concern in all my courses, whether on reform, the South, women, the Civil War, the family, the Great Depression, the nineteenth century, or a survey of American history. Without exception my students responded to this story with great interest and enthusiasm; their willingness to reevaluate their own preconceptions related to work and family life has sustained me through several years of research and writing. Each semester I was able to count on a receptive audience for my findings long before they were published. Therefore it is appropriate that I first acknowledge the help of my Wellesley students, who provided me with the initial inspiration for this study and who eagerly explored with me the various details and broad themes that ultimately gave the project its shape.

The National Endowment for the Humanities funded an initial year of research, and the Wellesley College Center for Research on Women provided a forum in which to present preliminary findings, both through its seminar series and its working papers list. Various grants administered by the center also enabled me to hire student research interns for three summers. The college faculty awards committee and history department made possible additional support for student assistants, and I was able to draw upon the talents of Carol Corneilse, Sherrie Inness, Carol Mapoma, Lydia Luz, Twinkle Shipes, and Chana Woods for data collection and preparation of numerous drafts of the manuscript (using, of all antiquated machines, an electric typewriter). Brian Drayton rescued me from a number of stylistic and organizational gaffes. The reference, circulation, and interlibrary departments at the Wellesley library managed to track down many obscure sources and helped me locate missing ones, including books I had forgotten were checked out to myself. I would also like to express special thanks to Jean C. Proctor (wily in the ways of the Wellesley bureaucracy), for she is as good a friend as she is skilled as an administrator in the Wellesley history department.

Several scholars were most generous with their time and expertise. My colleagues at Wellesley who read drafts and supplied much useful information on specific issues included Jerold Auerbach, Paul Cohen, Marsha Darling, Weldon Jackson, Julie Matthaei, Kathryn Preyer, and Susan Reverby. Nancy Gabin graciously allowed me to use some of the fascinating material she had gathered on women auto workers during the World War II era. Michael P. Johnson's thorough reading of the Federal Writers Project Slave Narrative Collection yielded some crucial examples in the chapter on slavery. Elizabeth Pleck and Milton Cantor read several chapters in draft form and offered a number of perceptive comments. Ira Berlin and Stanley Engerman provided helpful and detailed comments on drafts during the earliest stages of the project and helped me define the major issues more precisely. Ellen Fitzpatrick perhaps heard more about this project than she would have liked; but she was always willing to take time out from her own busy schedule of writing and teaching to lend a sympathetic ear, read drafts, and help sort out knotty theoretical issues. Her support has meant a great deal to me.

Three historians in particular lent me their wise counsel, and the project as a whole benefited enormously from their collective and individual insights. Nell Irvin Painter gave the entire manuscript a meticulous reading and encouraged me to think more carefully about the dynamics of class in relation to Afro-American history. Eric Foner also read the manuscript with painstaking care and urged me to place contemporary political issues into historical perspective. Steve Fraser has long had a commitment to this project. I shamelessly took advantage of his patience and detailed understanding of American labor history, and received invaluable encouragement in return. All three of these individuals were thorough and tough-minded in their criticism of various drafts; on more than one occasion after digesting their comments, I gave myself credit only for knowing a good suggestion when I saw one.

During the past few years I have had ample opportunity to ponder the relation between my own work and family life. Unlike many other working women today or in the past, I was able to count on friends and babysitters who provided my daughter with the most loving and reliable care possible. Without the services of Ingrid Kondos, Sigrid Bergenstein, Anne Gillis, and Eileen MacDermott in particular I could not have finished this book. Sarah Jones Abramson herself had a mixed effect on the process of research and writing. Too often she was happy just to drool on notecards and nibble on books. Yet her lovely presence was a constant reminder of what a luxury it is for a gainfully employed mother in this country to have a job that she enjoys and childcare arrangements she trusts. Sarah helped me to realize that the story that unfolds on the following pages has behind it the drama and force of everyday life.

The household that has two books in press at the same time is neither a very tranquil nor tidy one, but Jeffrey B. Abramson has endured the chaos with good humor and patience. He was busy writing his own book, and, unlike the traditional historian's spouse, he did not check any of my footnotes or type any of my drafts. But the elegant precision of his writing set a high standard for me, and he helped with the formulation of several sections of the study. Most important, his compassionate vision of a just and free society—a community based on political and economic equality for all its members, and on tolerance and respect for diverse cultures as well as individuals—has informed not only his own work but mine as well. I dedicate this book to him and to that ideal.

PREFACE TO THE NEW EDITION

Soon after I learned that Basic Books intended to reissue *Labor of Love, Labor of Sorrow* in a twenty-fifth anniversary edition, a number of friends, colleagues, and family members offered me advice (admittedly, most of it solicited) on revising the original text. Almost without exception they suggested that I add a new preface, and extend the epilogue to the present, leaving the rest of the chapters intact. They pointed out, correctly, that so much had been written on the history of black working women since the book was first published it would be virtually impossible to incorporate all of that new scholarship into a revised edition. Overall, the book's argument—the profound tension between black women's work for whites and the work they performed for their own families and communities—had withstood the test of time, classroom use, and reviewers. Of course the emergence of one particular black working wife and mother onto the public stage in late 2008 suggested the urgent need for an update; the family history of First Lady Michelle Robinson Obama, and the narrative of her life, would provide a fitting coda to the book, a way to survey the grand sweep of African American history over the last century and a half. Her great-great-grandfather Jim Robinson, an enslaved rice hand, was born in the South Carolina low country in 1850, a time and place discussed in Chapter 1. By the late twentieth century, Robinson Obama had graduated from Princeton University and Harvard Law School, and was working in a series of high-powered jobs as an attorney. Expanding the epilogue to include the Robinsons seemed to be a fitting way to highlight the crosscurrents of historical transformation and continuity from the antebellum period to the present.

For obvious reasons I found these suggestions for a minimal set of revisions appealing, but in the end I decided to overhaul the book in a more thorough way. The bibliography now includes over one thousand citations gleaned from manuscript collections and other unpublished materials, magazines and newspapers, books, government reports, and scholarly essays. A couple hundred of these citations are new to this edition. Though this expanded bibliography is by no means exhaustive, it does offer the student a place to begin for research on the history of black women, work, and the family. At the same time I have preserved the essential features of the original text—attention to the nation's political economy and changes in the social division of labor over time, enhanced by stories about the struggles of individual women and their families. Labor-force statistics contextualize discussions of individual women and the contours of their workdays inside and outside the home, and their labors waged and unwaged. Whenever possible I tried to let these women from the past speak for themselves. At the same time, in this edition I have added new information, based on recent scholarship, that revises, strengthens, or renders irrelevant material in the original study. Accordingly, in some places I have rewritten or discarded whole sections, and in other places I have supported the original passage with additional examples. Throughout, my intent is to introduce readers to individual African American working women, many of whom are remarkable in their own right, though they have remained largely anonymous to historians and other scholars. Other changes, which I describe in more detail below, include questioning some commonly used terms, highlighting the contrasts between various groups of black working women and their white counterparts, and placing the history described here into a larger framework of worldwide systems of labor dispossession and exploitation. This analysis now extends back in time to the origins of slavery in the British North American colonies, and forward to the Barack Obama presidential administration. Though Michelle Robinson Obama serves as the pivot for the last chapter, her story is balanced by a discussion of the enduring legacy of slavery on all black working women, especially the vulnerable and impoverished, who continue to struggle to provide their children with decent schooling, adequate health care, and meaningful job opportunities for the future.

When I began this book in the early 1980s, black women's history was a relatively new field, and I had few case studies to draw upon. Of course over the last three decades the field has grown exponentially, and has attracted the energies not only of historians, but also anthropologists, economists, sociologists, and literary scholars. I found that much of this new research added depth and texture to the broad themes originally presented in *Labor of Love*, but some of this research challenged my interpretations—of the prevalence of nuclear families in the slave quarters, for example—and some of it encouraged me to deepen my analysis of certain topics—such as black women's entrepreneurial impulses and the unwaged work of middle-class women fighting for social justice at the local and national levels.

Over the years I have discovered that the use of certain words and terms obscures rather than furthers our understanding of the past. This edition of *Labor of Love* modifies or eliminates certain word forms used throughout the original. In the pages that follow I term black women born into bondage "enslaved workers" rather than "slaves"; the word "slave" implies that their lives were reduced to a particular subordinate legal status, and the point of the book is just the opposite—that black women in their roles as family and community members resisted their masters' notion that they were only slaves and nothing more. In addition, I avoid use of the words "race" or "racism," preferring instead to focus on racial ideologies and the way they were deployed over time. In place of "Jim Crow," I have chosen to use instead "American apartheid" as a way to convey the pervasive institutional and cultural apparatus of segregation and disfranchisement. And too, I have refrained from labeling any one person or group "feminist" unless they themselves used that descriptor. In the last few decades, the term has been used to describe upper-middle-class women who fought for particular issues, but not necessarily on behalf of poorer women, or women of color. Throughout history, strong-willed African American women often spoke out against gender-based hierarchies in law and society; but these women expanded their call for justice to include hierarchies based on "racial" ideas and class, as well. The word feminism ignores those complex historical realities.

Since completing *Labor of Love* in 1985, I have focused my work on the role of racial ideologies in shaping the labor of all American workers, and not just people of African descent. By contrasting the status of blacks with that of their white counterparts, we can better understand the liabilities of black people as enslaved workers (to 1865), and as citizens, wage-earners, migrants, and family members. Published in 1992, my book *The Dispossessed: America's Underclasses from the Civil War to the Present* considered black and white households as units of economic production. *Labor of Love* argues that much of black women's work was shaped by family imperatives, but that in critical ways, those imperatives differed substantially from those faced by white people regardless of class. I am also mindful of the way that global economic systems have constrained black workers, and also rendered their plight similar to that of dispossessed peoples elsewhere. While American racial ideologies were unique, shaped by the nation's peculiar history of war, technological development, and class relations, those ideologies justified a kind of labor exploitation that found favor among elites all over the world.

One of the criticisms of the book when it was first released was that it presented an overly sentimental view of black families (as revealed in the title, as well as the text), oblivious to the realities of husband-wife and parent-child relations, especially as those relations played out in households under great stress. I agree with that criticism, up to a point. Yet the story told here focuses not on the social or psychological dynamics of black households, but on the historic forces that have shaped the labor patterns of black women at home, in communities, on antebellum plantations, and in the paid labor force. This edition supports the view that as a group, black working women through history have made heroic exertions to provide for their families and to resist the dehumanizing effects of a marketplace undergirded by white-supremacist ideologies.

The last quarter century has witnessed sea changes in the lives of Americans. The rise of the global economy, the proliferation of various electronic media, changing demographics fueled by foreign immigration, and the threat of terrorism have all shaped U.S. society in ways that could not have been predicted in 1985 when this book was first published. This updated, revised edition explores the effects of these developments and others on the labors and family lives of African American women. Heading into the second decade of the twenty-first century, middle-class black women have reached virtual parity with their white counterparts in terms of representation in the clerical work force, a trend that did not get underway until the late 1960s. In 2009, the Obama administration heightened the national visibility of distinguished black women scholars, policy-makers, politicians, and other professionals by hiring a number of them to work in and for the White House. Despite these developments, however, the plight of impoverished black women has not changed that much over the last twenty-five years, or over the last century and a half, for that matter. Denigrated and caricatured by politicians and employers alike, many black wives and mothers have had to make do with little in the way of material resources in the realms of housework, childcare, and waged work. Their labors consist not of "balancing" or "juggling" competing demands as much as coping daily with multiple responsibilities that threaten to overwhelm them. Therefore I end this book with a conclusion that is virtually the same as the last paragraph in the 1985 edition.

Finally, I would like to update the Acknowledgments. My daughter Sarah, who was drooling on notecards and nibbling on books in the early 1980s, is now a productive scholar in her own right, studying patterns of Jewish identity in London; and my daughter Anna, born the month this book was published in 1985, is about to embark on her own academic career, as a graduate student in the field of English literature. Our conversations about the material presented here have immeasurably enriched the revising of it.

At Basic Books, Lara Heimert's enthusiasm for a new edition of the book has helped sustain me through the daunting process of revising and updating the text. Her assistant, Brandon Proia; the project editor, Laura Esterman; and my copyeditor, Nancy King, all did an outstanding job seeing the manuscript through the production process. Geri Thoma, my agent, has offered much-appreciated and consistent support for my work in general. I am also appreciative of my excellent research assistants, Paul T. Conrad, Kyle Shelton, Cameron Strang, and Meredith Zide for their help in compiling bibliographical citations and summarizing recent scholarship for this edition. I would also like to highlight the contributions of my University of Texas colleagues in the field of modern African American history—particularly the work cited herein of Tiffany Gill, Laurie B. Green, and Juliet E. K. Walker.

I regret that my parents, Albert Jones and Sylvia Phelps Jones, are no longer here to share with me the pleasure of the publication of this new edition of *Labor of Love*, but their love for me through the years resonates in the pages that follow. Finally, I have left unchanged the Acknowledgments from the first edition, and I would also like to renew the dedication—to my husband of thirty years, Jeffrey Abramson. My emotional and intellectual debts to him, first recorded in 1985, have only grown and deepened over the last quarter century, and for that I am profoundly grateful.

INTRODUCTION

THIS BOOK IS about the work and family life of women whose foremothers were brought to this country in chains as enslaved laborers. The forces that shaped the institution of human bondage in the American South endured, albeit in altered form, long after the Thirteenth Amendment was ratified by the states; whether black women toiled in a sweltering Virginia tobacco factory in the 1890s or in the kitchen of a Chicago white woman in the 1950s, they felt the oppressive force of racial and gender ideologies, ideas of social difference that until the mid-1960s carried the weight of law. Throughout American history, black women's meager wages—and in the case of slavery, lack of any wages at all—stood in stark contrast to their strenuous labors in the workforce and at home. In their efforts to sustain family ties and preserve a vital group culture, they shared a common purpose with wives and mothers of all groups, a purpose that did not abate with the passage of time. This study seeks to offer more than a chronicle of changes in patterns of black women's labor as enslaved workers, wage earners, nurturers, and community activists from 1830 to the present; it is also a testament to the stubbornness of a mother's love in opposition to the dehumanizing demands of the marketplace.

Black women's work took place within three distinct spheres that were simultaneously mutually reinforcing and antagonistic. One workplace consisted of their own households, the locus of family feeling, and another consisted of their own communities, which remained largely segregated, in political if not spatial terms, from white people. The family obligations of wives and mothers also overlapped in the area of community welfare, as their desire to provide for their kin and neighbors expanded out of the private realm and into public activities that advanced the interests of black people as a group. In contrast to these kinds of work, which earned for black women the respect of their own people, participation in the paid labor force (or slave economy) reinforced their subordinate status as women and as blacks within American society. As defined by white men, "racial" and gender ideologies amounted to political strategies intended to keep white women and black people "in their place" by enforcing a social division of labor that relegated these groups to certain kinds of jobs. Because of their doubly disadvantaged status, black women were confined to two types of work that seemed ironically contradictory—the first was domestic and institutional service, vindictively termed women's work; the other was manual labor so physically arduous it was usually considered men's work. The vast majority of black female wage earners were barred from peacetime factory labor and from the traditional (white) female occupations of secretarial and sales work until well into the 1960s. Moreover, black married women have always worked in proportionately greater numbers than white wives; not until relatively recently did percentages of married workers begin to converge for women of the two groups. In fact, black women's economic position relative to white women is analogous to women's position relative to men, for black women have been limited to "black women's work" that paid much less than that performed by white women.

Indeed, a focus on white women exclusively will miss the significance of slavery as a labor system that exploited black women, and will miss the fact that black wives entered the work force in greater numbers, only to face a fundamentally different kind of prejudice, compared to their white counterparts. Whether based on detailed case studies or general overviews, a grand narrative will reveal that women's participation in the paid labor force has undergone tremendous changes over the last century and a half, but that an underlying current of continuity—in the form of inferior wages and jobs—has characterized women's work throughout the period. When young women entered the first New England textile mills in the early nineteenth century, when the clerical and sales sectors began to draw large numbers of women into the workforce around 1900, both the national occupational structure and the institution of the family registered profound effects. Nevertheless, women remained segregated in female jobs, and their pay remained but a fraction of men's. Although it is possible to generalize, noting that patterns of black women's work also underwent transformations over the years and that these women also endured a persistent form of inequality, the history of white women yields only a narrow conception of the larger forces that affected black women's work. The history of black working women does not constitute a subset of white women's history; rather, the history of white women remains incomplete without a full understanding of the ways racial and gender ideologies shaped the lives of all women—and all men, for that matter.

Throughout American history, the black family has been the site of a struggle between black women and the whites who sought to profit from their labor, slaveowners and employers who saw black mothers' family responsibilities as detrimental to their own financial interests. To these white people, the black family offered a steady and reliable source of new laborers; black women reproduced the supply of cheap labor at the same time they fed and nurtured their own kin groups. However, women's attention to family duties represented a diversion of their time, energy, and physical resources that might otherwise have been expended in the workforce. Slaveholders callously disregarded black familial relationships in order to pursue their own profit-making; but even after emancipation, the more time a sharecropping mother spent with her children at home, the less cotton her family was bound to produce. The large-scale withdrawal of black females from the cotton fields immediately after the Civil War made white planters realize that the tight control they formerly enjoyed over their field hands was gone forever. To cite another example, in the late nineteenth century, southern domestics defied the wishes of white housewives and refused to "live in." By returning home at night, black servants had an opportunity to see their own families for a brief time each day; in the process they deprived white women of a servant "on call" twenty-four hours a day. For these reasons, the welfare of the black family (as defined by its own members) could have explicitly negative implications for white landowners and housewives.

The political consequences of black women's family duties became dramatically apparent when slave cooks stole food from the master's kitchen to feed hungry runaways, and when grandmothers prepared feasts for civil rights workers in the South during the 1960s. A mother's love could yield clearly political, and explosive, consequences; Mamie Bradley Till insisted that the corpse of her beaten and mutilated son Emmett, murdered by two Mississippi white men in 1955, be displayed in an open casket so "the whole world could see" what they had done to her child.[1] On an everyday level, the social context of a woman's work determined the commitment and concern she brought to different tasks, and to the same task, like cooking, under different circumstances. Carried out in the home of a white family, preparing and serving meals signaled a servant's position as a lowly, ill-paid employee. Yet a woman notorious for her carelessness on the job might enjoy the praise of family and neighbors for her culinary skills and generosity. In an interview with anthropologist James Langston Gwaltney, May Anna Madison recalled with delight the "day-off get-togethers" hosted by rotating families in her native Kentucky neighborhood—Thursdays when friends would celebrate their day off from service with good food and companionship: "That was hard work, but people didn't mind because they wanted to do that and they were working for themselves. They were working with people they liked and at the end they made this grand meal. Now, they didn't work any harder for the white woman. As a matter of fact, they didn't work as hard for white people as they did for themselves. But when we worked for ourselves, everybody did what he could do best and nobody bothered you."[2] While May Anna Madison and other domestics were often present (as workers) at social gatherings of whites, no white people were ever privy to these Thursday get-togethers, a fact that highlights the social tensions between black women's divergent worlds of work.

A focus on black working women—not only what they did, but also what they desired for themselves and their children—reveals the intersection of African American, laboring-class, and female cultures, all of which tended toward a cooperative ethos: In the words of an Afro-American saying, "What goes around comes around." Black people demonstrated a communal solidarity that grew out of their African heritage on the one hand and the ruthless exploitation of their labor by whites on the other. While crucial to a full understanding of the origins and effects of the "racial" caste system, this perspective offers few insights into the complexities of male-female relationships as they manifested themselves within African American households and communities. Too often historians have used the gender-neutral term blacks (or "slaves") to mean men exclusively.[3] Yet an exploration of the gendered division of labor within black communities and households suggests how black people's attempts to structure their own social order were thwarted by oppression. Furthermore, historians of American women have outlined the dimensions of a female sensibility and a working-class ethos that contrasted with the individualism and self-seeking so lauded by middle-class white males. But if black women sought solace and support in the company of their sisters, if they took pride in a family well fed, a congregation led joyfully in song, or a child graduated from high school, they nonetheless maintained a group self-consciousness and loyalty to their kin (reinforced by white hostility) that precluded any putative bonds of womanhood with slave mistresses or white female employers. Moreover, the tendency of members of the white laboring classes to claim "racial" superiority over black people with whom they in some cases shared a lowly material condition suggests that an analysis based exclusively on class factors will not yield a full understanding of black women's work.

Over the last three decades, the field of American women's history has grown exponentially, with scholars exploring many different groups of women throughout the British American colonies and the United States, and many different aspects of their labor and family lives. Yet there remains a preoccupation with the roles of women in the development of industrial capitalism—as middle-class consumers, members of the industrial workforce, and socializers and caretakers of future laborers. This particular approach encompasses a wide range of white women, from factory workers to full-time homemakers and genteel reformers. Yet it overlooks female agricultural laborers throughout the nineteenth and halfway into the twentieth centuries, divorced as these women were from the mainstream of industrial development. This is not to suggest that black women remained outside the process of industrialization; to the contrary, their labor as cotton cultivators helped to produce the raw material that fueled the earliest stages of the Industrial Revolution, in the antebellum period, and the emergence of transnational capitalism beginning in the postbellum period. Moreover, their wage work as domestic servants freed middle-class white women to enter the labor force themselves, shop for consumer goods, or devote their leisure time to social-welfare activities that ameliorated the worst ills of the economic system, but kept it intact.

In recent years, scholars of black women's work have produced an impressive number and range of articles and monographs. It is no longer possible to suggest, as it was in 1985, that historians have neglected black women, or the theme of connections between work and family. At the same time, the insights emerging from this scholarship have had strikingly little impact on federal social policy. Indeed, it is a cruel irony that, over the generations, scholars and policymakers alike have taken the manifestations of black women's oppression and twisted them into the argument that a powerful black matriarchy exists.[4] The persistent belief that any woman who fulfills a traditional male role, either as breadwinner or household head, wields some sort of all-encompassing power over her spouse and children is belied by the experiences of black working women. These women lacked the control over their own productive energies and material resources that would have guaranteed them a meaningful form of social power. Perhaps they were "freed" or "liberated" from narrow gender-role conventions, but they remained tied to overwhelming wage-earning and child-rearing responsibilities. As spiritual counselors and as healers, black women did exert informal authority over persons of both sexes and all ages in their own communities. Yet when measured against traditional standards of power—defined in terms of wealth; personal autonomy; and control over workers, votes, or inheritances—black wives and mothers had little leverage with which to manipulate the behavior of their kinfolk.

Nevertheless, legislators and bureaucrats have failed to address black women's need for jobs in any systematic way. In the early twenty-first century, it was clear that large-scale structural unemployment among black men had taken an enormous toll on the integrity of lower-income black husband-wife, parent-child relationships. In pockets of concentrated poverty, women lacked access to good jobs and to quality education and daycare for their children. Single mothers had few choices but to accept public assistance, limited by law to five years' worth, or work for wages too low to support their families. Yet ideologues continued to condemn "lazy" mothers receiving welfare and at the same time urge middle-class white working wives to hearken back to hearth and home. Thus the persistent oppression of poor black women revealed all the prejudices and contradictions inherent in national welfare policy.

By this time, several striking developments had complicated the history of black working women—first, the emergence of a black upper-middle class and with it a cohort of well-educated, high-achieving professionals; second, processes of labor displacement that affected factory workers and middle-class secretaries, bank tellers, retail clerks, and telephone operators; and third, the proliferation of multicultural, impoverished populations located all over the country. The passage of the 1964 Civil Rights Act, which dismantled the legal basis of American apartheid, benefited a segment of the black community and paved the way for the election of an African American, Barack Obama, as president in 2008. Obama's wife, Michelle, a graduate of Princeton University and Harvard Law School, faced none of the legal, and few of the structural, barriers to success that had plagued the black women who came before her. Yet juxtaposed against her impressive achievements were the limitations faced by increasing numbers of poor people, particularly African Americans, rural whites, and recent immigrants, who lacked the formal education that would enable them to get secure, well-paying jobs and to provide their children with the kind of first-rate public education available by and large only to families in well-to-do suburbs.

Although in the pages that follow the concepts of work and the family are defined in the broadest possible way, they nonetheless yield a selective account of African American history. Fully one-half of this study deals exclusively with enslaved and rural and working-class women in the South (from 1830 to 1915), both because the vast majority of blacks lived in that region during those years and because such a focus provides a much needed corrective to the northeastern-urban bias implicit in much historical scholarship. Nevertheless, a comprehensive study of black women would necessarily involve a detailed examination of the religious and educational institutions that, together with the family, served as the linchpins of black community life. Black middle-class women have worked for pay outside their homes to a much greater extent than their white counterparts, and, as social workers, school teachers, and church and club members, often perceived themselves as civil rights activists in a way that middle-class white female professionals and reformers did not. Black women's community work had a subversive component, for it served to defy a white society that not only saw blacks as exploitable labor, but also withheld from them the benefits of public and private social-welfare programs. These women deserve fuller treatment than they receive here; they appear in this study primarily insofar as their labors benefited their less well-to-do sisters, and only insofar as they themselves benefited from the hard work and sacrifices of their own less well-to-do mothers.[5]

Though focused on black working women, this study illuminates larger historical forces shaping the labor of many other groups. Structural changes in the economy over the last century and a half have contributed to the marginalization of black and white rural and working-class people alike. The wives of white sharecroppers also bore many children and toiled in the fields, receiving little in the way of financial compensation and existing on the fringes of the developing consumer economy. Eastern European immigrant women worked in factories and at home for pitifully low wages and under the most degrading conditions. Mechanization and the decline of heavy industry in the 1970s and 1980s adversely affected blue-collar workers regardless of skin color or ethnic background, many of whom found it difficult to reintegrate themselves into the white-collar and high-technology sectors. Early twenty-first century undocumented immigrants, deprived of the protections afforded U.S. citizens, remained susceptible to workplace exploitation in ways that echoed the history of African Americans. Thus the forces that conspired to keep black women and men in their inferior place also helped to undermine the economic security of other non-elites as well. Nevertheless, the basic premise of this work remains a compelling one: In their poverty and vulnerability, black people experienced these historical economic transformations in fundamentally different ways compared with other groups regardless of class, and black women, while not removed from the larger history of the American working class, shouldered unique burdens at home and endured unique forms of discrimination in the workplace. This theme holds true up to the present time, despite some observers' claims that the United States has achieved "colorblind" and "post-racial" workplaces.

Any examination of the mechanics of prejudice risks reducing its human subjects to victims, helpless before a many-tentacled monster that invades every part of their body and soul. The cultural distinctiveness of black community life, and attempts by black working women to subordinate the demands of their employers to the needs of their own families, reveal the inherent weakness of the "victimization" perspective. Clearly, black people could live their lives apart from prejudice without being oblivious to or untouched by it. In her introduction to the richly textured and evocative memoir *Lemon Swamp and Other Places*, Karen Fields notes that while segregation and disfranchisement played "like a background Muzak unlistened to," her grandparents "went purposefully in and out the front door of their life."[6] By virtue of their education and relatively comfortable material circumstances,

Mamie and Robert Fields were able to maintain an emotional detachment from the mean-spiritedness of white neighbors and public officials. Though exceptional in terms of their class status, they reveal how all black women and men struggled, with varying degrees of success, to define their lives according to their own terms.

The history of black working women is too often and too easily reduced to the images of the long-suffering mother—in the words of the poet Langston Hughes, "Life for me ain't been no crystal stair,"[7] on the one hand—and the indomitable grandmother—pillar of strength and wisdom to all who know her—on the other. Literary critic Mary Helen Washington has observed that "there still remains something of a sacred-cow attitude in regard to black women that prevents exploration of many aspects of their lives." She adds that "adopting the attitude of reverence means that we must settle for some idealized nonsense about black women and remain deprived of real characters from whom we could learn more about ourselves."[8] In some ways, this book is a nonfictional response to Mary Helen Washington's challenge. In other ways, however, it falls short of her incisive critique of what other writers have called the "myth of the black 'superwoman.'"[9] While the historical data quite clearly reveal the broad range of black women's individual and collective responses to their various workplaces, it has been difficult not to focus on those wives and mothers who, enduring great hardship, put their "sassiness" to good use in defense of their families, or found the wherewithal to help a neighbor whose plight was even more desperate than their own. In this account of black working women, evidence of their bitterness and sorrow abounds; still, the stories of those who survived with faith and courage reveal certain truths about the human spirit—truths that remind us, blacks and whites, women and men, of what poet Audre Lorde has called "the lessons of the black mothers in each of us."[10]

ONE

"MY MOTHER WAS MUCH OF A WOMAN"

Slavery, 1830–1860

AH WAS BORN back due in slavery," says Nanny to her granddaughter in Zora Neale Hurston's novel *Their Eyes Were Watching God*, "so it wasn't for me to fulfill my dreams of whut a woman oughta be and to do." Nanny never confused the degrading regimen of slavery with her own desires as they related to work, love, and motherhood: "Ah didn't want to be used for a work-ox and a brood-sow and Ah didn't want mah daughter used dat way neither. It sho wasn't mah will for things to happen lak they did." Throughout her life Nanny maintained a silent faith in herself and her sisters, a faith silenced within the spiritual void of bondage: "Ah wanted to preach a great sermon about colored women sittin' on high, but they wasn't no pulpit for me," she grieved.[1]

Nanny's lament captures the essence of the antebellum South's hierarchical caste system shaped by racial and gender ideologies, and based on dramatic inequalities of wealth and power. A compact, volatile, and ultimately isolated society, the slaveholder's estate represented in microcosm a larger drama in which physical force, the hallmark of the region's political economy, sustained the power of whites over blacks, men over women, rich over poor. Here, then, without pretense or apology were notions of social difference wedded to the pursuit of profit. As blacks, enslaved women were exploited for their skills and physical strength in the production of staple crops; as women, they performed a reproductive function vital to individual slaveholders' financial interests and to the inherently expansive system of slavery in general. Yet they also worked to resist the demands of masters and mistresses, white men and women who placed their own material and economic well-being over the integrity of black family life.[2]

The peculiar configuration of enforced labor relations and reproductive imperatives under slavery converged most dramatically where the two forms of political domination overlapped—that is, in the experiences of enslaved women.[3] In the context of the social division of labor in early rural America, the plantation work of black men and white women conformed to certain broader labor patterns not unique to the antebellum South. For example, despite the rhetorical glorification of the slaveholder's wife as the embodiment of various otherworldly virtues, she remained responsible for conventional womanly duties in the mundane realm of household management.[4] Likewise, enslaved men performed duties similar to those of New England and southern yeomen farmers. They planted, weeded, and harvested crops, and during the winter months they burned brush, cleared pasture, mended fences, and repaired equipment. A few received special training and labored as skilled artisans or mechanics. Clearly, the size, spatial arrangement, and commercial orientation, as well as patterns of brutal physical abuse, set the southern plantation apart from northern and midwestern family farms. Still, the definitions of white women's work, and of black men's work, did not differ substantially within any of these settings.

However, the slaveowner took a more crudely opportunistic approach toward the labor of black women, revealing the interplay (and at times conflict) between notions of women *qua* black workers and women *qua* female reproducers and domestic laborers; hence a master just as "naturally" put his bondswomen to work chopping cotton as washing, ironing, or cooking. Furthermore, in seeking to maximize the productivity of his entire labor force while reserving certain tasks for women exclusively, the owner demonstrated how patriarchal and capitalist assumptions concerning women's work could reinforce each other.[5]

At the same time, enslaved women also worked on behalf of their own nuclear and extended families and their own communities—and therein lies a central irony in the history of their labor. In defiance of the slaveholders' tendencies to ignore gender differences in making assignments in the fields, men and women whenever possible adhered to a strict division of labor within their own households and communities. Consequently, black women's parental obligations, and affective relations more generally, played a key role in their struggle to combat oppression, for their attention to the duties of motherhood deprived whites of full control over them as field laborers, domestic servants, and "broodsows." Indeed, the persistence with which enslaved women sought to define on their own terms "what a woman ought to be and to do" would ultimately have a profound impact on American history long after the formal institution of bondage had ceased to exist.

WORKING FOR WHITES: ENSLAVED WOMEN'S LABOR AS A PROBLEM OF PLANTATION MANAGEMENT

The emergence of the institution of British North American slavery was by no means a foregone conclusion. Throughout the seventeenth century, young white men and women from England made up the bulk of the labor force in the staple-crop economy of the largest tobacco-producing colonies, Virginia and Maryland. These young people worked as indentured servants, laboring for a landowner for a stipulated number of years in return for gaining passage to the New World. Some Chesapeake plantations included small numbers of Native Americans and people of African descent (either enslaved or free) among their labor forces; but for the most part English masters and mistresses deployed their own countrymen and women in the tobacco fields. Regardless of skin color or ethnicity, all of these field-workers proved difficult to manage; indentured servants and other bound workers resisted the enforced pace of labor in the tobacco fields, spent their nights drinking and fornicating, shirked their household tasks, threatened their masters and mistresses, and ran away. English workers in particular demanded respite from labor-intensive tobacco cultivation on English holidays; they demanded English food; and most significantly, they demanded the rights of English men and women—the right to sue masters who beat and otherwise abused them. By the late seventeenth century, those servants who had gained their freedom, usually after seven years of "hard usage" in the fields, found themselves without prospects in the way of landownership or political rights. They formed a restless group of men and women on the margins of Chesapeake society. For all these reasons, tobacco planters began to consider the enslavement of Africans as a possible solution to their labor problems.[6]

Yet Chesapeake colonists held deep misgivings about incorporating large numbers of Africans, and people of African descent, into their plantation households. Deeply suspicious of all other ethnic groups (including the Spanish, French, and Portuguese), masters and mistresses resisted cohabiting with people who were not English, English-speaking, or Christian. For a number of reasons enslaved laborers were risky; they were expensive to buy, and the high mortality rates among them, especially during the seventeenth century, meant they made a poor investment for cost-conscious planters. Like their English-servant and Indian-hireling counterparts, they were potentially dangerous as resentful individuals and as members of rebellious groups. Moreover, the multicultural Atlantic basin, which brought together people from Europe, Africa, and the New World, militated against the idea of a "race"-based slave system, one that categorized persons as either "black" or "white." Equiano Olaudah, an enslaved seaman, noted the variable colors on display throughout the Atlantic, a place where, with exposure to the sun, Spaniards "become as dark colored as our native Indians of Virginia," and where blended cultures challenged the idea that ethnic identities based on skin color were forever fixed, immutable. Noted Equiano of the exchange of languages, religions, and folkways in general among peoples from Europe, Africa, and the Americas: "Understanding is not confined to feature or color."[7]

By the mid-eighteenth century several factors contributed to the rise of slavery as a labor system integral to the economy and society of the southern colonies. With the expansion of the international slave trade, a decline in the supply of available English indentured servants, and the improved mortality rates among bound Africans and their children, slavery became a viable source of laborers for landowners cultivating not only tobacco in the Chesapeake but also rice in the Georgia and South Carolina low country. Political theorists such as Thomas Jefferson began to develop racial ideologies that sharply differentiated "blacks" from "whites" in terms of their intellectual potential and fitness for citizenship rights. The invention of the cotton gin in 1791 opened the way for the spread of cotton cultivation, a development that increased the value of enslaved workers and imposed on those workers a harsh new regimen of forced gang labor in the fields.[8]

The first enslaved workers arrived on the North American continent not as Africans but as members of ethnic groups from the African continent. For several generations (and even after the closing of the African slave trade in the United States in 1808) they and their descendants retained their ethnic identities and homeland traditions related to all manner of religious beliefs and rituals, foodways, and folkways. Among some groups, their Islamic faith provided a form of social cohesion that transcended ethnic and linguistic differences. Slaves' African ethnic customs, combined with their unique subordinate legal status, set them apart from all whites, including the disfranchised and impoverished.[9]

Planters sought to exploit the agricultural knowledge of certain ethnic groups, especially those skilled in the production of rice. But before planting could commence, whites put Africans and their descendants to work at the arduous and dangerous tasks of cutting trees and clearing land, tasks unfamiliar to Early Modern English people. Although slave traders in the Americas valued male over female laborers, they understood that women were integral to the sustenance of enslaved populations in terms of food preparation, medical care, and the preservation of social and religious rituals such as mourning the dead. African women possessed a variety of other skills that enhanced their financial value to whites; many women produced baskets, pottery, and other household items; and some had experience marketing and trading goods. Yet over time slaveholders developed a set of ideas that held that people of African descent were best "suited" for manual labor, and unworthy of even the most basic human rights by virtue of their "race." At the same time, the growth of the southern mulatto population—primarily the children of enslaved women impregnated by white slaveowners or overseers—revealed whites' hypocrisy and cynicism in using the concept of race as a way of categorizing people into groups of either "blacks" or "whites."[10]

By 1830, slavery was an entrenched institution in the United States, vital to the political and economic life not only of the staple-crop South, but also the industrializing North, where textile mills processed the cotton picked by enslaved workers from South Carolina to Louisiana. As a labor system, slavery exhibited regional variations; enslaved laborers toiled in the workshops and sawmills of the upper South, on the sprawling absentee-owner rice plantations in the low country, on holdings large and small in the broad swath of the Cotton Belt, and on the docks of seaports and river ports throughout the South. At the same time, an emergent African American culture showed common characteristics throughout the South. A balanced sex ratio, especially on the largest holdings, provided the foundation for the black family under slavery. Ethnic identities gave way to a new, hybrid culture that blended African and European traditions. By the early nineteenth century, most enslaved persons, with the exception of low-country Gullah-Geechee speakers, spoke English. Slaves throughout the United States embraced a form of the Christian religion that included African elements of worship—the ring shout, for example—and downplayed European beliefs related to original sin and the damnation of souls. Reinforced through oral tradition, blacks' worldview stressed the arbitrary boundaries between the natural and spiritual realms, and highlighted the significance of funerary rites and other customs related to food and medicine as markers of a distinctive African heritage. Slaves remained without recourse to the law, and they endured massive forced migration; between 1820 and 1860, 10 percent of slaves in the upper South were sold to the lower South, and family separations were routine.[11]

During the last three decades of the antebellum period, slaveowners began to issue self-serving pronouncements defending the institution of bondage as a positive good, a way to care for "childlike" black people and incorporate them into white "households." Yet enslaved men and women were under no such illusion; slavery was a system of coerced labor, first and foremost. Interviewed by a Federal Writers Project (FWP) worker in 1937, the elderly former slave Hannah Davidson spoke reluctantly of her ordeal in Kentucky: "The things that my sister May and I suffered were so terrible . . . It is best not to have such things in our memory." During the course of the interview Davidson stressed the unremitting toil that had shaped her life under bondage. "Work, work, work," she said; it had consumed all her days (from dawn until midnight) and all her years (she was only eight when she began minding her master's children and helping the older women with their spinning). "I been so exhausted working, I was like an inchworm crawling along a roof. I worked till I thought another lick would kill me." On Sundays, "the only time they [the slaves] had to themselves," she recalled, women washed clothes and some of the men tended their small tobacco patches. As a child she loved to play in the haystack, but that was possible only on "Sunday evening, after work."[12]

Slaveowners experimented with various divisions of labor calculated to exploit black men, women, and children, and push them to the limits of human endurance. All slaves were barred by law from owning property or acquiring literacy skills, and although the system played favorites with a few, black males and females were equal in the sense that neither gender wielded legally enforceable economic power over the other. Some slaves, such as those in the Rice Kingdom of low-country South Carolina and Georgia, accumulated modest amounts of personal property, and kept chickens and tended gardens. And slaves throughout the South trafficked in goods they appropriated from their masters and sold to other blacks or whites for gain. Nevertheless, to a considerable extent, the types of jobs enslaved laborers did, and the amount and regularity of labor they were forced to devote to such jobs, were all dictated by the master.[13]

For a number of reasons, then, the definition of enslaved women's work is problematic. If work is any activity that leads either directly or indirectly to the production of goods or services, then these wives, mothers, and daughters did nothing *but* work. (An exception was late night revelry, which allowed women to use their bodies for pleasure rather than labor, and often left them too depleted and tired to work efficiently the next day.) Even their efforts to care for themselves and their families helped to maintain the owner's workforce and to enhance its overall productivity; virtually all forms of nurture contributed to the health and welfare of the enslaved population, thereby increasing the actual value of the master's property—that is, slaves as strong workers, marketable commodities, and speculative properties. White men warned prospective mothers that they wanted neither "runts" nor girls born on their plantations, and enslaved women understood that their owner's economic self-interest affected even the most intimate family ties. Of the pregnant bondswomen on her husband's large Butler's Island (Georgia) rice plantation, Fanny Kemble observed, "They have all of them a most distinct and perfect knowledge of their value to their owners as property," and she recoiled at their obsequious profession obviously intended to delight her: "Missus, tho' we no able to work, we make little niggers for Massa."[14]

The rhythm of the planting-weeding-harvesting cycle shaped the lives of almost all American enslaved workers, 95 percent of whom lived in rural areas. This cycle dictated a common work routine (gang labor) for slaves who cultivated the king of all agricultural products, cotton, in the broad swath of Black Belt that dominated the whole region. Patterns of labor organization varied in the other staple-crop economies—tobacco in the upper South, rice along the coast of Georgia and South Carolina, and sugar in Louisiana. The task system characteristic of low-country rice cultivation granted slave women and men an exceptional degree of control over their own time after the completion of their daily assignments; however, this system imposed additional, heavy burdens on workers, now forced to grow their own food as well as toil in the rice fields. In 1860, of almost 4 million slaves, about half labored on farms with holdings of twenty slaves or more; one-quarter endured bondage with at least fifty other people on the same plantation. In its most basic form, a life of slavery meant working the soil with other blacks at a pace calculated to reap the largest harvest for a white master.[15]

Under these conditions, the physical frailty that accompanied old age was unlikely to spare enslaved women from the demands of labor. The West African tradition of respect for one's elders found new meaning among African Americans; for most women, old age brought increased influence within the slave community even as their economic value to the master declined. Still, owners, fearful lest women escape from "earning their salt" once they became too infirm to go to the field, set them to work at other tasks—knitting, cooking, spinning, weaving, dairying, washing, ironing, caring for the children. (Elderly men served as gardeners, wagoners, carters, and stock tenders.) Nevertheless, the imperatives of the southern economic system sometimes compelled slaveowners to extract from feeble women what field labor they could. In other cases they reduced elderly persons' material provisions—housing and allowances of food and clothing—in proportion to their decreased productivity.

In his efforts to wrench as much field labor as possible from slaves of child-bearing age without injuring their reproductive capacity, the master made "a noble admission of female equality," observed Kemble, an abolitionist sympathizer, with bitter irony. Slaveholders had little use for sentimental platitudes about the delicacy of the female constitution when it came to grading their "hands" according to physical strength and endurance. Judged on the basis of a standard set by a healthy adult man, most women probably ranked as three-quarter hands; yet there were enough women like Susan Mabry of Virginia, who could pick 400 or 500 pounds of cotton a day (150 to 200 pounds was considered respectable for an average worker) to remove from a master's mind all doubts about the abilities of a strong, healthy woman field-worker. At the same time, he was putting into practice time-honored Anglo-Saxon notions about the types of work appropriate for impoverished women, thereby producing many a "very dreary scene" like the one described by northern journalist Frederick Law Olmsted: During winter preparation of rice fields on a Sea Island plantation, he saw a group of black women, "armed with axes, shovels and hoes . . . all slopping about in the black, unctuous mire at the bottom of the ditches." In essence, the quest for an "efficient" agricultural workforce led slaveowners to downplay gender differences in assigning adults to field labor.[16]

Dressed in coarse osnaburg gowns; their skirts "reefed up with a cord drawn tightly around the body, a little above the hips" (the traditional "second belt"); long sleeves pushed above the elbows and kerchiefs on their heads, female field-hands were a common sight throughout the antebellum South. Together with their fathers, husbands, brothers, and sons, black women spent up to fourteen hours a day toiling out of doors, often under a blazing sun. In the Cotton Belt they plowed fields; dropped seed; and hoed, picked, ginned, sorted, and moted cotton. On farms in Virginia, North Carolina, Kentucky, and Tennessee, women hoed tobacco; laid worm fences; and threshed, raked, and bound wheat. For those on the Sea Islands and in coastal areas, rice culture included raking and burning the stubble from the previous year's crop; ditching; sowing seed; plowing, listing, and hoeing fields; and harvesting, stacking, and threshing the rice. In the bayou region of Louisiana, women planted sugar-cane cuttings, plowed, and helped to harvest and gin the cane. During the winter, they performed a myriad of tasks necessary on nineteenth-century farms: repairing roads, pitching hay, burning brush, and setting up post and rail fences. Like Sara Colquitt of Alabama, most adult females "worked in de fields every day from 'fore daylight to almost plumb dark." During the busy harvest season, everyone was forced to labor up to sixteen hours at a time—after sunset by the light of candles or burning pine knots. Miscellaneous chores regularly occupied men and women around outbuildings and indoors on rainy days. Male and female enslaved laborers watered the horses, fed the chickens, and slopped the hogs. Together they ginned cotton, ground hominy, shelled corn and peas, and milled flour.[17]

In fact, throughout the South, enslaved women formed the bulk of the agricultural labor force (and an estimated 60 to 80 percent of all rice hands). Work assignments for men and women differed according to the size of a plantation, its crops, and its degree of labor specialization. On the largest holdings, masters trained men as artisans and then diverted the energies of husbands, fathers, and sons from the fields to the workshop. On smaller plantations, including one Virginia wheat farm, the men scythed and cradled the grain, women raked and bound it into sheaves, which children then gathered and stacked. Thomas Couper, a wealthy Sea Island planter, divided his slaves according to gender and employed men exclusively in ditching and women in moting and sorting cotton. Within the two gender groups, he further classified hands according to individual strength so that during the sugar-cane harvest, three "gangs" of women stripped blades (medium-level task), cut them (hardest), and bound and carried them (easiest). However, since cotton served as the basis of the southern agricultural system, general patterns of female work usually overshadowed local and regional differences in labor-force management. Stated simply, most women spent a good deal of their lives plowing, hoeing, and picking cotton. In the fields the notion of a distinctive "women's work" vanished as slaveholders realized that "women can do plowing very well & full well with the hoes and [are] equal to men at picking."[18]

However, it would be inaccurate to label female field-hands as unskilled hands in contrast to their menfolk working as carpenters, coopers, blacksmiths, brick masons, and boat pilots. To harness a double team of mules or oxen and steer, to guide a heavy wooden plow, to sow a rice field, or to pick hundreds of pounds a cotton each day was no mean feat for strong men, and yet slave women mastered these rigorous activities. White men and women from the North and South marveled at the skill and strength of female plow hands. Emily Burke of eastern Georgia saw men and women "promiscuously run their ploughs side by side and day after day . . . and as far as I was able to learn, the part the women sustained in this masculine employment, was quite as efficient as that of the more athletic sex." In his travels through Mississippi, Frederick Law Olmsted watched as women "twitched their plows around on the head-land, jerking their reins, and yelling to their mules, with apparent ease, energy, and rapidity." He failed to see "any indication that their sex unfitted them for the occupation."[19]

On another estate in the Mississippi Valley, Olmsted observed forty of the "largest and strongest" women he had ever seen; they "carried themselves loftily, each having a hoe over the shoulder, and walking with a free, powerful swing, like *chasseurs* on the march." In preparing fields for planting and in keeping grass from strangling the crop, women as well as men blistered their hands with the clumsy hoe characteristic of southern agriculture. "Hammered out of pig iron, broad like a shovel," these "slave-time hoes" were made to withstand worker-inflicted damage. Recalled one former slave of the tool that also served as pick, spade, and gravedigger: "Dey make 'em heavy so dey fall hard, but de bigges' trouble was liftin' dem up." Hoeing was backbreaking labor, but the versatility of the tool and its importance to cotton cultivation meant that the majority of female hands used it a good part of the year.[20]

The cotton-picking season usually began in late July or early August and continued without interruption until the end of December. Thus for up to five months annually, every available man, woman, and child was engaged in a type of work that was strenuous and "tedious from its sameness." Workers carried a bag fastened by a strap around their neck and deposited the cotton in it as they made their way down the row, at the end of which they emptied the bag's contents into a basket. Picking cotton required endurance and agility as much as physical strength, and women frequently won regional and interfarm competitions conducted during the year. Pregnant and nursing women usually ranked as half-hands and were required to pick an amount less than the "average" 150 or so pounds per day.[21]

Slaveholders often reserved the tasks that demanded sheer muscle power for men exclusively. These included clearing the land of trees, rolling logs, and chopping and hauling wood. On rice plantations, enslaved men engineered intricate systems of canals and ditches that allowed for the flooding of fields with fresh water from nearby rivers. Yet plantation exigencies sometimes mandated women's labor in these areas too. Generally, the smaller the farm, the more arduous and varied was women's fieldwork. Lizzie Atkins, who lived on a twenty-five-acre Texas plantation with only three other slaves, remembered working "until slam dark"; she helped to clear land, cut wood, and tend the livestock in addition to her other duties of hoeing corn, spinning thread, sewing clothes, cooking, washing dishes, and grinding corn. One Texas farmer, who had his female slaves haul logs and plow with oxen, even made them wear breeches, thus minimizing outward differences between the genders.

Enslaved women in the low-country rice fields dug ditches and otherwise contributed to the region's distinctive irrigation system. Still, FWP interviews with former slaves indicate that blacks considered certain jobs uncharacteristic of bondswomen. Recalled Louise Terrell of her days on a farm near Jackson, Mississippi: "The women had to split rails all day long, just like the men." Nancy Boudry of Georgia said she used to "split wood jus' like a man." Elderly women reminisced about their mothers and grandmothers with a mixture of pride and wonder. Mary Frances Webb declared of her slave grandmother: "In the winter she sawed and cut cord wood just like a man. She said it didn't hurt her as she was strong as an ox." Janie Scott's description of her mother implied the extent of the older woman's emotional as well as physical strength: She was "strong and could roll and cut logs like a man, and was much of a woman."[22]

At first it seems ironic that masters would utilize women fully as field laborers, but reserve most of the skilled occupations that required manual dexterity for men. Here the high cost of specialized and extensive training proved crucial in determining the division of labor. Although women were capable of learning these skills, their work lives were frequently interrupted by childbearing and nursing; a female blacksmith might not be able to provide the regular service required on a plantation. Too, masters frequently "hired out" mechanics and artisans to work for other employers during the winter, and women's domestic responsibilities were deemed too important to permit protracted absences from their quarters. However, many young girls learned to spin thread and weave cloth because these tasks could occupy them immediately before and after childbirth.[23]

The drive for profits induced slaveowners to squeeze every bit of strength from black women as a group. According to some estimates, in the 1850s at least 90 percent of all enslaved females over sixteen years of age labored more than 261 days per year, eleven to thirteen hours each day. Few overseers or masters had any patience with women whose movements in the field were persistently "clumsy, awkward, gross, [and] elephantine" for whatever reasons—malnutrition, exhaustion, recalcitrance. As Hannah Davidson said: "If you had something to do, you did it or got whipped." The enforced pace of work more nearly resembled that of a factory than a farm; Kemble referred to female field-hands as "human hoeing machines." The bitter memories of former slaves merely suggest the extent to which the physical strength of women was exploited. Eliza Scantling of South Carolina, only sixteen years old at the end of the Civil War, plowed with a mule during the coldest months of the year: "Sometimes me hands get so cold I jes' cry." Matilda Perry of Virginia "use to wuk fum sun to sun in dat ole terbaccy field. Wuk till my back felt lak it ready to pop in two."[24]

Although pregnant and nursing women suffered from temporary lapses in productivity, most slaveholders apparently agreed with the (in Olmsted's words) "well-known, intelligent and benevolent" Mississippi planter who declared that "Labor is conducive to health; a healthy woman will rear most children." (They obviously did not have the benefit of modern medical knowledge that links the overwork of pregnant mothers not only with a consequent decline in their reproductive capacity but also with Sudden Infant Death Syndrome affecting primarily children under six months of age.) Still, slaveowners faced a real dilemma when it came to making use of the physical strength of women as field-workers and at the same time protecting their investment in women as childbearers. These two objectives—one focused on immediate profit returns and the other on long-term economic considerations—at times clashed, as women who spent long hours picking cotton or harvesting rice or sugar cane, toiling in the fields with heavy iron hoes, and walking several miles a day sustained damage to their reproductive systems immediately before and after giving birth. In the sugar fields of Louisiana and the rice fields of the low country, heat, overwork, poor diet, and chronic illness conspired to limit fecundity levels among women. In these crop cultures, the twin demands of production of the crop and reproduction of the labor force proved mutually exclusive in ways that planters understood but refused to acknowledge in terms of modified work regimens for their female slaves. At the regional level, a decline in slave fertility and an increase in miscarriage rates during the cotton boom years of 1830 to 1860 suggest the heightened demands made upon women, both in terms of increased workloads in the fields and family breakups associated with the massive, forced migration of slaves from the upper to the lower South.[25]

The auction block revealed in graphic terms the value of enslaved women in both long-range and immediate financial terms. Traffickers in human bodies examined men and women for their "soundness"—that is, their health and ability to work hard. White men poked and prodded the "property" on sale, considering every part of a man, woman, or child—teeth, mouth, eyes, and limbs. Yet a woman's childbearing capacity set her apart from boys and men, as revealed by the preoccupation of auctioneers and buyers with women's breasts and genitalia. One seller exhorted potential buyers of the slave Betsy, "There's a breast for you, good for a round dozen before she's done child-bearing." In fact, women's unique ordeal under slavery derived from their capacity to bear children.[26]

Masters frequently suspected bondswomen, whether pregnant or not, of shamming illness and fatigue—"play[ing] the lady at your expense," as one Virginia planter put it. These fears help to account for the reckless brutality with which owners forced women to work in the fields during and after their "confinement"—a period of time that might last as long as four or six weeks, or might be considerably shortened by masters who had women deliver their children between the cotton rows. Indeed, in the severity of punishment they meted out to slaves, owners made little distinction between men and women. Since women attained parity with black men in terms of their productive abilities in the cotton fields, they often received a proportionate share of the whippings. In response to an interviewer's inquiry, a former Virginia slave declared, "Beat women! Why sure he [master] beat women. Beat women jes lak men. Beat women naked an' wash 'em down in brine."[27]

Agricultural journalists, travelers in the South, and planters themselves loudly condemned overseers—usually illiterate men of the landless class—for their violent ways. Yet despite the inevitable depletion of their workforce from illness and high mortality rates, slaveholders continued to search for overseers who could make the biggest crop. Consequently, overseers drove enslaved women and beat them mercilessly, with some victims achieving respite only in return for sexual submission. To a white man, a black woman was not only a worker who needed prodding, but also a female capable of fulfilling his sexual or aggressive desires. For this reason, a fine line existed between rape and work-related punishment, and an overseer's lust might yield to sadistic rage. The mother of Minnie Fulkes was suspended from a barn rafter and beaten with a horsewhip "nekkid 'til the blood run down her back to her heels" for fending off the advances of an overseer on a Virginia plantation. In his autobiographical *Narrative*, Frederick Douglass described a similarly gruesome scene, forever emblazoned on his memory: a master who whipped Douglass's aunt "upon her naked back until she was literally covered with blood. . . . He would whip her to make her scream, and whip her to make her hush; and not until overcome with fatigue would he cease to swing the blood-clotted cowskin."[28]

The whipping of pregnant and nursing mothers—"so that blood and milk flew mingled from their breasts"—revealed the myriad impulses that conjoined to make women especially susceptible to physical abuse. The pregnant woman represented the sexual activity of the enslaved community in general, and (in most but not all cases) that of her husband and herself in particular; she thus symbolized a life in the quarters carried on apart from white interference. One particular method of whipping pregnant slaves was used throughout the South: "They were made to lie face down in a specially dug depression in the ground," a practice that provided simultaneously for the protection of the fetus and the abuse of its mother. Enslaved women's roles as workers and as childbearers came together in these trenches, these graves for the living, in southern plantation fields. The uniformity of procedure suggests that the terrorizing of pregnant women was not uncommon, despite the fact that the fertility of these women was crucial to the well-being of every plantation.[29]

Impatient with slow workers and determined to discipline women whom they suspected of feigning illness, masters and overseers at times indulged in rampages of violence that led to the victim's death. Former Mississippi slave Clara Young told of her seventeen-year-old cousin, pregnant for the first time and unable to keep up with the rest of the workers in the field. The driver whipped her until she bled; she died the next morning. He had told the other slaves, "If dey said anything 'bout it to de marster, he'd beat them to death, too, so ever'body kep' quiet an' de marster neber knowed." Thus cruelty derived not only from the pathological impulses of a few individuals, but also from a basic premise of the slave system itself: the use of violence to achieve a productive labor force and to terrorize those laborers into a state of compliance.[30]

Upon first consideration, the frequency with which small boys and girls, pregnant women, mothers of as many as ten children, and grandmothers were beaten bloody seems to indicate that inexplicable sadism pervaded the Old South. In fact, whites often displaced their anger at particularly unruly blacks onto the most vulnerable members of the slave community. Douglass argued that "the doctrine that submission to violence is the best cure for violence did not hold good as between slaves and overseers. He was whipped oftener who was whipped easiest." Like the mistress who was "afraid of the grown Negroes" and beat the children "all the time" instead, many whites feared the strong men and women who could defend themselves—or retaliate. Historical sources contain innumerable examples of slaves who overpowered a tormenter and beat him senseless or killed him with his own whip. Referring to a powerful black man who "wouldin' 'low nobody ter whip 'in," one plantation owner told his overseer, "let 'im 'lone[;] he's too strong ter be whup'd." The overseer's hatred of this enslaved worker was bound to find some other form of release; by abusing a weaker person, he could unleash his aggression and indirectly punish the menacing relative or friend of his victim.[31]

In some cases, a woman would rebel in a manner commensurate with the work demands imposed upon her. In the words of former slaves, "She'd git stubborn like a mule and quit." Or she took her hoe and knocked the overseer "plum down" and "chopped him right across his head." When masters and drivers "got rough on her, she got rough on them, and ran away in the woods." She cursed the man who insisted he "owned" her so that he beat her "till she fell" and left her broken body to serve as a warning to others: "Dat's what you git effen you sass me." Nevertheless, a systematic survey of the FWP Slave Narrative Collection reveals that women were more likely than men to engage in "verbal confrontations and striking the master but not running away," probably because of their family responsibilities. A case study of a Georgia plantation indicates that when women did run away, they usually accompanied or followed spouses already in hiding.[32]

Family members who perceived their mothers or sisters as particularly susceptible to abuse in the fields conspired to lessen their workload. Frank Bell and his four brothers, enslaved on a Virginia wheat farm, followed their parents down the long rows of grain during the harvest season. "In dat way one could help de other when dey got behind. All of us would pitch in and help Momma who warn't very strong." This overseer discouraged families from working together because he believed "dey ain't gonna work as fast as when dey all mixed up," but the black driver, Bell's uncle, "always looked out for his kinfolk, especially my mother." James Taliaferro's father counted the corn rows marked out for Aunt Rebecca, "a short-talking woman that ole Marsa didn't like," and alerted her to the fact that her assignment was almost double that given to the other women. Rebecca indignantly confronted the master, who relented by reducing her task, but not before he threatened to sell James's father for his meddling. On another plantation, the hands surreptitiously added handfuls of cotton to the basket of a young woman who "was small and just couldn't get her proper amount." In the low-country Rice Kingdom, where a daily task consisted of hoeing a quarter acre, elderly, ill, and pregnant female rice hands at times relied on family members to help them complete their work, since masters rarely modified tasks to accommodate the health or age of a worker.[33]

No enslaved woman exercised authority over enslaved men as part of their work routine, but it is uncertain whether this practice reflected the sensibilities of the slaveowners or of the workers themselves. Women were assigned to teach children simple tasks in the house and field and to supervise other women in various facets of household industry. A master might excuse a woman from the fields and order her to manage a funeral observance, but he would not install her as a driver over people in the field. Many strong-willed women demonstrated that they commanded respect among males as well as females, but more often than not masters perceived this as a negative quality to be suppressed. One Louisiana slaveholder complained bitterly about a particularly "rascally set of old negroes"—"the better you treat them the worse they are." He had no difficulty pinpointing the cause of the trouble, for "Big Lucy, the leader, corrupts every young negro in her power." Throughout the South women were held responsible for instigating all sorts of undesirable behavior among their husbands and brothers and sisters. On Charles Colcock Jones's Georgia plantation, the slave Cash gave up going to prayer meeting and started swearing as soon as he married Phoebe, well-known for her truculence. Apparently few masters attempted to co-opt high-spirited women by offering them positions of formal power over black men.[34]

Work in the soil thus represented the chief lot of all slaves, female and male. In the Big House, a division of labor based on both gender and age became more apparent. Although women predominated as household workers, few were assigned full-time to this kind of labor, and even those who were remained unspecialized. The size of the plantation determined the degree women could labor exclusively as cleaners, laundresses, cooks, maids, and the caretakers of white children. As few as 5 percent of all antebellum adult slaves served in the elite corps of house servants trained for specific duties. Of course during the harvest season, all slaves, including those in the house, went to the fields to make obeisance to King Cotton. Thus the lines between domestic service and fieldwork blurred during the day and during the lives of enslaved women. Many continued to live in the quarters but rose early in the morning to perform various chores for the mistress—"up wid de fust light to draw water and help as house girl"—before heading for the field. James Claiborne's mother "wuked in de fiel' some, an' aroun' de house sometimes." Young girls tended babies and waited on tables until they were sent outside—"mos' soon's" they could work—and returned to the house years later, too frail to hoe weeds but still able to cook and sew. The circle of women's domestic work went unbroken from day to day and from generation to generation.[35]

Just as southern white men scorned manual labor as the proper sphere of slaves, so their wives strove, often unsuccessfully, to lead a life of leisure within their own homes. Those duties necessary to maintain the health, comfort, and daily welfare of white families were considered less women's work than black women's and black children's work. Slave mistresses supervised the whole operation, but on the largest plantations the sheer magnitude of the responsibility meant that black women had to supply the elbow grease. (Like white men, mistresses often described the work of enslaved women as work they themselves had accomplished. Wrote the mistress Dolly Lunt Burge in her diary, "laid by all of the corn . . . got a bag of cotton out.") For most enslaved domestics, housework involved hard, steady, often strenuous labor as they juggled the demands made by the mistress and other members of the master's family. Mingo White of Alabama never forgot that his mother had shouldered a workload "too heavy for any one person." She served as personal maid to the master's daughter, cooked for all the hands on the plantation, carded cotton, spun a daily quota of thread, and wove and dyed cloth. Every Wednesday she carried the white family's laundry three-quarters of a mile to a creek, where she beat each garment with a wooden paddle. Ironing consumed the rest of her day. Like the lowliest field-hand, she felt the lash if any tasks went undone.[36]

Though mistresses found that their husbands commandeered most bondswomen for fieldwork during the better part of the day, they discovered in black children an acceptable alternative source of labor. Girls were favored for domestic service, but a child's gender played only a secondary role in determining household assignments. On smaller holdings especially, the demands of housework, like cotton cultivation, admitted no finely honed division of labor, although masters always chose boys to accompany them on hunting trips and to serve as their personal valets. Until puberty, boys and girls shared a great deal in terms of dress and work. All children wore a "split-tail shirt," a knee-length smock slit up the sides: "Boys and gals all dress jes' alike . . . They call it a shirt iffen a boy wear it and call it a dress iffen the gal wear it." After the age of six or so, many received assignments in and around the Big House from one or more members of the master's family. Mr. and Mrs. Alex Smith, who grew up together, remembered performing different tasks. As a girl, she helped to spin thread and pick seed from cotton and cockle burrs from wool. He had chopped wood, carried water, hoed weeds, tended the cows, and picked bugs from tobacco plants. However, slave narratives contain descriptions of both boys and girls elsewhere doing each of these things. In the barnyard boys and girls alike gathered eggs, plucked chickens, drove cows to and from the stable, and "tended the gaps" (opened and closed gates). It was no wonder that Mary Ella Grandberry, a slave child grown old, "disremember[ed] ever playin' lack chilluns do today."[37]

Parents could hardly voice their objections when their children began their initiation into the arduous world of grown-up labor, and at times mothers and fathers acquiesced willingly, because masters increased accordingly the food allotments of youngsters now forced to work hard. And so black girls and boys followed the mistress's directions in filling wood boxes with kindling, lighting fires in chilly bedrooms in the morning and evening, making beds, washing and ironing clothes, parching coffee, polishing shoes, and stoking fires while the white family slept at night. They fetched water and milk from the springhouse and meat from the smokehouse. Three times a day they set the table, helped to prepare and serve meals, "minded flies" with peacock-feather brushes, passed the salt and pepper on command, and washed the dishes. They swept, polished, and dusted, served drinks, and fanned overheated visitors. Mistresses entrusted to the care of those who were little more than babies themselves the bathing, diapering, dressing, grooming, and entertaining of white infants. (One little girl, introduced to her new "young mistress," looked at the child in her mistress's arms and replied in disbelief, "No, I don't see no young mistress, that's a baby."). As tiny ladies-in-waiting, black children did the bidding of fastidious white women and little girls. Cicely Cawthon, age six when the Civil War began, called herself the mistress's "little keeper"; "I stayed around, and waited on her, handed her water, fanned her, kept the flies off her, pulled up her pillow, and done anything she'd tell me to do." Martha Showvely recounted a nightly ritual with her Virginia mistress. After she finished her regular work around the house, the young girl would go to the woman's bedroom, bow to her, wait for acknowledgment, and then scurry around as ordered, lowering the shades, filling the water pitcher, arranging towels on the washstand, or "anything else" that struck the woman's fancy. Mary Woodward, only eleven in 1865, was taught to comb her mistress's hair, lace her corset, and arrange her hoop skirts. At the end of the toilet, Mary was supposed to say "You is served, mistress!" Recalled the former slave, "Her lak them little words at de last."[38]

The privileged status and material comfort of mistresses rested squarely on the backs of their female slaves. Nevertheless, the system of bondage ultimately mandated the subordination of all women, both black and white, to masters-husbands whose behavior ranged from benevolent to tyrannical, but always within a patriarchal context. Wealthy southern planters, consumed with the rituals of "honor," lorded over their wives, children, and enslaved workers—and in some cases these last two groups overlapped. Mary Boykin Chesnut believed that slave mistresses were "abolitionists in their hearts and hot ones too." But if women's resentment toward slavery found only indirect, or private, expression, the causes for that resentment are readily apparent. The slaveholders' insatiable quest for more and better cotton lands mocked their wives' desire for a more settled, orderly existence. On a more immediate level, slavery rubbed raw the wounds of white women's grievances in two specific ways—first, it added greatly to their household responsibilities, and second, it often injected irreconcilable conflicts into the husband-wife relationship.[39]

As they went about their daily chores, mistresses repeatedly complained about the burdens imposed on them; they were, they felt, "slaves of slaves." To instruct youthful servants in the mysteries of table-setting, fire-stoking, and childcare; to cajole and threaten sullen domestics who persisted in sewing too slowly or carelessly; to keep track of those women assigned to duties in the yard, garden, or chicken house taxed the patience of the most lax white housewives. Impudence and recalcitrance among black women were recurring problems, but even more significantly, enslaved laborers could make a mistress's life miserable by literally doing nothing. A white woman might banish a particularly stubborn cook to the fields (indeed, some black women calculated upon that response in order to be near their families), only to find herself faced with an even more contentious replacement. Obviously, in these cases, lines of dependency blurred; a mistress might have served in a managerial capacity, but she relied on enslaved cooks and chambermaids to perform a tremendous amount of work that she was unwilling or unable to do herself.[40]

In their role as labor managers, mistresses lashed out at black women not only to punish them, but also to vent their anger on victims even more wronged than themselves. We may speculate that, in the enslaved woman, the mistress saw the source of her own misery, but she also saw herself—a woman without rights or recourse, subject to the whims of an egotistical man. At the same time, some evidence suggests that widowed slaveholding women, under intense pressure to fulfill the traditional male duties of labor managers, were particularly harsh in their dealings with their enslaved subordinates. Regardless of the source, white women's anxieties frequently spilled over into acts of violence. Severe chastisement did not necessarily guarantee the repentance of the offender. However, patterns of mistress-initiated violence toward black women suggest that such acts were just as often spontaneous outbursts of rage as they were deliberate measures to reform behavior. When punishing slave women for minor offenses, mistresses were likely to attack with any weapon available—knitting needles, tongs, a fork or butcher knife, an ironing board, or a pan of boiling water. In the heat of the moment, white women devised barbaric forms of punishment that resulted in the mutilation or permanent scarring of their female servants.[41]

Predictably, jealousy over their spouse's real or suspected infidelity led many white wives to openly express their anger and shame. Husbands who flaunted their predatory sexual behavior in the slave quarters essentially dared their wives to attack a specific woman or her offspring. When Roswell King's wife learned that he had fathered children by the slaves Judy and Scylla, she had the two women whipped and sent to the low-country estate's "penal colony" out of spite. Some promiscuous husbands made no attempts at gentlemanly discretion (or "transcendent silence") within their own households, but rather actively sought to antagonize their wives. For example, Sarah Wilson, the daughter of an enslaved woman and her white master, remembered that as a child she was "picked on" by the mistress. The white woman chafed under her husband's taunts; he would order her to "'let [Sarah] alone, she got big, big blood in her,' and then laugh."[42]

Divorce petitions provide one of the few sources that reveal white wives' outrage in response to their husbands' provocative behavior. A witness in a Virginia divorce case in 1848 offered the following testimony: A master one morning told his favorite slave to sit down at the breakfast table "to which Mrs. N [his wife] objected, saying . . . that she (Mrs. N) would have her severely punished." The husband then replied "that in that event he would visit her (Mrs. N) with a like punishment. Mrs. N then burst into tears and asked if it was not too much for her to stand." Like at least some other masters, Mr. N freely admitted that his initial attraction to his future wife stemmed from her "large Estate of land and negroes." (Thus a favorable marriage became one more consideration for the ambitious slaveholder.) However, this particular husband went out of his way to demonstrate his "strong dislike and aversion to the company" of his bride by sleeping with the black woman "on a pallet in his wife's room" and by frequently embracing her in the presence of his wife. Mrs. N's first response was to lay "her hands in an angry manner on the said servant." Her husband, besides threatening his wife with bodily harm, "told her if she did not like his course, to leave his house and take herself to some place she liked better." Although the outcome of this case is not known, the patriarchalism of the southern legal system dictated that the odds would be against the humiliated Mrs. N. In any case, the considerable dowry she brought to the marriage would remain in the hands of her spouse.[43]

Scattered evidence from other sources also indicates that slaveholders at times physically abused their wives. While this was hardly normative behavior, it appears to have been a natural by-product of a violent culture. Men who drank freely and whipped their slaves could hardly have been expected to respect the frail flower of white womanhood at all times. But again, the denigration of white women, whether manifested through physical force or in a more subtle, though no less painful way, was part and parcel of slavery. By directing their anger toward enslaved women, white wives achieved a fleeting moment of catharsis. Rarely in American history is there a more striking example of the way in which the patriarchal imperative could turn woman against woman, white against black.[44]

Not surprisingly, then, interviews with former slaves suggest that the advantages of domestic service over fieldwork for women have been exaggerated in accounts written by whites. Fetching wood and water, preparing three full meals a day over a smoky fireplace, or pressing damp clothes with a hot iron rivaled cotton picking as back-breaking labor. Always "on call," women servants often had to snatch a bite to eat whenever they could, remain standing in the presence of whites, and sleep on the floor at the foot of a mistress's bed, increasing the chances that they would sooner or later be bribed, seduced, or forced into sexual relations with the master. Peeling potatoes with a sharp knife, building a fire, or carrying a heavy load of laundry down a steep flight of stairs required skills and dexterity not always possessed by every enslaved woman, let alone little boys and girls, and injuries were common. Chastisement for minor infractions came with swift severity; cooks who burned the bread, and children who stole sweets or fell asleep while singing to the baby, suffered all kinds of abuse, from jabs with pins to beatings that left them disfigured for life. The master's house offered no shelter from the most brutal manifestations of slavery.[45]

For any one or all of these reasons, black women might prefer fieldwork to housework. During his visit to a rice plantation in 1853, Olmsted noted that hands "accustomed to the comparatively unconstrained life of the negro-settlement detest the close control and careful movements required of the house servants." Marriage could be both a means and an incentive to escape a willful mistress. Jessie Sparrow's mother wed at age thirteen in order "to ge' outer de big house. Dat how come she to marry so soon." Claude Wilson recalled many years later that "his mother was very rebellious toward her duties and constantly harassed the 'Missus' about letting her work in the fields with her husband until finally she was permitted to make the change from the house to the fields to be near her man." Other women, denied an alternative, explored the range of their own emotional resources in attempting to resist petty tyranny; their defiance rubbed raw the nerves of mistresses already harried and high-strung. A few servants simply withdrew into a shell of "melancholy and timidity."[46]

The dual status of a bondswoman—an enslaved laborer and a female—afforded her master a certain degree of flexibility in formulating her work assignments. When he needed a field-hand, her status as an able-bodied adult took precedence over gender considerations, and she was forced to toil alongside her menfolk. At the same time, the master's belief that most forms of domestic service required the attentions of a female reinforced the traditional role of woman as household worker. The authority of the master in adhering to or dispensing with a gendered division of labor was absolute, but at times individual women could influence his decisions to some extent. In certain cases, a woman's preference for either fieldwork or domestic service worked to her advantage. For example, the rebelliousness of Claude Wilson's mother prompted her removal from the Big House to the field, a change she desired. Similarly, a master might promise a woman an opportunity to do a kind of work she preferred as a reward for her cooperation and diligence. On the other hand, a slave's misbehavior might cause her to lose a position she had come to value; more than one prized cook or maid was exiled to the fields for "sassing" the mistress or stealing. A system of rewards and punishments thus depended on the preferences of individual men and women, and a servant determined to make life miserable for the family in the Big House might get her way in any case.[47]

Masters and mistresses allocated enslaved women's labor according to at least three different considerations—the whites' desire to increase staple-crop production; enlarge their workforce; and provide for the daily maintenance of, and childcare within, their own (white) households. As if it were not difficult enough to balance these competing objectives, the master often found that he and his overseer and wife were operating at cross-purposes when it came to exploiting the labor of black women. Profit-making was a "rational" basis upon which to set enslaved females to work in the fields, but long-term interests related to women's childbearing capacity at times yielded to the demands of the harvest at hand. Owners and overseers alike might easily slip over the boundary between chastising black women for work-related offenses and terrorizing them as a means of asserting control over the entire slave labor force. Moreover, the sexual exploitation of a black woman could produce concentric rings of bitterness that engulfed the white mistress, resulting in further (though economically "irrational") abuse of the victim herself. The slave master, armed with both a whip and legal authority over all plantation residents, was able to shield himself from the wellspring of hate that sprang from these peculiarly southern forms of inequality. Yet the slave community too had a claim on the energies of black women, and its own gendered division of labor helped to subvert the authority of the slaveowner in ways that he could not or would not fully understand.

WORKING FOR EACH OTHER: ENSLAVED WOMEN'S LABOR IN THE CONTEXT OF FAMILY AND COMMUNITY LIFE

In the field and the Big House, black women worked under the close supervision of white men and women at a forced pace. The slaves derived few, if any, tangible benefits from their labor to increase staple-crop profits and to cook, clean, and care for the white family. However, blacks' efforts on behalf of their own health and welfare often took place in spaces apart from whites, with rhythms more in tune with community and family life. For enslaved women, these responsibilities, though physically arduous, could offer a degree of personal fulfillment. As Martha Colquitt remarked of her slave grandmother and mother who stayed up late to knit and sew clothes "for us chillun": "Dey done it 'cause dey wanted to. Dey wuz workin' for deyselves den." Slave women deprived of the ability to cook for their own kinfolk or discipline their own children felt a keen sense of loss; family responsibilities revealed the limited extent to which black women and men could control their own lives. Furthermore, a strict gendered division of labor in the quarters openly challenged the master's purely opportunistic approach to slave women's fieldwork.[48]

In the eighteenth and early nineteenth centuries, enslaved women's notions of what a woman "ought to be and to do" derived from gender roles shaped by specific ethnic identities. For example, the slaves brought to Virginia included Igbos, Senegambians, and Akans. In Igboland (present-day southeastern Nigeria), women possessed considerable authority in the realms of commerce, defense, and family life. Igbo wives had control over their own farmland, and their community and kinfolk supported them if they sought to remove themselves from abusive spousal relationships. Historians speculate that in the British North American colonies, Igbo women earned a well-deserved reputation for running away, and even committing suicide, because they were imbued with a sense of independence that had been nourished in their homeland.[49]

More generally, throughout the antebellum period, African traditions continued to shape the lives of enslaved women in multiple ways. Descended from peoples of present-day Sierra Leone and Angola, slaves along the Georgia and Sea Island coast tended small garden plots with vegetables native to Africa—groundnuts, benne (sesame), and gourds. Wives and mothers used a traditional mortar and pestle to grind corn at night, an arduous task for women bone-tired from laboring in the fields all day. Techniques related to fishing, basket-weaving, cooking, and mourning the dead all derived from African practices. Men and women spoke a pidgin language, Gullah (in South Carolina) or Geechee (in Georgia), and called everyday items by their African names—*seraka* for rice cake, *juba halta* for water bucket, and *wah-hoo bahk* for slingshot.[50]

Though dimmed by time and necessity, the outlines of African work patterns endured among enslaved laborers. As members of traditional agricultural societies, most African women played a major role in the production of the family's food as well as in providing basic household services. The gendered division of labor was more often determined by a woman's childcare and domestic responsibilities than by any presumed physical weakness among females as a group. In some tribes a woman might engage in heavy, monotonous fieldwork as long as she could make provisions for nursing her baby, which often meant keeping an infant with her in the field. She cultivated a kitchen garden that yielded a variety of vegetables consumed by the family or sold at market, and she milked the cows and churned butter.[51]

West Africans brought with them competencies and knowledge that slaveowners readily exploited and that enslaved communities depended upon. Many black women had experience spinning thread, weaving cloth, and sewing clothes. Moreover, enslaved laborers often used methods and tools handed down from their ancestors—the mortar and pestle for pounding rice, for example. Whites frequently commented on the ability of women to balance heavy and unwieldy loads on their heads, an African custom. These skills and cultural practices enhanced enslaved communities as well as the master's overall operation.[52]

The primary difficulty in generalizing about African women's part in agriculture stems from the fact that members of West African tribes captured for the North American slave trade came from different hoe-culture economies. Within the geographically limited Niger Delta region, for example, men and women of the Igbo tribe worked together in planting, weeding, and harvesting, while female members of another prominent group, the Yoruba, helped only with the harvest. Throughout most of sub-Saharan Africa (and particularly on the west coast), women had primary responsibility for tilling (though not clearing) the soil and cultivating the crops; perhaps this tradition, combined with work patterns established by white masters in this country, reinforced the blacks' beliefs that cutting trees and rolling logs was "men's work." In any case, it is clear that African women often did fieldwork.[53]

In the United States, enslaved families assumed diverse forms that were, in many instances, the product of local economic and demographic patterns as much as black people's inclinations. Some families lived together in nuclear units of husband, wife, and children, while some lived together with kin, fictive kin (persons who had been adopted into an extended family), and other nonblood relations. Most large plantations were self-contained entities, but many slaves lived on holdings connected to other nearby estates through patterns of marriage and nighttime trade and socializing. Young single women lived with their parents, while older single women lived together in some instances. Family structure, though based upon the ideal of the nuclear family, shifted in response to outside pressures (the demands of the slaveowner) and internal needs. Still, some generalizations are warranted: Most enslaved households consisted of cramped quarters for adults and children. Social relations between husband and wife and parents and children were ultimately fragile, reflecting the imperatives of the slave trade and the family life-process of even "benevolent" slaveholders, who routinely willed bequests and gave gifts of enslaved persons to their own children. Indeed, the demand for slaves in the lower South broke apart families living in the upper South. The extraordinarily high mortality rates associated with rice and sugar cultivation produced cultures of grief suffered by wives and mothers in the Georgia and South Carolina low country and the lower Mississippi Valley. The practice of keeping children with their mother meant that many enslaved communities were matrifocal, with women responsible for childcare and the day-to-day chores of family life.[54]

The labors of enslaved women in the quarters constituted additional responsibilities for women already worked to the limits of human endurance in the fields or in the Big House. Indeed, it is difficult to distinguish with any precision work for the master on the one hand and work for one's family on the other, since basic sustenance activities—cooking, sewing, caring for children, tending gardens—ultimately benefited the owner by maintaining the health and welfare of his bound labor force. Quilting, corn shucking, and other "working socials" also served the interests of the master even as these events provided enslaved men and women, young and old, male and female, with the opportunity to enjoy one another's company.[55]

Enslaved women of all ages toiled in the quarters. Older women provided a variety of services either communally or centrally for the whole plantation. On smaller farms, a cook and her assistants might prepare one or all of the meals for the other slaves each day except Sunday. Likewise, an elderly woman, with the help of children too young to work in the fields, often was assigned charge of a nursery in the quarters, where mothers left their babies during the day. To keep any number of little ones happy and out of trouble for up to twelve to fourteen hours at a time taxed the patience of the most kindly souls. Enslaved children grew up with a mixture of affection for and fear of the grandmothers who had dished out the licks along with the cornbread and clabber. Other "grannies" usurped the position of the white physician (he rarely appeared in any case); they "brewed medicines for every ailment," gave cloves and whiskey to ease the pain of childbirth, and prescribed potions for the lovesick. Even a child forced to partake of "Stinkin' Jacob tea" or a concoction of "turpentine an' castor oil an' Jerusalem oak" (for worms) could assert years later that "Gran'mammy was a great doctor," surely a testimony to her respected position within the slave community if not to the delectability of her remedies.[56]

On many plantations it was customary to release adult women from fieldwork early on Saturday so that they could do the week's washing. Whether laundering was done in old wooden tubs, iron pots, or a nearby creek with batten sticks, wooden paddles, or wash-boards, it was a time-consuming and difficult chore. Yet this ancient form of women's work provided opportunities for socializing "whilst de 'omans leaned over de tubs washin' and a-singin' dem old songs." Years later, Mary Frances Webb remembered wash day—"a regu-lar picnic"—with some fondness; it was a time for women "to spend the day together," out of the sight and earshot of whites. Yet it is doubtful that these overworked older women shared the little girl's unalloyed affection for laundry day.[57]

Much of the work black women did for the slave community resembled the colonial sys-tem of household industry. Well into the nineteenth century throughout the South, en-slaved women continued to spin thread, weave and dye cloth, sew clothes, make soap and candles, prepare and preserve foods, churn butter, and grow food for the family table. They mastered all these tasks with the aid of primitive equipment and skills passed on from grandmothers. Looking back, blacks of both sexes exclaimed over their mothers' ability to prepare clothes dye from various combinations of tree bark and leaves, soil and berries; make soap out of ashes and animal skins; and fashion bottle lamps from string and tallow. Because of their lack of time and materials, wives and mothers rarely found in these activi-ties an outlet for creative expression, but they did take pride in their resourcefulness, and they produced articles of value to the community as a whole.[58]

Home textile production illustrates the ironies of women's community labor under slav-ery, for the threads of cotton and wool bound them together in both bondage and sister-hood. Masters (or mistresses) imposed rigid spinning and weaving quotas on women who worked in the fields all day. For example, many were forced to spin one "cut" (about three hundred yards) of thread nightly, or four to five cuts during rainy days or in the winter. Women of all ages worked together, and boys and girls helped to tease and card wool, pick up the loom shuttles, and knit. In the flickering candlelight, the whir of the spinning wheel and the clickety-clack of the loom played a seductive lullaby, drawing those who were al-ready "mighty tired" away from their assigned tasks.[59]

As the "head spinner" on a Virginia plantation, Bob Ellis's mother was often sent home from fieldwork early to prepare materials for the night's work: "She had to portion out de cotton dey was gonna spin an' see dat each got a fair share." Later that evening, after sup-per, as she moved around the dusty loom room to check on the progress of the other women, she would sing:

> Keep yo' eye on de sun,
> See how she run,
> Don't let her catch you with your work undone,
> I'm a trouble, I'm a trouble,
> Trouble don' las' always.

With her song of urgency and promise she coaxed her sisters to finish their work so they could return home by sundown: "Dat made de women all speed up so dey could finish fo' dark catch 'em, 'cause it mighty hard handlin' dat cotton thread by fire-light."[60]

Enslaved women's work for other community members challenged the master's authority in direct ways. As the persons in charge of food preparation for both whites and their own families, they at times clandestinely fed runaways in an effort to keep them out of harm's way for as long as possible. One elderly black man recalled that it was not uncommon on his master's plantation for slaves to go and hide after they were punished, and added, "I've known my mother to help them the best she could; they would stay in the woods and come in at night, and mother would give them something to eat." While the act of cooking might not differ in a technical sense when performed for blacks as opposed to whites, it certainly assumed heightened emotional significance for the black women involved, and, when carried out in such subversive ways, political significance for social relations on the plantation.[61]

In the quarters, the communal spirit was but an enlarged manifestation of kin relationships. Indeed, family, kin, and community blended into one another, for blood ties were often supplemented by fictive kin when the slaves defined patterns of mutual affection and obligations among themselves. Moreover, depending upon the size and age of the plantation, slave fertility and mortality rates, and the incidence of "abroad" marriages (formed by spouses who belonged to different masters), kinship might encompass a significant percentage of enslaved workers at any one time. For example, during the twenty-year period before the Civil War, the bondsmen and bondswomen on the Good Hope, South Carolina, plantation were related to three out of ten of their fellows. When calculated on the basis of household linkages, the average individual could find that fully 75 percent of all residences in the quarters "house[d] kin, or the kin of those kin." These linkages were often more numerous for women than for men, simply because "abroad" marriages, combined with masters' buying and selling practices, reinforced the matrifocality of family structure. In any case, a woman's sense of responsibility for her own blood relations often found expression through her service to the community of slaves.[62]

To varying degrees based on the proclivities of their owner and the type of crop culture in which they labored, enslaved women accumulated property and engaged in petty commodity production. Some planters gave their workers considerable leeway in tending a garden; keeping chickens, pigs, horses, and mules; marketing eggs, honey, and vegetables; and claiming ownership of a variety of things such as boats, animal traps, and fishing tackle. While making quilts and clothing often represented a burden imposed upon women exclusively, many wives and mothers welcomed the opportunity to market goods and foodstuffs, either openly to customers in the marketplaces of nearby towns, or illicitly to poor whites on back roads at night. Some planters, like the Manigaults (father and son) of Argyle Island, in the Savannah River, broke from local tradition and refused their overseers and enslaved laborers alike the privilege of keeping chickens; the planters believed that this type of economic activity caused inevitable squabbles over who owned what. Other owners, however, saw all kinds of work performed by enslaved laborers, including petty commodity production and other forms of enterprise, as both an enhancement of the plantation's larder and as a means of discouraging men and women from running away and leaving their possessions, variously defined, behind.[63]

At the same time, gender did matter in the quarters; out of the father-mother, husband-wife nexus sprang the slaves' beliefs about what men and women should be and do. On smaller holdings, especially, husbands and wives remained separated from each other, leaving women with the bulk of child-rearing obligations. On the largest plantations, the presence of extended kin networks in the quarters blurred lines between nuclear families and their relatives, many of whom lived nearby if not under the same roof. Nevertheless, the family was a common (if not the exclusive) form of cohabitation regardless of the location, size, or economy of a plantation, the nature of its ownership, or the age of its slave community. Because of the omnipresent threat of forced separation by sale, gift, or bequest, these families were not stable. Yet, in the absence of such separations, unions between husbands and wives and parents and children often endured for many years. Households tended to be large; families with eight living children were not uncommon.[64]

Within the quarters, the process of child socialization reflected both the demands made upon the slaves by whites and the values of an emerging African American culture. For most young women, sexual maturity marked a crucial turning point, a time when their life experiences diverged quite explicitly from those of their brothers. Until that point, boys and girls shared a great deal in terms of dress, play, and work. In early adolescence (ages ten to fourteen), a child would normally join the regular workforce in the fields as a half-hand. At that time (or perhaps before), he or she received adult clothing. This rite of passage apparently made more of an impression on boys than girls, probably because pants offered more of a contrast to the infant's smock than did a dress. Willis Cofer attested to the significance of the change: "Boys jes' wore shirts what looked lak dresses 'til dey wuz 12 years old and big enough to wuk in de field . . . and all de boys wuz mighty proud when dey got big enough to wear pants and go to wuk in de fields wid grown folkses. When a boy got to be man enough to wear pants, he drawed rations and quit eatin' out of de trough [in the nursery]."[65]

Whether or not slave girls received any advance warning from female relatives about menarche and its consequences is unknown. Despite the crowding of large families into small cabins, at least some parents managed to maintain a degree of privacy in their own relations and keep a daughter innocent until she acquired firsthand experience. It is possible that a "sizable minority" of girls became sexually active soon after they began to menstruate, though some scholars have argued that the average age of a slave woman at the time of the birth of her first child was twenty or twenty-one, four years after menarche and probably two years after the onset of fertility. The quality of that first sexual experience of course depended upon a number of personal factors, but all of these were overshadowed by the fact that enslaved women were always vulnerable to rape by white men.[66]

For young black people of both sexes, courtship was both a diversion and a delight. Enslaved men formally initiated the courting process. When a young man saw "a likely looking gal," he found the opportunity to woo her on the way to and from work, in the field behind the overseer's back (George Taylor was "too crazy 'bout de girls" to keep his mind on cotton chopping), or at Saturday night dances in the quarters. Chivalry covered a broad spectrum of behavior, from refraining from chewing tobacco in the presence of a sweetheart to protecting her from the lash. At times it was difficult for the two to slip away by themselves, and flirting was carried on by pairs in a group setting. Delia Harris remembered a teasing song sung by the young men on the Virginia plantation where she lived. They began with, "Hi, Ho, Johnson gal . . . Johnson gal is de gal fo' me," even though there was no such person; "De boys jus' start dat way to git all de gals to perkin' up." Then each youth proceeded to call the name of a favorite, and if any girl was left out she was bound to feel "mighty po'ly 'bout it, too." Rivalry among suitors—"setting up to a gal and [finding] there was another fellow setting up to her too"—prompted some to obtain magic potions from conjurers and herb doctors. And girls would encourage attention in all the familiar ways. "Gals always tried to fix up fo' partyin', even ef dey ain't got nothin' but a piece of ribbon to tie in dey hair." They played coy and "hard to get."[67]

When this process proceeded naturally and freely, the couple might eventually have a child, or if the girl had already had her first baby (perhaps by a different man), they might marry and settle into a long-lasting monogamous union. Husbands and wives expected each other to be faithful, and the slave community frowned on adultery. Not surprisingly, though, demographic conditions and cultural traditions specific to individual plantations could interfere with this romantic ideal. An unbalanced sex ratio, in addition to the slaves' exogamous customs, often limited the number of available partners. Moreover, many partners, like the two in Mississippi married in the field between the handles of a plow, were reminded in no uncertain terms that their master considered them primarily as workers, not as lovers or husband and wife. An owner might prohibit a marriage for any reason, and he might forbid a male slave to seek a wife elsewhere, since the children of their marriage would belong not to him but to the wife's owner. Andy Marion insisted that black men "had a hell of a time gittin' a wife durin' slavery. If you didn't see one on de place to suit you and chances was you didn't suit them, why what could you do?" He listed the options and stressed that the preferences of a number of parties had to be taken into consideration: "Couldn't spring up, grab a mule and ride to de next plantation widout a written pass. S'- pose you gits your marster's consent to go? Look here, de gal's marster got to consent, de gal got to consent, de gal's daddy got to consent, de gal's mammy got to consent. It was a hell of a way!"[68]

Whites often intervened in more direct ways to upset the sexual order that black men and women created for themselves, thereby obliterating otherwise viable courtship and marriage practices. That masters failed to engage in systematic or widespread breeding (as evidenced by the relatively late age at which slave women bore their first child, for example) does not negate the obvious conclusions to be drawn from the FWP slave narratives— that white men and women at times seized the opportunity to manipulate slave marital choices, for economic reasons on the one hand, out of seemingly sheer high-handedness on the other.[69]

At times, slaveholders took an unsolicited interest in a slave woman's love life. "Don't you ever let me see you with that ape again," one South Carolina mistress would say to young girls with contempt. "If you cannot pick a mate better than that I'll do the picking for you." Masters frequently practiced a form of eugenics by withholding their permission for certain marriages and arranging others. Some enslaved women bitterly rejected the proposed spouse. Rose Williams, forced to live with a man named Rufus because the master wanted them "to bring forth portly chillen," warned the slave to stay away from her "'fore I busts yous brains out and stomp on dem." Threatened with a whipping, she finally relented, but never married. Many years later Rose Williams explained, "After what I does for de massa, I's never wants no truck with any man. De Lawd forgive dis cullud woman, but he have to 'scuse me and look for some others for to 'plenish de earth." Some masters followed a policy of separating quarreling spouses and then "bestow[ing] them in 'marriage' on other parties, whether they chose it or not." These men and women often distinguished between their current mate and "real" husband or wife who had been taken from them.[70]

Enslaved women's bodies were the site of conflict between the women themselves and the owners and white physicians who sought to control their reproductive lives. Some white doctors went to extreme lengths to ensure a pregnant woman delivered a healthy baby; medical interventions could consist of a wide range of measures, including enemas, blister plasters, and drugs such as morphine and opium. At the other extreme were women who chewed the herb cotton root bar (*gossypium hirsutum*), an abortifacient, a practice that was well known throughout the South and one that masters sought to prevent at all costs. The former Texas slave William Byrd recalled that women would at times "slip out at night and get them a lot of cotton roots and bury them under their quarters." On a Tennessee plantation, according to William Coleman, the master "would almost kill a negro woman if he caught her chewing cotton root, but still that did not do much good[;] they would slip and chew it in spite of all he could do about it." Mary Gaffney attributed her childlessness to her own use of the herb: "Maser was going to raise him a lot more slaves, but still I cheated Maser, I never did have any slaves to grow and Maser he wondered what was the matter." Gaffney told her son, "I kept cotton roots and chewed them all the time but I was careful not to let Maser know or catch me." After she was free, she began to bear children.[71]

The economic significance of the American slave population's natural increase over the years obscures the centrality of children to the slave woman's physical, emotional, and social existence. Each new birth represented a financial gain for the slaveholder, but in the quarters the baby was a new member of the community. Some young girls had their first child out of wedlock, an event that proved functional to a girl's family since masters were less likely to sell a woman who early demonstrated her fecundity; young people in their late teens and early twenties were prime candidates for sale if an owner needed the cash. A long-lasting marriage (though not necessarily to the first child's father) often followed within a couple of years. After that, more children came with sustained regularity. Early in the nineteenth century, in areas of the upper South, fertility levels among slave women neared human capacity. A woman whose fertile years spanned the ages of eighteen to forty-five, for example, might conceive thirteen children and spend ten years of her life pregnant and almost the whole period nursing one child after another.[72]

Children were a source of a mother's pain as well as her joy. Extraordinary rates of slave infant mortality (twice that of whites in 1850) meant that many women regularly suffered the loss of a baby before or after its birth. Even more dramatically, on disease-ridden low-country rice plantations, infant mortality rates could reach as high as 90 percent; there, only one out of ten babies lived to see his or her first birthday. (Rice culture was especially hazardous to infants, who succumbed to gastrointestinal diseases and waterborne ailments.) If slaveholders faced a dilemma when they tried to maximize women's productive and reproductive abilities simultaneously, mothers suffered the emotional and physical consequences. New mothers had to walk long distances from field to nursery to feed their infants, and their overheated milk provided inadequate and unhealthy nourishment. For these and other reasons, in the South as a whole, fewer than two out of three black children survived to the age of ten in the years between 1850 and 1860; the life expectancy at birth for males and females was only 32.6 and 33.6 years, respectively. Excessive childbearing, malnutrition, and heavy manual labor left many women weak and susceptible to illness. A slave mother's love protected her children only up to a point: "Many a day my ole mama has stood by an' watched massa beat her chillun 'till dey bled an' she couldn' open her mouf." The reality or threat of separation from their families (a fact of slave life that became even more frequent during the late antebellum period) caused some women to descend into madness, the cries of "Take me wid you, mammy" echoing in their ears, while others donned a mask of stoicism to conceal their inner pain.[73]

Men shared the obligations of family life with women. In denying slaves the right to own property, make a living for themselves, participate in public life, or protect their children, the institution of bondage deprived black men of access to the patriarchy in the larger economic and political sense. Nevertheless, whether or not they cohabited on the same plantation, men and women worked together to support the husband's and father's role as provider and protector. In the evenings and on Sundays, men collected firewood; made shoes; wove baskets; constructed beds, tables, chairs, and animal traps; and carved butter paddles and ax handles. Other family members appreciated a father's skills; recalled Molly Ammonds, "My pappy made all de furniture dat went in our house an' it were might' good furniture too," and Pauline Johnson echoed, "De furn'chure was ho-mek, but my daddy mek it good an' stout." Husbands provided necessary supplements to the family diet by hunting and trapping quails, possums, turkeys, rabbits, squirrels, and raccoons, and by fishing. They often assumed responsibility for cultivating the tiny household garden plots allotted to families by the master. Some craftsmen, like Bill Austin's father, received goods or small sums of money in return for their work on nearby estates; Jack Austin, "regarded as a fairly good carpenter, mason, and bricklayer," was paid in "hams, bits of cornmeal, cloth for dresses for his wife and children, and other small gifts; these he either used for his small family or bartered with other slaves."[74]

These familial duties also applied to men who lived apart from their wives and children, even though they were usually allowed to visit only on Saturday night and Sunday. Lucinda Miller's family "never had any sugar, and only got coffee when her father would bring it to her mother" during his visits. The father of Hannah Chapman was sold to a nearby planter when she was very small. Because "he missed us and us longed for him," she said many years later, he tried to visit his family under the cover of darkness whenever possible. She noted, "Us would gather 'round him an' crawl up in his lap, tickled slap to death, but he give us dese pleasures at a painful risk." If the master should happen to discover him, "us would track him de nex' day by de blood stains," she remembered.[75]

Hannah McFarland of South Carolina recounted the time when the local slave patrol attempted to whip her mother, "but my papa sho' stopped dat," she said proudly. Whether or not he was made to suffer for his courage is unknown; however, the history of slavery is replete with accounts of husbands who intervened, at the risk of their own lives, to save wives and children from violence at the hands of whites. But in a more general sense, the sexual violation of black women by white men rivaled the separation of families as the foremost provocation injected into black family life by slaveholders. It is impossible to document with any precision the frequency of these encounters; the 10 percent of the slave population classified as "mulatto" in 1860 provides a very conservative estimate of the incidence of rape or concubinage on southern plantations. Scholars debate whether sexual relations between a master and an enslaved woman could ever yield true affection for either party, or whether the unequal power relations by definition precluded such affection. Yet it is true that the pervasive resentment on the part of black women as well as men, who knew that random or systematic assaults were always a possibility, cannot be quantified in any meaningful way. A women's acquiescence in the sexual advances of an overseer or owner might offer a modicum of protection for herself or her family—especially when a master vowed to "put her in his pocket" (that is, sell her) or whip her if she protested. Nevertheless, black women often struggled to resist, and their fathers, sons, and husbands often struggled to protect them.[76]

Regardless of the circumstances under which their womenfolk were sexually abused, black men reacted with deep humiliation and outrage, a reaction that at least some slaveholders intended to provoke. One Louisiana white man would enter a slave cabin and tell the husband "to go outside and wait 'til he do what he want to do." The black man "had to do it and he couldn't do nothing 'bout it." (This master "had chillen by his own chillen.") Other husbands ran away rather than witness such horrors. Recalled one elderly former slave, "What we saw, couldn't do nothing 'bout it. My blood is bilin' now at the thoughts of dem times." It would be naive to assume that the rape of a black wife by a white man did not adversely affect the woman's relationship with her husband; her innocence in initiating or sustaining a sexual encounter might not have shielded her from her husband's wrath. The fact that in some slave quarters mulatto children were scorned as the master's offspring indicates that the community in general hardly regarded this form of abuse with equanimity; hence the desperation of the young slave wife described by an FWP interviewee who feared that her husband would eventually learn of her ordeal at the hands of the master.[77]

The black man's role as protector of his family would find explicit expression in postemancipation patterns of work and family life. Until that time, the more freedom the slaves had in determining their own activities, the more clearly emerged a distinct division of labor between the sexes. During community festivities like log rollings, rail splittings, wood choppings, and corn shuckings, men performed the prescribed labor while women cooked the meals. At times, male participants willingly "worked all night," for, in the words of one, "We had the 'Heavenly Banners' (women and whiskey) by us." A limited amount of primary evidence indicates that men actively scorned women's work, especially cooking, house-cleaning, sewing, washing clothes, and intimate forms of childcare like bathing children and picking lice out of their hair. Some slaveholders devised forms of public humiliation that capitalized on men's attempts to avoid these tasks. One Louisiana cotton planter punished slave men by forcing them to wash clothes; he also made chronic offenders wear women's dresses in an effort to shame them in public.[78]

If gender mattered to the division of labor within the slave quarters, so too did age. The overwhelming youth of the general slave population between 1830 and 1860 (more than half of all enslaved persons were under twenty years of age) meant that most plantations had only a few considered elderly—the 10 percent over fifty years of age. For antebellum slaves, these revered (and sometimes feared) women served as a tangible link with the African past. Interviewed by a Federal Writers Project worker in 1937, a Mississippi-born former slave, James Brittian, recalled his own "grandma Aunt Mary" who had lived for 110 years. A "Molly Gasca [Madagascar?] negro," she was plagued by a jealous mistress because of her striking physical appearance: "Her hair it was fine as silk and hung down below her waist." Ned Chaney's African-born Granny Silla (she was the oldest person anyone knew, he thought) commanded respect by virtue of her advanced age and her remarkable healing powers: "Ever'body set a heap of sto' by her. I reckon, because she done 'cumullated so much knowledge an' because her head were so white." When Granny Silla died, her "little bags" of mysterious substances were buried with her because no one else knew how to use them. Yet Chaney's description of his own mother, a midwife and herb doctor, indicates that she too eventually assumed a position of authority within the community.[79]

As a little girl in Georgia, Mary Colbert adored her grandmother, a strong field-hand, "smart as a whip." "I used to tell my mother that I wished I was named Hannah for her, and so Mother called me Mary Hannah," she recalled. Amanda Harris, interviewed in Virginia when she was ninety years old, looked back to the decade before the war, when her grandmother was still alive: "Used to see her puffin' on dat ole pipe o' her'n, an' one day I ast her what fun she got outen it. 'Tain't no fun, chile,' she tole me. 'But it's a pow'ful lot o' easment. Smoke away trouble, darter. Blow ole trouble an' worry 'way in smoke." Amanda started smoking a pipe shortly before her grandmother died, and in 1937 she declared, "Now dat I'm as ole as she was I know what she mean." In the quiet dignity of their own lives, these grandmothers preserved the past for future generations of African American women.[80]

The formal task of spiritual leader remained a man's job, and women could not aspire to the title or recognition that accompanied the preacher's role. At the same time, women, especially older ones, exercised power through a variety of channels. Well into the antebellum period, elderly persons who had survived the horrific Middle Passage upheld Muslim traditions and religious practices. Midwives delivered babies and interpreted the signs that accompanied their birth—twins, seventh children, infants born with a caul. Plantation "doctresses" relied on a combination of herbs and other natural remedies, and liberal doses of social psychology, to treat all manner of ills. As conjurers, they used spells to ward off "hants" (ghosts and spirits) and witches, and insisted that couples intending to marry receive their permission even before they consulted the parents. Harriet Ware, a northern teacher assigned to the South Carolina Sea Islands, reported in 1862, "'Learning' with these people I find means a knowledge of medicine, and a person is valued accordingly." Many older women practiced the healing arts in their combined role of midwife, root doctor, healer, and conjurer. By interpreting dreams and strange occurrences, they brought the real world closer to the supernatural realm and offered spiritual guidance to the ill, the troubled, and the lovelorn. Slaveholders paid grudging respect to the influence of enslaved women by complaining about them. Writing of the low-country antebellum Rice Kingdom, Charles C. Jones Jr. noted the "difficulty and annoyance" caused by what he termed "the interference of these old negro women—conjurers—who, in plying their secret trade, gave rise to disturbances and promoted strife and disquietude."[81]

Within well-defined limits, enslaved men and women created—or preserved—an explicit gendered division of labor based on their own preferences. Husbands and wives and fathers and mothers had reciprocal obligations toward each other. Without a legal right to private property, men lacked the means to achieve economic superiority over their wives, one of the major sources of inequality in the ("free") sexual order. But if married couples shared duties related to household maintenance and community survival, they were nonetheless reduced to a state of powerlessness that rendered virtually meaningless the concept of equality as it applies to traditional marital relations, especially since black women were so vulnerable to attacks by white men.

Moreover, task allocation among enslaved workers themselves revealed a tension between two different attitudes toward "women's work." The first involved a profound respect for the labor that women did and their ability to meet the demands imposed upon them by competing parties. For example, in an 1840 speech before a northern audience, John Curry, a former slave who grew up in North Carolina, recalled that "My mother's labor was very hard." He went on to outline her daily responsibilities in the cow pen (she milked fourteen cows) in addition to caring for the children of mothers who worked in the fields. She also cooked for the slaves on the plantation, and did all the ironing and washing for the master's household as well as for her own husband and seven children (including three orphans she had adopted). At night, she "would find one boy with his knee out, a patch wanting here, and a stitch there, and she would sit down by her lightwood fire, and sew and sleep alternately." Echoes of this type of appreciation for women's work are found throughout the slave narratives, work recounted in loving detail by both sons and daughters.[82]

Although men might regard women's domestic labor as intrinsically valuable, this type of activity was nevertheless labeled "women's work" on the assumption that it was the special province of females. In this sense, black women and men performed complementary functions whenever possible within their own "sphere" of socially defined responsibilities. Yet a husband was not "equally" willing to wash clothes compared to a mother's "willingness" to gather firewood in the absence of her spouse. This twin impulse to honor the hardworking wife and mother and relegate "grannies" to positions of informal influence would help to shape the internal structure of the freed community after the Civil War.

PLACES AND PEOPLE THAT DEFIED THE RULE OF PLANTATION SLAVERY

The tight discipline of workers on southern plantations, where most black women toiled from sunup to sundown in the fields, was the hallmark of antebellum slavery. Yet some African Americans lived and labored outside these parameters of planter control, in the process mocking slaveholders' contentions that blacks were by nature dependent and incapable of taking care of themselves. In southern cities and in the northern states, black people sought to control their own productive energies, and to build their own communities apart from white interference.

The institution of bondage proved remarkably flexible. Along the fall line in the southeastern Piedmont region, textile mill owners cobbled together workforces of men, women, and children, black and white, enslaved and free, on the basis of complex calculations: Some owners employed whites as operatives on the theory that they could be easily fired when river levels dropped and the machines stopped, or when demand for their product was low. Other owners hired enslaved laborers and put them to work tending machines because they (in contrast to white wage earners) could not strike, arrive at work late in the day, demand schools for their children, or refuse to work without facing punishment. In southern seaports and river ports, black artisans both enslaved and free took advantage of the hiring-out system, and earned cash wages. Some masters allowed their enslaved carpenters, coopers, and brick masons, for example, to find work on their own, and even live on their own, as long as they turned over the bulk of their pay to their owner. In these cities, the occupations filled by black women were largely limited to domestic service, but a few skilled seamstresses and pastry chefs achieved a loyal white clientele for their handiwork. It was not unusual to see black women making their way through the dusty streets, carrying immense bundles of firewood or laundry on their heads, in the African manner. Through heroic exertions, some enslaved women, like their male counterparts, were able to save their meager wages and eventually buy themselves and even their own family members. In Chatham County, Georgia, Sarah Ann Block's mother worked as a nurse, and eventually bought herself and her two children, paying $500 for each person.[83]

In 1860, a quarter of a million southern blacks were free, compared to the nearly 4 million in bondage. This former figure had declined from 3 percent of the black population in 1830 to 1.5 percent in 1860. Most southern free people of color lived in cities, and some owned modest businesses—the men as draymen or butchers, the women as bakers, seamstresses, and caterers, and as peddlers of produce, brooms, and prepared foods. A handful of these entrepreneurs even owned enslaved workers, though it is difficult to tell whether individual holdings constituted exploited labor forces or shelters for relatives who would otherwise be forced to move out of state once they became free. The wives of the most successful of these entrepreneurs and artisans often dressed and conducted themselves in ways that alarmed whites determined to see all blacks as members of a dependent and impoverished class of people. In some places, black women were able to afford fancy clothes and expensive carriage rides; the Reverend Nehemiah Adams, a northern clergyman, visited

Savannah in 1854 and commented on the elegant clothing of the city's black church congregants, musing about "how impossible it must soon become to treat with indignity" any enslaved person who dressed so well. Yet Adams was mistaken in minimizing the vulnerability of even those black women arrayed in finery.[84]

In southern cities, black women led religious and missionary societies sponsored by independent so-called African churches, as well as benevolent and burial societies that remained largely out of the eye of white people. Some free women of color taught clandestine schools for black children. Yet even they remained closely monitored by whites; most cities required all free people of color to have a "guardian," a white man responsible for their good behavior. Though all black women in the urban South suffered under caste legislation intended to keep blacks from prospering, or learning to read or write, many managed to carve out for themselves lives that were less constricted than those of their sisters on the countryside. A rich associational life, marked by late-night parties and fancy balls no less than Sunday schools, provided urban women with a more varied existence than that of enslaved plantation workers.[85]

In the North, most individual state emancipation laws had eliminated bondage by 1830, though some states eliminated slavery completely only gradually—Pennsylvania not until 1847, for example. Some black women toiled in rural areas as field-hands and domestics; those in the dairy shops of Narragansett Bay, Rhode Island, were unusual by the virtue of their regimented labor—they produced a quota of rounds of cheese daily. By 1860, six out of ten of all northern blacks lived in cities. During this period of rapid industrialization, when textile and shoe mills sprang up along the rushing rivers of New England and the Mid-Atlantic, black women remained confined largely to domestic work, but laboring at a number of different tasks. Enterprising souls, such as Elleanor Eldrige, born free in Rhode Island in 1785, and the African-born Chloe Spear of Boston, pieced together a living through a patchwork of jobs—taking in boarders, working as a nurse or laundress, weaving, spinning, or finding work in a hotel or with a private family. Married women were forced to assume more and more responsibility for breadwinning as their menfolk faced increasingly dire employment possibilities. Traditionally, northern black men had worked as laborers, cartmen, mariners, shoemakers, waiters, barbers, cooks, blacksmiths, tailors, chimney sweeps, and nightmen; but between 1840 and 1860, 4.3 million Irish and German immigrants to the United States began to make inroads into some of these jobs—especially those of waiters and barbers, rendering entire black communities more vulnerable than ever before. In 1848, Frederick Douglass took note of the legal liabilities that transcended region and oppressed black men and women, enslaved and free, north and south: "In the Northern states we are not slaves to individuals, not personal slaves, yet in many respects we are slaves of the community . . . It is more than a figure of speech to say that we are, as a people, chained together."[86]

Fugitives from slavery such as Frederick Douglass, William and Ellen Craft, and many others found a public voice by writing and by speaking in public against slavery; their firsthand accounts of life under bondage transfixed northern whites and in the process transformed the abolitionist movement. Harriet Jacobs escaped from bondage in North Carolina in 1842, when she was twenty-nine years old; abused by her master, she hid in her grand-mother's tiny attic for seven long years. In the North, she electrified readers of the *New York Tribune* with a serialized account of her dramatic journey, an account that was pub-lished in book form (under the pseudonym Linda Brent), in 1861. In 1851, Sojourner Truth, born Isabella Baumfree, a slave, in New York in 1757, addressed the Ohio Women's Rights Convention in Akron, and urged her listeners to consider the way that racial and gender ideologies oppressed black women:

> Well, children, where there is so much racket there must be something out of kilter. I think that 'twixt the Negroes of the South and the women at the North, all talking about rights, the white men will be in a fix pretty soon. But what's all this here talking about?
>
> That man over there says that women need to be helped into carriages, and lifted over ditches, and to have the best place everywhere. Nobody ever helps me into car-riages, or over mud-puddles, or gives me any best place! And ain't I a woman? Look at me! Look at my arm! I have ploughed and planted, and gathered into barns, and no man could head me! And ain't I a woman? I could work as much and eat as much as a man—when I could get it—and bear the lash as well! And ain't I a woman? I have borne five children, and seen most all sold off to slavery, and when I cried out with my mother's grief, none but Jesus heard me! And ain't I a woman?

Harriet Jacobs and Sojourner Truth found their voices, and gained wider audiences, in a time and place that relegated black women to the role of household drudge exclusively.[87]

In other ways too black women bridged the divide between North and South, slavery and freedom, by their defiant actions that challenged the very foundations of bondage. The fugitive Harriet Tubman put her life on the line by returning to her native Eastern Shore of Maryland at least a dozen times and bringing out of slavery up to seventy individuals, many of them extended kin. In the late 1850s, the abolitionist John Brown sought her good coun-sel as he planned an attack on a federal arsenal in Harpers Ferry, Virginia; by that time Tub-man was well known for her skills as a scout and her intimate knowledge of the eastern seaboard, from Virginia to Canada. As a group, northern black women helped organize the Free Produce movement, which urged northern consumers to refrain from buying prod-ucts, including cotton, produced by enslaved workers. Boston and New York were home to substantial numbers of southern runaways. Together with white activists, most notably An-gelina and Sarah Grimke, the daughters of a wealthy South Carolina planter (and the stepsiblings of some of their father's slaves), the fugitives highlighted the routine sexual abuse of enslaved women, and the routine separation of enslaved families, as the most out-rageous of slavery's many horrors.[88]

Ultimately these antislavery appeals, whether to reason or to sentiment, moved few white Americans. By 1860 slavery as an institution was well entrenched in the South, and vital to northern manufacturing interests. Enslaved workers represented fully one-third of the South's total population, and in six lower-South states, the percentage of slaves ranged from 44 percent of the population (in Florida and Georgia) to 57 percent in South Carolina. Because slaveholders valued the reproduction of the plantation workforce just as highly as increases in their annual crop (in fact, the two objectives were inseparable), it would be difficult to argue that racial ideologies superseded gender ideologies as an ordering principle for this peculiar society. Rather than attempt to determine which was more oppressive, we would do well to remember that the two systems shared a dense, common tangle of roots, and that together they yielded bitter fruit in the antebellum South. Black women bore witness to that bitterness in ways different from those of black men on the one hand and white women on the other.

In their devotion to family ties—a devotion that encompassed kin and ultimately the whole slave community—black women and men affirmed the value of group survival over the slaveholders' base financial and political considerations. Black family life, as the cornerstone of African American culture, combined an African heritage with American exigencies; and within the network of kin relations, black women and men sought to express their respect for one another, for the community on a single plantation or on neighboring plantations, even as they resisted white intrusions.

The work of black women helped to preserve that community. Janie Scott's admiration for her mother, who was "much of a woman," sustained her through the conflagration of civil war, for freedom demanded of black women the same kind of strength and resourcefulness they and their mothers had demonstrated under slavery. As workers, many freedwomen would still have to pick cotton and wash dishes for whites. Yet as wives, mothers, workers, church members, and leaders, they would help to define the priorities of a freedpeople—or rather, affirm the priorities they had developed under slavery—and thereby transform the southern society and economy, and all of American society, during the postbellum years.

ENSLAVED WOMEN
BECOMING FREEDWOMEN

The Civil War and Reconstruction

IN APRIL 1866, a white man named M. C. Fulton confronted a vexing problem that threatened the viability of his cotton plantation located not far from Augusta, Georgia. During what should have been one of the busiest times of the year—the planting season—the married freedwomen on Fulton's place refused to go into the fields. Instead, he charged in a letter to a federal agent, these women were "as nearly idle as it is possible for them to be, pretending to spin—knit or something that really amounts to nothing[,] for their husbands have to buy them clothing." Fulton hoped that he would get a sympathetic hearing from the agent, who represented the United States Bureau of Refugees, Freedmen, and Abandoned Lands, created by Congress to oversee the transition between slavery and freedom among southern black people. Fulton was both puzzled and alarmed by the freedwomen's withdrawal from field labor: "Now these women have always been used to working out & it would be far better for them to go to work for reasonable wages & their rations—both in regard to health & in furtherance of their family wellbeing." By staying at home and having their husbands support them, the planter observed, the women severely diminished his labor supply, and their absence from the fields "must affect to some extent the present crop." Fulton considered the wives of his male workers "bad examples to those at work . . . [and] often mischief makers," but he did not judge them in exclusively racialized terms, for, he claimed, "Poor white women . . . have to work—so should all poor people."[1]

It is entirely possible that the bureau agent to whom Fulton sent his letter responded in a way that pleased the planter, by coming to the plantation and giving Fulton's workers a stern lecture about the virtues of field labor for women and men alike. Many agents aimed to put into practice a view common among white Northerners, whether missionaries, Union military officials, Republican politicians, or transplanted migrants newly arrived in the South. These whites believed that, now that the Civil War had destroyed the institution of slavery, it was essential that black men and women return to the cotton, rice, and sugar fields. As "free" laborers, the former slaves should be bound not by the institution of bondage but by labor contracts negotiated annually with a landlord. According to this view, black women "worked" only when they labored under the watchful eye of a white person in a field, or in a kitchen, but not when they cared for their own families at home. Missing from this equation was the fact that black women's domestic duties—as caretakers of children and producers of clothing and foodstuffs—nourished and sustained the South's labor force; in addition, their household labor lessened a landlord's obligations to supply cash, furnishings, or credit for the goods and services that wives and mothers provided on a routine basis.

For the former slaves, the Civil War destroyed the institution of bondage but opened a new fight for dignity and full citizenship rights. The conflict claimed as many as 700,000 lives; 620,000 northern and southern soldiers died, as did thousands of enslaved laborers forced to toil on the Confederacy's defenses. The war, initially fought over the preservation of the federal union, gradually evolved into a struggle against slavery and for freedom— the right of all individuals for self-determination. Throughout this era of military and political upheaval, though, black women demonstrated that they would seek to put the interests of their families first. To the extent that they could, freedwomen took control of their own productive energies in ways that thwarted the intentions of planters, the policies of the Freedmen's Bureau, and the prejudices of white Northerners and Southerners in general. As Fulton fumed, the black wives and mothers stayed at home with their children, working at housekeeping and childcare rather than planting cotton. Yet even bureau agents feared that the "evil of female loaferism"—the preference among wives and mothers to labor on their own terms and to attend to their own households—threatened to subvert the South's free labor experiment. Like the Irish and French-Canadian immigrant women who toiled in New England textile mills to help support their families, freedwomen were considered by whites exempt from the middle-class feminine ideal of full-time domesticity. Still, the irony did not escape the notice of one Yankee journalist: Of a planter who had come south from the North, employing freedwomen in 1866, the journalist wrote disapprovingly, "An abolitionist making women work in the fields, like beasts of burden—or men!"[2]

For their part, southern planters could not reconcile themselves to the fact of emancipation; they believed that "free black labor" was a contradiction in terms, that blacks would never work of their own free will. An unpredictable labor situation therefore required any and all measures that would bind the freedpeople body and soul to the southern soil. Black women—at least some of whom had reportedly "retired from the fields" in the mid-1860s—represented a significant part of the region's potential workforce in a period when planters' fears about low agricultural productivity reached almost hysterical proportions. Ultimately, southern whites embraced an authoritarian labor system, alternately accommodating, cajoling, and brutalizing the people whom they had once claimed to care for and know so well. Thus by the end of the Civil War, it was clear that the victorious Yankees and the vanquished Confederates agreed on very little when it came to rebuilding the war-torn South; but one assumption they did share was that black wives and mothers should continue to toil under the supervision of whites.[3]

Freed blacks resisted both the northern work ethic and the southern system of neoslavery: "Those appear most thriving and happy who are at work for themselves," noted one perceptive observer. The full import of their preference for family-based systems of labor organization over gang labor becomes apparent when viewed in a national context. The industrial North was increasingly coming to rely on workers who had yielded to employers all power over their working conditions. In contrast, sharecropping husbands and wives retained a minimal amount of control over their own labor and that of their children on both a daily and seasonal basis. Furthermore, the sharecropping system enabled mothers to divide their time between field- and housework in a way that reflected a family's needs. The system also removed wives and daughters from the reach of lacivious white supervisors. Here then were tangible benefits of freedom that could not be reckoned in financial terms.[4]

As workers or potential workers, freedpeople assumed the roles of political actors in an era marked by clashes over land, labor, and political rights. Because the former slaves preferred to labor in kin groups rather than gangs, the black family of necessity became enmeshed in larger questions about justice on the southern countryside; indeed, the relations between (working) husbands and ("nonworking") wives, and between parents and school-age children became subjects of larger debates about southern economic recovery and the status of freedpeople in general. Therefore it is difficult to disentangle family life—and the choices of, and constraints upon, black women in particular—from partisan political contests that pit Republicans against Democrats in the postbellum South. Although black women did not gain the right to vote when their menfolk did in 1867, they nevertheless participated in the great political debates of the day in their roles as workers and as fully engaged members of freed communities.

Emancipation was not a gift bestowed upon passive slaves by Union soldiers or presidential proclamation; rather, it was a process by which black people ceased to labor for their masters and sought instead to provide directly for one another. Control over one's labor and one's family life represented a dual gauge by which freedpeople measured true freedom. Blacks sought to weld kin and work relations into a single unit of economic and social welfare so that women could be wives and mothers first and laundresses and cotton-pickers second. The experiences of black women during these years revealed both the strength of old imperatives and the significance of new ones; in this regard their story mirrors on a personal level the larger drama of the Civil War and Reconstruction.

IN PURSUIT OF FREEDOM

The institution of slavery disintegrated gradually. It cracked under the weight of Confederate preparations for war soon after cannons fired on Fort Sumter in April 1861, and it crumbled—in some parts of the South many years after the Confederate surrender—when the former slaves were finally free to decide whether to leave or remain on their master's plantation. The effects of military defense strategy on the lives of blacks varied according to time and place; before the war's end a combination of factors based on circumstance and personal initiative opened the way to freedom for many, but often slowly, and only by degrees. Throughout the war, many enslaved workers remained alert to the dangers and the opportunities posed by military conflict and social upheaval. For women, the welfare of their children was often the primary consideration in determining an appropriate course of action once they confronted, or themselves created, a moment ripe with possibilities.[5]

Three individual cases suggest the varying states of awareness and choice that could shape the decisions of enslaved women during this period of violence and uncertainty. In 1862 a seventy-year-old Georgia bondswoman engineered a dramatic escape for herself and her twenty-two children and grandchildren. The group floated forty miles down the Savannah River on a flatboat and finally found refuge on a federal vessel. In contrast, Hannah Davidson recalled many years later that she and the other slaves on a Kentucky plantation lived in such rural isolation—and under such tyranny—that they remained bound to a white man until the mid-1880s: "We didn't even know we were free," she said. Yet Rosaline Rogers, thirty-eight years old at the war's end and mother of fourteen children, kept her family together on her master's Tennessee plantation, even after she was free to leave: "I was given my choice of staying on the same plantation, working on shares, or taking my family away, letting them out [to work in return] for their food and clothes. I decided to stay on that way; I could have my children with me." But, she added, the arrangement was far from satisfactory, for her children "were not allowed to go to school, they were taught only to work."[6]

The logic of resistance proceeded apace on plantations all over the South as slaveholders became increasingly preoccupied with the Confederacy's declining military fortunes. On a Mississippi plantation, Dora Franks overheard her master and mistress discussing the horror of an impending Yankee victory. The very thought of it made the white woman "feel lak jumpin' in de well," but, Dora Franks declared, "from dat minute I started prayin' for freedom. All de res' of de women done de same." Enslaved workers did not have to keep apprised of rebel maneuvers on the battleground to take advantage of novel situations produced by an absent master, a greenhorn overseer, or a nervous mistress uncertain how to maintain the upper hand. Under these conditions, black women, men, and children slowed their work pace to a crawl. "Awkward," "inefficient," "lazy," "erratic," "ungovernable," and "slack" (according to exasperated whites), they left weeds in the cotton fields, burned the evening's supper to a crisp, and let the cows trample the corn.[7]

Eliza Andrews, daughter of a prominent Georgia judge and slaveholder, expressed disgust when, a few days before the Confederacy's surrender, Lizzie, the family cook, stated emphatically that she would not be willing to prepare a meal "fur Jesus Christ to-day," let alone for two of her mistress's special friends. Aunt Lizzie and other enslaved women seemed to be fully aware of the effect their "insolence" had on mistresses "who had not been taught to work and who thought it beneath their standing to soil their hands." Safely behind Union lines, a Tennessee refugee told of an apocryphal encounter between her mistress and General Ulysses S. Grant: "Den she went back to the general, an' begged an' cried, and hel' out her han's, and say, 'General dese han's never was in dough—I never made a cake o' bread in my life; please let me have my cook!'" On some plantations, the startlingly open recalcitrance of female slaves seemed to portend greater evils, as white parents and children whispered in hushed tones about faithful old mammies who might spy for the Yankees and cooks who could "burn us out" or "slip up and stick any of us in the back."[8]

Their chains loosened by the distractions of war, many enslaved men and women challenged the physical and emotional resolve of whites in authority. For the vast majority, however, the war itself only intensified their hardships. As the Confederacy directed more of its resources and manpower toward the defense effort, food supplies became scarce throughout the region. Black men and women registered the effects of war when they were forced to abandoned familiar routines and grow corn instead of cotton. Planters and local government officials, anxious in the midst of black (and even white) rebels on their own soil and uncertain about the future of their new nation, reacted brutally to isolated cases of real and imagined insubordination. The owner of a Georgia coastal plantation was so infuriated by the number of his slaves who had fled to Union lines that he took special precautions to hold on to his prized cook; he bound her feet in iron stocks so that "she had to drag herself around her kitchen all day, and at night she was locked into the corn-house." Refugees arrived in Union camps with fresh scars on their backs told of masters and mistresses unleashing their bitterness on "blobber-mouth niggers [who] done cause a war."[9]

During wartime the responsibility for the care of children, the ill, and the elderly devolved upon enslaved women to an even greater extent than had been the case during the antebellum period. The services of white physicians were diverted away from plantations; before the war they had tried to keep the enslaved labor force "sound," and now they must attend to wounded and dying soldiers on battlefields and in hospitals. Black women healers stepped into the breach, utilizing their own folk methods and medicines to minister to the ill in the quarters.[10]

Confederate military mobilization and the lure of Union lines wreaked havoc on the already fragile ties that held families together. Efforts to restrict slave mobility prevented husbands from visiting their "broad" wives on a regular basis and discouraged cross-plantation marriages in general. Confederate impressment policies primarily affected enslaved men, who were put to work on military construction projects and in army camps, factories, and hospitals. The practice of "refugeeing" highly valued workers to the interior or to another state also meant that the strongest, healthiest men were taken away from plantation wives and children. On a western North Carolina plantation, a Confederate mandate that planters help feed the troops placed almost unbearable demands on young, old, and female enslaved workers, now forced to fill the places of black men impressed by the army. The effects of both refugeeing and impressments transformed slave communities in southwest Georgia, with long-standing members forcibly transported to Savannah and newcomers crowding plantations. One former bondsman later recalled that, when he was thirteen years old, his wartime master "put so much work on me, I could not do it; chopping & hauling wood and lumber logs." Some husbands and fathers made a bold bid for freedom, in some cases returning to free loved ones and spirit them away to safety—or at least to Union territory. Many freedwomen struggled to provide for their dependents while facing new and harsh demands from whites. These challenges tested the limits of a newfound freedom for wives and mothers.[11]

At times in different parts of the South, the approaching Union army provided black workers with both an opportunity and an incentive to flee from their masters. Soon after the Union forces took control of the South Carolina Sea Islands, Elizabeth Botume, a newly arrived northern teacher, observed a refugee mother and her three children hurrying toward a government steamer: "A huge negress was seen striding along with her hominy pot, in which was a live chicken, poised on her head. One child was on her back with its arms tightly clasped around her neck, and its feet about her waist, and under each arm was a smaller child. Her apron was tucked up in front, evidently filled with articles of clothing. Her feet were bare, and in her mouth was a short clay pipe. A poor little yellow dog ran by her side, and a half-grown pig trotted on before." From other parts of the South came similar descriptions of women travelers balancing bundles on their heads and children on their backs. These miniature caravans exemplified the difficulties faced by single mothers who ran away and sought protection behind Union lines.[12]

To women like the Louisiana mother who brought her dead child ("shot by her pursuing master") into a Yankee army camp "to be buried, as she said, *free*," Union territory symbolized the end of an old life and the beginning of a new one. But it was an inauspicious beginning. Crowded together, often lacking food, shelter, and medicine, these human "contraband of war" lived a wretched existence. Moreover, in 1863 the refugee settlements—and virtually any areas under federal control—became targets for northern military officials seeking black male conscripts. Black men wanted to defend their families and fight for freedom, and almost a quarter of a million served the Union war effort in some formal capacity—half as soldiers, the rest as laborers, teamsters, craftsmen, and servants. More than 110,000 black men from the Confederate states alone—14 percent of the black male population aged eighteen to forty-five—fought with the Union army. However, the violent wrenching of draftees from their wives and children caused great resentment among the refugees, especially those in the Georgia and South Carolina low country in the spring of 1863. The women of one camp, wrote Elizabeth Botume, "were proud of volunteers, but a draft was like an ignominious seizure." The scene in another one "raided" by Yankee soldiers hardly resembled a haven for the oppressed; wives "were crying bitterly, some looked angry and revengeful, but there was more grief than anything else."[13]

Whether southern black men volunteered for or were pressed into Union military service, the well-being of their families remained a constant source of anxiety for them. Wives and children who remained behind in Confederate territory on their masters' plantation, and even some of those who belonged to owners sympathetic to the northern cause, bore the brunt of white men's anger as the peculiar "southern way of life" began to recede. In Kentucky, Frances Johnson, whose husband was a Union soldier, reported that in 1864 her master had told her, "All the 'niggers' did mighty wrong in joining the Army." One day the following spring, she recalled, "My master's son . . . whipped me severely on my refusing to do some work for him which I was not in a condition to perform. He beat me in the presence of his father who told him [the son] to 'buck me and give me a thousand' meaning thereby a thousand lashes." The next day this mother of three managed to flee with her children and find refuge with her sister in nearby Lexington. In another case a Missouri slave woman wrote to her soldier husband, "They are treating me worse and worse every day. Our child cries for you," but added, "do not fret too much for me for it wont be long before I will be free and then all we make will be ours." In a Union camp in Virginia, a Union officer observed that black soldiers remained aware of the abuse suffered by their wives still enslaved: "A large number of them have families still remaining in servitude, who are most shamefully and inhumanely treated by their masters in consequence of their husbands having enlisted in the union army." Accounts like these impelled black soldiers to demand that the federal government provide their loved ones with some form of protection.[14]

In an effort to stay together and escape the vengeance of southern whites, some families followed their menfolk to the front lines. However, soldiers' wives, denounced as prostitutes and "idle, lazy vagrants" by military officials, found that the army camps offered little in the way of refuge from callousness and abuse. The payment of soldiers' wages was a notoriously slow and unpredictable process, leaving mothers with responsibility for the full support of their children. The elaborate application procedures discouraged even qualified women from seeking aid from the Army Quartermaster Department. A few wives sought jobs as laundresses and cooks in and around the camps, but gainful employment was not easy to come by during such chaotic times. Women fugitives found work in Union hospitals, but as nurses they were rarely granted the status or wages—and later pensions—accorded white women doing similar kinds of work. Meanwhile, not only did many families lack basic creature comforts in the form of adequate clothing and shelter; they were at times deprived of what little they did have by Union officers who felt that the presence of black wives impaired the military efficiency of their husbands. At Camp Nelson, Kentucky, in late 1864, white soldiers leveled the makeshift shantytown erected by black women to house their children and left four hundred persons homeless in bitterly cold weather. Such was the treatment accorded the kin of "soldiers who were even then in the field fighting for that Government which was causing all this suffering to their people."[15]

Although many women had no choice but to seek food and safety from northern troops, often with deeply disappointing or even horrific results, others managed to attain relative freedom from white interference and remain on or near their old home sites. In areas where whites had fled and large numbers of black men had marched—or been marched off—with the Union army, women of all ages grew crops and cared for each other. For example, several hundred women from the Combahee River region of South Carolina made up a small colony unto themselves in a Sea Island settlement. They prided themselves on their special handicrafts sent to their men "wid Mon'gomery's boys in de regiment": gloves and stockings made from "coarse yarn spun in a tin basin and knitted on reed, cut in the swamps." Together with men and women from other areas, the "Combees" cultivated cotton and potato patches, gathered ground nuts, minded the children, and nursed the ill.[16]

Such demonstrations of self-sufficiency amounted to political statements of defiance and determination among black fugitives. Indeed, within the context of armed conflict, news of a group of black men and women peacefully tilling the soil could strike fear in the hearts of low-country planters; such was the case when black refugees and fugitives established a colony on St. Simons Island, off the coast of Georgia, in the summer of 1862. Union officials initially encouraged the effort, which they believed could serve to provision Union troops in the area; wrote Commander S. W. Godon (aboard the *Mohican* in St. Simons Sound) to his superior, Flag-Officer DuPont: "Such a colony, properly managed, would do much good." And indeed the colonists set about growing crops and marketing foodstuffs and their own services to seamen in the area. Noted DuPont of the "contrabands": they "work for us in many ways and are very useful, and we pay them ten dollars a month and a ration." A list of "tariff of prices" charged to customers reveals black people *qua* provisioners for the Union navy and entrepreneurs in their own right. The tariff also suggests the eagerness among former slaves to put a specific price on goods and services they had provided their masters free of cost, and under duress. Among the foodstuffs they sold were milk (four cents a quart), corn (five cents per dozen), terrapins (ten cents each), watermelons (ten to fifteen cents each), chicken eggs (twelve cents per dozen), turtle eggs (five cents per dozen), as well as okra, beans, whortleberries, cantaloupes, and squash. The St. Simons colonists also raised chickens, trapped rabbits, and caught shrimp and fish, all of which they sold to seamen. Black laundresses charged fifty cents per dozen articles of clothing ("when soap and starch furnished"). By midsummer the colony consisted of six hundred men, women, and children.[17]

At the same time, the significance of St. Simons went beyond the obvious mutual advantage to both parties, buyers and sellers of goods and services. The colonists chose a leader from among themselves, Charles O'Neal; he was later killed in a skirmish with rebels on the island. In their attempts to establish a self-sufficient settlement, the colonists also brought together family members separated during slavery and the war. A Union chaplain, the Reverend Mansfield French, solemnized long-standing relationships as legal marriages, and presided over baptism ceremonies that included not only nuclear families but also "children presented by relatives or strangers, the parents being sold." Susie Baker, a literate fourteen-year-old refugee from Savannah, started a school on the island: "I had about forty children to teach, besides a number of adults who came to me nights, all of them so eager to learn to read, to read above anything else." The Reverend French made periodic appearances in the school to lecture the pupils on "Boston and the North," among other subjects.[18]

Yet the colonists' industriousness did not always mesh with federal officials' notions of black people's labor. The former slaves desired to control their own productive energies; they resisted orders from white men, and they concentrated their efforts on subsistence activities and not on cultivating staple crops such as cotton. DuPont acknowledged the blacks' "great dislike to do the work they have been accustomed to—that seems to make their condition the same as before. They will sit up all night and fish and catch crabs and go and catch horses and wild cattle and cross to the mainland on sculls and go and get corn and so on"; but they sought to free themselves of the enforced pace of fieldwork. This impulse—

toward self-direction and away from slavery—foreshadowed the development of freedpeople's settlements throughout the South after the war.[19]

For women who had accumulated modest amounts of household goods and other forms of property before or during the war, their first encounter with Union troops was hardly reassuring. Toward the end of the conflict, the federal armies lived off the land and appropriated food, clothing, household goods, and mules and horses from black and white Southerners alike. Into Yankee saddlebags and stomachs went the fruits of black people's labor for themselves. Rebecca Smith, a free woman of color in Beaufort County, South Carolina, lost pots, pans, and bedding to Union troops. When Sherman swept through Georgia from Atlanta to Savannah in late 1864, he authorized his troops, and specially appointed "bummers," to raid homesteads of all kinds in search of the provisions needed to keep his army of 60,000 well fed with the stores of honey, lard, rice, and chickens accumulated by enslaved workers along his route. Among the objects of Sherman's rapacious bummers were the black women of Savannah who had profited from wartime demands for lodging and food. Together with her partner, Moses Stikes, Binah Butler cultivated a seven-acre garden in the city; they paid their respective masters a certain amount for the privilege. Together they "worked there two years raising all kinds of Garden *truck* for the market" and selling chickens. They also managed to stockpile fifty bushels of potatoes and 2,500 pounds of fodder and hay.[20]

The end of the war signaled the first chance for large numbers of blacks to abandon the slave quarters as a demonstration of liberty. Asked why she wanted to move off her master's South Carolina plantation, the former slave Patience responded in a manner that belied her name: "I must go, if I stay here I'll never know I'm free." An elderly black woman turned her back on the relative comfort of her mistress's home and chose to live in a small village of freed people near Greensboro, Georgia, so that she could, in her words, *"Joy my freedom!"* These and other freedwomen acted decisively to escape the confinement of the place where they had lived as enslaved laborers. In the process they deprived the white South of a large part of its black labor supply.[21]

Amid the dislocation of civil war, then, black women's priorities and obligations coalesced into a single purpose: to escape from the oppression of slavery while keeping their families intact. Variations on this theme recurred throughout the South, as individual women, in concert with their kin, composed their own hymns to emancipation more or less unfettered by the vicissitudes of war. Though the black family suffered a series of disruptions provoked by Confederates and Yankees alike, it emerged as a strong and vital institution once the conflict had ended. The destiny of freedwomen in the postbellum period would be inextricably linked to that of their freed families.

BLACK WOMEN AS "FREE LABORERS," 1865–1870

Soon after he assumed the position of assistant commissioner of the Louisiana Freedmen's Bureau in 1865, Thomas W. Conway stated his policy regarding families of southern black Union soldiers. The northern federal agent found distressing the reports that former slaveowners near Port Hudson had, "at their pleasure," turned freedwomen and children off plantations "and [kept] their pigs chickens and cooking utensils and [left] them on the levee a week in a starving condition." Still, he remained firmly convinced that the government should not extend aid to soldiers' dependents; Conway wanted the "colored Soldiers and their families . . . to be treated like and expected to take care of themselves as white Soldiers and their families in the north." Moreover, the commissioner observed, the bureau "could not compel the planters to retain those women if their husbands were not on the place, unless contracts had been made with them." He appreciated the sacrifices that black soldiers had made for the "Noble Republic," but with their wages from military service (no matter how meager or unpredictable), "and the amount which can be earned by an industrious woman," he saw no reason why their families could not "be maintained in at least a comfortable manner." The freed people needed only to demonstrate "a little economy and industry" and they would become self-supporting.[22]

Viewing emancipation through a prism of their own self-interest, whether defined in ideological or material terms, whites in general showed a profound lack of understanding about the values and priorities that animated black men and women during the era of the Civil War. When Mobile came under Union control, a white woman, Ann Quigley, scornfully noted a dramatic change in the demeanor of black workers: "The insolence of servants is intolerable & those who have been treated with the greatest kindness, are the most insolent & ungrateful. . . . They have become so worthless, so demoralized."[23]

During the first fearful months of freedom, black families searching for loved ones and those seeking refuge in the city came in for much bitter criticism from whites who claimed the former slaves were wandering around the countryside aimlessly, avoiding work and creating havoc. Gradually many freedpeople returned to the general area where they had been enslaved in an effort to provide for themselves, and to claim, if possible, the lands upon which their forebears had labored and died. The degree to which the antebellum elite remained in power varied throughout the South. Nevertheless, the failure of the federal government to institute a comprehensive land confiscation and redistribution program, combined with southern whites' systematic refusal to sell property or extend credit to the former slaves, meant that the majority of blacks would remain economically dependent upon the group of people (if not the individuals) whom they had served as slaves. The extent of black migration out of the South during this period was negligible—and understandable, considering the lack of job opportunities for blacks elsewhere in the country. Most freedpeople remained in the vicinity of their enslavement; the proximity of kin groupings helped to determine precisely where they would settle.

Many whites felt that blacks as a "race" would gradually die out as result of their inability to care for themselves and work independently of the slaveholder's whip. The eagerness with which blacks initially fled the plantations convinced these white men that only "Black Laws" limiting their freedom of movement would ensure a stable labor force. The Yankees' vision of a free labor market, in which individual blacks used their wits to strike a favorable bargain with a prospective employer, struck the former Confederates as a ludicrous idea and an impossible objective.[24]

When it came to reconstructing southern society, Northerners were not all of the same stripe. But Republicans, and those in positions of political authority generally, tended to equate freedom with the opportunity to reap the profits from one's own toil, regardless of whether one owned land or worked for wages on someone else's land. Yankees conceived of the contract labor system as an innovation that would ensure the production of cotton necessary for the New England textile industry, and protect blacks against unbridled exploitation at the hands of their former masters. If a person did not like the terms or treatment accorded by an employer, he or she should look for work elsewhere, thereby (it was assumed) encouraging die-hard rebels to conform to enlightened labor practices. In time, after a thrifty household had accumulated a little cash, it could buy its own land and become part of the independent yeomanry. To this end northern Republicans established the Freedmen's Bureau, which oversaw contract negotiations between the former slaves and their new masters.[25]

The contract system was premised on the assumption that freedpeople would embrace gainful employment out of economic necessity if for no other reason. Still, the presumed baneful effects of generations of enslavement on blacks' moral character led Bureau Commissioner Oliver O. Howard to express the pious hope that, initially, "wholesome compulsion" would lead to "larger independence" for the masses. "Compulsion" came in a variety of shapes and sizes. For the Yankee general stationed in Richmond and determined to get the families of black soldiers off federal rations, it amounted to "hiring out" unemployed women or creating jobs for them in the form of "a grand *general* washing establishment for the city, where clothing of any one will be washed gratis." He suggested that "a little hard work and confinement will soon induce them to find employment, and the ultra philanthropists will not be shocked." In another case, after just a few months in the Mississippi Valley, one northern planter concluded that "many negro women *require* whipping." Indeed, even many "ultra philanthropists," including the northern teachers commissioned to minister to the freed blacks, believed that hard manual labor under the supervision of whites would refresh the souls of individual black women and men even as it restored the postwar southern economy.[26]

The bureau's annual contract system proved ill-suited as a means for the former slaves to achieve true freedom. Workers were required to sign up for a year's stint on January 1, and to remain with the same employer until December 31. Yet the calendar year did not jibe with the growing season, with its busy weeks in the spring and late fall; at dispute then were the slack periods when black families wished to work on their own, while planters were demanding that they repair fences, clear brush, and perform other duties not directly related to crop cultivation. Contracts often stipulated that families were forbidden from keeping chickens or tending gardens, an effort to render the household completely dependent on the supplies extended on credit by the landlord. Northern officials assumed that workers would exercise their right to leave a place when the contract expired, failing to anticipate that many landlords kept their workers in debt from one year to another, forcing them at gunpoint to labor to pay off the debt. Even families that did leave a plantation at "reckoning time" found that other employers down the road instituted the same exploitative labor policies. The Northerners' idea that planters would compete for workers through fair and reasonable working conditions and wage practices found no favor, or practical application, among white landowners.

If few enslaved women ever had the luxury of choosing between different kinds of work, freedwomen with children found that economic necessity bred its own kind of slavery. Their only choice was to take whatever work was available—and that was not much. Despite the paternalistic rhetoric of the antebellum period, planters quickly adjusted to a postwar calculus based on postwar financial considerations. Gone were the professions of concern for all the black members of "our family," including nonproductive workers such as the very young and the very old. In their place were demands only for the able-bodied, forcing freed mothers to make agonizing choices. These dilemmas surfaced during the war, and continued well after it. In Mississippi, the enslaved domestic Elsy had to choose between living with her husband, who lacked the means to support her and their four children, and with her mistress. She decided to remain with the white woman and earn wages, prompting her husband to complain that "she waits on the [mistress] and none of the others do; that she behaves as if she was not free." For understandable reasons, women who had to support their children were more likely to remain on a plantation after the war compared to those women who could count on the support of their husbands or other family members.[27]

Field-hands and domestic servants who decided to stay on or return to their master's plantation needed the children's help to make ends meet; at times it seemed as if only seasoned cotton-pickers would be able to eat. In May 1866, "a worn, weary woman with 11 children, and another, with three," spent ten days in the forest near Columbus, Georgia, before entering the city to seek assistance. "We was driv off, Misses, kase wese no account with our childer," they told two sympathetic northern teachers. In like manner, a mother of five, evicted from a North Carolina farm by a white man who declared their "keep" would cost him more than they could earn, responded that "it seemed like it was mighty hard; she'd been made free, and it did appear as if thar must be something more comin'." Prized by antebellum planters as reproducers of the enslaved workforce, black women with children were now reviled as parasites, a drain on the resources of the postbellum plantation.[28]

Virtually all black women had to contend with the problem of finding and keeping a job and then depending upon white employers for payment. The largest single category of grievances initiated by black women under the Freedmen's Bureau "complaint" procedures concerned nonpayment of wages, indicating that many workers were routinely— and ruthlessly—defrauded of the small amounts they had earned and then "run off the place." (See Appendix A.) Few southern planters had reserves of cash on hand after the war, and so they "fulfilled" commitments to their employees by charging prices for supplies so exorbitant that workers were lucky if they ended the year even, rather than indebted to their employer. Presley George Sr., near Greensboro, North Carolina, made a convenient settlement with two of his field-hands, Puss and Polly, for their performance as free laborers during 1865. Here are their final accounts:

Due Presley George by Polly:

For 4¾ cuts wool @ 75¢/cut	$3.50
22 yds. cloth @ 50¢/yd.	11.00
5 yds. thread @ 50¢/yd.	2.50
Boarding one child (who didn't work) for 5 months	12.00
10 bushels corn @ $1.00/bushel	10.00
30 bushels corn @ $1.00/bushel	30.00
TOTAL	$69.00

Due Polly by Presley George:

For 3 months' work "by self" @ $4.00/month	$12.00
For 4 months' work by son Peter @ $8.00/month	32.00
For 4 months' work by son Burrell @ $4.00/month	16.00
For 4 months' work by daughter Siller @ $2.25/month	9.00
TOTAL	$69.00

Due Presley George by Puss:

For 6 yds. striped cloth @ 50¢/yd.	$3.00
1¾ cuts wool @ 75¢/cut	1.25
10 bushels corn @ $1.00/bushel	10.00
TOTAL	$14.25

Due Puss by Presley George:

For 4 months' work @ $3.50/month	$14.00[29]

Polly and Puss had signed contracts with Presley George under the bureau's wage labor agreement system, but that act of faith on their part hardly guaranteed them a living wage, or even any cash at all. The bureau recommended that cotton field-hands receive a monthly wage ($10 to $12 per month for adult men, $8 for women) and that employers refrain from using physical force as a means of discipline. However, thousands of freed blacks contracted for rations, clothing, and shelter only, especially during the period from 1865 to 1867. Employers retained unlimited authority in using various forms of punishment, physical and otherwise, and felt free to disregard the agreements at the first sign of recalcitrance on the part of their laborers. In these contracts, prohibitions against movement on and off the plantation were routine; blacks had to promise to "have no stragling about their houses and not to be strowling about at night," and they needed written permission to go into town or visit relatives nearby. The bureau tolerated and even in most cases approved these harsh and restrictive terms. As the teacher Laura Towne noted, "enforcement" of the contracts usually meant ensuring that "the blacks don't break a contract and [then] compelling them to submit cheerfully if the whites do."[30]

The bureau arranged for the resolution of contract disputes, and agents often made unilateral judgments when one party sued with a complaint; in other cases arbitration boards or military courts handed down decisions. Word traveled quickly among whites when officials particularly sympathetic to planters' interests opened their offices for business. For example, Agent Charles Rauschenberg, stationed in Cuthbert, Georgia, had little free time once he responded energetically to charges like the one Ivey White lodged against his field-hand Angeline Sealy: "Complains that she is lazy and does not pick more than 35 to 40 lbs. cotton per day." The verdict: "Charge sustained—receives a lecture on her duties and is told that if she does not average from 75–100 lbs. cotton per day that a deduction will be made from her wages." Most Northerners in positions of formal authority during the Reconstruction period detested southern planters as Confederate rebels but empathized with them as fledgling capitalists attempting to transition to a "free labor" contract system. Moreover, few Union officials were inclined to believe that freedwomen as a group should contribute anything less than their full muscle power to the rebuilding of the region's economic system.[31]

High rates of geographical mobility (as blacks moved about the southern countryside, in and out of towns, and to a lesser extent, to the southwestern part of the region) make it difficult to pinpoint with any precision the number of black women in specific kinds of jobs immediately after the war. Charlie Moses's mother moved the family from one Louisiana farm to another in search of work; "We jus' travelled all over from one place to another," he recalled. Freedwomen accepted any work they could find; in Columbia, South Carolina, they took the places of mules and turned screws to press cotton. The seasonal nature of agricultural labor meant that families often had to locate new sources of employment. When the cotton-picking season ended, for instance, Mingo White and his mother cut and hauled wood on an Alabama plantation. Many women had no choice but to continue working as field-hands cultivating staple crops for white landowners, their former masters.[32]

Other freedwomen relied on their cooking, gardening, dairying, and poultry-raising skills in an effort to make money as petty tradeswomen. In Aiken, South Carolina, a roving Yankee newspaper correspondent noted with approval that a black woman given fifty cents one day had appeared the next selling cakes and fresh fruit purchased with the money. Some women peddled berries, chickens, eggs, and vegetables along the road and in towns. During the difficult winter of 1865, a Charleston open-air market was "presided over" by "eyesnapping 'Aunties'" who sold their produce from small stalls.[33]

Others tried to turn their special talents into a secure means of making a living. Nevertheless, former slaves were too poor to pay much for the services of midwives and seamstresses, and whites at times did not pay at all. Most freedwomen had to piece together seasonal or part-time labor in any case. Even the small number of literate women who aspired to teaching, an estimated half of all teachers of the freedpeople in 1868, had to rely on the fortunes of local black communities, most of which were unable to support a school on a regular basis. Susie Baker King (married to a Civil War veteran) taught pupils in Savannah soon after the war; she and other independent instructors could hardly compete with a free school operated by a northern freedmen's aid society, the American Missionary Association (AMA). As a result, she was eventually forced from teaching into domestic service. A tiny number of teachers did qualify for aid from the Freedmen's Bureau or a private group like the AMA. In Georgia between 1865 and 1870, for example, perhaps seventy-five freedwomen received a modest salary for at least a few months from a northern source. However, New Englanders eager to help the cause of freedpeople's education preferred to commission white teachers from the northern and midwestern states.[34]

Although blacks remained largely dependent upon whites for employment and supplies, strikes and other forms of collective action among workers began to surface soon after the Yankee invasion of the South. During the busy harvest season in the fall of 1862, female field-hands on a Louisiana sugar plantation in Union-occupied territory engaged in a slowdown and then refused to work at all until the white landowner met their demand for wages. The men on the plantation also struck within a week. The planter, fearful that his entire crop would be lost if it were not cut and processed immediately, finally agreed to pay them. And in 1866, the "colored washerwomen" of Jackson, Mississippi, organized themselves and established a price code for their services. Though the strike in June of that year was unsuccessful, it suggested the potential inherent in group solidarity where black women predominated in an industry—in this case, laundry work.[35]

Slowly and grudgingly some whites began to learn a basic lesson of Reconstruction: Blacks' attitudes toward work depended on the extent to which they were free from white supervision. Edward S. Philbrick, a shrewd Yankee planter masquerading as a missionary on the South Carolina Sea Islands, marveled in March 1862 over the ability of former slaves to organize themselves and prepare hundreds of acres for planting cotton "without a white man near them." (Under the same conditions the Irish would not have shown as much initiative, he thought.) Frances Butler, daughter of the renowned actress and abolitionist Fanny Kemble but more similar in temperament to her slaveholding father, Pierce, returned to the family's Georgia estate in 1866. The young woman soon discovered that the elderly freedpeople were "far too old and infirm to work for me, but once let them get a bit of ground of their own given to them, and they become quite young and strong again." She had discovered that the aged Charity—"who represented herself as unable to move"— walked six miles almost every day to sell eggs (from her own chickens) on a neighboring plantation. And there were other women who derived newfound physical strength from self-reliance. A woman helping to "list" her family's small plot of land on James Island, South Carolina, startled a northern observer with her "vehement" declaration: "I can plough land same as a hoss. Wid dese hands I raise cotton dis year, buy two hosses!"[36]

In their desire for household self-determination, blacks defied bureau agents and northern and southern planters alike, challenging both the northern ethos of individualism and the southern imperative of staple crop agriculture. And ultimately the annual contract system failed to yield the benefits anticipated by either group of whites. Northerners underestimated the extent to which black people would be prevented from accumulating cash and acquiring property. On the other hand, Southerners had not counted on the leverage wielded by workers determined to pry concessions out of them in the form of days off and garden privileges, and to press their own advantage during times of labor shortages. Some of this leverage assumed the form of meaningful political power at the local and state levels;

for example, South Carolina rice workers (as members of the Republican Party) played a vital role in that state's political process until Reconstruction ended in 1877. In making certain decisions about how family labor was to be organized, black people not only broke with the past in defiance of the white South, they also rejected a future of materialistic individualism in opposition to the white, middle-class North.[37]

THE POLITICAL ECONOMY OF BLACK FAMILY AND COMMUNITY LIFE IN THE POSTWAR PERIOD

The Northerners' hope that black workers would be able to pursue their interests as individuals did not take into account the strong family ties that bound black households together. More specifically, although black women constituted a sizable proportion of the region's labor force, their obligations to their husbands and children and kin took priority over any form of personal self-seeking. For most black women, then, freedom had very little to do with individual opportunity or independence in the modern sense. Rather, freedom had meaning primarily in a family context. The institution of slavery had posed a constant threat to the stability of family relationships; after emancipation these relationships became solidified, though the sanctity of family life continued to come under pressure from the larger white society. Freedwomen derived emotional fulfillment and a newfound sense of pride from their roles as wives and mothers. Only at home could they exercise a measure of control over their own lives and those of their husbands and children and impose a semblance of order on the physical world.

At the same time, black women engaged in protopolitical activity when they withdrew from fieldwork, protested exploitation at the hands of employers, and lent their support to grassroots campaigns on behalf of landownership and civil rights. They remained deeply engaged in the momentous question of the day—the true meaning of freedom. That question resonated in the cotton and rice fields of the South, and in the kitchens of white women, no less than in the halls of Congress.

Though the black family emerged as a durable and vital institution after slavery, the strains of war took a tremendous toll on relations between husbands and wives, parents and children. For many households and individuals, the transition between bondage and freedom was a wrenching one, provoking disputes over property, over the custody of children, and over the reciprocal obligations of family members to one another. Some women took advantage of local Freedmen's Bureau courts to file grievances against abusive husbands or other kin whom they felt had wronged them. Not surprisingly, the dislocations of war in the form of migrations, forced and otherwise, and the reconstitution of families prompted marital difficulties not easily resolved. Some partners refrained from formalizing marital arrangements initiated under slavery, instead preserving informal bonds—but in the process rendering more problematic a whole host of contested issues related to social relationships and property ownership.[38]

Nevertheless, as soon as they were free, most blacks attempted to set their own work pace and conspired to protect one another from the white man's (and woman's) wrath.

Plantation managers charged that freedpeople, hired to work like slaves, were "loafering around" and "lummoxing about." More than one postwar overseer, his "patience worn plum out," railed against "grunting" blacks (those "pretending to be sick") and others who sauntered into the fields late in the day, left early to go fishing, or stayed home altogether; "damd sorry work" was the result. Modern economic historians confirm contemporary estimates that by the 1870s, the amount of black labor in the fields had dropped to one-quarter or one-third pre-emancipation levels.[39]

This fact does not mean that all black women throughout the South were refusing to work, however. We have seen that many single women, especially those with children, continued to toil for whites, in some cases on the same plantation for their former master or mistress. In addition, women in specific crop economies sought to adjust their own work patterns in response to current or historic grievances. For example, in the sugar parishes of Louisiana, black wives constituted a supplemental force and went out into the fields during the busiest seasons, in contrast to their husbands, who labored for wages on a full-time basis. In Mississippi freedwomen broke from their slave past of gang labor and remained alert to wage-earning opportunities that varied with the season of the year—as hoers or as pickers of cotton, or as laundresses. Near Columbus nearly every wife took in washing, receiving nine dollars each month in return, her boiling kettle a testament to her desire to earn money and at the same time care for her children at home. In low-country South Carolina, black women continued to plant and harvest rice, but they refused to do mudwork, the cold and disagreeable wintertime tasks. In response, planters had to hire Irish immigrant day laborers from Charleston and Savannah.[40]

Thus withdrawal of black females from full-time labor in the fields—a major theme in both contemporary and secondary accounts of Reconstruction—constituted a "radical change in the management of [white] households as well as plantations" and proved to be a source of "absolute torment" for former masters and mistresses (in the words of a South Carolina newspaper in 1871). The female field-hand who labored day in and day out, all year long under the ever-watchful eye of an overseer came to symbolize the old order.[41]

Employers made little effort to hide their contempt for freedwomen who "played the lady" and refused to join male workers in the fields. To apply the term "ladylike" to a black woman was apparently the height of sarcasm; by socially prescribed definition, black women could never become "ladies," though they might display pretensions in that direction. The term itself had predictable "racial" and class connotations. Well-to-do white ladies remained cloistered at home, fulfilling their marriage vows of motherhood and genteel domesticity. But black housewives appeared "most lazy"; in the words of disapproving whites, these women stayed "out of the fields, doing nothing," demanding that their husbands "support them in idleness." At the heart of the issue lay the whites' notion of productive labor; black women who eschewed work under the direct supervision of former masters did not really "work" at all, regardless of their family household responsibilities.[42]

In their haste to declare "free labor" a success, even Northerners and foreign visitors to the South ridiculed "lazy" freedwomen working within the confines of their own homes. Hypocritically—almost perversely—these whites questioned the "manhood" of husbands whom they charged were cowed by domineering female relatives. South Carolina Freedmen's Bureau agent John De Forest, for example, wrote that "myriads of women who once earned their own living now have aspirations to be like white ladies and, instead of using the hoe, pass the days in dawdling over their trivial housework, or gossiping among their neighbors." He disdained the "hopeless" look given him by men told "they must make their wives and daughters work." George Campbell, a Scotsman touring the South in 1878, declared, "I do not sympathize with negro ladies who make their husbands work while they enjoy the sweets of emancipation."[43]

Most southern and northern whites assumed that the freedpeople were engaged in a misguided attempt to imitate middle-class white norms as they applied to women's roles. In fact, however, the situation was a good deal more complicated. First, the reorganization of female labor resulted from choices made by *both* men and women. Second, it is inaccurate to speak of the total "removal" of women from the agricultural workforce. Many were no longer working full-time for a white overseer, but they continued to labor according to seasonal demands of the crop, and according to the needs and priorities established by their own families.

An Alabama planter suggested in 1868 that it was "a matter of pride with the men, to allow all exemption from labor to their wives." He told only part of the story. Accounts provided by disgruntled whites suggest that husbands did often take full responsibility for deciding which members of the family would work, and for whom: "Gilbert will stay on his old terms, but withdraws Fanny and puts Harry and Little Abram in her place and puts his son Gilbert out to a trade," reported Mary Jones, a Georgia plantation mistress, in January 1867. Before the war, her clergyman husband had exhorted his enslaved workers to marry and be faithful to their spouses; now the family responsibilities assumed by black husbands and fathers appeared to threaten the material well-being of white households. At the same time, there is good reason to suspect that wives willingly devoted more time to childcare and other domestic matters, rather than merely acquiescing in their husbands' demands. A married freedwoman, the mother of eleven children, reminded a northern journalist that she had had "to nus' my chil'n four times a day and pick two hundred pounds cotton besides" under slavery. She expressed at least relative satisfaction with her current situation: "I've a heap better time now'n I had when I was in bondage."[44]

The humiliations of slavery remained fresh in the minds of black women who continued to suffer physical abuse at the hands of white employers, and in the minds of their menfolk who witnessed or heard about such acts. It was not surprising then that freedmen attempted to protect their womenfolk from rape and other forms of assault; as individuals, some intervened directly, while others went to local Freedmen's Bureau agents with accounts of beatings inflicted on their wives, sisters, and daughters. Bureau records include the case of a Tennessee planter who "made several base attempts" upon the daughter of the freedman Sam Neal (his entire family had been hired by the white man for the 1865 season). When Neal protested the situation, he was deprived of his wages, threatened with death, and then beaten badly by the white man and an accomplice. As a group, men sought to minimize chances for white male–black female contact by removing their female kin from work environments supervised closely by whites.[45]

At first, cotton growers persisted in their belief that gangs afforded the most efficient means of labor organization because they had been used with relative success under slavery and facilitated centralization of control. Overseers had only to continue to force blacks to work steadily. However, Charles P. Ware, a Yankee cotton agent with Philbrick on the Sea Islands, noted as early as 1862: "One thing the people are universally opposed to. They all swear that they will not work in a gang, i.e., all working the whole, and all sharing alike." Freed men and women preferred to organize themselves into kin groups, as evidenced by the "squad" system, an intermediary phase between gang labor and family sharecropping. A postwar observer defined the squad as "a strong family group, who can attach other labour, and bring odd hands to work at proper seasons"; this structure represented "a choice, if not always attainable, nucleus of a 'squad.'" The squad usually numbered less than a dozen people (seven was average), and performed its tasks under the direction of one of its own members. In this way kinship patterns established under slavery coalesced into work relationships after the war. Still, blacks resented an arrangement under which they continued to live together in old slave quarters grouped near the landowner's house and lacked complete control over the work they performed in the field. And black women played a pivotal role in the emergence of families and households as units of economic production after the war.[46]

In the late 1860s this tug of economic and psychological warfare between planters determined to grow more cotton and blacks determined to resist the old slave ways culminated in what historians have called a "compromise"—the sharecropping system. It met the minimal demands of each party—a relatively reliable source of labor for white landowners, and, for freedpeople (more specifically, for families), a measure of independence in terms of workplace decision making. Sharecroppers moved out of the old cabins and into small houses scattered about the plantation. Fathers and husbands renegotiated contracts around the end of each calendar year; families not in debt to their employers for equipment and fertilizer often seized the opportunity to move in search of a better situation. By 1870 the "fifty-fifty" share arrangement under which planters parceled out to tenants small plots of land and provided rations and supplies in return for one-half the crop predominated throughout the Cotton South.[47]

The cotton sharecropping system helped to reshape southern class and gender relations even as it preserved a backward agricultural economy. The linking of personal financial credit to crop liens and the rise of debt peonage enforced by criminal statutes guaranteed a large, relatively immobile labor force at the expense of economic and social justice. In increasing numbers, poor whites would come under the same financial constraints that ensnared black people. Before the war, white women of modest means had helped sustain self-sufficient households by keeping gardens, producing cloth, and engaging in other tasks similar to those of the colonial housewife. After 1865, many of these households had to rely on loans from creditors who insisted on crops of cotton as a "lien" on the debt. Poor harvests bankrupted these small farmers. With the descent of these previously independent households into landlessness and tenancy, women were drawn into the cotton fields to pursue single-mindedly the largest crop their family could produce.[48]

Although data from 1870 presents only a static profile of black rural households in the Cotton South, it is possible to make some generalizations (based on additional forms of evidence) about the status of freedwomen five years after the war. The vast majority (91 percent) lived in rural areas. Illiterate and very poor (even compared to their poor white neighbors), they nonetheless shared the mixed joys of work and family life with their husbands, children, and nearby kin. Fertility rates declined very slowly from 1830 to 1880; the average mother in 1870 had six or seven children. The lives of these women were severely circumscribed, as were those of other family members. Most of the children never had an opportunity to attend school—or not with any regularity—and began to work in the fields or in the home of a white employer around the age of ten or twelve. Young women found it possible to leave their parents' home earlier than did the men they married. As a group, black women were distinguished from their white neighbors primarily by their extreme poverty and by the greater reliance of their families on the work they did outside the realm of traditional domestic responsibilities. (See Appendix B.)[49]

Within the limited public arena open to blacks, the husband represented the entire family, a cultural preference reinforced by demographic and economic factors. In 1870, 80 percent of black households in the Cotton Belt included a male head and his wife, a proportion identical to that in the neighboring white population. (Future commentators who posited that female-headed households revealed an unbroken line between slavery and the twentieth century were mistaken.) In addition, most of the husbands were older than their wives—in more than half the cases, four years older; in one out of five cases, at least ten years older. Thus these men exercised authority by virtue of their age as well as their gender.

Landowners, merchants, and Freedmen's Bureau agents acknowledged the role of the black husband as the head of his family at the same time they encouraged his wife to work outside the home. He took "more or less land according to the number of his family" and placed "his X mark" on a labor agreement with a landowner. Just as slaveholders had dealt opportunistically with the slave family—encouraging or ignoring it according to their own perceived interests—so postbellum planters seemed to have had little difficulty adjusting to the fact that freedmen's families were structured "traditionally" with the husband serving as the major source of authority. Patrick Broggan, an employer in Greenville, Alabama, agreed to supply food and other provisions for wives and children—"those who do not work on the farm"—"at the expense of their husbands and Fathers," men who promised "to work from Monday morning until Saturday night, faithfully and lose no time."[50]

Freedmen's Bureau's guidelines mandated that black women and men receive unequal compensation based on their gender rather than their productive abilities or efficiency. Agents also at times doled out less land to families with female (as opposed to male) household heads. Moreover, the bureau tried to hold men responsible for their wives' unwillingness to labor according to a contractual agreement. For example, the Cuthbert, Georgia, bureau official made one black man promise "to work faithfully and keep his wife in subjection" after the woman refused to work and "damned the Bureau" saying that "all the Bureaus out [there] can't make her work." Left unstated in these contracts was the assumption that black women's domestic labors—tending gardens and keeping chickens for example—

provided substantial support for families and thereby lessened landlords' need to provide much in the way of cash compensation for a year's labor.[51]

A sharecropper usually purchased the bulk of the family's supplies either in town or from a rural local merchant, and arranged to borrow or lease any stock animals that might be needed in plowing. He received direct payment in return for the labor of a son or daughter who had been "hired out." (A single mother who operated a farm might have delegated these responsibilities to her oldest son or another male kin relation, or tried to assume responsibility for them herself.) Finally, complaints and criminal charges lodged by black men against whites often expressed the grievances of an entire household.

Thus the gendered division of labor that had existed within the black family under slavery became more sharply focused after emancipation. Wives and mothers and husbands and fathers perceived domestic duties to be a woman's major obligation, in contrast to the slave master's view that a woman was first and foremost a field- or houseworker and only incidentally the member of a family. Now women also worked in the fields when their labor was needed as gauged by husbands and wives. At planting and especially harvest time, they joined other family members outside. During the late summer and early fall, some would hire out to white planters in the vicinity to pick cotton for a daily wage. Seasonal fluctuations in labor patterns extended to men as well. In areas where husbands could find additional work during the year—on rice plantations or in phosphate mines or sugar mills, for example—they left their "women and children to hoe and look after the crops." Yet in general, women's agricultural labor partook of a more seasonal character than that of their husbands.[52]

The fact that black families depended heavily upon the fieldwork of women and children is reflected in the great disparity between the proportion of working wives in Cotton Belt white and black households; in 1870 more than four out of ten black married women listed jobs, almost all as field laborers. By contrast, fully 98.4 percent of white wives told the census taker they were "keeping house" and had no gainful occupation. Moreover, about one-quarter (24.3 percent) of black households, in contrast to 13.8 percent of the white, included at least one working child under sixteen years of age. Rates of black female and child labor are probably quite low, since census takers were inconsistent in specifying occupations for members of sharecropping families. In any case, statistics indicate that freedmen's families occupied the lowest rung of the southern economic ladder; almost three-fourths of all black household heads (compared to 10 percent of their white counterparts) worked as unskilled agricultural laborers. By the mid-1870s no more than 4 to 8 percent of all freed families in the South owned their own farms.[53]

The rural paterfamilias tradition exemplified by the structure of black family relationships after the Civil War did not challenge the value and competence of freedwomen as field-workers. Rather, a distinct set of priorities determined how wives and mothers used their time in terms of housework, field labor, and tasks that produced supplements to the family income. Thus it is difficult to separate a freedwoman's "work" from her family-based obligations; productive labor had no meaning outside the family context. These aspects of a woman's life blended together in the seamless fabric of rural life.

Slavery, Civil War, Reconstruction

As enslaved workers and as freedwomen, black wives and mothers labored for white masters and mistresses even as they sought to provide for the everyday needs of their own families. Most enslaved women toiled in the fields for a great part of their lives (1). They formed an integral part of the labor force within the cotton economy that dominated the South's staple-crop system of agriculture throughout the nineteenth and early twentieth centuries (2). During the Civil War, the advance of the Union army left intact the broad outlines of black women's work. Some worked as servants (3) or laundresses for soldiers in military camps (4), where patterns of enforced deference to white men resembled those on antebellum plantations. For families who sought refuge behind Union lines, life remained hard and uncertain. With slavery abolished and the last cannon silenced, an enduring image of black womanhood remained etched in the minds of white southerners—that of a servant who responded to the daily demands of white people of all ages (5). The postbellum sharecropping economy was characterized by high rates of residential mobility within a circumscribed area, as families sought out a new landlord, and a better contractual arrangement, after the annual "reckoning" at the end of December (6).

1. Enslaved man and woman plowing rice in the soft soil of the Georgia low country. Photo by O. Pierre Havens. Schomburg Center for Research in Black Culture, New York Public Library.

2. Enslaved workers of all ages picking cotton. Schomburg Center for Research in Black Culture, New York Public Library.

3. Union General Fitz John Porter and his staff of officers, with servant. Headquarters of the Fifth Army Corps, Army of the Potomac, Harrison's Landing, Virginia (1862). Photo by Mathew Brady. National Archives.

4. "Contraband of war" at Union army camp, Yorktown, Virginia (1862). Library of Congress.

5. Enslaved nurse with white baby (c. 1845). Massachusetts Historical Society.

6. A sharecropper on the move. National Archives.

Since husbands and wives had different sets of duties, they needed each other to form a complete economic unit. As one Georgia black man explained to George Campbell in the late 1870s, "The able-bodied men cultivate, the women raise chickens and take in washing; and one way and another they manage to get along." When both partners were engaged in the same kind of work, it was usually the wife who had stepped over into her husband's "sphere." For instance, Fanny Hodges and her husband wed the year after they were freed. She remembers, "We had to work mighty hard. Sometimes I plowed in de fiel' all day; sometimes I washed an' den I cooked." Cotton growing was labor-intensive in a way that gardening and housework were not, and a family's ability to obtain financial credit from one year to the next depended upon the size of past harvests and the promise of future ones. Consequently the crop sometimes took precedence over other chores in terms of the allocation of a woman's energies.[54]

Age was also a crucial determinant of the division of labor in sharecropping families. Participation in household affairs could be exhilarating for a child aware of her own strength and value as a field-worker during these years of turmoil. Betty Powers was only eight years old in 1865, but she long remembered days of feverish activity for the whole family after her father bought a small piece of land in Texas: "De land ain't clear, so we 'uns all pitches in and clears it and builds de cabin. Was we 'uns proud? There 'twas, our place to do as we pleases, after bein' slaves. Dat sho' am de good feelin'. We works like beavers puttin' de crop in." Sylvia Watkins recalled that her father gathered all his children together after the war. She was twenty years old at the time and appreciated the special significance of a family able to work together: "We wuked in de fiel' wid mah daddy, en I know how ter do eberting dere ez to do in a fiel' 'cept plow."[55]

At least some children resented the restrictions imposed by their father who "raised crops en made us wuk in de fiel." The interests of the family superseded individual desires. Fathers had the last word in deciding which children went to the fields, when, and for how long. As a result some black women looked back on their years spent at home as a time of personal opportunities missed or delayed. The Federal Writers Project Slave Narrative Collection contains examples of fathers who prevented daughters from putting their own wishes before the family's welfare during the postbellum period. Ann Matthews told a federal interviewer: "I didn't go ter schul, mah daddy wouldin' let me. Said he needed me in de fiel wors den I needed schul." Here were two competing "needs," and the family came first.[56]

The status of black women after the war cannot be separated from their roles as wives and mothers within a wider network of kinship. Like poor people in general, blacks in the rural South relied upon kin and community in ways that defied the liberal ethos of unfettered individualism. Local communities shaped people's everyday lives. Indeed, more than one-third of all black households in the Cotton Belt lived in the immediate vicinity of people with the identical (paternal) surname, providing a rather crude—and conservative—index of local kinship clusters. As the persons responsible for child nurture and social welfare, freedwomen cared not only for members of their nuclear families, but also for dependent relatives and others in need. This post-emancipation cooperative impulse was a legacy of a collective ethos developed under slavery, but also a characteristic of all kinds of impoverished rural communities.[57]

The former slaves' attempts to provide for one another's needs appear to have been a logical and humane response to widespread hardship during the 1860s and 1870s. Nevertheless, whites spared from physical suffering, including southern elites and representatives of the northern professional class, often expressed misgivings about this form of benevolence. They believed that any able-bodied black person deserved a "living" only to the extent that he or she contributed to the southern commercial economy. Blacks should reap according to the cottonseed they sowed, the rice they planted, the sugar cane they harvested. Soon after she returned to her family's Sea Island estate in 1866, Frances Butler thought there was nothing else "to become of the negroes who cannot work except to die." In this way she masked her grief over the death of slavery with professed concern for ill, young, and elderly freedpeople. But within a few months she declared with evident irritation, "It is a well-known fact that you can't starve a negro." Noting that about a dozen people on Butler's Island did not work in the cotton fields and so received no clothes or food supplies, the white woman admitted that she saw "no difference whatever in their condition and those who get twelve dollars a month and full rations." Somehow the field-workers and non-workers alike managed to take care of themselves and one another by growing vegetables, catching fish, and trapping game. Consequently they relied less on wages paid by their employer. The threat of starvation proved to be a poor taskmaster in compelling these freedpeople to toil for Frances Butler.[58]

Too many blacks, according to bureau agent John De Forest, felt obliged to look after "a horde of lazy relatives" and neighbors, thus losing a precious opportunity to get ahead on their own. This tendency posed a serious threat to the South's new economic order, founded as it was, in De Forest's view, on individual effort and ambition. He pointed to the case of Aunt Judy, a black laundress who barely eked out a living for herself and her small children. Yet she had "benevolently taken in, and was nursing, a sick woman of her own race . . . The thoughtless charity of this penniless Negress in receiving another poverty-stricken creature under her roof was characteristic of the freedmen. However selfish, and even dishonest, they might be, they were extravagant in giving." By calling the woman's willingness to share a "thoughtless" act, De Forest implied that a "rational" economic being would labor only to enhance her own material welfare.[59]

The collective self-consciousness demonstrated by black women and men within their own kin networks found formal, explicit expression in the political arena during Reconstruction. Blacks immediately demanded full citizenship rights with the end of slavery. After enfranchisement in 1867, freedmen actively participated in postwar Republican politics, and political leaders came to constitute a new and influential class within black communities, though rivalries among members of this group could at times be intense. Throughout the South, class relationships that had prevailed before the war now shifted, opening up possibilities of cooperation between the former slaves and non-elite whites. The two groups met at a historical point characterized by landlessness and economic dependence, but they were on two different trajectories—the freedpeople on their way up (no matter how gradually) from slavery, the poor whites on their way down from self-sufficiency. Nevertheless, the vitality of the political process, tainted though it was by virulent and violent racial ideologies, provided black men with a public forum, one that their womenfolk also embraced, albeit in relatively indirect ways.[60]

Black men predominated in this arena because, like other groups in nineteenth-century America, they believed that males alone were responsible for and capable of the serious business of politicking. This notion was reinforced by laws that barred female suffrage. However, black husbands and fathers, unlike their white counterparts, perceived the preservation and physical welfare of their families (including protection from terrorists) to be distinct political issues, along with obvious measures like land reform and debt relief. In partisan political activity, freedmen extended their role as family protector outside the boundaries of the household. Black women did not serve as formal delegates to the many political conventions held during this period—the local and state gatherings during which men formulated and articulated their vision of a just postwar society. At the same time, they often attended these gatherings and made known their strong convictions about specific issues such as land, labor, and education. In instances of labor struggle, for example when whites cut the wages of seasonal laborers, black women were the chief victims and reacted accordingly, lending their voices and their defiant demeanor to mass meetings. Indeed, both verbal and visual accounts of postwar partisan and labor politics reveal the active participation of black women in wide-ranging discussions about labor, land, and civil rights. The artist who drew a picture of a July 1868 political meeting (published in *Harper's Weekly*) showed a group of women listening intently to a male speaker. Still, the sight of black wives patiently tilling the soil while their husbands attended political conventions, at times for days on end, convinced at least one white teacher that freedwomen deserved to participate more actively and directly in the community's public life. Elizabeth Botume wrote in 1869:

> We could not help wishing that since so much of the work was done by the colored women,—raising the provisions for their families, besides making and selling their own cotton, they might also hold some of the offices held by the men. I am confident they would despatch [*sic*] business if allowed to go to the polls; instead of listening and hanging around all day, discussing matters of which they knew so little, they would exclaim,—
>
> "Let me vote and go; I've got work to do."

In praising black women and their potential for political leadership, Botume denigrated black men. Like so many Northerners, she could hardly express positive sentiments toward one gender without belittling the other.[61]

It is true that freedmen monopolized formal positions of power within their own communities during Reconstruction; approximately six hundred served in elected positions throughout the South, thousands voted, and many lobbied and petitioned, participating in the full realm of the partisan-political process. But that did not necessarily mean that women quietly deferred to them in all matters outside the home. For example, in some rural areas two sources of religious authority—one dominated by men, the other by women—coexisted uneasily. In these cases formal role designations only partially reflected the "influence" wielded by individuals outside their own households. In the process of institutionalizing clandestine religious practices formed during slavery and separating them from white congregations, freedpeople reserved church leadership positions for men. In other ways, individual congregations fashioned a distinctly inferior role for women; some even turned women out of the sanctuary "before the men began to talk" about matters of church policy. On the Sea Islands, whites reported the public censure of freedwomen who had committed marital transgressions by showing a lack of proper respect for their husbands' authority. The biblical injunction "Wives submit yourselves to your husbands" provided preachers with a succinct justification for church-based decisions that seemed arbitrary or unfair to the women involved.[62]

These examples must be contrasted with equally dramatic cases of women who exercised considerable influence over their neighbors' spiritual lives but outside of formal religious bodies and, indeed, of Protestant denominationalism altogether. Elderly women in the long line of African and Afro-American conjurers and herb doctors continued to wield considerable influence among persons of both genders. On the Georgia Sea Islands, African-born Maum Katie was "a great 'spiritual mother,' a fortune-teller, or rather prophetess, and a woman of tremendous influence over her children," as were other women whose pronouncements and incantations were believed to be divinely inspired. Rural communities had two (in all probability competing) sources of spiritual and secular guidance—one a male and formal, the other female and informal—and this pattern magnified the gender-role differentiation within individual households.[63]

Rejecting the forced pace of the slave regimen and embracing a family-based system of labor organization, freedpeople exhibited a preference for work patterns typical of a "traditional" rural society in which religious, regional, and kinship loyalties are the dominant values, as opposed to personal ambition and self-seeking. Indeed, very soon after emancipation emerged black households—set within larger networks of kin and community—that closely conformed to the "premodern" family model. In this case the terms traditional and premodern are misleading, however, because the sharecropping family that lived and worked together actually represented an adaptation, or a response, to postwar conditions rather than a clinging to old ways. This development, initiated so boldly by blacks, was particularly significant because it contrasted sharply with trends characteristic of late-nineteenth-century northern society, in which making a living was increasingly carried on by individuals for cash wages, apart from family life.[64]

NEW DRESSES, DEFIANT WORDS AND ACTIONS, AND THEIR PRICE

In the fall of 1865 a Freedmen's Bureau officer stationed in Wilmington, North Carolina, remarked to a northern journalist that "the wearing of black veils by the young negro women had given great offense to the young white women," who consequently gave up this form of apparel altogether. In recounting the story, Sidney Andrews asked his readers a rhetorical question: "Does this matter of veils and parasols and handkerchiefs seem a small one?" and then he proceeded to answer it himself: "It is one of serious import to the bitter, spiteful women whose passionate hearts nursed the Rebellion." Andrews shared with other Yankee travelers in the South the opinion that white women stubbornly remained Confederates at heart long after their husbands had admitted military defeat. More important, his comments suggest the larger social significance of clothing in an era when social relations were at least temporarily in a state of flux.[65]

Rossa Cooley, a New England white woman who taught on the Sea Islands in the early twentieth century, offered a most perceptive statement on the role of women's clothes during the transition from slavery to freedom:

> Slavery to our Islanders meant field work, with no opportunity for the women and girls to dress as they chose and when they chose. Field workers were given their clothes as they were given their rations, only the clothes were given usually as a part of the Christmas celebration, "two clothes a year," explained one of them as she remembered the old days. With the hunger for books very naturally came the hunger for clothes, pretty clothes, and more of them! And so with school and freedom best clothes came out and ragged clothes were kept for the fields. Work and old "raggedy" clothes were . . . closely associated in the minds of the large group of middle-aged Island folk.

Even for the women who never attended school, the old forms of dress—plain, drab, and heavy, serving only a practical and not an expressive function—were scorned in favor of more colorful, elaborate garments.[66]

If clothes served to announce a freedwoman's awareness of her new status, they also revealed the change in male-female relationships from slave unions to legal marriages. Black husbands took pride in buying fashionable dresses and many-colored ribbons, pretty hats, and delicate parasols for their womenfolk. When a freedman walked alongside his well-dressed wife, both partners dramatized the legitimacy of their relationship and his role as family provider. A white landowner in Louisiana reproached one of his tenants for spending all the proceeds of his cotton crop on clothing, "the greatest lot of trash you ever saw," but the black man assured his employer that "he and his wife and children were satisfied and happy," and added, "What's the use of living if a man can't have the good of his labor?"[67]

White city dwellers in particular often associated "insolent" behavior with modes of freedwomen's dress that defied the traditional code of black subordination. In his description of a Charleston street scene in the mid-1860s—"so unlike anything we could imagine [before the war]"—Henry W. Ravenel implied that there was more than a casual connection between the two: "Negroes shoving white persons off the walk—Negro women drest in the most outré style, all with veils and parasols for which they have an especial fancy—riding on horseback with negro soldiers and in carriages." The abandonment of deference and old clothes, plus the presence of proud black soldiers in uniform, signaled an imminent struggle over "social equality," according to apprehensive whites. Another South Carolinian stated the crux of the matter: "The airs which the negroes assume often interfere with their efficiency as laborers."[68]

Freedwomen throughout the South apparently adopted a pugnacious personal style that complemented their "disrespectful" forms of dress. In their descriptions of southern society during the fifteen years after the war, northern and foreign observers conveyed the distinct impression that black women were particularly outspoken and aggressive (by implication relative to black men and white women) in their willingness to confront white authority figures, "Freedmen's Bureau officers not excluded," noted one shocked Georgia agent. In December 1868, in the Ogeechee rice district near Savannah, freedpeople staged an uprising against exploitative planters, raiding the homes of whites and spiriting away large amounts of rice. Sent to investigate and quell disorder, a posse consisting of one of the planters and a local sheriff and his deputies arrived at the scene to find a group of black men armed with muskets, axes, and clubs. Their womenfolk, "with sticks and hatchets in their hands," threatened the white men. Recalled the planter, the women were "all jabbering together like a pack of magpies. They were striking the ground with sticks, flourishing them in the air, and other things of that kind." The sheriff refused to speak to the women, insisting on negotiating with the men instead. The incident culminated in the arrest and conviction of several of the men.[69]

Two possible explanations helped to account for this recurrent theme in contemporary sources. First, large numbers of freedwomen might in fact have found a release for their anger by publicly denouncing their white tormentors, taking their grievances to a local bureau agent, or goading into action other blacks more reticent or fatalistic than themselves. It is also possible that northern and southern white journalists, officials, travelers, and planters were intrigued by exceptionally strong-willed freedwomen and so tended to highlight individual cases and exaggerate their importance. Defenders of the notion of early Victorian (white) womanhood could not help but be struck by black women who openly challenged conventional standards of female submissiveness. Freedwomen were described as "growling," "impertinent," "impudent," "vulgar" persons who "spoke up bold as brass" and, with their "loud and boisterous talking," demanded fair treatment for "we people [left] way back." In the process of ridiculing these women, Northerners often indirectly revealed their ambivalent attitudes toward black men. Apparently an aggressive woman existed outside the realm of "natural" male-female relationships, with her own truculence counterbalanced by the weakness of her husband, brother, or father; but ironically in such cases, male relatives were often perceived to be much more "reasonable" (that is, prone to accept the white man's point of view) than their vehement womenfolk.[70]

For example, John De Forest later recounted the respective reactions of an elderly couple who had used up in supplies any profit they might have earned from a full year's labor. The man remained "puzzled, incredulous, stubborn," and insisted there must be some mistake. His wife was not about to accept the situation so politely: "trembling with indignant suspicion, [she] looked on grimly or broke out in fits of passion. . . . 'Don' you give down to it, Peter,' she exhorted. 'It ain't no how ris'ible that we should 'a' worked all the year and git nothin' to go upon.'" De Forest, who elsewhere complained of black "female loaferism" prevalent in the area, showed a curious lack of sympathy for this hardworking woman. In other cases, Yankee planters, professed abolitionists, responded to the demands put forth by delegations of female field-hands with contempt for their brashness.[71]

In the months and years immediately after the war, black women embraced their new roles as citizens. Domestic servants and laundresses waited patiently in line to open accounts in the new Freedman's Savings and Trust Bank, created by Congress in 1866. Susie Baker King's grandmother Dolly Reed, who established a successful trading business in and around Savannah, eventually deposited $3,000 in the bank, the fruits of, in the words of her granddaughter, "her hard labor and self-denial before the war," and her faith in the future. When the bank failed in 1874, the result of poor investments, Reed remarked, "I will leave it all in God's hand. If the Yankees did take all our money, they freed my race; God will take care of us."[72]

In other arenas too black women availed themselves of the services and benefits that were due them from the federal government, making claims not as dependents but as citizens entitled to certain rights and privileges. They resisted mightily, although not always successfully, the efforts of whites to "apprentice" black children and reduce them to slavery. We have seen that in some instances they took their grievances in the realm of social and labor relations to local Freedmen's Bureau agents for redress or negotiation. And while the bureau was in operation, from 1865 to 1868, women pressed for bureau-sponsored schools for their children, for rations for their families, and for protection from abusive landlords. Eventually, black nurses for the Union army and widows of Union soldiers would attempt to exercise their rights in applying for the pensions to which they were entitled. Yet these efforts were not always successful, compared with those of their white counterparts. For example, while 84 percent of white widows received pensions, the figure for their black counterparts was only 61 percent. Many black women were too poor to travel long distances to cities to fill out the requisite documents; lacking identification papers, they could neither meet official requirements nor persevere in the face of long delays imposed by indifferent clerks and pension officials.[73]

As a group and as individuals, freedwomen paid dearly for their assertiveness and for that of their sisters who dressed, spoke up, shouted, and acted like free women. Maria Mitchell was "talking loud"—"for her rights and would as much as she pleased and as loud as she pleased"; but the white man who was the object of her wrath hit her hard in the face five times and broke one of her teeth. One night in April 1867, Harriett Murray, a servant in the home of Dick Porter near Panola, Mississippi, was dragged from the house into the nearby woods by her employer and another white man. There "her hands were tied to the fork of a limb" and she was whipped "until the two men were tired out; two candles were burnt out in the time." Porter then took her down from the tree, stripped her of her clothing, and held her while the other man continued to beat her. The cause of the assault is unknown, although the advice given to the victim by a local magistrate—that she should accept $38 in pay from Porter and forget about the whipping—indicates that a wage dispute was involved. Neither assailant was arrested.[74]

Lacking any alternatives, some freedwomen continued to toil as they had under slavery and thus remained susceptible to "punishment" for any number of "offenses." The amount and quality of work performed by women, and disagreements over the compensation due them, provoked the rage of white men who were slave masters in all but name. In Athens, Georgia, Margaret Martin left her place of work to visit her niece one day in the spring of 1868 and was "badly beaten and choked" by her employer upon her return. The defiant freedwoman Caroline appeared before a Greensboro, North Carolina, Freedmen's Bureau official and reported that Thomas Price had failed to pay her for her services; when she next appeared on Price's plantation, the white man "knocked her down and Beat her with his fist" and ordered his overseer to bring him "the strap"; "then he whipped her with it holding her head between his knees on the bare flesh by turning her clothes up." The overseer also administered "a hundred lashes or more" after Price told him to "ware her out." Lucretia Adams of Yorkville, South Carolina, endured a night of terror initiated by eight drunken white men (she recognized all her assailants, including Oliver and Charles Boehmgart and Bill and Newman Thomas). They "just talked as anybody would" and told her, "We heard you wouldn't work. We were sent for . . . to come here and whip you, to make the damned niggers work."[75]

The incidents just described were exceptional only in that they were reported to northern officials. Like Mississippi's Harriett Murray, most women heeded the warnings issued by their attackers to remain silent or leave the area if they did not want to be killed. Victims or relatives who tried to prosecute these white men inevitably discovered that violence against freedpeople was not only sanctioned, but sometimes initiated by so-called law-enforcement authorities as well. Local officials often refused to make arrests despite overwhelming evidence against a man or group of men; most shared the view—expressed candidly by a Mississippi deputy—that "there was neither money nor glory" in making such arrests.[76]

Even if a white man were held to await trial, post-emancipation southern justice was less than forthright, rivaling mythical Wild West lawlessness for sheer outrageousness. In specific cases concerning freedwomen, a town mayor assisted in helping an accused rapist to make his escape; and a judge charged with beating a woman presided over his own trial, declared himself innocent, jailed his victim, and then forced her husband to pay for her release. Cases for black women plaintiffs were argued by drunken lawyers, and jury members stood up in the midst of proceedings to expound on behalf of the defendant. In June of 1868 an Upperville, Virginia, white man accused of assaulting a black woman leaped up during the trial and began beating her ferociously; he was acquitted. This last case revealed that a black woman who brought charges against her abuser often put herself in jeopardy. The Upperville white man was pronounced not guilty, the woman was fined court costs and remanded to jail because she was unable to pay.[77]

The viciousness aimed at freedwomen was particularly significant as a phenomenon in American women's history. Unlike the cold-blooded slaughter of Native Americans by U.S. army troops, these were personal attacks, carried out face-to-face by men who knew their victims and their families. Northern factory and sweatshop owners routinely exploited poor and immigrant women, but they rarely took up arms against a single recalcitrant worker. During Reconstruction, terrorist attacks against freed men, women, and children revealed all the anxieties related to gender roles and power that remained locked in the South's collective consciousness.[78]

OUT OF THE FIELDS: CITY LIFE AND SCHOOLING

Although only one out of ten southern blacks lived in towns with populations greater than 2,500 in 1870, the lives of urban freedwomen reveal variations on larger themes related to the postwar southern political economy. Connections between work and family patterns in the cities differed from those in rural areas, mainly because of the difference in demand for the labor of black men; but these connections were no less explicit. Moreover, as early as 1870, southern towns had begun to expose the dilemmas that would characterize African American urban communities for years to come, in the North as well as the South. In essence, family stability was sacrificed to the vitality and possibilities of city life. Under these conditions, black women's work, always accorded the least possible respect and remuneration by white employers, increased in importance to family survival.

The large urban in-migration among newly freed slaves and the predictably cynical reaction of southern whites to it have been amply documented in state and regional studies of Reconstruction. Black men, women, and children came to the city, whites charged, to partake of whiskey, and to avoid an honest day's work. But, in fact, many freedpeople (often referred to as "hordes" or "swarms" by whites) fled the war-torn countryside to seek food and safety in populated areas. Hostility among whites, many of whom believed that the city was "intended for white people," coupled with a lack of housing and employment for the newcomers, caused a black exodus back to the cotton fields in 1866 and 1867. Still, the urban black population increased markedly during the 1860–1870 decade (by a rate of 75 percent overall), especially in certain large cities. Five years after the war, for example, Atlanta, Savannah, Richmond, Montgomery, and Raleigh each had almost equal numbers of black and white residents.[79]

Women were overrepresented among freedpeople who remained in the cities permanently after the war and among those who participated in a gradual migration cityward throughout the South during the last decades of the nineteenth century. Single mothers in rural areas found it difficult to support themselves and their children by renting land or working as sharecroppers or wage laborers, and they sought employment in population centers. As a result, southern towns and cities were characterized by an unbalanced sex ratio in favor of women; in seven southern cities (1870 to 1880), women outnumbered men by ten to eight. In 1870 the ratio in both Atlanta and Wilmington, North Carolina, was about four to three. In New Orleans the number of black females aged fifteen to forty-five exceeded that of men in the same age bracket by more than 50 percent. Predictably, the percentage of female-headed households in the towns was greater than on the countryside—perhaps as high as 30 percent, twice the figure for rural households.[80]

Most black women secured jobs in only a limited number of occupations, all clustered at the bottom of the wage scale. These involved traditional "women's work"—(or rather, in the South, traditional *black* women's work)—domestic services performed for nonfamily members for nominal pay. A single woman could barely support a family of any size on her wages alone. Most urban freedwomen labored as servants or laundresses, with smaller numbers working as cooks, nurses, seamstresses, and unskilled laborers (in tobacco factories in Richmond, for example). In several cities, servants represented about half of all black working women, and laundresses another one-fifth. At the same time, as black people tried to provide for themselves and promote their own institutional life, the job options for women expanded accordingly. For example, the efforts of black communities throughout the South to establish schools opened up a limited number of teaching positions for women, some of whom had conducted clandestine schools for enslaved children before the war.[81]

For several reasons it is difficult to state exactly the number of urban freedwomen gainfully employed in 1870, though estimates for different places have ranged from 50 to 70 percent. Census data, probably the best single source, reveals a person's reported occupation but not necessarily her employment status at the time of the interview. The categories of cook, servant, and laundress were fairly flexible, and a woman might have worked in one capacity or another at different times of the year, or in all three simultaneously. The extent of seasonal work was not recorded; some women probably went out in the countryside during the late summer and early fall months to earn wages picking cotton. In the South's seaports and river ports, the busy season on the docks (late fall to late spring) created a high demand among longshoremen for the services of black laundresses, cooks, and the peddlers of fresh fruits and vegetables. Finally, those listed by summertime census takers as "at home" or "keeping house" might have been earning money by keeping boarders or selling garden produce even though they were not listed as part of the urban workforce.[82]

In cities, black women shouldered a heavy burden to support their children. Three times as many black women (proportionate to white) listed an occupation; in 1870 almost two-thirds of single black women but only one-quarter of single white women reported jobs. For married women the respective figures were 31 percent and 4 percent. An equal proportion (30 percent) of black and white households were headed by females. However, black family income amounted to less than 60 percent of white family income, and a black woman tended to remain in the workforce all her adult life, rather than entering or dropping out in response to other factors—such as changes in her husband's income or the number of children at home. Black children contributed relatively little to the overall family income because as a group they left home earlier than their white counterparts. In black and white families of similar structure and income, freedwomen with children were still more likely to work than white mothers.[83]

In financial terms, the quality of city life had little to offer the vast majority of freedpeople. Black men had a hard time finding steady work. Although about one-fifth made their living as artisans, they were bound to encounter the resentment of white competitors and the prejudice of potential white customers. Municipal ordinances imposed discriminatory licensing fees on black craftsmen, and vagrancy statutes limited their ability to move around in search of other possibilities. By the late nineteenth century these measures had the cumulative effect of reducing the proportion of skilled blacks in urban areas. For menial laborers the outlook was even grimmer; most probably worked on an irregular basis when they worked at all. The unpredictable labor demand in cities thus presented a striking contrast to the situation in rural areas ruled by King Cotton, where work cycles conformed to the ageless rhythm of the seasons and laborers were eagerly—and mercilessly—sought after by white landowners.[84]

Economic and political conditions had a crushing effect on the health, stability, and welfare of the urban black family. City life was hard and dangerous. White people's demand for cheap black labor was revealed in chain gangs consisting of women as well as men on streets all over the South. Yet at the same time, cities and towns afforded rich cultural, educational, and religious opportunities not available to blacks under slavery or to freedpeople scattered about the southern countryside. The social structure of black urban communities was much more complex than in areas where everyone made a living from the soil, and a favored few tradesmen and professionals in cities achieved a relatively comfortable standard of living. Large Baptist and Methodist churches provided religious and social services and a core of urban leadership devoted to both worldly and spiritual concerns. Like their counterparts all over the South, the freedwomen of San Antonio, Texas, sponsored a variety of fund-raising efforts to construct and further the mission of local churches. A variety of educational institutions—public and private, from elementary to college level—were concentrated in the towns. City children, freed from the never-ending demands of fieldwork and often near a school of some type, attended classes in greater numbers and with more regularity than their cousins in the country.[85]

Black women supported auxiliaries of the many fraternal orders and lodges founded by men immediately after the war. Cities such as Savannah and New Orleans had many societies dedicated to a wide array of political, labor, charitable, recreational, cultural, and religious purposes. Some of these were burial societies, while others brought together the members of a particular church, and still others had an overt political purpose—in Savannah, the Ladies Union League, for example. Women sponsored picnics, parades, dances, and other social events, and they pooled their modest resources to care for indigent community members. Mutual-aid societies reinforced black community solidarity in the face of overwhelming prejudice and violence. In Virginia, the freedwoman Mary Prout founded the Independent Order of Saint Luke three years after the war; a burial and mutual-aid association, the order institutionalized efforts by women to care for the ill and other vulnerable members of the community. Finally, working women found it less difficult to band together and stage collective job actions in the city. Striking laundresses in Jackson, Mississippi, in 1866, and in Galveston, Texas, in 1877, for example, demonstrated a high degree of class and group consciousness. Freedwomen helped to nourish urban communities in both social and economic terms.[86]

The social consequences of freedom—the coming together of families to work and live—were accompanied by changes in the way women worked, dressed, and thought about themselves. But if liberation from bondage brought tangible, immediate benefits to some women, for others it represented but a fervent hope that their children would some day live as truly free people. A mother's belief that the future might be better for her off-spring gave proof of the passing of slavery. The cook who "said she should die very happy, feeling that her children can spend 'the balance of their days in freedom, though she had been in bonds'" conceived of freedom in terms of her family's future welfare and not her current material condition. Black women throughout the South joined with men to form lo-cal education committees, build schoolhouses, and hire teachers at a time when their neigh-borhoods' resources were slim indeed.[87]

These mothers tried to prepare their children for a new kind of life. Poor but proud women refused to let their sons and daughters accept clothing (donated by whites) they considered ill-fitting or immodest; it was considered "highly indecorous to have the feet and ankles show below the dress," for example. Northern teachers and Freedmen's Bureau officials often lacked sensitivity toward these women who chose self-respect over conven-ience. Mary Ames, a Yankee teacher, recorded a revealing incident in her diary: "One girl brought back a dress she had taken home for 'Ma says it don't fit, and she don't want it.' It was rather large and short, but she was very dirty and ragged, and we told her she must keep it." In other instances, parents disciplined their children with the liberal use of the rod, but they reserved the right to decide how and whether it should be used. Two years after the war, a Georgia bureau agent sustained charges brought against Eliza James because she had "impudently" refused to punish her son at the behest of a white man "and said she would not whip her child for no poor white folks etc." For a white person to demand the punish-ment of a child smacked of slavery, and this freedwoman would not tolerate it.[88]

The elderly Sea Island evening-school pupil "who was much bent with rheumatism" but said she was "mighty anxious to know something"; the Savannah laundress who fastened her textbook to the fence so that she could read "while at work over the wash tub"; and the Greenville, South Carolina, dressmaker who attended classes in the morning and worked at her trade in the afternoon were three of the few freedwomen to receive some formal educa-tion soon after emancipation. (In 1870 more than eight out of ten southern blacks were illit-erate.) For most women, the rigors of childbearing and rearing, household chores, and outside employment represented a continuum from slavery to freedom, unbroken by schooling or other opportunities to expand their horizons beyond the cabin in the cotton field.[89]

The Alabama Freedmen's Bureau agents assigned to conduct a "Negro Census" for 1865 in the Athens-Huntsville area probably resented spending so much time and energy on what they considered bureaucratic nonsense. Before long they became careless in recording the ages and previous occupations of people they interviewed. However, for a while initially, they dutifully noted the required information: each person's name, age, gen-der, address, former owner, slave occupation, and "present employment." The first few pages of the census include these bits of data on about three hundred people. More than the gory details of an "outrage" report, or the tedious wording of a labor contract, this remark-able document chronicles the quiet revolution wrought in the lives of black women after emancipation.[90]

Consider the Jones family: Caroline, formerly a house servant, and her daughter, Savannah, both of whom had been owned by John Haws, were now reunited with husband William (previously owned by a white man named Crawford). Caroline reported no occupation but instead said she was "caring for her family." William continued to work in a railroad shop. Two months before the census interview they had celebrated their new life together with the birth of a son, James, who was listed as "Free born." Nearby, Nelson and Phoebe Humphrey and their five children came together from two plantations (Nelson from one and Phoebe and the children from another). Both former field-hands, Nelson was doing "Miscellaneous: for other people" and Phoebe took in laundry. Joanna (aged fourteen), who used to work as a house servant, was now attending school, and her thirteen-year-old sister, Elizabeth, no longer worked in the fields; she probably helped her mother with the washing.[91]

Not too far away two young women in the Hammond clan took up employment as laundresses so that Easter (sixty), a former domestic, would no longer have to work; she was listed as ill. The women, Nettie (thirty-three) and Ata (twenty-nine), had six children between them, but no husband was listed for either. In the same neighborhood resided a second Jones family, consisting of Gilbert (fifty) and Julia (forty-eight) and the children they had retrieved from two different slave masters. The father had found work as a blacksmith and son William (twenty-one) continued to labor as a field-hand. Gilbert Jr. (fourteen) stayed at home rather than work in the fields as he had before, and Amanda (eighteen), also a former hand but "subject to fits," was now able to "help her mother."[92]

Freedwomen like Phoebe Humphrey and Julia Jones would have had no difficulty listing the blessings of freedom: a reunion at long last with their families, the opportunity to devote more time to household affairs, and children attending school. Although it would be difficult to argue that their work was any less arduous than that of their enslaved mothers and foremothers, these women were now in a position to decide, together with their husbands, how and when various family members should contribute to the welfare of the household. Nettie and Ata Hammond probably had fewer alternatives when it came to supporting their children, but at least they were able to relieve the elderly Easter of her duties as a house servant.

Still, black women continued to occupy two distinct statuses that shaped their daily lives. In their neighborhoods they commanded respect as wives, mothers, and upholders of cultural tradition. In the eyes of whites busy laying the foundations for the "New South"—planters and federal officials—they were still workers who belonged to a despised caste, considered a lowly class apart from white women no matter how downtrodden. Yet freedwomen perceived freedom to mean not a release from back-breaking labor, but rather the opportunity to labor on behalf of their own families and kin within the protected spheres of household and community. In the late nineteenth century, southern black people would continue to define their interests as separate from those of white merchants and landowners.

THREE

"BENT BACKS AND LABORING MUSCLES"

In the Rural South, 1880–1915

FOR BLACK WOMEN in the rural South, the years 1880 to 1915 spanned the Civil War era and the "Great Migration" northward beginning with World War I. Although their domestic chores and fieldwork had not changed much since slavery, women during this period toiled with the new hope that their sons and daughters would one day escape from the southern staple-crop economy, with its attendant hardships and thwarted opportunities. Maud Lee Bryant, a farm wife in Moncure, North Carolina, spent long days in the fields chopping cotton, wheat, and tobacco, and long nights in the house, washing dishes and clothes, scrubbing floors, and sewing, starching, and ironing. She later recalled, "My main object of working was wanting the children to have a better way of living, that the world might be just a little better because the Lord had me here for something, and I tried to make good out of it, that was my aim."[1] Thus the substance of rural women's work remained the same compared to earlier generations, while its social context was transformed by the promise, but not necessarily the reality, of freedom.

Black sharecroppers rarely stayed on the same plantation for more than a year or two. With the "proverbial unacquisitiveness of the 'rolling stone,'"[2] they lived largely outside the mainstream of liberal, industrializing American society during the years from 1880 to 1915. Their quest for household and group autonomy represented the tangible legacy of slavery, for the former slaves and their children remained concentrated in the rural South, and their distinctive way of life became increasingly anomalous within the larger society.[3] Caught in the contradiction of a cash-crop economy based upon a repressive labor system, black households achieved neither consumer status nor total self-sufficiency. Consequently, the lives of black women were fraught with irony; though many had planted, chopped, and picked their share of cotton over the years, they rarely enjoyed the pleasure of a new cotton dress. Though they labored within an agricultural economy, they and their families barely survived on meager, protein-deficient diets. Within individual black households, this tension between commercial and subsistence agriculture helped to shape the gendered division of labor, as wives divided their time among domestic responsibilities, fieldwork, and modest trading and moneymaking activities.

The postbellum plantation economy reinforced the southern caste system but also undermined the economic status of an increasing number of non-elite whites. Landless sharecroppers and tenants of both groups labored to pick annual cotton harvests that by the last decade of the nineteenth century reached 1860 levels. These workers were part of a worldwide subordinate extractive-industrial labor force that fueled manufacturing (in this case cotton factory spindles); in 1891 the U.S. cotton crop supplied 60 to 80 percent of the markets in Britain, France, and Germany. Yet in the United States, the burdens of this exploitative system fell disproportionately on African Americans. By this time nine out of ten blacks lived in the South, and 80 percent of them resided in rural areas, primarily in the formerly slave Cotton Belt. Blacks represented one-third of the southern population and 40 percent of its farmers and farm laborers—but by no means its only poverty-stricken agricultural group. Up-country yeomen farmers were gradually drawn away from livestock and food production and into the commercial economy after the Civil War. In the process they lost their economic independence to a burgeoning system of financial credit. Yet on a social hierarchy that ranged from planters at the top to small landowners in the middle and various states of tenancy at the bottom—cash renters, share tenants, sharecroppers, and wage laborers—blacks monopolized the very lowliest positions. In 1910 fully nine-tenths of all southern blacks who made their living from the soil worked as tenants, sharecroppers, or contract laborers. Most barely eked out enough in cotton to pay for rent, food, and supplies. They did not own their own equipment or mules, nor could they market their crop independent of the landlord. As the price of cotton declined precipitously near the end of the century, landlords began to insist on a fixed amount of cash—rather than a share of the crop—as payment for rent. Thus individual black households bore the brunt of a faltering staple-crop economy.[4]

These years marked the emergence of American apartheid, a system by which a dominant group, whites, passed laws designed to humiliate a subordinate group, blacks, in public ways and in public places, including schools, parks, and theaters, and on public transportation. These new patterns of separation, combined with the systematic disfranchisement of black men, were enforced with state-sanctioned terrorism. As poor whites sank deeper into landlessness and poverty, whites of all classes sought to establish strict boundaries between white people and the descendants of slaves. And by the late nineteenth century, whites of all classes had joined together to demonize black men as a group, and to label all black women as immoral and sexually promiscuous. While white women of the laboring classes began to find work in textile factories, and unmarried white women of the middle classes took jobs in the emerging clerical sector, black women remained confined to traditional forms of task-oriented labor—agriculture work and domestic service. This system of apartheid lasted well into the twentieth century, and enjoyed the favor of the national government, as well as every southern state and many in the North as well.

The black women who emerged from slavery "knew that what they got wasn't what they wanted, it wasn't freedom, really," in the words of Ned Cobb, an Alabama sharecropper and political activist.[5] So wives and mothers constantly moved with their families every year or two to find better soil or a more reasonable landlord; or, bereft of a husband and grown sons, they travelled to a nearby town to locate gainful employment; or raised chickens so they could sell eggs and send their children to school. These women partook of the uniqueness of rural, late-nineteenth-century African American culture and at the same time bore the universal burdens of motherhood. They were the mothers and grandmothers of the early-twentieth-century migrants to northern cities, migrants who as young people had been reared in homes with primitive hearths, where women of all ages continued to guard the "embers of a smoldering liberty."[6]

THE TRIPLE DUTY OF RURAL WOMEN

For black Americans, the post-Reconstruction era opened inauspiciously. Between 1879 and 1881 as many as twenty thousand rural blacks fled the "young hell" of the lower South in search of the "promised land" of Kansas. Around this migration coalesced the major themes of African American history from 1880 to 1915: the forces of poverty and deprivation that enveloped all rural blacks, and the lure of land, education, and safety for their families that made them yearn for true freedom. The Kansas-fever exodus consisted primarily of families headed by former slaves desperate to escape neoslavery. Together with their menfolk, black women did their best to minimize the control that whites retained over their lives—a "New South" mandate succinctly summarized by the governor of North Carolina in 1883: "Your work is the tilling of the ground. . . . Address yourselves to the work, men and women alike."[7]

Although granted relatively more overall freedom than their enslaved parents, black men and women in the late nineteenth century had only a limited ability to make crucial decisions related to household and farm management. They inhabited the lowest rungs of the agricultural ladder—day labor and sharecropping—in contrast to poor whites, who had more opportunities to work as tenants and renters and to seek employment in textile mills. The nature of the sharecropping system meant that economic matters and family affairs overlapped to a considerable degree. Under optimal conditions, each family would have been able to decide for itself how best to use its members' labor, and when or whether to leave one plantation in search of better land or a more favorable contractual arrangement. These conditions rarely pertained in the Cotton South.[8]

By the early twentieth century, some plantations were so large and efficiently managed they resembled agricultural industrial establishments with hired hands rather than a loose conglomeration of independently operated family farms. The degree to which a sharecropping household was supervised determined its overall status in southern society, and blacks were systematically deprived of self-determination to a greater degree than their poor-white counterparts. For example, in an effort to monitor their tenants' work habits, large cotton planters often employed armed "riders" who were "constantly travelling from farm to farm." As agents of the white landowner, these men kept track of the size of each black family and had the authority to order all "working hands" into the fields at any time. Riders dealt with recalcitrant workers by "wearing them out"—that is, inflicting physical punishment. In fact, a government researcher noted that southern sharecroppers in general were "subjected to quite as complete supervision by the owner, general lessee or hired manager as that to which the wage laborers are subjected on large farms in the North and West, and indeed in the South."[9]

The more working families a planter had, the larger his profit; hence he would more readily withhold food from a family of unsatisfactory workers, or deny its children an opportunity for schooling, than turn them off his land. The planter thus sought to intervene in the black farmer's attempt to organize the labor of various family members. Usually the father assumed major responsibility for crop production, and he relied on the assistance of his wife and children during planting and harvesting. However, reported Thomas J. Edwards in his 1911 study of Alabama sharecroppers, if the father failed to oversee the satisfactory completion of a chore, then "the landlord compels every member of his family who is able to carry a hoe or plow to clean out the crops." Some very small households counted on relatives and neighbors to help them during these times; others had to pay the expense of extra laborers hired by the landlord to plow, weed, or chop the cotton on their own farms.[10]

Ultimately a white employer controlled not only a family's labor, but also its "furnishings" and food. By combining the roles of landlord and merchant-financier, he could regulate the flow of both cash and supplies to his workers—with whole families in some parts of the South receiving only $100 annually in credit. Annual interest rates as high as 25 percent (in the form of a lien on the next year's crop) were not unusual, and families had little choice but to borrow when they needed to buy seed, fertilizer, and clothes for the children. Some white men, like the planter who forbade sharecroppers on his land to raise hogs so that they would have to buy their salt pork from him, effectively reduced the opportunities for families to provide for their own welfare in the most basic way. To escape this vicious cycle of dependency required a good deal of luck, as well as the cooperation of each household member. The hardworking Pickens family of Arkansas, overwhelmed by debt in 1888, tried desperately to free themselves. Recalled William, the sixth of ten children: "In the ensuing winter Mother cooked and washed and Father felled trees in the icy 'brakes' to make rails and boards [to sell]." Their landlord removed temptation by closing the neighborhood school. Referring to that time, William Pickens remembered many years later that "very small children can be used to hoe and pick cotton, and I have seen my older sisters drive a plow." Yet a string of bad luck, including the death of a mule and torrential rains, thwarted the family's attempts to own and operate their own farm.[11]

Since plantation accounts were reckoned at the end of each year, sharecroppers had to remain on a farm until they received payment for their cotton (usually in December) or until they had discharged their debt to their employer. The tendency of families to move whenever they had the opportunity—up to one-third left for another, usually nearby, plantation at the end of any one year—caused apprehension among planters who wanted to count on a stable workforce for extended periods of time. In the end, the very measures used to subordinate black farmers served as an impetus for them to move away—to a plantation down the road, where they could be closer to their kinfolk or a school for their children; to a nearby town; or, after 1916, to a northern city. But until alternative forms of employment became available (the lack of free land and transportation halted the exodus to Kansas after a couple of years), most sharecroppers continued to move around within the plantation economy, but not out of it. Consequently, each December many sharecropping families made the trek from one plantation to another, a process called "shifting." Gradually, African American community life institutionalized these annual household migrations. Some families "were ever on the move from cabin to cabin," prompting the story about the chickens who "regularly presented themselves in the dooryard at Christmastime with their legs crossed for tying up before the next morning." Within such a circumscribed realm of activity, even a neighboring plantation seemed to beckon with opportunity, or at least the possibility of change.[12]

As productive members of the household economy, black women helped to fulfill the economic as well as the emotional needs of their families, factors to consider whenever a move was contemplated. These needs changed over the life course of individual families and clans. So too did the demands upon women fluctuate in the cabin and out in the cotton field, from season to season and from year to year. Thus the responsibilities of wives and mothers reflected considerations related to their families' immediate daily welfare, the fortunes of their kinfolk, and the staple-crop planting and harvesting cycle. Within this constantly shifting matrix of obligations, black women performed housekeeping and childcare tasks, earned small sums of cash, and worked in the fields. In the rural South, the nuclear family (consisting of two parents and their children) frequently cohabited within a larger, flexible household, and neighboring households were often linked by ties of kinship. These linkages helped to determine specific (but by no means static) patterns of reciprocal duties among household members, indicating that kinship clusters, rather than nuclear families, defined women's and men's daily labor.[13]

For example, a study of the black population in the Cotton Belt (based upon federal manuscript census data for 1880 and 1900) reveals that the "typical" African American household retained certain structural characteristics throughout this twenty-year period. At the core of this household were both a husband and wife (89.6 percent of all households in the 1880 sample, and 87.8 percent in 1900, were headed by a man; 86.4 percent and 82.5 percent, respectively, included both spouses). The typical household remained nuclear, although extended families (those that included blood relations) increased in importance over time (from 13.6 percent in 1880 to 23 percent in 1900). The average household had between four and five members. Significantly, a crude index of local kinship networks suggests that at least one-third of all families lived near some of their relatives. (See Appendix C.)[14]

Contemporary sources indicate that these networks played a large part in determining where sharecroppers' families moved at the end of the year and where small landowners settled permanently. For example, in-laws and distant cousins might try to induce a newlywed couple to join them by coaxing, "Nate, you a young fellow, you ought to be down here workin'." Moreover, the spirit of sharing that informed many small communities meant that a woman's chores extended out of her own household and into the larger community; indeed, some neighborhoods were composed entirely of kin, thereby making family and community virtually congruent. A woman might adopt an orphan or a newborn grandchild whose parents had not married. She and her husband helped out on a nearby farm when their neighbors found themselves shorthanded. She took over the domestic chores of a sister who just had a baby and consulted with other women in her family about the best remedy for a child wracked by fever. If she was particularly skilled in the art of folk medicine, she might serve as an herb doctor and prescribe cures for her neighbors suffering from anything from a toothache to a heartache.[15]

Kin networks also played a large part in the well-being of any particular individual or family, because husbands and sons often sought wage work off the plantation during "lay by" season (after the crop had been planted) and during the winter slack season, after the harvest. Rejecting the postbellum demands of landowners who expected their workforces to remain confined to the plantation year-round, black men periodically migrated in search of cash wages, essentially leaving their families in order to better provide for them. The women who stayed behind relied on close family and neighbors for childcare and for emotional and economic support. Thus the household was an elastic institution, expanding or contracting as circumstances demanded.

The needs of her kin had a direct bearing upon the number and ages of people a woman cooked and washed for under her own roof. Although the pattern changed somewhat during the late nineteenth century, in general the younger the husband, the more likely that he and his wife would live alone with their children. Older couples tended to include relatives to a greater degree than did younger couples. The sketchy data suggests that newlyweds quickly, though not necessarily immediately, established independent households, and years later a husband and wife might welcome kinfolk into their home. Perhaps these relatives worked in the fields, taking the place of older children who had left to begin families of their own. Or they might have needed the care and assistance that only a mature household could provide. In any case, it is clear that the boundaries of a household could expand or contract to fill both economic and social-welfare functions within the black community.[16]

Keeping in mind these transformations that occurred over the course of a generation, it is useful to begin a discussion of the farm wife's daily routine with the experience of a young married couple. She and her husband began their life together with very little in the way of material possessions, and they often had to make do with, in the words of Ned Cobb, the "sorriest land"—"Land so doggone thin . . . 'it won't sprout unknown peas.'" At least for the first few years, each new baby (probably five or six would survive infancy) meant an extra mouth to feed and body to clothe while the number of available "hands" in the family stayed the same. Consequently a young wife had to divide her time between domestic tasks and cotton cultivation, the mainstay of family life; she did "a man's share in the field, and a woman's part at home." As Rossa B. Cooley reported of a South Carolina Sea Island family, "Occupation: Mother, farming and housework. Father, farming."[17]

The primitive conditions under which these women performed household chores meant that the term housework used in the traditional sense is somewhat misleading. A small, rude sharecropper's dwelling was difficult to keep clean and tidy. Constructed by the white landowner usually many years before, the one- or two-room log or sawn-lumber cabin measured only fifteen or twenty square feet. It lacked glass windows, screens to keep out bugs and flies, running water, sanitary facilities, artificial illumination, cupboard and shelf space, and adequate insulation as well as ventilation. Most of the daily business of living— eating, sleeping, bathing—took place in one room where "stale sickly odors" inevitably accumulated. The ashes from a smoky fire used to prepare the evening meal had barely cooled before the children had to "bundle themselves up as well as they might and sleep on the floor in front of the fireplace," while their parents shared a small bed in the same room. Each modest addition to the cabin increased a family's living space and relative comfort—a lean-to, chicken coop–like kitchen; a wooden floor; efficient chimney; sleeping loft for the children; closets and cupboards; or an extra bedroom.[18]

Farm wives had little in the way of time, money, or incentive to make permanent improvements in or around a cabin the family did not own and hoped to leave in the next year or two. One Alabama mother summed up her frustration this way: "I have done dug holes in de ya[r]d by moonlight mo' dan o[n]ce so dat whah I stay at might hab a rose-bush, but I nebber could be sho' whose ya[r]d it would be de nex' yeah." Yet many women remained sensitive to their domestic environment; if they could not always find time to clean up the mud tracked in from outside each day, still they rearranged the house "very nice to meet the great Easter morning," whitewashed it for a Christmas celebration, dug up flowers in the woods to plant in the yard, or attached brightly colored pictures to the inside walls.[19]

Most families owned few pieces of heavy furniture; they invested their modest earnings in a mule, ox, plow, or wagon rather than domestic furnishings. In any case, households needed to remain portable in anticipation of the time when the family picked up and moved on to another place. These households also lacked artifacts of middle-class life, such as a wide variety of eating and cooking utensils, books, papers, pencils, bric-a-brac, and clocks. Black rural women relied on very few pieces of basic equipment in the course of the day; these included a large tub in which to bathe the youngsters and scrub the clothes, a cooking kettle, and a water pail. Their material standard of living was considerably lower than that of midcentury western pioneer families.[20]

The round of daily chores performed by a sharecropper's wife indicates that the arduousness of this way of life bore an inverse relation to its "simplicity." She usually rose with the roosters (about 4:00 a.m., before other members) to prepare breakfast over an open fire—salt pork (sliced thin and then fried), and molasses and fat on cornbread. She either served the meal in the cabin or took it out to family members who were by this time already at work in the field.[21]

During the planting season she joined her husband and children outside at tasks assigned on the basis of gender and age. For example, a typical division of labor included a father who "ran furrows" using a plow drawn by a mule or ox, a small child who followed him dropping seeds or "potato slips" on the ground, and "at each step the mother covering them with a cumbersome hoe or setting out the plants by piercing holes in the ground with a sharp stick, inserting the roots, and packing the earth with deft movements of the hand." Although she knew as much about the growing cycle as her husband, she probably deferred to his judgment when it came to deciding what she needed to do and when. More than one black person remembered a mother who "done anything my daddy told her to do as far as cultivatin' a crop out there."[22]

Harvest time consumed a substantial portion of each year; two to four cotton pickings lasted from August to December. Like planting techniques, picking had remained the same since the earliest days of slavery, and young and old, male and female, performed essentially the same task. Throughout the nineteenth and on into the twentieth century, the Cotton South was remarkable for its resistance to technological innovations compared to the industrial section of the Northeast, or commercial agriculture in the Midwest, a fact that weighed heavily on the shoulders of rural black women. Cotton picking was still such a labor-intensive task, few farm wives could escape its rigors. The critical significance of this operation to the well-being of the family—the greater the crop, the more favorable their economic situation at the end of the year—necessitated the labor of every able-bodied person and took priority over all but the most vital household chores.[23]

For the sharecropping family, children were a distinct economic asset. In 1880 nine out of ten southern black wives between the ages of twenty-one and thirty had at least one child aged three or under. Just as the agricultural system helped to influence family size, so the growing season affected an expectant mother's ability to refrain from fieldwork. In 1918 a Children's Bureau report noted that "to some extent, the amount of rest a mother can have before and after confinement is determined by the time of year or by the stage of cotton crop upon which depends the livelihood of the family." The birth of a child represented the promise of better times in terms of augmenting the household's labor supply, but for the time being it increased the workload of other family members and placed additional physical demands on the new mother herself.[24]

Compared to enslaved women, sharecroppers' wives had more flexibility when it came to taking care of their children during the day. Some women managed to hoe and keep an eye on an infant at the same time. But many, like the mother who laid her baby to sleep on a nearby fence rail, only to return and find "a great snake crawling over the child," found it difficult to divide their attention between the two tasks. Slightly older children presented problems of a different sort. For instance, the mother of five-year-old John Coleman had to choose between leaving him to his own devices while she worked in the field—he liked to run off and get into mischief in the creek—and coaxing him to help alongside her, "thinning the cotton or corn . . . picking cotton or peas." At the age of six or seven, oldest siblings often remained at home to watch over the younger children while their mother labored "in the crop."[25]

In preparation for the main meal of the day (eaten around 11:00 a.m.), a woman left the field early to collect firewood (which she might carry home on her back) and fetch water from a stream or well. Children could help her with water-toting, one of the worst forms of domestic drudgery; they would follow along behind her, carrying piggins, pails, or cups according to their size. The midday meal often consisted of food left over from breakfast, supplemented perhaps by turnip or collard greens from the family garden during the summer and early fall. The additional time required to fish, hunt for wild game, and pick berries, and the money needed to purchase additional supplies, meant that many sharecropping families subsisted on a substandard diet of meal, molasses, and fatty meat, especially in the winter and spring. The decline in black fertility rates during the late nineteenth century and the strikingly high child mortality rates during the same period were probably due at least in part to the poor health of rural women and their families.[26]

In the afternoon, work in the fields resumed. During the busy seasons of spring planting and fall picking, "the house was left out of order [as it was] in the morning, the cooking things scattered about the hearth just as they were used, and the few dishes on the old table . . . unwashed too." Indeed, travelers and social workers often remarked on the dirty dishes and unmade beds that were the hallmark of a sharecropper's cabin. Sympathetic observers realized that women who spent "twelve hours of the day in the field" could hardly hope to complete certain "homemaking" chores. The routine of meal preparation was repeated in the evening. After she collected firewood, brought up water, and milked the cow (if the family was fortunate enough to have one), a wife began to prepare the final meal of the day. Later that evening she might light a pine knot—"No lamps or oil are used unless some one is sick"—but usually family activity ceased around sunset. After a long day of physical labor, "nature overcomes the strongest and sleep is sought by all of the family"— for some, on mattresses stuffed with corn shucks, moss, or pine needles and pillows full of chicken feathers.[27]

Few rural women enjoyed respite from the inexorable demands of day-to-day household tasks or the annual cycle of cotton cultivation. Nursing a newborn child and cooking the family's meals; digging, hoeing, and chopping in the fields—these chores dictated the daily and seasonal rhythms of a black wife's life. Yet they represented only the barest outline of her domestic obligations. On rainy days, or by the light of a nighttime fire, she sewed quilts and mended clothes. "I worked many hours after they was in bed," recalled one mother of nine; "Plenty of times I've been to bed at three and four o'clock and get up at five the first one in the morning." During the day she had to carve out time to grind corn for meal, bathe the children, weed the garden, gather eggs, and do the laundry. Periodically she devoted an entire day to making soap out of ashes and lard or helping with the hog butchering.[28]

Unlike their enslaved grandmothers, most sharecropping women did not have the necessary equipment to spin cotton into thread and weave thread into cloth; the expense and bulk of spinning wheels and looms precluded household self-sufficiency in the area of textile production. Ironically, although the rural black family lived surrounded by raw cotton, its clothing had to be purchased from a local white merchant. A woman's freedom from the seemingly endless chores of spinning and weaving required a family's increased dependence on credit controlled by whites.

Her involvement with very poor women in the Alabama backcountry at the turn of the century convinced social worker Georgia Washington that "the mother has to hustle all through the winter, in order to get anything" for the family. The "wife and children are worked very hard every year" to pay for the bare necessities, but where "the family is large they are only half fed and clothed." As a result, most wives attempted to supplement the family income in a variety of ways, few of which earned them more than a few extra cents at a time. Some picked and sold berries or peanuts, while others marketed vegetables, eggs, and butter from the family's garden, chickens, and cow. A "midder" (midwife) found that her services were frequently in demand. Part-time laundresses took in washing and worked at home with the assistance of their older children.[29]

Although modest in terms of financial return, these activities were significant because they provided a bit of money for families that had to rely chiefly on credit. Combined with the wages a woman might earn at harvesttime, other moneymaking efforts could, over many years, yield enough cash to allow a family to buy its own land or escape sharecropping altogether. The Gillam family in central east Arkansas could never seem to break even at the end of the year, but Cora Gillam, wife and mother, made $1.50 per hundred pounds of cotton she picked in the fall, enabling the family to move to Little Rock. Women's moneymaking activities probably help to account for the peak of black landownership—in 1915, when 15 to 20 percent of black farmers owned their own land. Moreover, when women earned money by working at home, they were able to care for their small children, and at times engage in commercial exchange on a limited basis, in the process gaining a measure of self-esteem through the use of shrewd trading skills. This form of work contrasted with their husbands' responsibilities for crop production, which included not only field labor but also monthly and annual dealings with white landowner-merchants. Thus men's income-producing activities took place in the larger economic sphere of a regional cotton market, while women worked exclusively within the household and a localized foodstuff, seasonal-agricultural, and domestic-service economy.[30]

Husbands preferred that their wives work as laundresses at home, rather than under the direct supervision of whites in a kitchen or a yard. Still, out of economic necessity, a mother's moneymaking efforts could periodically compel her to leave her house. Although relatively few Cotton Belt women worked regularly as servants for whites (4.1 percent in 1880; 9 percent in 1900), some performed day service during the slack season. In addition, if a black household was relatively large and productive (that is, if it included a sufficient number of "hands" to support itself), a woman might hire herself out to a local planter for at least part of the year. In 1910, 27 percent of all black female agricultural laborers earned wages this way. One Alabama mother managed to combine childcare with wage earning; she took her stepson along when she "went and chopped cotton for white folks." He later recalled, "My stepmother wanted my company; but she also wanted to see me eat two good meals" provided each day by the landowner. As three-quarter hands, women could make about thirty-five cents per day for "full hours in the field."[31]

Children often helped in and around the house; they supplied additional (though somewhat unpredictable) labor and ideally stayed within their mother's sight and earshot. Youngsters of five or six also worked in the fields, dropping seeds or toting water. As mentioned earlier, white planters often shaped a family's priorities when it came to the use of children as workers; as a general rule, landowners believed that "the raising of children must not interfere with the raising of cotton," and they advanced food to a household in proportion to its "working hands" and not its actual members. W. E. B. DuBois, in his 1899 study, "The Negro in the Black Belt," found sharecroppers' children to be "poorly dressed, sickly, and cross," an indication that poor nutrition combined with hard work took their toll at an early age. Parents at times hired out children to white employers in order to lessen the crowding at home and bring in extra money.[32]

The gendered division of labor between boys and girls became more explicit as they grew older. For example, some families put all their children to work in the fields with the exception of the oldest daughter. Most girls served domestic apprenticeships under their mothers, but at the same time they learned to hoe and pick in the cotton fields and, in some cases, to chop wood and plow (these latter two were usually masculine tasks). In 1900 over half of all Cotton Belt households reported that at least one daughter aged sixteen or less was working as a field laborer. (See Appendix C.) Still, girls probably worked in the fields less often, and in proportionately smaller numbers, than boys, and their parents seemed more willing to allow them to acquire an education; school attendance rates among black females remained higher than those among males throughout the period 1880 to 1915, producing an early form of the "farmer's daughter effect." In the fifteen-to-twenty-year age bracket, only seven black males attended school for every ten females. By 1910 literacy rates among young people revealed that girls had surpassed boys in literacy, although the situation was reversed among elderly men and women.[33]

The financial imperatives of cotton sharecropping life produced rates of prolonged dependency for both sexes compared to those of wage earners in other staple-crop economies. Black youths who worked on the sugar plantations of Louisiana often grew resentful of having to turn over their wages to their parents, and struck out on their own when they reached the age of fourteen or fifteen. As a result, it was economically feasible for "both boys and girls [to] mate early, take houses, and set up for themselves." On the other hand, cotton sharecroppers' sons could draw upon little in the way of cash resources if they wanted to marry, forcing them "to wait for the home attractions." Men in the Cotton Belt married around age twenty-five, women at age twenty, reflecting, once again, the lessened demands made upon daughters as field-workers.[34]

The demographic and economic characteristics of rural black families demonstrate the continuous and pervasive effects of poverty. From 1880 to 1910 the fertility of black women declined by about one-third, due to disease and poor nutrition among females all over the South and their particularly unhealthful living conditions in urban areas. The life expectancy of black men and women at birth was only thirty-three years. If a woman survived until age twenty, she could expect to see one out of three of her children die before its tenth birthday and to die herself (around the age of fifty-four) before the youngest left home. Those women who outlived their husbands faced the exceedingly difficult task of trying to support a farm family on their own. Even women accustomed to plowing with a team of oxen and knowledgeable about the intricacies of cotton cultivation could find the process of bargaining with a white man for seed, supplies, and land to be an insurmountable barrier. Many widows therefore relied on the assistance of an older son or other male relative, consolidated their own household with that of neighbors or kin, or moved to the city in search of paid work.[35]

Women headed about 11 percent of all rural black southern households at any one time between 1880 and 1900, but not all of those who managed a farm or supervised the fieldwork of their children were single mothers or widows. As we have seen, some sharecropping fathers regularly left home to work elsewhere, resulting in a distinction between the "real" (that is, blood) family and the "economic" (cohabiting) household. In the Cotton Belt, men might leave their wives and children to till their land while they hired themselves out to a nearby planter or other employer. (In 1910 one-half of all southern black men employed in agriculture earned wages on either a year-round or temporary basis.) This pattern was especially common in areas characterized by non-cotton local economies that provided alternative sources of employment for men. In 1883, a Gadsden, Alabama, planter noted the lure of cash wages for his male croppers, and the disruption it caused his own operation: "You have your farm and your supplies, and your calculations made and your labor engaged, and think you are going to get along all right, but suddenly some man comes and says to your laborers, 'I want so many men to build a railroad; I will pay $1.50 a day, and pay every Saturday night'; and your laborer says to his wife, 'Sally, I am going off to work on the railroad,' and off he goes, leaving his wife and family behind him."[36]

On the South Carolina coast, some black men toiled as day laborers in the rice fields, while others left their farms for Savannah or Charleston in order to earn extra money (usually only a few dollars each week) as longshoremen or cotton-gin workers. Phosphate mining in the same area enabled husbands, fathers, and older sons to work together as "dredge han's." A poor harvest or a natural disaster (like the great hurricane of 1896) affecting the Sea Islands prompted an exodus of male household members old enough to work for wages; some went north, while most settled for indefinite periods of time in other parts of the South. Sugar plantations in Louisiana, sawmills and coal mines in Tennessee, lumbering and turpentine camps along the Florida and Alabama coasts, brickyards, and railroad construction projects all over the South provided income for men who sought to work for cash rather than "credit."[37]

While the "real" family never changed, the "economic" household responded to seasonal opportunities and to its own specific economic needs. Although the majority of black rural women were ruled by haggard King Cotton, some followed different seasonal rhythms and work patterns dictated by other forms of commercial enterprise—tobacco and sugar cultivation, truck farming, and oystering. Each of these economies had a distinctive division of labor based on both age and gender. The proximity of processing plants and marketing operations often meant that families employed in such work periodically or in some cases permanently crossed over from agricultural to quasi-industrial labor.

As older children began to leave their family, the economic gains achieved at the height of its productivity gradually dissipated. These established households sometimes took in boarders or relatives to offset the loss of departed offspring. No single pattern of either work or dependency characterized the rural elderly. For instance, DuBois noted of Black Belt communities in general: "Away down at the edge of the woods will live some grizzle-haired black man, digging wearily in the earth for his last crust; or a swarthy fat auntie, supported in comfort by an absent daughter, or an old couple living half by charity and half by odd jobs."[38]

Widows throughout the South represented extremes of hardship and well-being. An elderly woman living alone sometimes took in a young "mudderless" or "drift" (orphan) for mutual companionship and support. Like Aunt Adelaide, who "received less and less when she needed more and more" once her children left home, some of these women lamented their loss of self-sufficiency. "I ben strong ooman," said Adelaide, "I wuk fo' meself wid me han'. I ben ma[r]sh-cuttin' ooman. I go in de ma[r]sh and cut and carry fo' myself." At the other end of the spectrum was the widow Mrs. Henry; she supported herself by farming and "peddling cakes" until her health failed—or rather, faltered. After that she made a comfortable living selling sweet potatoes, poultry, hogs, and vegetables with the aid of two other women and a child.[39]

Regardless of their physical circumstances, these women formed a bridge of "bent backs and laboring muscles" between "the old African and slavery days, and the sixty difficult years of freedom" for their grandchildren and all younger people in the community. Although men headed individual households, it was not unusual to find an elderly woman presiding over a group of people who in turn cared for her. In Charlotte, North Carolina, the former slave Granny Ann lived alone but "everybody respected" her and "they never would let her cook for herself." She served as spiritual advisor to the neighborhood. To cite another case, according to the 1900 census, Winnie Moore, aged eighty and mother of ten children, lived alone in Perry County, Alabama, with no visible means of support. But at least five nearby households included Moores. Among them was that of John (aged thirty-four) and his wife, Sarah (thirty), who had a daughter of twelve named Winnie. Together grandmother and granddaughter Winnie reached from slavery into the twentieth century, and in their lives comingled the anguish of bondage and the ambiguity of freedom.[40]

Unlike cotton planters, white tobacco growers after the war resisted the idea of share-cropping for years, and throughout the late nineteenth century many blacks in the "Old Bright" belt of Virginia and North Carolina worked for wages (sixty to seventy cents per day). For example, in the Piedmont area of Virginia and the Carolinas, and in parts of Kentucky and Tennessee, black people toiled in tobacco fields as hired hands, tenants, or owners of small family farms. Children performed many of the basic—and most unpleasant—tasks related to the early stages of crop cultivation. Usually boys were hired out for longer periods of time and for a greater variety of operations than were girls. In the tobacco fields closer to home, children's and women's work often overlapped. For example, youngsters of both sexes, together with their mothers, spent long hours stooped over "worming" the plants—that is, examining the underside of each leaf and pinching the head off any worm they found. Conventional wisdom held that "women make better wormers than men, probably because they are more patient and painstaking."[41]

After 1900, when small tenant farms became more common (a trend linked specifically to the emergence of a single-crop commercial economy), women worked in the tobacco fields to a greater extent than they had previously. This change suggested that black men in tobacco-growing regions, like Cotton Belt freedmen, preferred that their womenfolk not perform fieldwork for wages under the direct supervision of whites. However, throughout the late nineteenth and early twentieth centuries, falling tobacco prices caused increasing numbers of farmers to abandon the land and migrate to nearby towns, where both sexes found menial jobs in tobacco-processing establishments.[42]

The sugar plantation economy of Louisiana, described as a "first cousin to slavery," also relied heavily on wage workers during the postbellum period. A persistent labor shortage in the industry between 1880 and 1900 resulted in "chronic labor disturbances" among workers whose pay was set very low (fifty cents a day for women; sixty-five cents for men) by white employers who colluded with one another over wage rates. In the spring and summer, women hoed in the fields; they plowed and ditched infrequently. The terse remarks made by a sugar plantation owner in his diary one day in 1888 revealed that women who worked under a wage (as opposed to family) system of labor organization remained vulnerable to rape and other forms of sexual abuse at the hands of white men: "Young Turcuit [the assistant overseer] is very objectionable from his 'goings on' with the colored women on the place."[43]

During the grinding season—October through January—hands from all over the state of Louisiana converged on centralized sugar factories. Wages ranged from twenty-five cents per day for children to eighty-five cents for women and a dollar for men. Families stayed in company-owned cabins (often converted slave quarters) and made their own decisions about when and how often wives and children should cut cane. Boys began to earn wages around the age of twelve or thirteen, girls not until three or four years later. Women set their own work schedules, much to the disgust of labor-hungry planters. Writing for the Department of Labor in 1902, one investigator found that on the Calumet plantation in St. Mary Parish, "Women make only about half-time. During the cultivating season practically none work on Saturdays and very few on Mondays. They do not work in bad weather. During grinding they lay off on Saturdays, but generally work on Mondays." In this way families managed to maintain domestic priorities within a wage economy.[44]

In the Tidewater region of Virginia around Hampton Roads and Norfolk, black truck farmers cultivated vegetables to be shipped to distant markets. Along the Atlantic coastline from Virginia to Georgia, oystering families included husbands who worked as gatherers and wives as shuckers. In Chatham County, Georgia, for example, fathers and brothers remained in their home villages during the winter harvest season, while their wives and daughters moved to the factory town of Warsaw to find employment in the seafood processing plants. Family members lived together in the off-season when the men fished and the women took in laundry or picked berries to sell.[45]

Despite the variations in these commercial economies, certain patterns of family organization remained characteristic of blacks in the rural South throughout the period from 1880 to 1915. For most households, a single, sudden misfortune—a flood, a summer drought, high prices for fertilizer, the death of a mule or cow—could upset the delicate balance between subsistence and starvation. Husbands and wives, sons and daughters, friends and kinfolk coordinated their labor and shifted their place of residence in order to stave off disaster—a process that was never-ending. Yet even the poorest families sought to preserve a division of labor between the genders so that fathers assumed primary responsibility for the financial affairs of the household, and mothers oversaw domestic chores first and labored as field-hands or wage earners when necessary. The heroic efforts among ordinary families to piece together a living went unappreciated among white landowners, who persisted in labeling their workers "shiftless." Ultimately, the remarkably varied patterns of work among these families—picking cotton and foraging for berries, hunting, fishing, and working for wages off the plantation—demonstrated that few rural black families could afford the "lazy" way of life too often attributed to them. And some forms of initiative could not be reduced to financial considerations.

WOMEN'S WORK AND ASPIRATIONS

To outsiders, rural life, set within a larger framework of pervasive poverty, seemed bleak indeed. DuBois himself asserted that the rural black person's "outlook in the majority of cases is hopeless." Perhaps on the surface, the struggle for a living was waged "out of grim necessity . . . without query or protest," as he suggested. However, below that surface ran a deep current of restlessness among even the least fortunate. In St. Meigs, Alabama, Georgia Washington worked with farm wives who "looked pretty rough on the outside." She soon discovered that these mothers were "dissatisfied themselves and anxious to change things at home and do better, but had no idea how or where to begin." They especially wanted the time and resources "to mend or clean up the children before sending them to school in the morning." According to Washington, their "dissatisfaction" was a hopeful sign, proof that they had not succumbed to a paralyzing fatalism.[46]

Two developments in late-nineteenth-century southern society—increasing literacy rates and a general urban in-migration among southern blacks—suggest that at least some families managed to wrench themselves from the past and look to the future. Neither books nor a home in the city would guarantee freedom, but these things did afford coming generations a way of life that differed in important respects from the neoslavery of the rural South. Black girls attended school in greater numbers than boys, and southern towns had disproportionately large black female populations. These developments were relevant to African American women's aspirations for their daughters and sons.

It was not uncommon for sharecroppers' children who acquired some schooling to credit their mothers later with providing them with the opportunity to learn. Speaking from experience, the educator William Pickens declared, "Many an educated Negro owes his enlightenment to the toil and sweat of a mother." The saying "chickens for shoes" referred to women's practice of using the money they earned selling eggs and chickens to buy shoes for their children so that they could attend school in the winter. Rossa B. Cooley pointed out that some black mothers were particularly concerned about rescuing their daughters from a fate they themselves had endured. For example, born and raised in slavery, the Sea Island woman Chloe had "one idea" for her daughter Clarissa and that was "an education that meant going to school and away from all the drudgery, the chance to wear pretty clothes any day in the week, and as her utmost goal, the Latin and algebra offered by the early Negro schools in their zeal to prove the capacity of liberated blacks." Female college graduates who responded to a survey conducted by Atlanta University researchers in 1900 frequently mentioned the sacrifices of their mothers, who, like Job, were "patience personified."[47]

Frances Ellen Watkins Harper, a black writer and lecturer, suggested that black mothers "are the levers which move in education. The men talk about it . . . but the women work most for it." She recounted examples of mothers who toiled day and night in the fields and over the washtub in order to send their children to school. One mother "urged her husband to go in debt 500 dollars" for their seven children's education. This emphasis on women's support for schooling raises the question of whether or not mothers and fathers differed in their perception of education and its desirability for their offspring.[48]

Although girls engaged in some types of field and domestic labor at an early age, parents excused them more often and for longer periods of time (compared to their brothers) to attend the neighborhood school. For instance, the George C. Burleson family listed in the 1900 federal manuscript census for Pike County, Alabama, included four children. Ida May, the oldest (aged sixteen), had attended school for six of the previous twelve months. Her younger brother, Clifford (aged eleven), had worked as a farm laborer all year and had not gone to school at all. In 1910 the Bureau of the Census remarked upon higher female literacy rates among the younger generation by observing, "Negro girls and younger women have received at least such elementary school training as is represented by the ability to write, more generally than have Negro boys and men."[49]

If literate persons—and they were more often women than men—prized their own skills highly, they might have felt more strongly about enabling their children to learn to read and write. Apparently, in some rural families the divergent experiences and immediate concerns of fathers compared to mothers prompted conflicting attitudes toward schooling. Perhaps the experiences of Martin V. Washington were not so unusual. Born in 1878 in South Carolina, Washington grew up in a household composed of his parents and ten siblings. His mother had received a grammar-school education, but his father had never gone to school. "Because of the lack of his education," explained Washington, "my father was not anxious for his children to attend school; he preferred to have them work on the farm." On the other hand, his mother, "who knew the value of an education," tried to ensure that all of her children acquired some schooling.[50]

For blacks in the rural South, even a smattering of education could provoke discontent and thereby disrupt family and community life. Martin Washington's father might have feared that his children would move away, and indeed, the younger man did eventually leave South Carolina for New York City. Ned Cobb put the matter succinctly: "As a whole, if children got book learnin enough they'd jump off of this country; they don't want to plow, don't want no part of no sort of field work." He believed that the "biggest majority" of literate blacks sooner or later moved to town to find a "public job" (i.e., wage work). If education was a means of personal advancement, then it could splinter families, as young people, eager to flee from the routine of rural life, abandoned the farms of their parents.[51]

The Pickens family of South Carolina moved from the country to the village of Pendleton in the late 1880s. The various factors that shaped their decision reveal how considerations related to both work and schooling attracted people to the towns. (The 1880s represented the peak period of black urban in-migration between 1865 and 1915.) Mrs. Pickens had a great desire "to school the children," but they could hardly attend classes on a regular basis as long as the family's white landlord "would not tolerate a tenant who put his children to school in the farming season." Working together, the Pickenses just barely made ends meet in any case; cotton prices had fallen to the point where a hand earned only thirty-five or forty cents a day for picking one hundred pounds.[52]

In Pendleton, the children could attend a better school for longer stretches at a time. Their father relinquished the plow in order to become a "man of all work," and their mother found a job as a cook in a hotel. She preferred this type of employment over field-work because it allowed her "somewhat better opportunities" to care for her small children (she probably took them to work with her). William Pickens believed that town life afforded a measure of financial independence for the family, compared to his experiences on a tenant farm, where "my father worked while another man reckoned." Pickens himself went on to become a scholar and an early official of the National Association for the Advancement of Colored People (NAACP).[53]

By 1910 about 18 percent of the southern black population lived in towns of 2,500 inhabitants or more (an increase of 11 percent over 1860). Since emancipation, small but steadily increasing numbers of former slaves had made their way cityward. As wives, widows, and daughters, black women participated in this gradual migration in disproportionately large numbers. Some women accompanied their husbands to town so that the family as a whole could benefit from the wider variety of jobs available to blacks. Unmarried women—including daughters eager to break away from the "dreary drudgery" of the sharecropper's farm, and widows desperate to feed and clothe their children—found an "unlimited field" of jobs, but only in the areas of domestic service and laundering. As a result, all of the major southern cities had an unbalanced sex ratio in favor of women throughout the late nineteenth century. The selection process at work in this population movement, like any other, indicates that black women possessed a spirit of "upward ambition and aspiration" at least equal to that of their menfolk.[54]

Throughout this period, then, some black women demonstrated a restlessness of mind as well as body. In their willingness to move from cabin to cabin and from country to town, they belied the familiar charge that women were more "conservative" than men, less quick to take chances or to abandon the familiar. Perhaps even more dramatic were mothers' attempts to school their children, for in the process they risked losing them. Ned Cobb never went to school because, he thought, "my daddy was scared I'd leave him, so he held me down." Cobb's father had his own priorities, and at least he never had to share the pain felt by a Sea Island mother who read in a note from her self-exiled son, "It pays a man to leave home sometimes, my mother, and he will see more and learn more."[55]

THE RURAL COOPERATIVE ETHOS IN AN INDUSTRIALIZING NATION

Late-nineteenth-century middle-class white women derived their status from that of their husbands. "Unproductive" in the context of a cash-oriented, industrializing economy, and formally unable to take part in the nation's political process, they enjoyed financial security only insofar as their spouses were steady and reliable providers. In contrast, black working women in the South had a more equal relationship with their husbands in the sense that the two partners were not separated by extremes of economic power or political rights; black men and women lacked both. Oppression shaped these unions in another way. The overlapping of economic and domestic functions combined with the pressures imposed by a surrounding, hostile white society meant that black working women were not so dramatically dependent upon their husbands as were middle-class white wives. Within black families and communities, then, public-private, male-female distinctions were less tightly drawn than among middle-class whites. Together, black women and men participated in a rural folk culture based upon group cooperation rather than competition and the accumulation of goods. The ways this culture both resembled and contrasted with that of poor southern whites helps to illuminate the interaction between class and racial-ideological factors in shaping the roles of women.[56]

Referring to the worldview of Ned Cobb's father, Hayes, the biographer-interviewer Theodore Rosengarten observed that "righteousness consisted in not having so much that it hurt to lose it." Ned himself remembered that his father as a young man had passed up promising opportunities to buy land because "he was blindfolded; he didn't look to the future." Ruled by "them old slavery thoughts," Hayes knew that "whenever the colored man prospered too fast in this country under the old rulins, they worked every figure to cut you down, cut your britches off you. So, it . . . weren't no use in climbin too fast; weren't no use in climbin slow, neither, if they was goin to take everything you worked for when you got too high." Rural black communities that abided by this philosophy sought to achieve self-determination within a limited sphere of action. In this way they insulated themselves from whites and from the disappointment that often accompanied individual self-seeking. They lived like Ned's brother Peter; he "made up his mind that he weren't goin to have anything and after that, why nothin could hurt him."[57]

Contemporary northern scholars and journalists, as well as southern planters, charged that rural blacks valued freedom of movement, "furious religious revivals," and community holidays—"none of which brings them profit of any sort." A Georgia landowner characterized in this way the philosophy of his tenants, who tended to "dismiss further thought of economy" once they had fulfilled their financial obligations to him: *"dum vivimus vivamus"* (while we are living let us live). Some white observers seized upon this theme and warned of its ramifications for the future of American society. Within a growing economy based upon the production of consumer goods, black people's apparent willingness to make do with the little they had represented not so much a moral transgression as a threat to employee discipline. Why should a black husband and father work hard if he was "content with a log cabin and a fireplace, and with corn, bacon, and molasses as articles of food"? How would he advance southern or national economic development if he was satisfied with "merely enough to keep soul and body together"? One contemporary scholar suggested that for the average household head to enjoy a higher standard of living, "his wants must be diversified"; otherwise he lacked the impulse to make, save, and spend money. Of course the issue was more complex than the "simple needs" or "wants" of blacks would imply. For example, a northern reporter pointed out that the preachers of the New South gospel of wealth inevitably clashed with the majority of white employers who vowed "to do almost anything to keep the Negro on the land and his wife in the kitchen as long as they are obedient and unambitious workers."[58]

Black settlements in remote areas—especially those that remained relatively self-sufficient through hunting and fishing—experienced the mixed blessings of semiautonomy. These communities existed almost wholly outside the larger regional and national economic system. For example, the people of the Sea Islands who "labor only for the fulfillment of the petition, 'Give us this day our daily bread,' and literally 'take no thought for the morrow,' working only when their necessities compel them," revealed the dilemma of a traditional subculture located within a modern nation. As independent, self-respecting farmers (a proportionately large number owned their own land), the Sea Islanders remained relatively unmolested by whites and managed to preserve West African traditions and folkways to a remarkable degree. Their diet, consisting of fowl, fish, shellfish, and fresh vegetables, was nutritionally superior to that of Cotton Belt sharecroppers. Yet they lacked proper medical care and the most basic household conveniences. (Water-toting women hailed the installation of a water pump in the early twentieth century as "a most spectacular innovation in domestic economy.") Floods and other natural disasters periodically wreaked havoc on their way of life, and pushed young people off the islands and into nearby cities, leaving behind primarily the elderly and the blind.[59]

Other rural communities possessed a strong corporatist ethos and a concomitant scorn for the hoarding of private possessions. As government researcher J. Bradford Laws wrote disapprovingly of the sugar workers he studied in 1902, "They have an unfortunate notion of generosity, which enables the more worthless to borrow fuel, food, and what not on all hands from the more thrifty." It is clear that these patterns of behavior were determined as much by economic necessity as by cultural "choice." If black household members pooled their energies to make a good crop, and if communities collectively provided for their own welfare, then poverty and oppression ruled out most of the alternative strategies. Individualism was a luxury that sharecroppers simply could not afford.[60]

Rural folk relied on one another to help celebrate the wedding of a young couple, rejoice in a preacher's fervent exhortation, mark the annual closing of the local school, minister to the ill, and bury the dead. Women participated in all these rites and communal events. In addition, they had their own gender-based activities, as well as societies that contributed to the general good of the community. On the Sea Islands, young women would "often take Saturday afternoon as a time for cleaning the yard or the parlor, for ironing their clothes, or for preparing their hair." (Their brothers gathered at a favorite meeting place or organized a "cornfield baseball game.") Quilting brought young and old women together for a daylong festival of sewing, chatting, and feasting. Supported by the modest dues of their members, female voluntary beneficial societies met vital social-welfare needs that individual families could not always afford; these groups helped their members to pay for life insurance, medical care, and burial services. Even the poorest women managed to contribute a few pennies a month and to attend weekly meetings. In turn-of-the-century Alabama, "The woman who is not a member of one of these is pitied and considered rather out of date."[61]

The impulse for mutual solace and support among rural African Americans culminated in their religious institutions and worship services. At monthly meetings women and men met to reaffirm their unique spiritual heritage, to seek comfort, and to comfort one another. Black women found a "psychological center" in religious belief, and the church provided strength for those overcome by the day-to-day business of living. For many weary share-croppers' wives and mothers, worship services allowed for physical and spiritual release and offered a means of transcending earthly cares in the company of one's friends and family. Faith created "a private world inside the self, sustained by religious sentiment and religious symbolism . . . fashioned to contain the world without." "Spiritual mothers" served as the "main pillars" of Methodist and Baptist churches, but they also exercised religious leadership outside formal institutional boundaries; elderly women in particular commanded respect as the standard-bearers of tradition and as the younger generation's link to its ancestors.[62]

Of course, "places behind God's back," where Mamie Garvin Fields taught a small school, were shaped as much by whites' prejudices as by black solidarity, and the "ethos of mutuality" that pervaded rural communities did not preclude physical violence or overt conflict between individuals. At times a Saturday night "frolic" ended in a bloody confrontation between two men who sought courage from a whiskey bottle and self-esteem through hand-to-hand conflict. Similarly, oppression could bind a family tightly together, but it could also heighten tensions among people who had few outlets for their rage and frustration. Patterns of domestic conflict reflected both historical injustices and daily family pressures. These forces affected black women and men in different ways.[63]

On a superficial level, the roots of domestic violence are not difficult to recognize or understand. Cramped living quarters and unexpected setbacks provoked the most even-tempered of household heads. Like their slave parents, mothers and fathers often used harsh disciplinary techniques on children, not only to prepare them for life in a white-dominated world where all blacks had to act cautiously, but also to exert rigid control over this one vital facet of domestic life. If whites attempted to cut "the britches off" black fathers and husbands, then these men would try to assert their authority over their households with even greater determination. At times that determination was manifested in violence and brutality.[64]

Ned Cobb's father epitomized the sharecropper who lorded over his wives (he married three times) and children. More than once the Cobb children watched helplessly as their father beat their mother, and they too were "whipped . . . up scandalous" for the slightest infraction. Hayes divided his time between his "outside woman"—an unmarried laundress in the neighborhood—and his "regular" family, and he made no effort to conceal the fact. He hired out his womenfolk or sent them to the fields like the children, and they dared not protest, while Hayes spent his days in a characteristically masculine fashion—alone, away from the house, hunting. According to Ned Cobb, his "daddy'd have his gun on his shoulder and be off on Sitimachas Creek swamps, huntin'," after commanding his wife to "'Take that plow! Hoe!'" The son remembered with bitterness years later that his stepmother (who had borne his father thirteen children) "put part of a day's work in the field" before she died one night.[65]

Ned Cobb's father was undoubtedly an extreme example of a domestic tyrant, but he and other husbands like him inspired white and black women community leaders, educators, and social workers to formulate a critique of African American family life in the late nineteenth century. Sensitive to the economic problems confronted by black marriage partners, these observers charged that black men enjoyed certain male prerogatives without the corresponding striving and ambition that those prerogatives were meant to reward. Juxtaposed with this "irresponsible" man was his wife—no doubt a "real drudge," but certainly "the greatest sufferer from the stress and strain attendant upon the economic conditions" faced by all blacks. The chief problem seemed to stem from the fact that black women played a prominent role in supporting the family in addition to performing their domestic responsibilities. In the eyes of their critics, black men as a group were not particularly concerned about "getting ahead" in the world and thus fell short of their wives' spirit of industry and self-sacrifice.[66]

White teacher-social workers like Rossa Cooley and Georgia Washington and black writers and educators like Anna J. Cooper, Katherine Davis Tillman, Frances Harper, and Fannie Barrier Williams focused on the domestic achievements of poor women and with varying degrees of subtlety condemned their "worthless" husbands. Their critique of black womanhood marked the emergence of the "black matriarchy thesis," for they suggested that the main problem in black family life was an "irresponsible" father who took advantage of his "faithful, hardworking womenfolks." By the mid-twentieth century, sociologists had shifted public attention to the "irresponsible" father's *absence*; the relatively large number of single, working mothers in the nation's urban ghettos seemed to lend additional credence to an argument that originally purported to deal with the problems of rural women. Thus the image of the strong, overburdened black mother persisted through the years, and it was usually accompanied by the implicit assumption that women wielded authority over men and children in these families.[67]

Yet the Cobb household was never a "matriarchy." The difficulty in conceptualizing black male-female roles derives from the fact that most observers (whether writing in the nineteenth century or later) have used as their basis for comparison the white middle-class model of family life. Black men headed the vast majority of southern rural families, and they self-consciously ruled their wives and children; hence the use of the term *patriarchy* to describe family relationships. But these households deviated from the traditional gendered division of labor in the sense that wives worked to supplement the family income, and fathers often lacked the incentive to try to earn money so that they could purchase property or goods and thus advance the family's status. These men worked hard—they had to, in order to survive the ruthlessly exploitative sharecropping system—but most realized that even harder work would not necessarily enable them to escape poverty. Those who confronted this dilemma hardly deserved the epithet "worthless manhood." Still, for husbands and wives, relative equality of economic function did not imply equality of domestic authority.

Although both partners made an essential contribution to the welfare of the household, they were compensated in different ways for their labor. This reward differential reflected their contrasting household responsibilities and produced contrasting attitudes toward work and its personal and social value. As a participant in a staple-crop economy, a black father assumed responsibility for a crop that would be exchanged in the marketplace at the end of the year. He supposedly toiled for future compensation in the form of cash. However, his physical exertion gained him little in the way of immediate reward: in fact he tilled the ground to repay one debt and to ensure that he would have another in the coming year. Under such conditions, most men took pride in their farming abilities, but worked no more strenuously than was absolutely necessary to satisfy white creditors and keep their own families alive in the process.

Their wives, by contrast, daily performed discreet tasks that yielded tangible results upon completion. Meal preparation, laundering, egg gathering—these chores had finite boundaries in the course of a day. Childcare was a special case; it was an ongoing responsibility that began when a woman had her first baby and ended years later when her youngest child left home. On a more mundane level, childcare was a constant preoccupation of mothers during their waking hours, and infants' needs often invaded their sleep. Yet a woman's exclusive authority in this area of domestic life might earn her emotional gratification. Her husband hardly derived a similar sense of gratification from his responsibility for the cotton crop; he "earned" only what a white man was willing to pay him. Hence, the distinction between work patterns simplistically labeled by some contemporary writers as male "irresponsibility" and female "self-sacrifice" actually reflected a complex phenomenon shaped by the different demands made upon black men and women and the degree of personal satisfaction resulting from the fulfillment of those demands.

Elites in the late-nineteenth-century South also stigmatized poor white men and women with charges of laziness and lethargy; together black and white sharecroppers and tenants endured a form of opprobrium traditionally directed at working people by their employers and social "betters." Like their black counterparts, propertyless whites valued self-sufficiency over cash-crop tenancy, and they too confronted new class relationships established after the war—relationships that turned on mortgages, credit, and crop liens as much as on "race" and kinship. By 1900 over one-third of all whites employed in agriculture were tenants, and even small landowners remained perched precariously on the brink of financial disaster, only a drought or a boll weevil plague away from indebtedness. As many as 90 percent of white farmers in Mississippi, Alabama, and Georgia owed money to a local financier at the end of the century. A gradual but significant decrease in domestic food production throughout this period meant that few laborers or tenants regardless of skin color could feed themselves without purchasing supplies from a planter-merchant. Thus all landless farmers, white and black, confronted uncertainties in a period of declining agricultural prices and general economic hardship. It seems likely then that southern poor people as a group deviated from the predominant (that is, white middle-class northern-industrial) culture, a way of life shaped by the powerful ideology of individualism and personal gain.[68]

A comparison of the experiences of poor white and black women in the rural South suggests that to a great extent, class and gender conjoined to determine what all sharecroppers' wives did and how they did it. For example, data on black and white households in the Cotton South for 1880 and 1900 indicate some striking similarities between the family structures characteristic of the two groups. Both types of "average" households possessed a male head, and a male head accompanied by his spouse, in the same proportions. Black and white wives shared the same age patterns relative to their husbands. Though slightly larger, white households had a similar configuration compared to black ones and lived near at least some of their kin to the same extent. (See Appendix C.)

Detailed descriptions of the work of poor white rural women are lacking for the nineteenth century. If we assume, however, that these women were no better off than their daughters and granddaughters who continued to live on farms—and there is no reason to believe that they were—we can extrapolate material about white tenant-farm women in the 1930s to learn about earlier generations. Margaret Hagood's study *Mothers of the South* (published in 1939), suggests that the basic responsibilities of these women had remained the same over the years. Like black women, poor white farm wives bore the domestic burdens characteristic of the economic system of southern staple-crop agriculture. They married in their late teens and had an average of six children (although large households of twelve or thirteen were not uncommon). Because the family was constantly in debt to a local merchant, husbands and wives felt glad if they broke even at the end of the year. Most women made do with very little cash in piecing together the family's subsistence. They performed all the household chores of washing, sewing, cleaning, cooking, and churning, often with the assistance of their eldest daughter, but a majority also helped out in the cotton or tobacco fields during the busy seasons. Wrote Hagood, "The customary practice is for the father's claim for field work to take precedence over that of the mother for help at the house." Like their black counterparts, these wives often supplemented the family income with the proceeds they earned from selling eggs, vegetables, or milk.[69]

In terms of earthly comforts, life offered little more to white tenant-farm wives than it did to blacks: white women lived in sparsely furnished two- or three-room cabins that lacked running water, and their Cotton Belt families tended to move every three years or so. Mothers were attended by a midwife during childbirth. Predictably, they knew nothing about modern contraceptive techniques, and although they took pride in their child-rearing abilities, they suffered from the consequent drain on their emotional and physical resources. Dreams and fortune-tellers explained the past and predicted the future for many of these illiterate women, but they seemed to lack the religious devotion and denominational loyalties exhibited by black wives and mothers. Undernourished and overworked, they had to remind themselves of the biblical dictate, "Be content with your lot."[70]

In a rural society that honored a code of neighborliness and mutual cooperation, black and white women had few opportunities for contact with one another. Husbands and fathers of all skin colors and classes observed a ritualized, "racialized" etiquette in the public arena—in town, at the post office, courthouse, or supply store—but their wives were largely excluded from these encounters. Middle-class white women acted out their own presumptions of racial superiority in their dealings with black servants and laundresses. Tenant-farm wives could not afford to employ black women for any length of time or exploit them in a direct way. A few women of the two groups did come together in situations that held the promise of enhancing mutual respect and appreciation—for example, when they participated in the Southern Farmers Alliance in the 1880s and 1890s, or when black "grannies" attended white women during childbirth. Yet these opportunities were rare, and for the most part women lacked a formal voice in the politics of rural protest.[71]

The fact that the labor of white sharecroppers' wives was so similar to that of their black counterparts is less significant than the social environment in which that work took place. For the outcast group, the preservation of family integrity served as a political statement to the white South, especially in an era marked by the continued exploitation of black workers, and the systematic disfranchisement of black male voters. To nurse a child, send a daughter to school, feed a hungry family after a long day at work in the fields, or patch a shirt by the light of a flickering fire—these simple acts of domesticity assumed special significance when performed for a people so beleaguered by human as well as natural forces. If white women also had to make soup out of scraps, at least they and their families remained secure from "bulldosers" (mobs) and Judge Lynch, and (at least some of) their menfolk voted and participated in a wider political arena. White women as well as white men demonized black men and expressed contempt for black women in ways that were both petty and devastating. The fact that black and poor white women shared the same work responsibilities means not that they shared a political consciousness, but rather that they lived parallel lives. In the end, white women and the daughters of women who had been enslaved sought to teach their children different lessons about the "southern way of life," its freedoms and its dangers.

On the surface, the extreme lengths to which southern elites went in order to preserve such a large, relatively powerless agricultural laboring class seems puzzling. To maintain elaborate rigid structures of American-style apartheid required time, money, and constant vigilance, financial and political burdens not embraced so eagerly by privileged people elsewhere. In northeastern and midwestern cities, employers valued both technological innovation and industrial workers who, though also exploited on the job, managed to embrace a consumerist ethos; if factories were to produce boots and dresses and bicycles, then workers must make cash wages and be able to buy these goods. In contrast, the South self-consciously followed another path; the immiseration of rural blacks served as the distinguishing feature of the regional economy, an indication that whites willingly sacrificed economic development and a more dynamic labor market, all in an effort to preserve traditional social ("racial" and class) hierarchies.

At the same time, the southern case appears not so unusual when viewed in relation to certain other labor systems in the United States and abroad. Whites considered Chinese immigrants and Native Americans similar to blacks in their ability to live off little, a rationale for paying these groups poorly, or (in the case of Native Americans) not at all. The more impoverished a group, the less it could buy and the less "fit" it seemed for the blessings of American citizenship. Meanwhile, around the world, investors were seeking out subordinate populations to grow the crops and mine the minerals and chop the trees to fuel a new, transnational capitalism. Together with landless Japanese and Filipinos toiling in the Hawaiian sugar cane fields, Puerto Ricans growing coffee or sugar cane, and Appalachian whites digging coal out of mine shafts, rural African Americans produced the raw materials that would help to feed, clothe, shelter, and warm the urban middle classes. In this respect the story of rural southern African American women is but a variation of histories of subordinate groups around the globe.

In a world where time-oriented labor increasingly represented a form of "progress," no matter how ambiguous, black women received pay on the basis of the tasks they performed in the fields and in the homes of white people. Despite the transition in labor organization from slavery to sharecropping, the work of black women in the rural South continued to respond to the same human and seasonal rhythms over the generations. By the early twentieth century, they still structured their labor around household chores and childcare, field and sporadic wage work, and community welfare activities. Moreover, emancipation hardly lessened the demands made upon females of all ages; young girls worked alongside their mothers, and elderly women had to provide for themselves and their families as long as they were physically able. Although women's specific duties reflected their variable priorities (determined by the cotton-growing cycle and the size and maturity of individual households), the need for a woman to labor rarely abated in the course of a day, a year, or her lifetime.

In its functional response to unique historical circumstances, the rural black household necessarily differed from the late-nineteenth-century middle-class ideal, which assumed that men would engage in individual self-aggrandizement. According to this ideal, women were to remain isolated at home, only indirectly sharing in the larger social values of wealth and power accumulation. In contrast, rural black women labored in harmony with the values of cooperation and sharing established by their own communities, even as their husbands were prevented from participating in the cash economy in a way that would answer to white-defined notions of masculinity.

Despite the hard, never-ending work performed by rural women—who, ironically, were labeled part of a "lazy" and "shiftless" culture by contemporaries—they could not entirely compensate for the loss of both a husband (through death or another form of permanent separation) and older sons or male relatives who established households on their own. The sharecropping family strove to maintain a delicate balance between its labor resources and its economic needs, and men, as both negotiators in the public sphere and as fieldworkers, were crucial to that balance. Therefore, during the latter part of the nineteenth century, single mothers, widows, and unmarried daughters had little choice but to look cityward.[72] Many of them discovered that while the southern countryside continued to mirror the slave past, in the towns that past was refracted into new shapes and images.

FOUR

BETWEEN THE SOUTHERN COTTON FIELD AND THE NORTHERN GHETTO

The Urban South, 1880–1915

LIFE IN THE turn-of-the-century urban South foreshadowed the conditions that black men and women would eventually encounter in northern and midwestern cities. Although southern towns remained uniquely southern—with all the historic liabilities that the term implies—they also shaped black household structure in ways that would come to characterize the northern ghetto. Husbands were deprived of the satisfaction of providing their families with a reliable source of income, while wives found their duties enlarged as they added full-time paid employment to their already considerable domestic responsibilities.[1]

Whenever rural black folk loaded their few simple possessions into a wooden cart and abandoned the sharecropper's cabin in favor of a new life in a nearby town, they entered a world that was not entirely unfamiliar to them. During the years from 1880 to 1915, these urban in-migrants underwent a less wrenching experience than the one faced by European immigrants or even rural native whites who entered the largest northeastern cities. For blacks in the South, movement out of the countryside was likely to take place incrementally, from plantation to village and then to town or city, and the vast majority remained concentrated in unskilled and service jobs. Still, black households in the placid crossroads of Covington, Louisiana (in 1910, total population of 2,601); in the bustling town of Athens, Georgia (14,913); or the venerable city of Richmond, Virginia (127,678)—all defined as urban areas by the U.S. Bureau of the Census—shared certain characteristics that differentiated them from their rural counterparts. These characteristics were shaped both by an urban labor market segmented on the basis of class, gender, and racial ideologies, and by the demographic characteristics of the migrants themselves. In contrast to labor-hungry cotton plantation owners, nonrural employers usually hired black men only for the duration of a particular construction project or contract. These sporadic wage-earning opportunities guaranteed husbands and sons only low wages and long periods of enforced idleness. In contrast, urban black women, who more often than farm wives served as their families' only provider, found relatively steady employment as domestic servants and laundresses. The city's cash economy in effect heightened individual household members' reliance on one another even as it facilitated the independence of those members who could earn enough to support themselves.[2]

Black women's adjustment to—or acquiescence in—patterns of southern urban life can best be described as uneven. Although they had little choice but to engage in wage-earning activities, female breadwinners resisted yielding completely to the industrial work ethic enshrined in the cities. Domestics sabotaged the best-laid plans of white housewives, tobacco workers declared their own holidays whenever family or community interests dictated, and laundresses continued to engage in a traditional, task-oriented form of labor carried out in their own homes apart from white supervision. At the same time, except for those employed by black businesses, black women found no job opportunities in the emerging clerical and retail sectors, a new, major source of economic opportunity for their white counterparts.

The trend toward growing concentrations of black people in the late-nineteenth-century urban South had significant political implications. Although migration into cities represented only a trickle of persons relative to the total southern black population—no more than 2 or 3 percent each decade during the period from 1880 to 1915—well over a million people participated. Southern blacks constituted a highly significant minority—about 30 percent—of the region's urban population between 1890 and 1910, and about one-fifth lived in towns or cities (the same proportion as southern whites). During this period, growing black urban neighborhoods, together with a new generation of outspoken black leaders (both women and men), began to challenge the emerging system of southern-style apartheid and other efforts by white politicians and employers to solidify their own power. As workers, wives, and club members, black women sought to assert themselves against the new wave of violent intimidation. Participants in the Atlanta washerwomen's strike of 1881, well-dressed Nashville demonstrators protesting segregation on railroad cars, and college graduates serving as the South's first generation of publicly supported school teachers all took part in the growing movement for group self-determination. This type of activism prompted ever more repressive measures on the part of the white South, which in turn spurred the great migration north, beginning in 1916. Ultimately, black refugees from the South during World War I made their own dramatic political statement on behalf of freedom and justice.[3]

WORK AND FAMILY IN A NONRURAL SOUTHERN SETTING

In southern towns, white households maintained a high, steady demand for private household services, and they reserved these jobs for black women. This simple fact had a profound impact on black family life, for it meant that many married black women (unlike the wives and mothers of any other group) rivaled their menfolk as primary breadwinners; the economic dependence that bound wife to husband no longer applied in these cases. Nevertheless, exclusive emphasis on the ways the urban black household deviated from the white middle-class norm obscures the adaptive strategies utilized by black rural in-migrants and urban natives to provide for their families and keep them together. Briefly stated, historians tend to oversimplify several complex demographic and social issues when they cite the male-absent family as conclusive proof of the city's debilitating effects on black people.[4]

The black urban household had readily identifiable structural characteristics. These included relatively high proportions of female-headed families, women in the paid labor force, widows, and fewer family members. The majority of black households consisted of both a father and a mother within the core family, but a significant minority did not. The percentage of female heads varied in cities throughout the South, but overall from 25 to 30 percent of all urban black families (proportionately twice as many as those in rural areas) lacked a husband or father at any one time between 1880 and 1915. Several facts of urban life account for this phenomenon. As a rule, households headed by women were most common among economically disadvantaged groups and among those with an unbalanced sex ratio in favor of females—two major characteristics of the black population in southern cities. Many female heads were over forty years of age, widows who had earlier cohabited with their spouses. The lack of job opportunities for black men caused some to leave their families periodically and search for work elsewhere. Recent in-migrants included large numbers of single women who could not support themselves and their children by working as field-hands or tenant farmers; these women had lost their spouses in the country, not in the city. Finally, some of the younger women who had sole responsibility for their children described themselves to census takers as single, an indication that they had borne children out of wedlock.[5]

Unlike sharecroppers, black urban women had to rely almost exclusively on wage labor in order to provide for their families or supplement their husbands' income. Most of these women—young single women and married, separated, or widowed mothers—toiled either as domestic servants or laundresses. In the largest southern cities, from 50 to 70 percent of all adult black females were gainfully employed at least part of the year around the turn of the century. Young unmarried women reported a job three times more often than similarly situated white women, while black married women entered the workforce five times more often relative to white wives. A case study of workers in Durham reveals that 100 percent of all black female household heads aged twenty to twenty-four were wage earners in 1900; 78 to 80 percent of female heads aged twenty-five to fifty-four reported jobs, as did 66 percent of those over fifty-five years of age.[6]

Census statistics present a portrait of the urban workforce that is frozen in time, one that misses the fluidity in black women's employment situation. Many patched together a living for their families by engaging in a variety of income-producing activities throughout the year. W. E. B. DuBois, for example, told of one city mother who "sells vegetables, chickens and eggs, milk and butter, to neighbors, washes and irons and sometimes cooks." In downtown areas, black women could often be found peddling cakes or hawking fresh flowers when the weather was good. In addition, the concentration of women in laundering and domestic service fails to reveal the increasing numbers who engaged in some form of labor on nearby farms, especially during harvest season. The womenfolk of a particular household often had to adjust their employment according to the family's needs, with grandmothers and daughters finding temporary work during a father's absence or a mother's confinement. The predictably high demand for field-hands during harvesttime encouraged some urban women to seek daily wage work in the countryside in the fall.[7]

Between 1880 and 1910, from 20 to 25 percent of black women in southern cities were widows (white proportions were considerably lower), the result of high death rates among black men and the tendency among older rural women to migrate to urban areas soon after the death of their husband. Elderly women in general worked for wages, if their household needed the extra income, though other members tried to provide for them if at all possible. (In 1880, 63 percent of widows and 49 percent of married women lived with either their children or other kin.) During this period, fully one-quarter of all black women sixty-five years and older in the urban South were gainfully employed, a figure five times higher than that for white women in the same age bracket.[8]

Despite the numerical significance of augmented and extended households (which tended to be larger than the nuclear type), black urban households were smaller than those of whites—about four persons compared to five in the 1890s. The fact that male-absent families on the average had fewer members than those with two parents helps to explain this phenomenon to a limited extent. However, the primary causes of smaller black households fall into four categories: first, the disproportionate number of in-migrants with few or no children; second, declining fertility rates among urban women; third, high mortality rates, especially among children and men; and fourth, the absence of older children, who often left home earlier than those in white families.[9]

Recently widowed sharecroppers' wives had the greatest incentive to move to the city if they had no other family members to help them operate their farms. A study of elderly black female in-migrants living in seventeen southern cities between 1880 and 1900 reveals that the rate of childlessness among this group was double that of their rural counterparts. Thus at least some smaller households reflected their original rural family status and not necessarily the baneful effects of urban life.[10]

A variety of statistical indicators reveals why black households were smaller than those of whites: Black fertility declined by one-third between 1880 and 1910, and overall urban black fertility rates were only half those in rural areas. As a result, southern black women had fewer children than white women of the same region. In 1910 wives of nonagricultural black workers in the South had borne an average of four to six children each, compared to an average of eight for farm wives. The prevalence of infectious diseases among black men and women alike; the nutritionally inadequate diets of all blacks, especially women of child-bearing age; the unbalanced sex ratio in favor of women, making potential mates more difficult to find; and the heavy physical labor required of washerwomen and domestics all contributed to lower fertility rates within urban settlements. For poor people, the various hardships related to city life conspired against proper prenatal care and led to miscarriages and spontaneous abortions. One black physician familiar with the living conditions and work responsibilities of black women in southern cities made this trenchant observation in 1896:

> As to still-births: Why should we be surprised at the great number of stillbirths among our women, since they do most of the work that is liable to produce this state of things? They do the cooking, the sweeping, the lifting of heavy pots; they carry the coal, the wood, the water; they carry heavy burdens on their heads; they do heavy washing, make beds, turn heavy mattresses, and climb the stairs several times during the day, while their more favored white sister is seated in her big armchair, and not allowed to move, even if she wanted to.

These involuntary constraints on normal, healthy childbearing call into question the assertion made by some historians that late-nineteenth-century urban blacks were in the process of "internalizing white fertility norms."[11]

Moreover, a relatively large number of black infants died soon after birth. Overall, black mortality rates in southern cities were consistently higher than those of whites—twice as high in cities like Montgomery, New Orleans, Alexandria, and Norfolk. In 1910 urban blacks were twice as likely to die from tuberculosis as whites, a reflection of the substandard, drafty housing in which they lived. (TB was not a "black" disease, but a poor person's disease.) Predictably, black child mortality ratios were proportionally high and, in some cases, startlingly high. For example, between 1882 and 1895, deaths of children under five in Atlanta accounted for more than one-third of the annual mortality rate for the city's black population. In a black ward of Richmond, about one-half of all the children born to black women who were living in 1900 had died. Although the situation began to improve somewhat around the turn of the century, black death rates remained substantially higher than those of whites. Polluted water supplies, inadequate medical care, crowded living conditions, and long working hours among wage earners all contributed to the unhealthfulness of urban communities. Segregated cemeteries stood in mute testimony to the forces that separated white from black residents, in dying as in living.[12]

City life encouraged and often forced young people from poor families to leave home at an earlier age than their country cousins. When teenage boys found that they could earn a wage and gain some independence from their parents, they often decided to set up housekeeping on their own. The city's cash economy thus shortened the length of time that young men and women were financially beholden to their elders. Consequently, a constant proliferation of new households headed by young men in their late teens or early twenties kept the average black family size relatively low compared to that of both black rural and white urban residents.[13]

Once they established a household and started a family, most black newlyweds found it difficult if not impossible to survive on the husband's earnings alone. Although the urban labor market was more diversified than that in the country, black men remained concentrated in low-paying, unskilled jobs that were temporary or seasonal in nature; in the late nineteenth century, most made less than $30 a month. After the Civil War, the small black artisan class that had emerged during the antebellum period gradually fell on hard times in the form of discriminatory licensing statutes, exclusion from white-controlled trade unions, and prejudice on the part of potential white customers. By the last decade of the century, the

skilled trades (through their unions) and the professions had shut out blacks to a large degree. In the urban South, the majority of black men depended upon short-term, seasonal, or
part-time "public work"—as draymen, construction workers, ditchers, or unskilled factory
workers—and thus lacked both a reliable or self-sufficient income. In 1880 seven black districts in New Orleans had male unemployment rates of from 4 to 55 percent annually, with
an average of almost one out of every five men out of work when the census was taken. An
Atlanta University study conducted in 1897 revealed that of 1,100 urban families, only 24
percent relied exclusively on a male household head's earnings; various combinations of
working wives, children, and relatives were needed to sustain individual households. During the first decade of the twentieth century, four out of five black male workers in Athens,
Georgia, "shift[ed] their employment as the public demand[ed]" and rarely had work for
more than nine months out of the year.[14]

Most men knew when and where to find available jobs—at a certain time in a local
foundry or sawmill, for example. In the off-season they often congregated during the day at
a neighborhood meeting spot, perhaps a grocery store or saloon. In this manner they could
make themselves visible to potential employers who needed day laborers and at the same
time socialize with one another. This "street-corner culture" combined elements of fatalism
with a raucous sort of male camaraderie based on gambling and drinking (and it was a culture that inspired the strong disapproval of black wives and mothers of all ages). In his 1908
report entitled "Negro American Family," DuBois attributed the "idleness and loafing"
among Covington, Georgia, black men who spent their time in "dives and gambling dens"
to "the irregularity of work at certain seasons of the year." At least one cynical observer
suggested that these men had little incentive to seek employment, supported as they were
"by the work of their wives, mothers, or sweethearts." A historically more accurate account
would replace such speculation with attention to the structural factors that limited the availability of work to black husbands, fathers, and sons.[15]

Black people in general remained conspicuous for their absence from textile mill machine-
operative work, though a few black women toiled as custodians in the mills and as domestics in the homes of white workers. And white women, especially those who were young
and unmarried, began to find work in the clerical and retail sectors, and other forms of employment in a relatively clean and safe environment. Trapped within the urban matrix of
discrimination and material deprivation, black wives and mothers often had to take whatever jobs they could find. Still, some did manage to supplement the household income with
a type of work that allowed them a modicum of control over their time and childcare responsibilities. For mothers, washing and ironing clothes provided an opportunity to work
without the interference of whites, and with the help of their own children, at home. In 1900
more women aged thirty-five and older performed laundry work than domestic service.
The arduousness of this type of work, and the contempt with which middle-class whites regarded manual labor of any kind—especially cleaning (whether floors, clothes, or infants)—meant that laundering was the province of black women exclusively.
Washerwomen ranked highest on the "racial exclusion" scale, even higher than domestics,
in the Cotton South by the late nineteenth century.[16]

Although laundering involved little in the way of equipment or initial investment, it hardly paid a woman a reasonable wage for her considerable expenditure of energy. Most women made no more than a couple of dollars a week for work that was exceedingly heavy and hot, and especially unpleasant in the South's already steamy summertime climate. A woman would usually collect clothes on Monday from two or three families. She set up a large pot in the yard of her house and instructed the children to help her draw water. The clothes had to be boiled in the pot, scrubbed on a washboard, rinsed, starched, wrung out, hung up, and ironed. (She had to pay for the starch and soap out of her own meager earnings.) On Saturday she would deliver the clothes and, she hoped, collect her money. A customer's complaints that her new wash powder had eaten a hole in his shirt, or that she had lost a sock, resulted in his refusal to pay for the entire week's load if she was lucky, her imprisonment if she was not.[17]

Women could also earn some money by taking in boarders. In Richmond, the nuclear family gradually declined in importance as black husbands and wives either accepted lodgers (to produce an augmented household) or kin (extended). In 1880, 65 percent of black households in the Jackson ward of Richmond included only a core of one or both parents and children; twenty years later that figure had shrunk to 41 percent, with 31 percent of all households extended and the rest augmented. This trend probably reflected the accelerated in-migration among blacks from the surrounding countryside, and the increasing reliance of a poverty-stricken population on members of its own group for housing and economic support.[18]

Despite the undeniable economic pressures on the family, few households were thrown entirely upon their own resources. Cramped quarters pushed people out into their tiny yards, the children to play, the wives to wash clothes and to chat with neighbors, allowing family members to merge with the community. Relatives looked after the offspring of working mothers during the day and welcomed into their homes eager newcomers fresh off the farm. The kin networks that gave shape to black rural life remained intact and in some cases even intensified in the urban environment. For example, elderly urban women more often lived with relatives than did elderly women in the country. Older female residents of extended households in the cities found their wage-earning responsibilities lessened to a considerable degree by younger people, revealing once again the inadequacy of judging the strength of family ties solely on the basis of nuclear family structure.[19]

The concentration of people promoted a cooperative ethos evident in institutional structures and informal activity. Benevolent and mutual aid societies flourished in urban areas where people had more cash and greater access to central meeting places. Of the twenty-two different voluntary societies in Petersburg, Virginia, in 1898, about half consisted exclusively of female members; these included the Sisters of Friendship (organized during the antebellum period), Sisters of Charity, Ladies Union, Daughters of Bethlehem, Loving Sisters, Ladies Working Club, Daughters of Zion, Young Sisters of Charity, Sisters of David, and Sisters of Rebeccah. Also, communication among workers affected the shape of local urban labor markets. The practice among men and women in some towns to refuse a job from which a neighbor had been fired illustrated the existence of a spirit of cooperation over and above economic self-interest. If the marital relationship experienced severe disruptions as a result of the vicissitudes of urban life, then neighborhoods sought to compensate with a tight network of both formal and informal, secular and church-related social welfare services.[20]

Whatever their trials and tribulations, black women continued to aid and be aided by their friends and relatives. Whenever husbands went off to look for work and older sons and daughters abandoned home to start life anew on their own, wives and mothers took in lodgers or consolidated households with the family next door. Kin and community could help, at least in some minimal way, to fill a gap left by the death or departure of a household wage earner. Consequently, family and community were separated only by a shifting, tenuous boundary, as one social institution expanded or contracted to compensate for the inadequacies (either temporary or permanent) of the other. In contrast to the movement inherent in this process, its purpose remained fixed: to provide people with the basic needs of everyday life—clothing, shelter, and emotional and physical sustenance.

"TOO PROUD TO BEND, TOO POOR TO BREAK"[21]: IN THE SERVICE OF WHITE FAMILIES

Domestic service recapitulated the mistress-slave relationship in the midst of late-nineteenth-century industrializing America. As paid labor became increasingly associated with the time-oriented production of goods, the black nurse, maid, and cook remained something of a labor-force anachronism in a national if not regional (southern) context. A traditional form of "women's work"—dirty, tedious, low-paying—service lacked the rewards of self-satisfaction and pride that supposedly accompanied such tasks when performed for one's own family. In fact, the system of paid household labor itself undermined the black woman's own role as mother and homemaker. It thus served as a tangible reminder of the days of bondage, when black women were (in the eyes of whites) servants first and family members only incidentally. Moreover, service made manifest all the tensions and uncertainties inherent in the personal interaction between the female members of two different classes. The mistress showed "all kinds of harshness and meanness in the kitchen" though she smiled in the parlor, while her servant retaliated with strategies perversely appropriate to the domestic battleground. Of the black women who earned wages in the late nineteenth century, fully 90 percent of them labored as domestic servants in private homes or in commercial settings such as hotels and boardinghouses.[22]

Under the southern system of apartheid, laws mandating "racial" segregation were meant to humiliate blacks, and not necessarily to keep black and white people apart from each other on a daily basis. Alfred Holt Stone, a Mississippi planter, made the case for legally enforced segregation when he highlighted the contradiction between the routine proximity of the two groups in the course of daily life on the one hand, and the abrogation of black civil rights on the other: Black and white people might interact, and remain in close and even intimate contact with each other, "provided it be upon terms which contain no equality of personal status." In the urban South, the work of black domestics came to sym-bolize that contradiction.[23]

In general, the younger the black woman, the more likely she worked in a white house-hold; married women worked as laundresses (in their own homes) in slightly larger num-bers. After the Civil War, day service—in contrast to living in—came to predominate, as black women refused to subordinate completely their own family interests to the demands of a white employer; the 15 or 20 percent of urban servants who lived in white households were probably young single women. Because they had virtually no other employment op-portunities, these women had to accept the most exploitative wages—$4.00 to $8.00 per month for cooks and maids, $1.50 to $3.00 for nurses (often girls who were children them-selves). In many cases, the length of the workday varied from day to day, with women ex-pected to remain under their employer's roof for twelve to fourteen hours at a time and even on call "from sunrise to sunrise, every day in the week" if they lived in the house or nearby. The cheapness of domestic labor meant that all but the poorest white families con-sidered some sort of "help" an affordable necessity.[24]

Household employees suffered from internal conflict and stress as a result of working very long hours for white families and spending proportionately less time caring for their own. A general description of their daily routine, compiled from a variety of firsthand ac-counts, social workers' reports, and contemporary urban studies, holds true for most women in a variety of situations: widows, wives whose husbands might or might not have steady employment, mothers with or without older children to help out around the house, daughters who felt some responsibility for the welfare of younger siblings left alone at home. At the same time, there is little evidence to suggest that unemployed black husbands took care of cleaning, cooking, or childcare while their wives were at work.

Most servants were expected to arrive at their employer's house quite early in the morn-ing to prepare or serve breakfast to the white family. In Chattanooga, "one of the first scenes in our streets between the hours of five and six o'clock in the morning is large num-bers of women rushing to their places of work for the day." Usually children would awaken with their mother, and she quickly gave them something to eat—"sometimes a piece of bread, sometimes it is a little molasses in a tin plate or old bucket top." This early-morning departure at times caused a mild uproar; the children, not quite awake, might quarrel among themselves and plead with their mother to stay home.[25]

Provisions for childcare depended upon a family's circumstances. Once in a while a mother might take a child to work with her, although this probably worked best only for women who labored in an institutional setting such as a hotel kitchen, where they were not so closely supervised as in a private home. Most women had to entrust the care of their offspring to a neighbor, nearby relative, or older sibling (in all likelihood these persons also had other responsibilities during the day), or leave them alone to fend for themselves. Many years later one black educator recalled that his mother, the cook for an "exacting" white family, could not always return home to feed her children at mealtime; "we would of-ten cry for food," he remembered, "until, falling here and there on the floor, we would sob ourselves off to sleep." Just as often, youngsters were left free to wander in or out of their own neighborhood, and they invariably got into mischief: "They ramble about until tired, fall down at almost any place, go to sleep, and wake up again only to continue the ramble, sometimes until late in the night." Some of the older ones found themselves in a jail cell at the end of the day. More than one observer even suggested that the high mortality rates among urban children were due to daytime accidents or diseases that their overworked, distracted parents failed to detect in time. For children of all ages, the city presented a "miry slough" of temptation and physical danger.[26]

Depending upon the proximity of her place of work to her own home and the whims of her employer, a woman might snatch some time and return briefly to check up on her household during the afternoon. Cooks in particular often insisted on time off after the noonday meal and nurses sometimes scheduled a midday stroll with their white charges so that they could look in on their own children (or siblings) at home. Because "white folks don't like to see their servants' children hanging around their premises," few mothers felt free to encourage their offspring to visit them at work. Whenever a mother returned home (usually in the evening around 8:00 p.m.), she brought with her leftover food from her employer's kitchen, commonly referred to as a "service pan." A well-established custom— "part of the oral contract, exprest or implied" between mistress and maid—the service pan expanded in proportion to a black woman's needs and resourcefulness. In any case, it was not until the end of the day that she had any time to spend with her own children, and then only if she could locate them quickly. At times a woman would have to scour the community for little ones who had gotten lost or fallen asleep in some tucked-away nook or cranny. Once recovered, they were bound to be cranky, tired, and hungry. A mother had to squeeze whatever attention and affection she could find time to give her children into these late-night hours and her day off. Yet their welfare remained a constant preoccupation with her as she fed, diapered, and amused white babies.[27]

One investigator noted that the more conscientious a domestic servant as a wife and mother, the poorer the quality of her performance in a white household. Lingering bitterness and guilt over necessarily neglected chores at home no doubt affected the way a woman or even young girl felt about her job. These angry feelings festered in a workplace full of mutual suspicion and hostility between employer and employee. White women perceived their relationship with their servants to be one of never-ending antagonism, and, as a matter of pride, principle, and practicality, they often felt compelled to extract as much labor as possible from their servants.[28]

Although mistresses dubbed their employees with the titles of maid, cook, or nurse, they in fact placed little value on labor specialization within their households. Thus a "nurse" could find herself "watering the lawn in front with the garden hose, sweeping the sidewalk, mopping the porch and halls, dusting around the house, helping the cook, or darning stockings." An unsuspecting black woman in Richmond responded to an advertisement for a "chambermaid in a small family," and soon after accepting the position discovered that she was "expected to answer the door bell, wait on the table, keep the rooms in order, and make herself generally useful as assistant cook or laundress"—for a family of ten. She quit after a week, adding to the growing list of "slovenly and unreliable" maids who had failed to sat-isfy the mistress. In response to a questionnaire distributed in 1913, a white woman in Athens, Georgia, expressed her disgust with the current state of service, because "the cook does not want to clean house and driver will not work the garden, or serve the table."[29]

For post–Civil War era black domestics, the work environment remained heavily laden with the trappings of slavery. Blacks had to "put a handle" to white folks' names. One South Carolina white man reported, "Occasionally a pert maid or man servant will address their employers as Mr. and Mrs. instead of Master or Miss, but the whites are very jealous of such innovations; I have known several nurses discharged because they refused to prefix Master to the names of the children." Yet a black woman, regardless of her age, was re-ferred to as "cook," "Mammy," or "Betty May" by all, including the youngest members of the household: "The child I work for calls me girl." Added to this enforced deference were the wildly erratic personalities of individual white women. Deprived of formal economic or political power, and convinced of their own "racial" superiority, they fiercely tried to main-tain the upper hand in governing sullen, recalcitrant servants. In the kitchen, bedroom, and parlor, in the course of a fourteen-hour day, a "disordered temperament" could find a mul-titude of opportunities to wreak emotional and physical violence upon another human be-ing so similar to yet so different from herself, especially when her husband and son considered a servant "their special prey." Thus the often-cited "closeness" between women of the two groups—at times mothers about the same age—was more illusory than real. Many black women, raised with the admonition "never to lie except to white people," kept their own counsel despite long years of "faithful" service to a single white household.[30]

Predictably, then, servants resisted providing their employers with unbroken hours (or days) of hard, steady labor. Indeed, a number of specific strategies enabled them to main-tain some control over the workplace and some self-respect in the process. The pervasive use of these tactics among blacks guaranteed that the mistress-servant relationship would be no less turbulent or hostile just because it was "personal." For example, in listing griev-ances about the work habits of their employees, white women used a standard stock of ad-jectives that dramatically conveyed the nature and form of black women's resistance to this "relic of slavery"—incompetent, worthless, untidy, indolent, wasteful. Not only did ser-vants have to be monitored constantly, "as negroes never do anything without being told," they rarely passed up an opportunity to irritate their employers. A white man in South Car-olina voiced common complaints: "Negro seamstresses always (except a few who were reared and trained in cultivated families) perform coarse sewing, and the washerwomen . . . badly damage the clothes they work on, iron-rusting them, tearing them, breaking off the buttons, and burning them brown; and as for starch!—Colored cooks, too, generally abuse stoves, suffering them to get clogged with soot, and to 'burn out' in half the time they ought to last." Writing in the Charlotte, North Carolina, *Chronicle* in 1889, a white woman voiced a familiar complaint about the attitude of her servants and their unwillingness to work cheerfully: "Those who consent to wait in the dining room are very apt to be disagreeably insolent," she noted. An Athens mistress summed up the problem when she described her employees as "thorough and reliable in nothing."[31]

Domestics arrived late to work, left early in the afternoon, or stayed away for days at a time to mark special events and holidays. Communal celebrations in their own neighborhoods took precedence over the needs and expectations of their employers. Revivals periodically inspired sinners to "get religion" and join with others in an ecstasy of newfound salvation. A circus in town often accounted for cold stoves and dirty parlors in white households. "Excursions"—the chartering of a train for pleasure and fund-raising on behalf of a church or benevolent society—proved to be the bane of many a mistress's existence. Moreover, the catchall explanation of "illness" masked a wide variety of activities that easily and frequently kept servants from their daily routine. Testifying before the U.S. Senate Committee on Education and Labor in 1883, one Alabama white woman noted of her servants' unreliability: "No matter how much they may be needed in the house, no matter how important the occasion may be, or how urgent the need for their services, they will just leave the cooking-stove . . . and go off." For the average southern housewife, the end of slavery signaled the onset of a "makeshift kind of life," the woman continued, and reminded committee members that absent servants meant "you have got to go and cook your own dinner, and another housekeeper has to go and wait on her own table, and so on."[32]

White women justified the low wages paid to domestics by arguing that "theft," as an institutionalized part of the job and extension of the legitimate service pan, entailed considerable loss of food and clothing. Most had no choice but to consider it "a kind of underhand commutation of wages," a price they paid for any service at all. When asked how she compensated her servants, one Georgia mistress responded, "We can add to the money wage, clothing, shoes, overcoats, rain coats, blankets, etc. Much that is new, much that is 'second hand' but the money is only part." Depending upon the degree of her employer's desperation to hold on to her, and her need to hold on to this particular job, the shrewd cook or maid tested the limits of her ingenuity. She spirited away from the kitchen not only scraps and leftovers but also the cakes, biscuits, and pies she had prepared that afternoon. She "borrowed" all sorts of staples from the neighboring household—food that never found its way onto the mistress's table. Servants considered "toting" as their right, a hard-earned form of "pay" for a distasteful job.[33]

During this period, white working-class women in the North clearly preferred the most grueling factory work over domestic service, and their entrance into the clerical and manufacturing sectors left an increasing proportion of black women to scrub floors, make beds, and cook meals for employers. In the South, black women had few alternatives to this kind of employment, but they too made it clear that almost any other kind of paid labor had its relative advantages. For example, seafood processing involved messy, smelly work, but one researcher noted that in Warsaw, Georgia, where it was available to black women, "domestic work is very hard to secure. Most of the women prefer to shuck oysters at higher wages with shorter hours of service and greater personal freedom." Similarly, white women in Litwalton, Virginia, found it difficult to hire day workers because black women there could make a minimum of forty cents a day in seafood-processing plants. In other areas, cotton-picking time in the surrounding countryside prompted a temporary exodus of domestic workers out of the towns.[34]

Despite their dependence on subsistence-level wages, black women had priorities that at times superseded work for whites. If a woman lived in a small town and cultivated an extensive garden, she might stay at home and feed her family fresh fruits and vegetables, and peddle the remainder at an open-air market. Some servants saved small sums of money during the year so that they would not have to spend summer days slaving over a stove "too hot for us." This impulse helps to account for the argument made by white women in favor of keeping servants' wages low—if they made more, it was assumed, they would readjust their work hours and days accordingly. Finally, black communities frequently demonstrated their own "code of color ethics," which stipulated that a person should not work for a white woman who was a well-known unscrupulous employer, or one who was particularly "'finicky,' or hard to please." Indeed, in Athens, according to one contemporary investigator, "So widely known are the methods of individual housekeepers, and so strange to the whites is the inner life of the darker half of the population, that it is believed by some that a blacklist is kept by the negro lodges, and that the servants keep 'tabs' in this way on their employers." In fact, mutual support and cooperation among blacks gave the appearance of an "organization," provoking among white women constant discussion of "the servant problem" and ways to combat it.[35]

During a period in American history when increasing numbers of people found work performing unskilled manual-labor jobs in an industrial setting, domestic service represented an enduring form of traditional, premodern employment for women. The job's hours and description varied according to the desires of the employer, and those might change in the course of an hour or a day. The intense relationship between mistress and maid, and the inevitable intrusion of temperamental factors into that relationship, differed significantly from the relatively anonymous factory shop, where a number of laborers toiled side-by-side at stipulated tasks. Factory workers were designated "hands"—they served as an extension of the machinery they worked with—but domestics were "help," a term that implied a certain amount of informality and interaction between employer and employee.

At the same time, the contrast between the industrial workplace and the white household invites certain intriguing comparisons. Like wage earners in the manufacturing process, domestics had potential power over their employers because they controlled the quality of their own labor and, either individually or collectively, the supply of that labor. The white mistress served as both the owner of an establishment and manager of her own workers; although she did not hire servants in order to make a profit, she did try to make them work as efficiently as possible. She could either resign herself to her workers' inadequacies or search for new ones—an almost universal dilemma among exasperated Victorian mistresses. Indeed, compared to northern industrial workers who challenged harsh working conditions in late-nineteenth-century factories, black domestics exhibited an equal if not greater amount of day-to-day resistance to the demands imposed upon them. Individually, these servants waged their own war against the slave legacy; collectively, they wielded an informal power that directly affected the basic human services provided within white households.

ALTERNATIVES TO DOMESTIC SERVICE, AND THEIR LIABILITIES

Whether they were oyster shuckers or tobacco stemmers, black women were not easily transformed into "modern" workers. As black people, they had not been given the chance to demonstrate a thoroughgoing commitment to the industrial work ethic of time-oriented factory discipline. As women, they sought to help make family ends meet, combining their role of budget-stretcher with that of on-and-off breadwinner. Inevitably they looked forward to the time when a small cash reserve, or a husband's steady income, would allow them to devote all their time to household chores and childcare responsibilities. Motherhood, not job status, served as their primary source of self-definition, and for this reason nurturing duties frequently won out over the foreman's insistence on punctual and regular work habits. Furthermore, the single-minded devotion to industry that only personal drive could instill was merely a useless expenditure of energy among workers automatically denied any chance of advancement because of rigid gender segregation in the workplace. But if southern black women had a great deal in common with unmarried white immigrant women toiling in the sweatshops of New York City, they also shared certain attitudes and allegiances with their menfolk in the African American community. In the midst of urban congestion, blacks maintained an aversion to closely supervised, strictly regimented labor—an aversion born in the cotton fields and hardened by the overseer's whip. Resistance to industrial work discipline thus amounted to resistance to the "racial" caste system itself. Unlike the white hill-country people employed in the cotton mills, blacks entered the factory not simply as rural folk, but as a distinct subgroup with a long history of enforced subservience.[36]

Black women who fled from the degradation of domestic service only to find themselves in the hot, humid tobacco stemmers' room paid a high price in terms of their general health and well-being; and in the process, they exchanged the mistress's capriciousness for the shop foreman's rules and regulations. Their experiences as tobacco workers in particular reveal that they played a necessarily limited role in postwar southern economic development without ever being truly integrated into the industrial workforce. Certainly southern blacks were not unique in their defiance of the factory bell. But the hardships imposed upon black women in the southern industrial work setting did represent a unique intersection of racial, gender, and class liabilities among one group of workers in late-nineteenth-century America.

Tensions that underlay the South's racial caste and economic class systems influenced industrialists' attitudes toward mechanization and hiring practices. The region's large supply of cheap black labor inhibited technological advances in several industries (including cotton cultivation and iron and tobacco) for many years. In deciding whether to hire blacks or whites, and in segregating their workers, employers manipulated "racial" antagonisms in order to inhibit unionization and bolster the status of poor whites at the expense of blacks.[37]

At first glance, the tiny number of black women cotton mill employees—883 (most were scrubwomen and custodians) out of a total of 728,309 southern black women engaged in nonagricultural pursuits in 1910—seems difficult to understand. Masters and mistresses used enslaved women extensively in small-scale textile production on antebellum plantations, and owners of textile mills put black men, women, and children to work as machine operatives. After the war freedwomen eagerly sought new kinds of employment as alternatives to domestic service and fieldwork. Yet New South textile lords hired virtually no black women as mill operatives or even menial laborers on a sustained basis. The few black men who found work in this industry—the cornerstone of the late-nineteenth-century southern "industrial revolution"—were confined to the periphery of the manufacturing process. Of the 6,333 black male textile mill employees in 1910, most swept floors and stairways, labored in the dye house, or served as teamsters. Some worked in the picker and card rooms, "where a large amount of floating lint, dust, and dirt is always found, and where the work is heavier and more disagreeable than in any other department in the mill." Black children, hired even less frequently than their mothers, worked as waste-gatherers and sweepers. In 1915, South Carolina passed a law barring blacks and whites from laboring in the same cotton-mill room, but by this time the exclusion of blacks from these worksites was a well-institutionalized practice throughout the South. In short, as one historian notes, "Cotton mills were reserved for whites."[38]

As the price of cotton declined throughout the last quarter of the nineteenth century and rates of farm tenancy among poor whites increased, agrarian radicalism emerged as a political force; both the rhetoric and grassroots activity of disaffected small farmers escalated during the 1880s and 1890s. The New South economic elite sought to defuse any possibility of biracial cooperation that might threaten the hegemony of planters and financiers. One tactic was to bring the families of impoverished Georgia and South Carolina "sandhillers" or North Carolina "clayeaters" into the new cotton mills, built in nearby locales (the Piedmont region). Thus a policy that had purely financial consequences during the antebellum period (enslaved operatives were relatively expensive) assumed a special political urgency after the war and shaped the demographic profile of mill workers until the early 1970s.[39]

Given the primacy of racial-ideological factors at work in this process, southerners' attempts to explain their refusal to hire black workers sound a bit hollow and even embarrassed. Once in a while a candid mill superintendent (like this one in Augusta, Georgia), dared to venture aloud, "Why, we have negro bricklayers, tailors, decorators, and these do handsome work; negro women are good seamstresses; there are negro dentists and doctors. I don't see why piccaninnies won't make good factory hands, spinning and weaving. There is nothing lacking in their capacity to learn." Other whites who agreed preferred to keep their opinions to themselves and only half-jokingly suggested that their "fellow-manufacturers would want to hang" them for voicing such heresy.[40]

New South propagandists routinely justified their decision to exclude blacks from the mills by insisting that the former slaves were "careless" and "not temperamentally adapted to monotonous, mechanical work." Furthermore, they suggested, "The negro women have not the deftness of white women and could not, therefore, economically take their place.

The same is true of the children." For the most part, however, neither southern industrial-ists nor the contemporary northern scholars who put the stamp of social-scientific re-spectability on their labor management decisions distinguished between black men and women when discussing their potential as mill workers. Racial ideologies overshadowed gender as the primary determinant of labor-force composition. Slaveholders who had put slaves to work at a variety of industrial and skilled tasks would have been surprised to hear their New South grandsons expound upon black people's congenital physical "unfitness for the exactions of manufacturing occupations."[41]

It is clear that, given the chance, black women would have accepted mill jobs regardless of the arduousness or unhealthfulness of the work. That some preferred even the worst in-dustrial jobs to domestic service is apparent from their relatively high participation in the manufacturing of tobacco. By all accounts, the processing of raw tobacco into cigars and chewing plugs represented the least desirable and lowest-paying type of factory work in the late-nineteenth-century South. For this reason, white employers in the eleven former Con-federate states were using, by 1910, up to 8,482 black women annually—2,138 unskilled and 6,344 semiskilled workers. Although this number accounts for less than 2 percent of all southern black women engaged in nonagricultural pursuits, it presents a striking contrast to the textile mill counterexample. If cotton manufacturers felt they had to articulate, if not put into action, paternalistic professions of concern for their white workers, then tobacco employers felt no such compunction. The result was a system of labor exploitation un-adorned by the veneer of paeans to progress or (white) "racial" self-interest.[42]

Enslaved workers had predominated in antebellum tobacco factories (most of them con-centrated in Virginia) that specialized in the production of cigars and chewing tobacco. Af-ter the war, black women continued to labor as "rehandlers," sorting, stripping, stemming, and hanging tobacco leaves—all part of the redrying process. Several factors in the late nineteenth century led to the rapid growth of tobacco manufacturing and the employment of greater numbers of white women as skilled operatives; these included the mechanization of the industry, an increase in demand for cigarettes, and the consequent shift in production sites from the old tobacco belt of Virginia to the "Bright Yellow" (cigarette) belt centered in North Carolina. But as more white women took jobs as cigarette rollers, black women retained their positions as rehandlers, the worst of all tobacco factory jobs.[43]

A complex system of group segregation remained in effect throughout the industry. Ci-gar factories tended to employ blacks as both laborers and operatives while cigarette manu-facturers used white women as skilled workers and blacks as manual laborers. In cigar factories black women sorted the tobacco according to a company grading system, stripped individual leaves of their central stem and hung them up to dry, and labeled the cigars or plugs and packed them into boxes. Black men converted the raw leaf (mixed with a sweet licorice mixture) into a finished product. When whites and blacks worked under the same roof in cigarette manufacturing, they toiled in separate work spaces, all of which were su-pervised by white foremen.[44]

The fact that black women were kept apart from both men and white women facilitated discriminatory working conditions in individual factories. Exempt from the social and political pressures that limited their counterparts in the textile business to an all-white work-force, tobacco manufacturers could well afford to ignore health and safety considerations and to keep wages at rock-bottom minimums, especially in the redrying plants. The average rehandler toiled five and one-half days a week, but the seasonal nature of her job limited most to less than nine months of steady work each year. In a study of 2,318 black female tobacco and cigar factory operatives, DuBois found that one-third were unemployed at least four months each year. In 1880 workers in North Carolina made from forty to eighty cents a day (often for twelve-hour days), and thirty-five years later the vast majority in the same state still took home less than six dollars a week in wages.[45]

Gender discrimination compounded "racial" prejudice in limiting the wages and prospects of black women. A survey of industry wage levels conducted during the first decade of the twentieth century revealed that adult female tobacco workers in North Carolina and Virginia earned only $154 to $180 annually, about two-thirds of average male wages. Few black women ever had the chance to advance to a better job and earn a living wage. Satisfactory workers were given "year round jobs," not promotions. Even an employer "who conceded that during an emergency when an experiment could be safely risked, 'Negro women made the prettiest cigars you ever saw,'" staunchly refused to promote his female workers on a permanent basis, "thereby following the path of least resistance."[46]

Emma Shields, an investigator for the United States Department of Labor's Women's Bureau, noted in her study of black women in the southern tobacco industry that these workers had been systematically deprived of those "industrial incentives and rewards which have proven beneficial and inspiring to other groups in industry." While engaged in the mind-deadening process of sorting and stemming, they had to work standing up in sweltering, poorly lighted workrooms, "where the rays of sunlight are shut out by an apron or an old burlap bag, and where even the fresh air cannot be admitted lest it dry the tobacco." In some factories, mingled with the particles of tobacco dust was the stench emanating from a tiny water closet—"a small space partitioned off from the work-room which supplies its only ventilation. The air in this room is usually so heavily laden with fumes that it is nauseating. It is not uncommon to see the workers with handkerchiefs tied over their nostrils to prevent inhaling the stifling, strangling air." The workplace lacked any facilities wherein a woman might hang her coat, dress in work clothes, rest, or eat her lunch; the short breaks found workers at their benches or out in the street. Dirt-encrusted floors—"Managers consider it a joke to even suggest scrubbing them"—and the communal drinking cup tied to a water barrel were also "typical of tobacco rehandling plants, which offer the principal factory employment to Negro women in the Southland," Shields observed. Laborers routinely contracted respiratory ailments and cankerous sores on their hands and lips.[47]

Many of these workers had to support their families, either alone or with the help of other household members. Of 4,639 black women employed as tobacco and cigar operatives in 1900, more than 55 percent were at least twenty-five years of age and either married, widowed, or divorced. (Women laborers included some who were "very old, others crippled.") The percentage of single women engaged in this type of work (45 percent) was lower than that in domestic service (53 percent) but higher compared to laundry work (23 percent).

Since a majority of these women were married, or had been at one time, they often had to make some provisions for childcare during the day. As a result, it was not uncommon for young children to assist in the rehandling process. Stemming and stripping "tended to become a family occupation, mothers bringing their children or young workers their younger brothers and sisters, these latter working sometimes only before and after school, and in other cases all through the day."[48]

Southern employers sometimes made contradictory statements regarding the efficiency of black women as tobacco workers. In an indirect way, at least, these statements reveal the internal struggle waged by black women who had no choice but to work, and yet refused to submit completely to the dehumanizing system of industrial work discipline. The fact that black women and girls were willing—or rather, desperate enough—to work under such wretched conditions caused factory owners and supervisors to declare that they were inherently suited for this type of employment. The tobacco industry as a whole enjoyed an oversupply of labor between 1880 and 1910, encouraging many women to try to hold on to their jobs; in return they earned praise for their "childlike loyalty to their employers."[49]

A large pool of women willing to work (at least temporarily) provided foremen with an opportunity to dismiss persons who committed the slightest infraction against factory discipline and to ignore the prevalence of occupational dangers. As Nanny May Tilley suggests in her history of the Bright Yellow tobacco industry, "Work in stemmeries involved numerous hazards including fires, falling elevators, cuts from drying fans, and collisions with drays. Yet it was not unusual for operators of plants to call for and secure large numbers of Negro workers on short notice." The reluctance of whites to accept this form of employment led superintendents to value black workers more highly than the poor wages or working conditions indicated. Still, industrialists persisted in bemoaning their own "dependence on shiftless and unreliable Negro women and children," and employers remained at the mercy of traveling fairs, berry-picking season, funerals, church socials, and their workers' impulse to visit rural kinfolk.[50]

Prevented from talking to one another or sitting in the workplace—foremen apparently believed that both conversation and chairs caused the pace to slacken—female rehandlers sang together. In this way they established a rhythm to make the repetitive tasks more bearable even as they collectively expressed feelings of hope and protest: "Oh, by an' by I'm goin' to lay down this heavy load." Ironically, this form of resistance to the monotony of industrial labor (apparently unique to black tobacco workers during this period in American history) convinced manufacturers that their employees were happy and content. Domestic and foreign visitors alike professed to be deeply affected by the sight and sound of stemmers moving back and forth in unison, "bodies swaying and fingers flying," their voices lifted in sorrowful lament. The novelty of the scene apparently distracted most observers from remarking upon the heat, dust, and dirt that the singers were trying to transcend. And few whites at the time would have been able to recognize the similarity between these workers and their enslaved foremothers who sang as they wove cloth or hoed the cotton fields together.[51]

It would be a mistake to assume that, just because black women had few other viable employment options, they accepted these jobs gratefully and uncritically. Indeed, the comments made by one elderly Danville woman who had worked as a stemmer and grader for sixty years indicate that at least some of these workers had a sense of their own worth even if their employers did not. Elviry Magee testified to the skilled nature of her labor:

> I tell you one thing, I knows tobacco. I knows all de grades an' blends. I knows bright tobacco an' burley tobacco an' Kaintucky tobacco an' all de rest. You 'members Old Man Hughes what built all dese here schools an' horspitals in town? Well, I learnt Mister John how to grade tobacco when he first come in de factory. Yes, Jesus, I give Mister John his start. I'm po' now an' I was po' den but he come to be a rich man. But it didn't do him no good. De Lawd called him away wi' Bright's misery. I believes one reason was case he didn't pay niggers nothin'. I was his best hand—he say so hisse'f—an' he didn't never pay . . . no mo'n fifty to sebenty-five cents a day.

Elviry Magee derived at least a measure of satisfaction from her own expertise. If life on earth was cruel and unjust, she took comfort in the belief that God would eventually vindicate her claim.[52]

Tobacco manufacturing was a distinctly urban enterprise, and black female tobacco workers suffered from the family disruptions and lack of employment alternatives characteristic of an urban setting in the late-nineteenth-century South. In contrast, employees of seafood-processing plants combined elements of both industrial and rural work patterns; they labored in factories for part of the year and then returned to fishing, farming, or other jobs during the off-season. Consequently their work and family experiences represented variations on both urban and rural themes.

Oyster gathering and processing engaged the energies of entire families that lived in coastal areas of the southeastern United States. The harvest lasted from September through April, though few persons employed in the industry worked steadily or full time even during these months. Husbands and fathers, some of whom owned their own boats, gathered the oysters in the course of ten-day fishing trips and arranged to have them shipped to nearby factories; for a week's work, gatherers near Savannah earned $5 to $7 in 1908. In the processing plants, women and children shuckers often outnumbered men. Depending upon their experience and the size of the oysters, they received from forty cents to $4 per day; women workers probably averaged $5 or $6 a week. One researcher found a preponderance of females in the coastal town of Warsaw, Georgia, during the winter months. They had migrated from the nearby Sea Islands, many to work in oyster factories: "Their fathers and brothers, remaining on these islands, are oyster gatherers for the factories. They are thus all members of the same economic group."[53]

Shuckers stood at workbenches all day and either steamed or pried open the shells. The smell of oysters permeated their hair, clothes, and bodies, even after they left the plant, and it could linger well after the season's end. Still, as we have seen, many black women preferred this type of work over domestic service; paid by the quart shucked daily, they could set their own pace with a minimum of white supervision and earn at least a dollar or two more each week than they could by catering to the demands of a white housewife. In seacoast towns with the "oyster alternative," domestics were as loudly condemned for their shoddy performance as they were eagerly sought after.[54]

During the off-season, families came together again and farmed, picked berries, peddled seafood, or found an assortment of odd jobs. Wives often took in boarders or washed clothes, while children assisted their parents or found work on their own. The ability of ten-year-olds to become financially independent of their parents prompted some of them to leave home, though the loss of one person's wages could throw off-balance a household that just barely managed to piece together an existence over the course of a year. A 1901 report on the Litwalton, Virginia, oyster-processing industry revealed that able-bodied husbands, wives, and children all contributed to the family's welfare in some way. One household of eight included a father unable to work; the fifty-five-year-old mother who, together with the four eldest children (two sons and two daughters aged eleven to twenty-one), shucked oysters and earned $18 per week; and the three youngest daughters who cooked and kept house. This family also received $10 weekly from boarders. When the oyster season ended, the four wage earners had to find other jobs as soon as possible.[55]

Like many other southern black families, members of oyster workers' households experienced periodic disruptions that separated fathers from mothers and children. Wage-earning teenagers followed the pattern of their city cousins who aspired to enjoy the fruits of their own labor as soon as they could support themselves. Yet, for blacks in coastal fishing villages, the ocean tides proved to be a reliable predictor of employment opportunities, compared to the uncertain rhythms of town life. Oyster shuckers and gatherers could count on working as hard as they wished during the harvest season; after that, the insatiable demand for domestic servants and laundresses assured them a makeshift existence, and fresh vegetables and fish were in relatively plentiful supply. Nevertheless, young people, eager to experience the city for themselves, gradually abandoned Warsaw for Savannah and Litwalton for Richmond. Leaving the stench of oysters behind, they soon discovered that what the city lacked in comfort and security it made up for in diversity and a more vital social life.

THE POLITICAL DYNAMICS OF MIDDLE-CLASS WOMEN'S WORK, WAGED AND UNWAGED

The small but visible and highly vocal black middle class that emerged in late-nineteenth-century southern cities played a large part in the development of African American political consciousness. This class owed its status and relatively comfortable circumstances to male household heads who managed—through luck, hard work, and determination—to maintain their tenuous positions as skilled craftsmen or entrepreneurs within a political environment increasingly hostile to the economic and educational aspirations of black men and women alike. Fathers and husbands commanded widespread respect in their communities through their positions of political, religious, or educational leadership.

Unlike white middle-class women, their wives and daughters often engaged in wage earning, both because the financial security of most black families remained precarious, and because they sought to put to good use their talents and formal schooling. Although skilled laborers and professionals accounted for no more than 3 or 4 percent of all gainfully employed black women in the urban South, they exerted considerable influence in their own neighborhoods. Sewing and school teaching were considered genteel occupations for black women during this era. The role of school teacher in particular shows how women of the black elite combined gainful employment with their own highly significant form of social activism, and how their sense of community responsibility inspired formal women's organizations that were ultimately political, and at times, radical, in nature.[56]

The job of garment-making covered a wide variety of skill levels and specialties, though the vast majority of black women engaged in this trade considered themselves "seamstresses" or "dressmakers." In at least some late-nineteenth-century cities (among them Charleston, Louisville, and New Orleans), this general category of working women constituted the largest group of "artisans," or skilled tradespeople, of either gender within the black population. Seamstresses tended to be younger than laundresses (they perhaps depended more heavily upon retaining nimble fingers and keen eyesight) and older than servants; the occupation was particularly suitable for mothers who needed to stay home with their children. Although data on wage levels are unavailable, a seamstress's pay probably reflected her age and experience, degree of specialization, and the class status of her clients. Like any other self-employed black person, she depended either upon black customers who could afford to pay very little or upon whites who chose to pay whatever they wanted. Demand for her services remained sporadic throughout the year, and it is unlikely that many seamstresses labored full time at their craft. At the same time, the slight increase in the percentage of black women who worked in the needle trades during the first decade of the twentieth century suggests that more women were either choosing or being forced into this work.[57]

Teaching constituted a special category of black women's work during this period in American history, for it implicitly involved a commitment to social activism. The young woman who guided exuberant abecedarians through their lessons—either in a drafty, one-room country school or in a dark and dank city classroom—could hardly help but remember that her enslaved forebears endured harsh punishment for trying to unlock the secrets of the printed word. After emancipation, the schooling of black children continued to have sinister connotations in the minds of white Southerners; the caste system generated its own forms of social control, rendering formal schooling unnecessary and indeed counterproductive within the context of the white-supremacist project. Consequently, teachers as a matter of course performed their duties with a certain political self-consciousness, and it is not surprising that the period's outspoken, national black female leaders (among them Fannie Jackson Coppin, Lucy Laney, Charlotte Hawkins Brown, and Fannie Barrier Williams) began their careers of lifelong public service as southern elementary school teachers.[58]

Census figures probably underestimate the total number of blacks engaged in teaching at any one time during these years. School calendars set by local, poorly funded district committees varied from year to year, especially in rural areas, where the majority of southern blacks lived. Many instructors taught only a couple of months each year and listed some other occupation—clergyman, seamstress, field-hand—when questioned by a federal census taker. Still, certain trends are unmistakable. The southern black teaching force reflected the general feminization of the profession that took place throughout the country in the nineteenth century. Like northern white teachers, black instructors tended to be young single women. Thus in 1900 almost 90 percent were thirty-four years or younger, and 72 percent were unmarried (this latter figure was low compared to whites). By 1910, 17,266 black females taught in the southern states. They outnumbered their male colleagues (who were older and more often married) by a ratio greater than three to one, and represented 1 percent of the region's black working women.[59]

The youthfulness and gender of the average black teacher reflected both the local school board's drive for economy, and the fact that teaching rarely paid enough to support a family or any dependents. Indeed, the lot of the black teacher was a particularly difficult one, for she relied upon either hostile white administrators or poverty-stricken black parents for her livelihood. And she contended daily with the baneful effects of the maldistribution of southern county school funds that worked to the detriment of black pupils. Compared to her white southern counterpart, the black instructor taught more children (an average of ninety-five as opposed to forty-five) in a smaller school. She had to make do with less in the way of essential equipment (books, pencils, and slates) and classroom time (a three- to four-month rather than five- to six-month school year). She made less money—usually no more than $25 or $30 per month—compared to white male, white female, or even black male teachers, in that order. And she knew that few, if any, of her pupils would find a job commensurate with their schooling.[60]

Teachers in the largest southern cities lived and worked on the political frontier of "racial" group consciousness during the period from 1880 to 1915. By the early 1880s, most of the schools established by the Freedmen's Bureau and northern freedmen's aid societies two decades earlier had been incorporated into fledgling urban public school systems administered by whites. School boards were determined to replace the hated Yankee teachers with native whites. This takeover of schools provided black children with only a nominal public education, for they remained segregated in cramped, poorly constructed buildings under the tutelage of hostile white teachers, often those judged unfit to teach pupils of their own color.[61]

Blacks in urban areas began to demand black teachers for their own schools as soon as the northern freedmen's aid instructors departed. Despite their formal political powerlessness, black parents and community leaders were at least partially successful in their efforts to petition and pressure school boards and city councils into hiring black teachers. Initially, most whites apparently feared that integrated staffs in black schools would foreshadow "social equality" and its corollary, "racial" warfare. The Readjuster biracial political movement in Virginia in the late 1870s won for black supporters teaching positions in local schools, prompting white fears of integrated schools and black teachers presiding over "mixed" classrooms. These fears, which over time and in various places reached hysterical proportions, suggested that white people believed that the whole "racial" caste system rested on a flimsy foundation, one easily undermined by black and white children sitting together in an elementary-school classroom. But in some places economic considerations trumped such anxieties, once white authorities realized that black teachers could be paid so little. A white school superintendent in Sampson County, North Carolina, instructed local officials: "None of the colored teachers deserve as large a salary as the white teachers, so adjust the teachers' wages as to give both races schools of the same length, and yet the white race gets more of the school fund to which they are entitled." Indeed, teaching paid so poorly that many black men abandoned the field to women altogether. In the end, the meager teacher's salary—less than laundry work, tobacco stemming, or domestic service in some instances—suggests that many black women considered the position as much social outreach as employment.[62]

Struggling to overcome these inequities and frustrations, black teachers (who made on average 60 percent of their white counterparts) made heroic efforts to attract and retain pupils at all levels. A surprisingly high percentage of urban school-aged children managed to attend classes at least sometime during the year; in Richmond, the names of 96.5 percent of all black children were recorded on teachers' class lists for the year 1890, although most probably attended on a sporadic basis at best. Educators in other cities noted that a lack of classroom space kept enrollments at artificially low levels. In 1910 the average black school attendance figures in the thirteen largest cities ranged from 65 percent in Charleston to 74.4 percent in Houston. School-related ceremonies and celebrations—dedication observances, and end-of-term exhibitions, for example—became an integral part of local community life.[63]

Ever since the end of the Civil War, southern cities had served as centers of black higher education, and that fact inevitably affected the quality of instruction available to black children outside rural areas. (Between 1890 and 1910, rates of female illiteracy in the six largest southern cities fell dramatically, from about 50 to 20 percent, rates almost identical to those of black men and about 15 percent lower than those of rural blacks.) In Atlanta, Nashville, and New Orleans, northern-sponsored normal (i.e., teacher-training) schools and colleges prepared young black people—by the turn of the century, a majority of them women—to be teachers and community leaders. Students taught in nearby schools during the summer vacation or settled permanently near their alma mater after graduation. In 1910 fully three-quarters of all Atlanta black teachers had graduated from the prestigious Atlanta University. Barred from pursuing careers in other professions (including the clergy), highly educated black women channeled their talents and energies into neighborhood schools.[64]

The story of Mamie Garvin Fields brings together many of the themes related to middle-class working women around the turn of the century. Born in 1888, she was part of the highly educated black "aristocracy" of Charleston, South Carolina. She graduated from Claflin University in Orangeburg, South Carolina, and later (both before and after her marriage to Robert Fields, a bricklayer) worked as a dressmaker and an elementary school teacher. Her job as teacher on the outlying Sea Islands combined elements of social work and diplomacy, as she firmly but deftly negotiated with tightfisted white school-board members for the supplies that her white colleagues took for granted. Fields's sense of social responsibility—which was inspired by her religious devotion and was an integral part of her family's self-definition—found formal expression through the City Federation of Colored Women's Clubs in 1916. This group, affiliated with the National Association of Colored Women (NACW, founded in 1896), worked to improve the living conditions of less fortunate black Charlestonians and engaged in a wide variety of other reform activities, always in opposition to the resistance and apathy of the white powers-that-be. "Do What You Can" was the motto and name of Mamie Fields's club, which focused on problems faced by homeless young girls: "We all could see that we had a responsibility for those girls: they were the daughters of our community coming up."[65]

Tennessee editor, businesswoman, and antilynching activist Ida B. Wells early articulated a theme that rapidly became the NACW's call to moral arms: in the words of historian Gerda Lerner, "a defense of black womanhood as part of a defense of the race from terror and abuse." More generally, in the lives of middle-class black women, gainful employment, entrepreneurial impulses, religious devotion, volunteer work, and political activism on behalf of families often blended seamlessly. A strong collective ethos promoting community welfare informed all of these activities. Elected executive secretary of the Independent Order of St. Luke in 1899, Richmond's Maggie Lena Walker opened the first bank organized by an American woman three years later. The order also established a cooperative department store, St. Luke Emporium, where black women could shop and work. Concerned about the welfare of the children in her Atlanta neighborhood, Lugenia Burns Hope (the wife of Atlanta University president John Hope) launched a community project that created play and day care facilities. Burns Hope was the founder of a social settlement, the Neighborhood Union, which sponsored campaigns on behalf of paved streets and public health, and sponsored investigations into a variety of social problems that plagued impoverished black Atlantans. All of these women were outspoken and uncompromising in their demand for equal justice.[66]

At the same time, many black women chose a more circuitous path in the quest for social change. Indeed, the theme of black women's club work and activism—famously expressed by Mary McLeod Bethune (clubwoman and founder of the Central Life Insurance Company of Tampa) as "Lifting as we climb"—proved problematic in certain key respects. Some women believed that "racial uplift," defined as instructing the poor in personal hygiene, personal deportment in public, thrift, and temperance, would go a long way toward convincing whites that black people were deserving of equal rights. Bethune and other black women activists tried to find common ground with white mothers and churchwomen in an effort to stem the rising tide of violence against blacks and to work together on a reform agenda of temperance and public health measures. Yet these efforts came to little or nothing, and ultimately placed the burden on poor blacks to change their personal behavior. A leader of black Baptist women, Nannie Burroughs declared in 1903 "that the masses of our sisters must hear the gospel of industry and heed its blessed principle before they can be morally saved." She cited as the means of countering white prejudice the tools of "soap and water, hoes, spades, shovels and paint." Lucy Wilmot Smith, an active member of the

American National Baptist Convention, urged black women to become self-supporting, whether they were wives, sisters, or mothers; yet in suggesting they eschew domestic service in favor of other pursuits such as truck farming, poultry raising, bee-keeping, lecturing, and nursing, she betrayed a lack of understanding of the severe constraints under which impoverished women lived and labored. Without fundamental transformations in the southern political economy, appeals for the "moral uplift" of black people would yield little in the way of meaningful social change.[67]

THE ROLE OF BLACK WOMEN IN SOUTHERN LABOR RELATIONS, 1880–1915

During the last quarter of the nineteenth century, the status of poor whites deteriorated and a new generation of blacks born after emancipation began to speak out and act against the caste system. In response, white lawmakers erected new forms of legal scaffolding to uphold American-style apartheid. "Racial" prejudice continued to be the prime determinant of the "southern way of life," but the manifestations of that prejudice gradually assumed new and monstrous forms—*de jure* segregation, disfranchisement, white-initiated riots, and lynchings of black men, women, and children. In the cities thus were compressed the forces of black assertion on the one hand and white reaction on the other, a dialectic that frequently culminated in bloodshed. Some urban black women entered this maelstrom as labor activists or determined opponents to hierarchies of caste and color, while others were forcibly drawn in as victims of physical violence. Yet in an era of public segregation, many continued to labor within white households, a seeming contradiction in the history of late-nineteenth-century southern labor relations.[68]

The potential of blacks to compete with whites for nonagricultural jobs drove the sharp wedge of prejudice into southern labor organizations. Even the Knights of Labor, theoretically committed to cooperation among black and white, male and female workers, usually abided by southern regional mores and thus surrendered whatever claim to power it had. In the late 1880s, Richmond's fifty-three Knights assemblies were segregated by "race" (twenty-three white, thirty black) and then, within the black group, by gender (twenty-four male, six female). Trade unions organized in individual cities often excluded skilled blacks in an effort to prevent them from securing apprenticeships or contracts. The United Mine Workers welcomed blacks into its ranks, but acquiesced in a social division of labor that reserved better jobs, including supervisory positions, for whites only. The emergence of the American Federation of Labor in the 1890s marked the abandonment of southern blacks by the mainstream national labor movement. The New Orleans general strikes of 1892 and 1907, supported by black and white workers alike, remain noteworthy exceptions.[69]

As blacks, females, and unskilled workers, the vast majority of southern black women had no role to play in trade and job-specific unions dominated by white men. However, when black male workers engaged in collective action, either with or in opposition to white men, their womenfolk made indirect but noteworthy contributions to the labor movement. Wives and daughters helped support striking husbands and fathers by finding gainful employment or assuming additional wage-earning responsibilities for the duration of the conflict. Domestics stepped up their raids on the pantries of white women (the wives of their husbands' employers), so that their families could eat and stave off complete financial disaster.[70]

For obvious reasons, black women and men during this period developed a long-standing, well-founded suspicion toward the white industrial working classes in general and white labor unions in particular. At times white working-class women used traditional means of labor agitation in efforts to rid their workplace of black employees. In 1897 the hiring of two black female spinners sparked a spontaneous protest by white women operatives in an Atlanta textile mill. "In sympathy," the Textile Workers Union staged a walkout among female employees at the factory—1,400 workers in all. The company fired the black women. Most other employers had by this time learned the lesson that deference to white workers' prejudices amounted to a good labor-relations strategy. Still, at times, some employers punished rebellious black hands by replacing them with whites; in 1889 a Danville tobacco manufacturer dealt with black strikers by shifting to an all-white workforce. Considering the creative ways that employers manipulated racial ideologies and the composition of workplaces, it was no wonder that black and white workers remained divided by mutual distrust and bitterness.[71]

Black women did participate in successful strikes sponsored by the National Tobacco Workers Union around the turn of the century. Stemmers in Florence and hangers, pickers, and stemmers in Danville enjoyed at least temporary victories in 1898, probably because few whites were interested in taking their jobs. Considering the inherent difficulties in forging an effective labor organization among either white women or black men and women in this period, the militant job action conducted by Atlanta laundresses in the summer of 1881 deserves special consideration. Organized through and strongly supported by black churches in the community, the Washerwomen's Association of Atlanta struck for a wage of $1 per twelve pounds of wash. Women who played an active part in the strike made an effort to bring others into the group. The spirit of resistance among so many women (about three thousand altogether at one point) was contagious, and the Atlanta *Constitution* noted apprehensively, "Not only washerwomen, but the cooks, house servants and nurses are asking an increase." The white establishment in Atlanta wasted little time in marshaling the full weight of both the private and public sectors in an effort to destroy the association. Landlords threatened to raise the strikers' rents to exorbitant levels, and the city council debated a resolution that would require every laundress to pay $25 for a business license. The washerwomen vowed they would pay the fee and declared in a public statement, "Then we will have full control of the city's washing at our own prices, as the city has control over our husbands' work at their prices." However, in reality few women could afford to buy such a license, and that fact, combined with the arrest and fining of the strike leaders, soon broke the back of the movement. The strike put white Atlanta on notice that laundresses would resist being treated like slaves, but it also impressed upon the black community the severity of its economic vulnerability and political weakness.[72]

Black urban women also challenged the tenets of white supremacy outside the workplace as well. During the first six years of the twentieth century, groups participated in boycotts against newly segregated public transit systems in twenty-five southern cities. Individual women refused to abide by southern custom and uphold the "deference ritual" enforced since slavery on public streets. Indeed, whites coupled their complaints about the poor service rendered by domestics with the observation that younger women lacked the obsequiousness and tractability of their slave mothers. Throughout the urban South, alleged crimes against the code of "racial" etiquette, especially those committed by young black girls, prompted nervous mutterings and promises of quick retaliation. The Chattanooga *Times* advised its readers: "Negro girls are apt to be extremely insolent, not only to whites of their own age, but to ladies. In the matter of collisions between school-boys, that may best be left to the police. The negro girls who push white women and girls off the walks can be cured of that practice by the use of a horsewhip; and we advise white fathers and husbands to use the whip. It's a great corrective." The call for white men to protect their ladies from "insolent" black girls revealed a growing preoccupation with the "virtue" of white women as a pretext for the persecution of all black people.[73]

The caste system of the nineteenth-century South strictly regulated sociosexual relations between black and white men and women. White men considered free and uninhibited access to black women as their prerogative and at the same time declared taboo any sexual activity between black men and white women. Under slavery, this code was enforced through the use of violence and intimidation. When, during the Reconstruction period, white men lost such tight control over black women, they feared that black men would "naturally" begin to sexually harass their former mistresses; after all (whites realized), the sexual abuse of women had always signified the hatred men of one group felt toward members of the other. Thus any hint of sexual impropriety on the part of black men met with swift retribution, and provided white men as a group with an opportunity to reaffirm their sense of racial superiority and "manhood." More deadly though was the tendency of many lynch mobs to use charges of rape as a blatant pretext for murdering black men. The mutilation and castration of lynching victims brought into explicit focus the tangle of "hate and guilt and sex and fear" that enmeshed all southerners well into the twentieth century.[74]

White men's persistent violation of black women constituted a more common phenomenon that served as a backdrop for periodic lynchings throughout the South, especially during the years 1890 to 1910. A woman or girl found herself in danger of being attacked whenever she walked down a country road—"The poorest type of white man feels at liberty to accost her and follow her, and force her." But her employer's home remained the source of her greatest fears. In 1924, Strom Thurmond, the son of a well-to-do white family in Edgefield, South Carolina, impregnated a fifteen-year-old maid of the family, Carrie "Tunch" Butler. Their relationship became public knowledge only after Thurmond's death, at age one hundred, in 2003. What made the case unusual was not the fact of the sexual abuse of this young girl by the son of her employer, but that his daughter by Butler, Essie Mae Washington-Williams, began to speak openly about her father, who by that time had earned a national reputation as a staunch segregationist. Denunciations of "miscegenation" thus rang hollow in a region where white men considered the abuse of black women to be their prerogative.[75]

Clearly, then, black domestics and their employers daily lived out the paradoxical south-ern system of public segregation and private integration (at times rendered in the form of intimate abusive relationships). Whites lacked an interest in—as well as access to—the dy-namics of black communities; the family life of blacks "touches that of the white people only in economic matters," in the words of DuBois. The two groups remained largely seg-regated in public pursuits. Yet black women constantly worked in the presence of whites of both genders and all ages. A black newspaper in Orangeburg, South Carolina, highlighted the irony in 1889. The blackest woman, it noted, can "cook the food for prejudiced throats" and hold "the whitest, cleanest baby," "but the angry passions rise when a well-dressed, ed-ucated, refined negro pays his own fare and seats himself quietly in a public conveyance." In the end, *de jure* segregation was a move designed to limit blacks' political power, and to humiliate them in public, rather than to curtail personal contact between members of the two groups.[76]

Around the turn of the twentieth century, nonrural southern workplaces became more highly politicized, reflecting the intensity of reaction among whites to the self-assertion of blacks at all levels of society. Middle-class black women began to challenge the eternal veri-ties of southern life through political agitation, but many of their working-class sisters de-cided to give up the old struggle in the South and embrace a new one in the North. They were all too familiar with the fate of elderly women like Elviry Magee, "po' now an' . . . po' den" while her employer "come to be a rich man." The creation of war-industry jobs in the Midwest and Northeast after 1916 released the floodgates of migration and revealed a deep wellspring of fear and discontent among blacks all over the South. This mass population movement heralded the beginning of a new era, and with it the first evidence of what would become a central fact in the history of blacks and white women during the twentieth cen-tury—that they gained greatest access to economic opportunities during periods of world-wide military conflict.

"TO GET OUT OF THIS LAND OF SUFRING"

Black Women Migrants to the North, 1900–1930

IN MAY 1917, soon after she arrived in Pittsburgh, a middle-aged black woman from Alabama wrote home and assured her friends, "You think I have forgotten you all but I never will." In the letter she told of her new home, the largest city she had ever seen—"45 miles long & equal in breath," built upon mountains of biblical grandeur and sprinkled with fruit trees just now "peeping out," triumphant over the long winter. Still, Pittsburgh's setting was marred by congestion and by a blanket of grimy smoke from nearby mines and steel mills. The woman's description of the city seemed to reflect her own experiences as a domestic servant, for her initial excitement over relatively high wartime wages soon gave way to a daily struggle to adjust to the economic realities of northern life: "They give you big money for what you do but they charge you big things for what you get." Indeed, she noted, in a way that combined images of the city with ambivalence about her job, "Some places look like torment . . . & some places look like Paradise in this great city."[1]

The northward movement of southern blacks during the early twentieth century had a unique, dramatic quality, and the participants often described their journey with religious metaphors; like the Jews of the Old Testament, they fled oppression in Egypt, bound for the promised land. The reasons for their flight from the South were obvious enough—an exploitative sharecropping system, state-sanctioned terrorism, disfranchisement, segregations, a plague of boll weevils working its way up the Cotton Belt. When World War I opened up employment possibilities in the industrial Northeast and Midwest, mass migration began in earnest; the lure of high wages and a freer life proved irresistible to a people limited to agricultural and domestic service in the land of neoslavery.[2]

Yet if the South embodied the explicit evil of Pharaoh's Egypt, the North eventually came to represent an ambiguous kind of promised land for the 2 million black people who joined in the exodus between 1900 and 1930. Industrial employers expressed a calculated preference for white foreign-born workers (most from southern and eastern Europe) over the downtrodden blacks in their own country; the latter group was accorded a conditional welcome only after the supply of immigrant labor had diminished, down from 1.2 million newcomers from abroad in 1914, to about 110,000 four years later. Meanwhile, wartime munitions, iron, steel, glass, food processing, railroad, and automobile industries desperately needed additional workers. The long-standing preference on the part of northern employers for immigrants indicated the depth of prejudice that black workers would encounter in their attempt to affirm the true meaning of their native citizenship.[3]

If the divergent experiences of black migrants and white immigrants offer an instructive comparison, so too does the contrast in experiences of Appalachian white and Deep-South black northbound migrants. During the Great Migration, between 1916 and 1927, when 1.2 million southern blacks moved north, 1.3 million southern white men, women, and children, many from the hills and hollows of Appalachia, made the same journey. White families registered the effects of a contracted labor market in the extractive sector of the region, as coal mining became mechanized. Like their black contemporaries, these white migrants had large families and practiced a fundamentalist Protestantism; both groups possessed little if any experience with factory work or other time-oriented, industrial-disciplined labor. Yet white men found jobs as semiskilled machine and assembly-line operatives in northern factories, while black men and women remained confined to menial work. White families had the opportunity eventually to move up and out of impoverished migrant neighborhoods, while black families remained confined to urban ghettos by the force of restrictive homeowners' covenants, bank redlining practices, and complicit white real estate agents.[4]

Rural folk, black and white, native-born and immigrant, had to "adjust" to a northern urban environment, but patterns of adjustment reflected their distinctive employment options. The families of Polish immigrant and black migrant meatpackers in Chicago, for example, faced similar exploitative housing and working conditions, and both groups sought to preserve their cultural traditions, relying on family and kin to ease the transition between rural and city life. Yet ultimately black people—even though they were native-born Americans and English-speaking Protestants—found themselves at a disadvantage in the northern labor force, despite their favorable levels of educational attainment compared to European peasants. Scholars who contrast the occupational mobility of white and black (im)migrants during these years usually focus on the job histories of men; by the 1920s, an increasing number of northern production sites were becoming mechanized, depressing the demand for unskilled labor that had benefited immigrants in the previous decades, and putting black male workers at risk. At the same time a good case can be made for including black wives and mothers in an analysis of this sort, for an extraordinarily high proportion of them (relative to their working-class white counterparts regardless of ethnic background) served as primary or supplementary breadwinners in their households, and unlike white women, they took home wages more nearly equal to those of their menfolk. The progress of African Americans as a group was clearly linked to the job status of black women, and thus the discrimination encountered by wives and mothers in the marketplace was a crucial factor in inhibiting the upward mobility of their families.[5]

Black female migrants from the South eagerly sought factory jobs that paid more money for shorter working hours compared with, and lacked the social stigma attached to, domestic service. One twenty-two-year-old woman interviewed by the Chicago Commission on Race Relations in 1920 was adamant in her determination to remain at work in a box factory: "I'll never work in nobody's kitchen but my own any more. No indeed! That's the one thing that makes me stick to this job." In all likelihood, her good fortune was only temporary, and within a year or so in the midst of the economic downturn, she would have to return to washing dishes and clothes for whites. While immigrant women continued to find expanded job opportunities in manufacturing, black women formed an ever larger proportion of laborers in the shrinking fields of hand laundry work and personal service. Yet it would be difficult to argue that a young woman fresh off the boat from southern Italy was better qualified to sort and pack candy compared to a recent black migrant from Georgia.[6]

Moreover, the systematic exclusion of black women from the growing sales and clerical sectors had little to do with any presumed handicap on the part of these women in terms of their education, physical proximity to downtown offices and stores, or willingness to work at "white women's" jobs. Indeed, the daughters of black migrant parents attained educational parity not only with second-generation immigrant women but also with native white women of native parentage, indicating that their struggle for self-improvement was as persistent as the prejudice that denied them the fruits of that struggle. Thus, suggestions that blacks as a group lacked the requisite qualifications for factory or clerical jobs, or shunned them out of some vague cultural preference for the undemanding pace of domestic service, do not accurately describe the experiences of black working women.[7]

In the urban North, black women worked in greater numbers, but for less pay compared to white wage earners. The fact that the overwhelming proportion of African American wives and mothers remained confined to domestic service served as a reminder that divisions of labor based on racial ideologies were national, and not regional, systems of power. At the same time, the migrants did manage to transform the nature of their labor to some degree, by turning what had been a patriarchal relationship between master or mistress and servant into one based on an employer-employee relationship. When black women insisted on "living out" and not in the homes of their employers, for example, they sought to retain some control over their work and family lives. At the same time, the institutional legacies of slavery, in the form of discriminatory job and housing policies, overshadowed their best attempts to carve a new future out of the urban landscape in the North.[8]

In the end, most migrants measured their success according to standards set by their old friends and neighbors who stayed behind. In the North, wives and mothers had to stretch tiny budgets to make ends meet; guard their children against new and frightening dangers; wash, cook, and scrub for lodgers; and do battle against dirt and faulty plumbing in cramped, dilapidated quarters. Nevertheless, these women rarely decided to return south for good. Though they "had gone from the fire into the frying pan,"[9] their children had expanded opportunities for schooling and, after 1920, they themselves could vote and participate in local and national politics. Whether a female migrant hailed from the fields of South Carolina or the alleys of Nashville, whether she took up residence in a Harlem tenement, Cleveland rooming house, or Pittsburgh bungalow, she and other newcomers soon learned that "half you hear [about the North] is not true."[10] But the half that *was* true continued to serve as a powerful inducement to those blacks still in the South.

PATHS NORTH

The hundreds of thousands of black women who followed husbands north, or threw meager belongings into pillow cases and ventured out alone, or donned men's overalls to get a free ride on a train headed for the Midwest, belied the words of a song sung by blacks in the Deep South around 1915:

> *When a woman takes the blues,*
> *She tucks her head and cries;*
> *But when a man catches the blues,*
> *He catches er freight and rides.*[11]

In fact, in myriad ways, women took the initiative and played a central role in the process of migration north. Beulah Nelson described how she "fired herself" from a domestic job with a white family as a first step in her decision to move to Washington, D.C., in 1922. Other women scrimped and saved for the trip from their meager earnings, and helped to organize the friends and family members who eventually made the trek together. Moreover, few women ceased to travel once they arrived at their destination; they continued to move in search of better jobs and living quarters, and made periodic visits south to visit friends. The self-selective nature of the migration process meant that migrating women were likely to be younger and better educated compared to other black women in the South. Still, regardless of their reasons for leaving, or their immediate family situation, most women could ill afford to lose time looking for a job when they reached the big city; the urban North would offer them no respite from gainful employment.[12]

Between 1870 and 1910, an average of 6,700 southern blacks moved north annually. The women who took part in this early movement tended to be young, single, separated, or widowed, and they often made the journey alone. Most left the mid-Atlantic or south Atlantic region (from Delaware and Maryland down through Virginia and the Carolinas) and traveled to Philadelphia, New York, or Boston in response to what they believed were specific job offers in domestic service. Some, like Essie Roberts of St. Helena's Island, South Carolina, relied on personal contacts for advice and encouragement. Roberts, a widow, learned from her white employer in Beaufort of a Massachusetts woman in need of a maid; in 1901 she left her children at home on the island with a relative who later took them up north to join her. Other women fell prey to unscrupulous northern employment agencies that promised them good wages and comfortable lodgings. These agencies became notorious among social workers for their exploitation of "fresh green country girls." More than one young black woman, lured north by the prospect of a cook's job and provided transportation at a nominal cost, found herself alone on the dock in New York or Boston and at the mercy of a "society official." After her luggage was confiscated, she might be "placed" in a brothel or with a white woman who only wanted a window washer or floor scrubber. Nevertheless, cheap steamship fares continued to attract young women who felt "stifled in the dead country town[s]."[13]

By the early twentieth century, black communities in the Northeast reflected the demographic characteristics of this young adult migrating population. Women who left homes along the southeastern seaboard helped to create unbalanced sex ratios in Philadelphia (116 black females to 100 males in 1900) and New York (124 to 100). In 1905 one-quarter of all adult black women in New York lived alone or in a lodging house (90 percent of the black working women in the city were domestic servants). Taken together, midwestern cities received only a few hundred black southerners each year, and most of them were young men without families.[14]

In the South, the "War to Make the World Safe for Democracy" galvanized African Americans as citizens, workers, and freedom fighters. Several wartime developments politicized black women's labor in new and even violent ways. Throughout the South, the issue of black women's wage work took on heightened significance when local draft registration boards targeted black men disproportionately; these boards ruled that black families were better able to cope without a father's wages than their white counterparts, because black women so routinely contributed wages to their households. In contrast, went the reasoning, white middle-class families relied to a greater extent on a breadwinning husband and father who should therefore gain an exemption from military service. Southern black women took advantage of high labor-demand during wartime, and participated in the labor militancy characteristic of a wide variety of wage earners those years; in 1916 the domestics in Houston organized themselves into a "Woman's Domestic Union . . . for the purpose of protecting ourselves against low wages, long hours and insanitary conditions." Black laundresses in Tampa demanded a minimum wage, and threatened that "any woman who works for less than $2 a day, the union scale, will be run out of town." Approximately 250 Mobile laundresses went on strike, and in an action that echoed the protests of field-hands in the rural South, brandished sticks at a protest against strikebreakers taking their jobs. These and other forms of collective action failed in the face of mass arrests, police brutality, and intimidation from law enforcement officials. For working women, then, migration north was a logical decision; even the power of their numbers was not sufficient to ensure them decent wages and working conditions in the South.[15]

The Great Migration of the World War I era represented a dramatic break with the past in several crucial respects. First, the sheer magnitude of the movement was striking. Between 1916 and 1921 an estimated half-million blacks, or about 5 percent of the total southern black population, headed north (this number was larger than the aggregate figure for the preceding forty years). Compared with their predecessors, the new migrants more often came from the Deep South; they traveled longer distances to their final destination and relied on overland (rail) transportation rather than water transportation, and a greater proportion than previously chose to go to midwestern cities. In 1920 more than a fourth of the North's black population was concentrated in New York, Chicago, and Philadelphia, and their black communities were larger than any in the South. Still, blacks numbered no more than 9 percent of the total population of any urban area in the North, and only 2 percent of all northerners were black.[16]

Contemporary observers, and especially nervous white southerners convinced that their entire supply of black labor was about to disappear overnight, provided melodramatic accounts of the initial population movement in the spring of 1916. Many assumed that the arrival of a train sponsored by a northern railroad company was enough to create havoc at a moment's notice and that black men, promised free transportation and outrageously high wages, would scramble aboard with only the shirts on their backs, without bothering to say good-bye to friends or family. In fact, the decision to leave was just as often a calculated one made by husbands and fathers as it was an impulsive act on the part of single men. In his survey of 506 male migrants to Pittsburgh in 1918, Abraham Epstein found that three hundred were married (though single people predominated in the eighteen-to-thirty-year age group). Thirty percent already had their families with them, and an almost equal number planned to have their wives and children join them as soon as possible.[17]

The Great Migration, then, was frequently a family affair. Significantly, black men mentioned the degraded status of their womenfolk as one of the prime incentives to migrate, along with low wages and poor educational opportunities for their children. Husbands told of sexual harassment of wives and daughters by white men and of other forms of indignities woven into the fabric of southern society. One migrant to Chicago expressed satisfaction that his wife could now go into a shop and "try on a hat and if she don't want it she don't have to buy it." Another man in the same city, a stockyard worker, told an interviewer that in Mississippi:

> Men and women had to work in the fields. A woman was not permitted to remain at home if she felt like it. If she was found at home some of the white people would come to ask why she was not in the field and tell her she had better get to the field or else abide by the consequences. After the summer crops were all in, any of the white people could send for any Negro woman to come and do the family washing at 75 cents to $1.00 a day. If she sent word she could not come she had to send an excuse why she could not come. They were never allowed to stay at home as long as they were able to go. Had to take whatever they paid you for your work.

Letters from potential migrants to the Chicago *Defender* (the largest black newspaper and an enthusiastic proponent of migration) indicate that most men expected their wives to continue to contribute to the family income, at least temporarily, in their new northern home. Husbands wrote to the weekly paper and inquired about employment possibilities, describing their wives as "very industrious," "a very good cook . . . [with] lots of references," or "a good launders." But a move out of the South, according to a Florida man in the spring of 1917, would be worth the trouble if only because "it will allow me to get my wife away from down hear."[18]

Some women during this period did have to make the decision to leave, find their way north, and locate housing without the aid of a trailblazing spouse. Single mothers from rural areas searched for a way north, because, as one South Carolina widow put it, "When you live on the farm, the man is the strength." Domestic servants in southern cities decided to find out for themselves the truth of reports that northern wages might be three or four times more than they were used to making. Strains on the household budget prompted daughters to strike out at an early age. A fifteen-year-old in New Orleans realized that her mother had "such a hard time" trying to make ends meet for a family of five and as the old- est child, she could lessen expenses at home and at the same time contribute extra cash to the family income by finding a job in Chicago. The plight of a Sea Island girl about the same age was less critical but no less compelling. In 1919 she left for New York City, hoping to escape from the loneliness of St. Helena's Island, where you "go to bed at six o'clock. Everything dead. No dances, no moving picture show, nothing to go to."[19]

More dramatic reasons to leave were instances of systematic violent attacks by whites on black men and women during this period; between 1882 and 1930, cotton-state lynch mobs murdered 1,663 black people, and state officials executed 1,299 more through the "legiti- mate" judicial process. In1918, Mrs. J. S. Harper, president of the Colored Federated Clubs of Augusta, Georgia, wrote to President Woodrow Wilson on behalf of herself and other club members. Together the women demanded justice in the case of Mary Turner, who was lynched on May 19 "for an alleged unwise remark" Turner had made in the wake of the killing of her husband by a white mob. Wrote Harper, "We the Negro Women of the state are aroused by this unwarranted lawlessness and are discouraged and crushed by a spirit of humiliation and dread; . . . we deplore the migratory movement of the Negro from the South, yet we cannot counsel them to remain in the light of these conditions under which we live." Upon arriving for the first time in Tuskegee, Alabama, to attend school, Hazel Starks was horrified to see on display a young black man who had been hanged by a mob for refusing to give up his seat to a white youth in a theater. Recalled Starks, the sight of the body was the catalyst that prompted her to make plans to move to Cincinnati. These grisly cases underscored the pervasive culture of violence in the South, a culture that brutalized black men and women in the course of their everyday worklives.[20]

It is clear then, that the Great Migration north among African Americans was not a movement borne exclusively of poverty. However, black women had unique grievances. Though reluctant to speak explicitly about their sexual vulnerability to black and white men alike, some women migrants told stories of abuse at the hands of a male kinsman, su- pervisor, or employer as they recounted their narrative of moving north. These women fled for their own physical safety, and for the safety of their children.[21]

Families and individuals differed in the way they timed their move and managed the transition between rural and urban work. Migration northward from the Mississippi Valley to the Midwest between 1916 and 1930 provides a useful, well-documented case study of these issues and highlights differences between men's and women's employment patterns. For example, interviewed by historian Peter Gottlieb for his study of Pittsburgh's mi- grants, Jonnie F., a black woman, explained why she had become part of the Great Migra- tion many years ago. As a child she had not minded picking cotton, or even hauling three-hundred-pound baskets of the crop with her brother: "It was fun then, you know, but when you commence to gettin' older and work, work, work, and stay the same . . . You know, you want a change." She and other rural teens were semidependent upon their parents. They lived at home most of the time, but often worked as nonagricultural wage earners when their labor was not needed on the farm (July and August, November and December)—the young women as domestic servants in towns, the young men as laborers in logging camps, cotton presses, or sawmills. When they returned to the family cabin, many of them had mixed feelings of pride and resentment as they turned over hard-earned wages to families that relied on this meager but valuable source of cash, and they chafed under the rule of fathers who wielded an iron hand in enforcing a specific division of labor based on gender and age within the household.[22]

For many migrants, the trip north unfolded in incremental steps. Their off-season work introduced them to a world apart from the cotton field and their own kin clusters. Short-range geographical mobility among "shifting" sharecroppers, combined with the small but steady flow of country blacks into southern cities, made movement a fact of life for even the most isolated rural folk. Compared to their sisters and wives, young men had more opportunities to hear about jobs in the North and to make contacts that would assist them in planning the journey. Indeed, men were much more likely than women to work their way north gradually, picking up a few dollars and some encouragement from friends along the way before breaking out of the South altogether. Yet many rural young people of both sexes had already had some experience with jobs not unlike the ones they would eventually find up north. At the same time, there is some evidence that single women went directly from the rural South to the urban North in one long-distance journey, as they left their family of origin and sought out kin in northern cities. In general, then, patterns of movement reflected the gender, age, and marital status of the migrants.[23]

The nature of employment opportunities in specific cities shaped the demographics of migration to those places. Men almost invariably led the way north to Pittsburgh and Detroit and other cities that offered industrial jobs for them but few positions outside domestic service for women. Chicago, with its more diversified female occupational structure, attracted single women and wives like Mrs. T of St. Louis, who preceded her husband to the city in order to investigate job conditions because, according to a Race Commission interviewer in 1920, she "doesn't always wait for him to bring something to her, but goes out herself and helps to get it." Mid-Atlantic and northeastern cities were more likely than midwestern manufacturing centers to have balanced sex rations of female and migrants; places such as Philadelphia, New York, and Boston offered only a small range of domestic service positions, but those positions, in commercial establishments as well as private homes, were open to men and women.[24]

Few migrants, male or female, abandoned the South totally or irrevocably. Some went back home frequently to join in community celebrations, to help with planting and harvesting on the family farm, or to coax friends north with their beautiful new clothes and stories of good pay. A constant flow of letters containing cash and advice between North and South facilitated the gradual migration of whole clans and even villages. For example, the records of a Detroit social-welfare agency include the case of a young Georgia widow who moved to the city in 1922 to care for her ill niece. The woman returned south the following year and then went back to Detroit with one of her children, leaving the other three in the care of her mother-in-law. In 1925 she managed to convince the older woman (aged seventy) and her sister-in-law (aged fifty-nine) to join her in the North. There the three women pieced together a living for themselves and the four children by doing "day work," domestic service on a daily basis. Thus the continuous renewal of personal ties through visits south and moves north meant that, at least for the first few years, the migrants maintained contact with their southern homes in both a physical and a cultural sense.[25]

The adjustment from a wartime to a peacetime economy led to a national recession in 1920–1921. Migration from the South slackened in response, but then picked up again in 1922 and reached a peak the next year. Despite the disillusionment of recent migrants, they sent home encouraging reports so that the stream of refugees continued unabated as long as economic conditions were favorable. Elderly people who remained in the South expressed remorse over the departure of their kin, and they lamented the severing, or at least loosening, of bonds that had traditionally held the generations together through love and obligation. Some, however, received much-appreciated cash from northern relatives on a sporadic or regular basis. One Mississippi woman who lived in a small town that had been decimated by the Great Migration told an investigator that she felt envious of her "friends who are in the North and prospering," and noted ruefully, "If I stay here any longer, I'll go wild. . . . There ain't enough people here I now know to give me a decent burial."[26]

WORK AND FAMILY LIFE IN THE URBAN NORTH

Paid Labor

The radical economic inequality of black working women in the urban North did not become apparent until the early twentieth century. Before that time, disproportionately large numbers of single and married black women worked for wages, but they and black men and unmarried white women were concentrated in essentially the same job category—domestic service. In a rough sense, all three groups were subjected to the same kinds of degrading working conditions characteristic of this form of employment. However, as household conveniences and electricity lessened the need for elbow grease, new forms of business enterprise opened clerical and sales positions for white women. Commercial laundries gradually replaced laundresses with machines. In the process, personal service became increasingly associated with black women exclusively. For the most part, black female wage earners remained outside the expanding industrial economy, and the few who gained a foothold in factory work remained in the lowest-paying jobs. Despite the significant shift in white working women's options, the paid labor of black women exhibited striking continuity across space—urban areas in the North and South—and time—from the nineteenth to the early twentieth century.[27]

Black women's gainful employment reflected their fathers' and husbands' job insecurity. Beginning in the 1880s, the arrival of large numbers of Eastern Europeans had a dramatic

The South, 1870 to 1930

The late-nineteenth-century economic revolution fundamentally altered the nation's job structure and created new employment possibilities for white women, but southern black women gained virtually no access to the positions of secretary, clerical worker, and retail salesperson. Some black wives, mothers, and daughters in urban areas peddled vegetables (1) or stemmed tobacco leaves (2) on a seasonal basis. The majority readily found full-time work as domestics, but their hours were long and their pay meager. Black communities (like the town of Mound Bayou, Mississippi) supported only a handful of female employees in sales, clerical, and communications work (3). Throughout this period of rapid economic change, the vast majority of black women lived in the rural southern hinterland, and their paid labor remained task-oriented well into the twentieth century (4). The availability of a large, subservient agricultural labor force rendered technological improvements superfluous, even threatening, in the context of the region's social order, so black women in the countryside continued to plow and hoe and pick cotton in much the same way as their enslaved grandmothers. Owners of large agribusiness plantations strove for high levels of crop productivity, and in the process emulated the policies of large industrial corporations; these policies mandated the close supervision of all laborers, whether hired hands, sharecroppers, or tenants (5). When World War I opened up northern industrial jobs to black men, large numbers of black families abandoned the South and sought out the "promised land" of the North (6).

1. Vegetable peddlers in Charleston, South Carolina (c. 1900). Library of Congress.

2. Tobacco worker (1922). National Archives.

3. Telephone operator in the all-black town of Mound Bayou, Mississippi. Schomburg Center for Research in Black Culture, New York Public Library.

TELEPHONE EXC.
OPERATOR, MOUND BAYOU   MISS. 92.

4. Workers with bambusa brooms, Latimer's plantation, Belton, South Carolina (1899). National Archives.

5. Picking cotton under the watchful eye of a mounted white overseer (1928). National Archives.

6. A southern family arrives in Chicago. Schomburg Center for Research in Black Culture, New York Public Library.

impact on the type and numbers of positions available to black men. Always just a tiny percentage of the total male population of any particular northern city, black men had never been able to dominate a single type of work; nevertheless, the displacement by successive waves of immigrant groups of black artisans, apartment house doormen, barbers, elevator operators, and waiters and cooks in expensive hotels was well underway by 1900.[28]

Although the war provided black men with their first opportunities in northern industrial employment, regardless of their personal talents or ambitions they rarely advanced beyond those jobs at the lowest rungs of the employment ladder. These were menial positions, subject to regular layoffs. Demobilization resulted in mass firings of black laborers in many plants, though some retained their low-level jobs in the metalworking, automobile, and food processing industries. For example, in the 1920s, black men composed up to 70 to 80 percent of all workers in Chicago meatpacking and slaughterhouses; there they were concentrated in jobs that no other group would take, so difficult and disagreeable were the assigned tasks. Black men still constituted a labor force of last resort, and they could not look forward to gradual advancement in the form of promotions for themselves or even for their sons. Moreover, black men's work patterns continued to diverge from those of white men, who moved into white-collar, managerial, and advanced technology jobs in increasing numbers. By 1930 two types of workers symbolized the status of all black male wage earners in the urban North—the New York City apartment house janitor and the Pittsburgh foundry worker who manned a blast furnace during the hottest months of the year.[29]

Because most male breadwinners suffered from chronic underemployment and sporadic unemployment, other household members had to supplement their irregular earnings. In 1930 from 34 to 44 percent of black households in the largest northern cities had two or more gainfully employed workers. Most striking among black families was the high percentage of wives who worked outside the home—in 1920, five times more than the women in any other "racial" or ethnic group. The different cities showed some variation in this regard: In 1920, for example, 25.5 percent of black married women in Detroit, but 46.4 percent in New York, worked for wages (rates for all cities remained stable over the following decade). Variations between cities can be explained by reference to the local job situation for black men. In general, where men had access to industrial employment—in Pittsburgh and Detroit, for example—fewer wives worked than those in cities where large numbers of men could find little work outside domestic service. Jobs in the latter category were just as insecure as those in the industrial sector, but with the added disadvantage that they paid much less.[30]

Black wives worked in greater proportion compared to white wives, but more significantly, they served as wage earners more often than immigrant wives of the same socioeconomic class. Not only did black husbands earn less than foreign-born men, their wives bore fewer children compared to immigrant women. The few children blacks had tended to establish independent households, or at least to retain wages for their own use, in greater proportion than the offspring of immigrant families. For example, based on her observations of black and immigrant neighborhoods in Manhattan in 1911, New York social worker Mary White Ovington suggested that the "marked contrasts" in the lives of women in the two groups derived primarily from their respective households' "different occupational opportunities." The young white wife, she wrote in *Half a Man: The Status of the Negro in New York,* rarely "journeys far from her own home"; she departs from "her narrow round of domestic duties" to seek day or laundry work only if "unemployment visits the family wage earner." As the household grows in size over the years, its income is augmented by the wages of older sons and daughters who, "having entered factory or store, bring home their pay envelopes unbroken on Saturday nights" and turn them over to their mother. Gradually the family's standard of living improves, and the number and quality of its material possessions increases. As children depart from the household to marry, and the father's wage-earning capacity dwindles in proportion to his physical strength, the family falls on difficult times and "the end of the woman's married life is likely to be hard and comfortless."[31]

The black woman had a quite different family history. Ovington noted that she often begins "self-sustaining work" at the age of fifteen and remains in the labor force after marriage because of her husband's inability to support his family ("save in extreme penury") on his wages alone. The working black wife's day is more diverse and varied than that of the white homemaker, but she must sacrifice time with her children in return. Wrote Ovington, "An industrious, competent woman, [the black mother] works and spends, and in her scant hours of leisure takes pride in keeping her children well-dressed and clean."[32]

A black woman must continue to work throughout her middle years because her wage-earning children tend to hand over to her "only such part [of their paychecks] as they choose to spare." Ovington disapprovingly noted what she called these young people's self-indulgent spending habits, and their tendency to neglect the needs of their parents and siblings. The types of jobs available to sons and daughters served to lessen parental control; many "go out to service, accept long and irregular hours in hotel or apartment, travel for days on boat or train." Moreover, "factory and store are closed" to young women. Consequently the mother "must continue her round of washing and scrubbing." Yet old age did not necessarily bring with it unremitting drudgery and sorrow. According to Ovington, an elderly black woman often spent her last years engaged in productive labor at home, "treated with respect and consideration" in the household of her children.[33]

Census data reveal that Ovington's analysis held true for the Great Migration period and after, as well. The percentage of black women gainfully employed in New England, the mid-Atlantic states (New York, New Jersey, Pennsylvania), and the east north-central region (Ohio, Indiana, Illinois, Michigan) increased slightly between 1900 and 1930, but stayed within the 40 to 50 percent range. Occupational patterns based on age were stable from 1900 to 1920; black women between the ages of sixteen and twenty-four worked in the greatest proportion, but while white women tended to drop out of the workforce in their early twenties, black women stayed in it for many years. In some cities, the percentage of employed older black women had actually increased by the time the first phase of the Great Migration ended around 1920. About six out of ten women in the twenty-five-to-forty-four-year-old category continued to earn wages throughout the period (56.5 percent in 1900, 62.7 percent in 1920), and that figure declined only slightly for women aged forty-five and over (53.5 percent in 1900 and 54.8 percent in 1920). (Few foreign-born married women in northern cities took jobs outside the home, with the exception of those in New England mill towns; in 1920 only 10 percent in the Northeast and Midwest were engaged in gainful employment.) Thus the need for black mothers and wives to work remained constant before and after World War I.[34]

In general, black women's work in the North was synonymous with domestic service; although the caste system was more harsh in the South, white Americans regardless of regional affiliation relegated black women to this lowliest of occupational statuses. In the three largest northern cities—New York, Chicago, and Philadelphia—the total number of servants declined by about 25 percent (from 181,000 to 138,000) between 1910 and 1920, but the proportion of black women in that occupational category increased by 10 to 15 percent. After World War I, black women constituted more than a fifth of all domestics in New York and Chicago, and over one-half in Philadelphia. Pittsburgh, with its heavy-industry jobs for black men, offered few alternatives for their wives and daughters; in 1920 fully 90 percent of black women in that city made their living as day workers, washerwomen, or live-in servants. The 108,342 servants and 46,914 laundresses not in commercial laundries totaled almost two-thirds of all gainfully employed black women in the North.[35]

In their efforts to secure cheap domestic labor from the South, white middle-class families at times engaged in deceitful practices. In the early 1920s, for example, a young Florida native was reduced to a state of involuntary servitude by a family in a Chicago suburb. She eventually managed to escape but not before her employer "had kicked, beaten, and threatened her with a revolver if she attempted to leave." Yet such cases of violence and overt intimidation were relatively rare. Like southern mistresses, northern white women tyrannized their servants in more subtle ways. Indeed, though a migrant might endure a scolding delivered in a Brooklyn accent, or even broken English, instead of a southern drawl, she was likely to discover that the personal dynamics of the employer-employee relationship differed little between North and South.[36]

Still, in the urban North the occupation of domestic service was shaped by the region's peculiar social structure and spatial arrangement and so diverged in certain ways from the southern case. For instance, in their new homes, migrant women for the first time encountered competition from white women, primarily immigrants, for service jobs. Moreover, developments in household technology affected the number and kinds of jobs available. As the work associated with cleaning, heating, and lighting homes became more efficient and less messy, and as the latest labor-saving devices were installed in modern, expensive apartment units, the demand for servants declined. And finally, the traditional social hierarchy characteristic of service collapsed into two or three categories of work, leaving little room for upward mobility within households.[37]

A profusion of new gadgets and technology, combined with domestic reformers' attempts to "professionalize" and "systematize" household management during this period, more often than not complicated the daily routine for servants and housewives alike. Illiterate cooks had no use for recipes, grocery lists, or filing systems. Gas and electric appliances could work miracles if used properly, but offered the resentful domestic an opportunity to wreak havoc on her employer's pocketbook and nerves. In 1922 a government researcher reported cases of laundresses who had either ruined clothes or broken equipment while using electric machines. Whirling washtubs and powerful clothes wringers endangered the arms and fingers of women accustomed to boiling clothes over an open fire or beating them on river rocks. Mistresses expressed their frustration toward employees who did not know "how to fold the clothes just so after they were ironed as well as wash them out according to rule." In sum, few white women were inclined to oversee the transformation of field-hands into practitioners of the new "scientific" principles of domestic labor.[38]

Like their southern sisters, black domestics in the North had their own strategies for coping with jobs they despised as much as needed. First and foremost, as a group they refused, whenever possible, to submit to the desire of white employers for live-in servants. Noted a study made by the Chicago School of Civics and Philanthropy in 1911, "[Married black women] are accused of having no family feeling, yet the fact remains that they will accept a lower wage and live under far less advantageous conditions for the sake of being free at night. That is why the 'day work' is so popular." Day work had distinct advantages; it conformed to the long-term checkered work schedule of most working mothers, and it allowed employees a certain amount of flexibility in choosing their mistresses and assignments. White women, who preferred a sustained commitment from "general houseworkers," retaliated against day workers with a variety of ruses to wring more labor from them at a cheap price. Employers advertised for a laundress to do a week's worth of washing, but then presented her with three times that amount—apparently freshly soiled—to launder for the agreed-upon wages. Some women promised but never delivered pay raises, while others insisted that the servant perform additional work for the employer's neighbors for one day's pay.[39]

When other kinds of jobs did become available, black women rarely hesitated to pursue them, though this fact is hardly reflected in occupational statistics for the first three decades of the twentieth century. For example, less than 3 percent of all black working women were engaged in manufacturing in 1900 compared with 21 percent of foreign-born and 38 percent of native-born white working women. By 1930 the comparable figures were 5.5 percent of gainfully employed black women (100,500 out of 1,776,922), 27.1 percent of foreign-born, and 19 percent of native-born white women. (These figures reveal the impact of the last group's opportunities in sales and clerical work.) Black women, about 10 percent of the total American female population, constituted only 5.4 percent of the country's female manufacturing workers and only 0.5 percent of all female employees in clerical occupations, though they were gainfully employed in disproportionately large numbers overall. Dressmakers who worked at home accounted for about one-fifth of all black women described under the heading "Manufacturing and Mechanical Pursuits" in the United States Census for 1930. The largest group of black female factory workers in the North included those in the clothing industry (16 percent of all black women factory workers). An equal number labored in cigar and tobacco factories in the South. Food-processing workers (11 percent) constituted the next largest group.[40]

Like their menfolk, black women entered the northern industrial labor force, at least temporarily, for the first time during World War I, and the war represented both a break and a continuation in black women's employment patterns in the North. The wartime job hierarchy was shaped by both gender and racial ideologies, producing social divisions of labor that were at once unprecedented and time-honored. In general, black men and some white women took the unskilled industrial and other blue-collar jobs left by immigrant men who had entered the army; white women replaced native-born white men who had served as clerks and other kinds of white-collar workers; and black women took the non-defense jobs abandoned by white women and boys. Nevertheless, private employers and government officials did their best to maintain segregated workforces despite rapid labor-force turnover. In 1917, the seemingly arbitrary exclusion of black women from clothing-factory work at the Charleston Navy Yard—in favor of white women—prompted protests among potential job applicants, who prepared for a "determined fight for what they consider their rights," in the words of a sympathetic black newspaper. Still, a relatively small number of black women made inroads into the garment industry and into processing jobs in leather, paper, and textiles; and as employees of the government, they worked as cleaning women in arsenals and on railroads. Most notably, some five thousand black women found wartime employment in federal offices as typists and stenographers.[41]

A 1922 Women's Bureau survey of 11,812 black female employees in 150 plants in nine states found that most of the women were young (sixteen to thirty years old), and they worked at a variety of jobs. In war industry plants, they had assembled munitions and manufactured gas masks, airplane wings, nuts, bolts, rivets, screws, rubber tires, tubes, and shoes. As railroad employees they cleaned cars, repaired tracks, sorted salvage, flagged trains, and worked in the yards. The needs of local industries shaped black women's employment patterns in different cities. Over three thousand black women in Chicago found jobs in meatpacking plants. In the Philadelphia area they worked in twenty-eight different industries, including glass, garment, and candy factories.[42]

These jobs paid higher wages and offered more in the way of personal freedom compared to domestic service. In 1918 one black woman explained the decision made by herself and her friends to take jobs in a railroad yard that paid $3 a day: "All the colored women like this work and want to keep it. We are making more money at this than any work we can get, and we do not have to work as hard as at housework which requires us to be on duty from six o'clock in the morning until nine or ten at night, with might [sic] little time off and at very poor wages." The garment and railroad industries, in addition to government munitions factories, offered the highest wages to black women in industry—up to $15 to $20 per week. The prospect of hundreds of thousands of black women escaping the drudgery of service and entering the new technological age inspired the title of one extensive study conducted in 1919, "A New Day for the Colored Woman Worker."[43]

Still, these new kinds of work remained contingent upon local economies; cities dominated by a single heavy industry, such as Pittsburgh, offered few prospects for black women wage earners. And for the most part, the return of soldiers to the domestic labor force reversed wartime patterns and deprived black women of their wartime gains. Indeed, three aspects of black women's industrial employment during World War I indicated that their "progress" in this area was destined to be temporary if not altogether illusory. First, only a small number of black domestics and laundresses found alternate employment in manufacturing. The percentage of semiskilled operatives increased threefold from 1910 to 1920, but that gain represented only a small proportion (4.3 percent) of all black female workers engaged in nonagricultural pursuits immediately after the war. (A similar trend was evident among factory laborers.) Of the black women who did not till the soil in 1920, fully 80 percent were still maids, cooks, or washerwomen. Second, black women employed as industrial workers remained at the lowest echelons of the labor force in terms of wages and working conditions; for the most part they replaced white women who had advanced, also temporarily, to better positions. Finally, demobilization eroded even these modest gains. In October 1919 a writer for *World Outlook* acknowledged that "war expediency opened the door of industry" for black women, but that "in most cases, the colored woman is the 'marginal worker.' She is the last to be hired, the first to go." Those who managed to hold on to industrial jobs faced a constant struggle. As a New York woman remarked, "Over where I work in the dye factory, they expect more from a colored girl if she is to keep her job. They won't give a colored girl a break."[44]

Evidence from different cities highlights the problems of black women workers throughout the North. During the war, *New York Age*, a black publication, conducted a "Complete Survey of Race Women in Local Industries" and reported that the 2,185 women it studied were "doing work which white women will not do." According to the Consumers' League of Eastern Pennsylvania, in glass factories black women "had proved specially satisfactory, owing partly to their ability to stand the heat without suffering." Black women employed in this industry often worked in the most dangerous departments, "where at times bits of broken glass were flying in all directions." In fact, most black women employed in industrial establishments were not machine operatives or even semiskilled workers; they swept factory floors, scrubbed equipment, and disposed of refuse.[45]

Larger factories segregated black women in separate shops with inferior working, eating, and sanitary facilities. Smaller plants often refused to hire any black women at all, claiming the provision of separate areas would have been inefficient or too expensive. In addition, in rejecting her application, employers offered the black woman a litany of excuses: "'You are smart for taking the courses, but we do not employ coloreds'; 'The training center from which you come does not satisfy plant requirements'; 'Your qualifications are too high for the kind of job offered.'" In other cases, the extent of white employees' prejudice dictated hiring practices. During the 1920s, for example, white women factory workers in Philadelphia and machinery manufacturing operatives in Chicago went out on strike to protest the employment of black women in their plants. (The Chicago garment workers union was exceptional in that it successfully organized black women after they had been used as strikebreakers during the labor dispute of 1917.) Other companies integrated their nonunion female personnel with small numbers of strategically assigned black women to put their white employees on notice that cheap labor was readily available in the event of a protest or job action.[46]

Because of segmented female workplaces, individual black and white women did not usually vie directly for the same jobs at the same time. However, the role of black women as a reserve labor force served to intensify intergroup animosity and fear; the fluctuating economy caused many white women to worry constantly about their ability to hold on to a non-service job. Employers readily took advantage of this situation. For these reasons, few white women embraced black coworkers (especially those who readily took better jobs—if only temporarily—as strikebreakers) in the struggle against industrial capitalism. Moreover, organized labor helped to perpetuate the lowly position of black women workers. As a trade union, the American Federation of Labor had no interest in the fate of unskilled wage earners. But even local chapters of internationals that had a potential black constituency (like the Amalgamated Meat Cutters and Butcher Workmen and the International Ladies Garment Workers Union [ILGWU]) for the most part perceived the elimination of black women from the labor force to be in their own best interest. Unlike the Chicago ILGWU, these locals made little effort to organize black women. They unashamedly boasted "integrated" organizations, when in fact they might have no more than one or two black members. Separate groups of black female laborers lacked an advocate equivalent to their menfolks' Brotherhood of Sleeping Car Porters and thus had to engage in informal methods of protest—absenteeism, high turnover rates, careless work habits, or spontaneous job actions like walkouts—in order to resist exploitation in the form of low wages and poor working conditions.[47]

Accounts of black women in two specific northern industries—meatpacking plants and commercial laundries—during the postwar decade reveal barriers to their advancement as factory workers. In the late 1920s Alma Herbst, a Chicago researcher, conducted a survey of 1,126 black female and 6,905 black male workers in twenty-four Chicago slaughterhouses and meat-processing plants. The industry as a whole, she reported, was characterized by a high percentage of unskilled laborers, seasonal variations in employment, and hiring practices determined by "racial" and ethnic loyalties. Black women were assigned to the "most unattractive and disagreeable department"—hog killing and beef casing—and labored "under repulsive conditions." They had no access to even very low-paying tasks carried out in "clean, light, and comfortable" rooms or to positions that involved work viewed by plant visitors. In the bacon room of one establishment, for example, "The walls are painted white and the workers are clad in white"; for "aesthetic" reasons, and to conform to the "public's wishes" that black hands never touch a product in its last stages of processing, black women were routinely excluded from this department.[48]

These women carried a double burden that ruled out the possibilities for wage and occupational advancement. The lack of promotions was "more pronounced for women than for men, and for Negro women than for white," according to Herbst. Foremen (invariably white males) complained that black women workers were "the most irregular in attendance" and cited a number of reasons, from "loose living" to caring for ill children. Nevertheless, as a group these employees earned praise "for their loyalty and reliability during labor troubles and for their willingness to do the dirty work which soon became distasteful to foreign women." Black women workers labored for longer hours but took home smaller paychecks than did white women in the industry.[49]

Employers in meatpacking plants "put a premium upon youthful agility and alertness," and younger women, with their "nimble fingers," had a competitive advantage over older ones when applying for jobs. This was not the case in commercial laundries, where, according to a report released by the Women's Bureau in 1930, "the older woman, experienced in housework" predominated. During the early twentieth century, commercial steam laundries began to take customers away from individual washerwomen who worked in their own or their employers' homes. By the mid-1920s, the industry had become a big business in the largest northern cities, as smaller establishments consolidated and the total number of employees increased. During that decade black women became a larger proportion of laundry operatives; in 1930 they numbered 20,463, or one-quarter of all women employed in steam laundries. In Cleveland and Chicago, they constituted at least half of the industry's female workforce. In the latter city, "The opportunity to work in a laundry was practically denied to Negro women until a labor shortage forced laundry owners to tap this reserve labor supply."[50]

Laundry work was hot and damp, and most plants were ill-equipped to provide artificial ventilation or sanitary and rest facilities. As a rule, black women performed the lowest-paying, least-skilled jobs—hand ironing and flat work, and in the Northeast and Midwest earned an average of $12 per week compared to the $14 made by white women. Moreover, black women bore the brunt of periodic layoffs and "worked full time less generally than did white women." Consequently, there was "little or no relation between hours and earnings, the factors influencing the medians being locality and race." These differentials in wages and work opportunities were all the more dramatic given the similarity between white and black women in terms of their demographic characteristics and economic status. About 40 percent of the women in both groups surveyed by the Women's Bureau were married, and one-third of the women in each group had children under fourteen years of age. They cited "failure on the part of the husband" as the main reason they were working. The bureau concluded that "with the Negro woman, as with the white, the need of support for herself or herself and family was the principle reason for her working."[51]

If the history of black women in factory jobs is one of discrimination even more profound than that faced by immigrant women, the history of black women in clerical and sales work is one of complete exclusion. The reasons why black women as a group continued to make beds and wash dishes while white women were being hired as switchboard operators, stenographers, and sales clerks illustrate the complicated ways in which racial ideologies could shape the hiring policies of industrial and commercial capitalists. Employers did not necessarily forfeit their economic interests to their own prejudices, though it is true that prejudice against women and blacks precluded an ideal, efficient workforce in which tasks were assigned on the basis of ability, rather than on physical or cultural characteristics. Rather, for many establishments, discrimination proved to be good business in terms of both employee and customer relations.[52]

Like industrialists, employers of clerical, telephone, and sales personnel had to balance the cheapness of black female labor with the high costs of physical segregation. But to these employers, the "sexy saleslady" factor served as the primary reason for limiting low-paying but relatively high-status positions to white women, usually those of native parentage. As the Victorian era drew to a close, companies that sold consumer goods and services became increasingly self-conscious about their public image. Businesses sought to exploit the link between consumption and ego gratification; the most effective medium between product and consuming public, according to advertising experts, was an attractive, well-spoken, and pliant young woman who invested whatever she was selling with her own charms. Tact and politeness were key ingredients in any successful public-relations position, but a pleasing physical appearance (or voice)—one that conformed to a native-born white American standard of female beauty—was an equally important consideration in hiring office receptionists, secretaries, department store clerks, and telephone operators.[53]

For these reasons even black female high-school graduates could find few positions commensurate with their formal education. Stories of highly educated black women condemned to a lifetime of menial labor were legion. For example, a young graduate of the Cambridge Latin and High School, Addie W. Hunter, fulfilled certification requirements for civil service and clerical positions in Boston, but she had to work in a factory while she chased "the will-o-the-wisp of the possible job." She invested all of her meager savings in an unsuccessful lawsuit to gain a position for which she was qualified. In 1916, "out of pocket, out of courage, without at present, any defense in the law," she stated the obvious reason why other young women like herself would inevitably find their formal training wasted: "For the way things stand at present, it is useless to have the requirements. Color—the reason nobody will give, the reason nobody is required to give, will always be in the way."[54]

The social division of labor in Chicago stores and offices during the 1920s provides additional confirmation of these points. A clothing store in the city hired both black and white women, but the latter served as salesclerks and ate in a lunchroom on the first floor, while black women worked as maids and ate in the basement. Significantly, the country's largest employer of black clerical workers (1,050 in 1920) was Montgomery Ward, a mail-order establishment whose personnel had no direct contact with the customers they served. Even this company ran into public-relations problems. When black women were first hired during World War I, they had to eat their meals in local Loop restaurants, prompting complaints from the owners of these establishments "fearing the loss of old patrons in handling this new business." The company eventually built its own cafeteria in order to shore up its image and remove its black employees from public view.[55]

Thus far, the discussion of black women's paid labor has focused on the machinations of white employers who were physically removed from the black ghetto. Yet some black women worked in their own neighborhoods and, in a small number of cases, for employers of their own color. During the post–World War I era, the compression of black community life in northern cities spawned group self-consciousness manifested through political and business activity and artistic creativity. Black people focused inward and transformed southern folkways of self-help into northern voluntary and commercial institutions. At the same time, the relatively small number of jobs available to women in the ghettos reveals the limited extent to which blacks as a group were able to provide educational, business, and entertainment services for themselves. For example, by the early twentieth century, the black public teaching force had been feminized; at the national level, women in the profession outnumbered men by a ratio of about five to one. This ratio was true for the North as well as the South, though the number of women involved rarely totaled more than a handful in any area. In 1920 Chicago had only 138 black female school teachers. It is difficult to generalize about these teachers, though they were probably young, single, confined to the lowest grades, and paid less than whites performing the same jobs. As black school attendance and political power gradually increased in neighborhoods like Harlem and Chicago's South Side, a few black teachers were appointed by highly politicized citywide school boards. Still, most of these positions in predominantly black schools would continue to go to white teachers, who showed little sensitivity to the special needs of their students and automatically labeled them inferior in mental aptitude.[56]

The growth of black enterprise in northern cities suffered a hiatus around the turn of the century when white barbers, restaurant owners, and shopkeepers successfully attracted white customers away from black entrepreneurs. The Great Migration spurred black business activity once more, and this time black men and women appealed primarily to members of their own group for patronage. By the 1930s almost all ghetto communities could boast at least a few black-owned businesses; for example, Chicago had two banks, two insurance companies, and three newspapers, as well as several florist shops, funeral parlors, and corner grocery stores. Nevertheless, women contributed to these ventures primarily as "sacrificing wives" (along with their "useful children") rather than as paid workers.[57]

Several factors help to account for the small number of black women employed within the ghetto itself. Most significant is the fact that the majority of stores and companies selling to blacks continued to be owned, managed, and staffed by whites. For example, in the 1920s less than 20 percent of Harlem businesses belonged to blacks. The few black firms that did exist were usually short-lived, small operations with few employees. Finally, whenever openings for blacks did occur in sales or clerical work, they often went to black men rather than women. In Chicago in 1920, 1,247 black men had jobs in trade compared to 734 women, and four times as many black males as females were clerical workers, the opposite of the trend in the larger white society. No more than 2 or 3 percent of the black workers in any northern city, male or female, fell into either of these job categories. Instances of successful black businesswomen, like Madame C. J. Walker, distributor of hair-straightening products and the first African American woman millionaire, and Mrs. Annie M. Turnbo Malone, manufacturer of "The Wonderful Hair Grower," were as spectacular as they were rare. The majority of female entrepreneurs were seamstresses and hairdressers who conducted modest businesses in their own homes.[58]

In most large cities during this period, commercial entertainment and vice districts were located in or near black residential areas. White law-enforcement officials sought to concentrate this type of activity—with its attendant drug and alcohol use, prostitution, gambling, and petty and organized crime—and keep it away from "respectable" (that is, white middle-class) neighborhoods. Many of the black people with jobs in the fields of legal or illegal entertainment were either employees of whites or consumers of services and goods marketed by whites. Young, attractive black women worked as dancers or waitresses in cabarets that catered to middle-class "slummers." This type of work provided little long-term financial security, but for some women it offered a glamorous alternative to laundry and kichen work.[59]

Predictably, the physical concentration of urban vice gradually created disproportionate numbers of black prostitutes. The "incentives" for young women to make their living this way were largely negative ones—inability to support oneself by other means, and force exerted by a pimp. Most of the domestic servants in brothels were young black women, at least some of whom were vulnerable to the seductive demands of madams and patrons. A study of prostitution in New York City from 1900 to 1931 conducted by a Brooklyn College sociologist highlighted a number of themes characteristic of the profession in other northern cities as well. During the first three decades of the century, the "social evil" had gradually coalesced in Harlem, a "civic twilight zone" that whites found to be "a convenient place in which to go on a moral vacation." Poor and without "influential friends," black women were arrested and convicted more often and received stiffer jail sentences compared to their white counterparts. No doubt many individual women struggled to preserve their self-respect under the most degrading of circumstances. Yet as a group, black prostitutes represented an extreme form of the victimization endured by all black women workers in terms of their health, safety, and financial compensation.[60]

In sum, the history of black women's paid labor during this period constitutes not a variation on patterns of work among their white counterparts, but a unique history in and of itself. To be sure, black and white female factory workers labored for low wages under the watchful eye of foremen who might seek to exploit them sexually, and members of both groups remained segregated from male workers. Yet black women's work experiences revealed larger patterns of social and economic discrimination. In factories, black women toiled apart from even those who were already making less than white men; they received task assignments more unpleasant and hazardous than those who already toiled under the worst of conditions. Marriage intensified the differences between black and white working-class women. Although many young working girls might have indulged in romantic fantasies about marriage, few black women could count on a wedding to end their days of sustained wage earning. And the white mistress–black maid relationship preserved the inequities of the slave system (in fact that is the analogy some domestics made), and thus a unique historical legacy compounded the humiliations inherent in the servant's job. In the end, a black female wage earner encountered a depth and form of discrimination never experienced by a Polish woman, no matter how poor, illiterate, or lacking in a "factory sense" she was.[61]

Household Responsibilities

Born in Mississippi, Maggie Comer was the stepdaughter of an abusive father, a drifter who refused to work for a white man and who showed little regard for the well-being of his wife and children. Maggie received only six months' worth of classroom schooling her whole life—her stepfather expressed his violent opposition to formal education of any kind, and yet she managed to teach herself, quickly coming to realize that "I'm not too much at education, but with my fingers I could beat some people with a pencil." In 1920, Maggie moved north, to East Chicago, to live with a relative, and shortly thereafter she met and married James Comer. A native of Alabama, Comer had arrived in the city in 1916, and found a job in a steel mill. Though Comer was fortunate to have a steady job, he paid a high price for his near-perfect attendance record; in 1949 he contracted emphysema as a result of the stifling, dusty foundry he had worked in for more than three decades. For her part, Maggie helped support her family, which included five children, by ironing, washing, sewing, and cooking for the household, and by operating a small grocery store, taking in boarders, working for a caterer, serving as a poll watcher on election days, and doing other "little jobs here and there." By dint of their parents' hard work and sacrifice, the Comer children eventually earned a total of thirteen college degrees. Maggie Comer's labor, both waged and unwaged, was a critical factor in the Comer's family history, a story of triumph laced with self-sacrifice and debilitating physical illness. Observed their son James, who graduated from medical school and went on to a faculty position at Yale University, "The steel mill had given us a small piece of the American dream that the cotton fields had not."[62]

Any discussion of women's work in the home must begin with a description of the material dimensions of household and community life, for these, together with a culturally determined gendered division of labor, shaped women's domestic responsibilities. Although the specific process of ghettoization varied from city to city, the Great Migration in general intensified patterns of segregation throughout the urban North. This trend was indicative of heightened white hostility toward black migrants, hostility that erupted into the antiblack riots of the "Red Summer" of 1919. Even before World War I, New York, Philadelphia, and Chicago had black communities that ranked among the ten largest in the nation. San Juan Hill and Harlem, the Seventh Ward, and State Street testified to the social ties that bound blacks together, as well as to whites' legal and violent strategies that curtailed residential expansion. The histories of ghetto development have been told in detail elsewhere; here it is necessary to note only that black migrants faced a severe housing shortage and that white landlords were as eager to charge exorbitant rents as they were unwilling to maintain or improve existing dwellings.[63]

Predictably, family and community considerations often, but not always, helped to determine not only when, and with whom, a woman left the South, but also the extent of her household responsibilities in the North. Some women left their children behind with kin or neighbors in the South and sought a new life up North. When Arlena Burch gave birth to her daughter, Elizabeth, out of wedlock in 1926 in Chester, Georgia, she decided to leave the baby with her maternal grandmother and settle in Albion, Michigan, a place she had lived before. And in fact, not all women depended on family members to travel north. As many as half of all women migrants either had no spouse, or were not accompanied by one on their journey. On the other hand, some went along with friends, neighbors, or fellow church congregants, and others blazed a path on their own. Single women, unlike their brothers who might "drif' an' creep" north, often had a specific destination in mind, but that did not always mean they could rely upon friends or relatives for a place to live.[64]

These women had few choices. Lodging with an unfamiliar family at least provided protection and companionship; many women preferred to share a tiny apartment with several other people rather than live alone in an employer's attic or a dreary closet of a boardinghouse room. In eastern cities, the problem was exacerbated by an unbalanced sex ratio in favor of women. For example, among native-born blacks in New York City during the 1920s, there were 10 females for every 8.5 males, and 30 percent of those women were lodging or living alone.[65]

The variable, ever-changing nature of black household structure in the North reflected the arrival of new migrants or the loss of employment among others. As E. Franklin Frazier pointed out in a study of Chicago's black neighborhoods, the housing situation of individual families often improved to some extent over time, with the most recent migrants inheriting the least appealing facilities. Residential stability was a process, achieved by increments. The story of a Georgia family illustrates this form of progressive geographical mobility. Mr. J, formerly a sharecropper, arrived in Chicago in February 1917. He found a job in the stockyards and then sent for his wife and daughter to join him. At first the family stayed in a rooming house that "catered to such an undesirable element that the wife remained in her room with their daughter all day." Mrs. J's initial impressions of Chicago were formed by her depressing surroundings: "She thought the city too was cold, dirty, and noisy to live in. Having nothing to do and not knowing anyone, she was so lonely that she cried daily and begged her husband to put her in three rooms of their own or go back home." They finally took up housekeeping in a single-family dwelling, but the house "leaked and was damp and cold," so they moved again to better, larger quarters. After three years in the city, Mrs. J was able to express at least relative satisfaction with life in the North, despite the bad weather and high prices: "You don't have an overseer always standing over you," she remarked.[66]

Small, congested, poorly equipped rooms, together with inclement winter weather and unfamiliar forms of household technology, changed the nature of housework for many migrant women. During his visits to the homes of Pittsburgh newcomers, Abraham Epstein noted that though an apartment might be equipped with gas, many women persisted in using coal and wood to fuel their fires for cooking and laundry purposes, even in July: "Being unaccustomed to the use of gas, and fearful of it, [they] preferred the more accustomed method of cooking." A similar situation existed in Philadelphia, where migrants continued to use familiar cooking equipment rather than feed coins into a kitchen meter for gas. Grease and soot from old kerosene or coal stoves smudged the few windows of tenement apartments and, by blocking out all light, necessitated the use of oil lamps day and night. The women who contributed to the family income by washing clothes worked under the most trying circumstances. Mrs. E. H. of Pittsburgh had to lug water from an outside pump up the stairs to her one-room apartment; it always seemed to be hot and damp and filled with ill children. On warm, sunny days, clothes might be hung outside in a back courtyard, but in cold or rainy weather, the laundry had to dry inside. Although not all migrants lived in the large, multiple-unit dwellings characteristic of New York, few had the front porches that even washerwomen in the urban South depended upon.[67]

Women who worked for money within their own homes faced a tradeoff of sorts between taking care of their own children and adding to the confusion in already overcrowded rooms. At home, laundresses, seamstresses, and hairdressers had relative flexibility in terms of hours of work and childcare provisions. Yet, at the same time, their tiny apartments became "hotter, more cluttered, and more unhealthful." Moreover, this type of work was often unreliable and failed to provide adequate support for a family with children.[68]

The duties associated with childcare were a significant factor in the working lives of many working women, as both an incentive for them to move north, and as a substantial component of their unwaged labor once they arrived. Geneva Robinson and her grandmother journeyed from Hodges, South Carolina, to Cleveland in 1926 because her working cousin needed someone to look after her children. When she moved to Washington, D.C., in 1914, Alabama's Esther Lawson worked not for a white woman but for her brother and his wife: "I did linen piecework while at Brother's. His wife worked by the week, but I helped a laundress and did for Brother's childrens. She'd send her big sons out, and early, too! They'd bring in the work, and I'd help her. Now a good part of the day I did Brother's house, and all day I had to mind his children." Childcare was women's work, even when menfolk were available to do it. Another migrant to Washington, Isetta Peters, recalled firmly, "Now, the father of the children never minded nobody. No, in them days a man didn't do no mindin' for no child. Maybe a half hour or so, but somebody'd be over there quick 'cause he wasn't staying in there with childrens long. No sir."[69]

Many black women had to care for their own offspring and those of relatives and friends, and try to earn wages at the same time. Yet northern social workers and politicians persisted in holding black working mothers responsible for a variety of social ills related to family life, from the extraordinarily high black infant mortality rates found in all northern cities to educational "retardation" and juvenile delinquency. Certainly, the gainful employment of mothers could at times adversely affect children, though through no fault of their own. Women with infants could not breastfeed regularly during the day; they had to substitute cow's milk or some other food (routinely prepared under less than ideal conditions) for this natural, nutritionally superior form of nourishment. Neighbors and relatives had their own domestic and financial responsibilities, and many could care for other children only sporadically. Some unattended children were locked in the home all day, while others took to the streets, "with keys tied around their necks on a ribbon" to seek out fun and mischief until their mothers returned from work. For older children, the hours between school and suppertime provided ample opportunity to explore the neighborhood with adventurous companions. Social workers lamented the fate of children like Pittsburgh's Harry, age eleven, a thief, left to his own devices by a mother earning $3 a week in a service job that consumed all her time but a few hours each morning.[70]

Anxious parents realized that ghetto life threatened the well-being of their children in ways never dreamed of back on the cotton plantation. One elderly black woman in Washington, D.C., commented upon the proximity of brothels, dance halls, saloons, and gambling dens to black residential areas: "I have lived here long enough to know that you can't grow a good potato out of bad ground," she said. "Dis sho is bad ground." Crowded homes and a lack of outside recreation facilities, combined with the enticements of popular music, alcohol, and easy money, pushed restless youngsters out of the house and into streetwise trouble. New forms of commercial entertainment—some legitimate, like moving pictures, others borderline, like pool halls—lured young people of all ages. Compared to the small-town South, northern ghettos were "wide open." If children strayed from the straitlaced ways of their elders, perhaps it was only because, as one Chicago woman observed of migrants in general, "They had to be good there [in the South] for they had nothing else to do but go to church."[71]

Like mothers, fathers feared for their children. In 1917 one man, recently arrived in Cleveland, complained about ghetto "loffers, gamblers [and] pockit pickers"; "I can not raise my children here like they should be," he declared, "this is one of the worst places in principle you ever look on in your life." Yet few men could exercise any regular, systematic control over their children's whereabouts. Like their wives, male servants and factory laborers worked long hours outside their own neighborhoods. In contrast to their women-folk, though, those who were laid off or otherwise unemployed often gathered in places familiar to white employers looking for workers—a certain street corner, vacant lot, lunch-room, or barbershop, for example. In other cases, Pullman porters, live-in domestics, and other men who could find work only in a distant city were absent from home for extended periods.[72]

Obviously the elusiveness of regular, well-paying jobs for black husbands—and for their sons, too, when they became husbands—created severe hardships for individual families. Not only were these families poor, but the affective ties that bound husband and wife were often strained. Interviewed by a Detroit welfare worker in the 1920s, a Georgia-born black woman chronicled her husband's work history since their marriage. Noted the report: "[The man] was unable to support a family but never had any special quarrel with [his wife]. He left on February 24, 1923 and has never been heard from since. [She] thinks he left because of his inability to support family." The wife herself had not worked until her husband was unemployed. After he went away, she moved in with her parents and worked first as a laundress and then as a day worker. Her mother cared for her five children. The departure of her husband had not left this woman totally bereft of emotional or material resources. Yet the fact remains that the father of her children and a potential source of support was gone, plunging the family into even more dire financial circumstances.[73]

As this case suggests, the lowly job status of black men exerted a powerful effect on the well-being and structure of black households; unemployed husbands who left their families, either permanently or temporarily, increased the proportion of female-headed households. Yet census data for the period 1900 to 1930 indicates that these households were only relatively more numerous than those among native-born white or immigrant groups. Indeed, the differences were not statistically significant during these early years. For example, in 1930 the percentage of black female–headed households outnumbered those of native and foreign-born whites by no more than six percentage points in New York, Chicago, and

Cleveland. Independent variables like sex ratio, adult mortality rates, and group socioeconomic status probably accounted for much of the differential. The fact that large numbers of single, widowed, and divorced women had migrated from the South during the pre-1916 period also had an impact on the demographic profile of these urban neighborhoods. It was not until later in the century, when black ghettos felt the full impact of massive long-term unemployment and when federal welfare policy institutionalized male desertion as a means for families to qualify for financial support, that the proportion of black female–headed families exceeded that of other groups to a striking degree.[74]

Fathers were not the only wage earners to make an untimely departure from the black household and thus create extra work for wives and mothers. In the northern city, eldest daughters still helped their mother with the housework and childcare, but they lacked the subservience characteristic of the rural paterfamilias tradition. An Urban League official outlined the substance of these new mother-daughter conflicts in an article entitled "The Migrant in Pittsburgh," published in the October 1923 issue of *Opportunity*, the league's monthly journal. In discussing ghetto crime statistics, John T. Clark noted that few of the black women arrested were migrants because "the women are busy trying to adjust themselves and their families to the uncomfortable surroundings. When these women do appear before the courts, it is usually to make complaints against erring husbands or daughters." Mothers considered clothes washing "as the proper share of housework" for adolescent girls; in some cases that meant that a ten- or twelve-year-old was responsible for doing the laundry for families with as many as ten members. Perhaps it was no wonder, then, that as more married women had to engage in day work during the recession of 1921–1922, rates of "juvenile delinquency" (usually defined as truancy, vagrancy, or sexual activity) among black girls aged ten to eighteen noticeably increased; without rigorous parental oversight, at least some girls chose the excitement of street life over scrubbing clothes.[75]

Given the instability of the household's income from day to day and from year to year, and the disproportionately large share of black as opposed to white immigrant household income consumed by housing costs, black mothers had to institute a hand-to-mouth budgeting system. Sadie Mossell's analysis of Philadelphia migrant families' budgets in 1919 reveals the basic dilemmas of the urban family. She noted that black mothers had to shop for groceries every day and buy coal in small quantities. Because they lacked the storage facilities for either food or fuel, they spent more for these commodities. The poorest families relied on credit and in the long run paid higher prices than those that could afford to pay in cash. Most had brought little furniture from the South and purchased beds, tables, and dressers at excessive interest rates. The size of a family's living quarters depended not upon the number of children or lodgers but on its economic status; thus the largest families, which tended to be the poorest, occupied the smallest houses and apartments.[76]

In supplying the household's necessities, migrant wives and mothers had to adjust to the North's cash economy. Observed one transplanted Sea Islander on the difference between the price of a dozen eggs in New York (sixty-five cents) and Beaufort, South Carolina (six cents): "Here in New York, you wake up in the morning and have $15 in your pocket, but no food. But you can buy that. On the Island you wake up with a pantry full of food, but not a dime." Southern sharecroppers lived on the landlord's credit, and in some cases grew their own vegetables and raised hogs, cows, and chickens; they rarely saw more than a few dollars each month. Even in southern towns and cities, blacks often kept a few chickens and tended a small garden. But in the North these hedges against hard times were no longer available, and furthermore, a whole host of new, expensive necessities had appeared—warm clothing, shoes (for "all feet at least ten months in the year"), and large quantities of coal, gas, or kerosene. The migrant woman found that she had moved from semi-self-sufficiency to a consumer society. As her "stores of 'hog and hominy,' corn meal, syrup, and sweet potatoes" brought from Alabama dwindled, "the corner grocery, with its bewildering bright-colored canned goods, and other dazzling shops offer[ed] unusual opportunities for getting rid of money."[77]

In the midst of all these difficulties, black wives and mothers sought, in Mary Ovington's words, "to live a life apart from the roughness about them, but close to their church and their children." In New York's black neighborhoods, she noted, women struggled to provide an air of "home-likeness" to their tiny apartments; they adorned walls with colorful cards and photographs and found places for knickknacks and other "pretty things." Most significantly, mealtime "carried with it an air of a social function"; the family sat down to eat together, and "the mother would use many dishes though she must take the time from her laundry work to wash them." This account, published in *Charities* in 1905, was echoed four years later by another white social worker, Helen Tucker, this time in reference to Pittsburgh blacks: "Even the very poorest Negro homes are usually clean inside and out and have a home-like air—[there is] always some attempt at ornamentation, oftenest expressed by a fancy lamp."[78]

Migrant mothers after 1916 probably had considerably more difficulty achieving "home-likeness" in quarters that were so congested and temporary. However, for these women, the act of housekeeping in and of itself served as a strategy for providing a highly mobile population with a sense of stability. In Chicago, gainfully employed single black mothers maintained independent households to a greater extent than similarly situated white women, who tended either to board with a family or live in a rooming house. For black women, "Maintaining a home seems to depend less upon having a husband to provide it, than upon the presence of children who need to have the home." These mothers worked for wages in order to preserve the integrity of family life.[79]

In the North, the amount of work associated with household maintenance increased dramatically as wives sought to meet the daily needs of lodgers, as well as those of their immediate families. Extended and augmented households served both economic and social functions. Because of the youthfulness of the migrant population and the unbalanced sex ratio among blacks in most northern cities (in favor of women in the East, men in the Midwest), ghettos contained an unusually large number of single persons, childless married couples, and parents with very few children. (Fertility rates of northern urban black women were lower than those of southern women, black or white, in cities or rural areas.) In seeking shelter for themselves, then, blacks as a group faced problems shaped by both demographic and economic considerations that made the enlarged household a compelling arrangement, if not an absolute necessity in many cases.[80]

At least one-third of ghetto households between 1915 and 1930 contained lodgers at any one time; in 1930 the rates varied from 28 percent of all black homeowners in Pittsburgh to 37 percent in Cleveland and New York, and from 30 percent of all renters in Pittsburgh to 44 percent in Detroit. According to a study of urban "adjustment" among blacks and Poles in Pittsburgh from 1900 to 1930, maturing black families relied increasingly on income from lodgers because they could not count on their own sons and daughters for financial support. Polish households, on the other hand, became more nuclear over the years; gradually children started to work and turn over their wages to their parents, thereby lessening the need for boarders. Moreover, black heads of household were less able than their Polish counterparts to provide "meaningful economic contacts" for either their offspring or friends, fostering a greater sense of individualism (with regard to finding and keeping jobs) among black wage earners who lived together.[81]

Female lodgers at times helped the mother of the household with babysitting, cleaning, and cooking. Indeed, case histories of extended and augmented families suggest that at a certain point at least one woman boarder became necessary to share the tremendous increase in housework. Large households simply added to the domestic obligations of wives who had little in the way of time, cash, and household appliances. Black women supported the lodging system by dint of muscle power and organizational ability, and in the process they demonstrated how their homemaking skills could help to supplement household income while benefiting the migrant community. In the urban North, as in the rural and urban South, the boundaries between family and kin, household and neighborhood remained flexible and ever shifting.[82]

Migrants from the South found the difficult journey to a new life in the North eased somewhat by services offered by middle-class black women. Members of the "Old Elite" (relatively prosperous natives or long-term northerners) and the wives of a new class of ghetto businessmen and professionals joined forces to help working women, and they served as the driving force behind social-welfare programs duplicated in cities throughout the North: day nurseries, homes for young working women and for the elderly, recreational facilities for girls. Many of their programs were coordinated by the National Urban League (founded in 1911), a coalition of several New York community groups, including the National League for the Protection of Colored Women. Like local branches of the Young Women's Christian Association (YWCA) and the National Association of Colored Women, the league took a great interest in the problems of ordinary black women; it offered instruction in nutrition and hygiene, organized social clubs for the wives of working men, sent social workers into the homes of the needy, and attempted to introduce domestic servants to northern standards of household maintenance. These efforts amounted to more than a parallel, segregated version of urban "Progressive reform"; rather, they derived from the historic self-help impulse that had characterized black communities since the era of slavery.[83]

At the same time, not all longtime, well-to-do black northerners welcomed the migrants unconditionally. Like the German Jews who had settled in the United States in the nineteenth century, and then cast a wary eye on their newly arrived Eastern European coreligionists, black northerners feared that the newcomers' personal appearance and comportment, and public performances, would bring disrepute to the whole group. As early as 1888, in Washington, D.C., the *Washington Bee*, a black paper, expressed disapproval of the periodic parades and processions that newly arrived southerners eagerly joined in: "The tinsel show, gaudy display and straggling procession; thrusting upon public view a vastly undue proportion of the most unfortunate, unimproved and unprogressive class of colored people, and thereby inviting public disgust and contempt, and repelling the more thrifty and self respecting among us, is a positive hurt to the whole colored population of this city." On into the twentieth century, middle-class northern blacks spoke out against black laborers who traveled home on public transportation wearing soiled work clothes, or talked loudly on street corners. Like their southern counterparts, northern blacks who had earned over time a hard-won "respectability" sought to distance themselves from the impoverished folk who seemed to confirm white people's worst stereotypes about black people. The Urban League for example took it upon itself to issue guidelines for governing the social etiquette of public spaces in northern cities.[84]

Yet for Beulah Nelson, it was not the disapproval of black elites that caused her so much mortification, nor was it the Urban League or a black women's club group that changed her behavior: She gradually adjusted to northern life on her own terms. Acutely self-conscious about her southern accent, she remembered: "My talking was so bad. . . . Oh, they [northern blacks] sounded so different and nice to me. It was clear and sweet to hear, like music." She also worried about her clothing, consisting of "Old things stuff from down home." For Nelson, assimilation to northern customs, fashions, and speech patterns would come painfully, and only over time. In the meantime, she maintained a skeptical attitude toward life in her new home: "Crowded, smelly streets, noise, and confusion was all I saw. And people talked liked it was somethin' near 'bout heaven."[85]

THE NORTHERN SYNTHESIS: OLD AND NEW WAYS IN THE GHETTO

Black migrants brought with them a way of looking at the world that originated in the rural South and set them apart from equally poor white country folk, as well as from city dwellers. Like other newcomers to the city, they had to learn how to find a job, sustain kin relationships, and spend money and free time. Yet the process of adjustment among blacks was shaped by long-standing African American traditions and customs, and thus contrasted with that of various Eastern European immigrant groups on the one hand and native-born white urban in-migrants on the other. As a goal, "adjustment" to northern life remained uniquely difficult for the migrants and their children; they might accommodate themselves to time-oriented jobs and to the crowded living conditions of the ghetto; but those accommodations did not necessarily imply an indifference or total acquiescence to discrimination in the workplace or the housing market.

In the North, patterns of socializing changed least of all among married women. Working for wages, commuting, and housekeeping for family and boarders left little free time. Noted one Chicago woman, "My daughter and I work for the same company—We get $1.50 a day and we pack so many sausages we don't have much time to play but it is a matter of a dollar with me and I feel that God made the path and I am walking therein." Outside of the job and the home, most wives could partake only in church services, benevolent society meetings, and visits with friends, though an occasional moving-picture show or concert provided special enjoyment. (When singer George Garner "returned from triumphs abroad to entertain the home folks in Chicago," included in his audiences was "many an old woman [who] struggled up the stairs of Orchestra Hall after the day's work to hear him sing.") Perhaps most revealing was the practice of ghetto women sitting on the front stoop of their house or apartment building; there they could enter into community street life while staying close to home and sleeping babies.[86]

"The street is the symbol of life," noted one observer of black neighborhoods in the 1920s; "it satisfies to some extent the craving for new and thrilling experience." The urban scene offered more in the way of excitement for those not tied down with housework. Husbands and fathers embraced a subculture apart from wives and children; among their peers, the qualities of aggressiveness and daring superseded the domestic virtues. Northern ghettos offered a wide variety of settings for camaraderie. The local barbershop was often a favorite place for men to meet, tell jokes, boast of their sexual prowess, and exchange gossip. As havens from whites, work, and women, poolrooms mixed alcohol and competitiveness, a dangerous combination that at times led to bloodshed. Organized sports allowed young men to demonstrate their athletic skills before admiring parents, siblings, and sweethearts. Finally, "pay dances" symbolized a new code of social etiquette between the sexes—a code shaped by urban openness, a general breakdown in Victorian morality, and the rise of commercial entertainment. For blacks, these forms of recreation were largely a northern phenomenon; southern urban life, characterized by a more easygoing pace and a higher degree of residential integration, lacked the ghetto's scale and sophistication of leisure-time activities.[87]

Young single working women more easily pursued urban entertainments compared to their mothers. They experienced a brief interlude between the end of their domestic apprenticeship at home and the beginning of their responsibilities as wives and mothers. On the job they probably talked about fashions and beaux, and in the evening they sought diversions from a long and tedious workday. Miss T. S., the Chicago box factory employee, admitted to a Race Commission interviewer, "I make more money here than I did down South, but I can't save anything out of it—there are so many places to go here, but down South you work, work, work, and you have to save money because you haven't any place to spend it." Restaurants, cafes, department stores, and theaters provided meeting places for young women and set standards related to consumerism. For most of these women, marriage would mean a radical retreat from their brief social and economic independence. But for a few months or years, they experienced a way of life never encountered by their mothers, who, as young women, had gone directly from their father's cabin to their husband's cabin.[88]

In the midst of myriad challenges to traditional southern mores, some residents in northern ghettos tried to re-create the intimacy of village life they left behind. Older and married women played a leading role in this effort. They provided the constituency for storefront churches, which offered smaller, more intense worship services than did the largest northern churches. Contemporaries noted that church attendance was the most important form of "recreation" for wives. In the sanctuary, women entered a world divorced from worldly cares; there they prayed together for the souls of wayward husbands and rebellious children, all those who had, in the words of one wife, "forgotten to stay close to God" and were therefore bound for destruction. Smaller ghetto churches in general showed a pronounced lack of interest in social-welfare issues during this period; they offered heavenly, not earthly, salvation. Their exhortations for the faithful to resist temptation appealed most strongly to the women who served as the foundation of community stability and order. Some migrants linked women's strong religious faith, as evidenced by church-going, to their ability to withstand the trauma of moving north and surviving in a strange new place. Noted Edith Gaines, a native of Lucknow, South Carolina, of her new life in Washington, D.C.: "We were living in apartments, and in little short streets and things like that. Back then you didn't have a whole lot to look forward to. People were so religious then because all their hope was in the Lord. That's how it was."[89]

At the same time, not all churches were equal, and migrants were likely to draw a stark distinction between modest storefronts, with their charismatic leaders and traditional forms of worship, and the larger, relatively more staid congregations of mainstream denominations. In the South, services and the preachers who conducted them were impervious to the clock, and hymns were sung and prayers recited from memory. In older northern churches, most congregants were literate, bringing to the fore the hymnbook and the prayer book, and services responded to the rhythms of urban life, bound by the clock. In smaller spaces, women might worship in the presence of kin and close family members, recreating a small-town southern worship experience as nearly as possible in the urban North.[90]

Black women passed on to their children those organizational impulses and folk beliefs capable of surviving the transition from a rural to an urban, southern to northern setting. Mutual aid societies, insurance and savings clubs, and auxiliaries to men's lodges benefited factory workers just as they had tenant farmers. The discriminatory practices of northern urban hospitals, together with the fact that many migrants had neither the money nor the inclination to seek formal medical care, heightened reliance on elderly women skilled in the ways of healing. Grannies continued to dispense potions and advice to cope with a multitude of ills: a baby's teething pains, a straying spouse, indigestion, and impotence. It is not clear where Harlem residents obtained rabbit brains or wood lice, necessary ingredients for certain magic recipes; "cockroach rum" was probably more easily prepared under the circumstances.[91]

As African American literary and musical culture began to emerge into the national (that is, white) consciousness, and as black ghetto leaders began to play increasingly prominent roles in local political affairs and black nationalist enterprises, working-class black women retained their private, but lost much of their public, influence. This is not to romanticize tight-knit southern plantation communities in which women exerted considerable social influence as midwives, healers, conjurers, and fortune-tellers. Rather, it is to suggest that "modern" forms of self-expression through commercialized leisure and consumer activities curtailed the influence of poorer women. Too, few older women had either the time or the resources to participate actively in formal organizations. For example, wives and mothers of all ages served as ardent supporters of and investors in Marcus Garvey's Universal Negro Improvement Association, a nationalist group founded in New York City in 1919, but with the notable exception of Henrietta Vinton Davis, no women held high leadership positions in this influential organization.[92]

In sum, the ability of individual women to retain a traditional way of living depended upon the proximity of hometown friends, the nature of their social intercourse, and the tractability of their children. New forms of public media also played a role in broadening the migrants' consciousness. (In 1930 Chicago had the highest percentage of black households with radios of any city in the country.) This suggests that many women had at least some opportunity to hear local and national news, jazz, ragtime, and dramatic programming, and that radio broadcasts expanded their world beyond family and friends.[93]

At times, long-standing values found room to grow and develop more freely in the ghetto than in the South. Throughout this period, black northern women retained a deep and abiding faith in the value of formal education. Although they failed to receive the financial rewards commensurate with their schooling, black Northerners sent their children to classes in the same proportion as white parents. By 1930 black women forty-four years and younger were literate to the same degree as northern white women and black men their age, though fully one-third of all black women in the ghetto over sixty-five still could not read and write. Left far behind were black women in the South, whose illiteracy rates were five times higher than those of women living in northern urban areas. Certainly these statistics indicate that northern black women had a chance to become more fully aware of the contemporary political debates that raged around them; the fact that they could vote after 1920 meant that they were free to participate in the political process, an opportunity that their southern sisters would not have until the 1960s.[94]

Spurred on by dynamic leaders like Ida Wells-Barnett and Fannie Barrier Williams, middle-class women during this period continued to organize around issues of national as well as community interest. Specifically, women's rights were major sources of concern for black women's organizations. The rebuffs and outright hostility they faced from white women, especially those affiliated with the General Federation of Women's Clubs and the National-American Woman Suffrage Association, only increased their determination to fight all forms of prejudice. Mary Church Terrell, president of the National Association of Colored Women, lobbied among white clubwomen, but found that they were too sensitive to the prejudices of southern whites to consider advancing the cause of black women.[95]

The expanded realm of political and educational activities in northern cities represented a tangible form of upward social mobility for middle-class black women migrants from the South. Few of these women could afford to define self-betterment (or even intergenerational advancement) according to the standards established by Eastern European immigrants and native-born whites—a move out of the congested city into the spacious suburbs, a move up from unskilled work into a semiskilled or white-collar position. Nevertheless, although black wives and mothers had to continue to toil for wages outside their own homes, doing traditional "black women's work," they reaffirmed cultural priorities that had significant social, if not material, consequences for black people as a group. Like their emancipated grandmothers, they worked for the educational improvement of their children, and like their emancipated grandfathers, they cast votes on behalf of the political integrity of their own communities. This is not to suggest that black women lacked an interest in striving for improved housing or jobs; to the contrary, their stubborn eagerness to seek out better living quarters, to leave domestic service for factory work, and to drop out of the workforce altogether whenever household finances permitted showed that they adhered to the family values shared by all women of the laboring classes. Yet the peculiar dynamics of racial ideologies in the North precluded a definition of upward mobility expressed in purely economic terms.

Gradually a national perspective began to break down the insularity of ghetto life, and a former rural peasantry directly confronted modern industrial society. Likewise, white northerners came to understand that racial ideologies were no longer an historical anachronism, or confined to the South, as they had once claimed. Noted the white journalist Ray Stannard Baker of the Great Migration: "On wide Southern farms [blacks] can live to themselves; in Northern cities they become part of ourselves."[96] His observation pertained primarily to growing black political influence, for in a cultural and economic sense, ghetto residents remained apart from the larger white society. When the depression of the 1930s threw white folks out of work, too, considerations of political expediency, not social justice, influenced the responses of most elected officials to the plight of black people. These responses affected black women both as wage earners and as family members; for the first time since Reconstruction the work of wives and mothers entered the purview of national policymakers. Yet once again economic upheaval would leave intact the legacy of unremitting toil handed down from mothers to daughters both north and south.

HARDER TIMES

The Great Depression

IN 1930, *Apex News*, the publication of Apex Beauty Products Company, told its readers, "No matter how hard times are, people must do four things—eat, be housed, clothed, and look well. The harder times are, the more people stress looks and appearance." The manufacture, selling, and use of cosmetics and other beauty products remained, according to the *News*, a "Depression-proof business," one that offered unparalleled opportunities for black women seeking to earn a decent living during the deepening economic crisis. The founder of Apex, Sarah Spencer Washington, personified the lucrative nature of the beauty industry, for out of her headquarters in Atlantic City, New Jersey, she built an empire of highly profitable, interconnected businesses; at its height, in addition to publishing *Apex News*, her company sold 75 different kinds of beauty products, employed 35,000 sales agents around the United States, and operated eleven beauty schools that produced 4,000 graduates annually, many of whom started their own beauty shops. In building one of the largest black businesses in the country, Washington was confident, "As long as there are women in the world, there will be beauty establishments."[1]

With her expansive entrepreneurial and philanthropic impulses, Washington resembled Madame C. J. Walker and other promoters of beauty products, long a mainstay of the black community. These businesswomen were dependent on no white man or woman. During the Great Depression, such enterprises, including product sales, beauty shops, and beauty schools, achieved heightened social and economic significance. Though laundresses and domestic servants earned little, they enjoyed patronizing neighborhood beauty parlors, where they could spend time and money on their appearance, socialize with friends, and support multiple black-owned businesses, including the hairdresser herself and the products she used. At the same time, black beauty-shop owners registered the effects of the Great Depression, for even the most successful—for example, those serving middle-class customers in Harlem—earned only $16 a week, not enough to pay their workers the minimum wage established by new federal legislation. Most black beauticians worked either out of their own homes or out of a small booth in a store, and, in contrast to the reassurances of

Apex News and other publications, barely, or rarely, made ends meet. Regardless of their circumstances, these working women labored for long hours for uncertain pay, and competition for clients was cutthroat. Operators lowered their prices—for example, halving the $1.50 to $2.00 they used to charge for shampooing and pressing—or bartered their services "for food, clothing, or anything else of use to them." Employees of small shops who managed to hold on to their jobs suffered a dramatic drop in wages, while their hours remained the same.[2]

Moreover, the nature of the work itself was not always an improvement over domestic service: One Harlem worker remarked, "We learned beauty culture to get away from sweating and scrubbing other people's floors, and ran into something just as bad—scrubbing people's scalps, straightening, and curling their hair with a hot iron all day, and smelling frying hair." And more than one beautician grew weary of hearing the incessant complaints of customers determined to take advantage of a captive audience to rail against their employers; "You'd think on their day off they'd forget their madams," lamented one beautician, who heard more than she wanted to know from each customer about "what my madam said." Nevertheless, by the 1920s and the 1930s, the African American beauty business had emerged as one of the few industries controlled exclusively from top to bottom by black women, a fact of considerable political import, especially after World War II.[3]

"Our people have always known how to season a pot," goes an African American saying that has special relevance for the period between 1929 and 1941. Depression-like conditions were not new for the vast majority of black Americans, and over the generations they had managed to get by with little in the way of material resources. Nevertheless, 1930s unemployment data reveal that they lost what little they already had more swiftly and surely than did whites. In 1932, the black unemployment rate had reached an estimated, unprecedented 50 percent in some parts of the country. Throughout this decade, black women's responsibilities increased in proportion to the economic losses suffered by their households; at home and on the job, wives and mothers were called upon to work even harder than they had in better times. At the same time, many women of modest means, in concert with middle-class allies, aggressively pursued their collective self-interest in the cotton fields, in urban neighborhoods, and at the highest echelons of the federal government. In the words of Mary McLeod Bethune, an influential member of President Franklin D. Roosevelt's "Black Cabinet" and an official of the National Youth Administration, "We have been eating the feet and head of the chicken long enough. The time has come when we want some white meat." For the first time since Reconstruction, many African Americans held out hope that the combined efforts of the president and Congress would promote meaningful social change.[4]

At the very bottom of a hierarchical labor force, black men and women lost their tenuous hold on employment in the agricultural, service, and industrial sectors; economic contraction eliminated many positions, and then spurred an unequal competition with whites for the ones that remained. Concentrated in the marginal occupations of sharecropping, private household service, and unskilled factory work, many black women's jobs had, by 1940, "gone to machines, gone to white people or gone out of style," in the words of activist-educator Nannie Burroughs. Although the financial needs of black families intensified during the depression, black women's labor-force participation dropped from 42 percent in 1930 to 37.8 percent ten years later, reflecting their diminished work opportunities. Wherever they did work—on farms, in white households, in the factory, and in their own homes—mothers and daughters found themselves subjected to speed-ups, performing more labor for the same or lesser rewards.[5]

The complex set of chain reactions that had such disastrous consequences for many Americans, and for black Americans in particular, originated with the stock market crash in October 1929 (though rural folk of both races and northern black people began to feel the effects of economic recession several years earlier). Still, patterns of black women's work derived not only from mechanistic economic forces during these years; for example, at the national level, the federal government served in some cases as an employer of black women, regulator of their industrial working conditions and wages, and provider of social services and relief. Local white administrators, especially those in southern states, used the federal resources at their disposal to reinforce the caste system, called by some "Jim Crow." "The job is JIM CROWED, the commodities are JIM CROWED, the very air you breathe under the Adams County Mississippi [Emergency Relief Administration] is contaminated with the parasite of JIM CROWISM," wrote one exasperated black man to the head of the Labor Department's Division of Negro Labor in 1935. Throughout this period, President Roosevelt remained hostage to the southern white Democrats who headed key congressional committees. Refusing to embrace antilynching legislation or black civil rights more generally, the president declared in 1933, "First things come first, and I can't alienate certain votes I need for measures that are more important at the moment by pushing any measures that would entail a fight." Nevertheless, the real benefits that some black families derived from federal programs, combined with highly visible gestures in the direction of egalitarianism made by Eleanor Roosevelt and a few New Deal officials, were enough to inspire a massive defection on the part of black voters from the Republican to the Democratic Party. In 1936, FDR received more than three-quarters of the black vote, a testament to the fact that northern black voters received their approximate fair share of jobs and relief, in contrast to southern blacks, the overwhelming majority of whom remained disenfranchised and thus powerless to counter the prejudicial decisions of local administrators.[6]

Labor unions revitalized and inspired by federal legislation in the mid-1930s, and radical political parties and community organizations galvanized by widespread social unrest, also shaped patterns of black women's work. Black women participated in broader labor and political struggles when they organized coworkers into a union affiliated with the Congress of Industrial Organizations (CIO), helped to build an organization of displaced sharecroppers, joined the Communist Party, or lobbied on behalf of the newly formed National Council of Negro Women (founded by Mary McLeod Bethune). According to writer Richard Wright, their initial, Depression-era encounters with a more expansive world, one that included in some cases white coworkers, represented for blacks "the death of our old folk lives, an acceptance of a death that enabled us to cross class and racial lines, a death that made us free."[7]

Yet Wright's epitaph for black folk consciousness was premature. Black nationalist and neighborhood welfare coalitions continued in the generations-old African American tradition of cooperation and group advancement. In addition, networks of kin and neighbors assumed critical significance among black women who had fewer resources with which to care for greater numbers of unemployed household members. As Annie Mae Hunt, a domestic, told her children in the 1930s, "You don't need no *certain* somebody. You need *somebody*. Somebody. That's all you need . . . but you got to have somebody that cares." Together, black sisters, mothers, grandmothers, and daughters relied on one another to get them through these harder times; as individuals many of them demonstrated strength and determination in ways they themselves did not always fully comprehend. The sole support of her three children, an East St. Louis black woman worked for meager wages as a meat trimmer during the day and did all her own housework and provided for a boarder in the evenings; in response to the queries of a government investigator in 1937, she admitted, "I don't hardly see myself how I make out."[8]

Thus black women's work in the 1930s took place within a matrix of federal action, class-based and black political activism, neighborly cooperation, and personal initiative. However, structural factors related to the American economic and political system inhibited meaningful change in the status of black women, relegated as they were to the fringes of a developing, though crippled, industrial economy. Most New Deal labor legislation targeted the employees of large industrial establishments; these employees were covered by new laws related to unemployment compensation, minimum wages and hours, and Social Security. Left out of these provisions were domestic servants, part-time workers, and agricultural laborers—that is, the vast majority of black men and women. Moreover, legislative measures that did ameliorate the condition of unemployed black working women at times could adversely affect their status as family members; for example, the welfare state provided minimal cash payments for single mothers with dependents, but it injected a new source of tension into marital relationships. In the end, trends related to national and regional economic development, combined with bureaucratic shortsightedness and prejudice, preserved the historic vulnerabilities endured by black women workers. Of the persistence of antiblack discrimination in the 1930s, one trenchant observer noted, "The devil is busy." But so too were hundreds of thousands of black women wage earners, community leaders, and housewives who faced "an old situation [with] a new name, 'depression.'"[9]

DIMINISHING OPPORTUNITIES IN THE PAID LABOR FORCE

High unemployment rates among their husbands and sons forced many white wives to enter the labor market for the first time in the 1930s. At the same time, black men were experiencing even higher rates of joblessness; their distress caused their wives to cling more desperately to the positions they already had, despite declining wages and deteriorating working conditions. During the Great Depression, most black women maintained only a precarious hold on gainful employment; their positions as family breadwinners depended upon, in the words of one social worker, "the breath of chance, to say nothing of the winds of economic change." Unemployment statistics for the 1930s can be misleading because they do not reveal the impact of a shifting occupational structure on divergent job options for black and white women. Just as significantly, the relatively high rate of black females' participation in the labor force obscures the highly temporary and degrading nature of their work experiences. Specifically, most of these women could find only seasonal or part-time employment; persistent forms of discrimination deprived them of a living wage no matter how hard they labored; and they endured a degree and type of workplace exploitation for which the mere fact of having a job could not compensate. During the decade, nine out of ten black women workers toiled as agricultural laborers or domestic servants. Various pieces of federal legislation designed to protect and raise the purchasing power of workers (most notably the National Industrial Recovery Act [1933], the Social Security Act [1935], and the Fair Labor Standards Act [1938]) exempted these two groups of workers from their provisions. In essence, then, no more than 10 percent of gainfully employed black women derived any direct benefit from the new federal policies designed primarily to cushion industrial wage earners against the regular upturns and downswings characteristic of a national market economy. Indeed, these policies were crafted not only by southern congressmen, but also by liberal New Dealers who believed that semiskilled assembly-line workers constituted the backbone of the American economy.[10]

Despite the rapid decline in a wide variety of indicators related to production and economic growth in the early 1930s, and despite the sluggishness of the pre-1941 recovery period, the numbers and kinds of job opportunities for white women expanded, as did their need to help supplement household income. The clerical sector grew (as it had in the 1920s) and would continue to do so in the 1940s, and in the process attracted more and more women into the workforce and employed a larger proportion of all white women workers. (The percentage of white women who were gainful workers steadily increased throughout the period 1920 to 1940 from 21.3 to 24.1 percent of all adult females.) At least during the early part of the depression decade, unemployment rates in the male-dominated industrial sector were generally higher than those in the female-dominated areas of sales, communications, and secretarial work. But the fact of gender segmentation in the labor force benefited white women, for black women had no access to white women's work even though (or perhaps because) it was deemed integral to both industrial capitalism and the burgeoning federal bureaucracy. In 1940 one-third of all white, but only 1.3 percent of all black, working women had clerical jobs. On the other hand, 60 percent of all black female workers were domestic servants; the figure for white women was only 10 percent.[11]

During the 1930s, a public debate over the propriety of working wives raged in city council chambers, state legislatures, union halls, and the pages of popular magazines, indicating that persons on both sides of the question assumed it was a new and startling development. As historian Alice Kessler-Harris has pointed out, "Issues involving male and female roles, allowed to pass unnoticed for generations because they affected mostly poor, immigrant, and single women, assumed central importance when they touched on the respectable middle class." Few congressmen or labor leaders evinced much concern over the baneful effects of economic dependence on the male ego when the ego in question was that of a black husband. Moreover, white female school teachers, social workers, and factory workers deprived white men of job opportunities in a way that black domestic servants did not. Working wives became a public issue to the extent that they encroached upon the prerogatives of white men at home and on the job.[12]

Women Who Daily "Hit the Sun"[13]: Black Farmworkers in the 1930s

Government programs that sought to limit crop production and raise the price of food had two major effects on black women: First, they hastened the displacement of sharecropping families that were now too costly to furnish (i.e., supply with credit) and that were no longer necessary to the staple-crop economy; and second, they enabled large planters to invest their cash subsidies in farm machinery, in the process reducing tenants and sharecroppers to the status of hired hands. Thus the Depression represented a major turning point in the history of southern farming, as the plantation labor system was transformed from sharecropping to wage labor, and the number of persons who made their living from the land declined rapidly. Of all black working women in 1940, 16 percent were employed in agriculture, down from 27 percent ten years earlier.[14]

A cornerstone of the early New Deal, the Agricultural Adjustment Act (AAA, passed in 1933), provided compensation for planters who grew less, and tenants were supposed to benefit from a portion of this allotment. In fact, plantation owners often failed to pass on to their tenants any of the money at all, arguing that the funds should be used to retire the (often concocted) debts of individual families. Others dispensed with the problem altogether by evicting tenants en masse or by "splitting" households to distinguish between productive and incapacitated or youthful members. National welfare policies indirectly encouraged this practice. For example, the Federal Emergency Relief Act of 1933 (FERA) made provisions for the distribution of relief funds by local private and governmental agencies to rural farm families. Thus an owner might agree to contract with individual able-bodied men and women (rather than a family unit) under the assumption that children needed very little anyway and that FERA would take care of the elderly. A confidential FERA report of July 1934 noted that "theoretically, [the average white planter] says that the landowner should maintain his tenants, if able, but actually, since he has had a taste of government relief, he is loathe to give it up."[15]

Together, these policies increased the fieldwork and family obligations of rural black women. Household members "dropped" by a landlord might not be "picked up" by a relief program, thus forcing wives and mothers to stretch their skimpy resources and provide for children or elderly kin and neighbors deprived of any direct source of income. As workers, these women found that the value of their labor had decreased, not only in terms of cash earned from the sale of cotton, but also in terms of the basic supplies—food, fertilizer, and equipment—furnished to each household by the landlord. At times new kinds of deprivation had wide-ranging and not fully anticipated consequences. A female sharecropper who testified before a national conference on economic recovery in the mid-1930s noted that her family's inability to purchase fertilizer meant that the children had no clothes to wear, since she was used to making their "aprons and dresses" from the rough burlap bags fertilizer came in. When it came to clothing the children, fertilizer sacks were better than nothing.[16]

Furthermore, black women's status declined relative to that of first, their poorest white neighbors, who were more likely to receive government assistance, and more of it; and second, industrial wage earners. Agricultural labor in the 1930s had an intensive, primitive quality, prompting one sociologist to suggest that "it seems to take a good deal of social pressure to get people to do this work." Mechanical advances had cut down on the amount of labor required for plowing furrows and hoeing rows of crops, but workers still did most of the harvesting by hand. Stooped over, moving slowly down long rows and picking cotton bolls or worming tobacco plants, or on their knees following a plow and "grabbling" in the earth for potatoes, those women who labored in the fields resembled their early-nineteenth-century foremothers in all but dress; now thinner, short-sleeved cotton dresses had replaced the hot, heavy osnaburgs of the antebellum period.[17]

In an effort to work their way out of chronic indebtedness, some black farm women took short-term, nearby jobs as wage laborers for the rate of forty to fifty cents a day. A 1937 Women's Bureau report noted that the female cotton-pickers of Concordia Parish, Louisiana, earned a total of $41.67 annually; most found, or accepted, gainful employment for less than ninety days each year. Those who continued to labor as sharecroppers of course received only a ramshackle room and meager board, but virtually nothing in cash. For some women, the stability and closeness of kin ties compensated for the lack of money. A thirty-eight-year-old mother who had left her husband and returned to her childhood home told an interviewer that though "she usually received nothing at the end of the year [it] was of no importance to her as long as she lived with her mother and brother and sister." Still, the irony of the situation was unavoidable. In her 1931 study of black female cotton laborers in Texas, Ruth Alice Allen calculated that they produced about one-eighth of the state's crop yet earned "no return but a share in the family living."[18]

Migratory labor represented an extreme form of farm workers' displacement. During the Great Depression, public attention focused on the white "Okies" who fled dust bowl conditions in the South and Southwest to seek an ever-elusive harvest of plenty on the West Coast. Blacks did not participate in this general population movement to any great extent because of the lack of mass (that is, rail) transportation and because they could not depend upon securing basic services such as food and gas en route in private automobiles. Yet in response to "reduced earnings in their usual work," family groups, for the first time on a large-scale basis, began to travel up and down the eastern seaboard, living in labor camps while working in Florida orange groves, Delaware canneries, and the fields of New Jersey truck farms. Recorded by the Women's Bureau in 1941, the story of the "A" family, a young Maryland couple, was typical. In 1939 Mrs. A had worked as a domestic and her husband as an oyster shucker, but "neither of these occupations afforded very full or steady employment." The next year between March and September they picked berries and canned tomatoes in Delaware, "grabbled" potatoes in Virginia, and harvested cucumbers in Maryland. Nine months of sporadic work had earned them only $330, one-third of which was Mrs. A's contribution. In their exploitative working and living conditions, seasonal employment, poor pay, and strong commitment to family ties, this husband and wife had much in common with all black agricultural laborers.[19]

Migrant laborers and sharecroppers did have advocates within the Roosevelt administration. Officials in the Resettlement Administration (1935), and in the Farm Security Administration (FSA) that replaced it in 1937, initiated a number of programs intended to offset the disastrous effects of the AAA on the southern and midwestern rural poor. These officials created and administered cooperative farming ventures, government-sponsored migratory labor camps, low-cost housing projects, and low-interest loans for tenants with an exceptional degree of egalitarianism. Many of these projects benefited black women as heads of households, farm wives, and day laborers. In addition, the documentary photography project sponsored by the FSA preserved striking images of working women for all posterity; these portraits in black and white, which conveyed both the dignity and the desperation of so many housewives, were stark reminders of the physical arduousness of a farm mother's daily labor. Yet the radical nature of FSA programs provoked the wrath of large landholding interests and budget-cutting congressmen, and so affected relatively small numbers of people. Always understaffed and underfunded, the administration made loans to only a few thousand farmers, compared to the estimated million people driven from the land during the decade.[20]

However, neither black nor white tenant farmers sat and waited passively for government aid. As early as 1931, the Communist Party helped to establish a Share Croppers Union (SCU) in Alabama, and party workers, like the young black woman Estelle Milner, were distributing copies of the party journal *Southern Worker* in the state's rural areas. This group never had many members, and it was superseded in 1934 by the Southern Tenant Farmers' Union (STFU), founded in Tyronza, Arkansas, with the help of the Socialist Party, in response to evictions precipitated by AAA programs. A year later the STFU claimed ten thousand members, at least half of them black, ample proof of its conviction that labor organizing among blacks as well as whites should begin with grassroots activity and not just rhetorical pronouncements from the upper echelons of the party. In its call for cooperative agricultural communities, the union posed an implicit threat to the southern plantation system. The efforts of southern senior politicians, landowners, and law-enforcement and judicial officials to crush the movement by any means possible—harassment, dynamite, and murder were among the tested strategies—provided a measure of that threat. AAA policymakers worked strenuously against the union and even purged its own ranks of its supporters. The STFU therefore lost much of its power after 1936. Years later Ned Cobb, who was active in the Alabama SCU and later imprisoned for his role in it, said that "it was a weak time amongst the colored people. They couldn't demand nothin'; they was subject to lose what they had if they demanded any more."[21]

Nevertheless, during its brief life, the STFU emerged as a vital political organization that relied on the commitment of women and men, blacks and whites. As one member later recalled, "Women were very active . . . and made a lot of decisions." Naomi Williams, a member of the Gould, Arkansas, local, cultivated a cotton patch of her own, daily picked up to three hundred pounds of a white landowner's crop, kept a vegetable garden, and taught school for her neighbors' children. "I done worked myself to death," she said as she explained to an interviewer why she became active in the union, and she spoke bitterly of the tremendous amount of labor necessary to keep her family together in a society that limited schooling for black children to seven months a year, "and the white kids . . . going to school all kind of every way." Other black women, like Carrie Dilworth and Henrietta McGee, earned long-lived reputations for their organizing and speaking abilities in the face of violent intimidation. Arkansas wives and mothers participated in the 1935 general strike of cotton-pickers and, together with their families, Missouri "Bootheel" women made national headlines when they camped out along a roadside in the winter of 1939. This mass demonstration did much to bring to public attention the plight of a "poor people in a rich land."[22]

In concert with their white neighbors and middle-class allies, black agrarian radicals in the 1930s left a legacy of resistance to their grandchildren but had little impact upon the emerging neoplantation system that relied on the labor of hired hands. All over the South, black families continued to yearn for economic independence, which they defined as a title to their own land, free of debt and government encumbrance. In rural eastern North Carolina, Gracie Turner stretched the $12 her husband earned each month digging up tree stumps on a public works project; she made it "do all it will" for nine people but resented the fact that public works took farmers away from the land: "Able-bodied landers has got no business a-havin' to look to de gover'ment for a livin'," she said. "Dey ought to live of'n de land. If 'twas fixed right dey'd make all de livin' dey need from de ground." A proud woman with her two feet rooted firmly in the southern soil, Gracie Turner believed that relief should come in the form of structural change, not piecemeal make-work; if the sharecropping system were only "fixed right," people could make a decent living on their own. During the 1930s, that possibility receded further and further out of sight.[23]

Kitchen Speed-Ups: Domestic Service

Contemporary literary and photographic images of a stricken nation showed dejected white men waiting in line for food, jobs, and relief. Yet observers sensitive to the racial-ideological dimensions of the crisis provided an alternative symbol—that of a middle-aged black woman in a thin, shabby coat and men's shoes, standing on a street corner in the dead of winter and offering her housecleaning services for ten cents an hour. If the migrant labor camp symbolized the black agricultural worker's descent into economic marginality, then the "slave markets" in northern cities revealed a similar fate for domestic servants. And in fact, the pressures on black women to earn a living increased in proportion to the rise in their menfolk's unemployment rates. Long accustomed to the role of breadwinner, black women of all ages now assumed even greater responsibility for the welfare of their families.[24]

"The 'mart' is but a miniature mirror of our economic battle front," wrote two investigative reporters in a 1935 issue of the NAACP's monthly journal, *The Crisis*. A creature of the Depression, the slave market consisted of groups of black women, aged seventeen to seventy, who waited on sidewalks for white women to drive up and offer them a day's work. The Bronx market, composed of several small ones—it was estimated that New York City had two hundred altogether—received the most attention from writers during the decade, though the general phenomenon recurred throughout other major cities. Before 1929, many New York domestics had worked for wealthy white families on Long Island. Their new employers, some of them working-class women themselves, paid as little as $5.00 weekly for full-time laborers to wash windows and clothes, iron (as many as twenty-one shirts a shift), and wax floors. These workers earned radically depressed wages: lunch and thirty-five cents for six hours of work, or $1.87 for an eight-hour day. They had to guard against various ruses that would deprive them of even this pittance—for example, a clock turned back an hour, the promised carfare that never materialized at the end of the day. As individuals they felt trapped, literally and figuratively pushed to the limits of their endurance. A thirty-year-old woman told federal interviewer Vivian Morris that she hated the people she worked for: "Dey's mean, 'ceitful, an' 'ain' hones'; but what ah'm gonna do? Ah got to live—got to hab a place to steh," and so she would talk her way into a job by boasting of her muscle power. Some days groups of women would spontaneously organize themselves and "run off the corner" those job seekers "who persisted in working for less than thirty cents an hour."[25]

Unlike their country cousins, urban domestics contended directly with white competitors pushed out of their factory and waitressing jobs. The agricultural labor system served as a giant sieve; for the most part, displaced farm families went to the city rather than vying for the remaining tenant positions. The urban economy had no comparable avenues of escape; it was a giant pressure cooker, forcing the unemployed to look for positions in occupations less prestigious than the ones they held formerly or, in the event of ultimate failure, to seek some form of charity or public assistance. The hardships faced by black men—now displaced by white men seeking jobs as waiters, bellhops, and street cleaners—were mirrored in the experiences of their wives, daughters, and sisters who had long worked as domestic servants. A 1937 Women's Bureau survey of destitute women in Chicago revealed that, although only 37 percent of native-born white women listed their "usual occupation" as domestic service, a much greater number had tried to take advantage of employers' preferences for white servants before they gave up the quest for jobs altogether and applied for relief. Meanwhile, the 81 percent of black women who had worked in service had nowhere else to go. Under these circumstances, the mere act of hiring a black woman seemed to some to represent a humanitarian gesture. In 1934 an observer of the social-welfare scene noted approvingly, with unintentional irony, that "From Mistress Martha Washington to Mistress Eleanor Roosevelt is not such a long time as time goes. There may be some significance in the fact that the household of the first First Lady was manned by Negro servants and the present First Lady has followed her example."[26]

The history of domestic service in the 1930s provides a fascinating case study of the lengths to which whites would go in exploiting a captive labor force. Those who employed live-in servants in some cases cut their wages, charged extra for room and board, or lengthened on-duty hours. However, it was in the area of day work that housewives elevated labor-expanding and money-saving methods to a fine art. General speed-ups were common in private homes throughout the North and South. Among the best bargains were children and teenagers; in Indianola, Mississippi, a sixteen-year-old black girl worked from 6:00 a.m.

to 7:00 p.m. daily for $1.50 a week. In the same town a maid completed her regular chores, plus those of the recently fired cook, for less pay than she had received previously. (A survey of Mississippi's domestics revealed that the average weekly pay was less than $2.00.) Some women received only carfare, clothing, or lunch for a day's work. Northern white women also lowered wages drastically. In 1932 Philadelphia domestics earned from $5.00 to $12.00 for a forty-eight- to sixty-seven-hour work week. Three years later they took home the same amount of money for ninety hours' worth of scrubbing, washing, and cooking, an hourly wage of fifteen cents.[27]

The deteriorating working conditions of domestic servants reflected the conscious choices of individual whites who took advantage of the abundant labor supply. Social workers recorded conversations with potential employers seeking "bright, lively" domestics (with the very best references) to do all the cooking, cleaning, laundry, and childcare for very little pay, because, in the words of one Pittsburgh woman, "There are so many people out of work that I am sure I can find a girl for $6.00 a week." Indeed, at times it seemed as if there existed a perversely negative relationship between expectations and compensation. An eighty-three-year-old South Carolina black woman, Jessie Sparrow, resisted working on Sundays because, she told an interviewer in 1937, "When dey pays you dat little bit of money, dey wants every bit your time." A southern white man demonstrated his own brand of logic when he "admitted as a matter of course that his cook was underpaid, but explained that this was necessary, since, if he gave her more money, she might soon have so much that she would no longer be willing to work for him." Well-educated black women contended with the machinations of employment agencies that signaled to potential employers that the applicant was white ("L-H-P" stood for "Long Haired Protestant"). In Seattle, Arline Yarbrough entered the job market armed with a high-school degree and training as a typist; yet she found her options so limited—"as soon as they'd [employers] seen we were black"—she ended up piecing together a livelihood, catch-as-catch-can: "little house jobs and baby sitting jobs, which would usually be for a day or two, a week at the most . . . it was a pretty cruel situation."[28]

The field of domestic service was virtually unaffected by national and state welfare policies. In the 1930s Women's Bureau officials sought to compensate for this inaction with a flurry of correspondence, radio and luncheon-meeting speeches, and voluntary guidelines related to the "servant problem." In her talks on the subject, bureau head Mary Anderson appealed to employers' sense of fairness when she suggested that they draw up job descriptions, guard against accidents in the workplace, and establish reasonable hours and wages. However, the few housewives privy to Anderson's exhortations were not inclined to heed them, especially when confronted by a seemingly compliant "slave" on the street corner. Consequently, black domestic workers in several cities, often under the sponsorship of a local Young Women's Christian Association, Urban League branch, or labor union, made heroic but unsuccessful attempts to form employees' organizations that would set uniform standards for service; but domestics in general constituted a shifting, amorphous group immune to large-scale organizational efforts. For example, founded in 1934 and affiliated with Building Service Union Local 149 (AFL), the New York Domestic Workers Union had only 1,000 (out of a potential of 100,000) members four years later. It advocated two five-hour shifts six days a week and insisted, "last but not least, no window washing." Baltimore's Domestic Workers Union (in the CIO fold) also welcomed all women and remained a relatively insignificant force in the regulation of wages and working conditions. Without adequate financial resources, leaders like New York's Dora Jones labored to organize women who "still believe in widespread propaganda that all unions are rackets." As a result, efforts by domestics to control wage rates informally through peer pressure or failure to report for work as promised represented spontaneous job actions more widespread and ultimately effective than official "union" activity.[29]

During the Depression, a long life of work was the corollary of a long day of work. Black women between the ages of twenty-five and sixty-five worked at consistently high rates; they simply could not rely on children or grandchildren to support them in their old age. The Federal Writers Project interviews with former slaves recorded in the late 1930s contain hundreds of examples of women in their seventies and eighties still cooking, cleaning, or hoeing for wages on a sporadic basis in order to keep themselves and their dependents alive. An interviewer described the seventy-seven-year-old widow Mandy Leslie of Fairhope, Alabama, as "a pillar of strength and comfort to several white households" because she did their washing and ironing every week. Living alone, her children gone, this elderly woman boiled clothes in an iron pot heated by a fire, and then rubbed them on a washboard and hung them on lines so they could be ironed the following day. Such was the price exacted from black women for the "strength and comfort" they provided whites.[30]

"On The Fly" in Factories

Black women's preference for factory jobs over domestic service became almost a moot issue during the Great Depression. In 1920, 7 percent of all black female gainful workers were classified as "manufacturing and mechanical employees"; in 1930, 5.5 percent; and in 1940, 6 percent. The fact that black women did not completely lose their weak hold on industrial positions reflected the segmentation of the labor force. Within specific geographical areas, certain jobs were earmarked not only for women, but also specifically for white or black or (in the Southwest) Hispanic women.[31]

Differentials in earnings, hours, and working conditions mirrored these various forms of segregation. For example, nationwide, black women earned twenty-three cents, and white women sixty-one cents, for every dollar earned by a white male. In Texas factories, the weekly wages of white women were $7.45, while Mexican women took home $5.40 and black women only $3.75. Comparing the hours of Florida female factory employees in 1930, the Women's Bureau found that black women outnumbered white in commercial laundries and certain food processing plants, and that they took shorter lunch hours and received about one-half the pay compared to white women industrial workers in general. In some establishments, a black woman's age and weekly hours were inversely related to her compensation; in other words, these employees were actually penalized for their experience and exceptionally long work week. Commenting on the low wages of fifteen to twenty-five cents per hour, and high productivity of southern tobacco stemmers (a traditional black female occupation), one government investigator noted sarcastically in 1934 that employers complained so much about the women's work habits that "it would seem that it was a charity to employ them, unless one remembered the thousands of pounds of tobacco that they were stemming and sorting."[32]

A sustained demand for their product through the early 1930s convinced tobacco manufacturers that it was they who presided over a truly "depression-proof" industry. Yet employers sought to press their economic advantage by imposing additional demands on workers who had no viable alternatives. Federally established minimum-wage guidelines exacerbated this trend. Stemming machines replaced some laborers and placed added strains on others, as if the constant heat, humidity, and stench of the workplace were not enough to make the job nearly unbearable. Interviewed by government officials, one black woman "described herself as crying at the machines because she could not quit in the face of high unemployment."[33]

Conditions were no better in other kinds of establishments characterized by high proportions of black women workers. Commercial laundry employees in New York City toiled fifty hours each week and "it was speed up, speed up, eating lunch on the fly" (that is, while they worked). Those in the starching department stood for ten hours each day "sticking their hands into almost-boiling starch." Complaints to the boss provoked a thinly veiled warning: "There ain't many places paying ten dollars a week now, Evie." The description of one black laundry press operator, published in a 1936 Women's Bureau report, would have seemed to verge on caricature had it not so accurately illustrated the deplorable work experience of so many women in need: The worker, who had only one leg, leaned on her crutches to depress the foot pedal, throughout the long, steamy day. (The garment industry reserved the position of presser for black women because of the intense heat and because the work required "unusual strength and endurance.") Burlap bag makers inhaled dirt and lint as a routine part of their job. Meatpacking and slaughtering plants kept black women in the offal and chitterling departments, which were cold, wet, and "vile smelling."[34]

This social division of labor was not new to American commercial establishments; the specific tasks assigned to black women had remained the same since they first entered northern factories in the World War I era. By the 1930s, however, it became clear that not only did individual positions lack advancement possibilities, but some jobs themselves (like those of tobacco stemmers) were well on the way to obsolescence. At the same time, federal child-labor legislation enacted as part of the New Deal necessitated the prolonged participation of mothers in the paid labor force. In North Carolina, laws restricting the labor of children under sixteen years of age meant that women often had to replace their offspring in the tobacco factories if families were to make ends meet, since two-thirds of all black households required the income of more than one worker. Under these circumstances the younger a woman's children, the more likely that she would have to seek and retain gainful employment.[35]

Because of the nature of their jobs, many black female industrial employees derived no benefits from New Deal wage and hour legislation. Even when black women came under federal guidelines, they did not necessarily enjoy improved wages or conditions. Voluntary

National Recovery Administration (NRA) minimum-wage codes set on an industry-wide basis institutionalized a variety of forms of discrimination (they were declared unconstitutional in 1935); workers received more or less pay depending upon their gender, "race," and geographical location—North-South and rural-urban. The NRA respected prevailing wage differentials that blatantly discriminated against blacks, women, southerners, and rural workers. Thus the black female industrial workers concentrated in southern commercial laundries and tobacco plants made the very lowest wages sanctioned by the NRA. The arbitrary distinctions enshrined by the codes at times led to gross inequities even between groups of black women within the same industry. Tobacco stemmers who worked in commercial factories made a median hourly wage of twenty-five to twenty-seven cents, but those who performed the same tasks in dealers' establishments (not covered by the NRA) earned only half that much, and usually no more than $6.55 for a fifty-five-hour week.[36]

In most cases employers found ways to circumvent minimum-wage-maximum-hours legislation that would have had a favorable impact on workers in general and black women in particular. Some steam laundries applied for and received exemptions from the codes on the basis of "labor scarcity" in the industry. Other employers reduced their hours and enforced speed-ups so that their employees would produce the same amount and take home the same weekly paycheck. If pressed on the issue, employers would fire their black women workers and either make do without them or replace them with machines. However, NRA codes ranked as a secondary factor in the displacement of black women; white competition played a much more important role in the process, simply because private industry failed to adhere to the voluntary standards in a way that would have made them effective. In any case, passage of the Fair Labor Standards Act of 1938, which made wage and hours standards mandatory, hardly solved the problem. For example, tobacco companies regarded the act as an incentive to mechanize the stemming operation that black women had traditionally performed by hand.[37]

The NRA's Section 7(a) and the Wagner Act had a much less ambiguous impact on the black women they directly affected. These two measures in particular spurred collective action by guaranteeing workers the right to organize and bargain collectively with their employers for the first time in American history. With the implicit backing of the federal government, laborers struggled to revive dormant unions and create new ones equal to the times. Nevertheless, looking ahead to World War II and beyond, it is clear that at least some unions organized blacks out of temporary expediency and not out of principled conviction; the fact that white labor leaders failed to challenge a discriminatory division of labor within their own industries reveals that even black union members would remain in the lowest paying jobs, uniquely vulnerable to layoffs and speed-ups alike.[38]

During the Depression, the American Federation of Labor persisted in organizing workers on the basis of their skills and pursued a less than aggressive policy in attracting and keeping black members. The history of the Tobacco Workers International Union (TWIU) in Durham, North Carolina, reveals the potentially divisive effects of the AFL's policies on a workforce composed of women and men, blacks and whites (locals organized their members according to task and then segregated them by skin color and gender). When the TWIU won a major strike against Liggett & Myers in June 1939, the company promptly installed machines in the stemming department, fired a large number of black women, and, for those who remained, cut back the number of workdays to four a week. The union readily sacrificed this group of workers to secure a contract. Annie Mack Barbee, a former L&M worker, spoke for other black women when she recalled, "The very day we quit working up there, here come the machines . . . Here come the machines and the white man was up there putting up signs for the bathrooms—'White Only' . . . I didn't get anything from Liggett & Myers . . . [T]he mass of black women didn't get a whole lot of nothing from them."[39]

What few gains the AFL did make in organizing blacks and whites came at least partly out of a sense of competition with its rebellious stepchild, the Congress of Industrial Organizations, which broke from the parent body in 1935. The CIO waged a series of pitched battles against recalcitrant employers in the steel, auto, and rubber industries, and its emphasis on industry-wide organizing provided a dramatic contrast to the AFL's exclusivity. The CIO's major campaigns spilled over into smaller businesses as well, and by 1940 it boasted 3.6 million members. Many of the 800,000 female union members in 1940 belonged to CIO affiliates.[40]

The International Ladies Garment Workers Union (which joined the CIO later in the decade) had its "racial" consciousness raised during the early 1930s. Mary Sweet, a black presser in the Boston garment industry, refused to participate in a 1933 strike organized by the ILGWU because it would not admit her as a member. Upon the successful completion of the strike, she noted, "Our shop signed a union agreement and the women pressers had to get out. They gave us four months to find other jobs." However, later the ILGWU asked her to help organize the black women who often served as strikebreakers. She attributed the local's new openness to orders received from headquarters in New York City, where a coalition of unions had formed the Negro Labor Committee to further the cause of black workers. By 1934 ILGWU locals in New York City, Boston, Chicago, and Philadelphia were integrated and some shops even boasted black "chairladies." The black dress-pressers in New York's Local 60 were among the best-paid women in Harlem, with wages of $45 to $50 for a thirty-five-hour week.[41]

The Amalgamated Clothing Workers of America not only welcomed black women into its ranks, it also spawned an affiliate, the United Laundry Workers (ULW), one of the most successful integrated unions in the 1930s. The ULW had 14,000 members in 1937, many of them black women. Evelyn Macon credited her own newfound militancy to a boss's order that she and other women in a New York laundry stop singing the spirituals that had distracted them from their slavelike conditions. He "said that was too much pleasure to have while working for his money, and the singing was cut out." As a result, she said, the workers then had an opportunity to contemplate their "miserable lot"—"that was where the boss made his mistake." After a few weeks, persistent picketing, combined with less than effective strikebreakers, helped them get a CIO contract, with a thirty-five-cent minimum wage and a five-day week.[42]

At least some black communities threw their support behind union activities for the first time, impressed with the relative openness of CIO policies and with the uncompromisingly egalitarian rhetoric of the Communist Party. (In fact the Communists conducted several dramatic, successful organizing drives that made full use of black women's leadership abilities, including the St. Louis nutpickers' strike against "Boss Funsten" in 1933.) The CIO represented a new era in the history of black women, and its significance went far beyond the number who were members. Black women served to advance the cause of workers' rights by supporting their husbands' decision to join and stick by a union. In some cases they helped to form women's auxiliaries, like the one associated with the Steel Workers Organizing Committee. The Women's Emergency Brigade played a pivotal role in the 1937 General Motors sit-down strike conducted by the United Automobile Workers in Flint, Michigan. And finally, black wives and mothers benefited materially whenever their husbands and sons won wage increases or job security through their participation in CIO-affiliated unions.[43]

Nevertheless, the CIO won its greatest gains for blacks who already had jobs, rather than for those systematically excluded from certain kinds of work, prompting one historian to call its policies "aracist." Especially large and cohesive communities formed their own advocacy groups (like the Harlem Labor Union) when white-dominated locals called upon black support and used it to win jobs for white workers exclusively. Moreover, affiliates' opportunistic approach toward black women workers would become abundantly clear at the end of World War II, when the interests of black men and white and black women were ignored by many white men in the union hierarchy, from shop-floor stewards to leaders of the internationals. If the CIO promoted a "culture of unity," that culture was a product of the Great Depression, rather than a long-term, principled commitment to full equality for black men and women workers.[44]

The success of industrial unions during the 1930s benefited only a small percentage of black workers overall. In contrast, black working women in general found strong advocates from several quarters during the Great Depression, groups that focused on a number of strategies, including vocational training, political advocacy, and organized protests. For example, in founding the National Council of Negro Women (NCNW) in 1935, Mary McLeod Bethune, a member of FDR's "Black Cabinet," brought together twenty-eight black women leaders, themselves heads of national groups, to form "an organization of organizations." The initial purpose of this new umbrella group was to coordinate the drive to place black women in federal agencies, but it soon expanded its reach. Bethune, with her stress on the role of government action, and her willingness to embrace the Democratic Party as an agent of change, presented a contrast with Mary Church Terrell, first president of the National Association of Colored Women's Clubs, who had supported a philosophy of "uplift" and the Republican Party. The NCNW sought to make alliances with other groups, such as the League of Women Voters, and to challenge discriminatory hiring—including the requirement that job applicants submit a photo of themselves—in federal agencies. The group also decried the exemption of domestics and agricultural workers from Social Security and other landmark pieces of social-welfare legislation. Complementing the work of the NCNW was the Ladies Auxiliary of the Brotherhood of Sleeping Car Porters—1,500 female relatives of the porters, who came together from scattered regional councils in 1938 to form a national organization. The auxiliary promoted the unionization of black men and women, in contrast to what it considered the middle-class professional bias of the NCNW. Also active were local groups, such as the Harlem branch of the Young Women's Christian Association, which sponsored a variety of services for black working women, including a trade school and nursing courses in an effort to open the way for more black secretaries and nurses. Yet the barriers to full and equal hiring policies remained seemingly insurmountable. In 1935, Cecelia Cabaniss Saunders, executive director of the Harlem Y, testified before a mayoral Commission on Conditions in Harlem, describing the intransigence of the local telephone company: "We asked for employment of telephone operators at least in the Harlem area. They objected to the voices of the colored girls. We said we had someone with a lovely voice. We asked to have her tried out. The telephone company didn't agree to that. These girls were reared in New York. No one would know whether they were colored or white." Faced with such blatant prejudice, the appeals of black women's advocacy groups would falter in the absence of federal mandates and the legal backing to enforce them.[45]

Women's Wage Work in the Black Community

Black women employed outside of agriculture, domestic labor, and industry represented a diversity of work experiences, not all of which lend themselves to close historical scrutiny. For example, the numbers racket, which offered the hope to many poor people that they could "gain through luck what had been denied them through labor," served as a major employer in some black communities. During the 1930s, the Chicago numbers business sustained as many as two hundred employees, at least some of them women in white-collar jobs, and boasted a $26,000 weekly payroll. Predictably, though, legitimate businesses operated by blacks suffered losses reflecting their clients' reduced circumstances; between 1929 and 1935 the sales of black-owned retail stores dropped by 51.6 percent, compared to a decline in the nation's overall payroll of 32.5 percent. As healers, religious leaders, and entrepreneurs, black women still offered their services to friends and neighbors, but in most cases they had to adjust their fees to bring them in line with the realities of depression life.[46]

Midwives and older women knowledgeable in folk medicine continued to occupy an honored place in African American culture. Their techniques represented an irresistible mixture of common-sense psychology and time-honored tradition. In the 1930s some midwives still "put a sharp knife under the pillow" of a woman in labor; "they say that cuts the pain." In Florida, Izzelly Haines prescribed concoctions of onions, gin, boiled mud, and worm-infested "dauber nests" to hasten the expulsion of the afterbirth. Southern midwives delivered up to 85 percent of all babies in parts of that region during the 1930s. Certainly these women were relatively affordable; in Texas even rural doctors charged up to $75 for attending a woman in labor, while the rate for a midwife was usually less than $10. Ultimately, however, "grannies" depended upon their patients for their own well-being, more often than not adopting the attitude of Haines; in 1939, in response to an interviewer's question, she noted, "As for pay, I takes whatever they give me."[47]

The northern ghetto opened some opportunities for female religious leaders to exercise power in a formal sense. Like midwives and grannies, female preachers served as "spiritual advisors" to their followers and as links to a southern past. But their style tended to be flamboyant as they competed with others for storefront "consumers," their words full of urgency as they exhorted worshippers to confront a crisis born of faithlessness more than economic depression. Here was Harlem's Mother Horn, attired in silk and presiding over a congregation of four hundred, a "dynamo of action" during old-time fundamentalist services in her Pentacostal sanctuary; or Elder Lucy Smith, "elderly, corpulent, dark-skinned and maternal," who during the 1930s transformed her tiny meeting place into the prosperous Church of All Nations in Chicago's Bronzeville. Lucy Smith began her career, she later recalled, "with giving advice to folks in my neighborhood." But unlike the vast majority of female "confessors," she had gone on to parlay into worldly success her ability to heal "all kinds of sores and pains of the body and of the mind."[48]

More conventional forms of female employment offered limited opportunities for black women during the Great Depression. Only a few nurses found jobs in local hospitals; instead, increasingly those with nursing credentials sought work in public-health agencies sponsored by cities or states. Henrietta Smith Chisholm graduated from Freedmen's Hospital in Washington, D.C., a degree that launched her on a career in public health in the early 1930s. Recalled Smith Chisholm, "Freedmen's was the only hospital at which Negro nurses could work." Like teachers, nurses benefited from specialized training that allowed them to earn steadier wages above those of a domestic, and at the same time gain the satisfaction of serving the community, characterized as it was by rigid patterns of segregation. Smith Chisholm noted, "I liked public health very much. This was brand new. . . . [It] was the right field for me because I enjoyed it because it wasn't all morbidity—you felt like you were giving people help before they got into trouble. We hoped we were. I especially liked the infant and maternity program and worked mostly in infant, maternal, and child welfare clinics." Her annual salary of $1,620 placed her among the best-paid black professionals during the Depression.[49]

As black businesses closed their doors or laid off employees, and white-owned ghetto establishments adamantly refused to hire black clerks, secretaries, or salespeople, black men and women launched "Don't Buy Where You Can't Work" campaigns. The struggles in Chicago, Baltimore, Washington, Detroit, Harlem, and Cleveland relied on boycotts sponsored by neighborhood "Housewives Leagues," whose members took their grocery and clothes shopping elsewhere, or did without, rather than patronize all-white stores. These campaigns captured an estimated 75,000 new jobs for blacks during the Depression decade, and together they had an economic impact comparable to that of the CIO in its organizing efforts, and second only to government jobs as a new source of openings. In the process, women's energies at the grassroots level were harnessed and given explicit political expression.[50]

Efforts to win jobs for Harlem residents revealed how the Communist Party in the North both fulfilled and fell short of community expectations during the Depression. Black people embraced the party when it responded to their needs for jobs and better housing—a conditional form of support that inspired mixed feelings in party members. One official later re-called that many of the poorer black women attracted to the organization needed work, "and we had to say to them: 'The Party is not a sewing club'" (referring to government-sponsored work projects). The party organized shop units among groups of women workers (like the nurses in Harlem hospitals) and helped to open a significant number of jobs for blacks in tele-phone and federal welfare offices. Yet despite its reliance on charismatic local leaders (in-cluding Bonita Williams and Rose Gauldens), it remained dominated by white men and aloof from the intense religious devotion of the black masses. Helen Cade Brehon, recalling her youth in Harlem, suggested that the party's aloofness from the church also indicated that it "underestimated . . . the importance of our women in the Black community."[51]

Women who relied upon public institutions and private businesses within their own neighborhoods for gainful employment during the Depression faced a double dilemma. The faltering enterprises operated by members of their own group needed fewer and fewer employees, while the federal government and white businessmen persisted in hiring whites for the other positions available. Only through collective action could black women and men win those coveted jobs that existed by virtue of their own patronage; the successful community boycotts of the 1930s would serve as a lesson for the next generation of black leaders—a lesson that revealed the economic and political power inherent in ordinary black housewives' commitment to justice.

The Partisan and Ideological Politics of Public Works Projects

If the labor movement touched only a fraction of all black women workers, it of course of-fered little solace to the large numbers out of work. For jobless black mothers, wives, and daughters in rural areas and in the city, North and South, the federal government proved to be a most grudging employer of last resort. Indeed, there was good reason to suspect that, left to their own devices, public works administrators would merely reflect the pref-erences of employers in the private sector. More often—usually—officials used their power to help whites at the expense of blacks. At the same time, some New Deal programs presaged the affirmative action policies of the 1960s and beyond. In 1935 President Roo-sevelt issued Executive Order 7046, outlawing discrimination by the Works Progress Ad-ministration (WPA). In response, Crystal Bird Faucet, a black woman and head of Philadelphia's Women's and Professional Project of the WPA, unilaterally raised the quota limiting black women's participation from one-third to one-half; as a result, three thousand black women, all former relief recipients, benefited from gainful employment. On another New Deal front, the Public Works Administration (PWA) took steps to en-sure that local building projects hired black construction workers and that local housing projects awarded black tenants their fair share of units. These initiatives were especially significant in the North, where Democratic politicians had an incentive to appeal to likely black constituents, a consideration irrelevant in the South, where black voters remained systematically disfranchised.[52]

In assessing the impact of New Deal public works programs on black women, it is diffi-cult at times to separate federal policy from local guidelines, prevailing national (white) public opinion from specific sectional biases. Southern sponsorship of work relief is especially revealing, for white Democrats found themselves in a quandary of sorts as they sought to take advantage of black women's "free" labor and at the same time cooperate with the private employers of field-hands and domestic servants. (Of course the boundary between public and private employers frequently blurred whenever local administrators relied on black labor in their own homes or fields.) Ultimately these whites were able to use federal funds provided by the Federal Emergency Relief Administration (1933–1935) and the WPA (1935–1941) to reinforce traditional social divisions of labor based on class considerations and racial and gender ideologies.[53]

The various works programs of the 1930s discriminated against white women and all blacks in terms of the number and kinds of jobs offered to applicants. Policymakers, bureaucrats, and social workers believed that jobs constituted a more dignified and respectable form of aid than direct relief (workers in general agreed) and that employment should therefore benefit men more than women, whites more than blacks. Most projects created heavy construction-type work for men on the assumption that priority would be given to the primary breadwinner in needy families. This policy ignored the wage-earning role of both single and married women and, in particular, severely limited the opportunities for female household heads. As part of his first annual report on "Negro Project Workers" in the WPA, Alfred Edgar Smith, an agency administrative assistant, noted that, during the year, "Some Negro women family heads subsisted on irregular issues of surplus commodities or not at all because of scarcity of projects for their employment." Between 1935 and 1941, less than 20 percent of all WPA workers were female, and only about 3 percent of all WPA workers were black women, although a higher—and in the South, much higher—proportion of all female family heads on relief were black.[54]

Few well-educated black women received job assignments commensurate with their talents or professional training. Margaret Walker, Zora Neale Hurston, and Catherine Dunham worked on the Federal Writers Project, and Hurston served as head of the black folklore unit of the Florida FWP from 1938 to 1939. A small number of black women benefited from relatively prestigious social work and clerical positions. For example, the large Washington, D.C., black population was in a favorable geographical location, near the seat of power; in 1938, 162 black women WPA employees were working as clerks and seventy-three as typists. Elsewhere, a handful served as supervisors for segregated projects, but like Jannie F. Simms of Louisa County, Virginia, they often had to rely on direct intervention from sympathetic federal officials in order to get and keep their jobs. Simms owed her appointment as "Garden Director for the Subsistence Garden of Louisa County, among colored people" to Forrester B. Washington, director of Negro work for the FERA. The WPA received well-deserved criticism for reducing skilled and well-educated blacks of both genders to menial labor.[55]

Over one-half of all women employed by the WPA worked on sewing projects, which required local sponsors to donate materials. In the absence of such a sponsor, black women in impoverished communities like Madison County, Alabama, found all WPA opportunities closed to them. Moreover, the administration of so-called sewing-room "tests" served to reduce the number of eligible black women applicants. Another program for women, "household demonstration training," provided instruction in domestic skills and supposedly helped to put WPA workers at a competitive advantage in the private job market. In fact, project managers often systematically excluded black women; in 1937 "only white women in St. Louis, Missouri, and white and Mexican women in San Antonio, Texas, were being trained in the Household Training Centers," while resources for black women remained suspended in a state of "contemplation." In any case it is unlikely that the few black women who received a certificate from short-term WPA household training programs found their chances for private employment markedly improved.[56]

Nevertheless, black women preferred public jobs because they usually paid more and required shorter hours compared to private work. Therefore, many southern whites objected to aid of any kind—cash or jobs—that would "take the pressure off the Negro families to seek employment on the farms or in the white households," under the assumption that the "standard of relief offered would compete too favorably with the local living standards of the Negroes." Sensitive to these criticisms, southern WPA officials routinely engaged in "clever manipulations" to reduce the wages to which black women were entitled. For example, in response to federally authorized pay hikes, they "reclassified downward" workers so that a "'raise' plus their new wages merely equaled their old wages." New Orleans officials went so far as to allow "two Negro women to share one WPA salary, so that instead of one worker receiving about $39.00 [monthly], two workers received about $19.50 each." Nevertheless, even this small amount was more than black women could earn as servants.[57]

Just as the private sector reserved certain kinds of work exclusively for black women, so WPA supervisors created special projects limited to either blacks or whites. For example, St. Louis industrial training programs remained closed to black women because they lacked the requisite "factory experience." In the South, only black women found employment on the euphemistically titled "Beautification" projects. White administrators in North Carolina, South Carolina, Georgia, Alabama, Virginia, and Texas justified these projects by arguing that they simply required the women involved to do "landscaping, [and] wild flower planting . . . pointing out that this is the only suitable form of employment for these Negro women, since they cannot sew, and 'cannot expect to get any other type of work when they return to private industry.'" Critics of these discriminatory policies charged that black women, unlike their white counterparts, were forced to perform "men's jobs" outdoors and that some even had to wear a special uniform "stamping them as some sort of convicts." From Florence, South Carolina, in February 1936 came a complaint from a local physician that revealed the true nature of the projects in question: "The Beautification Project appears to be 'For Negro Women Only.' This project is not what its name implies, but rather a type of work that should be assigned to men. Women are worked in 'gangs' in connection with the City's dump pile, incinerator and ditch piles. Illnesses traced to such exposure as these women must face do not entitle them to medical aid at the expense of the WPA." In Fayetteville, North Carolina, officials opened a "cleaning project" for black women and at the same time disbanded their sewing group. Thurgood Marshall, assistant special counsel for the National Association for the Advancement of Colored People, reported that WPA officials transported southern black women workers in open trucks during foul weather and "required [them] to do regular scouring and cleaning work as well as painting and chopping grass at the white schools." Black female construction workers in Jackson, Mississippi, toiled under the supervision of guards armed with guns. In Savannah, a black mother sent a letter to FDR and told him that white women received indoor assignments while "we are in the wood cutting down three [sic] and digging them up by the roots with grub hoe an pick ax[;] these thing aint fare."[58]

At times WPA officials (and welfare administrators in general) served as recruiting agents for local planters who complained that they could not find enough hands to pick cotton and worm tobacco plants. A "Workers Council for Colored" representative in Raleigh, North Carolina, denounced the recent dismissal of all black female household heads from federal jobs programs in October 1937; Mary Albright wrote to Harry Hopkins that the WPA wanted to "make us take other jobs . . . and white women were hired & sent for & given places that colored women was made to leave or quit." These "other jobs" included forcing mothers to stand in open trucks twenty miles each way, twice a day, to work in tobacco fields "beginning 6 to 6:30 a.m. till 7:30 & 8:00 p.m."—all for "such poor wages" that they could not possibly support their families. In Oklahoma, a WPA official closed a black women's work project upon the appearance of "an abundant cotton crop which is in full picking flower." By way of explanation, he wrote to his Washington supervisors that "these women are perfectly able to do this kind of work and there is plenty of work to do." Alfred Edgar Smith noted in his report for 1938 that black women in the urban and rural South had been denied WPA jobs because they were told "You can find work in kitchens" or "You can find work if you look for it." In response to one black woman's request for aid, a Mississippi official ordered her to "go hunt washings."[59]

Because they wielded a certain amount of political influence, black women and men in the North frequently received their proportionate share of Works Progress Administration jobs; in fact, this form of employment "provided an economic floor for the whole black community in the 1930s." Yet the actions of local federal administrators in the South indicated how little those white men's attitudes toward black female labor had changed since the days of slavery. Whether they were plantation owners or government officials, they saw black wives and mothers chiefly as domestic servants or manual laborers, outside the pale of the (white) gendered division of labor. During the Depression, southern administrators had access for the first time to large amounts of federal money, which they used on a large scale to preserve the fundamental inequalities in the former Confederate states.[60]

Domestics' daughters might have thrilled to the galvanizing power of a Mother Horn, or marveled over photographs of Mary McLeod Bethune in her Washington, D.C., office. But it was the entertainment field that fueled the dreams of black girls who yearned for a life's work of glamour and triumph. As the keepers of the flame of African American musical tradition, a handful of black female singers were rewarded by listeners both black and white in clubs or at home in front of the radio or Victrola, because, in the words of writer Richard Wright, "Those who deny us are willing to sing our songs." Hollywood for the most part reinforced stereotypes of black women as mammies, scatterbrains, or tragic mulattoes. Yet the recording industry gave expression to a full range of artistic styles—from the earth-moving spirituals of Mahalia Jackson, to Ella Fitzgerald's punchy jazz, Lena Horne's sultry pops, and the worldly blues of Billie Holiday and Bessie Smith. On Easter Sunday 1939, the contralto opera singer Marian Anderson, a granddaughter of former slaves, transfixed the nation with her concert on the steps of the Lincoln Memorial in Washington, D.C. When the Daughters of the American Revolution refused to let Anderson sing in Constitution Hall in that city—they had a "white artists only" policy—Eleanor Roosevelt resigned her membership in the group and arranged for Anderson to perform at the memorial, which she did to great acclaim. In the public spotlight, surrounded by musicians and their managers, famous black women singers beckoned listeners away from the routine of the white woman's kitchen and into a glittering world of public adulation. Yet in a song like Bessie Smith's "Washwoman's Blues," the cycle of black women's work came full circle, as the successful singer reminded herself of the fate from which luck and talent had rescued her. A wailing clarinet serenades the weary laundress: "All day long I'm slavin' / All day long I'm bustin' suds / Gee my hands are tired washin' out these dirty duds." The rhythm of the piece is slow, laborious, evocative of the work itself. In effect, the song lifted one woman's sorrows out of their time and place and transformed them into a universal lament of great dignity and beauty.[61]

In sum, as expendable members of the labor force, black women often suffered whenever government policies caused industrial employers to reduce the number of their workers or landowners to cut back on staple-crop production. Neither federal officials nor CIO leaders ever directly confronted the major problem that affected these workers—the fact that they were barred from the type of job that carried with it benefits and the promise of advancement and security. Moreover, by failing to include domestic and agricultural laborers in workers' legislation, the New Deal ensured that their status relative to other kinds of employees would decline even further. The necessary commitment on the part of government, unions, and private enterprise to open the nation's job structure to black women would not even begin to take shape until the mid-1960s. Thus while policymakers continued to patch up a faltering economic system, black women continued to work for themselves, their families, and their communities in defiance of the degradation implicit in so much of their paid labor.

THE MEANS OF SURVIVAL: UNWAGED HOUSEHOLDS AND COMMUNITY WORK

During the 1930s, eight or nine out of every ten black households lived on the thin edge between subsistence and complete economic disaster. Even in northern cities, no more than 10 percent of the black population maintained a relatively comfortable, secure material existence characteristic of the white middle class. Poor women were able to care for their own families to the extent that they could depend upon kin, neighbors, and friends for mutual assistance. Thus a mother who maintained a home characterized by "extreme poverty and social disorganization"—in the words of two sociologists—would nevertheless try to preside over "a few family rituals to give both variety and order" to the lives of her friends and dependents. Her child's birthday party, for example, mandated specific kinds of dress and behavior on the part of the guests in return for her hospitality. This simple event transcended the physical deprivation that threatened to overwhelm the household and leave its members bereft of all hope and security. Although white wives and mothers also served as a cohesive force within their own homes and neighborhoods, black women employed somewhat different strategies for survival—strategies that followed the well-worn grooves of a generations-old African American culture. "There is nothing—no ownership or lust for power—that stands between us and our kin," wrote Richard Wright in 1941, adding, "Our scale of values differs from that of the world from which we have been excluded."[62]

Fertility continued to drop among black and white women during the 1930s, and rates for both groups hit a low point in the 1940s. Black women bore slightly more children than their white counterparts during the decade, although this generalization masks significant rural-urban differentials. Black fertility declined most rapidly and reached its lowest level in northern cities, where in 1940 black women averaged three children compared to the 5.5 born to mothers in the rural South. (Comparable figures for white women were two for northern city dwellers and five for rural southerners.) Certainly women in both sections of the country had compelling reasons to limit the size of their families voluntarily; the collapse of the family sharecropping system and passage of child-labor laws meant that children no longer served an economically productive function in either southern rural or mill-town families.[63]

Despite great difficulties in making ends meet, many mothers derived extraordinary pride and satisfaction from the well-being of their children, and they viewed life according to the options available to their offspring. When she interviewed people in the small town of Indianola, Mississippi, in the late 1930s, Hortense Powdermaker found that the black women seemed "more buoyant and hopeful" than their menfolk. She offered this explanation: "The greater optimism of the women relates to their identification with their children both as cause and as effect. The children carry them ahead into a future where more may be possible; and the future seems more promising, more important, more worth struggling for, because of the children." Mothers thus saw the education of their children as the fulfillment of their own dreams. Of her only son, one Chicago domestic servant said, "He's my greatest joy and happiness in the world. I'm going to do everything in my power to see that he gets the very best education so he'll be able to make a mark for himself in life. He'll be able to tell the world that his mother took an interest in him." Such was the redeeming feature of black women's labor in their own eyes; it produced tangible rewards for the next generation. If, as the old saying went, "Children is shore nuff riches," then black women young and old were rich indeed.[64]

At the same time, limited resources meant that routine, repetitive housekeeping chores amounted to little more than sheer drudgery for most black (as well as poor white) women. The basic outlines of their household labor had changed little over the generations, but even more striking was the continuity in methods and equipment. Not until the late 1930s did southern tenant farmwives benefit from New Deal rural electrification projects (especially the Tennessee Valley Authority), and even then few could afford modern appliances like vacuum cleaners, electric irons, and refrigerators—conveniences readily available to middle-class residents of cities and suburbs. Southern black women still prepared meals with old-fashioned wood cookstoves and boiled the family's laundry in big iron wash pots outside. Washday entailed lugging an additional fifty gallons of water—four hundred pounds—from a nearby pump or distant stream. Though northern urban women used washboards and tubs instead of "dobbing" sticks and pots, they routinely suffered from backaches and bruised knuckles; the laundry was the bane of more than one daughter's existence.[65]

As their needs intensified and their cash dwindled, many black women turned to welfare agencies for assistance; some found the very prospect inherently degrading, while others accepted cash and jobs as their "due recompense" for a lifetime—and generations—of serving whites. Applying for government or private aid called for a certain amount of persistence and determination. Indeed, the application process was often a job in itself with no guarantee of pay. The white social worker–black applicant relationship provoked additional tensions that humiliated and angered wives and mothers. "When I go to them for help they talk to me like I was a dog," a Fort Valley, Georgia, black woman wrote in a letter to an official in 1935. In Greenwood, Mississippi, Pinkie Pelcher addressed her complaint directly to FDR in December 1936. White caseworkers served more to harass than help blacks, she declared: "We have been slaves for them all our lives and don' need them standing around over us telling us how to sweep the floor." Prominent black politicians criticized the "severe, scientific," bureaucratic method, while black nationalists denounced it as one more example of the "white devil's aptitude in tricknollogy." Nevertheless, by mid-decade, relief rivaled domestic service and agriculture as a source of income for black Americans; in 1933, for example, three or four blacks out of every ten in Pittsburgh, Cleveland, New Orleans, and Philadelphia received aid of some kind. Neither direct cash payments nor public jobs provided for luxurious living. Amounts varied from year to year and from place to place, but in general northern urban blacks faced less discrimination compared to those in the urban and especially rural South. Predictably, under FERA, blacks found it more difficult to qualify for aid and, once they did, received less money compared to their white counterparts. Local southern officials, both public and private, tended to assume "that the Negro is better adapted to the open country environment than is the poor white and hence in less need of relief." At the national level, FERA policymakers put their official stamp of approval on this view when they suggested that "food and clothing cost less for the Negro family not because the needs of the Negro are necessarily less but because he is accustomed to getting along on less."[66]

Disabled women and mothers with dependent children were the primary recipients of government relief, especially after the Social Security Act of 1935 provided for systematic and regular federal aid (on a matching-fund basis with the states) to qualified members of these two groups. Elderly, ill, and handicapped black women faced special hardships. A Women's Bureau study entitled "Unattached Women on Relief in Chicago, 1937" found that compared to white women in the same desperate situation—that is, "hungry all the time"—

World War I Through the Great Depression

During World War I, thousands of southern black women migrated north, eager to find heavy-industry jobs that offered higher wages and shorter hours compared to domestic service and agricultural labor. War workers often performed menial, unskilled labor deemed by employers to be too difficult or disagreeable for white women, and their lowly status was revealed by the heavy, coarse men's clothing they had to wear at work (1–3). Still, these jobs enabled black women to escape from the isolation of white women's kitchens and to share the rigors of the workplace with their friends and kinfolk (4). When the war ended, food-processing and meat-packing jobs were among the few factory positions available to black women (5), most of whom remained barred from machine-operative, retail, and clerical jobs. In the North and Midwest, burgeoning urban neighborhoods created employment possibilities for increasing numbers of female workers who provided services to members of their own group (6). Rural Americans in general early felt the tremors of impending depression, but black women and men in particular bore the brunt of the collapsing sharecropping system, and received less government assistance compared to their poor white neighbors in the 1930s (7). Farm Security Administration photographers sought out southern rural women, for the strength and dignity of farmers' wives seemed to symbolize the resilience of traditional values in the midst of a shaken nation (8). Forced to rely on their own resources, black women all over the country had to make do with less cash and more of their own hard work in these especially difficult times (9).

1. Women washing a locomotive on the Pennsylvania Railroad (c. 1918). Library of Congress.

2. Lumberyard workers (1919). National Archives.

3. Brickyard workers, McKees Rock, Pennsylvania (c. 1919). National Archives.

4. Workers weighing wire coils and recording weights (1919). Photo by F. P. Burke. National Archives.

5. Plucking chickens, St. Louis (1938). National Archives.

6. Beauty-parlor workers. Photo by H. A. Brown. Schomburg Center for Research in Black Culture, New York Public Library.

7. Laborers picking cotton in Tallulah, Louisiana. National Archives.

8. Cotton field-worker, Greene County, Georgia (1941). Photo by Jack Delano. Library of Congress.

9. Farmer's wife with her flock of chickens, guinea fowl, and turkeys, Putnam County, Georgia (1941). Photo by Irving Rusinow. National Archives.

the blacks tended to be migrants from the South, younger, and physically incapacitated. Most had worked their whole lives as domestic servants but were unable to do so now.[67]

Single mothers gain to benefit from the Aid to Dependent Children (ADC) program. This program potentially benefited the 20 percent of all black families with a female head and children under sixteen years of age. Honest need, however, did not always guarantee a place on the relief rolls; several states instituted eligibility guidelines in addition to those required by the federal government, and local administrators cited these as reasons for disqualifying children in "unsuitable" homes. In Georgia, for example, twenty-four thousand white and twenty-nine thousand black children qualified for aid in a technical sense in 1935, yet only 1.5 percent of the blacks (compared to 14.4 percent of the whites) were receiving assistance five years later. Most of the black children who were admitted to the program lived in Atlanta. In addition, striking regional variations in payments became a standard feature of ADC because of the matching-fund requirement. In 1939–1940, the average monthly payment per black child varied from $3.52 in South Carolina to $24.15 in New York. The attempt to encourage local initiative in providing for the poor thus came at the expense of children's welfare.[68]

While the ADC program as administered in the South probably could not sustain a family whose mother was unemployed, at least some black women in the urban North withdrew from the paid labor force when they received federal assistance that could materially improve the quality of family life. For example, a 1936 study showed that infant mortality declined in black neighborhoods where the number of relief cases was highest. In part the investigator attributed this to social-welfare services, including instruction in health care and nutrition, for destitute mothers; but E. Franklin Frazier, who summarized the study in a 1938 issue of *Science and Society*, listed an additional finding: "There is also the factor that the mother, if employed prior to the family's going on relief, worked several months during pregnancy and returned to work within a minimum time after the birth of the child whereas the mother on relief remains at home and is thus able to take greater precautions in regard to her own health during pregnancy, and devote more care to her child after its birth." For women like the Chicago mother who "had resigned herself to being lower-class, although she refused to take a job in domestic service," New Deal welfare programs afforded an opportunity to place family considerations over the demands of white employers.[69]

However, direct payments had contradictory effects on black households. They might have enhanced the black woman's role as mother, but they also at times dramatically changed her relationship with her husband. For example, the plight of a Pittsburgh woman, recounted by a National Urban League official in 1931, told a larger story. This mother of six children, all under sixteen years of age, had applied to the city's welfare office for aid when her husband lost the steel mill job he had held for several years. He was told that "he needn't trouble looking for a job as long as there is so many white men out of work." His wife commented with ill-disguised bitterness, "I guess us colored folks don't get hungry . . . like white folks." One day her husband left and never returned. "He told me once that if he wasn't living at home the welfare people would help me and the kids, and maybe he just went away on that account." A few years later the ADC program would help to institutionalize this phenomenon; some unemployed fathers "deserted" their families and provided for them indirectly, by enabling mothers and children to qualify for relief. Nevertheless, when a father left home he lost his function as provider and the status that went with it.[70]

By the mid-1930s about 40 percent of all husband-absent black families were receiving federal assistance. During the decade, the economic and affective ties that bound black women and men together were severed at a faster rate than in previous years, although it is difficult to estimate the relative significance of government welfare policy and male jobless-ness as causal factors. About 29 percent of all black households had a female head in 1930, and 31 percent in 1940. But the increase was most dramatic in northern cities, where the proportion grew from one-fifth in 1930 to one-quarter a decade later. Here it should be noted that men still headed a majority of black households and that nationally, the ratio of such households to those of whites was 90 percent.[71]

Even when a father remained at home and the family received relief from private or government agencies, the intrusion of a social worker into their lives could upset traditional role patterns and produce heated arguments between husband and wife. (This pattern was evident in white as well as black families.) One Watts, California, welfare official chroni-cled the breakdown in patriarchy within the "S" family in 1935. Formerly employed as a blacksmith, Mr. S was accustomed to ruling his wife and three children with a firm hand. When he prevented his wife from spending an allowance of $6 monthly (added to their wel-fare check) for milk, she rebelled and convinced the social worker to send the check directly to her instead of to him. "The S's almost separated. Mr. S insisted that he was head of the house. He could manage his own affairs and that no woman could manage his money." Moreover, the children vowed that they would "tell the [welfare] office" if their father abused them. Thus at times wives and children challenged their father's authority and chan-neled their energies into securing greater and more varied benefits from a source outside the family.[72]

In spite of—or perhaps to counter—these disruptive economic and emotional influ-ences, some women managed to provide homelike touches for even the most temporary of quarters. When sharecropping families in Georgia's Black Belt moved to a new plantation at the end of the year, the wife "puts up new clothes lines and clears the path to the spring or well and chops the weeds from the back door." Women who snatched some time from their daily round of chores to plant flowers around their cabins might have had to tend them at night, after the children fell asleep, but they could "be seen standing idle for a moment dur-ing the busiest part of the day to gaze across the even rows to where gaily colored zinnias flame among the white cotton." City dwellers prided themselves on their window boxes, and many women in the North and South sewed curtains, hung photographs of the cham-pion black boxer Joe Louis on the walls, and arranged their simple furniture in the most pleasing and practical manner possible. In Washington, D.C., alley dwellers' homes used space and equipment in highly imaginative ways to maximize their family's comfort under difficult conditions.[73]

The Depression placed additional financial strains on all black households, and women responded accordingly—by welcoming new members in a position to make an economic contribution, offering to care for kin or friends in need, and encouraging young people either to postpone marriage so that they could help support their siblings or to strike out on their own in order to lessen their parents' burdens. These adaptive strategies—often cited by scholars and government officials as evidence of black communities' social "disorganization" and instability—enabled black families all over the country to adjust their size and composition to match their resources. A 1934 FERA report showed hardship among cotton tenant-farmers had increased the number of "combined households" among rural Alabama blacks. In Texas, extended and augmented black families often included more than one adult woman to help with the additional domestic obligations imposed on mothers during the Depression. Nationally, black households contained greater numbers of "non-family members," and these households were more often either very large or very small compared to those in the white population.[74]

Most women continued to use familiar economizing measures, though the crisis forced them to get by with even less cash than they were used to spending. Some ordered clothes and household supplies through the Sears, Roebuck mail-order catalog in order to circumvent local white-owned department and grocery stores. They bought an inferior grade of produce at lower prices and passed up more expensive canned and processed foods. Increasing numbers of women sought to make do with virtually no money at all. Patrons of the general store owned by Maya Angelou's grandmother in Stamps, Arkansas, paid for supplies with their "welfare food," powdered milk and eggs. Residents of a tenement building in Chicago were fortunate that their landlord accepted maintenance services provided by black husbands and fathers in lieu of rent. Rural folk took advantage of natural resources and an abundance of space in ways reminiscent of their freed grandparents. In the absence of overt opposition from the landlord, they raised vegetables and their "main livin come out of the hog pen, come out of the cow lot." Women used customary methods to make purple dye from pokeberries; canned fruits and vegetables; scoured the surrounding countryside for nuts, berries, and edible plants; and fished local lakes and rivers for the evening meal.[75]

Urban housewives had more limited opportunities in this regard, but they too used their wits to compensate for a lack of cash. Few ghetto residents lived in sight of a tree, but that did not prevent women from exploiting nearby sources of firewood that could be used for cooking and heating purposes. A Washington, D.C., social worker recounted the activities of Auntie Jane, a "heavy set and strong" forty-year-old woman, who "one cold dark wintry day" in 1938, dressed "in her men's clothing," led an expedition of women and children to two partially demolished buildings and salvaged "the wooden planks as they were torn off the beams . . . Auntie Jane was full of vigor, joyous as a hunter or fisher securing food—she had secured *warmth* for the Court [alley]."[76]

Women often derived a great deal of satisfaction from these activities, but most housewives had to piece together a living that combined domestic self-sufficiency with wage labor. Later, appreciative daughters would recall their mothers who "struggle[d] trying to see that we had at least one meal a day and something to wear, things of that kind." A rural sociologist told of Sadie Thompson of Macon County, Alabama, who "had enterprise and initiative and both virtues were required to keep up her household," consisting of her own children and the orphans she had adopted. As a group they made fourteen bales of cotton one year, but since they received no money from the sale of it, only their tiny livestock holdings, together with some homemade syrup and an occasional dollar from the landlord, kept them alive.[77]

One FERA official showed unusual sensitivity in assessing the labor of sixty-one black female household heads dropped from relief rolls in Georgia in 1935: "Only one has secured a permanent job. But there is no dearth of genuine resourcefulness. In their effort to maintain existence, these people are catching and selling fish, reselling vegetables, sewing in exchange for old clothes, letting out sleeping space, and doing odd jobs. They understand how to help each other. Stoves are used in common, wash boilers go their rounds, and garden crops are exchanged and shared." Based on both impressionistic and statistical data, it appears that, of all women from poor households, blacks more often than whites could count on help from their friends and neighbors during the 1930s. Mutual assistance manifested itself in many forms. Grandmothers cared for their children's children and all three generations benefited; the elderly women gained companionship and, in some cases, a measure of economic support; their children were free to search for jobs elsewhere; and the grandchildren lived under the watchful eye of a relative who was often "as strict . . . and as kind as she knew how to be." Martha Colquitt's small family in Athens, Georgia, was part of an extended network (one not necessarily based on blood ties) consisting of individuals of all ages who cared for those in need. The eighty-five-year-old widow had four living children, three of whom resided out of state; the fourth, also a widow, lived with her mother and her baby. The elderly woman outlined for a Federal Writers Project worker in 1937 the links that bound the three of them to the rest of the community: "My neighbors helps me, by bringin' me a little to eat, when dey knows I ain't got nothin' in de house to cook," she said. "De storekeeper lets me have a little credit, but I owe her so much now dat I'se shamed to ax her to let me have anythin' else . . . de young gals in the neighborhood helps me to do washin'."[78]

During the Depression black housewives often found themselves to be a part of a cohesive community despite high rates of residential turnover. Discriminatory laws and zoning policies severely restricted the geographical size and location of black neighborhoods; families might move, but if they stayed in the same city they were bound to remain near their old friends. In the South, mobility among "shifting" sharecroppers was usually confined to a particular county, and kin groups often stayed intact. The collective ethos among neighbors sprung from necessity as much as physical proximity. Residents of a Chicago tenement had to share facilities like bathrooms, hot plates, stoves, and sinks because of the inadequacy of their individual apartments. They also exchanged goods and services among themselves: "A girl might 'do the hair' of a neighbor in return for permission to use her pots and pans. Another woman might trade some bread for a glass of milk. There was seldom any money to lend or borrow, but the bartering of services and utensils was general." Lillian Roberts recalled that her mother would distribute contents of her welfare box— "prunes and beans and things like that . . . soap and stuff that was supposed to last you for a month"—to other people she knew. In the South neighbors helped each other slaughter livestock, can fruit, make quilts, and pick wild grapes.[79]

As the militancy of black urban communities increased during the 1930s, this traditional cooperative impulse could bring black women into direct conflict with established authorities. Wives and mothers joined together and risked arrest and imprisonment to withhold their money from rent-raising landlords, block the eviction of a neighboring family, or protect a black fugitive from law-enforcement agents. These activities also represented a form of productive labor among women who sought to protect their families and friends from physical hardship and injustice.[80]

Finally, women played an important role in festivities that brought neighbors together in a secular communion of fellowship. During rent parties in northern ghettos and church socials in southern villages, the preparation and serving of food symbolized the spiritual component of collective survival. As Mary Mebane of Durham, North Carolina, noted, "People who would now be considered below the poverty level on any statistical chart still had enough sense of self, of human worth, to enjoy sharing what they had with others. The meal was the tie that binds." Mothers of all ages engaged in friendly competition; the delectability of their pies, cakes, corn bread, biscuits, fried chicken, and preserves were a tribute to the ways in which the poor could conduct a "rich exchange" among themselves.[81]

The Great Depression imposed additional psychological burdens upon black women already taxed to their emotional and physical limits. Individual women reacted differently to increased hardship. Some, like some white women, capitulated to drink and despair, while others entered a state of spiritual otherworldliness and simply went through the motions of day-to-day existence. On the other hand, the mundane, daily routine itself, no matter how strenuous and "fixed, without change, unvarying," offered solace to women like Mary Mebane's mother, Nonnie: "She more than accepted it, she embraced it; it gave meaning to her life, it was what she had been put here on this earth to do." But in Brooklyn, Paule Marshall's mother and her friends followed the most basic and commonplace of recipes for personal integrity and group self-affirmation. They knew "that you had to 'tie up your belly' [hold in the pain] when things got rough and go on with life." In the late afternoon, after putting in their time on a "slave market" street corner and then, if they were lucky, in a white woman's house, they gathered in the Marshalls' basement kitchen and talked—a form of group therapy that was also "an outlet for the tremendous collective energy they possessed." The warmth of human contact transformed them from day workers into poets, as their animated conversations ranged over the neighborhood, out into the larger world of politics, and back to the sanctity of their own hearts. They excoriated employers who paid them with only a pitiable lunch—"as if anybody can scrub floor on an egg and some cheese that don't have no taste to it!"—and they took pleasure in their own imaginative use of language, there "in the wordshop of the kitchen." A little girl of eight who delighted in the way these women talked, "endlessly, passionately, poetically," would later reach a wider audience with her own words that told what it was like to be a black woman in America.[82]

Although black working women in the 1930s faced speed-ups within their homes and communities as well as on the job, the social implications of these added burdens reflected the contrasts between the two kinds of workplaces. On the one hand, in their own households and neighborhoods, wives and mothers came to rely even more heavily on friends and kin than they had in the past. Cooperative work efforts inevitably possessed a strong emotional component, for they reflected feelings of loyalty and mutual affection as well as great material need. On the other hand, the contraction of the national economy undercut black women's already inferior position in the agricultural, domestic service, and industrial sectors. The number of waged jobs shrank, and some disappeared altogether, their elimination hastened by shortsighted federal programs and regulations. Meanwhile, black women received few of the governmental benefits designed to cushion the impact of economic fluctuations on working people in general. The 1930s marked the emergence of a two-tiered social division of labor, contrasting the decent wages and benefits and job security of employees of large manufacturing establishments with the poor pay and unpredictable employment of laborers in rural, seasonal, part-time, and domestic jobs. Clustered in the latter category of workers, black women as well as black men derived little immediate or tangible value from the historic social-welfare legislation of the 1930s.

World War II would lead the black community belatedly and temporarily out of depression, but black women's experiences during the 1930s would discourage them from relying exclusively on either the federal government or labor unions as their advocates in the marketplace. Instead, together with their husbands, sons, and brothers, they would increasingly come to identify their rights as workers with their rights as American citizens, and in the process affirm at home those democratic principles so integral to the war effort abroad.

SEVEN

THE ROOTS OF TWO
REVOLUTIONS, 1940–1955

IN 1943, Pauli Murray, a law student at Howard University in Washington, D.C., helped spearhead the country's first sit-in protests against segregated public eating places. Born in Durham, North Carolina, Murray had graduated from Hunter College in 1933. Five years later, she applied to the University of North Carolina (UNC) for a degree in social work; not only did the all-white university refuse to consider her application—"Members of your race are not admitted to the University"—but the NAACP refused to back her in her fight against discrimination. The venerable civil-rights group feared that Murray's application would not provide a compelling test case for a variety of reasons: She had attended college in the North, not in North Carolina; her years in Depression-era New York City had radicalized her (in 1936 she had joined a splinter group of the Communist Party); and she dressed and comported herself in a way that was not "feminine" enough for mainstream reformers. Though stung by the opposition she encountered from all quarters to her UNC application, Murray continued and expanded her activism when she embraced the March on Washington Movement (MOWM), an initiative intended to win for black men and women their fair share of defense-industry jobs during World War II. Murray, with other women students at Howard Law School, formed an "Action Corps" which intended, in her words, to coordinate "guerilla-like warfare" against segregation throughout the capital; this kind of "warfare" would rely on boycotts and peaceful demonstrations to expose the fundamental hypocrisies of a nation fighting fascism abroad. Launched in 1943, the D.C. protests provided a template for an ongoing civil rights movement that would begin to receive national press coverage in the mid-1950s.[1]

Murray and her classmates scored some notable successes opening up restaurants to the black citizens of Washington, but her personal struggles continued. In 1944, she distinguished herself as her class valedictorian, and applied to Harvard Law School for graduate work, only to receive a rejection that read, in part, "Your picture and the salutation on your college transcript indicate that you are not of the sex entitled to be admitted to Harvard Law School." Still stinging from the indignity inflicted upon her by UNC, Murray tried to restrain the deep emotions of humiliation and rage she felt. As she wrote in a newspaper article that summer, a woman activist must maintain a sense of integrity in the face of the most outrageous provocations; she must achieve "a quieting of the spirit . . . a pause before the conflict," which would in turn yield "the courage you need to hold fast to your self-control." In 1946 President Harry S. Truman appointed Murray to the newly formed President's Committee on Civil Rights, and she continued in her roles as activist and theorist of social change. By the time she helped found the National Organization for Women in 1966, she had long since linked the causes of equal rights for black people and for women. Her own encounters with discrimination informed a law article she published in 1965; in it she noted, "The rights of women and the rights of Negroes are only different phases of the fundamental and indivisible issue of human rights." Appropriately enough she titled the article "Jane Crow and the Law."[2]

World War II and the postwar decade were seedtime years for the modern civil rights and women's liberation movements. Both movements grew out of the promises of social change that the wartime economy made but peacetime society failed to deliver. Caught in a tangle of inequality created by gender and racial ideologies, black working women stood to gain much from this dual challenge to a caste system that transcended regional boundaries. Nevertheless, by the mid-1960s it had become abundantly clear that while black women of all ages all over the country embraced the struggle for justice on behalf of black people, they did not necessarily feel any affinity for its sister cause that professed to represent the interests of women regardless of color, class, or cultural background. During this era of military conflict and political and social turmoil, black women continued to share with black men specific grievances, even as the war propelled them to stake new claims to full citizenship in the arenas of jobs, housing, public accommodations, and voting. At the same time, black women's daily work and family lives bore little resemblance to those of the privileged white women who would later attempt to define national "feminist" priorities.[3]

The war enlisted the active participation of black wage earners around the country. In return they received paychecks that appeared fat enough by the lean, hungry standards set in the 1930s, but mean and contemptible when viewed in the context of national economic growth and the sacrifices of black men and women in the armed services. Writing from Michigan in 1941, Lutensia Dillard appealed to President Roosevelt, contrasting the new challenges for black men as soldiers with old patterns of discrimination—black men were still "not aloud [sic] to work and make a living for their wives and children." Dillard, writing on behalf of the local branch of the Colored Women's Democrat Club, maintained faith in the ability of the president's party to redress long-standing grievances, but other black activists abandoned the two major parties to embrace radical advocacy groups that were, they believed, equal to these perilous times. Meanwhile, the war years abounded in egregious examples of whites' contempt for black people—the humiliating treatment accorded black soldiers by white military personnel and civilians alike (Nazi prisoners of war held a higher status in some cases), the upgrading of whites at the expense of their black coworkers, violent efforts by white neighborhoods to deprive black families of access to public housing projects—these and other issues swelled the membership rolls of the NAACP, and, in 1943, contributed to the founding of the Congress of Racial Equality (CORE). The National Urban League also helped to dramatize the need for a "Double Victory" over racism at home as well as fascism abroad. Like the army nurse in wartime Alabama who dared to board a bus before white passengers and was beaten by police and then jailed, black Americans directly confronted the racial hypocrisy of a "democratic" nation at war. In the process, they demonstrated that "you can never tell when some black person has just had all he or she can stand!" Out of this commitment to civil rights activism in the 1940s came lunch-counter sit-ins, freedom rides, and challenges to voting restrictions, all of which presaged the civil rights revolution of the 1950s.[4]

With few exceptions, white politicians yielded to the pressure exerted by civil rights groups only to the extent that they depended upon black votes to maintain their own positions of authority, and only to the extent they feared that the brutality of police and segregationists represented a public relations disaster for their hometowns. Interviewed many years later, a black woman who had worked in a munitions factory during the war recalled the era's main lesson: "No one does anything—you never get anything—out of the goodness of people's hearts." She was referring specifically to the impetus behind the March on Washington Movement, the major offensive against discrimination in war industry plants that began in 1940. A. Philip Randolph, founder and head of the Brotherhood of Sleeping Car Porters, coordinated the protest that originated when a black woman delegate to a civil rights convention in Chicago that year suggested: "We ought to throw fifty thousand Negroes around the White House, bring them from all over the country, in jalopies, in trains and any way they can get there . . . until we get some action [on the integration of defense industries] from the White House." The threat of just such a demonstration as the country was beginning to mobilize for war provoked President Franklin Roosevelt to issue Executive Order 8802 (outlawing discriminatory hiring practices by defense contractors) and to establish an investigative but ultimately relatively ineffectual agency, the Committee on Fair Employment Practices (FEPC), in June 1941. The intense demand for labor, and not the imprecations of the FEPC, opened up some previously all-white jobs for blacks during the war. President Truman's rhetorical flourishes in the direction of egalitarianism—his order to desegregate federal offices and the armed forces in 1948 notwithstanding—offered little tangible support for people lodged in wretched housing and plagued by inferior educational and employment opportunities. His successor, Dwight D. Eisenhower, continued to honor (southern) states rights in the tradition of chief executives. White employers slowly and grudgingly lowered the barriers against blacks when wartime imperatives and black political demands left them no choice, but they hastily erected the same barriers at the first sign of peace. In 1945 the writer-poet Maya Angelou sensed the angry mood of former black war heroes, now "hanging on the ghetto corners like forgotten laundry left on a back yard fence." She wrote, "Thus we lived through a major war. The question in the ghettos was, Can we make it through a minor peace?" It was a question that resonated as loudly through the segregated North as through the segregated South.[5]

White working women also had to fight for fair and equal seniority, promotion, and wage policies during and after the war, but compared to black women, they had different perspectives on the issue of gainful employment. Little is revealed about black women's specific challenges by the narrative of a generic "Rosie the Riveter"—the white housewife who heeded appeals to her patriotism and donned denim overalls for the duration of the conflict, to "do the job *he* left behind." The war won, so the story goes, Rosie eagerly relinquished her riveting gun in 1945 to take up a new duty, the production of a baby boom on a full-time basis. From 1940 to 1945 married and older white women did join the labor force in increasing numbers (total female participation climbed from 14.8 million to 19.5 million in the five-year period), and many took blue-collar "men's jobs" for the first time. Yet these developments were less war-specific than they appeared, since three-quarters of all wartime working women had joined the job market before 1941, and many sought to retain their jobs once the military conflict ended. Rosie and her new husband most likely found a modest house in a new suburb, where they shared in a postwar prosperity marked by new patterns of consumption—of houses, appliances, entertainment, and higher education for their children. She probably took a job as a secretary to pay for a family vacation or a second car. As American citizenship came increasingly to be identified with middle-class affluence, black women contended with barriers to equality on all fronts.[6]

The growing proportion of married women in the labor force during World War II signaled a trend toward the convergence of black and white female employment rates. In 1944 three out of ten white women and four out of ten black women worked. Despite the similarity of these statistics, however, the story of black working women departs substantially from that of their white counterparts during these years. Black women entered (and reentered) the labor force at a slower rate because they encountered persistent discrimination. With the exception of a decline in agricultural labor (from 16 to 8 percent of all gainfully employed black women) and an increase in the proportion of machine operatives (from 4 to 16 percent), their occupational structure remained intact during and after World War II. By 1950, 60 percent of all black working women (compared to 16 percent of all white working women) were concentrated in institutional and private household service jobs, and 40 percent of all white working women (compared to 5 percent of black women) had clerical or sales jobs.[7]

Spread out in the suburbs, frantically balancing child-rearing with new economic responsibilities or eschewing gainful employment in favor of full-time family work, some middle-class white women began to suffer from what Betty Friedan would later label "the problem that has no name." But black women, with more and more of their families (in the words of writer Ann Petry) "crammed on top of each other—jammed and packed and forced into the smallest possible space"—could claim no mystique that inspired public celebration. In their ability to combine wage earning with the care of their families, they did, however, maintain the respect of their communities' opinion makers in a way that white women often did not. For women of the two groups, poverty and prosperity inspired separate strategies for change and, at least during the third quarter of the twentieth century, created histories that were separate and unequal.[8]

THE ELUSIVE "DOUBLE V FOR VICTORY" DURING WORLD WAR II

During World War II, when her white employer suddenly started to substitute the word "colored" for "nigger" in her presence, Ruth Shays accounted for the change this way: "You see, these Japanese and Germans was threatening to cut their toenails too short to walk, so she called herself being friendly by not using that word 'nigger' because she knows I hate and despise it." Shays, a domestic worker, believed her own experiences reflected the dynamics of American military-defense politics: "Whenever they [whites] get a little scared they try to act like they might be decent, but when that war was over you didn't hear much about freedom and the equal rights, and what you heard didn't have much to do with what was going on." Ruth Shays's cynicism about the impact of a temporary shortage of domestic servants was justified. Yet if black women did not achieve any long-lasting economic gains as a result of the war, together with their menfolk they did begin to test the limits of their own collective strength in ways that would reverberate into the future.[9]

The wartime experience of black Americans reflected both economic progress and stubborn prejudice, and this apparent paradox spurred widespread social conflict. Government officials and private employers seemed bent on achieving efficient labor mobilization without disturbing fundamental inequities in American life, but black women and men enjoyed a newfound material well-being, if relative only to their meager conditions in the past. Several major unions—most notably the United Automobile Workers (UAW)—made dramatic efforts to consolidate their gains from the late 1930s, and win the support of all workers; black union membership increased from 200,000 in 1940 to 1.25 million five years later. Yet violent "hate strikes" instigated by white workers over the hiring of blacks took place within this broader context of labor union militancy. Meanwhile black women labored in defense-industry jobs, toiled as domestics for white-women workers, served as members of the segregated Women's Army Auxiliary Corps, and cared for their families while their husbands fought in the war. Writing in *Opportunity*, the magazine of the National Urban League, Leotha Hackshaw demonstrated the twin impulses of outrage and determination when she wrote in April 1943, "We brown women of America need victory so much, so desperately. We must prove it to white Americans as well—that our country can't get along without the labor and sacrifice of her brown daughters."[10]

In search of well-paying defense jobs, blacks responded to a new openness in defense hiring in 1942, and over one-half million migrated out of the South in the next three years. But as they doubled and tripled up in already congested tenements in the North and Midwest, and in some cases filled the housing left vacant by interned Japanese Americans in the Far West, social tensions worsened. Competition for jobs and housing between blacks and whites exploded in urban riots that raged in Harlem, Detroit, and twenty-five other cities during the summer of 1943. As further evidence of their ambivalent status during the war, black men served in the armed forces in the same proportion as white men, providing their families with much-needed regular monthly checks, all the while segregated and subjected to verbal and physical attacks from their white compatriots.[11]

Most black women measured the impact of the war on their own lives primarily in terms of the quality of their jobs and living quarters. Lillian Hatcher, one of the first black women hired above the service level in the Detroit auto industry, recalled that her new job paid double what she had been making as a cafeteria worker:

> I was working not for patriotic reasons, I was working for the money. The 97 cents an hour was the greatest salary that I had earned. Going up to $1.16 an hour—that was going to be my top rate. And I really needed that money, because my son was wearing out corduroy pants, two and three pair a month, gym shoes and all the other things my daughters too had to have, you know, clothing and shoes and all that stuff. And our house rent was the whole price of $32.50 a month and we had to save for that, in order to pay $32.50 and keep the light and gas.

Despite the high cost of living, the North afforded expanded economic opportunities the rural South did not. Julia Mathews left Elm City, North Carolina, and found work in Baltimore in food-packing plants and an arsenal, among other places. She periodically returned to visit family in North Carolina, but her wartime wage work led her to vow that she "wasn't going to work nobody's farm." For years to come, many black women workers would recall the defense-industry "utopia" of high wages.[12]

A 1945 publication of the U.S. Women's Bureau lauded "Negro Women War Workers," and listed those who contributed directly to the war effort—Brooklyn Navy Yard mechanics, and workers in the electrical equipment and machinery-manufacturing business, steel mills, foundries, and aircraft assembly lines. Yet this report revealed in indirect ways at least the uphill battles that black women fought throughout the war. For example, as late as July 1942, fewer than thirty black women were employed in Detroit-area defense industries; a year and a half later the number had exploded to fourteen thousand. The latter figure was the result of a vigorous push by local and national black groups to open these jobs to nonwhites, but it was still only a tiny fraction of Detroit jobs. Moreover, the Women's Bureau also lauded those black women workers in "essential civilian industries," including domestic servants, migrant laborers, employees in canneries, railroad workers, and employees in gas stations. The report thus highlighted black women's relatively late date of entry into defense jobs, and their persistent role as "support workers" for the white men and women who enjoyed substantial benefits in the queue for good jobs and good wages.[13]

From the beginning of the war onward, official United States government recruitment propaganda, from posters to short stories in popular women's magazines, was aimed exclusively at white women of both the middle and working classes. Initially at least, when black women were mentioned in connection with the national manpower crisis at all, they were exhorted to enter "war service" by taking jobs that white women most readily abandoned—laundry, cafeteria, and domestic work. The Women's Bureau contended that many black women "do not even realize that they are doing war work, work which affects directly the country's war production"; a large defense employer made the point explicitly: *"We think every worker we can place in a laundry is worth three new workers in our own plants."* Shop-floor supervisors complained that while male workers might absent themselves from the factory as a result of overindulgence the night before, (white) female workers stayed home periodically to catch up on their washing, cleaning, and grocery shopping. In this respect white wives' household duties threatened the defense industry, and by extension, the whole war effort. Black women thus were supposed to form a behind-the-scenes cadre of support workers for gainfully employed white wives.[14]

The private service sector shrank by one-fifth nationwide during the war, as all women eagerly sought better-paying jobs. Labeled "kitchen mechanics," black women found that they could command a higher wage from white housewives in regions where alternative sources of employment kept the supply of domestics low. For example, a Baltimore arsenal that employed four hundred black female gas-mask assemblers caused maids' wages to rise and working conditions to improve; "The Whip Changes Hands," announced the headline of a 1941 newspaper article on the predicament of the city's white housewives. In the South, where the relatively few industrial establishments refused to hire black women in operatives' positions, most wives and mothers continued to labor in someone else's kitchen. Even in this area of the country, however, the air was filled with rumors of mysterious "Eleanor Clubs" (named for the notorious busybody of a First Lady)—groups of black women who colluded to withhold their labor from the job market in order to demand unprecedented wage concessions. Observers reported that white wives exerted pressure on their businessmen-husbands not to hire black women and in the process "'spoil' good domestic servants." One sociologist reported that a general restlessness on the part of southern black women workers "has proved to be one of the most intimate effects of the war in many [white] households . . . [and] one of the most serious barriers to interracial tolerance and good will."[15]

By 1944 black women constituted 60 percent of all private household workers (up 13 percent over the figure for 1940), reflecting white women's hasty flight from service as soon as the Great Depression ended. Black women also filled a disproportionate number of institutional service jobs as a result of the "secondary boom" in the restaurant, lodging, and custodial services industries. For the first two and a half years of the war, if and when defense plants hired any black women at all, they usually used them as scrubwomen or janitors and kept them in these jobs for the duration of the conflict. Institutional service offered more in the way of higher wages and on-the-job companionship than private domestic employment; even better, a blue-collar job beat making beds or "busting suds" for anyone. In general, labor-hungry employers hired either white women or black men first, depending upon the industry, but black women always last. This ranking of "racial" and gender priorities obscures the fact that many blacks, male or female, could not find work at all until the war was well underway. For instance, in late 1941 Kansas City defense-plant personnel officers claimed they needed one thousand operatives but refused to hire available black women. Employers still preferred to await an influx of white southern migrants to the area, or to speed up their current workers, rather than take advantage of local blacks who stood ready and waiting.[16]

During the first part of the war, blatant discrimination in federal and privately sponsored training programs created a "bottleneck" that limited the number of blacks qualified for skilled and semiskilled jobs. As a result of the more egalitarian policies of the National Youth Administration, that situation had changed by midwar. But in August 1943 the personnel manager of a Detroit bomber plant was still telling one of many black women who had just completed a formal training program that "when a department is nice and peaceful they don't go around looking for trouble by putting colored people in the department." Other employers recited the familiar litany of excuses—the plant did not yet have segregated bathrooms, there were not enough applicants for a separate shift of black workers, white female employees would cause trouble. "But my wife needs a maid" was another common refrain.[17]

The federal government made only nominal efforts to ensure that blacks received their fair share of wartime jobs, and the unadorned discriminatory policies of several major agencies tended to cancel out any gains in that direction. Despite the national publicity surrounding the creation of the Fair Employment Practices Committee in 1941, the agency engaged primarily in "jawboning" as a means of pressuring defense contractors to hire blacks; it handled grievances on an individual basis only, and its cumbersome bureaucratic machinery made careful investigation time-consuming, and meaningful enforcement almost nonexistent. (Local black labor and civil rights groups had to take the initiative in securing FEPC action against defiant employers.) Other government offices made no pretense of following egalitarian policies; the United States Employment Service and the War Manpower Commission, together with its weak Women's Advisory Commission, actually catered to the preferences of individual employers for whites over blacks.[18]

Faced with this kind of intransigence, black women had to struggle for each and every job above the lowest service level, and then, if they were successful, struggle to hold on to it. During the war Maya Angelou became the first black streetcar conductor in San Francisco, but not before she had journeyed to the personnel office with "the frequency of a person on salary" and endured endless runarounds from the complacent white receptionist. She finally wore down her antagonist's resolve with dogged persistence and a suitably contrived application form. Thus the young black woman managed to fulfill a promise she had made to herself, the initial announcement of which "made my veins stand out, and my mouth tighten into a prune": "I WOULD HAVE THE JOB. I WOULD BE A CONDUCTORETTE AND SLING A FULL MONEY CHANGER FROM MY BELT. I WOULD."[19]

More often than not, individual resolve was insufficient to crack long-standing barriers, and then would-be workers would have to rely on their collective strength and well-placed allies, usually civil rights groups and working brothers and husbands. The Detroit automobile industry provides a dramatic case in point. The largest manufacturers, paternalistic Ford Motor Company included, openly refused to hire blacks in general and black women in particular for work in establishments converted to war industry. In late 1942 Detroit-area defense plants had only one hundred black female production employees out of a total female work force of ninety-six thousand; the converted auto industry had hired only nine hundred black women in nonproduction work. However, the UAW was anxious to retain its support among the city's black community, which had proved crucial in the union's successful strike against Ford in 1941. Although skeptics still believed that the CIO in general had admitted blacks "for the same reason that Lincoln freed the slaves—to save the union," a core of determined black foundry workers in Local 600 maintained some leverage over UAW union policies.[20]

With the backing of the NAACP, Urban League, Double Victory clubs, and Negro Youth Council for Victory and Democracy, male workers and potential female workers staged protests and mass meetings to publicize the hiring issue, beginning in early 1942. That fall a large group met in a downtown hotel to endorse a "Victory Plan" that would result in the employment of ten thousand jobless black women in Detroit, at least one thousand of whom had received job training. A delegation of black leaders went to Washington, D.C., to demand action from the FEPC, while picketers daily demonstrated outside the gates at various plants. Finally, manufacturers made token concessions, though they persisted in their preference for uneducated white southern migrants, both women and men. In April of 1943, black women constituted only 3 percent of the female workers in Detroit-area auto plants. Several large companies still had not hired any at all, leaving as many as twenty-five thousand black women in the area unemployed.[21]

Often black women found that their hard-won jobs in industry were not only segregated, but the most dangerous and grueling ones that a factory had to offer. During the war, certain men's jobs were converted to women's work and in the process downgraded to a lower pay and status, but others were converted to black women's work of even greater inferiority. In airplane assembly plants, black women stood in stifling "dope rooms" filled with the nauseating fumes of glue, while white women sat on stools in the well-ventilated sewing room. "Where women were employed in the sintering plants [in which ore dust mixed with the heat of blast furnaces], they were chiefly Negroes," according to the Women's Bureau, "and were reported as moving as much dirt and material as men." Elsewhere black women worked with ammunitions and gunpowder, poisonous plastics and acetone, sealing mud, and hazardous equipment—all without the prospect of job advancement or promotion. Furthermore, they were routinely assigned "discouraging" night-shifts that imposed additional burdens on them as wives and mothers.[22]

When it came to protecting the rights of white women and black workers, labor unions had a mixed record during World War II. Some organizations, like the Boilermakers, steadfastly refused to admit blacks as equal members at all, and others, especially in the South, kept locals strictly segregated. Yet the largest and most militant groups affiliated with the Congress of Industrial Organizations instituted relatively progressive policies and the machinery to enforce them. The CIO created a Committee to Abolish Racial Discrimination with counterparts in ten affiliated unions, and through state political action committees lobbied for permanent FEPC legislation at the war's end. The UAW maintained at least a rhetorical commitment to equality for blacks and white women, and in 1944 it formed its own Women's Bureau (with Lillian Hatcher as a codirector) to monitor cases involving discrimination in seniority, wages, and promotion.[23]

Various unions' public statements were not always matched by shop-floor vigilance, however. Maida Springer Kemp of the International Ladies Garment Workers Union (ILGWU) estimated that nine out of ten executive officials in her union supported the ideal of equality, but that only a third of those showed any willingness to work actively on behalf of it. Some black women even faced the novel task of begging to join a union local. New to their wartime jobs, a group of women autoworkers approached the chief steward of the UAW and inquired about membership. He demurred, explaining, "You don't have to join . . . I just want to save you some money, you don't have to pay your money in." They insisted and paid their dues anyway.[24]

Not all black women were so determined to participate in union activities. Many claimed priority for family responsibilities over and above the time and energy that union membership would entail. Lillian Hatcher recalled that during the war her coworkers had no difficulty getting to work on time, but when it came to attending a Sunday union meeting, "They would give most any excuse: they didn't feel good, they had to cook dinner for their husband, they had a sick child, they had to visit the grandmother, they had guests in, or they had to wash, they had to do some work." Hatcher acknowledged that a supportive family was indispensable if a woman was to survive the constant intrusion of union affairs into her household. Yet she and other black women ultimately decided to join a union and pursue collective action in an effort to improve the quality of family life. Already on the 11:00 p.m. to 8:00 a.m. shift, she first became active in her UAW local when a new shift assignment interfered even more drastically with getting her children ready for school: "Trying to get back home in time to get them off to school at quarter to nine . . . was a hardship. . . . They were about to change the hours to suit the company, not the workers."[25]

The black women workers who emerged from this crucible of hardship to become union leaders themselves were an especially hardy lot, and in many cases their outspokenness during the war signaled a lifelong commitment to social justice for all people, on and off the job. Given the revered place in African American culture for "sassy" women, it was not surprising that many acquired a reputation for verbal aggressiveness in dealing with managers, union officials, and rank-and-file workers. Theodosia Simpson, operator of a stemming machine, assumed a leading role in the June 1943 strike against the R. J. Reynolds Tobacco Company in Winston-Salem, North Carolina. At one point she startled a personnel official by challenging his contention that federal wage controls limited what management could do for its workers. Simpson caught him "off guard" with the declaration, "Mr. Whitaker, according to the 'little steel' formula, you can give us a wage increase without filing a petition to the National War Labor Board." When a foreman confronted another woman worker, Ruby Jones, and asked her what she wanted, Jones shot back, "I want your respect. That's all I ask." As one of the male union leaders recalled of Theodosia Simpson, Ruby Jones, and other active women like Velma Hopkins and Moranda Smith, "The black women made that union possible. We could never have beaten them [Reynolds] without them. It was the militancy among those black women."[26]

On the shop-floor, black female union leaders at times faced difficulty mediating between different ethnic groups, let alone between blacks and whites. In New York City one ILGWU local education director observed of her shop's multicultural membership, "While they hated one another sometimes, they jointly hated anything black." Elected shop steward in an aviation plant, Sylvia Woods averted a threatened walkout by whites when she told them that if they objected to the hiring of a black woman, "Fine. We'll fill your places before you get home." She and officials like Massie Eberhardt, a worker in an Orange, New Jersey, laundry, won the grudging respect of white union members by pressing grievances vigorously: "I mean because if you get in trouble, Sylvia goes in there and wrecks the place." In these situations the door to mutual understanding swung both ways. A black woman might shift from open fear and suspicion of her white coworkers, to an attitude of "You didn't have to love one another, but you [all] wanted decent wages, hours, conditions of work," and perhaps even to a prized friendship with a white woman.[27]

Nevertheless, most workplaces remained segregated throughout the war, diminishing the prospects for meaningful relationships that cut across the color line. Many white women workers sought to retain their privileged position and resist any contact at all with black women; these exclusionary impulses could at times erupt into "hate strikes" when white women considered their long-standing privileges to be rights. The Bell Telephone system enshrined those privileges in a traditional division of labor that reserved the job of telephone operator for "white ladies" only, using the resistance of their current employees to work or cooperate with or to train blacks as a rationale for maintaining an exclusionary workplace. Black advocacy groups organized systematic campaigns to open these workplaces. For example, in St. Louis in the summer of 1943, members of the local March on Washington Movement began to picket the offices of Southwestern Bell, carrying signs that read "Discrimination in employment is undemocratic—*I protest it!* Hire Negroes now." Yet the union of white operators, the Telephone Employees' Association, launched wildcat strikes, work stoppages, and walkouts—not only in response to the hiring of token black women, but also to the possibility that black women might someday be hired. The union vowed to "safeguard the interests of all [current] workers." Bell officials charged that the threat of strikes effectively prevented them from hiring black women. It was not until December 1944 that New York Telephone hired its first black operators.[28]

In a number of industries, corporate management played a key role in determining the outcome of tense worksites during the war. Prejudiced personnel officials implicitly encouraged hostile white workers by not hiring blacks in the first place, or by firing those newly employed at the slightest provocation. In 1943 a Murray Body plant foreman in Detroit used a minor dispute (provoked when a white woman took a black coworker's sandwich) as a pretext to get rid of four black women in a department; since they were still on probation, they were not covered by union job security guidelines. Similarly, in the summer of 1944, a large Virginia cotton mill quickly capitulated to the collective protests of white women and dismissed the few black women it had recently hired. In contrast, other employers, like the Winchester Repeating Arms Company in New Haven, Connecticut, simply told their white female employees at the outset to "work together or else" and received "fine cooperation" from them in return.[29]

During the war years, day-to-day struggles on the job received less attention than the "Negro Women Pioneers," a phenomenon that writer Alice Walker would later call "the Exception, the One." Indeed, at the time, publicity surrounding the hiring of the first black nurses in New York City hospitals and of the first black female mechanics at the Brooklyn Navy Yard could divert attention from the larger pattern of persistent discrimination. Statistics were also misleading. For example, the percentage of black women in the clerical sector doubled from 1940 to 1944, but they still represented less than 2 percent of the total number of workers in that field and most of them remained invisible to white business customers and concentrated in government jobs around Washington, D.C. The much-heralded black members of the Women's Army and Auxiliary Corps (renamed the Women's Army Corps [WAC] in 1943) revealed the ambiguous nature of black women's professional and social advancement during the war. About four thousand served in the corps (10 percent of all WAACs), but like officers in the Army Nurse corps, they were placed in separate units, reflecting the strict "racial" segregation of the armed forces in general, and rarely sent overseas. In 1942, Zelda Webb Anderson eagerly reported for duty and quickly mastered the M-1 rifle as well as the challenges of basic training. Yet she soon found that regardless of their education or talents, most black WACs were assigned to menial jobs in the laundry or hospital unit—"very demeaning," she recalled. In response to a Fort Breckinridge, Kentucky, post commander, who told her that she was assigned to the kitchen, she replied "Sir, I have not had any mess training." He countered, "All you nigras know how to cook," which prompted her to say, boldly, "You just met one who does not know how to cook." At Fort Devens, Massachusetts, six black WAACs were court-martialed when they refused to accept kitchen and custodial assignments, while their white counterparts worked in the motor pool and related divisions. (The four who received dishonorable discharges were later exonerated by higher officials.) Despite pressure from black women's organizations like the National Council of Negro Women and Alpha Kappa Alpha Sorority, the Women's Reserve of the U.S. Navy excluded black women altogether until October 1944, too late to see active duty.[30]

White-supremacist impulses shaped the jobs of black soldiers as well as WACs. In his autobiography, *Colored People*, Henry Louis Gates Jr. highlights the convergence of gender and racial ideologies on the military bases, where women were in short supply and therefore black men were assigned traditional women's work: "Because the Army replicates the social structure of the larger society it defends, almost all black draftees were taught to cook and clean. Of course, it was usually women who cooked and cleaned outside the Army, but *someone* had to do the work, so it would be black men." Military officials thus persisted in the customary exclusion of black men and women from machine work, which included the use of typewriters, cars, and trucks. Moreover, whether or not they worked in the military or in defense industries, most black employees could not aspire to supervisory positions, or even to meaningful promotions of any kind. World War II did little to disrupt the nation's traditional "racial" division of labor.[31]

At the same time, a preoccupation with the job structure can obscure the dramatic, if relative, improvements in black people's standard of living. Higher wages and lower unemployment rates compared to depression days meant that many—"from prostitutes to preachers"—prospered during the war. The internal dynamics of family life reflected this new prosperity, for better and worse. A study conducted by the Harlem Children's Center in 1942 indicated that the conflict was having a significant impact on the black community, as the number of households on relief and the number of malnourished children significantly diminished. The war had "proven beneficial to Harlem's teenage youngsters," the report concluded. "It has removed a great deal of the anxiety and frustration common to submarginal income families, which inevitably affected children." With more and better employment opportunities, black men gained a new measure of self-respect, which in turn affected family relationships. Mary Mebane said her father felt "proud and happy" when he got a job as a carpenter at a nearby military base; before that he had pieced together a living selling junk and cleaning cesspools. But the war did cause social dislocation and thereby introduce new anxieties—or at least exacerbate long-standing ones—that disrupted family life. The entry of black men into the armed services and the lure of easier money elsewhere actually increased the proportion of female-headed households, leaving more women (though not necessarily to a greater extent than among whites) "lonely and looking." Whole families scattered; younger children stayed with their grandmother while older siblings struck out on their own, hardly knowing whether they would eventually hit the jackpot of a good job or end up in a junkyard commune.[32]

For the migrating households that remained intact, a trek up north or out west could mean stepping "out of the frying pan into a hornet nest." Migrants' quarters were often primitive and cramped, and women's responsibilities multiplied accordingly. Viola Johnson arrived in Las Vegas in 1942 and joined her family in a tent where seven of them lived. Throughout the day and night, male members of the family rotated on and off different shifts at the nearby Basic Magnesium Corporation. Recalling the heat and rain and crowded conditions, Johnson said, "It was awful living there." Precious Mack remembered that first her uncle and then her father had ventured out of the South before the rest of the family followed them to the San Francisco Bay Area. Arriving in the land of lemon trees, the twelve-member family took up residence in a one-room trailer—"honest, and no facilities—no running water, no inside toilet." The four oldest children and their father alleviated the cramped sleeping situation by working the "graveyard" shift in a nearby shipyard. Precious Mack's mother stayed home with the youngest children and thus managed to avoid a form of wartime domestic conflict immortalized in black singer Huddie Ledbetter's song "National Defense Blues": "Just because she was working / Making so much dough / That woman got displaced / Did not love me no more." Black men working in California had inspired Ledbetter with the observation: "The women are working on that defense and they's making lots of money, just quitting their husbands." The bigger a wife's paycheck, the less dependent financially she was on her spouse, but the greater her total work obligations during her doubly busy days. Some wives managed to juggle new and inconvenient working hours with the routine demands of a husband who "propped his feet up and got a can of beer while you fixed dinner." Others decided they were better off with just one, instead of two "bosses"—especially if one job paid nothing at all.[33]

When their landlord was a city or the federal government, black women expanded their arena of struggle in order to care for families beleaguered by the strains of war. In 1943, Lottie Hall, a leader of the tenants' council at the Gilmor Homes in Baltimore, highlighted the sacrifices of women who labored in defense industries by day, only to return home at night and find that their apartments lacked heat or hot water. Representing 587 other black families in the housing project, Hall waged a frustrating battle with officials remarkable for their hostility, or at best indifference, to the living conditions of war workers. Throughout the United States, black women tenants of public housing contended with city councils and federal agencies that resisted providing adequate, or even "emergency," housing for blacks, as urban black populations grew exponentially during the war. White voters insisted that public projects remain segregated and outside of white neighborhoods. Claimed one white person in Baltimore, "We the people bought our homes in this section to get away from ne-groes, and the slums and filth that follow them." This person echoed the argument of whites who claimed their fight to maintain all-white worksites was part of the fight against tyranny and fascism: "We are fighting for freedom to live as we see fit but freedom doesn't, I hope, mean indiscriminate racial mixing." Faced with intransigence from local project managers, Lottie Hall and other members of the Gilmor Homes Tenant Council appealed directly to the federal government, a move that by February 1944 had won them some mea-sure of success—in the form of limited amounts of additional heat and hot water. The many black women who became active in tenants' rights protests during this period did so out of a need to claim their due not only as workers and as wives and mothers, but also as citizens contributing to the war effort.[34]

Yet authorities at all levels failed to heed the urgent call of Lottie Hall and others for the fair treatment they deserved and needed in order to care for their families. Throughout the war, black women supported the Office of Price Administration and Civilian Supply (OPA), a federal agency charged with controlling the costs of rent, food, and other necessi-ties. However, that support did not earn them fair treatment in the form of representation on local price boards, nor did it protect them from the skyrocketing price hikes associated with local grocery stores in the ghettos. The federal government did little to stem the ex-pansion of exclusionary selling practices that barred black men and women from buying at white stores. As southern migrants moved to the West Coast and the Pacific Northwest in search of wartime jobs they found signs posted in store windows reading "We Do Not So-licit Colored Trade." Indeed, as black people moved into predominantly white regions of the country, the system of American apartheid spread and grew outside the confines of the South and the urban North. These practices guaranteed that black wives and mothers would continue to lack the basic consumer choices enjoyed by their white counterparts.[35]

In other ways, too, black women's labors were compounded by a government unable or unwilling to challenge prevailing practices that endangered the health and well-being of families. National and local politicians, in concert with private employers, resisted the idea of federally subsidized childcare for mothers stretched to the limit. Most employers and public officials believed that married working women were a temporary fixture in the wartime economy. The few private and public facilities that did exist were usually inconve-niently located or closed to black children. The need to combine child-rearing with gainful employment was not a new one for many black mothers, of course, but the war in several respects actually intensified their difficulties. Women who moved to a different area of the country left behind kin support networks, including babysitting aunts and grandmothers. Unlike domestic service jobs, those in the public sector were often situated outside residential areas, necessitating longer commuting times for already harried mothers. In a prizewinning essay submitted to a National Urban League competition in 1943, Leotha Hackshaw detailed her nerve-wracking days living in the Bronx and working at a Long Island ordnance plant. She rose at 5:30 a.m. to prepare herself for work and her toddler son for his babysitter. If the sitter arrived late, she had to make a mad dash to the subway. Eventually, a transfer to the midnight to 8:00 a.m. shift eased the morning mayhem, but then she found it difficult to get any rest: "I never realized how many different noises there are until I tried to sleep in the daytime," she wrote. Unsympathetic employers were the rule, and they routinely docked the pay of mothers who missed work to look after family matters, whether emergency or routine. For single mothers like foundry worker Wanita Allen, it was "Rush, rush, rush. . . . It just got to be too much."[36]

The frenetic pace of life in the North and Midwest contrasted with conditions in the South, which lacked comparable defense-industry jobs and public-housing opportunities for black women. There a World War I migration pattern reestablished itself; displaced sharecroppers sought the domestic jobs abandoned by their city cousins, who left the region altogether. A study conducted with the cooperation of Atlanta welfare agencies in 1943 gave an indication of the malnutrition and chronic depression that plagued poor black women in that city. Forced to live in their employer's home as a condition of their job, some mothers were completely at a loss when it came to caring for their own children and even sought to institutionalize their offspring rather than see them try to fend for themselves day in and day out. For these women the war years brought little in the way of economic security or hope.[37]

Middle-class black women's groups responded to these wartime political and social injustices by publicizing myriad urgent issues, from the disruption of black family life to the entrenched prejudice at the highest levels of the federal bureaucracy. Composed of members located all over the country, the National Council of Negro Women, together with the black sororities, initiated aggressive lobbying efforts aimed at federal policies that perpetuated and reinforced stubborn inequities. Local welfare agencies and national groups like the Urban League and the YWCA relied on relatively well-educated black women as volunteers or paid staff members in their efforts to ease the adjustment of migrant families moving long distances. For example, Frankie V. Adams, a consultant to the National Board of the YWCA from 1944 to 1945, helped blacks new to the West Coast learn "when Negroes could work, what they could work at, where they could do it and where they could eat." Thus black women's efforts in the area of social welfare were "survival oriented" (concerned with jobs and housing) and characterized by a high degree of group consciousness, in contrast to white middle-class women's focus on a push for representation in the professions.[38]

While the increasing social stratification reflected in club membership and volunteer work foreshadowed the rise of a relatively secure, if small, postwar black middle class, the NAACP grew in stature among women of all backgrounds. Bold challenges to discrimination, whether sanctioned by government or private employers, were now the order of the day. Ella Baker, a friend of Pauli Murray's and, as of 1943, national director of branches of the NAACP, helped ensure that her organization was "on the cutting edge of social change." Claiming a broad-based membership, the association enlisted the services of large numbers of school teachers and welders, social workers and cafeteria employees during World War II. As a sponsor of economic boycotts and legal challenges to discriminatory housing and employment practices, the association spoke to the basic needs of black women who worked, and it offered a comprehensive plan for civil rights in a way that the UAW, or the YWCA, or the Republican or Democratic parties did not.[39]

BLACK WOMEN WORKERS DEMOBILIZED AND REDOMESTICATED

White women quickly lost their jobs in 1945—some positions went to returning soldiers and others disappeared entirely in the reconversion process. Yet as early as 1944, black women had begun to feel the full impact of "powerful forces at work . . . to repopulate the abandoned kitchens of Southern, and Northern, white women." The ambitions of one white housewife revealed the impetus for postwar consumer-oriented technology on the one hand and a return to the prewar social division of labor on the other: "First thing I'm going to do after the war is to get a vacuum cleaner. And a maid to run it." The chances were greater in 1950 than in 1940 that the maid would be black.[40]

All of the mechanisms that employers and union leaders used to deprive white female war defense workers of their jobs were used with a vengeance against black women—mass firings and layoffs, separate seniority lists based on "race" and gender, harassment of women who fought desperately to retain their blue-collar wages. These insults to black women knew no regional bounds. Confronting a Chrysler personnel officer who told her the company had no jobs—at least "not for *you*," one migrant from the South, Christine Denby, remarked, "I like it up North and I wouldn't go home to stay. But I don't like the Northerners." In general, black women who lacked the backing of a powerful, sympathetic union were at the mercy of employers who favored hiring returning GIs; even Richmond tobacco workers and Detroit metal polishers who belonged to their respective unions received no support when they were fired for no reason. In contrast, UAW member Silretha Love decided that she would not acquiesce in discriminatory treatment at the Dodge main plant after the war. When she was laid off, along with thirty other women, black and white, she led the way for the whole group by filing a grievance against Chrysler. The women won their case, and back pay, but Love returned to work only to face daily harassment from the superintendent of the plant, who proceeded to charge her with shoddy work. At a hearing Love pointed out, "Its [sic] funny. I was all right during the war. What's wrong with my work now?" With UAW backing she won her job back again, and received $1,684 in back pay.[41]

At times, though, even women members of the UAW in Detroit could not be assured of fair treatment at the war's end. When lone nighttime custodian Josephine McCloudy was fired for requesting to use the white restroom in a Packard plant in June 1945, she compared the insulting treatment she received from the white foremen with that parceled out to blacks "in the time of slavery." And yet an official at UAW Local 190 also "raised his voice" to her and refused to represent her at a grievance hearing. She persisted and eventually brought her case before the Fair Practices Department of the UAW, but the outcome is unknown. Many others shared a humiliating experience akin to that of McCloudy's. And a year after the war's end, the starkly disadvantaged position of black workers in a peacetime economy had become obvious once again. A government researcher noted that "reconversion affected Negroes more severely than white workers: from July 1945 to April 1946, for example, unemployment rates among nonwhites increased more than twice as much as among whites." (This ratio held constant through the late 1980s.) By 1948 most of the gains that blacks had derived from the wartime boom had been wiped out, and labor analysts predicted that, given the persistent marginality of black workers, their well-being depended almost entirely upon a strong economy. Meanwhile, the most powerful unions were turning their attention to negotiating with large manufacturers in order to win more generous benefits for their current employees, rather than taking up the cause of employees fired unfairly.[42]

Although 38 percent of white women found jobs as secretaries and retail clerks after the war, only 5 percent of black women were similarly employed. In 1946, New York City's Hilda Fortune, like other members of the National Council of Negro Women, expressed alarm at the prospect of black women war workers once again forced to enter white households through the back door; said one reluctant domestic, "I could stand the work if I were just treated respectfully by the family and the children." Interviewed by a roving reporter for the *Washington Post* on the "postwar servant problem," Bernice McCannon, currently still employed at a Virginia army base, said she planned to return to household employment shortly. The thirty-year-old black woman told a familiar story: "I have always done domestic work for families. When war came, I made the same move many domestics did. I took a higher paying job in a government cafeteria as a junior baker." Pressed to reveal her feelings on the subject, McCannon replied, "If domestic work offers a good living, I see no reason why most of us will not return to our old jobs." Then she added, "We will have no alternative."[43]

Bernice McCannon's comments revealed the dilemma faced by many black women workers during the period of demobilization. Like their white coworkers, they were loathe to leave relatively well-paying jobs and gainful employment in general; but unlike white women, they had few options other than institutional or domestic service when it came to providing for their families. After the war, as the opportunities for white women expanded and as black women became an even greater proportion of all service employees, the status of the job declined even further. The 41 percent of gainfully employed black women who worked in private households in 1950 still derived no benefits from national worker legislation—minimum wage or hours laws, unemployment compensation, or Social Security. Another 19 percent worked for long hours and meager pay as office building scrubwomen and restaurant and hotel help.[44]

As early as 1944, it was clear that black women would not rush back to the white woman's kitchen if they could avoid doing so. Those who were eligible preferred to take advantage of their twenty-six weeks' worth of unemployment compensation benefits, and to wait to find jobs in factories converted to peacetime production. In September 1945 Myrtle Ackies of Brooklyn noted her high pay as an automotive factory employee—twice the wages she had made in a laundry before the war—and declared confidently that "her days as a laundry worker [were] over." The refusal of Ackies and other women workers to return immediately to "the old rut" kept postwar domestics' wages at a higher level than many employers had expected. Reports abounded of housewives who immediately lowered the pay of servants as soon as the Japanese surrendered, only to find themselves without any help the next day. The Buffalo *Courier Express* reported in October 1945 that even women whose unemployment benefits had expired were staying out of the domestic job market; the result was a "revolution—a quiet, bloodless one" that enabled workers to set "their own hours and select . . . their own working conditions." By 1946 weekly wages for domestics were about $30 in the North (sixty cents to $1 per hour, compared to Depression-era slave-market rates of a fifth that amount). An article in the Chicago *Defender* compared the pay of maids favorably to that of factory and laundry workers. Nevertheless, inflation continued to erode some of these financial gains, and many women felt that the price of their pride was just too high to pay for any domestic job.[45]

For these reasons, as the war drew to a close, the Women's Bureau began making plans "to attract some of the women released from war jobs back into service." Reports from the field indicated "that girls and women do not want to go into domestic service (especially household employment) except as a last resort." In December 1944 Mary V. Robinson, chief public service and editorial director of the bureau, suggested that the bureau sponsor training classes for workers and mobilize local groups, like clubs affiliated with the National Council of Negro Women, "to show that household or domestic service is not necessarily a blind alley job." But of course, for black women, it was.[46]

Bureau officials seemed motivated by, on the one hand, the anxieties of upper middle-class white women, and, on the other, their own concern for black women who would find it difficult if not impossible to support their families if they continued to scorn this type of employment. As usual, the bureau demonstrated an abundance of good intentions, but its postwar campaign to improve the image of household service predictably faltered because of its reliance on the presumed goodwill and cooperation of prospective employers. Household Employment Committees composed of "representatives of responsible local groups," both black and white, were supposed to educate the general public about the need for uniform standards in the field. In its efforts, the bureau relied on articles in popular women's magazines, like the one in a 1946 issue of *Family Circle* ("What's Wrong With the Word 'Servant'?"), which went so far to suggest that "Even President Truman is a servant—of the people—and no one thinks any less of him for that." But an internal bureau report from that same year observed that the committee's program had "proved weakest in gaining employer cooperation," and that fact testified to its overall ineffectiveness.[47]

Some black communities initiated projects to ensure that relatively high postwar wage levels would not disappear as the supply of domestics increased. An Atlanta training center established in 1945 aimed to provide training and placement services for maids "so that higher wages can be earned, not demanded." Ruby Blackburn, one of the leaders of the center and herself a domestic worker, knew that the well-being of her entire community depended upon the ability of cooks and laundresses to earn a living wage. Like the Atlanta project, other community-sponsored placement bureaus kept track of delinquent employers and refused to honor their requests for workers once a pattern of complaints against them had been established.[48]

Relegated once again to service jobs, black women sought to retain their sense of dignity and self-worth. A study conducted by sociologist Bonnie Dill of twenty-six women employed in New York and Philadelphia during the 1940s and 1950s suggests they realized that they were trapped for the foreseeable future in these traditional jobs, and so they relied on workplace strategies of survival and resistance. On one level they exercised some control over their choice of employer: One woman responded to the unreasonable demands of a white housewife by declaring, "This job is not the type of job that I have to live with the rest of my life. I lived before I ever came here and I could leave here and go back to the city and find another job." On a daily basis they set limits on their work assignments ("Well, you said your girl cleans the floor, and I'm not your girl . . . and I don't scrub floors on my hands and knees") and used their own judgment when it came to handling tantrum-prone children ("If he kicked me on the shins, I'd kick him back"). Jewell Prieleau recalled that in the postwar period she and other domestics formed their own social clubs that met every Thursday night. These support groups served to inform job hunters of openings and to shield members against the snobbery of their neighbors who worked in institutional settings; "the girls [who] work in bars and . . . in restaurants, they always look down at domestic workers." Confronted each day with white people who knew "nothing about a hard life" and who were able to provide their own children with the finest educational advantages and material possessions (if not always firm discipline), the interviewees in the study varied in their ability to deal with the rigors of their job. But for all of them, the end of the war meant a return to age-old battles within white households.[49]

BLACK WORKING WOMEN AT MIDCENTURY

The Allies' defeat of the Axis powers in 1945 ushered in a new era fraught with peril and promise for African American women and men. Within a matter of months the United States had begun to wage a new war—this one "cold," not only against the Soviet Union but also against radicalism more generally. During the 1930s and 1940s, Pauli Murray and others had embraced collective action well to the left of mainstream Democratic and Republican politics; now, with the beginning of the cold war, these civil-rights activists had to defend themselves against charges of disloyalty to the United States. Yet for returning soldiers and all other black people who had contributed directly or indirectly to the war effort between 1941 and 1945, the promise of full and equal American citizenship still seemed remote. Increasingly, the country defined itself in terms of material well-being: Unlike Soviet citizens, the argument went, Americans could choose from a vast array of consumer items—from suburban tract houses so new and gleaming the paint was hardly dry, to fashionable cars and clothing. Between 1947 and 1953, the U.S. suburban population grew by 43 percent, in contrast to the growth rate of the general population, which was a quarter of that figure. Isolated from the new office parks that sprung up on the periphery of cities, restricted to inner-city all-black neighborhoods, black people entered the postwar period with a mixture of apprehension and determination inspired by their wartime experiences.

A combination of federal initiatives, technological innovation, and the hiring practices of private employers bode ill for black workers throughout the nation at midcentury. With the wartime FEPC, the federal government had broken with its own past of unapologetic support for exclusionary hiring practices. However, after 1945 black families continued to register the effects of federal policies that either explicitly or implicitly promoted white supremacist racial ideologies. The segregation of public housing projects, and in some cases the razing of whole black neighborhoods to make way for such projects, consigned black households to cramped and inferior living quarters. The Servicemen's Readjustment Act (GI Bill) of 1944 paid the college tuition of war veterans, but black servicemen did not benefit from this program compared to their white counterparts; the vast majority of white colleges and universities refused to admit black students, and black colleges and universities often lacked the necessary accreditation, or the space, that would enable black men to take advantage of the tuition program. At the same time, transformations in regional economies called into question the notion that the United States was rapidly becoming an "affluent society." In the South, the mechanical cotton-picker continued to displace thousands of sharecroppers and tenant farmers, forcing them up north or out west, where they found contracting job markets borne of assembly-line automation, and rigidly segregated job markets borne of old prejudices and practices.[50]

Like white migrants from the South, black men and women who traveled north after the war relied on kin for information, contacts, and housing. Yet northern-born blacks and southern-born migrants alike found themselves at a distinct disadvantage when competing with rural whites for entry-level factory jobs, whether in Bakersfield, California, or Cincinnati, Ohio, or Middletown, Connecticut. Everywhere it seemed, whites were often able to count on the help of friends and kin who had already found jobs as industrial laborers, while blacks usually had to rely either on more formal devices, such as employment agencies, or on friends and family who could provide an entrée into only the most menial jobs a region had to offer. In 1953, Lucille Bryant of Tallulah, Louisiana, was working in the cotton fields for $2.50 a day, or earning a fraction of that amount for putting in long hours as a servant in a white household. In October of that year she moved to Las Vegas, lured to the booming city by kin and by the promise of good wages on a booming "strip" fueled by the gambling business. Taking over the job of her cousin, who had found a better one, Bryant described her gratitude at finding employment as a hotel maid: "I got on my knees and gave God thanks, eight dollars a day and working in the shade!" Like thousands of other African Americans, Lucille Bryant escaped both the cotton field and the white woman's kitchen, but she remained confined to the service sector while white women workers took jobs as secretaries and store clerks. At the same time, aided and abetted by an aggressive service workers' union, Culinary Workers Local 226, Bryant and her cousin parlayed the chronic labor shortage in Las Vegas into their own modest form of upward mobility.[51]

In 1955 the population of Las Vegas's Westside numbered 16,000, a substantial black neighborhood of migrants from Arkansas and Louisiana, a black community where none had existed fifteen years before. To a considerable extent, the political and economic position of black women between 1945 and 1955 reflected their migration patterns, and more specifically their continued movement out of the cotton fields and into southern, and especially northern, cities. (Although black migration levels remained high in the immediate postwar years, by 1950, 68 percent of African Americans still lived in the South; 28 percent lived in the North and 4 percent in the West.) The migrants tended to be young (a majority were under twenty-nine) and male (107 men for every 100 women)—facts that would later help to shape the demographic profile of the civil rights movement. As whites dispersed to the suburbs, black people became even more concentrated in the cities, until by 1960 blacks as a group were urbanized to a greater degree than whites.[52]

Black families that remained in the rural South witnessed a transformation of the region's agricultural system but derived few tangible benefits from it. The introduction of new kinds of farm machinery in the 1940s, especially the mechanical cotton-picker, rendered the sharecropping system obsolete. As a result tenants were converted to hired hands at a rapid rate after the war, until 1954, when additional technological innovations lessened the need even for cheap, sporadic labor. Hence the most striking change in patterns of black women's work during the century after slavery resulted from contraction in the agricultural sector of the economy. On the eve of the one-hundredth anniversary of the Emancipation Proclamation, fewer than 10 percent of all black women made their living from the soil.[53]

Despite these changes in the southern landscape, rural black women in the 1940s and early 1950s lived in a world that their slave grandmothers would have recognized in its broad outlines. Sharecroppers' cabins, once scattered around plantations, disappeared in the wake of tractor exhaust, as landowners regrouped dwellings in a central location—usually on the edge of a road, so that they could more efficiently gather up their hands and truck them to the fields. Pockets of peonage dotted the region, now controlled by large national corporations rather than enterprising local companies. Under such exploitative working conditions, kin ties retained their social significance. Recalling her childhood in Georgia, a Newark, New Jersey, woman proudly told an interviewer that after her father had a stroke that left him incapacitated in 1951, family members kept him with them at all times, until his death three years later: "When we worked, we carried him to work. Many times when we picking cotton, carry him in the truck, carry the food and everything, keep him in the shade." With its enduring forms of oppression and its long tradition of household and community solidarity, the rural black South stood on the brink of revolt in the early 1950s.[54]

Five years after the war, southern black men made on average half as much as southern white men, and that figure declined to 46 percent by 1959. In the North the ratio remained about the same, though absolute annual wages were $300 to $500 higher. In Detroit and other manufacturing cities, black men early felt the effects of automation and other forms of labor-saving machinery designed to eliminate unskilled and manual laborers from as-sembly lines once and for all. Nationally, women workers as a whole received less than two-thirds the pay of their male counterparts, but black women took home yearly paychecks amounting to less than half of white women's, indicating that the postwar economic boom had not altered the unequal pay scale inherent in a labor force segregated by skin color or gender. In 1950 the average weekly pay of black women was $13; although inflation guaran-teed them higher hourly wages than they had received in the 1930s, their marginal status as workers continued to deprive them of steady gainful employment throughout the year.[55]

In the absence of outside intervention in the marketplace—whether through govern-ment action or union pressure—these unequal pay rates and employment opportunities were bound to persist. Employers found that they could gradually decrease the number of unskilled factory jobs and that they could count on white women to take lower-level white-collar jobs at relatively low pay. In other words, they had few economic incentives to hire black women. Black groups and the CIO had urged President Truman to enact a perma-nent FEPC into law, and he expressed support for the idea in 1945, but did nothing to en-sure its implementation. However, in late 1946 he established a President's Committee on Civil Rights, which one year later (with the input of Pauli Murray) produced *To Secure These Rights,* a scathing report on discrimination. Soon after, Truman desegregated the federal workforce (Executive Order 9980) and the armed services (Executive Order 9981). These moves prompted the defection of the southern conservative wing of the Democratic Party in 1948, into the Dixiecrats, or States Rights' Democratic Party, under the leadership of South Carolina senator Strom Thurmond.[56]

Truman's executive orders left intact the segregation of public housing, public educa-tion, and private employment. Unchecked by the federal government, the dynamics of dis-crimination that originated in the era of the Great Migration had taken a devastating toll on the majority of black northerners by 1950. For example, the relatively favorable educational position of blacks compared to "New Immigrants" in the second decade of the twentieth century had largely eroded thirty years later. In the nation's largest cities, black male unem-ployment rates were two to three times higher than those of foreign-born whites. Black women were likely to suffer joblessness at a rate three to four times greater than foreign-born white women in Chicago, Cleveland, Detroit, New York, and Philadelphia. Black wives with husbands present continued to work in higher proportions than their white counterparts (30.2 percent versus 19.6 percent). Black female labor force participation re-mained steady from 1940 to 1950 (about 37 percent), while that of white women edged up-ward from 24.5 percent to 28.4 percent in the course of the decade. These figures reflected the expansion of job opportunities for white women. Almost half of all black women re-mained in private household employment, which was one of the most "female" of occupa-tions; the prestige of a job was directly related to the percentage of men in it.[57]

Among African Americans, mortality rates were always higher in the city than in the countryside; deteriorating housing conditions in northern ghettos certainly helped to ac-count for the prevalence of disease and assorted health problems. During and after the war, hundreds of thousands of black migrants annually swelled northern cities, and white neighborhoods used all the means at their disposal—from restrictive covenants to dynamite—to keep the newcomers and long-term black residents confined within inflexible boundaries. The result was the emergence of a postwar ghetto in cities like Chicago. There "kitchenette" apartments proliferated as the proportion of nonwhites living in overcrowded housing increased (24 percent in 1950) and the proportion of whites actually declined. Cramped living quarters heightened the possibility of fires, made adequate means of garbage disposal nearly impossible, and bred rats. The rodents, "big enough to ride on," according to one black woman, at times invaded apartments in groups—"enough for a ball game," according to another—and attacked children. Less than 30 percent of project residents had a toilet in their apartments; they used communal bathrooms in the hallways. Yet the families living in these apartments were not necessarily bereft of all resources; at midcentury, six out of ten residents of Chicago public housing projects were gainfully employed. Nevertheless, "slum-clearance" projects further destabilized Chicago black families; fully ten thousand of the families affected by such programs were African American, the majority of which could not qualify for public housing.[58]

Throughout the years from 1945 to 1955, black women bore proportionately more children than white women and more often had to care for them without the support of a spouse. After reaching a low point in 1935, the fertility rate of both black and white women began a steep rise, peaking in 1957. In 1950 black fertility rates were 33 percent higher than those of whites. That year 25.3 percent of all black wives were either separated, divorced, or widowed, compared to 10 percent of all white women who had ever been married. About equal proportions of these previously married women of both races—four out of ten—were heads of households that included children. The fact that the separation rate for black women was four times as high as for white women (16 versus 4 percent) bore a direct relationship to the persistently high rates of black male unemployment and chronic underemployment throughout the postwar years.[59]

Black female household heads existed on the fringes of the much-vaunted "consumer society" of the 1950s, and they were held accountable for their own poverty and for the effects of poverty on their families. As middle-class white society prospered, single black mothers came to represent a pathological ghetto culture that white politicians and policymakers condemned in no uncertain terms. Social workers and other professionals argued that white unwed mothers suffered from psychological problems; in contrast, their black counterparts, so the argument went, reflected the social deviance of black families and black communities. Individual states institutionalized prevailing prejudices against so-called black "welfare chiselers" in their Aid to Dependent Children programs (after 1950 referred to as Aid to Families with Dependent Children [AFDC]). Specifically, several southern states authorized caseworkers to deny benefits to any woman who had a man in her home or who herself appeared "employable." Theoretically, this rule rendered all but ill and handicapped black mothers ineligible for aid, especially during harvest season in rural areas. Indeed, the "employable mother" provision had originated in Louisiana in order to deny assistance to families headed by women capable of fieldwork. Georgia passed its own version in 1952, mandating that all welfare recipients accept "suitable" employment regardless of the level of compensation. Other measures discriminated against the children of unwed mothers and others who lived in what white officials-considered "unsuitable" homes, and their proponents expressed concern specifically about the black population. These rules helped to keep AFDC rolls in the South relatively stable, though the number of recipients in the country as a whole increased dramatically after 1945. Nevertheless, even AFDC households in the relatively "generous" northeastern states subsisted on monthly payments considerably below the poverty line.[60]

To many white Americans obsessed with the threat of communism in the postwar period, government aid to the poor smacked of socialism, and efforts to overturn the caste system portended the country's imminent takeover by foreign agents. Labor unionists were not immune to this hysteria, and in the late 1940s and early 1950s, the AFL and CIO both scrambled to prove their patriotism by disassociating themselves from Communists and fellow travelers. In the minds of many established labor leaders, organizing black and white workers together had a distinctly "Red" taint to it.[61]

Labor's anticommunist impulses worked at cross-purposes with its renewed organizing drives in basic industries and throughout the South (the "Operation Dixie" campaigns). Restricted by a "no-strike" pledge during the war, the unions moved soon after VJ Day to consolidate their gains over the last decade and safeguard their members' purchasing power against inflation; in 1946 over one million workers were on strike sometime during the year. Black employees shared the determination of their white coworkers in these struggles, but they were expected to gratefully embrace "second-class membership" in many unions. Their demands for increased representation among the union leadership at the local and national levels, and for the fair implementation of union promotion and job security policies, went unheeded in all but a few progressive organizations. Thus black workers were caught between the outward militance of white unionists and the discriminatory policies they supported.[62]

In 1949 the CIO expelled eleven of its unions whose leaders were suspected of being Communists or Communist sympathizers. As a group, these unions had among the best records as advocates for blacks and, in some cases, for black women in particular. A case in point was the Food, Tobacco, Agricultural, and Allied Workers Union (FTA). One of its affiliates, the United Tobacco Workers, became the bargaining agent for the victorious tobacco workers in Winston-Salem, North Carolina (Local 22), after their strike in 1943. The wages of these workers, confined to the most disagreeable in the tobacco industry, did not keep pace with the rising cost of living, and in 1947 they readied themselves for another strike. The desperate need of black mothers to feed their children translated into union solidarity. For example, Estelle Flowers, a single parent with four children, detailed her regular expenses: "My six months old baby has to have milk—one can of evaporated milk—15 cents a can a day. It takes $2 a week for coal and that doesn't keep the home warm." With a wage increase she planned to "buy the clothes the children need—more food and I could give more to the church." In May 1947 Flowers and over ten thousand of her white and black coworkers won their fight for higher pay and shorter hours after a thirty-nine-day strike. By this time Moranda Smith, who played a prominent part in the 1943 struggle, had become widely known as a particularly "determined and militant" leader and later went on to serve as southern regional director of the FTA. As a result, she occupied the highest position any black woman had held to that time in the American labor movement.[63]

CIO leaders took alarm at a controversy surrounding Local 22; the famous black singer and leftist Paul Robeson had appeared at a rally during the strike, and the House Un-American Activities Committee launched an investigation of the "Communist-dominated union." Consequently the CIO's Executive Council decided to sponsor a competitor to Local 22 (the United Transport Service Employees), and the ensuing battle for loyalties left the FTA stripped of its status as bargaining agent for the workers. The AFL also tried to capitalize on the situation, though its Tobacco Workers International Union, with a long history of segregated locals, found no favor with black employees like Luanna Cooper. She noted, "They're trying to have jimcrow unions. But I'm telling you jimcrow unions aren't good. They wanted me to join. I told them: 'I get jimcrow free. I won't pay for that.'"[64]

The history of Local 22 revealed the potentially decisive—and divisive—role that unions could play in the black struggle for jobs and civil rights. Moranda Smith addressed the national convention of the CIO in 1947 and condemned antiunion legislation currently under consideration in the U.S. Congress that was later passed in the form of the Labor-Management Relations Act of 1947. Known as the Taft-Hartley, the act severely restricted the ability of unions to organize workers and protest unfair employer practices. "I live where men are lynched, and the people that lynch them are still free," Smith told the delegates. The Ku Klux Klan terrorized blacks who tried to join a union as well as those who tried to vote; economic exploitation and political oppression were two sides of the same coin. Smith urged the CIO to take an unequivocal stand in favor of black civil rights: "When the civil liberties of Negroes in the South are interfered with [and] you do nothing about it, I say to you you are untrue to the traditions of America. . . . We will call on you again, and we ask you not to fail us." But it was leaders like Moranda Smith and Luanna Cooper, not the CIO, who would take credit for the registration of eight thousand new voters in Winston-Salem and the election of the first black alderman in the twentieth-century South.[65]

Black women workers in the North also had to contend with red-baiting and with the less than wholehearted support of union officials. Florence Rice, a New York garment worker, joined the ILGWU soon after the end of the war. After complaining to a shop steward that her work assignment speed-up violated union guidelines, she learned the hard way that "the union wasn't for us blacks, that's one of the things you recognize." ILGWU Local 125 had no blacks in leadership positions and white union members passively—and at times aggressively—accepted wage scales and hiring policies biased against blacks. Rice's protests earned her the reputation of "a troublemaker," and "naturally I was known as a Communist," she said later. "That was a way of putting you down." Intense competition among black, Puerto Rican, and Italian women—many of the black women wives who felt "their first duty is to their family"—prevented them from risking their jobs to reform union policies. Still, Florence Rice remained committed to the ideal represented by an egalitarian labor organization: "I see hopes for unions as long as they practice true democracy. The fact is, the democracy that they talk about has never been practiced in this country in anything."[66]

Not every black woman worker saw her own union as "running [her] life," proof that "whites were in control of black people and we could never be able to do anything." The United Packinghouse Workers of America (UPWA, CIO) not only resisted anticommunist pressure from international headquarters but remained in the forefront of unions "fighting racial discrimination in and out of the plant," according to Bessie Coleman, member of Chicago's Local 28. Born in Mississippi, Coleman had moved to Chicago with her family and had almost finished high school when she had to drop out and work first as a maid and then as a clerk. During the war, she became active in the UPWA, impressed with its enlightened policies. Her coworkers elected her first steward in her department and then recording secretary of the local. During a major strike of packinghouse workers in 1946, Coleman served as a counselor for families in need of emergency aid and referred them to various service agencies in the city. Of her responsibilities in the area of social welfare, she said, "No other job that I do gives me as much satisfaction."[67]

Disillusioned by Taft-Hartley and the AFL's and CIO's complacency on "racial" issues, black labor leaders formed their own group in 1951, the National Negro Labor Council (NNLC); one member, Coleman Young (who would serve as mayor of Detroit from 1974 to 1993), termed the new group a modern variation of the "leftist labor movement . . . smaller, peskier, and more focused than ever." Women played a critical role in the formation and leadership of the NNLC; over one-third of the delegates to the council's initial conference were women, and Octavia Hawkins, a Chicago garment worker and member of the Amalgamated Clothing Workers, served as its first treasurer. Along with other organizers, she helped to open up positions for black women in St. Louis, Newark, Los Angeles, and Chicago (in this last city a year-long consumer boycott cracked the clerical-sales barrier in the Sears, Roebuck Company for the first time). As part of its own Operation Dixie, the NNLC targeted southern factory jobs for black women and men and helped sponsor a strike among Louisiana sugar workers in 1953. Nevertheless, the council, created at least partly in response to CIO red-baiting, eventually fell victim itself to accusations of Communist influence. Threatened with the prospect of being listed as a "Communist-front organization" by a federal investigative agency in 1956, the NNLC decided to forego a costly defense and disbanded. Meanwhile, black leaders remained justifiably skeptical of the recent AFL-CIO merger, a development that promised little in the way of genuine change for black workers.[68]

In the NNLC, black women and men came together to advance their collective interests in the face of institutionalized white intransigence. As individuals and as members of other black pressure groups, black women helped to sow the seeds for the national protest movement soon to come. During World War II, Ella Baker, the NAACP field secretary, contributed to the establishment of an NAACP youth group in Greensboro, North Carolina, the scene of the first student sit-ins in 1960, while NAACP staff member Ruby Hurley prepared the way for other chapters in parts of the Deep South. At midcentury, eighty-seven-year-old Mary Church Terrell capped a six-decades-long fight against injustice when she challenged discrimination in the restaurants of the nation's capital. Her attempt to buy a bowl of soup at the Thompson Restaurant led to a Supreme Court decision three years later that upheld Washington's previously unenforced antidiscrimination laws. The Atlanta voter registration drive of 1946 that added the names of eighteen thousand new voters to the city's registration lists, the first freedom ride sponsored by CORE in 1947 (called the Journey of Reconciliation)—these were efforts that called upon the energies and courage of women as well as men.[69]

By 1950 civil rights leaders realized that the Supreme Court had the potential to be a key ally. In *Smith v. Allwright* (1944), the Court declared the all-white primary unconstitutional. As a result in the South, black veterans in record numbers attempted to vote, but many encountered blatant resistance on the part of registrars and poll watchers; moreover, participation in the Democratic primary was often an exercise in futility, since many white political candidates remained outspoken in their prejudices and contemptuous of the interests of blacks in general. Nevertheless, the Supreme Court held out hope that the forces of justice could overcome the tyranny of a white majority throughout the country. By the 1940s and early 1950s, the court had already laid the groundwork for the historic *Brown v. The Board of Education* decision (1954) outlawing segregated public schooling. The successful outcome of these lawsuits had depended upon the strength of black community institutions—the NAACP, CORE, all-black colleges, churches, and women's clubs—that were themselves products of the repressive forces they sought to challenge.[70]

The prospect of school integration included a number of different scenarios, not all of which lived up to the promise of equal treatment. In the North, the strategy of integrating local schools proved problematic in urban areas where neighborhoods remained hypersegregated. Soon after the war, the Milwaukee school board hired Ruby Young, an experienced teacher with a master's degree from Teachers College of Columbia University. The board limited her assignments to black schools, as they did for all applicants of her skin color. Since Young was married, she did not qualify for full-time employment, but only substitute work. Moreover, more often than not, integration also meant the firing of black teachers and the installation of whites in predominantly black classrooms. Carolyn Reed, a New York City domestic, told an interviewer in the 1970s that she had grown up in a segregated neighborhood, but that the "teachers then . . . were marvelous—black teachers that were really interested in helping children." The lesson taught by one English instructor in particular had stood out in her mind over the years: "You are as good as anyone—you're just as good as anyone, but you're not better than anyone." Whether or not Carolyn Reed would have learned the same lesson from a white teacher in the early 1950s is of course open to question. Over the generations, black teachers had served as de facto activists in their own communities; now school integration, administered by white board members, threatened to deprive these teachers of both their livelihoods and their influence. In workplaces such as the classroom, "equality" came at a price.[71]

AN EBONY ALTERNATIVE TO THE WHITE FEMININE MYSTIQUE

In her book *The Feminine Mystique* (1963) about "this nameless aching dissatisfaction" suffered by so many American wives in the fifteen years after the war, Betty Friedan exposed the myth of the "happy housewife." The notion that women could and should derive self-fulfillment exclusively from child-rearing and homemaking permeated postwar popular culture and induced guilt and anxiety in those women who deviated from the stereotype. Friedan found that women's magazines, in particular, portrayed their readers as "brainless, fluffy kittens," unable to comprehend the complexities of international politics, interested only in turning yesterday's leftovers into tonight's gourmet dinner. In keeping with this mid-twentieth-century version of the Victorian Cult of True Womanhood, *Ladies' Home Journal, McCall's,* and other publications "printed virtually no articles except those that serviced women as housewives, or described women as housewives, or permitted a purely feminine identification." However, if the nineteenth-century women who failed to live up to the ideal were condemned as sinful, career women and childless wives in the mid-1950s were diagnosed as suffering from personality disorders. Friedan quoted one woman's magazine editor as saying, "If we get an article about a woman who does anything adventurous, out of the way, something by herself, you know, we figure she must be terribly aggressive, neurotic." Whether well-to-do and restless, or impoverished and pregnant, white women who defied middle-class norms apparently exhibited the symptoms of psychological distress.[72]

Friedan's analysis focused on the unarticulated longings of upper-middle-class white women who did not work; well educated, financially secure, but desperately unhappy, they needed reassurance that, in Friedan's words, "a baked potato is not as big as the world, and vacuuming the living-room floor—with or without makeup—is not work that takes enough thought or energy to challenge any woman's full capacity." Another group of women also felt victimized by the "feminine mystique" during this period—white middle- and working-class women who bore baby-boom children but also worked outside the home. These wage-earning housewives were keenly aware of the contradiction between the pervasive image of serene motherhood on the one hand and their exhausting efforts to juggle PTA bake sales with the demands of gainful employment on the other.[73]

Black women of course had a long history of combining paid labor with domestic obligations. In 1950 one-third of all black wives were in the labor force compared to one-quarter of all married women in the general population. A major study of the period 1940 to 1960 concluded that black mothers of school-aged children were more likely to work than their white counterparts, though part-time positions in the declining field of domestic service inhibited growth in their rates of labor-force participation. To most black women regardless of class, work seemed to form an integral part of the female role; the chances were good that their friends and close relatives all worked at least part of their adult lives, even if they did not. A survey of black women college students in the 1950s indicated that about half of the members of this relatively privileged group planned to work after graduation. Seventy percent of them had mothers who were wage earners, though the daughters hoped to avoid the menial occupations in which these older women were concentrated.[74]

Economic hardship compelled black wives and mothers to seek employment outside the home and compounded their domestic chores, since for the most part they lacked modern household conveniences and labor-saving gadgets. Yet their status as wage earners commanded great respect within the black community. The way that the nation's largest-circulation black magazine, *Ebony,* treated the issue of women's work provides a useful measure of this respect. Though *Ebony* indulged in its own brand of image-making and its portrayal of women hardly reflected their actual socioeconomic status, this monthly publication consistently presented working wives and mothers in a positive, and frequently positively heroic, light. Black working women had to contend with a myriad of problems, but the gnawing fear that they were neurotic was probably not one of them.

Founded in 1945 by John H. Johnson, a black Chicagoan in the insurance business, *Ebony* soon became widely recognized as "an Afro-American version of *Life* magazine." By the early 1950s, it claimed a monthly circulation of 500,000 and attracted more black readers than any other black or white periodical. In terms of content, the analogy with *Life* was not wholly accurate, for while it would have been difficult to identify a *Life* editorial policy of any substance, *Ebony* served as a militant advocate of black civil rights. Along with articles on sports, cinema, famous people, and human interest themes, the publication regularly addressed major political issues in a forthright, uncompromising way. Features ranged from South African apartheid and Caribbean poverty to the displacement of southern farmworkers, discrimination against blacks in labor unions, the plight of black veterans, and health problems affecting ghetto residents. Its stance can best be described as aggressively integrationist, similar to that of the NAACP. (In the words of a 1946 headline, that association remained "No. 1 Champion of Full Negro Freedom.") The magazine's editors scorned Roosevelt's "spineless and inept" political heirs for their failure to enact bold FEPC, antilynching, and public housing legislation. Filled with both optimism and rage at the end of the war, *Ebony* proclaimed that "Uncle Tom and Aunt Jemima are headed for oblivion as surely as Jim Crow," and drew attention to black and white Americans who labored on behalf of equality and against apathy and despair.[75]

In the decade after the war, the magazine approached the subject of black women and their work from several different perspectives. (Here it is appropriate to mention that its editorial board was composed entirely of men.) Although the lavish use of photographs and variety of news stories made it primarily a general-interest magazine, it is clear that the editors assumed that women constituted a significant, and probably even a majority, of their readership. The bulk of the publication's considerable advertising space was devoted to food products, beauty aids, and clothing. Regular features like "Fashion Fair" ("What's New in Spring Hats") and "Date With a Dish" ("How to Glorify the Apple") were similar to those in white women's magazines. In addition, issues of *Ebony* often contained stories listed under the headings of Marriage ("What Kind of Woman Should Ministers Marry?") and Family ("800,000 Negro Girls Will Never Go to the Altar," an analysis of geographical variations in the sex ratio).[76]

At first glance, *Ebony's* literary content and visual images appear contradictory in terms of women's issues. Photos of scantily clad bathing beauties frequently graced the cover, and some stories were obviously sensational. Yet in its numerous profiles of black women leaders, female entertainers who defied prejudiced whites, and ordinary women who attained professional success against all odds, *Ebony* stressed the intelligence and diverse accomplishments of black women. The July 1949 issue included an article entitled "Women Leaders: Their Century-Long Pilgrimage for Emancipation of Their Sex and Their Race is a Historic Battle," a moving account of the "courage, persistence and pioneering" of women from the slave Harriet Tubman to contemporary businesswomen, government officials, lawyers, and NAACP activists. Juxtaposed to this paean to black womanhood was a piece illustrated with the photo of a bobby soxer—"How to do the Bop Hop."[77]

Ebony had no single editorial policy on women's issues. However, one 1947 editorial entitled "Goodbye Mammy, Hello Mom" offered a twist on the postwar mainstream idea that Rosie the Riveter should retreat into the home. The writer pointed out that historically black women, whether enslaved or waged war workers, had never had the opportunity to devote their full attention to family life. But now, for the first time "since 1619," wives and mothers were enjoying the benefits derived from their husband's high wages: "Just ask Junior, who's been getting his bread and butter sandwiches regularly after school and [now] finding that rip in his blue jeans mended when he goes out to play." At last black mothers' domestic skills were being put to their proper use: "The cooking over which the 'white folks' used to go into ecstasies is now reserved for her own family and they really appreciate it."[78]

Ebony's articles about women often focused on those who had managed to break into not only predominantly white, but also predominantly male, occupations: "In every field, every occupation, individual Negro women excel." The magazine proudly featured black woman "firsts"—federal judge Jane M. Bolin; Dr. Helen O. Dickens, member of a professional society for surgeons; Jean Harris, the first black student to graduate from a medical school in Virginia; Mary Jones King, a bank manager. In its major stories, as well as the monthly "Speaking of People" column, the magazine regularly profiled "Lady" professionals and skilled workers, including dentists, detectives, justices of the peace, shoemakers, attorneys general, pharmacists, disc jockeys, auto mechanics, real estate agents, fingerprint technicians, professors of medicine, magazine editors, policewomen, car sellers, mechanical engineers, and photographers. Other articles dealt with women artists—sculptors, fashion designers, and novelists; as well as successful entrepreneurs—wholesale dealers, florists, and gemologists; and activists and administrators—labor organizers and Red Cross workers.[79]

The magazine offered its wholehearted endorsement of husbands and wives who followed careers and at the same time enjoyed a happy home life together. A story entitled "Medical Family: Two Doctor Daughters Carry on Tradition of Dr. Louis T. Wright" dealt with Jane and Barbara Wright, both graduates of a Seven-Sister college and medical school, both married to lawyers, and both able to attend to "the needs of their husbands and children at home." "Husband Wife Teams" examined the marriages of prominent dual-career couples, including psychologists Kenneth and Mamie Clark, and other lawyers, academics, business leaders, physicians, and journalists. The article concluded that "each couple is daily proving joint interests and twin careers to be both profitable and stimulating."[80]

Ebony editors were not interested in mirroring black women's occupational patterns in their magazine. To the contrary, their purpose was to counter the image of black women as domestic drudges and to emphasize their potential for work that was better paying and more challenging and prestigious. Indeed, maids were featured only when their employers were persons of note and their daily routines filled with glamour and excitement. Lilian Moseley told her "Secrets of a Movie Maid" in the November 1949 issue and gave readers an inside look at her "warm relationship" with film stars Loretta Young and Gene Kelly. The Roosevelt family maid, Elizabeth McDuffie, wrote an account of life in the White House in her April 1952 story, "FDR Was My Boss."[81]

The entertainment industry was a popular *Ebony* theme. In swank New York nightclubs and in glittering Hollywood, black women achieved fame and wealth. Actresses, singers, and dancers received journalistic attention far in excess of their actual numbers, and the magazine's treatment of this group suggested in especially dramatic terms the bittersweet meaning of success in white America. On one level, stories about these women resembled those published about white performers in white women's magazines during the same period; although photographs conveyed the glamour of show business, texts frequently emphasized performers' homemaking abilities. For example, Hazel Scott, nightclub singer and bride of Congressman Adam Clayton Powell Jr., was "a typical housewife. She says she always seems to use red thread for black hose." A story on Marian Anderson stressed the peace she found in her new home, an estate in Connecticut, alone with her husband and away from adoring concertgoers. Lena Horne liked "to think of herself as a working mother—even though her income . . . sometimes hits the $10,000 a week mark."[82]

Stories about Lena Horne in particular reveal the appeal of female performers who were outspoken in their support of civil rights. In the story just cited, Horne went on to observe that "this may be the first generation in the history of our race where Negro families will have something to leave to their children." Active in liberal politics (she campaigned for Henry Wallace and the Progressive Party in 1948), openly contemptuous of prejudice in all its forms, and widely admired for her singing ability, Horne, according to *Ebony*, embodied female beauty and set a high standard for all women regardless of their color. *Ebony* readers had an opportunity to learn not only about her newest gorgeous ball gown, but also about her ability to handle with dignity the snubs of a white waitress in an Alabama restaurant, and her rejection of lucrative acting roles that she considered demeaning to blacks.[83]

Other entertainers told stories that ordinary black women and men could understand and appreciate. The actresses Butterfly McQueen, Hattie McDaniel, and Ethel Waters faced the dilemma of accepting parts as domestic servants in movies or not working at all. Pearl Bailey refused to take "dialect" roles in films. (*Ebony* condemned the trend in the film industry apparent after the war: "Eight New Hollywood Films Backtrack to Hack Racial Stereotypes Casting Negro Actors as Usual Maids and Menials.") Juanita Hall and Joyce Bryant, both singers, also recounted their experiences "with racial bias in the entertainment world" and how they defied it. One of the most dramatic accounts involved Josephine Baker, who in 1951 returned to perform in her native country after a self-imposed exile in France. Baker insisted that her contract with a Miami nightclub include a "nondiscrimination clause" stipulating that the club would admit black patrons during her performances. (The club's owner had to check with his lawyer to make sure that such a clause would not violate Florida law.) This daughter of a St. Louis washerwoman thus made a triumphant entry into the United States, taking one more step, in her words, in "the Negro's march to freedom."[84]

Obviously not all black female entertainers were as outspoken as pianist Dorothy Donegan—in 1946 a journalist who interviewed her reported that her "political thinking is on the left, [and she] believes there should be radical reforms in America"—but *Ebony* chose to spotlight those who were. Nightclub, stage, movie, and concert stars had attained a high degree of public visibility among whites as well as blacks, and they were in a position to openly discuss and act upon issues of great significance to all black Americans. Therefore, *Ebony*, while devoting due attention to the glamorous and unconventional lifestyles of these women, also portrayed them as particularly committed and effective political activists.[85]

With its emphasis on professional and well-paid women workers, and on leaders in the mainstream of American politics (educator and government official Mary McLeod Bethune, Democratic politician Jeanetta Welch Brown, United Nations delegate Edith Sampson, for example), *Ebony* reflected rather traditional middle-class attitudes toward the nature of personal accomplishment. The magazine rarely featured women outside the realm of established black or white institutions; the articles on faith healers Vera Boykin and Lucy Smith were highly unusual. Still, though it did not reflect the day-to-day reality of black working women in postwar America, it did look to the future, when white and black women and black men could aspire to jobs that suited their talents and sensibilities. In this sense, it differed radically from its white counterparts, which were intent on promoting a unidimensional image of women's work. Indeed, *Ebony* anticipated the shift in the white press in the 1970s and 1980s, when the stereotype of the "superwoman"—the highly paid professional woman who was also a perfect wife and mother—became popular. This image was (and is) an unrealistic goal for the vast majority of women, but for black Americans at the time, it conveyed a message laden with political significance—that civil rights and good jobs went together, and that black women were equally entitled to both.[86]

The rights of white women and black women and men had always been intimately connected, from the time that abolitionists had inspired suffragists in the early nineteenth century. In the 1960s, with the women's liberation movement following so closely on the heels of civil rights demonstrations, this connection became manifest once again. Blacks and white women had gained temporary access to better jobs and pay during the war, and afterward they were not about to acquiesce in age-old forms of subordination. A focus on women of the two groups made the underlying impulses for radical change in both movements seem even more strikingly similar; white wives' labor force participation steadily increased in the postwar period, introducing greater numbers of them to specific inequities that had plagued black women for years—jobs and wages inferior to those of white men, the double duty of wage and housework. Yet the sexism encountered by white women during these years differed qualitatively from the prejudice that black women had endured for centuries. Black wives and mothers remained disfranchised and terrorized in the South, confined to northern inner-city ghettos, and systematically excluded from white women's jobs.[87]

Later some observers would accuse middle-class white women of seeking to advance their own, relatively petty, self-interests at the expense of bloodied black protesters. That charge was somewhat misleading, for it implied that racial and gender ideologies were unrelated forces, readily distinguishable from one another and unrelated to class factors in shaping patterns of oppression. Beginning in 1955, the revolutions and reactions of the next thirty years would reveal that civil rights depended not only on legal equality, but also on economic opportunity, as the plight of poor black women became ever more distinct from that of their more well-to-do sisters regardless of skin color.

EIGHT

THE STRUGGLE CONFIRMED AND TRANSFORMED, 1955–1980

IN HER 1981 prose-poem hymn to black women of the South entitled "My Black Mothers and Sisters, or on Beginning a Cultural Autobiography," Bernice Johnson Reagon recounted their centuries-long, everyday work to "deliver the goods for the survival" of all black people. A veteran of the earliest student demonstrations in the 1960s civil rights movement, Reagon noted in particular the remarkable story of Fannie Lou Hamer, a plantation worker who emerged as one of the preeminent leaders of the struggle. Of Hamer's initial decision to challenge the white people and procedures that kept Mississippi ballot boxes locked to blacks for so many years, Reagon wrote that it was not a matter of "one day suddenly going to register and vote." Rather, Hamer "was changing jobs to go on carrying out her real work." On one level, then, the movement represented a "continuance" in the history of black working women, but on another level it marked the beginning of a new era: "What is revolutionary about registering to vote in Mississippi in the sixties is you know you're going to get killed."[1]

By the mid-1950s, the time was ripe for southern black men and women to launch an all-out assault on American apartheid, and their push for full equality shook the national two-party system to its core. Liberal Republicans were hopeful they could recapture the descendants of former slaves who hailed Abraham Lincoln as "the Great Emancipator," but in just a few years conservative Republicans would begin eyeing southern white Democrats disillusioned with the multiple upheavals associated with inner-city and countercultural rebellions. Meanwhile, northern Democrats confronted the dilemma of keeping ghetto residents within the same fold as lily-white Southerners. The large-scale mechanization of southern agriculture had eliminated the historic need for a large, subservient, rural black workforce within the regional economy, thus loosening the grip of the white supremacist imperative. In southern towns and cities, business groups such as the Chamber of Commerce sought to moderate the actions and rhetoric of die-hard segregationists in an effort to lure federal investment and northern businesses to the South. Nevertheless, the renewed drive for civil rights originated with black people themselves; bolstered by recent Supreme Court decisions, a new class of well-educated and economically independent professionals, together with college students, farm laborers, and urban workers, engaged in a wide variety of protests throughout the South. Their tactics of peaceful, mass direct action, in contrast to the fury these acts provoked among white Southerners, created nationally broadcast images that shocked many whites in the North, where the individual and institutional forces of discrimination were no less real but considerably more elusive. Various civil rights groups adhered to an overall program that was deceptively simple: to build upon the existing resources of southern black communities and coordinate, in the words of Ella Baker, "a very simple reaction" to injustice.[2]

At the same time, black neighborhoods in the North escalated their attempts to combat the forces that shaped that region's variation on the "urban plantation"—poor housing, de facto residential segregation, workplace discrimination, and police brutality. Economic transformations in the North devastated black households, rendering even more urgent black people's demands for political and economic rights. During the 1950s, whole inner-city neighborhoods went from nearly all white to nearly all black, as white families continued their move to new subdivisions in leafy suburbs. Many businesses abandoned the city as well, seeking educated workforces and cheap land for expansive office parks. Large manufacturers hastened the process of technological innovation, leading to layoffs for black men and women who lacked the seniority rights that unions guaranteed to longer-term white employees. As a result of all these developments, many impoverished black women found themselves dependent on Aid to Families with Dependent Children; these "welfare" recipients remained at the mercy of government administrators who decided whether or not clients could qualify for aid in the form of cash or food stamps, and how clients could or could not spend the little money they had. In cities across the country, black women stepped up agitation for their rights, casting those rights broadly to reflect their own interests as mothers, workers, neighbors, consumers, citizens. Clearly, patterns of activism in the North and South reflected long-standing trends among black women who had for generations pressed for change within workplaces, housing projects, and local communities. At the same time, that activism was garnering headlines and the attention of a mass audience as well as political leaders at the highest echelons of government. When, in 1955, Chicago's Mamie Bradley Till insisted on an open coffin for the mutilated body of her son Emmett, murdered by two white men in Mississippi—so that "the whole world can see"—she ignited a political firestorm and revealed the explosive power of a mother's love, and rage, on a national stage.[3]

Black people's protests—from boycotts to sit-ins and freedom rides—culminated in the Civil Rights Acts of 1964 and 1965, legislation designed to integrate the paid workplace and to protect the voting rights of Americans regardless of the color of their skin or the place where they lived. Black women benefited from these measures in a number of immediate ways. As employees, they posted striking gains in retail sales, clerical work, and certain kinds of factory labor. The proportion of southern black women who had never cast a vote in an election dropped from 87 percent in 1952 to 28 percent a quarter of a century later.

Among black and white men and women, they as a group felt the most alienated from main-stream American life because of their highly disadvantaged position. Yet they voted in numbers proportionately larger than either black men or white women, and constituted a higher percentage of all black elected officials compared to white women within their own group. Two political scientists, Sandra Baxter and Marjorie Lansing, concluded that "black women have come to see themselves as a special interest group fighting to overcome the twin barriers of racial and sexual discrimination," and these women maintained a relatively intense political commitment despite their estrangement from "the system" in general.[4]

Although enfranchisement and integration constituted the iconic goals of the civil rights movement, southern black people mobilized on a number of fronts. Indeed, it was difficult to neatly categorize the protests, which could range from calls to bring white rapists of black women to justice, to efforts to establish black-owned businesses. Moreover, the move-ment overall had profound implications for black women's work broadly defined. In many areas of the South, the century-long fight for good jobs at decent wages presaged and paved the way for the political campaigns that burst into the national consciousness in the 1950s; in this respect the grievances of ill-paid black women wage earners represented but a subset of persistent grievances among the black community in general over education, housing, and health care. As workers, women (such as Montgomery's domestic servants during the bus boycott there) led and participated in mass demonstrations that highlighted the inter-twining of political and economic oppression. Meanwhile, black women's historic, unwaged work within their own communities came to the fore, as they contributed in myriad ways—as cooks and caretakers no less than community organizers—to the advancement of the movement for all black people's full inclusion in American life.

During this period, the economic status of black wage-earning women diverged dra-matically along class lines. Antidiscrimination legislation had mixed results on their chances for new kinds of, and more, secure jobs. After 1964, affirmative action and equal opportunity programs enabled significant numbers of black women to enter the white woman's pink-collar ghetto for the first time in American history. A well-educated few—the "golden cohort" of college graduates—found their way into business and professional positions. In some industries, employers hired black women for the first time in an apparent effort to comply with new federal mandates, but then seized the opportunity to pay these new workers far less than their white counterparts. Yet many new good jobs remained out of reach of inner-city residents, and unskilled and uneducated workers of both genders felt the weight of a faltering economy descend upon them, as the need for a marginal work-force dissipated.[5]

In 1980 a variety of demographic and economic indicators revealed that poverty had been both ghettoized and feminized. One-third of all black households, 70 percent of them headed by women, fell below the poverty line (about 10 percent of white families were poor). One-half of all black children were living in homes without a father. Teenagers had a high proportion of the 55 percent of black babies born out of wedlock, and if as single mothers they decided to establish independent households, they joined a group of women who had more children to rear and only 40 percent of the financial resources compared to their black sisters in married-couple situations. As AFDC recipients, many of these single women were in effect wedded to a mean-spirited provider, and they chafed under the dependency enforced by what welfare-rights advocate Johnnie Tillmon labeled this "supersexist marriage." Over the years, the collective and personal hardships endured by these women receded further out of the reach of underfunded and piecemeal social welfare programs.[6]

The ideological basis of black protest changed during the 1960s and 1970s, a change that mirrored the various roles played by different social groups over time. The elderly "mama," her religious devotion laced with defiance, came to represent the movement that originated on southern soil, and she was joined by well-dressed, clean-cut college students in the early 1960s. By the middle of the decade, these activists had yielded to militant Black Power advocates, often young men from the ghetto who called upon their brothers and sisters to concentrate on building their own economic and political institutions and to cease their demeaning attempts to gain entry into the white world. The militants, determined to assert their manhood at all costs, urged black women to eschew positions of authority within private households as well as the wider black community. At least partially in response to this call for self-abnegation, black women's rights advocates began their ascendancy in the late 1960s and early 1970s. They pointed to the bruised knees and calloused hands of their foremothers—proof, they claimed, not of woman's inferiority nor of her "castrating" aggressiveness, but of a strength that defied the boundaries of gender. Black women of all ages and backgrounds would help to define the national politics of protest in the 1980s, when the plight of poor black women, the children they cared for, and the husbands they lost, revealed the stubborn legacy of slavery.

BLACK WOMEN IN THE CIVIL RIGHTS MOVEMENT, 1955–1965

The indignities encountered daily by Rosa Parks in the course of making a living were hardly unique to her situation as a southern black woman in the 1950s. Each day the Montgomery, Alabama, seamstress rode in the back of a bus to a downtown department store, where she labored in a hot, steamy room and altered clothing for white customers. But one day in December 1955, on her way home from work, this longtime local NAACP member and activist refused to yield her seat to a white passenger; later folks would say that Rosa Parks "sat down and the world turned around," for hers was a timely challenge to a historic injustice. Rosa Parks was both a work-weary woman and a member of a black community long dedicated to the fight against discrimination. The movement she came to symbolize sprang not fully formed out of post–World War II society, but rather represented the latest chapter in a struggle that had been ongoing for generations, a struggle that combined agitation for political rights with a broader push for decent jobs and housing.[7]

The history of the Montgomery Improvement Association (MIA)—a local group formed in early 1956 to coordinate black citizens' boycott of the city's buses—told a larger story about the nature of social change in mid-twentieth-century America. Like a traditional African American call-and-response song, the Montgomery movement harmoniously blended individual initiative and grassroots support, dynamic leadership and well-disciplined followers. The MIA provided the first opportunity for a brilliant young Baptist preacher named Martin Luther King Jr. to fuse old-time religion with a newfound hopefulness born of the 1954 Supreme Court decision that declared segregated public schools unconstitutional. The protest tactics endorsed by King had deep roots in black culture, but they also attracted wide admiration outside the black community. And the boycott tapped a wellspring of energy and commitment among Montgomery's ordinary black working women as well as among leaders such as Rosa Parks and Jo Ann Gibson Robinson, a founder of the MIA; in the future, as in the past, male leaders would ignore the dynamic potential of black women's activism at their own peril.[8]

Drawn to King's emphasis on love and nonviolence, female domestic and service workers refused to ride the Montgomery buses for 381 days and thereby threw white household arrangements into disarray. These women had long endured the humiliation of standing in the back of city buses while the "white" seats remained empty, of paying their fare and then walking to the back door to board the bus, of listening to the driver scream epithets at them and even physically abuse those who angered or defied him. Not all women had borne this treatment quietly. Just nine months before Parks refused to give up her seat to a white man, a fifteen-year-old named Claudette Colvin did the same; as she was dragged off the bus and into the police station, the teenager protested, "It's my constitutional right!" Ever attentive to the dynamics of public relations, though, local NAACP officials decided that Colvin, who had a well-known rebellious streak, would not put the best public face on this new phase of the movement. Instead these leaders valued Parks's high status within the black community, her participation in civil rights workshops conducted by the Highlander School in Tennessee, and her "respectability" in the eyes of whites.[9]

During the boycott, white women served as reluctant allies when they drove maids to work and back home again rather than watch their dirty dishes and laundry pile higher. The marches and mass meetings ended only with federal intervention in the form of a Supreme Court ruling that outlawed segregated buses; mass direct action could crack but not crumble the southern caste system. Yet the MIA sponsored a potent protest that conformed to the cultural values of southern black people, in large measure because it respected black women's roles as workers and church members.

Throughout the South, black women played a prominent part in the boycotts, mass demonstrations, acts of civil disobedience, and voter registration drives conducted by the Southern Christian Leadership Conference (SCLC), the Congress of Racial Equality, and the Student Nonviolent Coordinating Committee (SNCC) between 1955 and 1965. Middle-class black women in the North watched with horror as southern whites escalated their attacks; in 1963, the National Council of Negro Women sponsored an investigation, conducted by their own members, of police assaults of and brutality toward female demonstrators in Selma, Alabama. Regardless of where they lived or labored, black people could relate to a major theme of the movement, expressed by striking sanitation workers in Memphis in 1968: "I *AM* a Man," a rallying cry that expressed outrage over the hardships endured by these men, who wore white people's cast-off clothing and worked long hours under degrading and dangerous conditions. Indeed, that slogan resonated throughout the North as well as the South, and among women as well as men.[10]

The issue of black women's work, waged and unwaged, served a lynchpin for many specific campaigns. Women came to the fore as unpaid community organizers when they helped to coordinate, mobilize, and inspire boycotters and demonstrators. In Memphis, Eddie May Garner and other women who had become active in predominantly black labor unions during the 1940s served as leaders of protests two decades later; Garner, an organizer for Furniture Workers Local 282, had protested poor working conditions at the city's major workplaces, including Loeb Laundry-Cleaners and Memphis Furniture. Black women employees toiled for long hours at low pay, and endured racist white supervisors, coworkers, and even international representatives of their own union. Garner's early activism primed her for the more high-profile strikes and demonstrations in the 1960s. Yet the very fact that they were employed also made women vulnerable to white backlash, which could take the form of pay reductions, firings, or worse. Indeed, throughout the South, most black women regardless of age depended upon white employers for their livelihood, rendering their commitment all the more remarkable in the face of vengeful landlords and spiteful housewives.[11]

Elderly black women, as prophets and protagonists, exercised a traditional form of informal religious leadership that found new channels of expression during this modern fight for human rights. Maya Angelou stated the matter succinctly when she noted the values among southern blacks: "Age has more worth than wealth, and religious piety more value than beauty."[12] In the rural South, women had both years and piety in abundance. Working women of all ages and classes enlisted their modest resources and special talents in the cause; since many members of the dominant caste considered the housing and feeding of civil rights workers to be a politically subversive act, even black women's domesticity assumed great value. Women professionals such as Ella Baker and Jo Ann Gibson Robinson drew upon their formal education and organizing skills to provide crucial logistical support to the campaign, often behind the scenes and out of the limelight. And finally, black working women—wage earners as well as family members—served as living testaments to the strength of African American culture and the depth of southern-style oppression.

These themes converged when black and white men and women described the lead taken by "mamas" in lending aid to the movement. "There is always a 'mama,'" wrote one black worker for SNCC in September 1962. He was referring not only to his gracious hostess in the Georgia town of Albany, but also to the general grassroots support for the movement he found among ordinary black women throughout the South. "She is usually a militant woman in the community, outspoken, understanding, and willing to catch hell, having already caught her share." She was also by definition an idealized figure, a working woman with a legendary capacity to chop cotton all day long, prepare a feast for a dozen folks in the evening, and then sit on her front porch until midnight, a shotgun spread conspicuously across her lap to protect the white and black canvassers lodged in her home.[13]

Observers frequently noted that southern black women formed the "backbone" of the movement—from the bus-boycotting domestics of Montgomery and the prisoners of the Albany jail, to the Mississippi hosts of SNCC workers and congregants in Monday-evening church rallies held all over the South; these women "took the lead in the struggle for dignity." Sympathetic outsiders were uncertain how to interpret this phenomenon. Some suggested that these women lacked the economic vulnerability of their menfolk, but this interpretation was clearly inadequate since the vast majority depended on wage work well into advanced age. Others speculated that women had the "calm courage necessary" for such dangerous work, or that they ran less risk of physical abuse, apparently unaware of the frequency with which black women verbally assaulted white law-enforcement authorities and suffered from violent retaliation for their boldness.[14]

In fact, for both demographic and cultural reasons black women participated in the movement in disproportionately large numbers compared to men. During the 1940s and 1950s, more black men than women migrated out of the South, and that fact, combined with the higher mortality rates among black males, left the region with an unbalanced sex ratio in favor of women. Even more significant was the custom of informal female leadership within southern black communities. From the grannies, healers, and conjurers under slavery to the nine pioneering "steady and determined" voter registrant applicants in Indianola, Mississippi, in 1964, black women had had to assume responsibility for the care and protection of their larger "family." Like Selma's female elders, these women still commanded respect in 1965: "them old women usually know."[15]

The black church was the chief vehicle of protest, and as the traditional bulwark of the church, southern black women were particularly sympathetic to the movement's philosophy of nonviolence, a strategy compatible with their role as family nurturers. In protest meetings and on the picket line, religious rhetoric, imagery, and rituals suffused the movement, making it at times indistinguishable from an exuberant, protracted church revival. Women felt at home in the Baptist and Methodist churches where they cried *Amen!* to clergy-activists who railed against the South's modern-day pharaohs. Northern and white participants became swept up in the fervor of it all and watched in wonder as an exposition on local black voter strength gave way to an impassioned "shout" led by an elderly woman who shunned the attempts of well-meaning bystanders to restrain her.[16]

Over the years, the black church had offered a special kind of sanctuary to women. Eleven o'clock Sunday morning was "the most segregated hour of the week" in the South, and during that time churchgoers regained the sense of self-worth denied to them during the work day. Observed the Reverend Joseph L. Roberts Jr., pastor of the Atlanta church where Martin Luther King Sr. had once preached, "I've got women in my congregation who go out five days a week wearing white uniforms, which says they are nobody, but when they dress on Sunday morning and come to Ebenezer, they are dressed to kill, naturally." Moreover, for women, the church represented a refuge from the evils that seemed to plague black men and young people in particular—the temptations of the flesh and of the spirit. Thus, as a place of peaceful resistance to the white world, the church melded together the tribulations that wives and mothers encountered on the job and at home, and provided the means for these women to triumph over them—or at least endure them.[17]

Both inside and outside of churches, black women led the singing of old-time gospel songs and new-style freedom songs that confounded menacing sheriffs and deputies. These were concise statements of faith and hope offered up in unison, and more than any other tactical device they linked the singers to an African American past and to one another. Bernice Johnson Reagon recalled of the Albany movement, "We became visible, our image was enlarged, when the sounds of freedom songs filled all the space in the church." The women in the audience who sang over and over, "Ain't nobody gonna let nobody turn me 'round" revealed a collective determination that was not necessarily new, but rather transformed. Fannie Lou Hamer's voice, "the rich powerful sound of an indomitable spirit," would ring out, "I've got the light of freedom . . . I'm gonna let it shine . . . tell Senator [James] Eastland [of Mississippi] . . . I'm gonna let it shine." In this way were women's energies ordinarily released during Sunday morning services harnessed to the civil rights cause.[18]

Church members found the message as well as the medium of the movement appealing, and they had no difficulty connecting spiritual with earthly forms of salvation. "God is so *just,*" said Mrs. Amos of Greenwood, Mississippi, and she juxtaposed pictures of Jesus and SNCC leader Robert Moses on her living-room wall. The ideals of love, charity, and brotherhood took on new meaning as whites reacted with tear gas, police dogs, and obscenities to singing demonstrators. Each act of passive resistance became one more step in the pilgrimage to justice. Topsy Eubanks felt like she had "been born again" after she attended a voter registration school in Dorchester, Georgia, and other black women donned their "churchgoing best" when they tried to register for the very first time.[19]

Ever since the days of slavery, male preachers had functioned as the most powerful leaders of black southern communities, and their role in the protests of the 1950s and 1960s revealed the breadth of their mission. Martin Luther King Jr. exerted tremendous influence from the time he emerged as the compelling spokesman of the Montgomery boycotters in 1956 to his assassination twelve years later. By the time of his death, younger and streetwise male leaders had already begun their ascendancy in the national spotlight. Still, throughout his public career, King attracted a mass following, especially among older black women, who appreciated his powerful, authentic preaching style and impeccable Baptist credentials. Lillie Jones, an elderly resident of Philadelphia, Mississippi, and many of her friends marched the whole route in a 1964 demonstration because "Dr. King was there"; "If he could risk his life for Neshoba County, they could too."[20]

This preponderance of clergymen leaders with female followers replicated a larger cultural pattern and at times seemed to stifle the potential of women who might have successfully served in positions of more responsibility and visibility. Born in Virginia in 1903, Ella Baker had joined the NAACP in 1938, rising to the position of head of branches in 1943. One of the early staff members of the SCLC (founded in 1957), she was widely admired for her organizational and rhetorical skills; at the same time, she realized from the beginning that "as a woman, an older woman, in a group of ministers who are accustomed to having women largely as supporters, there was no place for me to come into a leadership role." Harmony within the movement, not personal ambition, was her ambition: "The competition wasn't worth it," she noted. Yet Baker did "compete" with King when she offered an alternative vision for leadership and decision making, a vision that depended less on charismatic leaders and more on tapping the ideas and strengths of ordinary people regardless of their age or their station in life. Eschewing egotism, Baker had a profound effect on many young people, who felt inspired by her efforts to implement a non-hierarchical radical democracy through the auspices of the Student Nonviolent Coordinating Committee. Noted SNCC member Mary King, "Miss Baker tempered my natural tenacity and determination with flexibility and made me suspicious of dogmatism. . . . She taught me one of the most important lessons I have learned in life: There are many legitimate and effective avenues for social change and there is no single right way."[21]

For the most part, younger male leaders, especially those involved with the early SNCC, had a relatively egalitarian relationship with female organizers their own age, like Ruby Doris Smith Robinson, Diane Nash, and Cynthia Washington—strong, outspoken women who had proved themselves as effective field secretaries. Stokely Carmichael's infamous observation, uttered in a 1964 SNCC staff meeting, that the best position for women in the organization was "prone," later caused him a great deal of embarrassment; he claimed he had been joking when he said it. Certainly black women workers had more authority—and accordingly commanded more respect—within SNCC offices than their white counterparts, who were mostly young, middle-class volunteers from the North. But Carmichael's general attitude reflected the male posturing evident in the organization during the early 1960s and foreshadowed the overt sexism of the Black Power movement later in the decade.[22]

An assessment of black women's contributions to the civil rights movement between 1955 and 1965 must therefore take into account their formal and informal leadership responsibilities, as well as the generational differences between older, battle-scarred NAACP veterans like Charleston's Septima Clark and Little Rock's Daisy Bates, and young female college students. A large group of women who came of age in all-black colleges around this time rebelled against not only the southern caste system, but also against the conservative school administrators who enforced rigid codes of campus behavior and catered to white philanthropists. Anne Moody at Tougaloo, Bernice Johnson at Albany State, Ruby Doris Smith at Spelman, and Gwendolyn M. Patton at Tuskegee all incurred the wrath of school officials when they made no attempt to hide their disdain for the "Uncle Toms" in charge of their formal education. Yet at the same time, college had heightened their consciousness of social injustice and provided an organizational base for collective action.[23]

Following Ella Baker's urgings, some activists deferred to the "people who'd felt the heel of oppression" and encouraged them to take control of their own lives. Fannie Lou Hamer is perhaps the best example of a natural leader whose militant stance earned her the admiration of her neighbors long before the movement provided her with a national forum. Born in 1918 to sharecropping parents in Montgomery County, Mississippi, she was the youngest of twenty children. As a child and a young woman, she performed labor for whites that served as a constant reminder of her exploitation. If she could hardly make $4 for a day of backbreaking cotton-picking ("I was gettin' as much as the men 'cause I kept up with the time"), then "things wasn't right." She vividly remembered the time when she had to scrub a bathroom in her landlord's house that was reserved for his dog, while she and her husband had no inside plumbing in their own house: "Now they got they dog higher'n us." Her attempt to vote on August 31, 1962, cost her her home and her job as a plantation time-keeper in Ruleville, and the sounds of gunfire in the night punctuated her weeks-long search for safety. The Hamers would henceforth find no gainful employment from the whites of Sunflower County.[24]

Yet Fannie Lou Hamer did eventually find her true calling, and she became active in an SCLC citizenship program and later served as a SNCC field secretary. In the summer of 1963 she and several other women workers were beaten in a county jail in Winona. The blows left her permanently disabled, a measure of the threat she posed to the southern caste system.

> And let me tell you, before they stopped beatin' me, I wish they would have hit me one lick that could have ended the misery that they had me in. . . .
>
> So they had me lay down on my face, and they beat me with a thick leather thing that was wide. And it had sumpin' in it *heavy*. I don't know what that was, rocks or lead. But everytime they hit me, I got just as hard, and I put my hands behind my back, and they beat me in my hands 'til my hands . . . my hands was as navy blue as anything you ever seen . . . that blood, I guess, and then beatin' it 'til it just turned black.

Hamer went on to help found the Mississippi Freedom Democratic party, and presented televised testimony on behalf of all disenfranchised black voters at the Democratic National Convention in 1964. She quickly came to symbolize for blacks and whites alike the rich, largely untapped human resources in the Mississippi Delta.[25]

Fannie Lou Hamer's role in the southern civil rights drama was an especially dramatic one, but many other women matched her daring and commitment. On the front lines of freedom, when bodies were needed to endure the wrath of white mobs, young girls and women volunteered. Autherine Lucy faced down an angry mob in February 1956, when she became the first black student admitted (for graduate study in library science) to the University of Alabama. Elizabeth Eckford was only fifteen when she, together with eight other black students (the "Little Rock Nine"), entered Little Rock's all-white high school in 1957, amid the shrieks of white women: "Get her! Lynch her. . . . Get a rope and drag her over to this tree." Freedom rider Lucretia Collins, a Fisk College student, completed the violent journey from Nashville to Birmingham and then on to Jackson in the spring of 1961. Albany's Bertha Gober, together with a fellow student from Albany State, set off the Albany movement later that year when they attempted to buy bus tickets at the white counter in a Greyhound bus station. Women like Ruby Doris Smith and Diane Nash, who became cellmates after the Rock Hill, South Carolina, protest in 1960, also participated in the lunch-counter sit-in campaigns.[26]

Women professionals frequently lent their prestige and expertise to local struggles. Jo Ann Gibson Robinson, an English professor in Montgomery, jump-started the boycott when she labored with other members of the middle-class Women's Political Council to co-ordinate the effort and the mass rallies that sustained it. Lawyer Ruth Harvey represented twenty-seven defendants arrested for protesting the segregated public facilities in Danville, Virginia, in the early 1960s. Trois J. Latimer, a teacher at Albany State College, "ran the class out of the room into our demonstration line," recalled one of her admiring students. She told them, "Get out. Go do something for your freedom. You ain't doing nothing here." On the other hand, "Tom-teachers and chicken eating ministers"—relatively well-off community leaders too fearful to lend their support—earned nothing but the scorn of their former admirers, who began to exercise a newfound authority on their own.[27]

These women displayed courage "on a day-to-day basis, far from the glory and occasional glamour of the civil rights hierarchy," and provided the groundwork for new projects and institutions. In the late 1950s a Charleston beauty parlor operator named Mary Davis opened her shop to classes for illiterate adults. Around the same time Birdie Keglar of Tallahatchie County, Mississippi, defied local tradition when she attempted to pay her poll tax and, faced with official opposition, successfully sued the county sheriff. New Orleans's Virginia Collins organized a voter registration drive from 1960 to 1964; it offered instruction for potential voters and coordinated mass protests against discriminatory voting laws. Along the route of the historic Selma to Birmingham trek in 1965, a seventy-eight-year-old widow, Rosie Steele, allowed weary marchers to camp on her property: "I almost feel like I might live long enough to vote myself," she said. Meanwhile, a group of Selma women worked sixteen hours a day to prepare meals for the demonstrators.[28]

Indeed, throughout the South, civil rights workers heaped praise upon black women's cooking, revealing once again how traditional women's work could replenish a people under siege. The Mississippi Summer volunteers in particular filled their letters home to friends and relatives with the descriptions of feasts recently devoured. A Fourth of July celebration in Ruleville included "spicy chicken and this woman's or that woman's special ham and potato salad and sweet bread and cotton bread and hot muffins and peas cooked in bacon and onion sauce and home-made applesauce and sodas and punches and grape juice and potato casseroles and more and more and more until the pies and the cakes and the ice cream came and we could not refuse." This was truly "soul food" that nourished the spirit as well as the body.[29]

Later, when civil rights workers testified to the source of their commitment, or to the strength that enabled them to hold fast in the face of overwhelming opposition, many of them would allude to the image of the black working woman, in some cases their own mother. A CORE staff worker in Canton, Mississippi, Anne Moody remembered her mother's history of struggle. The young woman later wrote, "My whole childhood came to life again. I thought of how my mother suffered with us when we had been deserted by my father," and how at one point the older woman had labored as a field-hand every day but Sunday, at another time dragged her pregnant self out of bed each day to work in a local cafe, and later scrubbed for a white woman who "worked her so hard that she always came home griping about backaches." Alabama's Sallie Mae Hadnott, an NAACP member and voter registration activist (described by admirers as the "stabilizing factor, the upsetting factor; the bulwark and the pacifier [who keeps] Prattville alive") always remembered that her mother cooked white people's food but ate their scraps. Georgia Mae Turner, a share-cropper evicted from her home in Fayette County, Tennessee, defined her childhood of physical deprivation in these terms: "My mother did all she could," making dresses for the children out of cotton sacks, picking cotton "in those old raggedy pieces of shoes in the cold" for a landlord who cheated them anyway. According to one interviewer, Fannie Lou Hamer "was indelibly impressed with the figure of her mother, whom she repeatedly refers to as 'a strong woman,'" who was blinded while working for a white man. "And her clothes—they's been patched and patched over so much till they looked too heavy for her body to carry. All I could think was why did it have to be so hard for her. Then I vowed that when I got bigger, I'd do better by her."[30]

Black men and white women also marveled at the stamina of southern grannies and their daughters. Black men at times invoked the fierceness of their slave great-grandmothers who "cried for joy and shouted hallelujah when old master got the cold, cold ground that was coming to him." For middle-class white allies of the movement, often several generations removed from hard manual labor of any kind, the *"Choonk! Choonk! Choonk!"* of a hoe raised by "ancient arms . . . [in] their tireless assault on the rich soil of the Delta" was an in-sistent reminder of the broader continuities that shaped American society. Young white women wrote compassionately of field-hands like the twenty-two-year-old mother who toiled for twelve hours a day, and of service workers like the one who labored seventy-seven hours a week for whites "takin' care of their children, and my own jus' havin' to stay home all day."[31]

Long known for their verbal feistiness, black women supplied another source of inspira-tion for the movement: pithy quotations that eventually found their way into sermons, cam-paign speeches, newspaper articles, and scholarly monographs. Martin Luther King Jr. liked to cite the words of a seventy-two-year-old "oppressed, battered" woman who in-sisted on walking during the Montgomery boycott—"My feets is tired but my soul is rested"—as evidence of his people's great physical stamina and religious faith. The down-to-earth folk wisdom of black women at times seemed to eliminate the need for elaborate theories concerning the plight of the oppressed ("You know, we ain't dumb, even if we are poor. We need jobs. We need food. We need houses. But even with the poverty program we ain't got nothin' but needs"), and its solution ("Tax the rich and feed the poor"). Stokely Carmichael conveyed his contempt for middle-class black reformers when he repeated the observation of a woman from Alabama: "The food that Ralph Bunche eats doesn't fill my stomach."[32]

Women who used their sharp tongues as weapons against menacing whites acted within a tradition of verbal aggressiveness. These confrontations also quickly became part of the canon of struggle. Fannie Lou Hamer lost her job but had the last word when her boss told her he did not want her to register to vote: "'But you don't understand,' she said (with a passion that surprised them both). 'I'm not registerin' for *you*, I'm registerin' for *me!*'" Fed up with harassment from the Canton, Mississippi, police, Mrs. Chinn strode over to a patrol car one day and demanded, "You cops don't have anything better to do than sit in front of this [CORE] office all the time? If you don't, I wish you would find something. I get tired of looking at you." A demonstrator in a Philadelphia, Mississippi, march responded to the shocked expression of a white bystander with the cry, "Yes! It's me and I've kept your children. I could've spit in their milk for all you know!"[33]

Most women accepted the practical and philosophical justifications for nonviolence and limited their overt expression of anger to words. In contrast, some white southerners resorted to physical or economic retaliation against even peaceful demonstrators who were in many cases their own employees. Indeed, the violence directed against blacks during this period recalled the reign of terror unleashed against freedpeople during the post–Civil War era. If white authorities and vigilantes now patrolled the streets in cruisers and used more sophisticated firearms, they still made late-night attacks on the homes of activists and their sympathizers. Other forms of reprisal were more subtle but no less effective. When blacks in Tennessee's Fayette and Haywood counties tried to vote in 1959 and 1960, they were evicted from plantations, denied medical care, and barred from local food and supply stores. White physicians refused to deliver the babies of mothers on the local white Citizens Council blacklist ("Let's change that word to *white list*," wrote SNCC leader James Forman). In Ruleville, female field-hands who relied on the government's surplus commodities program during the slack season found that they were suddenly declared "ineligible" by white bureaucrats. To deprive an "uppity" woman of her livelihood was as easy as it was common, whether she was a well-educated school teacher like Septima Clark or an illiterate sharecropper like Georgia Mae Turner. Because of her activism, Clark was fired from her job and denied her pension benefits as a result. Not all women workers were willing or able to take such risks or endure such sacrifices.[34]

For these reasons, when dealing with whites face to face, some female employees engaged in the time-honored "deference ritual" perfected by their slave grandmothers. This strategy could at times enable a movement supporter to keep her job. A Montgomery domestic told her white employer that she walked to work not out of sympathy for the boycott but because she wanted to "stay away from the buses as long as that trouble is going on." Anna Mae, "one of the best block captains and most militant civil rights workers in Greenwood," sang freedom songs at night, but in the day, queried by a suspicious white housewife, she would profess ignorance of "silver rights workers" and deny with a hearty "No *ma'am*" that she knew "anythin' about freedom."[35]

The threat of economic or violent retaliation could keep some black women from joining the movement or offering public support to those who had. Franklin McCain, a black student who participated in the first lunch-counter sit-in at Greensboro, North Carolina, in February 1960, recalled that he and his three friends were taken aback when "a middle-aged black dishwasher behind the counter" called them "rabble-rousers, troublemakers." She lashed out angrily, "That's why we can't get anyplace today. . . . So why don't you go on out and stop making trouble?" Years later the woman appeared at a ceremony marking the historic protest and admitted to McCain, "Yes, I did say it and I said it because, first of all, I was afraid for what would happen to you as young black boys. Secondly, I was afraid of what would happen to me as an individual who had a job at the Woolworth store." Fear spawned its own brand of politics, and the South had its share of "beaten down" black women and men, people who acted out of "sheer self defense" when confronted with the possibility of social upheaval. "I can't sign no paper," a Mississippi woman in a "terrible house" told a voter registration canvasser. "I ain't no Negro, I'm a nigger. The Boss Man, he don't say nothing but nigger girl to me. I'm just a nigger, I can't sign no paper." In other cases, mothers worn from the care of too many children appeared too distracted even to contemplate a better way of life.[36]

Within this context, southern beauty shop owners possessed an unparalleled freedom of movement and action compared to women who depended on whites for a livelihood. Bernice Robinson, a Charleston beautician, contrasted her situation to that of her cousin, Septima Clark. By essentially outlawing NAACP membership among public employees in 1955, the South Carolina state legislature created "quite a lot of fear among teachers and other public employees" who otherwise might have become active participants in the movement. Robinson attributed the drop in the membership of the state's NAACP (between 1954 and 1957, a decline from 7,889 to 2,202) to these intense pressures on all wage workers beholden to whites. "That's the way it was all over the South. The whites would chop you down in a minute if you were dependent on them for a job." In contrast, Robinson noted, "I had my own business, supplied by black supply houses, so I didn't have to worry. Many people did." She could afford, literally, to become a leader in the citizenship-education movement. With control over her own time and workplace, Robinson managed to devote considerable time and resources to the movement and still keep her business. She recalled, "It got to the point where we were working so hard getting people to register to vote, that I would leave people under the dryer to take others down to the registration office to get them registered. I would say, 'If you get too hot under there, just cut her off and come out!'" By this time, then, beauty shops had emerged as a remarkable site of resistance to the white supremacist imperative.[37]

In their reaction to the movement, southern white women brought to the civil rights issue quite different perspectives compared to those of black women. The factors of age and class helped to shape white women's attitudes, which spanned a broad ideological and political spectrum. An oversimplified typology might highlight at one end the upper-middle-class Virginia Durrs, Anne Bradens, and Lillian Smiths active in organizations like the liberal NAACP or the radical Southern Conference Educational Fund, and at the other the inevitably anonymous women who clawed the faces of freedom riders with their fingernails, screamed obscenities at the Little Rock Nine, sprayed insecticide at Selma marchers, or angrily insisted that reports of the murder of three civil rights workers near Philadelphia, Mississippi, in 1964 were a Communist-inspired plot to destabilize American society. This analysis, however, would ignore the crucial role played by more privileged white women in subverting the cause of equal rights. Predictably, some female landlords evicted elderly black women from their homes, and housewives replaced activists with more docile servants. Moreover, a new, menacing figure emerged from the white middle class during this period—the voting registrar. Relatively well educated, adept at the classic techniques of intimidation and delay, she turned down many prospective black voters and discouraged many others from trying. Transparently discriminatory literacy tests gave white women like Martha Lamb, the "terror of Greenwood," full authority to reject applicants and summarily call for their arrest if they objected. Like their menfolk, white women believed that citizenship rights were finite, and to the extent that black people won their rights, those of whites would be diminished accordingly. At the same time, white women's fury over school integration in particular seemed to represent a perverse form of mothering, an attempt to preserve for their own children the advantages which depended on denying those advantages to others.[38]

On the other hand, critical aid to the movement could come from unlikely corners of white society. Female employers, anxious to retain black maids and laundresses, might pressure their husbands to capitulate to a black community's demands. Acting as chauffeurs, the white housewives of Montgomery enabled some black women to keep their jobs and at the same time remain faithful to Martin Luther King Jr. during the bus boycott. Many years later, white women informers—including the relatives of Ku Klux Klan members—played a key role in the conviction of at least one man responsible for the 1963 Birmingham church bombing that killed four black girls. Robert Chambliss's wife and her niece provided information to the authorities out of personal dislike for the man; the question remains just how many white women, inspired by religious sentiment or their own love of the human family, worked clandestinely on behalf of the civil rights movement.[39]

In any case, it is clear that blacks remained sensitive to nuances of support or hostility exhibited by white women. To Franklin McCain, the angry words of the black lunch-counter dishwasher seemed all the more biting when juxtaposed with those of a "couple of old [white] ladies [who] . . . came up to pat us on the back sort of and say, 'Ah, you should have done it ten years ago. It's a good thing I think you're doing.'" But black women continued to perceive white women in general as "lazy"; "That was why all white women had colored women working for them." This theme would figure prominently in the literature of black feminism during the late 1960s.[40]

Those heady days when blacks and whites linked arms and sang "We Shall Overcome" endured through the 1960s and on into the "Me Decade" of the 1970s. Labor activists, both black and white, embraced the ideology and rhetoric associated with "movement days" to wrench concessions from grudging southern employers. Martin Luther King Jr. helped to make the connection between jobs and civil rights explicit during his last days in Memphis, when he lent his support to striking sanitation workers. In 1969 the triumphant Charleston, South Carolina, female hospital workers credited their union victory after a 113-day-long strike to "a winning combination of 1199 union power and SCLC soul power." In the late 1970s Joan Griffin, a chief shop steward for a New Orleans local of the American Federation of State, County, and Municipal Employees, derived courage from the realization that "people like Dr. King weren't afraid" when they challenged southern mores two decades earlier. The one thousand Memphis furniture workers (mostly black women) who struck for ten weeks in 1980 sang "We Ain't Gonna Let Nobody Turn Us Around" on the picket line. Reported one union member, their enthusiasm "was just like you would see in a revival at a church," and they relied on preachers to publicize their cause. In towns and villages throughout the South, in unheralded ways, black women continued to fight for better schools and wages in a manner that undermined white notions of submissive black womanhood. Anna Mae Dickson, a fifty-five-year-old domestic servant and crusader for integrated schools in Grimes County, Texas, described her own quiet determination by quoting an elderly slave woman who had been punished for praying; said the woman to her master, "You don't know what my heart is doing."[41]

On an emotional level, many black women were profoundly affected by the events of the decade. Interviewed in the 1970s, Dorothy Cotton recalled that she had had her disagreements with coworkers over the years; for example, "I mean, I've gotten really mad at [the Reverend] Hosea [Williams], really wanna put him in a trunk and shut the door and sit on it sometimes, but," she added, "there is a bond." She noted, "We love each other, and I think we always will. It was my family."[42] The "beloved community," after all, recapitulated the relationships within the black family—mamas and preachers, sisters and brothers united against a common enemy, and women justifiably felt that they were an integral part of that community. In calling out the time-tested strengths of black women, and in sustaining their roles as life-givers, the movement represented an historic moment, the culmination of the black family's resistance to racial ideologies enshrined in laws and in workplaces. This moment was made all the more precious by its relatively brief life span, for in the years to come, under the stress of persistent economic deprivation, the public and private black family would enter a new period of divisiveness and fragmentation.

CROSSCURRENTS OF CHANGE: THE DIVERGENT STATUS OF BLACK WORKING WOMEN IN THE 1960s AND 1970s

While black women continued to labor for their own people, federal legislation, combined with transformations in the national economy, fundamentally altered their status as wage earners. Despite the turbulence of the 1960s, it is possible to discern the crosscurrents of change that buoyed some black working women up and into the middle class during this period and left others behind in a slough of poverty, mired in welfare and low-wage dependency. By the late 1970s, the social structure of the black population had expanded both upward and downward, as class variables as much as the legacy of oppression shaped patterns of household organization.

A collection of federal initiatives known as the Great Society, promoted by President Lyndon Johnson, included a number of programs that affected the status of black working women. As components of the so-called War on Poverty, federal health plans were intended to cover the elderly (Medicare) and poor children (Medicaid). Welfare rights activists seized the moment to make certain impoverished mothers received the benefits due them under AFDC regulations; in the early 1960s only one out of every three eligible families was receiving this form of aid, but by the 1971 the proportion was nine out of ten. The Model Cities and other urban programs aimed for "maximum feasible participation" among poor residents eager to participate in local decisions related to education, housing, economic development, and public health. The Manpower Development and Training Act of 1962 and projects established by the Economic Opportunity Act of 1964 created the Neighborhood Youth Corps and the Job Corps. None of these programs attacked the structural roots of poverty; in fact, private employers were shedding urban manufacturing jobs while the federal government was expanding cash payments to the poor. At the same time, federal money did encourage local black women leaders to organize and lobby on their own behalf. In Memphis, for example, the Memphis Area Project-South (MAP-South) enlisted seventy-five low-income black women in an effort to counter such public health problems as child malnutrition and child mortality. The women, working as neighborhood aides, raised awareness about prenatal and postnatal issues including low birth weights. The Memphis hospital system was segregated, and black infant mortality rates remained 50 percent higher than those of whites; 36.6 percent of infants died out of every 1000 born among blacks, 24.4 percent among whites. Under these distressing conditions, the neighborhood aides fulfilled black women's historic roles as community healers, now under the auspices of a federal program.[43]

Yet it was Title VII of the Civil Rights Act of 1964 that had the most demonstrable impact on black women workers. The measure outlawed discrimination in hiring on the basis of race, color, religion, gender, or national origin, and it established the Equal Employment Opportunity Commission (EEOC) to enforce the law. Together with other factors, by the late 1960s this legislation enabled black women as a group to approach parity with white women in terms of their wages and concentration in clerical service (when the figures are computed on a nationwide basis). Between 1960 and 1970, for example, the percentage of black women in the clerical and sales sector increased from 3 to 11 percent in the South and from 17 to 33 percent in the North. In 1980, 34 percent of all gainfully employed black women worked in the areas of technical, sales, and administrative support, compared to 36 percent of all white women. Six years after the passage of Title VII, northern black women's median earnings were about 95 percent of white women's (up from 75 to 80 percent at the beginning of the decade). However, the gains in southern black women's relative earnings were more scattered—up from 45 to 55 percent of white women's in Virginia, North Carolina, South Carolina, and Tennessee, but down from 55 to 45 to 50 percent in Mississippi and Louisiana.[44]

While Title VII legislation was in its formative stage, Pauli Murray was adamant that any workplace antidiscrimination law must apply to all women as well as black people in general. Breaking with other black leaders who argued that black men should remain the first and foremost beneficiaries of federal initiatives, Murray countered: "Negro women *especially* need protection against discrimination," especially considering that they headed more than 20 percent of black households. Because so many black women were breadwinners, then, employment opportunities were crucial for the well-being of black families in

particular and black communities in general. Murray had begun her activist career by lobbying First Lady Eleanor Roosevelt; now, in 1963, she contacted Lady Bird Johnson, the
U.S. attorney general, and (through a memorandum) every member of Congress to press
for the inclusion of "sex" in any upcoming bills.[45]

The effects of Title VII and various other affirmative action measures (including Executive Order 11246 in 1965 and subsequent Supreme Court decisions) revealed that it would
be easier for black women to advance occupationally within the realm of traditional white
women's work than it would be for them (and white women and black men) to approach the
job and pay levels of white men. For example, American Telephone and Telegraph lowered
its barriers against black women in the 1960s, and by 1970 it employed five times as many as
ten years earlier. However, these workers remained concentrated at the lowest rungs of the
occupational ladder as clerical workers and telephone operators. According to one researcher, "Black women were better able to compete with white women for such [entry-
level operator and secretarial] jobs than were black men able to compete with white men for
entry-level jobs as telephone installers and craftsmen." Court action, in the form of a consent decree handed down by a U.S. district court in 1973, forced the company to consider
women as well as black men for jobs in and promotions to skilled and professional positions. Nevertheless, white men increased their overall relative economic advantage in the
1970s. In 1976 the median-income ratios for the four gender-racial groups held constant
among persons with the same level of education: Black women made nearly as much as
white women (among high-school graduates, $8,028 vs. $8,381) but less than black men
($10,832) and much less than white men ($14,366). Black female college graduates made
only half the annual income of their white male counterparts.[46]

Not unexpectedly, several studies in the 1970s found that black women in general had
high levels of motivation but low aspirations when it came to planning their careers; they
hoped to go into traditional fields like social work and teaching, for example. High school
and college students alike were engaging in a realistic appraisal of the labor market; at the
same time, counselors and teachers were making a conscious effort to track young women
into these jobs. Female students in prestigious, predominantly white colleges gradually became more likely to train for careers in the traditional male fields of law, medicine, and
business. They constituted the first generation of highly educated black women to have
some (though still not necessarily equal) opportunity to compete with whites at the upper
echelons of the wage scale. Stigmatized with the imprint of affirmative action quotas, these
women also partook of a "special kind of [corporate] stress in a setting dominated by
whites."[47]

Black women pressed the case for equal employment rights by taking advantage of the
new Equal Employment Opportunity Commission, initiating and joining in class-action
lawsuits aimed at employers who ignored Title VII altogether. Beginning in 1966, Sallie
Pearl Lewis tried unsuccessfully for five years to get an entry-level job with the textile manufacturer J. P. Stevens. In 1973 she became the lead plaintiff in lawsuits challenging Stevens
and another large textile company. Lewis testified not only to the lack of economic opportunity, but also to the humiliation that black job applicants felt when they were arbitrarily

turned away by personnel officials: "You see, every time we go [to apply for a job], the black folk had to leave with a hanged head down, aching heart and we had to wonder [where] we was going to get another meal at."[48]

Clearly, then, the gains that black women did achieve rarely came easily. Lucy Sledge, a young woman in Roanoke Rapids, North Carolina, got a $1.25-per-hour job in a nearby J. P. Stevens textile mill in 1966. When she was later laid off, her white coworkers with less seniority received preferential treatment in the rehiring process. (Stevens feared that black workers, as strong supporters of unionization, would inevitably ignite a new round of labor organizing.) Inspired by civil rights protests in other parts of the South, the young woman decided to initiate the first suit charging racial discrimination against the company: "It was always what was happening somewhere else—Selma, Birmingham, Montgomery—not here. So my sisters and me just wanted to do something here." In 1970 Sledge filed a complaint with the EEOC, and the evidence related to her case formed the basis of a class action suit, *Sledge v. J. P. Stevens and Co.* Although her lawyers proved that Stevens was guilty of segregating its workers, Sledge had to appeal to a higher court before she won the right to press her own claim. "I did do right. I know I did," she remarked later. "I'd go down for this, if I had to, for my black brothers and sisters."[49]

For many black women, domestic service in homes and institutions formed their point of reference, and blue-collar and clerical jobs represented significant intergenerational advancement. Enrolled as an apprentice in a program for skilled workers, one black woman embraced the challenge: "I've always wanted to get ahead. All my life I've wanted to do something—like whatever I start, even today, I want to finish it, whether I'm right or wrong." In the mid-1970s Opallou Tucker, an older domestic, observed that "the doors are open now"—at least for younger black women. She realized that when she was in school, "You could have been the greatest typist in the world, but you would never have gotten a job." She expressed satisfaction that her niece would be able to put her clerical skills to good use now. The two women might well have perceived clerical work from different perspectives—the older one contrasting it with the arbitrary open-endedness of household work, the younger resenting the mind-numbing tyranny of routine, unchallenging tasks. Yet both would have agreed that secretarial jobs were superior to service because they paid better, provided Social Security and other benefits, allowed greater opportunities for unionization, and afforded less isolation from other workers. Nevertheless, clerical work and retail sales in general held little promise for the future, as a whole host of machines, from computers to automatic teller machines and price-scanning machines would render more and more workers superfluous.[50]

The public sector in particular developed relatively egalitarian hiring policies, and government jobs tended to pay higher salaries and offer greater advancement possibilities compared to those in private business. Black female government employees at all skill levels benefited from an assertive and rapidly expanding union, the American Federation of State, County, and Municipal Employees (AFSCME). At the same time, government work in general remained vulnerable to cost-cutting imposed by recessions, taxpayer revolts, and regular waves of local, state, and federal budget-slashing. Regardless of a woman's job description, the workplace still served as the locus of her resistance to injustice and exploitation. Recounting her decision to become an active union member, a state hospital worker in South Carolina remarked in 1974, "The main thing that got me involved, which is what makes every person get involved, was when I got on the job and into trouble."[51]

Black women who advanced as a result of equal opportunity legislation constituted a select group. They were likely to be young and well educated. (In 1970 black and white women between the ages of twenty-five and thirty-four had completed almost exactly the same number of years of formal schooling—12.0 and 12.6. Seventeen percent of all white women, however, had at least a college degree, compared with only 6 percent of black women.) Many came from families, either nuclear or extended, that supported their efforts in school and in the job market, whether through financial aid or enthusiastic encouragement. A young woman's place of residence also affected her ability to take advantage of job opportunities. The Bell system became a major employer of black women in the 1960s and 1970s because many of its offices were located in downtown areas (though by the late 1970s some companies had joined the out-migration to the suburbs). Finally, a variety of intangible factors affected a woman's chance of getting a job for which she was otherwise qualified. To some extent her future depended upon whether or not her prospective employer approved of her looks or found her personality to his liking—in other words, whether or not he considered her worthy to become one of his first (and few) black employees. Of J. P. Stevens's hiring preferences soon after the passage of Title VII, Lucy Sledge noted that "they weren't hiring any 'ugly blacks.'" An applicant had to conform to the expectation of white personnel managers in terms of skin color and overall physical attractiveness. The women who did not meet all or any one of these qualifications were readily identifiable—they were older, poorly educated, and lacking the skills and access to transportation that might allow them to get and retain better-paying jobs.[52]

By the 1970s, the ironies and limitations associated with Title VII had become manifest, revealing the mixed gains that accrued to black women workers with a high school diploma or less. For industries such as telephone systems and southern textiles, the integration of workforces meant depressed wages for employees as workforces gradually became predominantly black. White workers in the South could afford to quit low-wage jobs to take cleaner, safer, better paid positions associated with the economic growth of the Sun Belt—in financial services and banking for example. Within an emerging global economy, then, poorly paid black workers could boost the competitiveness of U.S. companies. Reversing an historic trend that excluded blacks from positions of machine operatives, by 1980 15 percent of gainfully employed black women worked as machine operatives in factories, but primarily in the least desirable positions within that category—as employees of dry-cleaning establishments for example. Companies that complied with federal mandates did not necessarily integrate all levels of the workforce, leaving blacks at the lower echelons of unskilled and semiskilled work, and whites predominating in managerial and supervisory positions. In the Bell System in 1969, only .06 to .09 percent of black workers were managers. In unionized workplaces, whites retained their seniority rights, in contrast to newly hired black employees. As more businesses introduced automation and advanced technologies, more jobs became stressful, with workers forced to meet daily quotas and endure verbal abuse heaped upon them by customers dissatisfied with the speed or quality of service they were receiving.[53]

Some employers expressed an overtly opportunistic stance toward integration. In 1969, for example, a Bell official acknowledged the spatial considerations that made black employees necessary to the business: Because the inner cities lacked "enough white, middle-class, success-oriented men and women," he claimed, "we need nonwhite employees. Not because we are good citizens. Or because it is the law as well as national goal to give them employment. We need them because we have so many jobs to fill and they will take them"—and because "they" would work for "as little as $4,000 to $5,000 a year." Other employers hoped that by tapping a vast reserve of black labor they might discourage unionization among white workers, and still others merely circumvented the law by requiring a picture of each job applicant, or insisting that three applicants be considered for each opening, thus preserving flexibility in whom was hired. And some employers and shop-floor supervisors showed indifference toward the abusive working conditions experienced by the black employees they hired, perhaps in the hope that the newcomers would quit in disgust. Many women in nontraditional blue-collar jobs had to balance the pride they felt at cracking all-male workplaces on the one hand, and dealing with degrading forms of verbal and sexual abuse by male coworkers on the other. Among the first generation of women coal miners, Patricia Brown had to contend with white men who "would take my bucket, or my jacket, and they would put them in a hangman's noose." Thus the dynamics of individual workplaces, the fortunes of specific industries, technological innovation, the emerging global economy, and hostile white coworkers all affected the way that Title VII affected black working women.[54]

Increasing numbers of black wives and mothers had to make do without paid jobs at all, prompting a dramatic new dimension of community organizing and protest. In Las Vegas, in the early afternoon of March 6, 1971, a procession of African American women stretched for two miles as it wended its way through the streets, ending when the demonstrators marched through the cavernous casino of the Caesars Palace Hotel. They were protesting the decision of Nevada's welfare administrator to cut almost nine hundred families from the state's Aid to Families with Dependent Children rolls—nearly three thousand individuals, all charged with "cheating" the system. Around the country, such budget cuts had become increasingly common, as local administrators deemed unmarried mothers "unsuitable" as mothers and hence ineligible for aid, and as welfare guidelines called for eliminating from the rolls those women who lived with a man whether or not he was able to support her and her children. By the early 1960s, politicians of both parties believed they could score points among white taxpayers, north and south, by demonizing impoverished black mothers. In California, the governor labeled single mothers "a bunch of prostitutes."[55]

In response to the Nevada cuts, members of the local National Welfare Rights Organization coordinated the March 6 protest; at the head of the line were the Reverend Ralph Abernathy, president of the Southern Christian Leadership Conference; the actress Jane Fonda; the head of the National Welfare Rights Organization, George Wiley; and national

NWRO organizer, Johnnie Tillmon. Yet the backbone of the Las Vegas movement was Ruby Duncan; she and other black mothers living in Las Vegas's Westside neighborhood had formed an organization called Operation Life, an advocacy group for women receiving AFDC. Operation Life embraced a broad agenda that encompassed the rights of poor women as consumers and as recipients of federal and state aid. Its members believed they were well suited to act on behalf of neighborhood concerns of all kinds; in Duncan's words, "Because living in the community, I could see what was needed next" They too were civil rights activists, and their protest that day in March highlighted the unique and growing vulnerabilities of impoverished women outside the South.[56]

The NWRO consisted primarily of black mothers, yet white women also suffered the humiliation that accompanied each AFDC check. In absolute terms, more white than black women received AFDC (60 percent of total recipients), yet by the 1960s "welfare" had become associated in the public eye with poor black inner-city mothers. It is possible that black women's long tradition of community activism helped to propel them into the forefront of this poor women's campaign. Mary Childers, a white woman, recounted the hardships of her own mother, a single mother of seven living in the Bronx. According to Childers, her mother felt overwhelmed by her own responsibilities; distrustful of bureaucrats, "too distracted to follow through on much, too anxious to be a member of any political group," she was unable to muster the courage or energy to protest her own straitened circumstances—until in the summer of 1963, local caseworkers refused to let her and other women have telephones. That decision prompted her to gather up her children and engage in a spontaneous protest against high-handed caseworkers and policymakers.[57]

In general, though, black and white women registered the effects of a transformed economy in the 1960s and 1970s in different ways. Despite the apparent convergence of black and white women's labor force participation, with 50 percent of each group working in 1980—similar proportions in clerical work—and their median earnings reaching near parity, they continued to follow different patterns and life histories of employment. For example, in the late 1970s, 60 percent of all black women living in households together with their husbands had jobs, compared to 48 percent of similarly situated white wives. At all education levels, black women's unemployment rates were higher than those for white women (among high-school graduates, 12 versus 5 percent). About 30 percent of black working women were still employed in either private or institutional service; the figure for white women was 18 percent. Moreover, black women worked after marriage and after the birth of their first child in greater proportions than white mothers. Though up until the late 1960s they were less likely to work full time (reflecting their concentration in seasonal and other irregular forms of employment), they made a greater contribution to the income of their households relative to white female wage earners.[58]

Indeed, much of the research comparing the economic status of the two groups in the 1960s and 1970s stressed "racial" differences rather than gender similarities. Detailed studies also highlighted the contrast between wives of different classes within their respective groups. In the late 1970s, for example, one investigation showed that 69 percent of black wives from middle-class families were in the paid labor force, compared to 42 percent of their white counterparts, and 51 and 29 percent of black and white working-class wives respectively. Because of the low job status of black men, even middle-class families remained just a paycheck away from financial disaster. Moreover, those households more often than white ones maintained a connection with impoverished kin by making loans to vulnerable family members, and in general black middle-class households did not have the real-estate equity that came with generations-long patterns of homeownership. All this is to say that black middle-class wives did not necessarily replicate the experiences, or family obligations, of white women of the same class. It was not surprising then that sociologists found that black women had incorporated both traditional (homemaking) and nontraditional (paid employment) roles into their personal ideologies of work, without needing to identify themselves exclusively in terms of either one role or the other the way white wives often did.[59]

The most striking contrast between patterns of black and white women's work reflected trends in their marital status. The percentage of black households headed by a woman grew at a rapid rate, from 17.6 percent in 1950 to 28.3 percent in 1970 and 40.2 percent in 1980—half of these in the South. Comparable figures for white households were 8.5, 10.9, and 14.6 percent. Black female heads were more likely to be young and separated (rather than divorced) mothers of children under eighteen, and unemployed, compared to whites; in 1980 only 49 percent had jobs. Their age and lack of education, combined with a traditional division of labor and employers' prejudices, tended to keep their earnings very low when they did work—a median income of $7,510 in 1981—while wives in two-parent black families had household incomes of $19,620.[60]

Several factors accounted for these trends. First, a large percentage of the rise in husband-absent households resulted from increases in black male unemployment rates in the 1960s and 1970s (at least twice as high as whites' throughout the period and Depression-era levels during the recession of 1975), and from their inferior wages; in 1970 southern black men made only 55 percent, and northern black men only 75 to 80 percent of white men's median earnings. Second, census statistics revealed a declining sex ratio, reflecting some combination of higher male mortality rates with the inability of census takers to locate men who were unsettled and, therefore, probably not part of the pool of eligible spouses. Third, a rising number of non-college-educated young men were in prison (in 1995, the figure would reach 16 percent). Taken together, these forces had a particularly devastating impact on young black women. Black eighteen- and nineteen-year-olds had a fertility rate two times as great as that of white women the same age. Meanwhile, older black married women as a group were having fewer children; their fertility rate dropped so precipitously after 1960 that the percentage of all children born to unwed mothers climbed from 38 percent to 55 percent ten years later. With one-half of all teenage male job seekers unable to find employment (and an unknown number too discouraged even to look), young mothers could expect little in the way of financial security from the father of their children.[61]

Several factors account for the spurt in women receiving AFDC during this period: An increase in female-headed households, the advocacy work of activists, and liberalized eligibility guidelines instituted in the 1960s (for example, some states took advantage of a 1962 provision that allowed them to aid families with an unemployed father still at home). From

1960 to 1975, AFDC caseloads grew tremendously, from 3 million to 11.4 million recipients. Among the most significant factors for this increase was the new assertiveness of poor mothers through the agency of the NWRO, which served to educate eligible persons not receiving aid, and to win for recipients additional benefits to which they were entitled. Formed in 1967 (and based on a prototype called Boston's Mothers for Adequate Welfare founded two years earlier), NWRO had eight hundred affiliates in fifty states by 1971. The group initially held great promise as a vehicle for grassroots ghetto organizing, but gradually dissolved in the face of external pressures as well as internal inconsistencies. Although its main constituency was female household heads, leadership remained in the hands of paid professionals—a black male executive director, George Wiley, and a host of white male staff members—throughout its nine-year history. Blending issues articulated by both the civil rights and the emerging women's movements, the group nevertheless attracted only nominal support (and in some cases open hostility) from middle-class organizations such as the NAACP, National Urban League, and National Organization for Women (NOW), all of which found the slogan "Welfare is a right" embarrassing or irrelevant to their own programs. Most mainstream black male leaders considered the issues of unwed motherhood and welfare dependency to be anathema to their agenda of portraying black people in general as hardworking and upright citizens. Founded in 1966, NOW too sought respectability as it appealed to state and federal legislators. Soon after helping to start the group, Pauli Murray resigned, convinced it represented the narrow interests of well-educated suburban women and women professionals. Arguing for a "unifying" movement that would bring together all exploited workers regardless of gender or skin color, Murray noted, "As a human being, I cannot allow myself to be fragmented into Negro at one time, woman at another, or worker at another." The NWRO remained a poor women's organization.[62]

Inner-city residents had a formidable ally on its executive committee—Johnnie Tillmon, a black mother of six from Watts, a neighborhood of Los Angeles. Born in Arkansas in 1928, she had picked cotton and worked in a laundry before she became too ill to hold a job. In 1963 she began to organize Watts AFDC mothers, and later, as an NWRO officer, she did battle with a federal bureaucracy that seemed bent on encouraging female dependency. In her incisive essay "Welfare Is a Women's Issue," Tillmon pointed out that welfare bureaucrats tried to control recipients' sex lives, economic resources, consumer purchases, childcare provisions, and choice of housing. In return, public assistance granted only a pittance—"barely enough for food and clothing." ("Having babies for profit is a lie that only men could make up, and only men could believe," she noted.) Politicians who chastised "lazy welfare cheaters" implicitly condemned poor women with children, according to Tillmon, for AFDC constituted the bulk of welfare entitlement programs. Yet "women's work is real work," and the ability to care for children with so little in the way of money and material resources belied the charge of laziness among AFDC mothers. Certainly application and follow-up procedures could involve considerable expenditures of time and energy, as women worked their way through the "humiliating and frustrating" maze of interviews, questionnaires, and visits from social workers. Observed Barbara Dugan, an aid recipient, "You mustn't believe them when they say we get something for nothing . . . You don't get anything for nothing. They make it hard as dirt." In order to receive their fair share of benefits, groups of women had to mobilize and push for "fair hearings" to receive authorization for certain kinds of basic expenditures such as household appliances, telephones, and furniture; and they had to picket and boycott establishments in order to gain access to the credit cards and credit plans that would free them from the usurious interest rates charged by local merchants and grocery store owners. To apply for and continue to receive not only public aid but also financial credit required perseverance and a certain amount of ingenuity; certainly in that respect all AFDC mothers worked outside the home in an effort to provide for their families.[63]

Politicians of both parties, together with federal officials, lacked a fundamental understanding of the challenges faced by poor women in terms of seeking decent employment, childcare, and health care. Perhaps most revealing was the Work Incentive Program (WIN). Designed in 1967 specifically to decrease the rolls of AFDC recipients, it required most of them to register for job training and placement services; women caring for children under school-age in their own homes were among those exempt. Because the number of registrants far exceeded the program's resources, persons most likely to be reintegrated into the workforce received priority; consequently men and whites fared best under WIN. Even those black women who completed classes and managed to find jobs often failed to leave AFDC entirely, since their unskilled positions rarely paid enough to bring them up to the poverty line. Neither did welfare. In effect, WIN helped to subsidize low-wage jobs for women; many turned eagerly to work, at least partly because AFDC payments were so meager, but they also had to fall back on AFDC when their jobs paid so little. And for too many, the inability to find quality childcare, or the high price of that care, made it impossible for them to keep a job—or even locate one in the first place.[64]

Several investigators noted the great desire to work among poor mothers. According to a Department of Labor researcher in 1977, "Enrollees [in WIN] wanted skilled jobs with wages that would enable them to live well above the welfare standard." Sar Levitan, a perceptive critic of the welfare system, observed that "there would be no shortage of willing takers for good jobs." Most poor mothers continued to combine work and welfare either simultaneously or alternately. In 1976 the number of AFDC recipients without wage work was only 25 percent higher than those who subsisted on some sort of combination of the two sources of income. Sixty percent of the wage earners (compared to 94 percent of those who received AFDC payments exclusively) still fell below the poverty line. A government investigator noted in 1978 that only one-tenth of AFDC mothers were "hard-core unemployed who spend most of all their working years on welfare." The others "move back and forth between low-income employment and welfare" (40 percent), or were "temporarily on welfare because they are down on their luck" (50 percent). Under the Nixon administration, the Comprehensive Employment Training Act of 1973 phased out WIN's job-training component along with other relatively costly programs that had targeted women, including the Neighborhood Youth Corps, and reduced it to the level of a placement agency only.[65]

The enormous amount of public indignation directed at the relatively small proportion of cases of fraud (the Commission on Civil Rights reported they were no more than 3 percent of the total) overshadowed concern for the large number of persons who qualified for aid but lacked the information and resources to apply successfully for it. In the late 1960s many eligible people were nonetheless not receiving benefits. The individual states, which retained a great deal of discretion over eligibility guidelines and bureaucratic procedures, of course had a vested interest in easing the pressure on their limited budgets; as a result, clients and potential clients often needed highly trained advocates to navigate their way through masses of red tape and administrative intransigence. Yet public resentment of "welfare" mothers, fueled by official misinformation and the posturing of politicians of both parties, only grew through the 1960s and 1970s.[66]

Meanwhile, very poor mothers struggled to get by without much in the way of outside governmental assistance. The work of urban anthropologist Carol Stack illuminated the social networks that allowed kin and neighbors to rely on each other for everything from childcare to food, clothing to cash. This exchange process within kin clusters followed the lines of cooperation evident among southern rural blacks immediately after emancipation. Stack found that in the Flats, a black neighborhood in a midwestern city, people "do not turn anyone down when they need help. The cooperative life style and the bonds created by the vast mass of moment-to-moment exchanges constitute an underlying element of black identity in the Flats." These modern-day kinship obligations were no less compelling because they facilitated the use of a car to get to an interview rather than a mule and a wagon to take a cotton bale to town.[67]

Likewise, community self-help organizations closely resembled the mutual benefit societies established a century earlier among rural blacks. The purpose of these groups was to aid individuals confronted with emergency situations. For example, Charleszetta Waddles founded the Perpetual Mission for Saving Souls of All Nations in Detroit in 1957. Twenty years later the mission was serving 100,000 people through its branches in the United States and ten African countries. An ordained minister in the International Association of Universal Truth, the mission of "Mother" Waddles grew out of her early, informal prayer meetings with other women. "We were all poor women with a house full of children, most of us," said this mother of ten, "and I felt that you are never too poor to help someone." The Detroit mission offered a wide variety of services, from a restaurant to legal and medical clinics, and emergency shelter and job placement counseling, and it existed solely on donations. The founder explained her mission this way: "If you just want to keep [the poor] alive, so to speak, well, this is fine. But if you want people to come up out of the ghetto, if you want people to reach out and be somebody, then there is more that has to be done, you know." The mission spoke to the needy's sense of pride and self-worth. It enabled a woman who had just gotten a job to buy some new clothes, and it paid for the prom dress and pictures of a teenager whose mother was on welfare. These services were all outside the reach of the government bureaucracy.[68]

In the end, however, these cooperative efforts amounted only to "holding back the ocean with a broom"; they enabled wives and mothers to make it safely through another day, or year, but they did not affect the larger economic and political structures that deprived them and their men of gainful employment or a living wage. The reversal of half-century-long patterns of south-north migration, evident in the late 1960s and fully apparent by the middle of the next decade, indicated that black people were once again beginning to move long distances in search of jobs. For some families, the Sun Belt of the 1970s and 1980s was the promised land that their grandparents had sought in New York and Chicago and their parents in the San Francisco Bay Area. Still, national occupational trends bode ill even for these new migrants, as increased foreign immigration and technological innovation produced "a declining middle" within the job structure of the near future.[69]

Black population movements to the North highlighted the persistent inequalities, and the deepening economic distress, that characterized the "Promised Land" so appealing to early-twentieth-century southern migrants. The civil rights movement was not an exclusively southern phenomenon, but rather marked by regional variations in the Northeast, Midwest, and Far West; regardless of these variations, black women played a prominent role as leaders. In 1960, four out of ten black people lived outside the South, and as a group they were more urbanized than whites. As more and more cities shed manufacturing jobs, the politics of jobs, neighborhood development, public health, housing, schooling, police brutality, and industrial pollution ignited protests that directly affected the quality of life among black women and their families. Well-educated women, including Constance Baker Motley, an attorney, assumed pivotal roles in challenges to all-white suburbs. Vera Bradley, a native of Knoxville and migrant to Detroit, served as the lead plaintiff for the Supreme Court case *Bradley v. Milliken* challenging the de facto school segregation so common throughout the northern states. The mother of two sons, Bradley had engaged in community work in Detroit ever since she had arrived in 1942. In Philadelphia, Roxanne Jones, a single mother and migrant from North Carolina, began her political career as head of the Philadelphia Welfare Rights Organization in 1967; a resident of the dank and deteriorating Southwark Plaza projects, Jones was in the forefront of tenants' rights and poor mothers' demands for credit. She noted of her initial encounter with the welfare bureaucracy, "The social worker made me feel like I had committed murder when I first asked for help." In 1976 she cofounded Philadelphia Citizens in Action to bring better health-care and schooling opportunities to her impoverished northern Philadelphia neighborhood, which was 98 percent black and 50 percent poor. Seven years later she won a seat in the Pennsylvania state senate, a journey that took her on a path by now familiar in black women's history—from a commitment to the welfare of her own family to a position of political influence in her larger community, and then on to the state level.[70]

Using a variety of tactics ranging from protesting and petitioning to litigating and community organizing, northern activists continued to encounter challenges that were not always vulnerable to the political strategies of mass disobedience as used in the South. In northern small towns and inner cities, the forces of discrimination were more difficult to pinpoint, more difficult to overcome, compared to the raw prejudice of the local police chief or the bigoted mayor or employer. In addition, northern activists faced the dilemma of pushing for integration on the one hand, or the more difficult task of agitating for structural change on the other. For example, in Milwaukee, local activists had much more success getting black teachers hired by the local school board than they did dismantling the de facto segregation that produced schools that were either virtually all white or all black. Too, the visibility of poor black mothers in so many different kinds of campaigns related to welfare rights and housing fueled resentments among some male leaders who saw their own interests as different from those of their wives, sisters, and mothers. By the late 1960s such tensions had spilled out into the open. Ironically, then, in a movement that blurred the boundaries between struggles in the North and South, between workplaces and households, and between "public" and "private" concerns, gender emerged as a divisive force within the ranks of black activists, especially among young women and men.[71]

IDEOLOGICAL BASES OF PROTEST: BLACK POWER AND BLACK FEMINISM, 1965–1980

Implicit in much black protest thought from slavery to the 1980s was a recognition of the value of African American community institutions and respect for the women who sustained them. How these institutions should be strengthened or altered, and the role black women should play in those transformations, were more controversial issues. During the 1960s and 1970s these questions assumed heightened urgency as the shortcomings of federal equal-opportunity legislation became more obvious. The bitter disillusionment felt by many black citizens—so evident in the widespread destruction that northerners wrought upon their own neighborhoods in Watts and elsewhere—found political expression in the Black Power movement, beginning in 1965. Young militants repudiated the "effete" liberal goals espoused by Martin Luther King Jr.; he was considered "out of place, out of season, too naive, too innocent, too cultured, too civil for these times." These young men charged that nonviolence had not only proved to be an ineffective strategy, but that it had also played into the hands of whites bent on tormenting long-suffering black mothers and children. A separatist movement safeguarded by armed men, not by pious pronouncements or biblical forbearance, would shield all blacks from the oppression and genocide institutionalized in American life, whether manifested by the trigger-happy white policemen who preyed upon men and women, young and old in the ghetto, or draft boards that routinely sent "brothers" to their deaths in Southeast Asia.[72]

At the same time, calls for black women to eschew their own interests as wives, mothers, and workers in favor of the interests of black men as freedom fighters were not limited to young militants. At the August 28, 1963, March on Washington for Jobs and Freedom, when the Reverend Martin Luther King Jr. delivered his famous "I Have a Dream" speech, women were conspicuous for their absence from the podium. Represented were black nationalists (Malcolm X), mainstream civil rights organizations (Whitney Young), the Black Panther Party (Huey Newton), and the Baptist clergy-activists (King). Gloster Current, a planner for that program, later acknowledged that he and others "hastily put together 'a tribute to women freedom fighters' but . . . it was an afterthought." Mainstream male reformers also made explicit the call for black women to step aside in the fight for equality. Declared Roy Wilkins, executive director of the NAACP, "Biologically, they ought to have children and stay home. I can't help it if God made them that way." And some women echoed this theme. Dorothy Height, head of the National Council of Negro Women, urged black women to focus their labors on promoting the well-being of their menfolk, in politics, on the job, and at home.[73]

It was among younger activists that the debate over women's role in the freedom struggle became most fierce. If Black Power advocates sought to distance themselves from the southern civil rights movement, then women in, or sympathetic to, militant groups soon began to advocate their own form of identity politics, distinguishing their interests from those of both black men and white women. Self-identified black feminists sought on the one hand to embrace all-inclusive humanity ("the enemy" consisted of "our urgent need to stereotype and close off people, places, and events into isolated categories"[74]) and on the other to maintain a collective sense of identity that actively scorned other aggrieved groups, especially white women. But whatever their ideological orientation, black men and women during this period inevitably confronted the problem of black women's labor—what it had represented in the past, what it signified for the future. In the process, this generation of leaders defined in new terms an old debate about the political significance of black women, work, and the family.

When Malcolm X spoke at a Harlem rally in 1964 along with Fannie Lou Hamer, he told his listeners that they "need to know more, first hand, about what's happening down there, especially to our women." After hearing of the vicious beating Hamer took in Winona, Mississippi, the year before, the Black Muslim leader charged, "I ask myself how in the world we can expect to be respected as *men* when we will allow something like that to be done to our women, and we do nothing about it?" In the 1960s Malcolm X and other militant black men who rejected the goal of racial integration often spoke and acted out of anger over the abuse that their womenfolk had endured at the hands of all whites—employers and terrorists, bureaucrats and "pigs." This impulse to protect black womanhood originated during slavery, when husbands and brothers risked death to save their loved ones from the slaveholder's whip, or his lust; in mid-twentieth-century political terms, especially in northern communities, the same impulse was used to justify the dominance of black men in leadership positions and to relegate black women to the fringes of the fight for civil rights. Although they espoused different strategies and cultivated different personal styles, too often male Black Power advocates—from activists to scholars—wanted their female kin to get out of the white man's kitchen and back into their own.[75]

Ironically, southern black women in SNCC helped to initiate the Black Power movement beginning in 1964 when their animosity toward white female volunteers from the North, among other reasons, led them to join with their male coworkers in an effort to purge the group of whites. By the time public attention had shifted from the grassroots black political organization in Lowndes County, Alabama, with a black panther as its symbol (in 1965), to the founding of the Black Panther Party for Self-Defense in Oakland, California (in 1966), prominent young black women leaders in SNCC had begun a precipitous descent into oblivion. They found their places filled by men like Huey Newton, who felt that the black man "must recapture his balls" at all costs. Still, this rejection of women had at its source an attitude more complex than a crude misogyny. For example, Newton and

other Black Panthers could excel at the ghetto's masculine ritual of "playing the dozens"—
"by talking about sexual liberties they have taken with the opponent's mother"—and yet still
glorify "the beautiful and noble Black woman" who supported her family through love and
hard work. They acted, they claimed, in defense of their women, who were urged to abandon political and economic competition with men and "take care of business" at home.[76]

The notion that black women—and more specifically, gainfully employed women—had
deprived males of all ages of their self-respect received the imprint of scholarly respectability in the form of the Moynihan Report. The study, entitled "The Negro Family: The Case
for National Action," was prepared for the United States Department of Labor by Daniel
Patrick Moynihan, a Harvard University sociologist, and released in March 1965. Moynihan blamed a "tightening tangle of pathology" within the black community on female-
headed black households. Single mothers, he charged, bequeathed a female culture to their
children and thereby lessened their sons' chances for healthy sex-role development. Consequently, black men needed to retreat to "an utterly masculine world . . . a world away from
women, a world run by strong men of unquestioned authority, where discipline, if harsh, is
nonetheless orderly and predictable, and where rewards, if limited, are granted on the basis
of performance." In sum, "In the U.S. Army you get to know what it means to feel like a
man." Black and white male scholars took up this theme, and in their virulent condemna-
tions of black "momism" blamed the "church-going, overworked . . . harassed, cranky,
frustrated" mother for the "disorganization" of the black family in general and the antiso-
cial tendencies of ghetto youth in particular.[77]

Black Power advocates rejected out of hand Moynihan's contention that military life
would redeem black men from their mothers; fighting the white man's war against people of
color in the jungles of Vietnam hardly offered black men any kind of redemption. And
Stokely Carmichael, a founding theorist of Black Power, accused Moynihan of "playing the
dozens" with black men. "To set the record straight," Carmichael wrote in 1966, "the reason we are in the bag we are in isn't because of my mama, it's because of what they did to
my mama." Still, other outspoken black men tacitly endorsed Moynihan's analysis and rev-
eled in their own male worlds, whether it was the Black Muslim temple or the ghetto street
corner. Militant black nationalist and Black Power groups in the 1960s agreed upon the importance of male-dominated leadership in the struggle for liberation and the need to establish a conventional sexual division of labor within the black household.[78]

Many black women expressed admiration for the Panthers' "posture and program," especially their willingness to answer the white man's arrogance with gunfire; and a woman,
Angela Davis, came to symbolize the angry defiance of the militant ethos. Indeed, members
of both sexes responded to the Black Power movement with a newfound sense of pride in
the beauty of their own blackness and with a collective determination to resist the superficial gains often associated with "racial integration." Older women at times criticized the
style but supported the substance of their demands. In Orange County, California, an elderly black woman told Eldridge Cleaver, "I like what you're saying, Mr. Cleaver, but your
bad words hurt my ears." Bobby Seale's own mother assured him, "I'm with y'all, I'll al-

ways be with you . . . ," but she feared for his safety and wished the Panthers would "stop cussin' just a little bit."[79]

More generally, Black Power advocates, black nationalists and feminists, and civil rights activists shared much more than media images seemed to suggest. Regardless of gender, age, or place of residence, most black people supported tenants' rights and black entrepreneurship, a focus on police brutality, and a determination to protect black women from white men. The southern civil rights movement was not as free of violence, and the Black Panther Party not as violent, as contemporary and subsequent caricatures would imply. The large number of points of inflection around which communities were organized calls into question the assertion that the push for more black businesses in the ghetto was an exclusively black nationalist goal. Was the rape of black women by white police officers a civil rights issue or a feminist issue? Clearly, starkly drawn categories of analysis and action did not reflect the reality of mass organizing in the North or South, among men or women. And in basic ways, different strands of political ideology and strategy only served to mask a broader, more inclusive struggle for civil rights and dignity—for human rights—and for the empowerment of black people as individuals and as a group.[80]

At the same time, many women activists felt that egocentric male militance endangered all the good work they had done and offered nothing constructive in its place. Dorothy Cotton, in charge of Citizenship Training Projects in Georgia during the late 1960s, told of "the so-called black militants—you know, the guys who were black power with their fists and berets and the jackets and the boots"—who advised her group to destroy public school buildings "and 'off' the superintendent." To Cotton, all the "cussin'" and threats provided little of real value for black people in the area; she concluded, "If you want to have change, of course, the bottom line is that the folk for whom the change is meant must be involved in it."[81]

Looking back on their own experiences as members of the Black Panther Party, in the early 1970s some young black women began to express resentment over the cult of virility that had pervaded the organization. Assata Shakur (formerly Joanne Chesinard) later termed herself and other female party members "moderately liberated"; they "were allowed to wear pants and expected to pick up the gun" (Erica Huggins was a good example), all the while giving "doe-eyed looks to our leaders." Sisters tended the children "while the Brotha was doing his thing, or had moved on to bigger and better things." A veteran of SNCC organizing drives before she became communications secretary for the Panthers, Kathleen Cleaver felt her skills went unappreciated in the party: "It seemed that it had something to do with the egos of the men involved," she told an interviewer in 1971.[82]

In fact, as early as 1964, Pauli Murray warned that the impending Black Power revolt of "ambitious men" would unleash "the backlash of a new male aggressiveness against Negro women." By this time, women active in SNCC had seen the handwriting on the wall. Their work in the organization proved crucial to the development of female civil rights workers' political consciousness, but as Cynthia Washington, a black organizer, pointed out, black and white women arrived at that consciousness after starting from "different ends of the spectrum." White women grew restive as they languished behind office desks, assigned to menial clerical tasks, while black women intimidated their male colleagues with their competence in the field. Sexual relations between black men and white women proved painful to many black women in SNCC. Frances Beal founded the Black Women's Liberation committee of SNCC and condemned the blatant male chauvinism of "so-called revolutionary organizations." Ruby Doris Smith Robinson, Kathleen Cleaver, and Angela Davis also spoke out against the tendency of men in SNCC to cry "matriarchal *coup d'etat*" "whenever we women were involved in something important." Cynthia Washington suggested that these men were motivated by a desire to rid themselves of female rivals for leadership positions when they called for black women in general to begin "producing children for the black nation." Though she served as the chair of the Black Panthers from 1974 to 1977, Elaine Brown decried the fact that, as she put it, women in the organization were largely "considered, at best, irrelevant. A woman asserting herself was a pariah. A woman attempting the role of leadership was . . . making an alliance with the counter-revolutionary, man-hating, lesbian, feminist white bitches." Ultimately, then, the Black Panthers merely confirmed the fears of young women who had served as the civil rights movement's backbone—with an emphasis on "back."[83]

When black women began to attempt to forge a political consciousness out of their unique interests in the 1960s, they found that they had little in the way of ready-made theories or strategies to build upon. The ideology of black feminism, ultimately, sprang not from abstract theoretical formulations, but from self-scrutiny and self-understanding. As Toni Morrison put it, the black woman "had nothing to fall back on: not maleness, not whiteness, not ladyhood, not anything. And out of the profound desolation of her reality she may very well have invented herself." The literature of black feminism took many forms—poetry, fiction, and autobiographies; scholarly articles and monographs; "rap-aloud" and stream-of-consciousness pieces; polemical tracts; personal interviews and dialogues. It ranged over a wide variety of topics, from paeans to a mother's flower garden (grown "as if by magic") and best friend Bella's cooking, to studies of gender and "racial" stereotyping in advertising, denunciations of hypocritical white women and abusive black husbands, an evocation of Billie Holiday's blues, and explorations of black lesbianism. Obviously, then, as an ideology it was characterized not by a few key works of widely recognized or self-appointed leaders, but by the interweaving of protests and laments from women who come from the farm and the ghetto, the factory and the university.[84]

Black feminists rejected the Moynihan thesis and the black male conservative NAACP leaders and Black Panthers who promoted it one way or another. Pauli Murray put the matter delicately when she suggested that the report "impliedly censured" black mothers "for their efforts to overcome a handicap not of their own making and for trying to meet the standards of the country as a whole." Some of her sisters were not so restrained. Did a welfare mother's "measley check" make her a castrating matriarch? Where was the power born of poverty and hunger? Observed one woman, "I've heard a lot of women wish they were men but I never heard no man wish he was a woman." The emotional strength of black women, their "highly functional" role and "mother wit," was labeled bitchy aggressiveness by men, too many of them black. In Alice Walker's words, "Our plainer gifts, our labors of fidelity and love, have been knocked down our throats." Black women social scientists amassed statistical and demographic evidence to refute the notion of black women's "privileged status" in American educational and economic life; this idea was advanced by black male leaders who contended that wives and lovers should remain "ten paces" behind their men, at least for the time being.[85]

Nevertheless, with near unanimity black women activists agreed that racial ideologies, rather than gender prescriptions, were the primary source of their oppression. Thus it was much easier for them to denounce white women instead of black men, and white feminism in particular quickly attracted much criticism. Certainly poor women of both races shared common interests in terms of their need for better jobs and wages, decent health care, reform of the welfare system, and elimination of discriminatory legislation. Yet these basic concerns, and a sensitivity to the unique vulnerabilities of minority women, did not inform the national white women's liberation movement (here defined primarily by NOW) until well into the 1970s. Thus, although Pauli Murray was one of its founders and Aileen Hernandez served briefly as one of its early presidents, many black women activists and academics shunned NOW as the representative of middle-class white women.

Overall, in its earliest stages, black feminism tended to equate white feminists with students, housewives, and upper-echelon professionals—that is, with women who either did not hold jobs at all or, if they did, made a comfortable and independent living from them. Black feminists pointed out that their experiences amounted to "more than a parenthetical remark in a chapter" of women's history, that the interests of white middle-class and black women were qualitatively different. (Nancy White quoted her mother—"the black woman is the white man's mule and the white woman is his dog"—to indicate her contempt for both white male supremacy and white female complacency.) Members of NOW and other white-dominated organizations, they charged, "suffered little more than boredom, gentle repression, and dishpan hands," and engaged in trivial and silly forms of self-aggrandizement when they burned their bras and insisted on the title "Ms."[86]

Moreover, white women had served as the active agents of racist America. Noted one middle-aged domestic, "Black men will make a fool out of me if I let them, but it was a white woman who had me crawling around her apartment before I was thirteen years old, cleaning places she would never think of cleaning with a toothbrush and toothpick!" White women were typified by, on the one hand, the plantation slave mistress and, on the other, the liberal Manhattan lawyer, active in NOW, with an underpaid black mother as her housekeeper: "What do you do with the fact that the women who clean your houses and tend your children while you attend conferences on feminist theory are, for the most part, poor and third-world women? What is the theory behind racist feminism?" Indeed, their divergent working lives formed the greatest gulf between black and middle-class white women. Diane K. Lewis asked, "Was staying at home proof of sexism or a privileged status?" A Mississippi single parent, a mother of eleven, dismissed women's liberation advocates as "just a bunch of women that don't know what they want. . . . If they so tired of staying at home, let them change places with me for a while and see how tired they get." Alice Walker rejected the term altogether—it evoked in the public imagination white-middle-class college students and housewives—and offered in its stead the term "womanist," to refer to black women acting on their own behalf.[87]

The tendency on the part of many black women to dismiss a supposedly monolithic women's liberation movement as an exercise in self-indulgence by spoiled white housewives was understandable, but misguided. Some black feminists accepted uncritically the images popularized by unsympathetic print and electronic-media journalists who sought to sensationalize equal rights protests without delving into the injustices that lay behind them. Moreover, by lumping all white women together under the rubric "middle class," black feminists downplayed the role that class played in shaping social relationships of all kinds. For a while at least, it seemed as if much of the rage felt by black women was being directed at other groups of women—ironic indeed considering that the very system they condemned had flourished, at least partly, as a result of the "racial" and class antagonisms that divided exploited workers of both sexes.

In the process of formulating a positive ideology, and not just one that reacted to the inadequacies of other interest groups, black feminists encountered three dilemmas that made the task of finding a "way out of no way" particularly hazardous. The first dilemma involved the formulation of a critique of black male sexism that would not automatically estrange black women from their fathers, husbands, and sons. White feminists might easily indulge in anti-male diatribes, but, as Gloria Joseph put it, "Black women cannot operate with a philosophy whose dynamics include separation, rejection, or exclusion of men." (Even black lesbians walked carefully around this "deeply taboo" subject.) Nevertheless, many black feminists continued to argue strenuously that black men shared with white men a lust for sexual power in ways that led to the gross abuse of black women's bodies and spirits. In her book *Ain't I a Woman?* bell hooks charged forthrightly that "many black men have shown that they were far more concerned with exerting masculine privilege than challenging racism."[88]

Perhaps Barbara Smith put her finger on the problem when she argued, "We don't have a language yet or a framework as to what is the true nature of women's oppression, given where it takes place and who it comes from and how." The mere description of black women's plight did not necessarily entail a rigorous analysis of the mechanics of gender and racial ideologies, or an understanding of the ways those ideologies reinforced each other. Ultimately, the interplay between institutional structures and personal initiative lay at the heart of the issue: Should black men and women be held morally accountable as individuals for the ways in which capitalism and patriarchy had twisted their expectations of one another? If not, who would explain this to a mother neglected by the embittered, unemployed father of her children?[89]

Black feminists faced a second major dilemma when they sought to celebrate black women's strengths—"that championship tradition"—without minimizing the corrosive effects of prejudice on their ability to function as free and healthy individuals. Black women, with their "culturally shaped resilience, strategic coping and defense mechanisms" had "tried to spell able" and keep the African American community intact. From their "work-worn, sexually abused bodies" had come a tender, creative impulse that in its most humble form—a song or a handmade dress—lifted the spirits of a people. However, during the latter part of the 1970s, black feminists began to examine in depth the high price that they and their mothers had paid for the constant stress under which they lived—hypertension; "drinking the blues away"; unwanted pregnancies; and higher rates of diabetes, breast cancer, and obesity than white women. Drained of their emotional energies by those dependent upon them, some women found it difficult to replenish their strength. Bernice Johnson Reagon recounted her own mother's work in the cotton fields and in the kitchen and then noted:

> *My father had a turning place*
> *Mama*
> *We had a turning place*
> *Mama*
> *White folks had a turning place*
> *All of us*
> *There was nobody for Mama to turn to*
> *She was it*

This issue once again highlighted the inadequacy of commonly used terms to explain black women's situation. They might be "liberated" from total financial dependence on their husbands ("there is a very few black women that their husbands can pocketbook to death because we can do for ourselves and will do so in a minute!"); but in some cases they were still locked within a prison of poor health and deep despair that might manifest itself in mental illness or domestic violence. May Anna Madison's observation, "There are some lives that people just shouldn't have to live" applied equally to the overburdened mother and the abused child.[90]

Black feminists' third dilemma was to organize themselves in a way that maximized their collective political strength by joining with other groups but without compromising their own integrity and identity. At the local level, feminist study groups and cooperatives began to spring up in the mid-1960s, and these ad hoc arrangements continually shifted and reconstituted themselves in response to crisis situations and the force of individual personalities. But black feminism was not yet a coherent political position from which to launch a national movement. Founded in 1973, the National Black Feminist Organization (NBFO) sponsored the path-breaking Eastern Regional Conference of Black Feminism the same year and gave birth to several branches throughout the country. But it had disappeared by the late 1970s, condemned as a "black NOW"—"like a white woman's conception of what a Black feminist organization should be"—too integrationist-minded, dominated by women in the professions. In reality, the NBFO and other groups like the Black Women Organized for Action (founded in San Francisco in 1973) had a much broader class-interest base than NOW. But they attracted relatively few active members and remained vulnerable to conflicts between lesbians and heterosexuals, poor and middle-class women. In 1982 Michele

Wallace observed, "Despite a sizable number of Black feminists who have contributed much to the leadership of the women's movement, there is still no Black women's movement, and it appears there won't be for some time to come." Yet she underestimated the growing influence of black women in labor unions, public-housing tenant councils, and city and state governments, all working to erase the residue of centuries of slavery and American apartheid.[91]

By the mid-1970s the larger women's liberation movement in the United States had become more diverse in terms of class and ethnic differences, more sensitive to racial ideologies and to the needs of women who cast their lot with traditional family and marital arrangements, and less dominated by the 55,000-member NOW. The high visibility of feminist theoreticians within the humanities and social sciences, and the respectability of women's rights as an issue among women of both major political parties, made it no longer possible to generalize blithely about "white feminists." Under these conditions, some black women became actively involved in white-dominated organizations relevant to their own interests—such as the Coalition of Labor Union Women (formed in 1974)—but they continued to stress the theme that their own work and family experiences were fundamentally different from those of white women. In fact, prospects for aggressive coalition-building among black women (who were, after all, only 5 percent of the total U.S. adult population), white feminists, third-world men and women, and the white working class seemed bleak. External factors played a major role: In the early 1970s various law-enforcement agencies violently eliminated the Black Power movement, while the New Left disintegrated in the face of the U.S. withdrawal from Vietnam, and the massive infusion of private and public funds into social-welfare programs tapered off. Social activism receded as a focus for journalists of all kinds. Yet weakness also sprang from internal forces, for black feminists still felt they needed to maintain their distance from other groups they feared would taint their cause. In effect, their self-realization depended upon the existence of negative reference groups.[92]

In the 1960s and 1970s emerged a new phenomenon in the history of black working women—the national recognition accorded a small number of them. Both New Yorker Shirley Chisholm, who served seven terms in the U.S. House of Representatives (1969–1983), together with Texan Barbara Jordan (1973–1979), achieved a national audience when they denounced the enduring effects of prejudice and described the hardships endured by African Americans in late-twentieth-century America. Chisholm noted prophetically in 1971: "Each black male and black female, white female and white male must escape from his or her own historical traps before they can be truly effective in helping others to free themselves."[93] Writers Maya Angelou, Toni Morrison, and Alice Walker wrote unflinchingly of the plight and the strength of black women. Coretta Scott King kept alive the legacy of her husband, pressing for a national holiday in his honor (approved by Congress and signed into law by President Reagan in 1983) and, in the 1980s, embarking on a new career as an outspoken opponent of the South African system of apartheid. However, it would be unfortunate if the high visibility of this group of women were juxtaposed with the struggles of poor women in the ghettos, as if this contrast encapsulated all the ambiguities related to black women's modern political and economic status. Instead, it would be more fruitful to note the ways in which these well-known women fit into a larger historical pattern: how the eloquence of their lives served to reflect those of their unsung grandmothers and sisters, and how they, like other black women of achievement throughout American history, often blended paid and unpaid work in the fields of education, politics, and literature. Moreover, in the stories they wrote about themselves, or about other women, they echoed rhythms characteristic of the experiences of so many black working women: stark, episodic confrontations with prejudice, followed by a reconsecration of the spirit with the help of friends and kin, and a rededication to a cause, or to a life.[93]

For those who hoped that their testimony would inspire a radical new national commitment on behalf of those women who demonstrated impressive accomplishments quietly, within the fold of family and community, the signs were not encouraging. Noted Hattie Gossett, a writer, at the beginning of the new decade: "You aint nothing but a black woman! who told you anybody wanted to hear from you? its the 80s. dont nobody care nothing about black folks these days, we is definitely not in vogue, this season we are not the rage, aint nobody even seriously courting our vote during this presidential year."[94] In fact, the "Reagan Revolution" would reinforce those very economic trends that continued to adversely affect black people. A cadre of influential white ideologues would initiate new assaults on the welfare of black working women and their children—all in the name of preserving family integrity. Increasing numbers of white people would call for "color-blind" public policies that would leave intact the legacy of generations of discrimination and prejudice—particularly the clustering of the impoverished black people in the rural South and northern inner-cities. And a largely indifferent white constituency would acquiesce in the injustice of this "new redemption."

NINE

CROSSCURRENTS OF PAST AND PRESENT, 1980–2009

IN MARCH 2009, a forty-five-year-old African American woman living in Washington, D.C., arrived in London and caused an international sensation. Michelle Robinson Obama, wife of the recently elected president of the United States, had come to town. One of the highlights of her visit was an address she made to a group of teenaged schoolgirls, most of whom were members of minority ethnic groups and residents of London's poorer neighborhoods. Robinson Obama nonetheless clearly felt an emotional connection with her young audience. In her talk, she reflected on her newfound celebrity status: "Nothing in my life's path ever would have predicted that I would be standing here as the first African-American First Lady," she said. "I was not raised with wealth or resources or any special standing to speak of." In denying the predictive power of her own history, her own "life's path," Robinson Obama was both right and wrong. She was right because in certain fundamental ways her family's journey over the last several generations represented the major themes in the history of African Americans from the antebellum period to the present. Her great-great-grandfather Jim Robinson was born into slavery on a rice plantation in the South Carolina low country (in 1850), and his grandson Fraser (born in 1912), like thousands of other southern blacks, had moved north, to Chicago. Michelle Robinson grew up in a two-parent household of modest means, in a brick bungalow on the city's South Side. In certain ways, then, her family narrative was familiar—typical of a broad swath of striving black families—without much to suggest that any particular member was destined for wealth or fame.[1]

At the same time, the First Lady was wrong in suggesting that her background betrayed no clues to her own achievements in life. After graduating from Princeton University and Harvard Law School, she held a series of high-level jobs—as an associate in a private law firm; an assistant to Mayor Richard M. Daley of Chicago; executive director of the Chicago Office of Public Affairs, a nonprofit agency that encourages young people to pursue careers in the nonprofit and governmental sectors; and vice president for community and external affairs for the University of Chicago Medical Center. In 1992 she married another ambitious lawyer named Barack Obama, and together they started a family. In her talk at the London school that day, the First Lady urged the pupils to value education, and to cultivate within themselves the qualities of fortitude, confidence, and hard work. These were the very qualities that had helped her achieve success in school and in the working world, eventually propelling her into the international spotlight with her husband's historic presidential campaign and election in the fall of 2008. Clearly, Michelle Obama's intelligence, drive, and self-discipline helped to account for her remarkable life story.[2]

The new First Lady came from a family shaped by the sharp contours of African American history. After a stint in the army in World War II, her grandfather found work as a mail carrier for the U.S. Postal Service, and with his wife raised their children in a cinderblock public housing project. Their son Fraser Robinson III (Michelle's father) tended boilers at a Chicago water-filtration plant. Public-works and civil-service jobs had secured for the Robinsons a place in the small, emerging mid-twentieth-century black middle class. Jobs held by men in previous generations of the family also included those of servant, shoemaker, newspaper salesman, soldier, and sawmill employee, all of which bespoke both the limited options available to black men in the wake of slavery, and the efforts of these particular husbands and fathers to avoid work as field-hands. In learning of her roots in low-country slavery, Michelle Obama cited the process of "uncovering the shame, digging out the pride that is part of that story—so that other folks feel comfortable about embracing the beauty and the tangled nature of this country." Indeed, it was out of the ordinariness of her own background that Michelle Obama emerged as an extraordinary woman.[3]

Beginning in January 2009, the White House became the workplace for a group of noteworthy African American women, modern-day successors to the maids, cooks, laundresses, and cleaning women who had served previous presidents. Born in 1937, Marian Robinson, Michelle's mother, helped care for her granddaughters Malia Ann, born in 1998, and Natasha (Sasha), 2001. She took the girls to and from school, and made sure they did their homework. A widow since 1991, Robinson had worked as a secretary in a Chicago Spiegel catalogue store and in a bank. Together with her husband (who suffered from muscular dystrophy for much of his adult life), she had raised two high-achieving children, Michelle and her older brother, Craig; he also graduated from Princeton and, in 2009, was serving as head men's coach for the Oregon State University basketball team. Although initially hesitant about leaving her Chicago home and moving to Washington, Robinson soon embraced life in the White House and the cultural liveliness of the capital. Observed her daughter, "She has a very full social life, so much so that sometimes we have to plan our schedule around her schedule."[4]

Also working in and around the White House was a group of Obama appointees—highly educated women with impressive resumes testifying to years of collective experience in government, politics, nonprofit organizations, private enterprise, and philanthropy. They represented the pinnacle of the 200,000 black working women employed by the federal government (out of a total 1.7 million) in 2009: Mona Sutphen, the president's deputy chief of staff; Desiree Rogers, White House social secretary; Cassandra Butts, deputy White House counsel; Valerie Jarrett, senior adviser and assistant to the president for Public Engagement and Intergovernmental Affairs; Susan Rice, U.S. ambassador to the United Nations; Melody Barnes, director of the White House Domestic Policy Council; and Margaret Hamburg, head of the Food and Drug Administration. Never before in the nation's history had so many black working women served in so many high-profile and senior positions in a presidential administration.[5]

And so it was not surprising that soon after Barack Obama assumed the presidency, commentators and journalists began to herald a new day in the history of black working women, and a new day in American "race relations." Writing in the *Nation*, Patricia J. Williams suggested that Michelle Obama had transcended the historic stereotypes that had plagued so many black women over the centuries—the household drudge; the sexualized, compliant concubine; the lazy welfare mother; the hard-edged career woman. Wrote Williams (a *Nation* columnist and a professor at Columbia Law School), "Hers is a well-rounded life, one of multiple roles and layered humanity. She is powerful yet approachable, highly educated yet colloquial, bare-armed but modest, playful but consummately civilized." Observers praised the new First Lady for her efforts to reach out to the impoverished African American community, especially school children, in the nation's capital, and at the same time keep her children's lives as normal as possible, with sleepovers in the White House and a new puppy to care for.[6]

Soon after the election, the Gallup Poll published a story under the headline "Americans See Obama Election as Race Relations Milestone." Among the findings: "Over two-thirds of Americans say Barack Obama's election as president is either the most important advance for blacks in the past 100 years, or among the two or three most important such advances," and "67% of Americans say a solution to relations between blacks and whites will eventually be worked out, the highest value Gallup has measured on this question." Seven out of ten Americans believed that "race relations in this country will get at least a little better as a result of Obama's election, including 28 percent who say they will get a lot better." Concluded the pollsters, "The data reviewed also show that Americans believe Obama's election represents a highly significant milestone in the history of race relations in this country." In a related vein, major newspapers published interviews with blacks and whites alike who seemed ready to put the nation's past of slavery and discrimination behind them and move forward. A headline in the *New York Times* declared: "In Obama Era, Voices Reflect Rising Sense of Racial Optimism," with two-thirds of Americans saying that "race relations were generally good," and a dramatic rise between summer 2008 and spring 2009 in the number of African Americans who felt that way.[7]

Yet the term "race relations" offers little insight into the status of African Americans: Where and under what conditions were whites and blacks "relating" to one another? The new president recognized as much; he understood that even the election of a man who identified himself as black (the son of a black Kenyan father and a white American mother) could not in and of itself guarantee a reversal of historic trends affecting African Americans. In his best-selling 1996 book, *The Audacity of Hope*, Obama noted stubborn stresses on the black family since the mid-twentieth century: the decline in the marriage rate among black women; the rise in the number of black children living in single-parent households (Obama had been one of them); and persistent rates of black poverty, especially among those trapped in the rural South and northern central cities. Indeed, so-called "post-racial" America afforded abundant evidence of the legacy of slavery, and the burdens that many African Americans still shouldered, even compared to white people of similar income levels. The economic crisis that hit the nation with such force beginning in the fall of 2008 disproportionately devastated blacks as homeowners and as workers compared to their white counterparts. Obama's victory in November 2008 carried with it great symbolic significance, yet larger structural forces in the economy rendered black working women and their families vulnerable in unique ways, even as the ranks of the poor swelled to include many "Fourth Wave" immigrants.[8]

Beginning in the 1970s, national and global economic developments adversely affected poor people everywhere, now forced to compete among themselves on a "level playing field" that nonetheless offered little in the way of good wages or decent benefits. The baneful effects of corporate restructuring and the universal search for cheap labor abided no color line, as immigrants from Southeast Asia and Latin America soon discovered. The domestic economy offered fewer and fewer jobs for workers who possessed little in the way of skills or formal education; well-paid jobs for high-school graduates were gradually disappearing, depleting in size and influence the industrial unions that for generations had represented large numbers of relatively well-paid, semiskilled machine operatives and assembly-line workers. Title VII of the 1964 Civil Rights Act cracked open many historically all-white workplaces, but at the same time, whole industries such as textiles and autos came under extreme pressure from foreign competitors, and jobs in those industries began to disappear. Affirmative-action policies challenged long-standing discriminatory traditions among white employers and university admissions officials, but the new openness affected primarily black men and women who were already well-educated or considered exceptionally promising in terms of their potential. These tensions—between a new "colorblind" American society on the one hand and stubborn forms of inequality on the other, would shape the lives and labors of black working women well into the future.[9]

THE REAGAN REVOLUTION AND THE "NEW FEDERALISM"

During the 1980s, the plight of the single black mother became a pivotal source of contention between Republicans and Democrats. For Republicans, now under the leadership of President Ronald Reagan, Aid to Families with Dependent Children (AFDC) served as a symbol of Great Society excesses—a federal program that, in the eyes of its critics, condemned the poor to perpetual dependence, rewarded immorality in the form of out-of-wedlock births, tolerated fraudulent practices, and actually increased rates of poverty by discouraging women from seeking employment and taking responsibility for their children. The ideological construct of the "welfare queen" (invariably a black woman living in a northern inner-city) apparently represented the culmination of all these vices, for, according to the caricature, she had too many children, spent her food stamps and other taxpayer-subsidized aid on alcohol, drove a fancy car, and raked in thousands of dollars through bogus claims processed by gullible and incompetent caseworkers. Republicans found that they could win white votes by tarring their Democratic opponents as reflexive proponents of "welfare," and, by implication, as supporters of sexual immorality and crime. Not until 1996, when President Bill Clinton, a Democrat, kept his campaign promise and ended "welfare as we know it," would this image of the black mother begin to lose some of its cultural resonance, at least in national politics.[10]

Despite the revolutionary nature of the Civil Rights Acts of 1964 and 1965, only a minority of black families could afford to move out of the ghetto and into suburban neighborhoods. Beginning in the 1970s and continuing through the 1980s, rising unemployment rates (reaching Depression-era levels for black men, especially young men) continued to wreak havoc on whole communities. In 1980, 40 percent of all black households were headed by a woman (compared to only 14 percent of all white households), and only about 50 percent of black female household heads were gainfully employed. These disastrous trends were largely impervious to notable gains in black voting and political strength. By the mid-1980s, black office seekers were claiming their fair share of power, especially at the local level in predominantly black rural counties and central cities: In 1985, for example, 6,016 black people, 1,358 of them women, won public office. Still, even the election of northern big-city black mayors could not change the fundamental equation of economic growth and development, characterized by the continued flight of jobs and middle-class families to the suburbs, and declining urban tax bases that led to the decay of minority neighborhoods, their schools, and housing stock.[11]

Specific policies enacted under the Reagan administration affected the well-being of impoverished women and their families in dramatic ways. Reagan initiated the "New Federalism," which called upon the states either to accept or reject responsibility for many of the social-welfare functions currently claimed by the federal government. The "New Federalism" reflected the mood of white suburbanites; they had become increasingly resentful at the idea that government was taxing them to fund an expanded version of President Johnson's "Great Society," with its attention to the poor, whether in northern ghettos or the hills and hollows of Appalachia. Subsequent cutbacks in public services led to a corresponding decline in public-sector jobs at the federal, state, and local levels, the mainstay of the black middle class. For black men and women who had established a "niche" in public employment, and counted on these jobs as vehicles of upward social mobility, the "New Federalism" represented an assault on their livelihoods and on the well-being of their families. In addition, the president trumpeted his "pro-family" stance through new regulations covering parent-child relations, but at the same time evinced little concern for black infant mortality rates twice as high as white rates. New Federalists in general sought to prune federal and state budgets of funds allocated to social-welfare programs for the poor. In the federal budget for fiscal 1984, the administration signaled its intention to reduce AFDC, school lunch, and food stamp benefits, and to substantially reduce the modest Special Supplementary Nutritional Program for Women, Infants and Children (WIC) that provided prenatal care for low-income pregnant women. These proposals were part of a larger political agenda that mandated that poor men and women fend for themselves, regardless of the immediate, drastic consequences for their children.[12]

Conservative anti-tax principles exacerbated the plight of inner cities. In 1980, the Philadelphia neighborhood surrounding the headquarters of the Philadelphia Citizens in Action (cofounded by the activist Roxanne Jones) had a population that was virtually all black, with half its residents impoverished and one-quarter unemployed. Like other ghettos around the country, this area of concentrated poverty was impervious to piecemeal reform projects. Food stamps and welfare payments could not compensate for the loss of jobs when urban factories and other businesses shuttered their doors, locked their gates, and relocated in the suburbs. Moreover, with the implicit and persistent backing of the federal government, several groups and institutions preserved the historical inequalities that had created distressed central cities—banks "redlined" black neighborhoods and refused to provide mortgages to their residents no matter how hardworking or well-off; neighborhood improvement associations and real estate agents worked to preserve the lily-white character of suburbs; local public-housing planners built segregated high-rise projects and massive interstate highways that blighted already beleaguered communities. In the early 1980s, Pennsylvania joined with other states to cut welfare benefits and tighten eligibility requirements. In June of 1983, Jones led a protest at Philadelphia Gas Works in response to the company's decision to deny service to all who failed to pay their bills. Two years later she won election to the Pennsylvania state senate, but economic and political realities could not alter the fact that poor people, even those employed full-time, simply could not make enough money to support their families.[13]

At the same time, an overall post–World War II trend reducing the gap between the rich and poor showed signs of reversal. Among the contributing factors was a renewed attack on labor unions. Reagan himself demonstrated a profoundly antiunion stance. His firing of 11,359 striking air-traffic controllers in 1981 revealed new threats for unions already under siege by global economic forces (the United Automobile Workers) as well as government policies (the American Federation of State, County, and Municipal Employees)—this at a time when it was becoming abundantly clear that labor unions were one of the most effective antipoverty strategies available to working people. Union successes in Las Vegas, the site of the fastest growing labor movement in the nation, demonstrated that good, secure jobs with decent wages and benefits were the key to stable families and upward mobility among even workers with limited education. In the 1960s, Ruby Duncan and Johnnie Tillmon had organized poor mothers to challenge restrictive eligibility requirements for AFDC; a generation later, African American women such as Hattie Canty were emerging as leaders of aggressive labor unions—in Canty's case, the one that represented thousands of chambermaids, bartenders, casino workers, and waitresses. Union members enjoyed not only decent pay and secure jobs, but also the opportunity to move up the ladder within workplaces to better positions, as far as their talent and experience would take them. Of her efforts to organize forty thousand employees of Las Vegas's largest casino hotels, Canty said, "It has not been a picnic for me, but I don't think I'd like to go on a picnic every day. I have enjoyed the struggle. I'm not the only Hattie. There's lots of Hatties out there." Nevertheless, unions faced an uphill battle as the Reagan and George H. W. Bush administrations imprinted their opposition to collective bargaining in their appointments to the National Labor Relations Board. Opined one of Reagan's appointees to the NLRB, "Collective bargaining frequently means labor monopoly, the destruction of individual freedom, and the destruction of the marketplace as the mechanism for determining the value of labor."[14]

During the 1980s, national political discourse echoed the contradictions in racial ideologies first apparent a century and a half earlier, in the antebellum North. On the one hand, whites as a group objected to affirmative action policies as "unfair" practices bound to reduce white workers to poverty. In fact, "affirmative action" encompassed a wide range of policies, from workplace quotas (receding over time as a result of Supreme Court rulings and public outcry) to outreach efforts to attract promising minority candidates to certain schools, colleges, or workplaces. Many job openings elicited an excess of fully qualified candidates, both blacks and whites. Yet whites held that hiring in general was a zero-sum game—for every good job taken by a black person one would be denied to a white person. Supporters of affirmative action pointed out that whites had for generations benefited from "preferences" themselves, laboring in all-white workplaces that excluded blacks as a matter of policy and principle; black people were now claiming their due. Yet coexisting simultaneously with the stereotype of the predatory job applicant was the stereotype of the lazy welfare recipient, an image fueled by Reagan's frequent (and fictional) invocation of a prototypical, cunning welfare mother living high off taxpayers' dollars. Thus these two seemingly contradictory images remained part of the political landscape—the black person determined to deprive whites of good jobs, and the black person determined to avoid gainful employment at all costs. These images were invariably gendered, with men representing the first category and women—mothers—representing the second.[15]

By this time, the structure of the workforce belied many of the claims by whites who believed black job seekers threatened their own well-being. It was larger economic forces, and not the hiring of small numbers of blacks in previously all-white workplaces, that led to the dramatic displacement of whites in certain industries. In fact, because of their relatively limited educations, many blacks remained confined to menial, low-paying labor in the service or social-service sectors; these workers were largely unaffected by affirmative action policies of universities, fire and police departments, and large corporations.

Moreover, "new immigrants" were challenging conventional black-white views of the American workplace. Certainly, many cities were already diverse places, with large numbers of Puerto Ricans in New York and large numbers of Chinese in San Francisco (for example). However, the immigration reform act of 1965 spurred the growth in numbers of political and economic refugees from Southeast Asia and Latin and Central America. Most found employment as factory workers or as unskilled laborers. By the mid-1970s, for example, Chinese women workers accounted for fully 80 percent of all members of New York City's International Ladies Garment Workers Union Local 23–25. Black working women in manufacturing felt economic pressure from these newcomers, achieving few if any substantial gains from affirmative action policies. Undocumented immigrants in particular undercut the wages of the lowest echelon of black workers, for without the protection that legal status conferred, these immigrants had virtually no recourse if and when they were denied over-time pay or the minimum wage, or forced to work long hours without benefits or days off. Eager to trim their own payrolls, employers from agribusinesses to sweatshop owners ea-gerly sought out such vulnerable men, women, and children.[16]

All over the country, employers began to make invidious comparisons between immi-grants and African Americans. Indeed, by virtue of their historical and present-day resistance to various forms of labor exploitation, blacks as a group bore the stigma of "troublemak-ers," in contrast to recent immigrants who were believed to be more compliant (as undocu-mented immigrants assuredly were). These employer preferences revealed a whole new set of stereotypes. Thus, managers of chicken hatcheries claimed that "only Asians have the physical dexterity and small hands needed to feel a chick's tiny sexual organs and determine whether they're male or female." Manufacturers of computer components and other kinds of electronic equipment offered similar rationales for their hiring practices, whether at home or abroad. Pockets of immigrants were tapped for specific low-wage jobs; for exam-ple, hotel owners recruited Vietnamese and Hmong immigrants for jobs as chambermaids and buspersons, regardless of whether or not they spoke English. In out-of-the-way places like Storm Lake, Iowa, employers found Hispanic and Laotian hands willing to do the dirty work that more settled groups shunned—a hog slaughterhouse offered "lots of knife work" ("not a pleasant job"), while Somalis found employment in the local turkey-packing plant. Meanwhile, some employers circled the globe, looking for workers who would not protest disagreeable and dangerous working conditions. This new, mean, global economy placed downward pressure on the pay of African American women engaged in low-wage work.[17]

Though times were changing in a "post-civil-rights" society, the challenges faced by many black women resembled those of their forebears. Donna Bazemore was sweltering in hundred-degree temperatures in a North Carolina chicken processing plant during the night shift, and attending school in the mornings; she had to leave her children in the care of her grandmother by day and her mother by night. Her long hours on the eviscerating and trimming lines left her with a crippling case of carpal tunnel syndrome. Bazemore eventu-ally quit her job, and became an organizer of poultry workers. Meanwhile, in Chicago's massive, blighted Henry Horner housing project, LaJoe Rivers spent her days trying to keep her family together; just venturing out to the grocery store—once a month, in a hired cab, to buy enough food for thirteen people with $542 worth of food stamps—constituted a task of heroic proportions. An AFDC recipient, Rivers had little choice but to remain de-pendent on the whims of social workers and bureaucrats for the well-being of her family. It was during this time, in the late 1980s and early 1990s, that women like Wilhelmina Green, a resident of St. Helena Island off the coast of South Carolina, were spending up to five hours a day on a bus commuting to jobs as kitchen workers on the nearby island of Hilton Head. Her husband disabled, Green was responsible for earning a living for her children and a grandchild. On the road or at work for thirteen hours each day, she earned $260 per week serving whites at an exclusive island "plantation." For Donna Bazemore, LaJoe

Rivers, and Wilhelmina Green, the effort to provide for their families with little in the way of financial resources partook of a certain timeless quality.[18]

As the United States suffered the wrenching effects of global transformations, and as impoverished multiethnic, multiracial communities proliferated throughout the country, black women, along with other wage earners (and would-be wage earners), confronted the liabilities of a deindustrialized economy. Progressive leaders emphasized the common plight of workers regardless of race or gender, black and white men and women who had been displaced from, or shut out of, the paid labor force. The northern inner city was just one of several distressed communities shaped by foreign competition, technological innovation, and global free trade. In their poverty and lack of access to health care and quality education, black women in South-Central Los Angeles shared hardships with Sioux Indians on the Pine Ridge Reservation in South Dakota; with rural Kentuckians piecing together a living from hunting, foraging, and wage work; and with residents of mill towns that had been kept alive by a single factory, now closed. During his 1988 presidential campaign, the Reverend Jesse Jackson offered a "universalizing vision" to all workers when he noted, "When the plant lights go out, we all look the same in the dark." In a speech to the National Urban League, Hugh Price, the president of the group, acknowledged the "still well-documented and undeniable reality" of prejudice based on skin color, but went on to declare, "We must not let ourselves, and especially children, fall into the paranoid trap of thinking that racism accounts for all that plagues us . . . The global realignment of work and wealth is, if anything, the bigger culprit." The decline of labor unions and the erosion of the heavy manufacturing, blue-collar sector; the shrinking payrolls and runaway shops; the robots and computers that decimated the demand for labor in certain industries—all of these developments directly affected thousands of black women typists, textile sewing machine operators, bank tellers, and office-machine operators. In 1990, fully a third of all black working women were concentrated in jobs that were not only low-paying, part-time, and unstable, but also vulnerable to the downsizing and corporate consolidations that characterized the new world economic order. Yet these female employees constituted but a subset of a larger group of American wage earners who paid a personal price for workforce restructuring.[19]

As workers within the home (toiling without pay) and outside the home (toiling for little pay), black and white women together continued to share the time-honored burdens of the double day, a day characterized by unequal treatment in the workplace and an unequal division of labor at home. For women in general, the challenges that came with working in low-paying pink-collar jobs, coping with sexual harassment, securing their reproductive rights, and finding quality and affordable childcare transcended class and color lines. In an economy marked by massive layoffs of high-tech executives as well as assembly-line workers, 3.5 million black women, together with 35 million other American women, took minimum-wage jobs in banks, nursing homes, beauty parlors, day-care centers, and fast-food restaurants. These women earned wages that served for their families "as a cushion between welfare and getting by."[20]

Clearly, then, more and more white women were confronting the inequalities of the modern workplace, and feeling the frustrations of the ill-paid breadwinner, frustrations that had defined the plight of black working women for generations. At the same time, issues related to female wage earning constituted only part of the political gender gap in the mid-1980s; public opinion polls indicated there was a distinct female sensibility on a wide range of issues, including nuclear weapons, defense spending, and education. Nevertheless, purveyors of a New Right ideology—including leaders of the "Moral Majority" movement founded and led by the Reverend Jerry Falwell—argued that women (and by women he meant by and large white women) should abide by traditional gender roles and refrain from working at all, whether that meant taking a secretarial job or aspiring to run companies or whole countries. Though the New Right attracted an inordinate amount of media attention, and though it claimed among its supporters many policymakers at the highest reaches of government, its attempts to revive the patriarchal family foundered on working women's rights, among other issues. In 1982, conservatives rejoiced when efforts to incorporate the Equal Rights Amendment (first proposed in 1923) into the Constitution failed to receive support from the necessary number of states. Yet the world of work now held a profound appeal for many wives over and above their frantic efforts to keep pace with inflation. Very few enjoyed well-paying prestigious jobs, but many increasingly saw wage earning as a source of self-identification and as a hedge against future financial disaster. Regardless of their own station in life, women of all classes, skin colors, and political loyalties had female friends and relatives who, suddenly widowed or divorced or separated, found themselves in substantially reduced circumstances and unable to get a good job or any job at all. When they pressed for divorce, middle-class white men produced their own share of displaced homemakers, a reminder that the full-time wife and mother, paeans to her domestic virtues notwithstanding, remained dependent on the good favor of her husband, regardless of economic status. Thus in condemning all feminists, whom they charged had badgered otherwise sensible housewives into the labor force, the New Right ignored two facts: First, these wives were making rational decisions based on their own marital and economic situations; and second, to an ever greater extent, American businesses were relying on the labor of wives and mothers for their profits. And many outspoken female conservatives, including the attorney Phyllis Schlafly, founder of the Eagle Forum, were themselves working women, too numerous to give the calls for women to return to full-time homemaking much political traction.[21]

Despite the common interests of workers of various demographic groups, prejudice—with all its subtle and not-so-subtle manifestations—remained a vital determinant in shaping black women's lives at home and on the job. Even compared to uneducated white women, black women were disproportionately poor; in 1989, 29.5 percent of white women who worked full-time and lacked a high school diploma headed households below the poverty line, compared to 38.7 percent of similarly situated black women. In 1991, 43.6 percent of all white women between the ages of twenty-five and thirty-four who had never graduated from high school were poor, but the figure for black women was 65.1 percent. Among women high school graduates, disparities still existed on the basis of skin color; 14.1 percent of all white women with a high school diploma were poor, but four out of ten black women with a similar education were impoverished. Black women continued to labor under a double disadvantage; as workers, they made less on a weekly basis ($336) compared to white men ($518), white women ($388), and black men ($380). As wives and mothers, compared to their white counterparts, they could less often count upon their spouses and the fathers of their children to lift the household out of poverty. Moreover, a United States Census Bureau study released in 1991 indicated that even black married couples were vulnerable to economic distress within a nationally depressed wage economy; between 1991 and 1992, black two-parent households registered "a significant increase" in their poverty rates—up to 13 percent from 11 percent—due to, among other factors, the decline in real wages for black men. After the recession of the early 1990s, employers began to hire again; but even a relatively low national jobless rate of 6 percent (in 1994) masked the problems of African Americans—an unemployment rate twice as high for blacks in general, and a rate of 30 percent for black teenagers. Still, employment per se constituted only part of the problem of poverty; the quality of that employment in terms of stability, pay, and benefits constituted the other part of the equation.[22]

Despite the employer mandates implied in Title VII, black women still faced overt skepticism, if not downright hostility, from some employers. A study conducted between July 1988 and March 1989 focused on the hiring preferences of 185 employers in Chicago and surrounding Cook County. Investigators found that personnel officials tended to identify young applicants by "race," relying on "class and space markers" to do so. White applicants from the suburbs (one kind of "space") were assumed to be middle class, well educated, hardworking, and responsible; black applicants from black neighborhoods (another "space") were assumed to be poor, ill-educated, lazy, and untrustworthy. No matter how well prepared or determined to succeed, black women had to contend with the negative attitudes of potential employers in a way that white women (regardless of their formal qualifications) did not. Few black working women in America needed the verifying data of a scholarly study to confirm the point and its relevance to their own lives and the welfare of their children.[23]

As the labors of black working women became even more arduous, attacks on their personal integrity in the political arena became even more ugly. This disjuncture between the manifold obligations of poor black wives and mothers, and the scorn heaped upon them in the guise of public debates over "welfare reform" was striking. Politicians and policymakers painted the distinction between wage work and homemaking, between "means-tested" social programs (AFDC) and "entitlement" social programs (Social Security) in black and white terms: Caring for one's family was not really "work" at all. Interviewed in Wisconsin in the 1980s, Denise Turner, a young African American mother who received AFDC and also worked part-time in a toy store, noted:

> I mean if you got a family, what're you talkin' about lazy?! A woman is on it [AFDC]
> because she's got some children. And if she's at home and she's doin' for her family,
> how the hell is she lazy? . . . To me that's not laziness. If she's doing a good job at that,
> she has to use a lot of skills. And she's putting in more than forty hours a week when

World War II to the Present

The booming World War II economy lifted black Americans out of the Great Depression, but recovery could not ensure them either sustained prosperity or political equality; these advances depended on the organized efforts of black working women and men themselves. Prized war-industry jobs were opened to black women only after national and local civil rights groups pressured employers to engage in fair hiring practices (1). Black working women, even members of the Women's Army Auxiliary Corps, remained segregated from their white counterparts, an affront to the ideals professed by the Allies in the international arena of war (2). Relatively few black women found work in the industrial sector; most contributed to the war in seemingly modest but essential ways—in jobs traditionally reserved for women (3), or in outdoor work traditionally reserved for men (4). After VJ Day, black women resisted going back into institutional or private domestic service, but they had few alternatives (5). However, by the 1960s, the civil rights revolution fought in both the North and the South had forced the federal government to outlaw discrimination in employment. For the first time in American history, significant numbers of black women in the arts and professions began to gain opportunities, and in some cases national recognition, commensurate with their training and talents (6–8). In 2009, Michelle Robinson Obama became the First Lady of the United States. An accomplished lawyer, she was the descendant of enslaved low-country South Carolina rice workers (9).

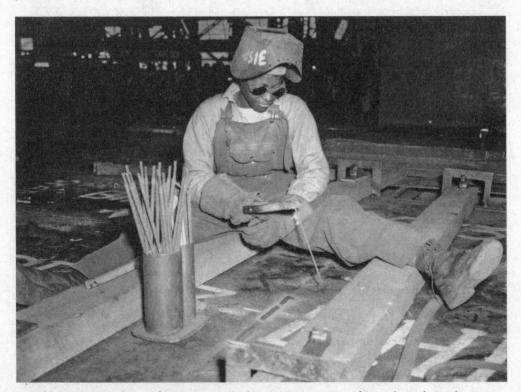

1. Welder-trainee worker on the SS *George Washington Carver*, Kaiser Shipyards, Richmond, California (1943). Library of Congress.

2. Members of the Thirty-third Post Headquarters Company of the Women's Army Auxiliary Corps, Fort Huachuca, Arizona. Schomburg Center for Research in Black Culture, New York Public Library.

3. Seamstress hand-stitching sleeves on an army overcoat (1942). Schomburg Center for Research in Black Culture, New York Public Library.

4. Gardeners in the Botanical Gardens, Washington, D.C. (c. 1943). Schomburg Center for Research in Black Culture, New York Public Library.

5. Cleaning woman. Schomburg Center for Research in Black Culture, New York Public Library.

6. New York City teacher (c. 1955). Schomburg Center for Research in Black Culture, New York Public Library.

7. Velma James, head chef at the Roosevelt Hotel, New York City (1976). Coreen Simpson.

8. Mabel Mercer in a performance at Cleo's, New York City (1978). Coreen Simpson.

9. Official portrait of First Lady Michelle Robinson Obama. Natalia Kolesnikova/AFP/Getty Images.

she's taking care of her family. And that's not laziness! Let some of these men that
work in the government, let some of them stay home and do that. They'll find that a
woman is not lazy when she's taking care of her family.

In the overheated rhetoric about "welfare queens" was lost the fact that many poor women
did not work outside the home for a number of interrelated reasons—because they or family members were in poor health and in need of care; because they were attending school;
because in a particularly dangerous neighborhood they wanted to stay at home with their
children. Still, under ideal conditions—a good job and the requisite social support systems—many poor women, like more and more middle-class women, expressed a desire to
work for wages outside the home.[24]

In the mid-1990s, the euphemistic call for "welfare reform" represented yet another
mean-spirited attack on poor black women. On the campaign trail, politicians appealed to
the basest instincts of an ill-informed public in vying with each other for the most Dracon-
ian "solution" to the "welfare crisis" (a "crisis" that consumed no more than 2 or 3 percent
of the national budget, a "crisis" characterized by stable welfare rolls for the previous two
decades). Grandstanders argued for rigid time limits imposed on AFDC recipients, for ex-
cluding extended kin from the children eligible for aid in a household, and for sending the
children of poor mothers to state-operated orphanages. Effective and quality childcare provisions and job-training programs quickly fell by the wayside in the heat of congressional
politicking. "Reforms" that tightened eligibility requirements (thus reducing the number of
poor children covered by AFDC) required aid applicants to fill out fifty-page-long questionnaires, imposed stringent work requirements, reduced food stamp and Medicaid funding, and forced mothers to report to state authorities the names of fathers with whom they
preferred to deal on an informal basis—only increased the workloads of impoverished
mothers.[25]

Although some observers stressed the significance of the global labor market in shaping
the lives of American workers, the fact of the matter was that the plight of poor women reflected local conditions as well. The tendency of Chicago employers and other whites to
conflate class, "racial," and space "markers" served as a reminder of the enduring significance of place in American life. Historical inequalities enshrined in residential patterns
throughout the United States prevented many black women and their children from rising
into the stable working class or the privileged middle class. Poor people tended to be concentrated in poor communities, whether in the South Bronx or in Tunica County, Mississippi, and those communities lacked good schools, good jobs at decent wages, quality health
care, and adequate police and fire protection. Poor communities were plagued by violent
crime and poisoned by polluted air and water. The nexus of overpriced and dilapidated
housing, understaffed and underfinanced educational institutions, and meager employment
opportunities represented a mockery of the American ideal of equal opportunity for all people. And the large number of impoverished black communities in particular stood as dramatic testimony to the failure of national civil rights legislation—supposedly ushering in a
"colorblind" society—to ensure political and economic equality for African Americans.

In the 1980s, sixteen metropolitan areas in the Northeast, Midwest, and South qualified as "hypersegregated" areas by virtue of their large, concentrated black populations. The social ills confronting ghettos claimed a great deal of prime-time media attention, leading many middle-class white Americans to conclude that all black people were poor, and that all poor black people inhabited a distinctively different "culture" from themselves. Social conflict was a natural consequence of these misguided assumptions. Black women in poor neighborhoods daily lived out a fundamental principle of late-twentieth-century "race matters" as defined by the philosopher Cornel West: "The persistence of poverty generates levels of *despair* that deepen social conflict; the escalation of paranoia produces levels of *distrust* that reinforce cultural division."[26]

THE END OF WELFARE, THE PERSISTENCE OF POVERTY

Battered with the "welfare" issue, the Democratic Party, on the defensive and under the leadership of President Bill Clinton, resolved to take AFDC off the political table once and for all. Beginning with the Franklin Delano Roosevelt administration and continuing through Lyndon B. Johnson and beyond, the Democrats faced increasing liabilities as the party of "welfare cheaters" and "welfare queens." Landmark legislation passed by Congress and signed by Clinton in 1996 abolished AFDC, created in 1935, yet the new program put in its place not only failed to attack the roots of poverty, it also imposed stringent new demands on impoverished women, making it nearly impossible for them to care for their families and provide adequate day care and health insurance for their children.[27]

The inaptly named Personal Responsibility and Work Opportunity Reconciliation Act (PRWORA) served as a fitting coda to the Reagan administration's New Federalism. The act devolved responsibility for poor families to the states, providing each with a block grant known as Temporary Assistance to Needy Families (TANF). States retained a great deal of discretion in deciding how to use the money, but the overall purposes of the funds included:

> (1) Provide assistance to needy families so that children may be cared for in their own homes or in the homes of relatives; (2) end the dependence of needy parents on government benefits by promoting job preparation, work, and marriage; (3) prevent and reduce the incidence of out-of-wedlock pregnancies and establish annual numerical goals for preventing and reducing the incidence of these pregnancies; and (4) encourage the formation and maintenance of two-parent families.

TANF also included a number of provisions that contrasted sharply with AFDC. Under the new program, recipients were required to find gainful employment after receiving two years of aid, were limited to a total of five years of payments, and were obligated to work a certain number of hours per week. Unlike the upper-middle class, full-time suburban homemakers glorified for their commitment to parenting, impoverished mothers must find gainful employment as soon as possible, regardless of the effects of that employment on their children. Indeed, implicit in TANF's goals were inherent contradictions: The legislation supported "traditional" marriage, but at the same time subjected children to a reality at odds with this type of marriage—long hours in all too often substandard day-care facilities, or no facilities at all. And because of their limited prospects and their daily worries, most overworked and impoverished mothers were reluctant to take on the additional burden of marriage to a man who had no gainful employment himself.[28]

The flexibility allowed states in spending TANF money contrasted with the inflexibility of requirements imposed upon the recipients. Added to the new regulations were budget cuts in food stamps and tightened rules about the eligibility of legal immigrants to receive food stamps, Social Security insurance, and Medicaid. Between 1996 and 2002, for example, programs benefiting low-income families were reduced by $55 billion. The Deficit Reduction Act of 2005 raised states' work participation targets and at the same time defined more narrowly the kind of work that recipients must engage in. In general, TANF regulations provided that mothers should seek gainful employment rather than attend school and thereby gain the skills and training that would eventually enable them to compete for better jobs.[29]

Within five years of the bill's passage, supporters of TANF felt vindicated, pointing to evidence that the number of families receiving some kind of government aid had declined sharply—down to 2 million in 2003 compared to 4.4 million in 1996. Yet behind the numbers lay disturbing developments that became clearer over time: For example, in 2002 just 48 percent of eligible recipients were actually receiving aid, compared to a participation rate of 80 percent under AFDC. The relatively few women (90 percent of adult TANF recipients were mothers) applying for aid revealed the counterproductive effects of new administrative hurdles in terms of meeting requirements and filling out forms, as well as a heightened level of intrusion into the lives of recipients by caseworkers. Remarked one harried mother, commenting on some caseworkers who had canceled appointments and others who insisted on mounds of paperwork: "I mean, dang! I'm draggin' kids on the bus to the baby-sitter, come back to you guys and you can't give me an hour? You can't squeeze me in?!? Everything has to be, like, procedures, procedures, procedures. It took me two weeks to get my food stamps because my light bill was not in my name. I had to go in three times, get the buses, get the childcare, just to show them."[30]

Meanwhile, poverty rates remained constant; in 2004, the Census Bureau reported that about 13 percent of all Americans were poor—11 percent of whites, 24.7 percent of blacks, and 22 percent of Hispanics. These figures underestimated the extent of the working poor, but they did provide a sense of the differential in rates among the four groups. Researchers puzzled over an apparent paradox: Many fewer families were receiving aid, yet the poverty rate was staying the same. In 2003 estimates revealed that as many as a million single mothers were receiving no kind of governmental aid whatsoever (whether TANF or Social Security insurance), and that these mothers were not living with anyone else who was receiving aid of this kind. Researchers called these women the "Disappeared": How were they and their children getting by?[31]

The daily struggles of poor women provide clues to this apparent paradox, and reveal another: The welfare-to-work path could actually end up harming the children it was meant to help. Some women found gainful employment just too expensive to make it worthwhile; keeping a job required bus fare, babysitting services, and money for lunch and in some cases a uniform. Almost all recipients lacked formal education, and this simple fact condemned them to menial, ill-paying jobs that lacked benefits such as health insurance and childcare. Leaving welfare often meant giving up the health insurance that TANF provided. In addition, most of these menial positions, some of them contrived, lacked any possibility for advancement, no matter how hard a woman worked or how long she stayed on the job. Many single mothers engaged in the heroic exertions necessary to keep their jobs— taking the children to school or day care in the morning, relying on unpredictable bus service to commute long distances to jobs, running back to pick up the kids during a work break. Exhausted, these women had no time for PTA meetings or shopping. A study of three mothers in Milwaukee revealed that they favored under-the-table arrangements, not employment, and found other additional resources by relying on boyfriends, extracting rent money from informal boarders, and doubling up with kin. This unsettled existence took a toll on children. One mother who moved a series of times remarked, "It's very shameful being in that situation with three kids, running from pillar to post, in and out of hotels. It was hard and I lost everything—clothes, the whole nine yards, even shoes." She continued, "My kids lost a whole lot; it took a lot from them and it took a lot from me. My kids were devastated . . . They couldn't play right, couldn't adjust right. The kids were always fussing and fighting with each other and homework got misplaced." Such was the nature of welfare "reform" in the interests of needy families.[32]

The failures of TANF were a reminder of the commodification of education and health care, two resources essential to the well-being and advancement of all workers and their families. In the 1990s, more and more critics raised their voices to protest the fatal flaw in American public education—the financing of schools with the local property tax. As future—or at least potential—wage earners, children in the poorest school districts daily learned lessons about the likely kind of life in store for them. For example, the children in the public schools of Camden, New Jersey, faced a multitude of obstacles that ruled out much learning on a meaningful scale. At Pyne Point Junior High School they came to class with dental and medical problems that remained undiagnosed and untreated. Located near an illegal dump site and a foul-smelling paper factory, the school lacked sports equipment and playing fields. At nearby Camden High School, students who hoped to find a job in the clerical or technical sector took classes in a "historical museum of old typewriters"; computers were too expensive for the school district to buy. Fifteen minutes away, the predominantly white district of Cherry Hill boasted modern schools and high rates of professional success for its white graduates. Ruthie Green-Brown, the principal of Camden High, recounted for author Jonathan Kozol a conversation she had had in her office with a ninth-grade girl. The student told Green-Brown, "'I'd like to have an office like this someday.' I said to her, 'You can!' But I was looking at this little girl and thinking to myself, 'What are the odds?'"[33]

In the mid-1990s, the issue of universal health care for Americans took center stage in a larger debate over national social-welfare policy. However, few observers bothered to articulate, or even recognize, the fact that this debate had critical relevance for black working women. Indeed, the problem of health was emblematic of the difficulties faced by poor black women in particular as they tried to hold down a job outside the home and simultaneously care for themselves, their children, and extended kin members within communities ill-serviced by physicians and health-care professionals of all kinds. Federal programs such as Medicaid (for the poor) and Medicare (for the elderly) provided only haphazard care for the very young and the very old; at risk were young and middle-aged women who worked but received no health benefits from their employers. In 1992, 17 percent of all Americans, but 22 percent of all African Americans, lacked health insurance; poor southern black women were among the groups most likely to lack coverage, and fully one-third of all African Americans without insurance were between eighteen and twenty-four years old.[34]

The story of one young woman's tribulations in providing for her ill and disabled family members, as recounted in Laurie Kaye Abraham's book *Mama Might Be Better Off Dead*, offers a case study of "a resourceful woman who tried to work the health care nonsystem to the best of her ability." A resident of one of Chicago's poor neighborhoods, North Lawndale, Jackie Banes was the granddaughter of Cora Jackson, who suffered from high blood pressure and diabetes; the wife of Robert Banes, who needed kidney dialysis three times a week to stay alive; the daughter of Tommy Markham, who had a stroke from high blood pressure when he was forty-eight; and the mother of three small children. Taking care of these family members was a full-time albeit unwaged job for Jackie Banes. She alone was responsible for seeing that her grandmother and husband followed special dietary restrictions and took their medications on time; she made arrangements to transport her wheelchair-bound grandmother to her medical appointments; she patiently familiarized an endless succession of different doctors with the older woman's condition; she met with the social workers who periodically appeared and then disappeared; and she called the ambulance for late-night trips to the emergency room and then arranged regular excursions to visit ailing kin in the hospital. Jackie Banes's working days were exhausting and never-ending:

> Once a day, Jackie washed the wound where her grandmother's leg was amputated and changed the dressing on her foot ulcer. Before meals, she tested Mrs. Jackson's blood sugar with a home kit. She tried to remember to give her a high blood pressure pill in the evenings. She gave her sponge baths, changed the pads in her bed, and emptied her catheter when Mrs. Jackson was given one in the fall. She washed her grandmother's soiled sheets and nightgowns and fixed her a plate of food when she called. She dragged her out of bed once a day so she could sit in the living room. She collected bills from hospitals, medical suppliers, and ambulance companies so that her grandmother might meet her spend-down and become eligible for Medicaid [a monthly process].

Banes's labors at home on behalf of her grandmother represented a bargain for the American taxpayers, who footed the bill for a jumble of inefficient and shortsighted medical programs known as Medicare; she received no compensation for working long hours and negotiating a convoluted maze (a "nonsystem") within the public and charitable health-care bureaucracies.[35]

Concentrated in the service and sales sectors, black working women were less likely to carry health insurance compared to other groups of Americans with better jobs; at the same time these women were more likely to live in areas plagued by hazardous waste sites—places like the Mississippi Delta's "Cancer Alley," or the toxic dumping grounds of Warren, North Carolina. Despite the proclivity among well-to-do Americans to romanticize rural (as opposed to inner-city) poverty, in fact, families outside of metropolitan regions lacked the minimal amount of health care resources of poor people in cities. All over the country, in urban neighborhoods as well as in the countryside, black folks of all ages and both sexes suffered from exposure to dirty air and water; these environmental factors, combined with the lack of regular medical care and preventive medicine, produced high rates of disease. Black women and men also suffered from serious complications from uncontrolled high blood pressure (for example, a high rate of kidney failure) and from diabetes (for example, amputations). Moreover, African American working women were disproportionately represented in jobs with obvious and dramatic health hazards—in the textile industry, where workers contracted brown lung, and in seasonal agricultural labor, with its high rates of tuberculosis and exposure to toxic pesticides.[36]

The development of the Mississippi catfish industry reveals how business innovations borne of the late-twentieth-century American entrepreneurial spirit could simultaneously depart from, and confirm, the history of black working women in the region. Where their foremothers had once picked cotton, women like Rose Ross in Leland, Mississippi, now processed fish on the "kill line" at the Delta Pride catfish processing plant. Observed a journalist, "She worked for the company for six years, ripping and gutting fish as they sped by on a conveyor belt—33 fish a minute, 1,980 fish an hour, as many as 20,000 fish a day. Finally, unable to work because of carpal tunnel syndrome, she was fired. Recalled Rose Ross later, "They didn't give me no worker's compensation or nothing. . . . They told me I was terminated because I couldn't do the job for Delta Pride. Then they walked me to the gate. They just showed me the door and told me to get stepping." (In the fall of 1990 nine hundred catfish workers in Indianola—most of them poor, black, and female—struck for higher wages and better working conditions. Despite modest gains, theirs was a Pyrrhic victory, since the industry was in the midst of cutbacks provoked by a saturated market.) In the days missed from work, in the employment opportunities forgone, and in untimely "early retirements" were reflected the occupational hazards of black working women and the chronic illnesses suffered by their families. The fact that many of these workers still labored outside the safety net of worker-legislation passed in the 1930s, and lacked employer-paid health insurance, revealed that slavery cast a long, menacing shadow over the late-twentieth-century United States.[37]

LIMITS OF THE "POST-RACIAL" WORKPLACE

In 1986, journalist Jill Nelson gave up her job as a freelance writer and relinquished "the freedom to be a full-time, at-home single parent" to her teenage daughter in order to work as a staff writer for the *Washington Post*'s new Sunday magazine. Over the next four years

Nelson negotiated her way around a variety of white editors, always self-conscious about the conflict between her desire to look "out for numero uno, like most people," and her mission to live as a "race woman . . . compulsively, irrevocably, painfully responsible not only for herself, but for her race." Burdened by her "bourgeois roots," Nelson launched a quest for an "authentic Negro experience," only to feel thwarted at every turn. At the office she contended with coworkers whose "smugness," she wrote, "comes from years of simply being Caucasian and, for the really fortunate, having a penis. . . . Up close, most white folks, like most people, are mediocre. They've just rigged the system to privilege themselves and disadvantage everyone else." At home, Nelson found her daughter, Misu, to be preoccupied with her own friends, to the detriment of her mother's role as a "race woman"; for example, Misu showed a distinct indifference toward the suggestion that mother and daughter spend a weekend in nearby Virginia "touring local slave plantations," visiting "the slave shanties, the shackles, the land our ancestors slaved on, died for." The fifteen-year-old responded to this itinerary "with the offhand viciousness of adolescence": "Mom, get a life. . . . This weekend, the mall's where it's at."[38]

Paid a good salary and at the peak of her profession, Nelson nevertheless felt weighted down by history, wondering, "Am I a freed black who has made it or a slave struggling to free herself and her people?" In her memoir, *Volunteer Slavery,* she cast herself in the tradition of black liberators, all the while battling the stereotypes that surrounded her: "The white lager [a "bunch of circling white wagons" reacting to black newcomers] at the magazine realizes that not only am I not Mammy, I may be part of Nat Turner's gang." In 1990, the thirty-seven-year-old Nelson resigned from her job, "tired of fighting," resentful because she felt she was held to a higher standard than white employees, and bitter over what she perceived to be her editors' determination to lump the capital city's entire black population into one vast, pathological underclass. Like her foremothers who quit the white woman's kitchen and abandoned the white man's cotton field, Nelson deprived a white employer of her labor; and so finally, she concluded, she was "free to imagine myself." Turning her back on a white boss, she decided, was her "authentic African-American experience."[39]

If sliding out from under the thumb of a white employer constituted an "authentic Negro experience," it is uncertain whether many black working women at the end of the twentieth century ever enjoyed one, or even could afford to seek after one. With a challenging job that paid well and demanded a good deal in the way of talent and initiative, Nelson would seem to have had little in common with other more representative black working women. Although Nelson worried that "most of us corporate Negroes aren't helping anyone but ourselves," in all likelihood most black working women were forced to contend with a different set of worries—that discriminatory pay rates and harsh working conditions constituted their own "authentic Negro experience," but one that they just as soon would have done without.[40]

Still, even highly paid black working women faced challenges that were at once unique to them and typical of the pressures faced by women who labored in high-powered, demanding workplaces. In his book *The Audacity of Hope*, Barack Obama wrote candidly of the strains on his own marriage, especially when the children were small: "Tired and stressed, we had little time for conversation, much less for romance." Coping with demands at work during the day, he returned home in the evening only to engage in "endless negotiations about every detail of managing the house, long lists of things I needed to do or had forgotten to do, and a generally sour attitude" on the part of his wife, Michelle. He believed that "my love should be enough, or so I thought. As far as I was concerned, she had nothing to complain about." Certainly for this young family, plenty of love and money was not enough to alleviate tensions at home. Only gradually did Obama realize the fact that "when children showed up, it was Michelle and not I who was expected to make the necessary adjustments. . . . She was the one who had to put her career on hold." She was the one who had to miss work when the kids got sick, and she was the one who managed day-care arrangements and playdates. For the first time in history, black couples were facing a brand new set of challenges, those of wealthy households that depended on the earning power of both husband and wife.[41]

Like Jill Nelson, some privileged black women "pioneers," felt they were still experiencing a modern-day form of American apartheid. In 1994, two thousand black women academics convened a conference at the Massachusetts Institute of Technology in Cambridge; tellingly, they called the gathering "Black Women in the Academy: Defending Our Name." They testified to the additional burdens of women intellectuals encouraged to serve as token minorities on university-wide committees, and forced to justify their research in the field of black studies to skeptical white colleagues, liabilities that affected their chances for tenure. No matter how accomplished, they remained vulnerable to vicious stereotyping in the mainstream media. For example, Professor Lani Guinier, a professor at Harvard Law School and civil rights scholar, fell victim to a concerted smear campaign that labeled her "Clinton's Quota Queen" (no doubt related to her sister "queen" on welfare). Attacks on her included this passage from an article in *U.S. News and World Report*: "Strange name, strange hair, strange writing—she's history."[42]

In the business and nonprofit sectors, organizations made a show of hiring highly educated black applicants, but then relegated them to separate departments where they were concentrated in personnel, community-outreach, human resources, and "diversity" offices. Using residential segregation as an analogy, Vikki Pryor, senior vice president at Blue Cross Blue Shield headquarters in Boston, noted in 1995, "Certainly there is a ghettoization of jobs in corporate America." These jobs carried with them certain liabilities. In contrast to mainstream positions, lines in the human resources or community outreach divisions were often the first ones affected by cutbacks; they tended to keep blacks separate from whites in the same organization; they rarely offered opportunities for promotion up and out of the "racialized" realm; and they failed to confer the credentials necessary to make the move into more traditional management positions in private companies. In the process of applying for a management position, the director of a community center or the affirmative action officer at a large corporation would inevitably founder on the query from a potential employer: "Have you ever run a profit and loss operation?"[43]

And black women did not need to be highly paid professionals to face the new and daunting task of "code-switching" or "shifting" between predominantly white workplaces during the day and predominantly black neighborhoods in the evenings and on weekends. "Code-switching" referred to the ability of workers to modify their behavior—the way they talked, dressed, laughed—according to the setting. In mostly white workplaces, black women battled new variations of historical stereotypes fueled by the misogynistic lyrics of "gangsta" rap, a kind of music that was becoming increasingly popular in the 1980s and 1990s. A survey of black working women in 2000–2003 found that about six out of ten claimed that they took pains to act differently around white people than around their friends, family, and neighbors. Among some women, whites called out mixed emotions of defensiveness and assertiveness. One Harvard graduate remarked, "With certain white crowds, I need to be a bit more pretentious and full of myself than I would ordinarily be." It was no wonder then that black working women reported that their jobs caused them levels of emotional stress that their job descriptions or pay alone could not account for.[44]

These were secretaries as well as corporate executives who had to navigate their way through a cultural minefield every day at work. Some wrote of the "rage of a privileged class" still facing on a day-to-day basis virulent prejudice and mistrust on the part of whites. In the suites of elite law firms and in the boardrooms of Fortune 500 corporations, black graduates of Ivy League schools remained ever vigilant, on a "race watch"; white supervisors and coworkers might applaud their individual achievements, and yet, "what you do poorly—well, that's when what you do will be dumped on the whole race." Certainly few whites felt the weight of responsibility for a whole people on their shoulders; when they faltered at work, they did not have to fear that they indicted all whites in the process.[45]

From a variety of quarters came the voices of relatively privileged black working women who suffered from a form of "racial fatigue" brought on by serving not only as workplace mediators but also as interpreters of black history and culture for white audiences of various kinds. The literary critic and scholar Ann duCille described her own work in the field of black feminist studies as placing her in the middle of a "suddenly busy, three-way intersection" of gender, race, and class issues, one of the dangers of which was "the likelihood of being run over by oncoming traffic"—such was the fate of scholars who toiled in a "once isolated and isolating" field that had taken on a "magnetic" quality. Marian Wright Edelman, the head of the Children's Defense Fund, spoke to the difficulties faced by black women workers in the presence of white clients or coworkers: "The daily stress of nonstop racial mindfulness and dealings with too many self-centered people who expect you to be cultural and racial translators and yet feel neither the need nor responsibility to reciprocate . . . is wearing." The "racial" nature of their jobs, combined with the pressure of serving as "race women" in the presence of whites, fueled the resentment that exploded in print in the 1990s—an anger that reflected personal variations on the tension between, on the one hand, the "roots" that they shared with other descendants of precolonial Africans, and, on the other, a desire to live life on their own terms, without the encumbrance of "racial exhaustion."[46]

As they neared or achieved job and wage parity with white coworkers, some "code-switchers" continued to distance themselves from problems they associated with white women exclusively—the guilt of working mothers and its opposite, the resentment of stay-at-home mothers. These "mommy wars" seemed far removed from the everyday tasks faced by black working women worried about protecting their children from a raw street culture, and worried about providing money and other kinds of support for extended kin still living in impoverished central cities. Of white working women's grievances, black attorney Robin Rucker Gaillard noted, "They don't speak to my reality. We don't generally have the time or luxury for the guilt and competition that some white mothers engage in." Pamela Walker, a Chicago business-school professor, agreed: "My family can afford expensive things, but why would I think about spending hundreds on a stroller when I could help a cousin buy textbooks for college? That's not my world." Of course, it would be inaccurate to claim that no middle-class white women professionals ever responded to less fortunate kin in need, or to claim that all black women professionals felt as responsible for extended family members as Walker. At the same time, the fact that many black middle-class families had only recently achieved some measure of success in moving to the suburbs or buying a house suggested that black women regardless of class were much more likely to have close kin in modest circumstances compared to their white counterparts.[47]

In fact, statistics that seemed to show parity between black and white women workers hid persistent differences between the two groups. Black college-educated women with children under the age of eighteen were more likely to be working than similarly situated white women (83.7 percent compared to 74 percent). Even highly compensated African American women maintained a precarious existence, since in many cases their families had little in the way of inheritances or real estate holdings to rely upon. Frances Luckett, a school principal in Maryland, expressed reservations about her well-educated daughter's decision to stay home with her children full time. "A lot of financial sacrifice went into helping her get her two degrees," Luckett noted, adding, "There are no guarantees in life, and I worry that if she just gives up her career, is just a wife and a mother, she will have nothing to fall back on."[48]

History, then, continued to shape black women's working lives and culture in profound ways. By the late twentieth century it was clear that many black people's long-standing (and in certain respects well-founded) suspicion of white physicians and medicine was taking a toll on the health and welfare of the community in general and of black women in particular. That tradition of mistrust, combined with the fact that many wives and mothers remained overwhelmed by family responsibilities and money worries, meant that they often ignored their own physical well-being. Here again the beauty shop emerged as a significant institution. Historian Tiffany Gill suggests that beauticians play a critical role in what she calls the "politics of dignity" by encouraging their customers to the spend time and effort on themselves; having one's hair and nails done was just one step in taking care of one's total self—a necessity, not a luxury. In South Carolina, salon owner Mary Louise Fant decided that she could best honor the memory of her aunt, who died of breast cancer in 1988, by joining the Beauty and the Breast campaign. Sponsored by the Susan G. Komen Breast Cancer Foundation, the campaign targeted women who failed to get regular checkups; Fant's aunt learned that she had cancer when she saw a doctor for the first time after more than fifteen years. Noted Fant: "We [black women] don't take care of ourselves because we're taking care of everybody else." The beauty shop was a real and potential site of "health activism," a place where women could encourage one another to get annual mammograms and conduct regular self-examinations. In black communities, the Beauty and the Breast campaign built upon a historical relationship between beauty workers and their customers, a relationship forged in a site where women felt comfortable coming together to concentrate on their own well-being, apart from men and white women. Observed Fant, "The relationship that a beautician has with her clients is the right atmosphere. We talk about any and everything. It's just easy to talk." Fant accepted the Beauty and the Breast challenge to talk to fifty women about breast cancer in one year; but it took her only two weeks to meet her quota. Of course white shops participated in the challenge, too, but they lacked the political and cultural resonance of their black counterparts, which had been shaped in part by a social division of labor that mandated that the vast majority of black women wage earners work for and under the supervision of whites.[49]

At the end of the twentieth century, two strikingly different images of African American women were created by and dominated the entertainment and news media. The overwhelmed welfare mother in a northern big-city ghetto coexisted on the nightly news, and in the consciousness of middle-class white Americans, with the high-powered, successful "information manager"—the TV reporter and anchorwoman, the corporate executive, the outspoken activist and policy spokesperson, and the big-city mayor. Still, even well-paid professionals remained vulnerable to larger changes in the economy because of their concentration in certain kinds of jobs: Human resources officers of large corporations found pink slips in their mailboxes when management sought to trim the managerial "fat" out of personnel; public service employees' positions were contingent on federal funding; and nonprofit-sector workers depended on the whims and personal fortunes of individual and corporate donors. Even those who managed to retain their jobs often saw their way to career advancement blocked by the forces of "racial" tokenism. In colleges and universities, as well as corporations and government offices, workers specializing in minority personnel issues found little room to move up the career ladder once they were typed by a restrictive job description; assistant professors agreed to serve on innumerable committees as a token "black representative" only to discover that tenure committees devalued such contributions; and some journalists resented the assumption that they were hired only to cover "black" stories to the exclusion of all other kinds of news. Finally, even large, broad-based civil rights organizations put in place "glass ceilings" that blocked the advancement of women professionals within those organizations.[50]

Structural issues affecting elite black women workers represented a form of "racial" prejudice that was pervasive but difficult to pinpoint with precision. The fact that certain white workers also chafed under tyrannical bosses meant that not all workplace difficulties could be reduced to "racism"; some supervisors were unreasonable in their dealings with all employees regardless of skin color. Nevertheless, in her book, Jill Nelson commented upon the emotional strain she felt as a bearer of "race secrets, never letting anyone know that maybe we're not the perfect Negroes, the ones most likely to be chosen to integrate this, be the first that, the ones whose lives are so neatly, perfectly repressed that we can withstand the scrutiny of the media, the crackers, and each other." This form of heightened self-consciousness among African American "pioneers" of the late twentieth century and their determination to resist racist stereotypes help to account for the assertiveness with which they pressed their case in the public forum.[51]

On the eve of the millennium, 5.3 million black women over the age of sixteen worked for wages in the United States. Yet despite the relatively high rate of black wives' participation in the labor force—67 percent compared to 59 percent for white wives—black families remained disproportionately poor; one out of three black households versus one out of ten white families was below the poverty line in the mid-1990s. On the other hand, more than one million black women managers and professionals testified to a tentative progress wrought by the combined effects of the previous three decades' antidiscrimination legislation, as well as affirmative action and equal-opportunity programs sponsored by employers in the public and private sectors. Younger black women reached parity with their white counterparts in the clerical category. However, more than half of all black working women labored as technical, office support, service, agricultural, and factory workers, most at low-paying jobs with little in the way of employment security or benefits. Still, the ill-paid wage work performed by black women only partially explained the relatively low incomes of black households. High rates of unemployment and underemployment among black men in the nation's largest cities and in the South's rural areas damaged the viability of the two-parent black family as an economic unit. Black female–headed households in the United States represented one-fourth of all the poor families in the country (although blacks made up only 11 percent of the total population), and female-headed households constituted 75 percent of all poor black families. More than 50 percent of all black female–headed households were poor, compared to 28.4 percent of families headed by white women. Poor black communities had uniquely high sex-ratio imbalances, reflecting the relatively large numbers of young black men either incarcerated or killed by violent means. Under these conditions, fewer and fewer black women could expect to marry, or to find a mate possessed of a job that would help to support the family. Within the black community, some men charged that whatever benefits resulted from Title VII and affirmative action policies, they accrued primarily to black women.[52]

In addition, it is true that certain workplaces revealed less a black-white divide than the tensions between black men and black women. Among the most famous black working women of the late twentieth century was law professor Anita Hill. Her charges of sexual harassment against Supreme Court nominee Clarence Thomas (her former boss at the Equal Employment Opportunity Commission) continued to inform public debate about a variety of issues long after the conclusion of his confirmation hearings before the Senate Judiciary Committee in the fall of 1991. This confrontation, which pitted a politically conservative, Yale Law School–educated black woman against a politically conservative, Yale Law School–educated black man, defied simple analysis; instead, in the words of Kimberle Crenshaw, "the drama's mystifying images, its misplaced pairings, and its baffling contradictions" served as a prism through which were refracted the issues of sexual harassment, affirmative action, and class and gender relations.[53]

The Hill-Thomas controversy churned the waters of political debate, waters made turbulent by the roiling of loyalties based on "race," gender, and class. In fact, the controversy was part of a wider contemporary discussion of the very idea of "race"—its historical significance (was Clarence Thomas just one in a long line of "uppity" black men "lynched" for their "intrusion" into the white halls of power?); its function as a source of self-identification (were black women placing their interests *qua* women over their interests *qua* blacks if they sided with Hill?); and its cultural meanings (was it possible that Hill and Thomas interpreted his behavior from two radically different perspectives?). By this time, the context for this debate had become more complicated; conventional assumptions about racial ideologies were coming under attack, as persons of mixed-race backgrounds challenged the American dyad of either/or, black or white, and as scholars suggested that race was "not an essence, but rather a metaphor pointing to cultural and historical differences." Historian Evelyn Brooks Higginbotham took this reasoning a step further when she argued, "Although racialized cultural identity has clearly served blacks in the struggle against discrimination, it has not sufficiently addressed the empirical reality of gender conflict within the black community or class differences among black women themselves." Ideas based on "race" offered little insight into the dynamics of gender relations within black households and communities.[54]

By virtue of her congressional testimony, Anita Hill was the unwilling recipient of high-profile media scrutiny, but by this time accomplished black women attorneys were not completely unknown figures on the cultural landscape. Running on network TV from 1984 to 1992, the wildly successful *Cosby Show* introduced millions of American viewers to Claire Huxtable (played by Phylicia Rashad), a high-powered New York City attorney married to a physician. With their five adorable children, the Huxtables represented an appealing blend of old-fashioned family feeling within a modern setting—two highly educated, professionally successful parents committed in equal measure to their children, their marriage, their careers, and the preservation of African American history and culture. Some observers would later claim that the Huxtables helped pave the way for Barack Obama's political career by countering stereotypes of impoverished inner-city residents with the reality of a new class of black professionals.

In any case, it is true that by the 1990s, a few black women artists and entertainers had achieved a level of public recognition and material success unknown to their talented forebears. Toni Morrison, winner of the Pulitzer and Nobel prizes in literature; Whitney Houston and Janet Jackson, both popular singers and movie stars; and Whoopi Goldberg, a film "superstar," all attracted large audiences that cut across lines of race, gender, and class. Goldberg's renditions of black working women represented a range of types—the noble, sensitive housekeeper who offered spiritual redemption to (various members of) a white family in the 1950s (*The Long Walk Home* [1990], *Corrina, Corrina* [1994]); the feisty nightclub singer on the run from the mob (*Sister Act* [1992]); a savvy but sensitive inner-city teacher (*Sister Act II* [1993]); a shrewd, fast-talking police detective (*The Player* [1993]); and a professional "race woman," the flamboyant owner of a store selling Afrocentric products (*Made in America* [1993]). As a leading box-office attraction, Goldberg had the freedom to pick and choose from among any number of film scripts; her career bore little resemblance to that of Butterfly McQueen or Hattie McDaniel, actresses restricted to demeaning domestic-service roles two or three generations earlier. Yet Goldberg's success could not compensate for the fact that Hollywood continued to offer few substantial parts to black women as a group. Despite some observers' pronouncements that the United States had finally achieved a "colorblind" society, the erasure of apartheid legislation from the legal code was insufficient to overcome the residue of four centuries of economic discrimination and cultural stereotyping. And that fact remained true for black working women at the top of the workforce, as well as at the bottom.

While the debates over the meaning of racial "ideologies" and "discourses" seemed on the surface to have little relevance to the efforts of ordinary women trying to keep their jobs and provide for their families, in fact these discussions had profound political implications. If race was but a social construction, then the problem of whiteness—the sense of superiority with which whites so arrogantly cloaked themselves—served as the centerpiece of "race relations"; it was up to white folks to shed their own prejudices, and not up to black folks to "fit in" to a system built on white people's prejudices. The conflict between policymakers over "universal" programs that would affect all workers (an increase in the minimum wage, for example) as opposed to race-specific programs (that targeted African American ghetto residents, for example) went to the heart of practical meanings of class and racial ideologies. More generally, the feminist theorist bell hooks suggested that these postmodern debates contained the seeds of alliances among a number of disaffected groups: "Many other groups now share with black folks a sense of deep alienation, despair, uncertainty, loss of a sense of grounding even if it is not informed by shared circumstance." The "shared sensibilities" of those groups "could be fertile ground for the construction of empathy—ties that would promote recognition of common commitments, and serve as a base for solidarity and coalition." Yet achieving that empathy would remain an uphill battle for men and women who still labored in workplaces that bore the deep imprint of past discrimination and suffering.[55]

THE EARLY TWENTY-FIRST CENTURY AND THE DAWN OF THE OBAMA ERA

The status of black working women in the early twenty-first century admitted of no easy generalizations. George W. Bush, who assumed office in January 2001, after the contested election of the previous November, was forthright in his admiration for Ronald Reagan. He and other social conservatives remained committed to a "starve the beast" policy that would deny tax revenue to the federal government and thus make the evisceration of social-welfare programs an economic necessity and presumably a political boon to the Republican Party. In the wake of the terrorist attacks on New York City and Washington, D.C., in September 2001, many Americans came to support calls for a new military buildup, and the ensuing wars in Afghanistan and (after March 2003) Iraq diverted billions of U.S. dollars away from domestic programs and toward conflicts in the Middle East. The first eight years of the new century witnessed new political upheavals—the strains associated with warfare;

the increasing politicization of foreign immigration; the introduction and refinement of new forms of sophisticated communications media; and the growing gap between the poorest and richest Americans, a reflection of rising inequality around the world. All of these developments affected different groups of black working women, though not always in ways that could be predicted.

As American culture shifted to a preoccupation with various forms of electronic media, visionary businesspeople seized the opportunity to innovate, and some built media empires accordingly. Among the richest and best known of these visionaries was Oprah Winfrey, mother-confessor to the masses on her afternoon TV talk show (syndicated in 138 cities in 1986), and in 1998 named by *Time* magazine as one of the one hundred most influential people in America. By the early twenty-first century she had become the nation's first black woman billionaire, a testament not only to the popularity of her weekday show, which attracted 33 million viewers, but also to her talent in promoting "synergy," the integration of different types of media. She herself expanded into acting; film production (via the Harpo Entertainment Group in 1988); multimedia online and print publications, including *O, the Oprah Magazine*, which made its debut in 2000 as part of a larger enterprise, Oxygen Media; and philanthropy. Her consolidated holdings thus spanned TV, film, and print and online publications.[56]

Winfrey also sought to bridge the divide among various components of modern life, including personal self-help and well-being, literature, culture, politics, and public affairs. Born in Mississippi in 1954, she grew up in inner-city Milwaukee, where her mother worked as a maid. She began her professional career as a news anchor in Nashville in 1972, and six years later began cohosting a talk show in Baltimore, *People Are Talking*. Her move to Chicago in 1984 allowed her to exercise her savvy as a television producer; she early recognized the potential in syndication, and before long her daily show was broadcast in 119 different countries. Winfrey's brilliance as a businesswoman was revealed not only in her shrewd strategies of raising and making money, but also in her understanding of the essential fungibility of everyday interests; on her show she focused on concerns alternately mundane and profound, matters that could not be confined within boundaries separating, for example, social welfare from entertainment, or popular fiction from political issues. Her reach extended deep into American culture. In 1993, President Clinton signed the National Child Protection Act, which became known as the "Oprah Bill"; herself the victim of abuse when a child, she had used her celebrity star-power to push for this legislation, which required performing criminal background checks on child care providers. At times Winfrey's pronouncements on current affairs had startlingly swift and far-reaching consequences, as in 1995, when one of her shows turned a spotlight on mad cow disease, causing the price of beef to plummet and Texas cattle ranchers to denounce her for contributing to widespread, unfounded public anxiety surrounding the issue. Her choice of a book for her on-air book club could propel obscure works of fiction to the top of the best-seller list. Winfrey was not the only black entrepreneur to profit from the synergy of mass media; the actor, comedian, and producer Bill Cosby, and Robert L. Johnson, founder of Black Entertainment Television, showed equally impressive reach and foresight in their business dealings. Yet in terms of day-to-day influence, Winfrey remained their superior; fabulously wealthy, she was not merely "successful," but a cultural phenomenon in her own right, reaching a daily audience that knew no boundaries of skin color, class, ethnic background, or even national borders.[57]

Winfrey joined a rarefied group of American billionaires who rose from humble beginnings to great wealth and influence. She overcame history to parlay her personal will and determination into a place at the very top of the country's business and philanthropic realms; in certain key respects, she was the quintessential individualist, her self-discipline and drive (in addition to her modest origins) akin to those of Franklin, Carnegie, and Rockefeller. At the opposite end of the economic spectrum was the African American working woman who rose to meet the challenges in the twenty-first century within the confines of a transformed workplace; for this worker, collective action was the means of political influence and financial well-being. Computers and robotics were slowly eroding the great American middle class, thrusting a favored few into the reaches of financial and information management—the financiers, lawyers, academics, doctors, scientists, and entertainment specialists—and pushing large numbers of former factory workers, bank tellers, and secretaries into part-time work that provided little in the way of compensation or security. Like the Las Vegas culinary, hotel, and restaurant employees, service workers began to organize, and in the process shifted the direction of the national labor movement from unions of semiskilled factory operatives to a variety of advocacy organizations for the laboring classes. For example, Tenants and Workers United began sponsoring community centers that, from Chicago to Florida, from Alexandria, Virginia, to Los Angeles, served as advocates for immigrants and all kinds of workers confronting low wages, dangerous jobs, high medical bills, and employers who engaged in systematic fraud. Black women assumed leadership positions in a number of these new organizations, including the Service Employees International Union (SEIU), and UNITE-HERE, which merged unions of restaurant and hotel employees (the first founded in 1891) with a coalition of garment workers (founded in 1995).[58]

One of the dispiriting ironies confronting the American labor force was the fact that increasing numbers of families with two full-time workers could not make ends meet. Though the official poverty rate hovered at about 14 percent (25 percent of African Americans), this figure woefully underestimated the number of working poor, and it is probable that at least one-quarter of the total U.S. population lived just one paycheck, or one health care crisis, from utter ruin. As a result, living-wage campaigns initiated in the mid-1990s proved especially effective in redressing the hardships faced by the working poor. These campaigns brought together labor unions, religious groups, foundations, and grassroots organizations to pressure local municipalities and states, and the contractors they hired, to offer their workers wages considerably higher than the minimum wage. In mid-2007, the federal minimum wage was just $5.15 an hour, reflecting both Congress's apparent indifference to the plight of the poor, and employers' claims that an increase in the wage would force them to cut their workforces and thus increase the ranks of the unemployed. Still, a number of cities raised the wage they paid to their own employees—Santa Fe to $9.50 an hour, for example. At the same time, the SEIU took the lead in sponsoring broad-based movements to lift wages and improve benefits for service-sector workers. Initiated in 1985 under the umbrella of the SEIU, the Justice for Janitors campaign was notable for organizing nearly a quarter of a million custodians in thirty cities around the country. These movements highlighted the fact that the struggle for decent working conditions and pay knew no barriers between men and women, blacks and whites, immigrants and the native-born, in southern or northern, rural or urban workplaces. Nevertheless, by the early twenty-first century, only 8 percent of all private-sector non-farmworkers belonged to unions, a decrease from a high of 33 percent in the early 1950s.[59]

Clearly, historical distinctions between types of work had receded, to be replaced by distinctions between the benefits packages (if any) offered to different kinds of employees, and between safe and unsafe workplaces. In this new world of downsizing and corporate mergers, employer-sponsored health benefits as much as wages served as a defining issue of a multitiered job structure. A few received generous benefits packages, but many low-skill and part-time workers received none at all. These developments eroded traditional differences that separated agricultural field-workers from indoor workers. In the early 1900s black women had hoped to move out of the fields and into well-lit office spaces that afforded better wages and cleaner working conditions. Certainly multicultural migrant agricultural labor forces, including those that annually wended their way out of Florida and up the Eastern Seaboard, others northward into Michigan from Texas, and still others out of Mexico and into California, all suffered from historical liabilities afflicting these kinds of laborers, including backbreaking work at piecemeal rates. They also found themselves at risk for nervous-system disorders, among other maladies, illnesses brought on by the use of pesticides in the fields. Yet offices and many other kinds of indoor worksites were dangerous places too. In California, Silicon Valley workers endured exposure to toxic chemicals. Keypunch operators and other clerical employees suffered from eyestrain and carpal tunnel syndrome. New standards of comfort in some of the nation's most expensive hotels added to the burdens of chambermaids. Lifting mattresses as heavy as 115 pounds and wrestling with ever-growing layers of bedding, including duvets, bedskirts, and extra pillows, comforters, and blankets, taxed the physical resources of the most experienced and energetic women, who now had to rely on daily doses of medication to ease back and shoulder pain. In 2006, housekeepers were earning an average of only $17,500 a year, despite their increasingly arduous labor—stooping and twisting and bending their bodies, completing bedmaking routines that required they lift mattresses as many as 150 to 200 times a day. In many cities, these workers suffered from rising injury rates, while rates of injuries in hotel kitchens and other hotel spaces were declining. When union officials attempted to raise the issue with management, they received a sharp rebuke: A spokesman for Hilton Hotels suggested the issue was a "smokescreen" designed to pressure managers to recognize the union.[60]

The ethnic background of chambermaids varied from city to city, with women of virtually all ethnicities and skin colors employed in these jobs throughout the country. Backbreaking manual labor was no longer the exclusive province of the descendants of slaves. Yet many black workers regardless of pay continued to filter their experiences through the lens of history, and saw their coworkers primarily as competitors. In some poor places, including Compton, California, where the local public school was the largest employer, black and Hispanic workers vied for a variety of jobs, from teacher to custodian and cafeteria worker, with both groups determined to install their own members in the key positions of principal, district superintendent, or school-board member. More generally, about three-quarters of the nation's estimated 11 million undocumented immigrants were concentrated in unskilled jobs in cleaning, construction, food preparation, manufacturing, and transportation, historically the worksites of blacks in general and black men in particular. U.S. employers of all kinds remained endlessly resourceful and creative in locating vulnerable workers denied fundamental rights of citizenship.[61]

In some cities the drive among Hispanic and Asian job applicants for positions in public schools and in police and fire departments replicated the drive among African Americans for those same positions decades earlier. In May 2006, massive street demonstrations and marches focused the nation's attention on the exploitation of Hispanic immigrants, especially those who were undocumented. These included men and women who worked long hours not only for low pay, but also for uncertain pay; in some cases forced to toil for long hours, they had little or no recourse if they were fired without receiving any compensation at all. In their militant rhetoric and their civil-disobedience tactics, the protests evoked the African American civil rights demonstrations of the 1950s and 1960s. Despite or perhaps because of this similarity, some black leaders reacted angrily, charging that even the most downtrodden immigrant at least had more legal protections than black workers under American apartheid, and that immigration posed a grave threat to the well-being of the black population, especially the residents of northern cities at the mercy of the low-wage job market. Linda Carter-Lewis, a human resources manager and the head of the NAACP branch in Des Moines, Iowa, minced no words when she said, "We [African Americans] will have no power, no clout. That's where I see this immigrant movement going. Even though many thousands and thousands of them have no legal status now and no right to vote right now, that day is coming." Certainly she was correct in the sense that in several areas of the country, including Texas, Florida, and California, the growth of the Hispanic population made them an increasingly powerful political force to be reckoned with. In these areas, demographic change would continue to shape the future in dramatic ways.[62]

Yet a substantial proportion of the African American population continued to shoulder the burdens of history in their everyday lives. For example, in general, black households lagged well behind their white counterparts in terms of net financial assets. The reason for this fact was easy enough to comprehend: Freed from slavery with little if anything in the form of material resources, many blacks in the rural South had remained landless, trapped in the peonage and sharecropping systems, beholden to white employers for jobs and housing. Moving north, the descendants of slaves continued to rent overpriced apartments, and even middle-class "strivers" found themselves shunned by the largest banks, which arbitrarily refused to lend to anyone who lived within predominantly black neighborhoods. The white poor could move around the urban North, out of migrant clusters and into working-class or eventually even suburban communities; residential mobility allowed them to ride a crest of homeownership they could pass on to subsequent generations. By the late twentieth century, household income indicators were less accurate than median net financial assets in providing a true picture of the long-term vulnerability and dependence of even middle-class black families. Poverty and wealth had a "racial" (which was actually an historic-structural) dimension, with the highest earning black households worth only 23 percent of similarly situated high-income white households. In fact, poor whites controlled about the same median level of assets as high-income blacks, indicating that well-to-do black professionals had not yet been able to amass the kinds of real estate assets that even modest white families had long taken for granted.[63]

The historical vulnerability of black families regardless of class became abundantly clear during the economic crisis that began in the fall of 2008. The financial-markets meltdown grew and festered into the most severe economic downturn since the Great Depression. The collapse of Chrysler and General Motors had a devastating impact on autoworkers, one-fifth of whom were African American. These workers, the sons of men assigned to the dirtiest work in foundries in the first half of the twentieth century, had made their way into good assembly-line jobs that paid $28 an hour and included generous benefits in terms of health care and vacation time. They had bought their own homes and sent their children to college. Now neither of their long-term allies, the United Automobile Workers or the Democratic Party, could stave off the crushing effects of a competitive global car market that offered American consumers cheaper, more fuel-efficient vehicles than the Big Three American makers could provide. At the same time, other job niches of the black middle class eroded in the wake of local and state budget-cutters who targeted teachers and clerical workers. The recession was in fact an inexorable process that hit certain segments of the workforce—those segments in which African Americans were overrepresented—in predictable ways. For the past forty years, black unemployment rates had been consistently higher than those for whites, sometimes twice as high. Now, in the late spring of 2009, almost 10 percent of Americans were out of work; the figure for whites was 8.6 percent; for blacks, 14.9; and for Hispanics, 12.7. By summer, in New York City black unemployment rates were rising four times as fast as those of whites, the result of contractions in the public, service, and retail-sales sectors. Whenever the stock market seemed to rally, observers talked about a "jobless recovery," one that would presumably leave the nearly 30 million "underutilized workers" bereft of employment. These men and women included those working part-time but seeking full-time jobs, those too discouraged to look actively for a job, and those officially unemployed; it was doubtful that the end of the downturn would restore their jobs or benefits to more than a quarter of them. Some observers warned that a significant proportion of a whole generation of children would grow up without health insurance, without a stable home life, without a place to live. Under these conditions, black workers and their families would suffer disproportionately.[64]

In June of 2009 the city of Baltimore initiated a lawsuit against Wells Fargo Bank, claiming that it systematically targeted the black community for high-interest subprime mortgages. Testimony from former loan officers suggested that the bank took pains to curry favor with black church leaders in hopes they would encourage their congregants to take out these risky kinds of loans. Meanwhile, the NAACP filed a class action lawsuit against more than a dozen banks, Wells Fargo among them, charging that discriminatory loan policies were routine nationwide. By this time boarded-up houses in weed-choked, poor, and even formerly middle-class neighborhoods stood as mute but bitter testament to the free-wheeling practices that represented the mirror image of redlining in decades past (and indeed, the aggressive marketing of subprime mortgages became known as "reverse redlining"). In New York, defaults on mortgages in predominantly minority (black and Latino) neighborhoods occurred at three times the rate as defaults in predominantly white neighborhoods. Most striking was the fact that even seemingly middle-class black families were victimized by this kind of predatory lending; black households making $68,000 per year were almost five times as likely as whites similarly situated, or even poorer, to take out subprime mortgages, which some bank officers called "ghetto loans."[65]

A detailed study of the foreclosures in middle-class neighborhoods in the New York City area, including Queens and Long Island, enumerated the domino-like effects of high rates of foreclosure: Drug dealers rushed in to take control of abandoned buildings, leading to a spike in crime. Housing values in the affected areas plummeted. Just as dramatic was the psychic toll taken on community residents—among them Lakisha Brown, a working mother of two in Jamaica, Queens, worried sick about losing her home to the bank, and Antoinnette Coffi, who had her work hours cut but still had to pay two mortgages, including a variable loan at 11 percent. Colvin Grannum, president of the Bedford-Stuyvesant Restoration Corporation in Brooklyn, explained that middle-class borrowers were more likely to turn to local brokers for loans because of previous generations' experiences with conventional banks. "I don't want to say it's in the cultural DNA, but a lot of us who are older than 30 have some memory of disappointment or humiliation related to banks," he told a reporter, referring to the preference given to customers with white skin. Grannum grimly noted the cumulative effects of generations of discriminatory bank policies: "Rather than helping to narrow the wealth and home ownership gap between black and white," he said, "we've managed in the last few years to strip a lot of equity out of black neighborhoods."[66]

Statistics related to housing foreclosures and unemployment meant that black families, whether middle class, working class, or poor, would suffer the brunt of the crisis. These facts reflected the enduring legacy of slavery in the form of long-standing patterns of segregation in schools, neighborhoods, and workplaces. And those patterns remained largely untouched by the impressive achievements of a cohort of African American women and men, the unprecedented amount of power wielded by Barack Obama notwithstanding. (Indeed, by May of 2009, African Americans as a group were voicing their skepticism about the effects of the Obama presidency on "race relations"; the optimism of the previous November had shriveled in response to the downturn.) If extraordinary talent and drive could help to propel certain women into positions of influence, for the vast majority a good education remained key. Like many African American mothers before her, Michelle Obama's mother, Marian Robinson, had exhorted her two children to study hard in school: "When you acquire knowledge, you acquire something no one could take away from you," she said. In the twenty-first century, the radical inequality in the American public education system, a product of local impulses fueled by invidious racial ideologies, served as the greatest barrier to the aspirations of many African American women who hoped to combine rewarding employment with a secure family life.[67]

Clearly, only a new moral vision of community could guide the unorthodox and far-reaching social changes necessary to the well-being of black women as wives and as wage earners. Time-bound political and social advocacy organizations were unequal to this task. In all but a few industries, unions were disappearing as a force capable of protecting workers from the ravages of a formerly freewheeling capitalism, now reliant on trillion-dollar government bailouts. Civil rights and women's rights organizations proved ineffective in altering the shape of a political economy that relegated increasing numbers of poor people to the margins of American society. In response to the devastation wrought by Hurricane Katrina in 2005, Americans might have seized the opportunity to conduct such a wide-ranging national conversation about a new moral vision—specifically, what the wealthiest nation on earth owes to its most vulnerable citizens. Nevertheless, politicians of both parties as well as policymakers chose to squander that opportunity. Here in the aftermath of the country's most destructive natural disaster were compressed a large number of familiar if dispiriting themes—the concentration of impoverished African Americans in the Lower Ninth Ward, the legacy and current reality of federal indifference toward the poor, the devastating effects on public health by environmental degradation, the plight of persons (in this case over one million) displaced from their homes and dispersed to other parts of the country. More than 1,800 men, women, and children lost their lives, and whole neighborhoods suffered contamination from a toxic stew of sewage, chemicals, bacteria, and oil. Even heroic efforts to rebuild the city could not promise its residents decent housing, public schools, or jobs in the future. Those structural issues underpinning patterns of concentrated poverty remained outside the purview of any national political conversation.[68]

Together, black and white working men and women were in a position to help redefine national priorities, and their common interests would inevitably yield a political program of benefit to black working women, one that spoke to the needs of breadwinners and nurturers, as well as parents and children. Reeling from the economic collapse and dealing with bailouts for banks and automakers, few politicians or policymakers showed an inclination to address the foundations of radically unequal American labor markets. For the foreseeable future, at least, the resourcefulness of black wives and mothers would continue to grow in proportion to the hardship they faced, and their labor would continue to represent that particular combination of love and sorrow that had for so long endured at home and on the job.

APPENDIX A*: DATA FOR CHAPTER 2

The 1868 Register of Complaints for the state of Louisiana—records kept by the Freedmen's Bureau provost marshal general—provides data on 1,990 cases and includes the following information: the name, sex, and race of the person against whom the charge was filed; and a summary of the issues involved in the case. The following types of cases were examined: charges initiated by black women against whites, black men, and other black women; and charges brought by black men against black women.

This register is one of the single most complete and extensive sources on the Freedmen's Bureau complaint system and how it affected, and was affected by, black women. Patterns illustrated by the results summarized in the following tables, however, have been confirmed by impressionistic analysis of other records regarding complaints. In general, the percentage of cases initiated by freedwomen (as opposed to freedmen) increased along a rural-urban continuum, reflecting the fact that a larger proportion of city women bore complete responsibility for their own welfare and that of their children.

1868 Register of Complaints, Louisiana
Provost Marshal General of Freedmen

TABLE A.1.
Source of Complaints by Initiator's Race (N = 1990)

	Total	Percentage
Black women	693	35
Black men	1077	54
White men and women (against blacks)	220	11
	1990	100

* Source: 1868 Register of Complaints for the State of Louisiana, vol. 136, ln #1372, Bureau of Refugees, Freedmen, and Abandoned Lands, Record group 105, National Archives, Washington, D.C.
Of all complaints initiated by blacks, 39 percent were brought by women.

TABLE A.2.
Nature of Complaints Initiated by Black Women and by Black Men
Against Black Women (N = 741)

	Total	Percentage
a. Black women's complaints against whites	466	
Issues:		
a. Nonpayment of wages; dispute over working conditions or compensation	411	88
b. Seizure, theft of property	29	6
c. Holding children by force against mother's wishes	8	2
d. Violence against black women	12	3
e. Miscellaneous	6	1
b. Black women's complaints against black men	125	
Issues:		
a. Nonpayment of wages or fees for services rendered	56	45
b. Dispute over child custody	7	6
c. Abandonment and/or abuse by husband	32	26
d. Dispute over property ownership	21	17
e. Seduction/abuse by man other than husband	4	3
f. Miscellaneous	5	4
c. Black women's complaints against black women	102	
Issues:		
a. Nonpayment of wages or fees	63	62
b. Dispute over child custody	10	10
c. Dispute over property ownership	22	21
d. Miscellaneous	7	7
d. Black men's complaints against black women	48	
Issues:		
a. Nonpayment of wages or fees	35	73
b. Dispute over child custody	3	6
c. Abandonment by wife	6	12
d. Dispute over property ownership	2	4
e. Miscellaneous	2	4

SOURCE: 1868 Register of Complaints for the State of Louisiana, vol. 136, In. #1372, Bureau of Refugees, Freedmen, and Abandoned Lands, Record group 105, National Archives, Washington, D.C.

APPENDIX B*: ADDITIONAL DATA
FOR CHAPTER 2

Black and White Household Structure in
Twenty-seven Cotton Belt Counties, 1870 (N = 614)

TABLE B.1.
Does the Household Include Both a
Husband and Wife? (N = 559)

No %	Yes %	Total	
20.7	79.3	309	*Black*
18.8	81.2	250	*White*
19.9	80.1	559	

TABLE B.2.
Sex of Household Head, By Race
(N = 613)

Female %	Male %	Total	
16.3	83.7	338	*Black*
13.5	86.5	275	*White*
15.0	86.5	613	

TABLE B.3.
Wife's Age Relative to Her Husband's, By Race (N = 446)

Same %	1–3 Yrs. Younger %	4–6 Yrs. Younger %	7–10 Yrs. Younger %	11 Yrs. and Younger %	1–3 Yrs. Older %	4–6 Yrs. Older %	7 Yrs. and Older %	Total	
10.2	18.9	22.5	14.8	16.8	9.0	4.5	3.3	244	*Black*
6.9	22.8	19.3	16.8	22.3	7.4	3.5	1.0	202	*White*
8.7	20.6	21.1	15.7	19.3	8.3	4.0	2.2	446	

* SOURCE: United States Department of Commerce, Bureau of the Census, Manuscript Population Schedules for the Ninth Census (1870), National Archives, Washington, D.C. For method of sample selection, see chapter 2, note 47.

TABLE B.4.
*Does the Household Have Relatives
Living Nearby? (N = 613)*

No %	Yes %	Total	
65.6	34.4	337	Black
71.4	28.6	276	White
68.2	31.8	613	

TABLE B.5.
Literacy of the Household Head, By Race (N = 447)

Cannot Write %	Cannot Read or Write %	Can Read and Write %	Total	
3.3	80.2	16.6	338	Black
3.3	21.7	75.0	276	White
3.3	53.9	42.8	614	

TABLE B.6.
Spouse's Literacy, By Race (N = 447)

Cannot Write %	Cannot Read or Write %	Can Read and Write %	Total	
2.0	81.6	16.3	245	Black
5.9	22.8	71.3	202	White
3.8	55.0	41.2	447	

TABLE B.7.
Occupations of Black Household Heads, By Sex (N = 338)

High White Collar %	Low White Collar %	Skilled %	Farmer %	Semi-skilled/ Service %	Laborer %	Keeping House %	None %	Total	
.0	.0	.0	.0	18.2	32.7	45.5	3.6	55	Female
.4	.7	5.3	18.4	1.1	73.1	.0	1.1	283	Male
.3	.6	4.4	15.4	3.8	66.6	7.4	1.5	338	

TABLE B.8.
Occupations of White Households Heads, By Sex (N = 275)

High White Collar %	Low White Collar %	Skilled %	Farmer %	Semi-skilled/ Service %	Laborer %	Keeping House %	None %	Total	
.0	.0	.0	13.5	2.7	2.7	78.4	2.7	37	Female
6.7	7.1	5.9	66.4	.4	11.3	.0	2.5	238	Male
5.5	6.2	5.1	59.3	.7	10.2	10.5	2.5	275	

TABLE B.9.
Size of Households (N = 338 black households; 276 white)

	N		Total Percent		Cumulative Percent	
	Black	White	Black	White	Black	White
1 Person	10	5	3.0	1.8	3.0	1.8
2 Persons	44	28	13.0	10.1	16.0	12.0
3–4 Persons	126	81	37.3	29.3	53.3	41.5
5–8 Persons	133	128	39.3	46.4	92.6	88.0
9–12 Persons	18	30	5.3	10.9	97.9	98.9
13+ Persons	7	3	2.1	1.1	100.0	100.0

TABLE B.10.
Household Type, By Race (N = 534)

Single Person %	Nuclear %	Ext. %	Aug. %	Ext./Aug. %	Unrelated Adults %	Total	
3.1	80.7	14.4	1.4	.3	.3	290	Black
2.1	71.3	7.4	17.6	1.2	.4	244	White
2.6	76.4	11.0	8.8	.7	.4	534	

TABLE B.11.
Spouse's Occupation, By Race (N = 408)

Skilled %	Semiskilled/ Service %	Laborer %	Keeping House %	Total	
.4	3.1	37.7	58.7	233	Black
.0	.0	1.6	98.4	185	White
.2	1.7	21.3	76.7	408	

APPENDIX C*: DATA FOR CHAPTER 3

Black and White Household Structure in Twenty-seven Cotton Belt Counties, 1880 and 1900
(N = 679 for 1880; 644 for 1900)

TABLE C.1.
Sex of Household Head, By Race
1880 (N = 679)

Female %	Male %	Total	
10.4	89.6	357	*Black*
9.1	90.9	320	*White*
9.7	90.3	677	

Raw chi-sq. = .325; sig. = .576; DF = 1.

1900 (N = 644)

Female %	Male %	Total	
12.2	87.8	353	*Black*
7.9	92.1	290	*White*
10.3	89.7	643	

Raw chi-sq. = 3.122; sig. = .073; DF = 1.

TABLE C.2.
Are Both Spouses Present in the Household? By Race
1880 (N = 644)

No %	Yes %	Total	
14.0	86.0	338	*Black*
12.5	87.5	304	*White*
13.3	86.8	642	

Raw chi-sq. = .388; sig. = .825; DF = 1

* SOURCE: United States Department of Commerce, Bureau of the Census, Manuscript Population Schedules for the Tenth and Twelfth Censuses (1880 and 1900), National Archives, Washington, D.C. For method of sample selection, see chapter 2, note 47.

1900 (N = 607)

No %	Yes %	Total	
17.5	82.5	332	Black
14.9	85.1	275	White
16.3	83.7	607	

Raw chi-sq. = .723; sig. = .600; DF = 1.

TABLE C.3.
Type of Household, By Race
1880 (N = 679)

Single Person %	Nuclear %	Ext. %	Aug. %	Ext./ Aug. %	Unrelated Adults %	Total	
3.7	74.2	13.6	5.9	1.7	.8	353	Black
3.1	62.7	13.5	15.7	5.0	.0	319	White
3.4	68.8	13.5	10.6	3.3	.4	672	

Raw chi-sq. = 26.725; sig. = .000; DF = 5.

1900 (N = 644)

Single Person %	Nuclear %	Ext. %	Aug. %	Ext./ Aug. %	Unrelated Adults %	Total	
5.7	64.9	22.9	4.0	1.7	.8	353	Black
3.4	65.2	19.0	.7	1.7	.0	290	White
4.7	65.0	21.2	7.0	1.7	.5	643	

Raw chi-sq. = 15.622; sig. = .008; DF = 5.

TABLE C.4.
Do Persons With the Same Surname Live Nearby? By Race
1880 (N = 559)

No %	Yes %	Total	
70.2	29.8	299	*Black*
69.2	30.8	260	*White*
69.8	30.2	559	

Raw chi-sq. = .066; sig. = .793; DF = 1.

1900 (N = 643)

No %	Yes %	Total	
65.6	34.4	352	*Black*
70.4	29.6	291	*White*
67.8	32.2	643	

Raw chi-sq. = 1.697; sig. = .190; DF = 1.

TABLE C.5.
Size of Household, By Race
1880 (N = 679)

1 Person %	2 %	3-4 %	5-8 %	9-12 %	13+ %	Total	
3.9	12.3	25.1	49.0	9.5	.3	359	*Black*
3.1	7.5	25.6	48.1	14.7	.9	320	*White*
3.5	10.0	25.3	48.6	11.9	.6	679	

Raw chi-sq. = 9.265; sig. = .098; DF = 5.

1900 (N = 644)

1 Person %	2 %	3-4 %	5-8 %	9-12 %	13+ %	Total	
5.7	14.2	30.6	35.7	13.3	.6	353	*Black*
3.4	11.7	26.5	44.7	12.7	1.0	291	*White*
4.7	13.0	28.7	39.8	13.0	.8	644	

Raw chi-sq. = 7.126; sig. = .210; DF = 5.

TABLE C.6.
Wife's Age Relative to Her Husband's, By Race
1880 (N = 557)

Same %	1–3 Yrs. Younger %	4–6 Yrs. Younger %	7–10 Yrs. Younger %	11 Yrs.+ Younger %	1–3 Yrs. Older %	4–6 Yrs. Older %	7 Yrs. and Older %	Total	
4.5	20.9	21.2	17.8	19.2	7.5	5.1	3.8	292	*Black*
4.9	23.4	24.5	17.7	17.7	5.3	3.4	3.0	265	*White*
4.7	22.1	22.8	17.8	18.5	6.5	4.3	3.4	557	

Raw chi-sq. = 3.569; sig. = .829; DF = 7.

1900 (N = 504)

Same %	1–3 Yrs. Younger %	4–6 Yrs. Younger %	7–10 Yrs. Younger %	11 Yrs.+ Younger %	1–3 Yrs. Older %	4–6 Yrs. Older %	7 Yrs. and Older %	Total	
6.6	26.9	22.1	12.9	19.9	7.4	2.6	1.5	271	*Black*
7.7	23.2	27.0	15.5	16.3	8.6	1.3	.4	233	*White*
7.1	25.2	24.4	14.1	18.3	7.9	2.0	1.0	504	

Raw chi-sq. = 6.283; sig. = .508; DF = 7.

TABLE C.7.
Literacy of Household Head, By Race
1880 (N = 676)

Cannot Read %	Cannot Write %	Cannot Read or Write %	Not Given/ Literate %	Total	
.3	6.7	70.0	23.0	357	*Black*
.3	2.5	16.3	80.9	319	*White*
.3	4.7	44.7	50.3	676	

Raw chi-sq. = 277.503; sig. = .000; DF = 3.

1900 (N = 640)

Cannot Read %	Cannot Write %	Cannot Read or Write %	Not Given/ Literate %	Total	
.0	6.8	55.0	38.2	351	*Black*
.0	3.5	9.7	86.9	289	*White*
.0	5.3	34.5	60.2	640	

Raw chi-sq. = 160.006; sig. = .000; DF = 2.

TABLE C.8.
Spouse's Literacy, By Race
1880 (N = 559)

Cannot Read %	Cannot Write %	Cannot Read or Write %	Not Given/ Literate %	Total	
.0	2.7	82.3	15.0	293	*Black*
.4	1.9	13.5	84.2	266	*White*
.2	2.3	49.6	47.9	559	

Raw chi-sq. = 273.637; sig. = .000; DF = 3.

1900 (N = 504)

Cannot Read %	Cannot Write %	Cannot Read or Write %	Not Given/ Literate %	Total	
.0	5.5	56.8	37.6	271	*Black*
.0	2.6	9.0	88.4	233	*White*
.0	4.2	34.7	61.1	504	

Raw chi-sq. = 137.973; sig. = .000; DF = 2.

TABLE C.9.
Type of Household, By Age of Household Head
Black Households, 1880 (N = 351)

Single Person %	Nuclear %	Ext. %	Aug. %	Ext./Aug. %	Unrelated Adults %	Total	
.0	62.5	.0	2.5	.0	25.0	8	*Under 20 Yrs.*
4.0	77.4	10.5	5.6	1.6	.8	124	*21–30*
2.3	77.0	11.5	8.0	1.1	.0	87	*31–40*
1.7	75.9	12.1	6.9	3.4	.0	58	*41–50*
6.8	75.0	11.4	4.5	2.3	.0	44	*51–60*
7.4	48.1	44.4	.0	.0	.0	27	*61–70*
.0	66.7	33.3	.0	.0	.0	3	*71+*
3.7	74.1	13.7	6.0	1.7	.9	351	

Raw chi-sq. = 90.356; sig. = .000; DF = 30.

White Households, 1880 (N = 317)

Single Person %	Nuclear %	Ext. %	Aug. %	Ext./Aug. %	Unrelated Adults %	Total	
.0	100.0	.0	.0	.0	.0	2	Under 20 Yrs.
3.4	64.8	14.8	2.5	4.5	.0	88	21–30
3.2	62.1	10.5	18.9	5.3	.0	95	31–40
3.1	56.3	18.8	18.8	3.1	.0	64	41–50
.0	71.4	4.8	11.9	11.9	.0	42	51–60
4.8	61.9	23.8	9.5	.0	.0	21	61–70
20.0	40.0	20.0	20.0	.0	.0	5	71+
3.2	62.8	13.6	15.5	5.0	.0	317	

Raw chi-sq. = 23.129; sig. = .512; DF = 24.

Black Households, 1900 (N = 350)

Single Person %	Nuclear %	Ext. %	Aug. %	Ext./Aug. %	Unrelated Adults %	Total	
.0	75.0	12.5	.0	.0	12.5	8	Under 20 Yrs.
8.7	60.0	25.2	4.3	1.7	.0	115	21–30
2.6	80.5	7.8	5.2	2.6	1.3	77	31–40
5.1	66.1	23.7	3.4	1.7	.0	59	41–50
1.8	61.8	27.3	5.5	1.8	1.8	55	51–60
7.7	57.7	34.6	.0	.0	.0	26	61–70
20.0	20.0	60.0	.0	.0	.0	10	71+
5.7	64.9	22.9	4.0	1.7	.9	350	

Raw chi-sq. = 50.807; sig. = .010; DF = 30.

White Households, 1900 (N = 287)

Single Person %	Nuclear %	Ext. %	Aug. %	Ext./Aug. %	Unrelated Adults %	Total	
14.3	57.1	14.3	14.3	.0	.0	7	Under 20 Yrs.
5.6	68.5	14.8	5.6	5.6	.0	54	21–30
1.5	67.6	14.7	16.2	.0	.0	68	31–40
2.9	67.1	18.6	11.4	.0	.0	70	41–50
5.6	59.3	27.8	7.4	.0	.0	54	51–60
.0	61.5	23.1	11.5	3.8	.0	26	61–70
.0	62.5	12.5	12.5	12.5	.0	8	71+
3.5	65.2	18.8	10.8	1.7	.0	287	

Raw chi-sq. = 28.080; sig. = .256; DF = 24.

TABLE C.10.
Number of Children in Household Who Attended School During the Previous Twelve Months, By Race
1880 (N = 679)

None %	1 %	2–3 %	4–5 %	6–7 %	8+ %	Total	
76.3	10.9	10.9	1.4	.3	.3	359	Black
66.9	11.3	18.4	2.5	.9	.0	320	White
71.9	11.0	14.4	1.9	.6	.1	679	

Raw chi-sq. = 12.071; sig. = .033; DF = 5.

1900 (N = 644)

None %	1 %	2–3 %	4–5 %	6–7 %	8+ %	Total	
69.4	12.5	13.6	3.7	.8	.0	353	Black
54.0	16.8	20.3	7.9	1.0	.0	291	White
62.4	14.4	16.6	5.6	.9	.0	644	

Raw chi-sq. = 17.636; sig. = .002; DF = 4.

TABLE C.11.
Job of Household Head, By Race
1880 (N = 665)

High White Collar %	Low White Collar %	Skilled %	Farmer %	Semiskilled/ Service %	Laborer %	Keeping House %	Total	
.3	2.0	2.6	42.1	3.2	47.0	2.9	347	Black
6.3	8.2	5.3	63.8	.9	10.4	5.0	318	White
3.2	5.0	3.9	52.5	2.1	29.5	3.9	665	

Raw chi-sq. = 131.066; sig. = .000; DF = 6.

1900 (N = 626)

High White Collar %	Low White Collar %	Skilled %	Farmer %	Semiskilled/ Service %	Laborer %	Keeping House %	Total	
1.4	.6	1.7	70.8	4.3	21.2	.0	349	Black
2.5	13.0	7.2	70.4	1.8	5.1	.0	277	White
1.9	6.1	4.2	70.6	3.2	14.1	.0	626	

Raw chi-sq. = 83.138; sig. = .000; DF = 5.

NOTES

INTRODUCTION

1. Feldstein, *Motherhood in Black and White*, 86–110.

2. Gwaltney, *Drylongso*, 173.

3. Higginbotham, "African-American Women's History and the Metalanguage of Race"; Hull, Scott, and Smith, eds., *All the Women Are White, All the Blacks Are Men*. See the pioneering literary-historical study by Noble, *Beautiful, Also, Are the Souls of My Black Sisters*, as well as the invaluable collections of documents edited by Lerner, *Black Women*, and Sterling, *We Are Your Sisters*.

4. See, for example, Moynihan, *The Negro Family*.

5. See, for example, Royster, *Lugenia Burns Hope*; Harley and Terborg-Penn, eds., *The Afro-American Woman*; Hine, *When the Truth is Told*; Terborg-Penn, "Discontented Black Feminists," in Scharf and Jensen, eds., *Decades of Discontent*; Jones, "Mary Church Terrell"; Davis, ed., *Contributions of Black Women to America*, 2 vols.; Hine, ed., *Black Women in Nursing*; special issue on black women in education in *Journal of Negro Education* (Summer 1982); Giddings, *When and Where I Enter*; White, *Too Heavy a Load*.

6. Fields and Fields, *Lemon Swamp*, xiv.

7. Langston Hughes, "Mother to Son," in Hughes and Bontemps, eds., *Poetry of the Negro*, 186.

8. Washington, ed., *Black-Eyed Susans*, xxxi.

9. Ladner, *Tomorrow's Tomorrow*; Wallace, *Black Macho*.

10. Lorde and Rich, "An Interview with Audre Lorde," 729.

CHAPTER 1

1. Hurston, *Their Eyes Were Watching God*, 31–32. Novelist, folklorist, and anthropologist, Hurston (b. 1901, d. 1960) had collected a massive amount of primary data on the culture and folklore of black Americans before she began work on *Their Eyes Were Watching God*. In 1938 she served as supervisor of the Negro Unit of the Florida Federal Writers Project, which compiled interviews with former slaves. Her various writings are finally receiving long-overdue literary attention and critical acclaim. See Hemenway, *Zora Neale Hurston*, and an anthology: Hurston, *I Love Myself When I Am Laughing*, ed. Walker.

2. General works on slavery include Young, *Domesticating Slavery*; Smith, *Mastered by the Clock*; Dew, *Bond of Iron*; Berlin and Morgan, eds., *Cultivation and Culture*; Oakes, *The Ruling Race*; Gutman, *The Black Family*; Genovese, *Roll, Jordan, Roll*; Owens, *This Species of Property*; Blassingame,

The Slave Community; David et al., *Reckoning With Slavery*; Escott, *Slavery Remembered*; Webber, *Deep Like the Rivers*.

3. For works that focus on enslaved women in particular, see, for example, Berry, *Swing the Sickle*; Camp, *Closer to Freedom*; Wood, *Women's Work, Men's Work*; Schwalm, *A Hard Fight for We*; Schwartz, *Birthing a Slave*; Morton, ed., *Discovering the Women in Slavery*; White, *Ar'n't I a Woman?*; Gaspar and Hine, *More Than Chattel*; Davis, "Reflections," and Obtiko, "'Custodians,'" in Hiller and Sheets, eds., *Women and Men*, 256–259; Hine and Wittenstein, "Female Slave Resistance," in Steady, ed., *Black Woman*, 289–300; hooks, *Ain't I a Woman*, 15–49. The volumes edited by Lerner, *Black Women in White America*, and Sterling, *We Are Your Sisters*, include material on the history of slave women.

4. Clinton, *Plantation Mistress*; Scott, *Southern Lady*; Fox-Genovese, *Plantation Household*; Wiener, *Mistresses and Slaves*; Wyatt-Brown, *Southern Honor*.

5. On women's "productive-reproductive" functions and the relationship between patriarchy and capitalism, see Kelly, "Doubled Vision of Feminist Theory," Hartmann, "Capitalism, Patriarchy, and Job Segregation," and Eisenstein, "Developing a Theory of Capitalist Patriarchy" and "Relations of Capitalist Patriarchy" in Eisenstein, ed., *Capitalist Patriarchy*; Kuhn and Wolpe, "Feminism and Materialism," and Beechey, "Women and Production" in Kuhn and Wolpe, eds., *Feminism and Materialism*.

6. See, for example, Jones, *American Work*, 23–80; Morgan, *American Slavery, American Freedom*; Galenson, *White Servitude in America*.

7. "become . . . color": Allison, ed., *Life of Olaudah Equiano*, 45–46. See also Piker, "Indians and Race in Early America," 3; Stewart, *'What Nature Suffers to Groe'*; Silver, "Learning to Live with Nature"; Spear, "Race Matters in the Colonial South"; Gallay, *The Indian Slave Trade*.

8. Berlin, *Many Thousands Gone*; Morgan, *Slave Counterpoint*.

9. Gomez, *Exchanging Our Country Marks*; Diouf, *Servants of Allah*.

10. Smallwood, *Saltwater Slavery*; Jones, *American Work*, 64–76.

11. Stevenson, *Life in Black and White*; Sidbury, *Becoming African in America*; Gomez, *Exchanging Our Country Marks*; Berlin, *Many Thousands Gone*; Creel, *"A Peculiar People."*

12. Interviews with former slaves have been published in various forms, including Rawick, ed., *American Slave*; Social Science Institute, Fisk University, *Unwritten History of Slavery*; Perdue and others, *Weevils in the Wheat*; Cade, "Out of the Mouths of Ex-Slaves"; Blassingame, ed., *Slave Testimony*. The narratives as a historical source are evaluated in Escott, *Slavery Remembered*, 3–18 ("The slave narratives offer the best evidence we will ever have on the feelings and attitudes of America's slaves"); Goodson, "Introductory Essay"; Woodward, "History from Slave Sources"; Bailey, "A Divided Prism"; Sekora and Turner, eds., *The Art of Slave Narrative*. The Davidson quotation is from Rawick, ed., *American Slave*, series 1, *Ohio Narratives*, 16:26–29. Hereafter all references will include the series number, name of the state, and volume and page numbers. The other major source of slave interview material taken from the Federal Writers Project (FWP) collection for this book— Perdue and others—will be referred to as *Weevils in the Wheat*. The Fisk University study is listed as *Unwritten History of Slavery*. Jacobs has compiled a useful index to the FWP narratives: *Index to the American Slave*.

13. Penningroth, *The Claims of Kinfolk*; Dusinberre, *Them Dark Days*; Pruneau, "All the Time is Work Time."

14. Supp. Series 1, *Mississippi Narratives*, pt. 2, 7:350; Supp. Series 1, *Oklahoma Narratives*, 12:110; Davis, "Reflections," 8; "they . . . Massa": Kemble, *Journal*, 60, 92. See also *Unwritten History*

of Slavery, 286; Camp, *Closer to Freedom*. For discussions of women's work and the inadequacy of traditional economic and social-scientific theory to define and analyze it, see Acker, "Issues," in Stromberg and Harkess, eds., *Women Working*; Brown, "Division of Labor."

15. Schwalm, *A Hard Fight for We*; Pruneau, "All the Time is Work Time"; Wood, *Women's Work, Men's Work*; Berlin, "Time, Space, and the Evolution," 66; and Morgan, "Work and Culture."

16. Kemble, *Journal*, 28; Olmsted, *Slave States*, 470. Gray, *History of Agriculture*, 533–548; *Weevils in the Wheat*, 199; Series 1, *Florida Narratives*, 17:305; Sydnor, *Slavery in Mississippi*, 20. See also Rivers, "'Dignity and Importance'," 422–423; Sterling, ed., *We Are Your Sisters*, 13–17.

17. Olmsted, *Slave States*, 387; Series 1, *Alabama Narratives*, 6:87. Work descriptions were gleaned from the Federal Writers Project Slave Narrative Collection (Rawick, ed., *American Slave*, and Perdue and others, *Weevils in the Wheat*) and Gray, *History of Agriculture*. Goodson ("Introductory Essay") has indexed a sample of the interviews with women by subject (for example, candlemaking, carding wool, fieldwork, splitting rails.) See also Bruchey, ed., *Cotton*, 174. See the documents under the heading "Making Cotton" and "The Routine of the Cotton Year," 171–80. For pictures of early-twentieth-century black women of St. Helena's Islands, South Carolina, wearing the second belt, see photographs in Dabbs, *Face of an Island*. The caption of one photo entitled "Woman with Hoe" reads: "Adelaide Washington sets off for her day's work in the field. The second belt or cord tied around the hips lifted all her garments a little and protected the long skirts from both early morning dew and contact with the dirt. . . . [According to] an African superstition . . . the second cord also gave the wearer extra strength" (no pp.). Olmsted, in *Slave States*, 387, includes a sketch of this form of dress.

18. Pruneau, "All the Time is Work Time," 4; *Weevils in the Wheat*, 26; Gray, *History of Agriculture*, 1:251; planter quoted in Owens, *This Species of Property*, 39.

19. Berry, *Swing the Sickle*; Genovese, *Roll, Jordan, Roll*, 495; Burke quoted in Gray, *History of Agriculture*, 549; Olmsted, *Back Country*, 81. For former slaves' descriptions of women who plowed, see Series 1, *Oklahoma Narratives*, 7:314; Series 1, *Florida Narratives*, 17:33.

20. Olmsted quoted in Sydnor, *Slavery in Mississippi*, 68; *Weevils in the Wheat*, 77. Of the women who worked in the South Carolina Sea Islands cotton fields, Harriet Ware (a northern teacher) wrote, "They walk off with their heavy hoes on their shoulders, as free, strong, and graceful as possible." Pearson, ed., *Letters from Port Royal*, 52.

21. Bruchey, ed., *Cotton*, 174. See the documents under the heading "Making Cotton" and "The Routine of the Cotton Year," 171–180. For examples of outstanding female pickers see Series 1, *Alabama Narratives*, 6:275 ("Once I won a contest wid a man an' made 480 pounds"); *Weevils in the Wheat*, 199.

22. Supp. Series 2, *Texas Narratives*, pt. 1, 2:93–96; Supp. Series 1, *Mississippi Narratives*, pt. 1, 6:235–236, and pt. 2, 7:404; Series 1, *Texas Narratives*, pt. 3, 5:231; Series 1, *Indiana Narratives*, 6:25; Series 1, *Georgia Narratives*, pt. 1, 12:113; Series 1, *Oklahoma Narratives*, 7:314; Series 1, *Alabama Narratives*, 6:338, For additional examples, see *Unwritten History of Slavery*, 203, 217, 241.

23. For a general discussion of slave artisans in the South, see Gray, *History of Agriculture*, 1:548, 565–567; Sydnor, *Slavery in Mississippi*, 9; Newton and Lewis, eds., *The Other Slaves*. Ransom and Sutch, in *One Kind of Freedom*, discuss "Occupational Distribution of Southern Blacks: 1860, 1870, 1890" in appendix B, 220–231. The works of Starobin (*Industrial Slavery*) and Brewer (*The Confederate Negro*) focus almost exclusively on male slaves. See also Gutman and Sutch, "Victorians All?" in Davis and others, *Reckoning with Slavery*, 160; Gutman, *Black Family*, 599–600. The "hiring out" of men and children frequently disrupted family life.

24. Ransom and Sutch, *One Kind of Freedom*, 233; Olmsted, *Slave States*, 388; Series 1, *Ohio Narratives*, 16:28; Kemble, *Journal*, 121; Series 1, *South Carolina Narratives*, pt. 4, 3:78; *Weevils in the Wheat*, 223–224. Genovese describes the plantation system as a "halfway house between peasant and factory cultures" *(Roll, Jordan, Roll*, 286). For further discussion of the grueling pace of fieldwork, see Gutman and Sutch, "Sambo Makes Good," in Davis and others, *Reckoning with Slavery*, 55–93.

25. Olmsted, *Back Country*, 58–59; Johnson, "Smothered Slave Infants"; Schwartz, *Birthing a Slave*; Tadman, "Demographic Cost of Sugar," 1536; Follett, "Heat, Sex, and Sugar." See also Gutman and Sutch, "The Slave Family," in Davis and others, *Reckoning with Slavery*, 94–133; Eblen, "New Estimates"; Gray, *History of Agriculture*, 562, 888–907.

26. Johnson, *Soul by Soul*; "there's a": quotation in Schwartz, *Birthing a Slave*, 72.

27. Savitt, *Medicine and Slavery*, 115–120; planter quoted in Olmsted, *Slave States*, 190; Gutman and Sutch, "Sambo Makes Good," in Davis and others, *Reckoning with Slavery*, 67; Series 1, *Virginia Narratives*, 16:51. See also Owens, *This Species of Property*, 38–40.

28. Douglass, *Narrative*, 42; Oakes, *Ruling Race*, 24, 156, 174–175; Olmsted, *Back Country*, 61; Series 1, *Virginia Narratives*, 16:11. See also Kemble, *Journal*, 121. For other descriptions of overseers and their treatment of slaves, see Olmsted, *Back Country*, 56–61, 81–82, 207, and *Slave States*, 438–439; Gray, *History of Agriculture*, 1:245–246; Escott, *Slavery Remembered*, 87–89. Slaves recall overseers (among them, "the meanest men that ever walked the earth") and their disciplinary techniques in Series 1, *Oklahoma Narratives*, 7:146; *Florida Narratives*, 17:88, 118; *Texas Narratives*, pt. 4, 5:210.

29. Grandy, *The Life of Moses Grandy*, 18; Series 1, *Alabama Narratives*, 6:66; Series 1, *Indiana Narratives*, 6:200. See also Supp. Series 2, *Louisiana Narratives*, 6:1939–1943, 2025, 2299. I wish to acknowledge Professor Michael P. Johnson for bringing to my attention additional examples of this practice.

30. Series I, *Mississippi Narratives*, 7:171.

31. Douglass, *Life and Times*, 52; Owens, *This Species of Property*, 218–219; Series 1, *Oklahoma Narratives*, 7:347; Series 1, *Tennessee Narratives*, 16:9.

32. Series 1, *Alabama Narratives*, 6:46; Series 1, *Florida Narratives*, 17:185; *Weevils in the Wheat*, 259, 216; Series 1, *Virginia Narratives*, 6:51; Escott, *Slavery Remembered*, 86–93; Faust, "Culture, Conflict and Community," 90. Escott includes an extensive discussion of resistance as revealed in the FWP Slave Narrative Collection and provides data on the age, gender, and marital status of registers and the purposes and forms of resistance. Gutman argues that the "typical runaway" was a male, aged sixteen to thirty-five years *(Black Family*, 264–265). See also M. E. Obtiko, "'Custodians of a House of Resistance': Black Women Respond to Slavery," in Hiller and Sheets, eds., *Women and Men*, 256–259; Owens, *This Species of Property*, 38, 88, 95; Sterling, ed., *We Are Your Sisters*, 56–84.

33. Pruneau, "All the Time is Work Time"; *Weevils in the Wheat*, 26, 157, 282. According to Gutman, plantation work patterns "apparently failed to take into account enlarged slave kin groups, and further study may show that a central tension between slaves and their owners had its origins in the separation of work and kinship obligations" *(Black Family*, 209). See also Webber, *Deep Like the Rivers*, 2; Faust, "Culture, Conflict, and Community," 87.

34. Series 1, *Florida Narratives*, 17:191; slaveholder quoted in Gutman, *Black Family*, 263; Starobin, ed., *Blacks in Bondage*, 54.

35. Genovese, *Roll, Jordan, Roll*, 328, 340; Series 1, *Alabama Narratives*, 6:273; Supp. Series 1, *Mississippi Narratives*, pt. 2, 7:400; Series 1, *Texas Narratives*, pt. 3, 5:45; *Unwritten History of Slavery*, 51. Some historians have emphasized that the distinction between house and fieldwork was not al-

ways meaningful in terms of shaping a slave's self-perception or defining his or her status. See Owens, *This Species of Property*, 113; Escott, *Slavery Remembered*, 59–60.

36. Burge quote in Wood, "Broken Reeds and Competent Farmers," 45; Series 1, *Alabama Narratives*, 6:416–417.

37. Series 1, *Texas Narratives*, pt. 4, 5:11; Series 1, *Indiana Narratives*, 6:183. See also Supp. Series 1, *Mississippi Narratives*, pt. 1, 6:54–55, 216, 257, 365, 380–381; *Unwritten History of Slavery*, 56, 60; King, *Stolen Childhood*; Schwartz, *Born in Bondage*.

38. The FWP Slave Narrative Collection and *Unwritten History of Slavery* provide these examples of children's work and many more. See Series 1, *Alabama Narratives*, 6:157; *Unwritten History of Slavery*, 263; Genovese, *Roll, Jordan, Roll*, 502–519; Supp. Series 1, *Georgia Narratives*, pt. 1, 3:185; *Weevils in the Wheat*, 264–265; Series 1, *South Carolina Narratives*, pt. 4, 3:257; Schwartz, *Born in Bondage*.

39. Wyatt-Brown, *Southern Honor*, 226; Woodward, ed., *Mary Chesnut's Civil War*, 255.

40. Clinton, *Plantation Mistress*, 16–35; Genovese, *Roll, Jordan, Roll*, 333–338; Olmsted, *Slave States*, 421; Series 1, *South Carolina Narratives*, pt. 4, 3:126; *Florida Narratives*, 17:356.

41. Wood, "Broken Reeds and Competent Farmers," 46. For specific incidents illustrating these points, see Series 1, *Oklahoma Narratives*, 7:135, 165–166; *Tennessee Narratives*, 16:14; *Weevils in the Wheat*, 63, 199; Blassingame, ed., *Slave Testimony*, 160–161, 131, 149. See also "A Seamstress Is Punished," in Lerner, ed., *Black Women in White America*, 18–19.

42. Wyatt-Brown, *Southern Honor*, 285, 288–91, 308, 321; Series 1, *Oklahoma Narratives*, 7:347. See also *Unwritten History of Slavery*, 261; Brent [Harriet Jacobs], *Incidents in the Life of a Slave Girl*; Jones, *Saving Savannah*, 83.

43. Johnston, *Race Relations*, 246–247.

44. Wyatt-Brown, *Southern Honor*, 281–283; Clinton, *Plantation Mistress*, 80–81.

45. See, for example, Blassingame, ed., *Slave Testimony*, 132.

46. Olmsted, *Slave States*, 421; Series 1, *South Carolina Narratives*, pt. 4, 3:126; Series 1, *Florida Narratives*, 17:356; Escott, *Slavery Remembered*, 64; Kemble, *Journal*, 98; Genovese, *Roll, Jordan, Roll*, 346–347; *Unwritten History of Slavery*, 201.

47. Series 1, *Florida Narratives*, 17:356; Gutman and Sutch, "Sambo Makes Good," in Davis and others, *Reckoning with Slavery*, 74; Kemble, *Journal*, 153; Gray, *History of Agriculture*, 1:553; Owens, *This Species of Property*, 113; Faust, "Culture, Conflict, and Community," 86.

48. Series 1, *Georgia Narratives*, pt. 1, 12:243; Davis, "Reflections," 4–7. For general discussions of women's work as it related to slave communal life, see also Owens, *This Species of Property*, 23, 225; White, *Ar'n't I a Woman?*; Polly Cancer recalled that, when she was growing up on a Mississippi plantation, the master "wudn't let de mammies whip dey own chillun [or "do dey own cookin"] . . . ef he cum 'cross a 'oman whuppin' her chile he'd say, 'Git 'way 'oman; dats my bizness.'" Supp. Series 1, *Mississippi Narratives*, pt. 2, 7:340–341.

49. Gomez, *Exchanging Our Country Marks*, 127.

50. Stewart, *'What Nature Suffers to Groe,'* 102; Pollitzer, *The Gullah People*; Turner, *Africanisms in the Gullah Dialect*.

51. For a theoretical formulation of the sexual division of labor in preindustrial societies, see Brown, "A Note on the Division of Labor by Sex."

52. Wood, *Black Majority*, 59–62; Lloyd, "Osi fakunde of Ijebu," in Curtain, ed., *Africa Remembered*, 263; Marguerite Dupire, "The Position of Women in a Pastoral Society," in Paulme, ed., *Women of Tropical Africa*, 76–80. Kemble, *Journal*, 42; Pearson, ed., *Letters from Port Royal*, 58, 106.

53. Herskovits, *The Myth of the Negro*, 33–85; Wood, *Black Majority*, 179, 250; Baumann, "The Division of Work." On the role of women in hoe agriculture, see also Mullings, "Women and Economic Change," in Hafkin and Bay, eds., *Women in Africa*, 239–264; Leith-Ross, *African Women*, 84–91; Boserup, *Woman's Role in Economic Development*, 15–36; Goody and Buckley, "Inheritance and Women's Labour." No tribes in precolonial Africa used the plow. See also Griffin, "West African and Black Working Women."

54. Stevenson, *Life in Black and White*; Kaye, *Joining Places*; White, *Ar'n't I a Woman?*; Malone, *Sweet Chariot*, 5, 256–262.

55. Berry, *Swing the Sickle*.

56. Fett, *Working Cures*; Gray, *History of Agriculture*, 1:563; Olmsted, *Slave States*, 424–425, 697–698; Owens, *This Species of Property*, 47; Series 1, *Florida Narratives*, 17:175; Series 1, *Alabama Narratives*, 6:216; Supp. Series 1, *Mississippi Narratives*, pt. 1, 6:10, 23, 25, 123; Supp. Series 1, *Georgia Narratives*, pt. 1, 3:27. Savitt (*Slavery and Medicine*) includes a section on black medicine (171–184) and confirms Rebecca Hooks's recollection that "on the plantation, the doctor was not nearly as popular as the 'granny' or midwife." Series 1, *Florida Narratives*, 17:175.

57. Series 1, *Georgia Narratives*, pt. 1, 12:70; *Oklahoma Narratives*, 7:314–315; White, *Ar'n't I a Woman?* 22–23; Supp. Series 1, *Texas Narratives*, pt. 1, 2:98. Group quilting projects served the same functions for women. See Webber, *Deep Like the Rivers*, 236.

58. The FWP Slave Narrative Collection contains many descriptions of slaves engaged in household industry. Earle details comparable techniques used by white women in colonial New England in *Home Life in Colonial Days*.

59. See, for example, Series 1, *South Carolina Narratives*, pt. 3, 3:15, 218, 236; *Texas Narratives*, pt. 3, 5:20, 89, 108, 114, 171, 188, 220; Supp. Series 1, *Mississippi Narratives*, pt. 1, 6:36; *Unwritten History of Slavery*, 56.

60. *Weevils in the Wheat*, 88–89. (George White of Lynchburg reported that his mother sang a similar version of this song to women while they were spinning. See p. 309.) White, *Ar'n't I a Woman?*

61. *Unwritten History of Slavery*, 53. See also Faust, "Culture, Conflict, and Community," 91.

62. Gutman, *Black Family*, 220–227; Wetherell, "Slave Kinship"; Edwards, *Scarlet Doesn't Live Here Anymore*, 140.

63. Penningroth, *Claims of Kinfolk*; Clifton, ed., *Life and Labor on Argyle Island*; Kaye, *Joining Places*, 106–111, 147–149, 161–162.

64. Genovese, *Roll, Jordan, Roll*, 319; Gutman, *Black Family*.

65. Series 1, *Georgia Narratives*, pt. 1, 12:203. For other examples of change from children's to adults' clothing, see Series 1, *Texas Narratives*, pt. 3, 5:211, 275; pt. 4, 5:109–110; *Georgia Narratives*, pt. 1, 12:277; Genovese, *Roll, Jordan, Roll*, 505. On childhood in the quarters, see also Schwartz, *Born in Bondage*; King, *Stolen Childhood*; Webber, *Deep Like the Rivers*; Wiggins, "The Play of Slave Children."

66. Gutman and Sutch, "Victorians All?" in Davis and others, *Reckoning with Slavery*, 146; Gutman, *Black Family*, 61–67, 75–80; Escott, *Slavery Remembered*, 52–53; Genovese, *Roll, Jordan, Roll*, 415, 459, 465–467; Trussell and Steckel, "The Age of Slaves at Menarche."

67. Escott, *Slavery Remembered*, 59–65; Genovese, *Roll, Jordan, Roll*, 339; Series 1, *Oklahoma Narratives*, 7:322; *Alabama Narratives*, 6:370; *Weevils in the Wheat*, 49, 131–132; Series 1, *South Carolina Narratives*, pt. 3, 3:106. For examples of courting practices, see Owens, *This Species of Property*, 195–196; Series 1, *South Carolina Narratives*, pt. 3, 3:78, 106, 167; pt. 4, 3:249; *Texas Narratives*, pt. 3,

5:15; *Indiana Narratives*, 6:139–140; *Oklahoma Narratives*, 7:264; *Mississippi Narratives*, 7:87; *Georgia Narratives*, pt. 1, 12:164; *Weevils in the Wheat*, 122; Sterling, ed., *We Are Your Sisters*, 31–43.

68. Gutman, *Black Family*, 50, 67–68; Gutman and Sutch, "Victorians All?" in Davis and others, *Reckoning with Slavery*, 139–142; Genovese, *Roll, Jordan, Roll*, 466–467; Series 1, *South Carolina Narratives*, pt. 3, 3:167–168. In *Black Family*, Gutman points out that "violence, even murder, sometimes followed suspected or actual infidelity" (p. 67). The aggrieved husband was almost always the aggressor. Webber suggests that "more community disfavor probably fell upon female than male adulterers," *Deep Like the Rivers*, 149. The marriage ceremony in the fields is described in Sydnor, *Slavery in Mississippi*, 63.

69. Sutch argues in "The Breeding of Slaves," in Engerman and Genovese, eds., *Race and Slavery*, that slaveowners in the breeding states "fostered polygamy and promiscuity among their slaves" and sold the children ("predominantly as young adults") to planters in the southwestern slave states (p. 198). Cf. Trussell and Steckel, "Age of Slaves"; Fogel and Engerman, *Time on the Cross*, 78–86.

70. Series 1, *South Carolina Narratives*, pt. 4, 3:53; *Texas Narratives*, pt. 4, 5:176–178; Kemble, *Journal*, 167, 205. Botume, *First Days*, 161–163; Escott, *Slavery Remembered*, 43–44; Series 1, *Texas Narratives*, pt. 4, 5:189; *Alabama Narratives*, 6:134, 221; *Mississippi Narratives*, 7:4; *Florida Narratives*, 17:167.

71. Schwartz, *Birthing a Slave*, 67; Gaffney quote in Perrin, "Resisting Reproduction," 261–262.

72. Gutman, *Black Family*, 75; Sutch, "The Care and Feeding of Slaves" in Davis and others, *Reckoning with Slavery*; Gutman and Sutch, "Victorians All?" in Davis and others, *Reckoning with Slavery*, 231–301 and 134–162; Owens, *This Species of Property*, 38.

73. Owens, *This Species of Property*, 40–41; Eblen, "New Estimates," 301–319; Steckel, "Slave Mortality"; Kiple and Kiple, "Slave Child Mortality," 284–309. Kiple and Kiple attribute the high rates of slave infant mortality to "a conspiracy of nutrition, African environmental heritage, and North American climatic circumstances rather than planter mistreatment" (p. 299). But see also Johnson, "Smothered Slave Infants." On the high fertility rates of slave women in the upper South, see Sutch, "Breeding of Slaves," in Davis and others, *Reckoning with Slavery*, 173–210. Quotations from *Weevils in the Wheat*, 150; Botume, *First Days*, 164. For discussions of the demographic effects of the cotton boom, see Owens, *This Species of Property*, 38; David, "Time on the Cross," in Davis and others, *Reckoning with Slavery*, 339–357; Eblen, "New Estimates," 312.

74. Series 1, *Alabama Narratives*, 6:9; Supp. Series 2, *Texas Narratives*, pt. 5, 6:2036–2037; Series 1, *Florida Narratives*, 1:22–23; Kaye, *Joining Places*, 51–118; Webber, *Deep Like the Rivers*, 112–113, 167–171; *Unwritten History of Slavery*, 251. On naming practices in the quarters, one scholar observes, "One function of naming a child for his father or paternal kin was to assert the child's place in slave society." See Cody, "Naming, Kinship, and Estate Dispersal," 203.

75. Gutman, *Black Family*, 67–68, 142, 267–268; Genovese, *Roll, Jordan, Roll*, 318, 482–494; Series 1, *South Carolina Narratives*, pt. 3, 3:192; Supp. Series 1, *Mississippi Narratives*, pt. 2, 7:382.

76. Series 1, *Oklahoma Narratives*, 7:210; Escott, *Slavery Remembered*, 49–57, 87; Owens, *This Species of Property*, 201; Genovese, *Roll, Jordan, Roll*, 512; Gutman and Sutch, "Victorians All?" in Davis and others, *Reckoning with Slavery*, 152; Steckel, "Miscegenation." For accounts of the rape of slave women, see Supp. Series 2, *Mississippi Narratives*, 7:2531, *Louisiana Narratives*, 4:1238–1240. See also Williamson, *New People*; Reed, *Hemingses of Monticello*.

77. Supp. Series 2, *Texas Narratives*, pt. 2, 2:23–24; *Weevils in the Wheat*, 207; Steckel, "Miscegenation," 251; Brown, "Sexuality and the Slave Community," 8; Series 1, *Florida Narratives*, 17:89–90. See also *Unwritten History of Slavery*, 44; Olmsted, *Slave States*, 619, 622; *Weevils in the Wheat*,

202, 207–208; Kemble, *Journal*, 141, 210. The social-scientific literature on rape reveals the antipathy toward the victim on the part of husbands or lovers who feel personally humiliated by the incident. See, for example, Notman and Nadelson, "The Rape Victim." This issue is complicated by the fact that the rape of slave women by black drivers did occur on occasion. As the supervisor of a gang of field-workers (sometimes of women exclusively), the driver had temptations and opportunities similar to those of white overseers, and not all of them showed the respect toward their fellow slaves that Frank Bell's uncle did. Some apparently harbored feelings of resentment that found at least partial release in attacks upon enslaved women. See Kemble, *Journal*, 228; Series 1, *Mississippi Narratives*, 7:13; Gutman, *Black Family*, 83–84; Olmsted, *Slave States*, 430, 436–38, 470, and *Back Country*, 81; Series 1, *Oklahoma Narratives*, 7:50; *Mississippi Narratives*, 7:171; Owens, *This Species of Property*, 123–125.

78. Gutman and Sutch, "Sambo Makes Good," in Davis and others, *Reckoning with Slavery*, 63; Owens, *This Species of Property*, 195; Supp. Series 1, *Mississippi Narratives*, pt. 1, 6:59–60. For mention of corn shuckings in particular, see Genovese, *Roll, Jordan, Roll*, 318; Series 1, *Mississippi Narratives*, 7:6; Series 1, *Oklahoma Narratives*, 7:230. In the context of traditional male-female roles, what Genovese calls the "curious sexual division of labor" that marked these festivities was not "curious" at all (p. 318).

79. Eblen, "New Estimates," 306; Pearson, ed., *Letters from Port Royal*, 25; Genovese, *Roll, Jordan, Roll*, 522–523; Andrews, *Journal of a Georgia Girl*, 101; Escott, *Slavery Remembered*, 108–109; Owens, *This Species of Property*, 140; Gutman, *Black Family*, 218; Olmsted, *Slave States*, 433; Gray, *History of Agriculture*, 548; Kemble, *Journal*, 164, 247; Douglass, *Narrative*, 76–78. According to Genovese, the ability of these elderly enslaved persons "to live decently and with self-respect depended primarily on the support of their younger fellow slaves" (*Roll, Jordan, Roll*, 523). See also Supp. Series 1, *Mississippi Narratives*, pt. 1, 6:242; Pollard, "Aging and Slavery"; Series 1, *Alabama Narratives*, 6:216, 256, 334; Supp. Series 2, *Nebraska Narratives*, 1:319–320; Webber, *Deep Like the Rivers*, 175–176.

80. Series 1, *Georgia Narratives*, pt. 1, 12:214; *Weevils in the Wheat*, 128.

81. Stevenson, *Life in Black and White*, 228; Fett, *Working Cures*; Jones, *Gullah Folktales*, 171; Blassingame, "Status and Social Structure," in Owens, ed., *Perspectives*, 142. See also Raboteau, *Slave Religion*, 238, 275; Webber, *Deep Like the Rivers*, 226; Genovese, *Roll, Jordan, Roll*, 225–227.

82. Blassingame, ed., *Slave Testimony*, 133.

83. Jones, *American Work*, 222–232; Jones, *Saving Savannah*, 3–116; Goldin, *Urban Slavery*; Wade, *Slavery in the Cities*; Southern Claims Commission, Chatham County Claim no. 18222, RG 217 (M1658), National Archives.

84. Adams, *South-Side View*, 29–30; Hunt, "The Struggle to Achieve" in Morton, ed., *Discovering the Women in Slavery*; Johnson and Roark, *Black Masters*; Koger, *Black Slaveowners*; Lightner and Ragan, "African American Slaveholders"; Walker, ed., *African American Business*, 50.

85. See, for example, Johnson, "African American Women" and "Free Blacks."

86. Melish, *Disowning Slavery*; Jones, *American Work*, 245–272; White, *Somewhat More Independent*; "In the Northern": Douglass quoted in John P. Pittman, "Douglass's Assimilationism and Antislavery," in Lawson and Kirkland, eds., *Frederick Douglass*, 72.

87. Truth quoted in Painter, *Sojourner Truth*, 126; Yellin, *Harriet Jacobs*; Yee, *Black Women Abolitionists*.

88. Larson, *Bound for the Promised Land*; Clinton, *Harriet Tubman*; Humez, *Harriet Tubman*; Walker, ed., *African American Business*, 601.

CHAPTER 2

1. Berlin and Rowland, eds., *Families and Freedom*, 185–187.

2. "evil": De Forest, *A Union Officer*, 94; "an abolitionist": Whitelaw Reid quoted in Powell, *New Masters*, 218; Foner, "Crisis of Free Labor," in Foner, *Politics and Ideology*. For a discussion of the Republican Party's "free labor" ideology, see Foner, *Free Soil, Free Labor, Free Men*. On the northern work ethic, see also Rodgers, *Work Ethic*. The party's postwar southern economic program is placed in political context by Gerteis, *From Contraband to Freedman*, and McFeely, *Yankee Stepfather*, 149–165. For a case study of the bureau, see Cimbala, *Under the Guardianship*.

3. Roark, *Masters Without Slaves*; "retired": Loring and Atkinson, *Cotton Culture*, 4. This work is a compilation of data based on an 1868 survey of labor and economic conditions in the South. See also Wiener, "Class Structure," 970–992.

4. "Those": Trowbridge, *The South*, 23; Robinson, *Bitter Fruits of Bondage*.

5. Litwack, *Been in the Storm So Long*, 162. Several studies are particularly useful in their treatment of the deinstitutionalization of slavery at the regional, state, and local levels: Mohr, *On the Threshold of Freedom*; Ripley, *Slaves and Freedmen*; Engs, *Freedom's First Generation*; Robinson, "In the Shadow of Old John Brown"; Cimprich, "Slave Behavior." See also Sterling, ed., *We Are Your Sisters*, 237–261.

6. Higginson, *Army Life*, 247. The quotations from former slaves are taken from Rawick, ed., *American Slave*, Series 1, *Ohio Narratives*, 16:29; Series 1, *Indiana Narratives*, 6:165–166.

7. Series 1, *Mississippi Narratives*, 7:52; Litwack, *Been in the Storm So Long*, 3–63.

8. Andrews, *War-Time Journal*, III, 127–128, 355; Series 1, *Florida Narratives*, 17:74; Haviland, *A Woman's Life-Work*, 266; Litwack, *Been in the Storm So Long*, 162; O'Donovan, *Becoming Free*, 94–95, 103.

9. Botume, *First Days*, 140; Series 1, *Texas Narratives*, pt. 4, 5:193–194. See also Haviland, *A Woman's Life-Work*, 254, 268; Towne, *Letters and Diary of Laura M. Towne*, 24; Litwack, *Been in the Storm So Long*, 10–11, 13, 54, 58, 182–183; O'Donovan, *Becoming Free*, 113. Mohr documents the effects of wartime food shortages and the escalation of antiblack violence in *On the Threshold of Freedom*.

10. Schwartz, *Birthing a Slave*, 295–296.

11. "put so much": quoted in Dunaway, *African-American Family*, 185; O'Donovan, *Becoming Free*, 21, 86–88. Durden, *The Gray and the Black*; Brewer, *The Confederate Negro*; Ripley, *Slaves and Freedmen*, 9–16, 151–157; Campbell and Pickens, "Document: 'My Dear Husband.'"

12. Botume, *First Days*, 15. Compare the description of a black woman on her way to Columbia, South Carolina, in December 1865 by Dennett, *The South As It Is*, 233: "She was a middle-aged woman, and appeared to be accompanied on her pilgrimage by her family. A little boy was following her, a little girl she led by the hand, and on her back was an infant slung in a shawl. A heavy bundle was balanced on her head. They all seemed weary as they trudged along through the mud, and their clothing was too scanty for the winter weather." See also Mohr, "Before Sherman"; Ripley, *Slaves and Freedmen*, 150; Gutman, *Black Family*, 268–269; Engs, *Freedom's First Generation*, 27.

13. Haviland, *A Woman's Life-Work*, 304; Botume, *First Days*, 55; Towne, *Letters and Diary*, 45; Taylor, *Reminiscences*, 16–21; Gutman, *Black Family*, 22–24; Series 1, *Virginia Narratives*, 16:43; Berlin, Reidy, and Rowland, eds., *Black Military Experience*, 12. On the willingness of black men to fight on behalf of their families, see also Gutman, *Black Family*, 371–385; Mohr, "Before Sherman," 339–341. Recruitment policies and tactics are discussed in Rose, *Rehearsal for Reconstruction*,

264–269; Ripley, *Slaves and Freedmen*, 108–109, 153–155; Gerteis, *From Contraband to Freedman*; Berlin, Reidy, and Rowland, eds., *Black Military Experience*, 37–299. Mathew Brady, the Civil War photographer, was primarily interested in corpses, cannon, and Union officers, but his *Illustrated History of the Civil War* contains pictures of black refugees (pp. 24, 146) and black laundresses at the camp in Yorktown (p. 141). The women in the picture on p. 146 are wearing kerchiefs; the two men are wearing different kinds of hats. The picture shows eight women, two men, and eight children.

14. "all the": "Affidavit of a Kentucky Black Soldier's Wife"; and "they are": "Missouri Slave Woman to Her Soldier Husband," in Berlin, Reidy, and Rowland, eds., *Black Military Experience*, 87, 686–687, 694–695; " large": quoted in Dunaway, *African-American Family*, 198.

15. "Affidavit of a Northern Missionary"; "Commander of a Tennessee Black Regiment to the Headquarters of the Department of the Mississippi and a Report by the Superintendent of Freedmen in West Tennessee"; "Superintendent of the 'Refugee Home' at Camp Nelson, Kentucky, to the Freedmen's Bureau Commissioner," in Berlin, Reidy, and Rowland, eds., *Black Military Experience*, 715–719; Howard, "The Civil War in Kentucky," 250–252; Schultz, *Women at the Front*, 37, 200–202. See also Litwack, *Been in the Storm So Long*, 64–103; Ripley, *Slaves and Freedmen*, 155; Taylor, *Reminiscences*, 16. For other firsthand accounts of black soldiers' families and their living conditions, see Trowbridge, *The South*, 288; Pearson, ed., *Letters from Port Royal*, 41; Higginson, *Army Life in a Black Regiment*. Issues related to the health of refugees in particular and freedpeople in general are discussed in Raphael, "Health and Social Welfare"; Legan, "Disease and the Freedmen."

16. Botume, *First Days*, 53–63.

17. "Such a colony": *Official Records of the Union and Confederate Navies* (hereafter *ORUCN*), Series 1, 12:634; Heard, "St. Simons Island"; Hayes, ed., *DuPont Letters*, 336.

18. "I had about": Clinton, ed., *Reminiscences of My Life*, 11; "children presented": quoted in Mohr, *On the Threshold of Freedom*, 82–83.

19. "great dislike": Hayes, ed., *DuPont Letters*, vol. 2: *The Blockade, 1862–63*, 71; *ORUCN*, Series 1, 13:145.

20. Schwalm, *A Hard Fight for We*, 124; "worked": Moses Stikes and Binah Butler, Chatham County Claim no. 17563, Southern Claims Commission, National Archives; Penningroth, *The Claims of Kinfolk*, 82; Jones, *Saving Savannah*, 204–214.

21. Patience quoted in Burton, "Ungrateful Servants?" 136; Andrews, *The South Since the War*, 353.

22. "Commander of the Post of Port Hudson, Louisiana, to the Louisiana Freedmen's Bureau Assistant Commissioner and the Latter's Reply," in Berlin, Reidy, and Rowland, eds., *Freedom*, 701–702.

23. "the insolence": quoted in Fitzgerald, *Urban Emancipation*, 33–34; Johnson, "Looking for Lost Kin," in Clinton, ed., *Southern Families*, 15–34; Foner, "Thaddeus Stevens, Confiscation, and Reconstruction," in Foner, *Politics and Ideology*; Wiener, *Social Origins of the New South*; Wayne, *The Reshaping of Plantation Society*; Ransom and Sutch, *One Kind of Freedom*.

24. Cohen, *At Freedom's Edge*; Roark, *Masters Without Slaves*, 111; Taylor, *Reconstruction of Virginia*, 105–110; Richardson, *Negro in the Reconstruction in Florida*, 53–54; Taylor, *Louisiana Reconstructed*, 324, 331–32.

25. McPherson, *Abolitionist Legacy*; Foner, "Crisis of Free Labor," in Foner, *Politics and Ideology*, 101; Rose, *Rehearsal for Reconstruction*; McFeely, *Yankee Stepfather*; Gerteis, *From Contraband to Freedman*, 65–82.

26. Howard, *Autobiography*, 221; "Commander of the Department of Virginia to the Commander of the District of Eastern Virginia," in Berlin, Reidy, and Rowland, eds., *Black Military Experience*, 721–722; planter quoted in Powell, *New Masters*, 117; Hancock, *South After Gettysburg*, 218. See also Ripley, *Slaves and Freedmen*, 75, 90–101; Engs, *Freedom's First Generation*, 106–108.

27. "she waits": quoted in Frankel, *Freedom's Women*, 21–22; Dunaway, *African-American Family*, 223; O'Donovan, *Becoming Free*, 112, 155–173.

28. "a worn, weary": Sarah E. Chase in Swint, ed., *Dear Ones at Home*, 203–204; Dennett, *South As It Is*, 105. Sarah E. Chase and her sister Lucy served as teachers in Columbus (and other parts of the South) under the sponsorship of the Boston Educational Commission, later the New England Freedmen's Union Commission. For other accounts of persons unable to work turned off plantations, see Gutman, *Black Family*, 210; Kolchin, *First Freedom*, 58.

29. "A Settlement Made Between Presley George, Sr., and his Freedmen by W. H. Gentry . . . ," Jan. 23, 1866, Reports of Outrages, Greensboro, N.C., Subass't. Comm. (Box no. 36, In. #2656), Bureau of Refugees, Freedmen, and Abandoned Lands (hereafter BRFAL). Record Group 105. See National Archives for Note.

30. Towne quoted in McFeely, *Yankee Stepfather*, 157. See also Andrews, *The South Since the War*, 100; Litwack, *Been in the Storm So Long*, 183–184; Richardson, *Negro in the Reconstruction of Florida*, 56–58. Richardson writes that in Florida, "The Bureau literally forced some of the freedmen to work on plantations, and the contracts approved by the agents often specified inadequate payment to the worker" (p. 59). Contract between A. B. Littlejohn and Bettie and Patsy, July 15, 1865, Contracts, Jacksonville, Alabama, Subass't. Comm. (Box no. 32, In. #137), BRFAL.

31. Case 104 (Sept. 9, 1867, p. 78), Register of Complaints, Cuthbert, Georgia, Agent (No. 238; In. #859), BRFAL. A "moderate" position was stated by Maj. George D. Reynolds, acting assistant commissioner for the Southern District of Mississippi in a letter to his "lieutenants" in the field, Aug. 12, 1865, District of Vicksburg: "Allow no cruelty or abuse of employees. Prevent or discourage as far as possible all Freedmen from leaving their present places of employment and show them the necessity of work." Records Relating to the Division of Crops on Cotton Plantations, 1867–68, Vicksburg, Miss., Subcommissioner (In. #2366), BRFAL. Gerteis discusses the "pattern of repression" that characterized the labor contract system from its inception in *From Contraband to Freedman*, 83–98.

32. Series 1, *Mississippi Narratives*, 7:116–117; Series 1, *Alabama Narratives*, 6:420–421; Dennett, *South As It Is*, 247; Trowbridge, *The South*, 413–414; Sitterson, *Sugar Country*, 235–245; Handy, "In a Tobacco Factory." See also Sterling, ed., *We Are Your Sisters*, 309–344.

33. Andrews, *South Since the War*, 224; Swint, ed., *Dear Ones at Home*, 181. For other examples of petty tradeswomen after the war, see Dennett, *South As It Is*, 278; Towne, *Letters and Diary*, 19; Campbell, *White and Black*, 338; King, *The Great South*, 554.

34. Clinton, ed., *Reminiscences of My Life in Camp*, 54; O'Donovan, *Becoming Free*, 173–177; Williams, *Self-Taught*, 96–125; Jones, *Soldiers of Light and Love*, 63–65, 69–76, 238–239. See also Lerner, ed., *Black Women in White America*, 103–107; Sterling, ed., *We Are Your Sisters*, 261–305; Perkins, "The Black Female," in Crow and Hatley, eds., *Black Americans*, 122–136; Ronald Butchart, "'We Can Best Instruct Our Own People',", and "Perspectives."

35. Ripley, *Slaves and Freedmen*, 22–23; Foner, *Women and the American Labor Movement: From Colonial Times to the Eve of World War I*, 124–25.

36. Pearson, ed., *Letters from Port Royal*, 11; Leigh, *Ten Years*, 57–58; Trowbridge, *The South*, 543; Botume, *First Days*, 228. Foner discusses the relative autonomy of Sea Island blacks before and after emancipation in *Nothing But Freedom*.

37. See, for example, O'Donovan, *Becoming Free*, 137–147, 226; Wayne, *Reshaping of Plantation Society*, 116–132; Armstrong, "From Task Labor to Free Labor"; Foner, *Nothing But Freedom*, 74–110.

38. See, for example, Penningroth, *Claims of Kinfolk*; Shaffer, "In the Shadow of the Old Constitution," in Clinton, ed., *Southern Families*, 59–75; Crouch, "The 'Chords of Love.'"

39. Record and Account Book of Mrs. Bayner's Plantation, Feb.-Dec. 1867, 5, 20, 23, Pine Bluff, Arkansas, Subordinate Field Office (vol. 148, In. #422), BRFAL. This record book chronicles the difficulties of overseer O. B. Nichols in managing his workforce during the entire cotton-growing season of 1867. Women were often listed as absent from the field, "waiting on their children." Some days Nichols reported that the women and children had "done nothing" in the fields. See also pp. 3, 5, 9. For other examples, see Leigh, *Ten Years*, 25, 57; Brooks, *Agrarian Revolution*, 20; Powell, *New Masters*, 109. Estimates of postbellum labor force participation rates are included in Ransom and Sutch, *One Kind of Freedom*, 232–236.

40. Schwalm, *A Hard Fight for We*, 222; Rodrigue, *Reconstruction in the Cane Fields*, 90–91; Frankel, *Freedom's Women*, 76.

41. Newspaper article quoted in Burton, "Ungrateful Servants?" 347. For evidence of the withdrawal of female labor from the fields between 1865 and 1875, and the reaction of Southern whites, see the following examples: Loring and Atkinson, *Cotton Culture*, 4, 13, 14, 15, 18, 20; Nordhoff, *The Cotton States*, 72, 99; Somers, *Southern*, 59, 272; De Forest, *Union Officer*, 94. Secondary accounts include Kolchin, *First Freedom*, 62–63; Wiener, *Social Origins of the New South*, 47; Ransom and Sutch, *One Kind of Freedom*, 44–45, 55, 195; Gutman, *Black Family*, 167–168; Litwack, *Been in the Storm So Long*, 244–245, 341, 393, 434; Taylor, *Louisiana Reconstructed*, 326–327; Powell, *New Masters*, 60, 108. A survey of contracts contained in the Freedmen's Bureau archives indicates that fewer women than men signed labor contracts. However, this is not necessarily an accurate measure of female participation in the labor force because husbands and fathers often signed for entire families.

42. Richardson, *Negro in the Reconstruction of Florida*, 63; Litwack, *Been in the Storm So Long*, 244–245; Loring and Atkinson, *Cotton Culture*, 15; Wiener, *Social Origins of the New South*, 47.

43. "myriads": De Forest, *Union Officer*, 94; Campbell, *White and Black*, 145.

44. Planter quoted in Loring and Atkinson, *Cotton Culture*, 13; mistress quoted in Myers, ed., *The Children of Pride*, 1370; freed woman quoted in Trowbridge, *The South*, 394.

45. Neal quoted in Gutman, *Black Family*, 393. See also pp. 22–25, 393–412. For the dramatic account of a husband who was wounded in an attempt to protect his wife from white men, see W. W. Woodward to Pvt. Maj. L. Walker, May 7, 1868, Labor Contracts, Anderson Court House, South Carolina, Acting Subass't. Comm. (Box no. 50, In. #3073), BRFAL.

46. Pearson, ed., *Letters from Port Royal*, 112; Somers, *Southern States Since the War*, 120; O'Donovan, *Becoming Free*. The records of settlements between planters and freedpeople supervised by bureau agents include examples of squads. For example, in the case *Freedmen v. Carland Graham*, near Baton Rouge, Louisiana, an agent wrote, "The Freedpeople were working the plantation in two separate squads, comprising four different families." The squads included, first: Jack and Ann Gray, Jack Gray Jr. and William Randolph; second: David and Victoria Butler, Frank and Celestine Benjamin, Lewis, Ed, Benjamin, Harriet, and Delia Buckner. "Freedmen v. Carland Graham," Dec. 13, 1867, 12–13, Register of Complaints, Baton Rouge, Louisiana, Assistant Subass't. Comm. (vol. 2231/2, In. #1499), BRFAL. For examples of other squads and lists of their members, see Register of Complaints, 2–6, Bayou Sara, Louisiana, Agent and Subass't. Comm. (vol. 234, In.

#1523), BRFAL. See also Shlomowitz, "Origins"; Kolchin, *First Freedom*, 46; Gutman, *Black Family*, 209; Wayne, *Reshaping of Plantation Society*, 124.

47. De Forest, *Union Officer*, 94; Ransom and Sutch, *One Kind of Freedom*, 87–88. Roark states that "sharecropping was a compromise, and it satisfied neither planters nor freedmen" (p. 142). See also Wynne, "Role of Freedmen."

48. Ransom and Sutch, *One Kind of Freedom*, 88. On the rise of the sharecropping system, see (in addition to Shlomowitz, "Origins" and Ransom and Sutch, *One Kind of Freedom*) Reid Jr., "White Land, Black Labor"; Mandle, *The Roots of Black Poverty*; Wiener, *Social Origins of the New South*; Wayne, *Reshaping of Plantation Society*, 123–129; Davis, *Good and Faithful Labor*; Higgs, *Competition and Coercion*, 37–61; Hahn, *The Roots of Southern Populism*. For a contemporary account of the transition from gang labor to sharecropping on a Georgia plantation, see Barrow Jr., "A Georgia Plantation."

49. This analysis is based on a sample of 338 black households in the twenty-seven counties in eight states that formed the basis for Ransom and Sutch's study of the postbellum Southern economy. The states and counties were: Alabama—Lowndes, Perry, Pike, Russell; Florida—Gadsden; Georgia—Coweta, Gwinnett, Terrell, Thomas, Twiggs; Louisiana—Claiburne, Grant; Mississippi—Attala, Clay, Jefferson, Lincoln, Pike, Rankin, Tunica, Washington, Yalobusha; North Carolina—Nash; South Carolina—Barnwell, Union; Texas—Cherokee, Red River, Robertson. The households were selected from the 1870 (and, for Chapter 3, the 1880 and 1900) federal population census at specific intervals. Data analyzed included information on the "race" (black, white, or mulatto), size, and type of household; presence, occupation, literacy, and age of household head and spouse; number and sex of working children and adults; number and sex of children who attended school; age of youngest person in the household; and listing of persons with the identical surname near the household in question. For confirmation of the findings discussed in the text (based on studies of other parts of the rural South), see, on two spouses present: Burton, "Ungrateful Servants?" 325; Kolchin, *First Freedom*, 69; on male-headed households: Smallwood, "Emancipation and the Black Family," 859; Burton, "Ungrateful Servants?" 321, 328–29, 331; on relative ages of spouses: Escott, *Slavery Remembered*, 170–171 (Escott found that among slave-narrative interviewees, the men married at an average of 27.6 years, the women at 19.5 years); on fertility rates: Kolchin, *First Freedom*, 69; Higgs, *Competition and Coercion*, 15; Eblen, "New Estimates," 306.

50. Nordhoff, *Cotton States*, 38; Series 1, *Tennessee Narratives*, 16:29; Contract between Patrick Broggan and freedpeople: "Carter-Dock and family—wife Diana and 2 daughters Flora and Bella," Miscellaneous Record Book, 1865–1867, Greenville, Alabama, Subass't. Comm. (vol. 127, In. #106), BRFAL.

51. Case 29 (May 30, 1868, pp. 104–105), Register of Complaints, Cuthbert, Georgia, Agent (vol. 238, In. #859), BRFAL; Regosin, *Freedom's Promise*, 12. See Labor Contracts for Spartanburg District, Spartanburg, S.C. (Box no. 87, In. #3343), BRFAL, for examples of women with dependents who were given less land than men with similar-sized families under a sharecropping arrangement on various plantations from 1865 to 1867.

52. Campbell, *White and Black*, 150, 156, 297; Taylor, *Negro in South Carolina*, 72; Botume, *First Days*, 241; Dennett, *South As It Is*, 326, 331; Nordhoff, *Cotton States*, 21, 38–39, 72. According to Shlomowitz, "The higher value placed on labor during the months from April to July can probably be attributed to the fact that female labor was a much closer substitute for male labor in picking than in plowing, planting, and cultivation" ("Origins," 568). After the war, Willis Cofer and his father

worked in the fields and his mother wove cloth "for all de folkses 'round 'bout" for fifty cents a day. Series 1, *Georgia Narratives*, pt. 1, 12:209–210.

53. Compare other studies on household size: Burton, "Ungrateful Servants?" 336; Kolchin, *First Freedom*, 67–70; Smallwood, "Emancipation and the Black Family," 853; on working spouses and children: Smallwood, "Emancipation and the Black Family," 855–856. See also Magdol, "Against the Gentry," in Magdol and Wakelyn, eds., *Southern Common People*, 191–210. According to Ransom and Sutch, *One Kind of Freedom* (based on 1880 data), "Whites could afford greater leisure and have a smaller fraction of the family at work than could blacks" (pp. 184–185). Higgs, *Competition and Co-ercion*, includes estimates (made by the United States Department of Agriculture) of black land own-ership for 1876: Tennessee and Alabama: 4 percent; North Carolina and Georgia: 4–5 percent; South Carolina and Texas: 5 percent; Mississippi, Louisiana, and Arkansas: 5–6 percent; Florida: 8 percent. These figures, he states, are based on "admittedly incomplete returns of information" (p. 52). See also Smallwood, "Emancipation and the Black Family," 855.

54. Campbell, *White and Black*, 376; Series 1, *Mississippi Narratives*, 7:70; Ransom and Sutch, *One Kind of Freedom*, 108, 113, 123–124, 130–131, 147, 161–163; Richardson, *Negro in the Reconstruc-tion of Florida*, 61, 65; Taylor, *Louisiana Reconstructed*, 87–88, 393, 402–406.

55. Series 1, *Texas Narratives*, pt. 3, 5:192; Series 1, *Tennessee Narratives*, 16:77. See also Ransom and Sutch, *One Kind of Freedom*, 232–236; Botume, *First Days*, 234; Loring and Atkinson, *Cotton Culture*, 14; Nordhoff, *Cotton States*, 21, 38, 39, 99; Campbell, *White and Black*, 156; Litwack, *Been in the Storm So Long*, 244; Dennett, *South As It Is*, 132.

56. Series 1, *Tennessee Narratives*, 16:44, 64. See also Jones, *Soldiers of Light and Love*, 128–133; Mack, *Parlor Ladies and Ebony Drudges*, 135–136.

57. Gutman, *Black Family*, 213, 224–229; Magdol, *A Right to the Land*, 11. Magdol discusses the ways the African American associational impulse was manifested in the social, economic, and insti-tutional life of freedpeople. The following procedure was employed to estimate the extent of local kin groupings: Each household for which data were coded was the first complete household on a cer-tain census page. That page, plus the previous and subsequent pages (a total of three), were exam-ined for individuals with a surname identical to that of any member of the household in question. If such a person or persons were located, the answer to the question "kin living nearby?" was coded 1 for "yes." This index is necessarily crude for several reasons. It takes into account only paternal rela-tionships. Identical surnames do not necessarily indicate blood ties. The households involved might have been a considerable distance from one another, precluding frequent contact among family members. Finally, the order of listing was determined by the route taken by a census taker (up one side of a road and down the other, or across the road to the next house, and so on).

58. Leigh, *Ten Years*, 24, 124.

59. De Forest, *Union Officer*, 29, 99.

60. Harding, *There Is A River*; Robinson, "Realm of Social Consensus"; Hahn, *Roots of Southern Populism*; McDonald and McWhiney, "Self-Sufficiency to Peonage"; Woodman, "Postbellum Social Change," 229. According to Foner, "Reconstruction allowed scope for a remarkable political and so-cial mobilization of the black community," and "for a moment, American freedmen had enjoyed an unparalleled opportunity to help shape their own destiny" *(Nothing But Freedom*, 72–73.) On black politicians during this period, see Rabinowitz, ed., *Southern Black Leaders*; Dray, *Capitol Men*.

61. Botume, *First Days*, 273; Kelly, "Black Laborers, the Republican Party, and the Crisis of Re-construction." Litwack, *Been in the Storm So Long* (pp. 502–556), provides an overview of freed-men's conventions throughout the South. See also Harding, *There Is a River*, 277–297. In "Sources

at the National Archives," Drago states, "In 1869, a convention of Georgia's top black leaders declared that women should not be subject to the same kind of work as men and urged 'upon the laboring men of this state, in behalf of their wives and daughters . . . that they take their wives from the drudgery and exposure of plantation soil as soon as it is in their power to do so'" (p. 82). See the drawing in *Harper's Weekly*, July 25, 1868, reproduced in Edwards, *Scarlet Doesn't Live Here Anymore*, 141.

62. Ames, *New England Woman's Diary*, 92; Leigh, *Ten Years*, 164; Botume, *First Days*, 166. The role of Sea Island religious institutions in ordering relations between the sexes is discussed in Gutman, *Black Family*, 70–73. See also Levine's discussion of "Freedom, Culture, and Religion," in Levine, *Black Culture and Black Consciousness*, 136–189.

63. Towne, *Letters and Diary*, 144–145; Pearson, ed., *Letters from Port Royal*, 43–44; Litwack, *Been in the Storm So Long*, 434.

64. The analytical framework developed here for studying the sharecropping family is based on Tamara K. Hareven's critique of modernization theory as it applies to family history. Hareven, "Modernization and Family History." Jonathan Wiener suggests that the black rejection of gang labor and preference for family share units "represented a move away from classic capitalist organization." See Wiener, "Class Structure and Economic Development," 984.

65. Andrews, *South Since the War*, 187.

66. Cooley, *Homes of the Freed*, 169–170; Fitzgerald, *Urban Emancipation*, 33–34.

67. Nordhoff, *Cotton States*, 72. See also Campbell, *White and Black*, 264; Brown, *My Southern Home*, 168–170; Knox, *Camp-Fire and Cotton-Field*, 410; Swint, ed., *Dear Ones at Home*, 33; Litwack, *Been in the Storm So Long*, 258, 315; Myers, ed., *Children of Pride*, 1308.

68. Ravenel quoted in Litwack, *Been in the Storm So Long*, 259; "A South Carolinian," "South Carolina Society," 677. See Taylor, *The Negro in the Reconstruction of Virginia*, for the example of a black woman who was charged with stealing a dress and described by the Richmond *Enquirer* in September 1866 as "a walking fashion plate in borrowed plumage" (p. 46). See also Leigh, *Ten Years*, 94.

69. Powell, *New Masters*, 109; Case 121, Sept. 16, 1867, Register of Complaints, Cuthbert, Georgia, Agent, BRFAL; "with sticks . . . kind": *Savannah Morning News*, Jan. 18, 1869; "all jabbering": *Savannah Morning News*, Jan. 20, 1869; Drago, "Militancy and Black Women." Litwack, *Been in the Storm So Long*, for example, includes many examples of women who defied Southern whites and asserted their rights in the workplace. See also Foner, *Nothing But Freedom*, 87.

70. Dennett, *South As It Is*, 292; Pearson, *Letters from Port Royal*, 53, 88; Knox, *Camp-Fire and Cotton-Field*, 374.

71. De Forest, *Union Officer*, 74–75, 94. See also Trowbridge, *The South*, 544; Campbell, *White and Black*, 134, 146; Pearson, *Letters from Port Royal*, 88, 250, 300–301; Stearns, *The Black Man of the South*, 43–46. In January of 1865 Edward Philbrick wrote of a group of black women who confronted him and, "like a flock of blackbirds all talking at once," protested the terms he had stipulated for their work for the corning year. He listened impatiently to their complaints that, despite growing a good deal of cotton for him, they were paid very little. His response: "I told them . . . that if some of those people who made so much noise didn't look out, they would get turned off the place, just as Venus and her gang got turned off last year. The fact is, they are trying to play brag, as such people often will; but they will all go to work in a few days, I feel sure" (Pearson, ed., *Letters from Port Royal*, 303–304).

72. Clinton, ed., *Reminiscences of My Life in Camp*, 27.

73. Shaffer, *After the Glory*, 56, 64, 121–123, 132, 137, 206; O'Donovan, *Becoming Free*, 193; Krawl, "For Better or for Worse," in Clinton, ed., *Southern Families*, 35–58; Edwards, *Scarlet Doesn't Live Here Anymore*, 143–147; Crouch, "The 'Chords of Love'"; Regosin, *Freedom's Promise*; Rosen, *Terror in the Heart of Freedom*.

74. "talking . . . pleased": quoted in Edwards, *Scarlet Doesn't Live Here Anymore*, 143. D. S. Harriman to Merritt Barber, Panola, Mississippi, Dec. 3, 1867, Registered Letters Received, Office of the Assistant Commissioner for Mississippi (In. #2052; Microfilm series M826, reel 31), BRFAL.

75. Athens, Wilkes County, October 31, 1868, Reports Relating to Murders and Outrages, Letters Received, Georgia Assistant Commissioner (In. #631; microfilm series M798, reel 32), BRFAL. Senate Testimony of Lucretia Adams, *Joint Select Committee to Inquire into the Affairs in the Late Insurrectionary States*, Report 41, Pt. 5 (South Carolina), 3:1577–1578. See also the case of a freedwoman whipped with a leather strap because she left her employer's residence to look for her brother. Report dated April 10, 1866, Reports of Outrages, Trial Records of Assistant Superintendent, June 1867–Oct. 1868, Greensboro, North Carolina, Subass't. Comm. (Box no. 36, In. #2656), BRFAL; Report dated Sept. 23, 1865, Reports of Outrages, June 1867–Oct. 1868, Greensboro, North Carolina, Subass't. Comm., BRFAL.

76. Deputy quoted in D. S. Harriman to Merritt Barber, Panola, Mississippi, Registered Letters Received, Office of the Assistant Commissioner for Mississippi, BRFAL.

77. These examples are based on cases in the Freedmen's Bureau archives for Georgia, Louisiana, North Carolina, South Carolina, and Virginia. An agent's account of the last case includes the following information: "States that Fanny Murry [*sic*] was severely beaten by Robert Singleton without any cause, then when the case was tried before John Can, J.P., Singleton did again strike Fanny in the presence of the Court, that in the face of incontestable proof of guilt Singleton was discharged and costs charged to Fanny." Case 35, June, 1868, Upperville, Virginia, Report of Outrages, Jan. 1, 1868–Dec. 31, 1868, Office of the Virginia Assistant Commissioner (Vol. 43, In. #3810), BRFAL. See also Sterling, ed., *We Are Your Sisters*, 344–355.

78. Rosen, *Terror in the Heart of Freedom*; Trelease, *White Terror*; Clinton, "Freedwomen, Sexuality, and Violence," in Clinton, *Half Sisters of History*, 136–153.

79. Howard N. Rabinowitz, *Race Relations*, 18–30. For further discussion of urban in-migration during this period, see Taylor, *The Negro in the Reconstruction of Virginia*, 111–120; J. G. Taylor, *Louisiana Reconstructed*, 326; Huffman Jr., "Town and Country in the South" in Magdol and Wakelyn, eds., *Southern Common People*, 239–251.

80. Goldin, "Female Labor Force," 92, 99; Somers, *Southern States*, 36; John W. Blassingame, *Black New Orleans*, 94–95; Kolchin, *First Freedom*, 62–63, 75; Burton, "Ungrateful Servants?" 359; Harris, "Work and the Family," 323; Reiff, Dahlin, and Smith, "Rural Push and Urban Pull." Goldin compared the black female populations of Atlanta, Charleston, Richmond, Mobile, New Orleans, Norfolk, and Savannah.

81. Williams, *Self-Taught*; Goldin, "Female Labor Force," 94–99; Rabinowitz, *Race Relations*, 72. In *Women and the American Labor Movement*, Foner points out that free black women dominated urban laundering even during the early colonial period. The occupation of course required little equipment or capital investment and could be carried out in the woman's home (p. 10).

82. Goldin, "Female Labor Force," 94; Blassingame, "Before the Ghetto," 466. See also Woodman's "Comment" [on Goldin].

83. Goldin, "Female Labor Force," 94–100; Somers, *Southern States*, 52, 66; Rabinowitz, *Race Relations*, 120; Blassingame, "Before the Ghetto," 468–469, and *Black New Orleans*, 164–167; Higgs, *Competition and Coercion*, 21–24; Woodman, "Sequel to Slavery." Goldin's argument con-

cerning the primacy of "race" (as opposed to class) as a determining factor in a woman's decision to work is somewhat weakened by her assumption that black and white men with identical jobs earned the same amount of money and by her low estimates of urban unemployment rates for black men. Very few black men could afford not to have their spouses work. John Blassingame ("Before the Ghetto," 466) argues that Savannah artisans who made from $1.80 to $3.50 per day (probably about the same amount earned in a week by a day laborer, servant, or laundress) refused to let their wives seek employment, out of a sense of pride. The seasonal and unpredictable nature of black men's employment might have meant that almost all urban families—regardless of the husband's occupation—relied in varying degrees on the small sums contributed regularly by wives who washed clothes, cleaned, or cooked for whites. In addition, the finding (Goldin, "Female Labor Force," 96–97) that 20 percent of all women worked as servants and that as many as 75 percent of these (15 percent of all black working women in the seven southern cities) lived in the homes of their white employers merits further investigation to determine whether they were young, unmarried women, or mothers with children.

84. Ransom and Sutch, *One Kind of Freedom*, 34–36; Rabinowitz, *Race Relations*, 61–96; Blassingame, *Black New Orleans*, 49–77; Burton, "Ungrateful Servants?" 348–353; Taylor, *Negro in the Reconstruction of Virginia*, 114–120.

85. Hunter, *To 'Joy My Freedom*, 67; Barr, "Black Urban Churches"; Rabinowitz, *Race Relations*, 152–181; Blassingame, "Before the Ghetto," and *Black New Orleans*, 107–171; Taylor, *Louisiana Reconstructed*, 455–479.

86. Brown, "Womanist Consciousness"; Walker, ed., *African American Business*, 589; Jones, *Saving Savannah*, app. 2; Rabinowitz, *Race Relations*, 227; Blassingame, "Before the Ghetto," 473–474, 485, and *Black New Orleans*, 146–147; Foner, *Women and the American Labor Movement*, 124, 176, 188.

87. Swint, ed., *Dear Ones at Home*, 41; Williams, *Self-Taught*; Jones, *Soldiers of Light and Love*, 49–84; Morris, *Reading, 'Riting, and Reconstruction*.

88. Botume, *First Days*, 236, 250; Ames, *New England Woman's Diary*, 38; Case 121 (Sept. 16, 1867), Register of Complaints, Cuthbert, Georgia, Agent, BRFAL. For examples of working mothers who washed, scrubbed, ironed, and sewed so that they could send their children to school "looking respectable," see Lemer, ed., *Black Women in White America*, 102.

89. Ames, *New England Woman's Diary*, 33; Andrews, *The South Since the War*, 338. De Forest, *Union Officer*, 117. See also Kolchin, *First Freedom*, 185–186.

90. Census of Black Citizens (1865), Huntsville and Athens, Alabama, Claims Agent (No. 79 1/2, In. #123), BRFAL.

91. Ibid.

92. Ibid.

CHAPTER 3

1. Interview with Maude Lee Bryant in Wilson, *Hope and Dignity*, 42.

2. Pickens, *Bursting Bonds*, 26–27.

3. Wiener contrasts the "Prussian Road" of southern postbellum economic development with the "classic capitalist path" taken by the North in his article "Class Structure," pp. 970–992. See also Ransom and Sutch, "Growth and Welfare"; Kousser, *Shaping of Southern Politics*; Michael Perman, *Struggle for Mastery*.

4. Logan analyzes the deterioration of black people's social and political status during this period in *Betrayal of the Negro*. Woodruff, *American Congo*; Beckert, "Emancipation and Empire"; Flynn

Jr., *White Land, Black Labor*; Mandle, *The Roots of Black Poverty*, 11; Jones, "Negroes of the Southern States"; U.S. Dept. of Commerce, *Negro Population*, 1790–1915, 503–523; Higgs, *Competition and Coercion*, 30–33, 77; Hahn, *The Roots of Southern Populism*; Woodman, "Comment," 997–1001, and "Postbellum Social Change"; McDonald and McWhiney, "The South From Self-Sufficiency to Peonage"; Jones, *The Dispossessed*.

5. Rosengarten, *All God's Dangers*, 7–8. The autobiography of this remarkable black man, Ned Cobb (Nate Shaw was a fictitious name used to protect Cobb while he was still living), is a major source of primary material related to black sharecroppers' family and community life. The text is in the form of transcribed interviews conducted by Rosengarten with Cobb.

6. Cooley, *Homes of the Freed*, 71. A Vassar College graduate, Cooley began her work as a teacher–social worker on St. Helena (South Carolina Sea Islands) in 1906.

7. Painter, *Exodusters*, 184, 194, 196; Gutman, *The Black Family*, 435, 437; North Carolina Governor James S. Jarvis quoted (from a speech he made at the opening of the Colored Industrial Fair in Raleigh in 1883) in Logan, *Negro in North Carolina*, 75; Steven Hahn, *A Nation Under Our Feet*.

8. For relevant studies, see Ransom and Sutch, *One Kind of Freedom*; Wiener, *Social Origins*; Mandle, *Roots of Black Poverty*.

9. Woodman, "Postbellum Social Change"; Baker, *Following the Color Line*, 76; U.S. Dept. of Commerce, *Plantation Farming in the United States* (1916), 17; Edwards, "Negro Farmers," 536.109. Edwards, "Negro Farmers," 536. In his study of sharecroppers, Kelsey notes, "The size of a man's family is known and the riders see to it that he keeps all the working hands in the field," *The Negro Farmer*, p. 48. (Although written from a racist perspective, this work contains much useful information pertaining to the daily routine and material condition of rural southern blacks around 1900.) For evidence of planters who compelled sharecropping families to pay for additional workers to harvest their crop, see Edwards, "The Tenant System and Some Changes Since Emancipation," American Academy of Political and Social Science *Annals* 49 (September 1913).

11. Wilkison, *Yeomen, Sharecroppers, and Socialists*; Pickens, *Bursting Bonds*, 26–27; Baker, *Following the Color Line*, 99; Holmes, "The Peons of the South"; Rosengarten, *All God's Dangers*, 115, 124.

12. Mandle, *Roots of Black Poverty*, 16, 23–25; Booker T. Washington's story about the chickens quoted in Dillingham, "Black Belt Settlement Work," 441.

13. Krech, "Black Family Organization"; Darling, "Growth and Decline."

14. This analysis is based on a study of 359 black households in 1880 and 353 black households in 1900 selected from the federal manuscript census (at specific intervals) for twenty-seven Cotton Belt counties (see Chapter 2). See also Drago, "Sources at the National Archives," 83–85; Gutman, *Black Family*, app. A.

15. Rosengarten, *All God's Dangers*, 117; DuBois, "The Negro in the Black Belt," 410; Gutman, *Black Family*, 212–214; Krech, "Black Family Organization."

16. Shifflett, "Household Composition," 241; Hareven, "The Family Process." Shifflett finds that in Louisa County in 1880, nine out of ten black newlywed families included relatives or boarders (p. 242). He suggests that very young as well as mature households "often became caretakers of aged dependents and homeless outsiders" (p. 258).

17. Rosengarten, *All God's Dangers*, 108–109 (Shaw used these terms to describe the first parcel of land he worked as a married man in 1907); Harper, "Coloured Women of America"; Cooley, *Homes of the Freed*, 146–147; Terrell and Hirsch, eds., *Such As Us*, 34–37. Shifflett discusses the consumer-to-worker ratio and its significance for household structure in "Household Composition," 245.

18. DuBois, ed., "The Negro American Family," Atlanta University Study no. 13, 50–54 (hereafter AUS with number). This description is compiled from Barrow, "A Georgia Plantation," 832; DuBois, "The Problem of Housing the Negro"; Kelsey, *Negro Farmer*, 45; Baker, *Following the Color Line*, 100; Cooley, *Homes of the Freed*, 33–34, 129–130.

19. Housewives quoted in Dillingham, "Black Belt Settlement Work," 442; and Cooley, *Homes of the Freed*, 64–65, 143. See also Tindall, *South Carolina Negroes*, 95. See also Walker, *In Search of Our Mothers' Gardens*; Glave, "A Garden So Brilliant with Colors."

20. Clowes, *Black America*, 124; Faragher, *Women and Men*, 45. The latter work facilitates comparison between mid-nineteenth-century white commercial-agriculture families in the Midwest and late nineteenth-century southern sharecropping blacks.

21. Kelsey, *Negro Farmer*, 45; Cooley, *Homes of the Freed*, 77–78; Kiser, *Sea Island to City*, 254; Drago, "Sources at the National Archives," 88; Wilson, *Hope and Dignity*, 42.

22. Kiser, *Sea Island to City*, 71; Rosengarten, *All God's Dangers*, 9; Baker, *Following the Color Line*, 100. For photographs of women field-workers during this period, see Willets, *Workers of the Nation*, 2:717; and Dabbs, *Face of an Island*.

23. Rosengarten, *All God's Dangers*, 9; Willets, *Workers of the Nation*, 716; Kelsey, *Negro Farmer*, 73; Barrow, "Georgia Plantation," 834.

24. Bradley and Williamson, *Rural Children*, 34.

25. Pickens, *Bursting Bonds*, 13; Kiser, *From Sea Island to City*, 253; Tindall, *South Carolina Negroes*, 95.

26. Kelsey, *Negro Farmer*, 45; Thomas J. Edwards, "Negro Farmers of Alabama. pt. 2: Sharecroppers." *Southern Workman* 40 (September 1911): 536. Water-toting women and children are described in Barrow, "Georgia Plantation," 832; Cooley, *Homes of the Freed*, 120; Washington, "Condition of the Women," 74. This last article provides an invaluable description of the sharecropping wife's daily schedule. On the diet of rural blacks, see Higgs, *Competition and Coercion*, 105–109; Brown, *Southern Home*, 189; Kelsey, *Negro Farmer*, 45. Child mortality rates are discussed in Gutman, *Black Family*, 450, 502; Clowes, *Black America*, 108–110; Higgs, *Competition and Coercion*, 21–24; Laycock Jr., "Infantile Mortality," 78–81. The fertility of American black women fell by one-third from 1880 to 1910. See Higgs, *Competition and Coercion*, 16; Eblen, "New Estimates," 312. Cutright and Shorter argue that the decline was the result of the poor health of black women as a group, "The Effects of Health." See also McFalls Jr. and Masnick, "Birth Control."

27. Washington, "Condition of the Women," 74, 77; Baker, *Following the Color Line*, 100; Brown, *Southern Home*, 189; Kelsey, *Negro Farmer*, 74. See the detailed description of individual families' living and working conditions in DuBois, ed., "Negro American Family," AUS 13, 134–137.

28. Wilson, *Hope and Dignity*, 42.

29. Washington, "Condition of the Women," 75; Cooley, *Homes of the Freed*, 59–62, 90–91; Kelsey, *Negro Farmer*, 30, 34, 37, 50; Harper, "Coloured Women"; Hammond, *The Cotton Industry*, 187–189; DuBois, "Negro in the Black Belt," 403; Janiewski, "From Field to Factory," 38–39, 44.

30. Holt, *Making Freedom Pay*; Biggert, "Legacy of Resistance," 80. Faragher includes a description of this type of petty commercial activity and its significance for farm wives in the Midwest. He suggests that "cross-cultural studies indicate that the responsibility for exchanging goods and services with persons outside the family tends to confer power and prestige." See *Women and Men*, 62.

31. Janiewski, "From Field to Factory," 46–47; Rosengarten, *All God's Dangers*, 14–15; Edwards, "Wage Earners"; Tindall, *South Carolina Negroes*, 99; U.S. Dept. of Commerce, *Negro Population*,

1790–1915, 506. Only 13.2 percent of all white women engaged in agriculture worked for wages for even part of the year in 1910.

32. Pickens, *Bursting Bonds*, 11; Kiser, *Sea Island to City*, 253–254; Kelsey, *Negro Farmer*, 30; DuBois, "Negro in the Black Belt," 403; Edwards, "Wage Earners," 459. In "Negro American Family," AUS 13, DuBois notes that the "whole tendency of the sharecropping labor system is to separate the family group—the house is too small for them, the young people go to town or hire out on a neighboring farm" (p. 129).

33. Kiser, *Sea Island to City*, 249, 253–254; Rosengarten, *All God's Dangers*, 15, 19–20, 56–58, 128; Kelsey, *Negro Farmer*, 62; Pickens, *Bursting Bonds*, 27; DuBois, ed., "Negro American Family," AUS 13, 135–137; United States Department of Commerce, Bureau of the Census, *Negro Population*, 403–415, 377–387; Fairclough, *A Class of their Own*. E. Wilbur Bock defines the "farmer's daughter's effect" as the willingness of black parents to enable their daughters to attend college in greater numbers compared to their sons. According to Bock, parents have a "clearer picture of occupational opportunities for their daughters than their sons, and greater assurance that aspirations for their daughters will be realized." Bock, "Farmer's Daughter Effect," 18–19.

34. Laws, "Negroes of Cinclare Central"; Cooley, *Homes of the Freed*, 110; DuBois, ed., "Negro American Family," AUS 13, 129, 134–147; Janiewski, "From Field to Factory," 22. The age at marriage among males and females was identical to that of rural midwestern whites in the mid-nineteenth century. See Faragher, *Women and Men*, 58.

35. Eblen, "New Estimates," 301–319; Cutright and Shorter, "Effects of Health," 191–218; Jones, "Social Studies," 317–318; Meeker, "Mortality Trends."

36. Planter quoted in Cohen, *At Freedom's Edge*, 232; Laws, "Negroes of Cinclare Central," 114. See also U.S. Dept. of Commerce, *Negro Population, 1790–1915*, 506; Greene and Woodson, *Negro Wage Earner*, 26–27.

37. Kiser, *Sea Island to City*, 65, 89–91, 105, 119, 126; Cooley, *Homes of the Freed*, 90–91; Kelsey, *Negro Farmer*, 37, 42, 50; Tindall, *South Carolina Negroes*, 125–127; Greene and Woodson, *Negro Wage Earner*, 30, 61, 72–73; Laws, "Negroes of Cinclare Central," 114; Lamon, *Black Tennesseans*, 132.

38. Shifflett, "Household Composition," 255; DuBois, ed., "Negro American Family," AUS 13, 129.

39. Cooley, *Homes of the Freed*, 72, 76; Harper, "Coloured Women," 12. Photographs of Aunt Adelaide are featured in Dabbs, *Face of an Island*.

40. Cooley, *Homes of the Freed*, 95, 72–77, 90–91, 93–101; Wilson, *Hope and Dignity*, 49; Kiser, *Sea Island to City*, 67; Barrow, "Georgia Plantation," 834; DuBois, ed., "Negro American Family," AUS 13, 129. For the Moore family example, see the federal population manuscript census for 1900, Perry County, Alabama, subdistrict 5, enumeration district 72, sheet 4, National Archives of the United States (available on microfilm). Other Moores are listed on the pages immediately following and preceding. See also Pickens, *Bursting Bonds*, 5–6.

41. Tilley, *The Bright Tobacco Industry*; Byrne, "Child Labor," 12, 23; Handy, "On the Tobacco Plantation," 653.

42. Tilley, *Bright Tobacco*, 93–102; Janiewski, "From Field to Factory," 7–62.

43. George W. Henderson, "Life in the Louisiana Sugar Belt." *Southern Workman* 35 (April 1906): 209; Sitterson, *Sugar Country*, 313, 320; Laws, "Negroes of Cinclare Central"; Kelsey, *Negro Farmer*, 58–60.

44. Sitterson, *Sugar Country*, 253–263; Kelsey, *Negro Farmer*, 59; Laws, "Negroes of Cinclare Central," 110, 115–116.

45. "Truck Farming in Tidewater Virginia"; Thorn, "The Negroes of Litwalton, Virginia"; Work, "The Negroes of Warsaw, Georgia"; Williams, "Local Conditions Among Negroes."

46. DuBois, ed., "Negro American Family," AUS 13, 129; Washington, "Condition of the Women," 76.

47. Pickens, *Bursting Bonds*, 17; Cooley, *Homes of the Freed*, 79–80, 174; DuBois, ed., "The College Bred Negro," AUS 5, 53–54.

48. Harper, "Coloured Women," 10–11.

49. For the Burleson example, see the federal manuscript population census for 1900, Pike County, Alabama, subdistrict no. 3, enumeration district no. 120, sheet 11. See also U.S. Dept. of Commerce, *Negro Population, 1790–1915*, 405; Woofter, "The Negroes of Athens, Georgia," 22–26; DuBois, "The Negroes of Farmville," 13.

50. Kiser, *Sea Island to City*, 248.

51. Rosengarten, *All God's Dangers*, 26. See also DuBois's story-essay, "Of the Coming of John" in DuBois, *Souls of Black Folk*, 228–249.

52. Pickens, *Bursting Bonds*, 11, 16–17; Higgs, *Competition and Coercion*, 32–35. See also DuBois, "Negroes of Farmville," 2–11.

53. Pickens, *Bursting Bonds*, 11–13.

54. Miller, "Surplus Negro Women"; DuBois, "Negro in the Black Belt," 403–411; Ransom and Sutch, "Growth and Welfare," 211; Reiff, Dahlin, and Smith, "Rural Push and Urban Pull."

55. Rosengarten, *All God's Dangers*, 26; Cooley, *Homes of the Freed*, 127–128. Compare the role of black women in the southern urban in-migration with the reluctance of pioneers' wives to begin the journey on the Overland Trail. Faragher suggests that the decision of midwestern farm families to move to the West Coast was invariably made by the husband, often over his wife's strenuous objection. *Women and Men*, 163–168.

56. This discussion utilizes the definition of "culture" provided by Howe in his essay, "American Victorianism": "An evolving system of beliefs, attitudes, and techniques, transmitted from generation to generation, and finding expression in innumerable activities people learn: religion, politics, child-rearing customs, the arts and professions, *inter alia*" (p. 509).

57. Rosengarten, *All God's Dangers*, xxi, 28; Lamon, *Black Tennesseans*, 118. Compare this attitude to the ambitiousness of even poor (white) commercial farmers on the midwestern frontier. See Faragher, *Women and Men*, 41.

58. Laws, "Negroes of Cinclare Central," 117; Baker, *Following the Color Line*, 77, 87; Barry, "Slavery in the South To-Day," 488; Woofter, "Negroes of Athens," 55. For a discussion of the "New South" ideology, see Woodward, *Origins of the New South*, 142–174; Gaston, *The New South Creed*.

59. Rowe, "The Negroes of the Sea Islands," 709; Cooley, *Homes of the Freed*, 22–24, 99, 124. See also Kiser, *Sea Island to City*, 58, 63–65, 81; Kelsey, *Negro Farmer*, 43.

60. Laws, "Negroes of Cinclare Central," 117; Shifflett, "Household Composition," 259.

61. Kiser, *Sea Island to City*, 206; Washington, "Condition of the Women," 75; DuBois, "Negro in the Black Belt," 403. In "Negro American Family," AUS 13, DuBois includes a section entitled "The Social Life of the Country," 130–132. See also DuBois, ed., "Some Efforts of American Negroes," AUS 3, "Economic Cooperation," AUS 12, "Efforts for Social Betterment," AUS 14, and "Morals and Manners," AUS 18.

62. This assessment of the importance of religion to black women is offered by Loewenberg and Bogin, eds., in their introduction to *Black Women*, 4, 8–14. See also Cooley, *Homes of the Freed*, 90;

DuBois, ed., "The Negro Church," AUS 8, 161; Washington, "Condition of Women," 75; Tillman, "Afro-American Women"; Brooks, "The Women's Movement."

63. Fields and Fields, *Lemon Swamp*, 123. Mamie Fields describes James Island, South Carolina, as "very poor and very neglected . . . a place behind God's back"; "ethos": Magdol, *A Right to the Land*, 11.

64. For evidence of domestic violence among rural blacks, see Kelsey, *Negro Farmer*, 62; Baker, *Following the Color Line*, 100. In his study of sharecroppers in DeKalb County, Georgia, DuBois describes a poverty-stricken family with twenty-one members in which "Now and then the father and mother engage in a hand-to-hand fight"; "Negro in the Black Belt," 403.

65. Rosengarten, *All God's Dangers*, 5, 9, 13, 23–25.

66. Washington, "Condition of the Women," 74; Cooper, "Colored Women as Wage-Earners."

67. Relevant essays and books by these women include Cooley, *Homes of the Freed*; Washington, "Condition of the Women"; Tillman, "Afro-American Women"; Harper, "Coloured Women"; Williams, "Employment for Negro Women," 432–437; Cooper, "Colored Women as Wage Earners," and *A Voice from the South*. For excerpts from the writings of Harper, Williams, and Cooper, see Loewenberg and Bogin, eds., *Black Women*. See also Jefferson, "The Southern Negro Women," for a succinct statement of this view. The best known example from the mid-twentieth-century literature on the black family is of course Moynihan, *The Negro Family*.

68. Fields, "Ideology and Race," in Kousser and McPherson, eds., *Region, Race, and Reconstruction*, 165–166; Woodman, "Sequel to Slavery"; Hahn, *Roots of Southern Populism*; McDonald and McWhiney, "South from Self-Sufficiency"; Ransom and Sutch, *One Kind of Freedom*, 153, 159, and "Growth and Welfare," 218–224; Flynn, *White Land, Black Labor*; Temin, "Patterns of Cotton Agriculture." For a discussion of the northern-industrial work ethic, see Rodgers, *Work Ethic in Industrial America*.

69. Hagood, *Mothers of the South*, 87.

70. Ibid., 23.

71. Jones, "Encounters, Likely and Unlikely." For examples of agrarian radicalism during this period, see Postel, *Populist Vision*; Ayers, *Promise of the New South*; Goodwyn, *Democratic Promise*; Schwartz, *Radical Protest and Social Structure*; Kremm and Neal, "Challenges to Subordination"; Holmes, "The Demise of the Colored Farmers' Alliance."

72. In "From Field to Factory," Janiewski details this process in relation to North Carolina tobacco tenants (pp. 7–62).

CHAPTER 4

1. Goldfield, *Cotton Fields*.

2. DuBois, ed., "The Negro American Family," AUS 13, 54. Gottlieb describes the incremental nature of intra- and interregional migration in "Making Their Own Way"; see the chapter entitled "The New Economic Structure" in Rabinowitz, *Race Relations*, 61–96.

3. U.S. Dept. of Commerce, *Negro Population, 1790–1915*, 87–98; Johnson and Campbell, *Black Migration in America*, 57–70. Cities with the largest proportions of blacks included New Orleans (26.3 percent), Nashville (33.1), Atlanta (33.5), Richmond (36.6), Birmingham (38.4), and Memphis (40.0). With the exception of New Orleans (total population 339,075), each of these cities had fewer than 155,000 residents, only a fraction of the size of the largest northern population centers. See also Rabinowitz, *Race Relations*, 329–339; Henri, *Black Migration*.

4. The percentages of all southern black women gainfully employed who worked as servants or laundresses in 1910 are:

STATE	% SERVANTS	% LAUNDRESSES
Alabama	12	13
Arkansas	11	10
Florida	19	28
Georgia	14	18
Louisiana	21	16
Mississippi	8	7
North Carolina	16	16
South Carolina	9	10
Tennessee	27	28
Texas	17	20
Virginia	34	27

The rest were mostly agricultural workers. Totals for the entire South include 253,464 servants and 257,738 laundresses. U.S. Dept. of Commerce, *Negro Population, 1790–1915*, 521–522.

5. Gutman, *Black Family*, 442–450; Janiewski, "From Field to Factory," 8–9; Blassingame, *Black New Orleans*, 236–238; Burton, "Ungrateful Servants?" 347–375; Miller, "Surplus Negro Women"; Reiff, Dahlin, and Smith, "Rural Push and Urban Pull." In his study of post–Civil War Atlanta, Harris holds class variables constant and finds "no significant differences" between black and white skilled workers' families in terms of household structure, number of children, or frequency of school attendance among children ("Work and the Family in Black Atlanta," p. 323). Of all black males over twenty years of age in Atlanta in 1880, 97.4 percent were manual laborers and 2.1 percent were nonmanual workers. The figures for white males were 40.4 and 55.8 percent, respectively.

6. Goldin, "Female Labor Force"; Rabinowitz, *Race Relations*, 64–67; Gutman, *Black Family*, 442–450, 483–484; Janiewski, "From Field to Factory," 125, 127. In the Durham case, comparable employment figures for white female household heads included 50 percent of all women aged twenty and over with the exception of those in the twenty-five- to thirty-four-year age bracket, 100 percent of whom worked in 1900.

7. DuBois, ed., "Negro American Family," AUS 13, 147; Rabinowitz, *Race Relations*, 77; Woodman, "Comment [on Goldin, "Female Labor Force"]."

8. Reiff, Dahlin, and Smith, "Rural Push and Urban Pull," 39–48; Miller, "Urban Blacks in the South," in Schnore, ed., *New Urban History*, 184–204.

9. DuBois, ed., "Social and Physical Conditions," AUS 2, app. A, 1–6; Blassingame, *Black New Orleans*, 236.

10. Reiff, Dahlin, and Smith, "Rural Push and Urban Pull," 39–48.

11. For the demographic data, see Engerman, "Black Fertility"; Lantz and Hendrix, "Black Fertility and the Black Family"; Cutright and Shorter, "Effects of Health"; Higgs, *Competition and Coercion*, 18–19; Eblen, "New Estimates"; McFalls, and Masnick, "Birth Control." The physician's quotation is from H. R. Butler, "Negligence a Cause of Mortality," in DuBois, ed., "Mortality Among Negroes," AUS 1, 21.

12. U.S. Dept. of Commerce, *Negro Population, 1790–1915*, 298–372; Jones, "The Negroes of the Southern States," 461; Rabinowitz, *Race Relations*, 120; DuBois, ed., "Social and Physical Conditions of

Negroes in Cities," AUS 2, app. B, 11, 12; Gutman, *Black Family*, 502; DuBois, ed., "Mortality Among Negroes in Cities," AUS 1; Higgs, *Competition and Coercion*, 20–23; Meeker, "Mortality Trends."

13. Goldin, "Female Labor Force," 100–101.

14. Gutman, *Black Family*, 441–443; Rabinowitz, *Race Relations*, 61–96; Ransom and Sutch, *One Kind of Freedom*, 31–39; DuBois, ed., "The Negro Artisan," AUS 7, 95, 116–117 (see the chart on p. 97 for a comparison between the wages of black and white artisans in Memphis); Blassingame, *Black New Orleans*, 63, 238; DuBois, ed., "Social and Physical Conditions of Negroes in Cities," AUS 2, app. A, 6; Hopkins, "Status, Mobility, and the Dimensions of Change" in Jackson and Schultz, eds., *Cities in American History*, 216–231. In his study of Athens, Georgia, in 1913, Woofter found that the uncertainty of public work "means that in many instances some other member of the family besides the father has to seek some steady source of income, such as washing or domestic service"; Woofter, "The Negroes of Athens" 41–42. The problem of chronic unemployment among construction and unskilled workers was not limited to southern black men during this period. For an overview of the subject, see Garraty, *Unemployment in History*, 103–145.

15. Janiewski, "From Field to Factory," 210; DuBois, ed., "Negro American Family," AUS 13, 57; Fleming, "Servant Problem," 2. See also Engs, *Freedom's First Generation*, 181, 183; DuBois, "The Negroes of Farmville," 22. Janiewski makes this crucial distinction between the "male 'public' sphere" and women's domestic activities in her discussion of Durham tobacco workers, "From Field to Factory," 210.

16. English, "I Have . . . a Lot of Work to Do"; Dorsey, *To Build Our Lives Together*, 42; U.S. Dept. of Commerce, *Statistics of Women at Work* (1916), 166; Ransom and Sutch, *One Kind of Freedom*, 37–38.

17. Fleming, "Servant Problem," 4–5; Rabinowitz, *Race Relations*, 74; Janiewski, "From Field to Factory," 38, 174; Woofter, "Negroes of Athens," 42, 44–45; Pickens, *Bursting Bonds*, 41.

18. Gutman, *Black Family*, 448, 500. For an analysis of the social-welfare functions performed by black families for needy kin and neighbors, see Shifflett, "Household Composition."

19. Krech III, "Black Family Organization"; Reiff, Dahlin, and Smith, "Rural Push and Urban Pull," 39–48.

20. DuBois, ed., "Some Efforts of American Negroes," AUS 3, 17–18; Blassingame, *Black New Orleans*, 167–171; Blassingame, "Before the Ghetto," 476–477. According to Fleming ("Servant Problem," p. 3), when an Auburn, Georgia, black "goes regularly (one or two days in a week) to a place to work, it becomes known as 'his place,' and if discharged, no amount of persuasion will induce another 'to take his place.'" This article demonstrates Fleming's antiblack bias, but it contains useful information revealing the ways in which blacks' customs and preferences could affect the employee-employer relationship in a nonrural setting.

21. Maya Angelou, "When I Think About Myself," in *Just Give Me A Cool Drink*, 25. Reprinted by permission of Hirt Music.

> *Sixty years in these folks' world*
> *The child I work for calls me girl*
> *I say 'Yes ma'am' for working's sake.*
> *Too proud to bend*
> *Too poor to break,*
> *I laugh until my stomach ache,*
> *When I think about myself.*

Also, for a theatrical presentation on the same themes, see Tony Kushner's musical, *Caroline, or Change*.

22. Katzman, *Seven Days a Week*, 184; Williams, "The Problem of Employment," 434; Hunter, *To 'Joy My Freedom*, 111.

23. "provided": Stone, *American Race Problem*, 224.

24. U.S. Dept. of Commerce, *Statistics of Women at Work* (1916), 41–55, 59; Katzman, *Seven Days a Week*, 198–199. As one white southerner noted of black women's preference for living out, "'They think it is more like being free to have their own home.'" Quoted in Katzman, 198–199. Information on wages is compiled from Women in Industry Committee, "Conditions of Women's Labor in Louisiana"; DuBois, "Negro in the Black Belt," 407; Woofter, "Negroes of Athens," 47. See also Clark-Lewis, *Living In, Living Out*. A "Negro Nurse" describes her "treadmill life" in an article entitled "More Slavery" (though this is probably a composite view provided by a social worker or academic).

25. Smith, "The Care of Neglected Children," in DuBois, ed., "Social and Physical Conditions," AUS 2, 41; Woofter, "Negroes of Athens," 62.

26. Butler, "Need of Day Nurseries," Smith, "The Care of Neglected Children," and Bass, "Need of Kindergartens," in DuBois, ed., "Social and Physical Conditions" AUS 2, 41–43, 63–68; Butler, "Mortality Among Negroes in Cities," Bass, "Poverty as a Cause of Mortality," and Laney, "General Conditions of Mortality," in DuBois, ed., "Mortality Among Negroes in Cities," AUS 1, 20–25, 30–34, 35–37; Holtzclaw, "A Negro's Life Story"; Terrell, "Club Work of Colored Women," 437 ("The infants of wage-earning mothers are frequently locked alone in a room from the time the mother leaves in the morning until she returns at night"). According to Rosa Bass, "We find great mortality among the children of the poor. Even before they can make their wants known, the mother is compelled to leave them daily, and a surprising number are burned to death"; in DuBois, ed., "Mortality among Negroes in Cities," 31.

27. Negro Nurse, "More Slavery," 197; Fleming "Servant Problem," 5–7; Holtzclaw, "Negro's Life Story," 79–89; DuBois, ed., "Morals and Manners," AUS 18, 85–90.

28. Woofter, "Negroes of Athens," 44; Williams, "Problem of Employment," 432–437; Negro Nurse, "More Slavery," 196–197; Katzman, *Seven Days a Week*, 185.

29. Negro Nurse, "More Slavery," 196; Burrell, "Report of the Committee," 44–45; Woofter, "Negroes of Athens," 60; Katzman, *Seven Days a Week*, 201.

30. Janiewski, "From Field to Factory," 39, 206; Angelou, "When I Think About Myself" in *Just Give Me a Cool Drink*; Burrell, "Report of the Committee," 44; A Southern Colored Woman, "The Race Problem," 587; Katzman, *Seven Days a Week*, 200–220. "Occasionally a pert": A South Carolinian, "South Carolina Society," 675.

31. DuBois, "Negroes of Farmville," 21; A South Carolinian, "South Carolina Society," 679; Charlotte woman quoted in Logan, *The Negro in North Carolina*, 89. See the revealing responses of Athens mistresses to Woofter's questionnaire in "Negroes of Athens," app. D, 59–62 ("Remarks on Domestic Service, Taken from Answers to Questionnaire Sent to Housekeepers").

32. "no matter . . . and so on": Senate testimony quoted in Katzman, *Seven Days a Week*, 192–193; Woofter, "Negroes of Athens," 35; Fleming, "Servant Problem," 13; Renoff, *Under the Big Tent*.

33. Fleming, "Servant Problem," 8; Woofter, "Negroes of Athens," 62; Negro Nurse, "More Slavery," 199; Hunter, *To 'Joy My Freedom*, 132.

34. Katzman, *Seven Days a Week*, 3–43, 241; Campbell, *Prisoners of Poverty*, 222–231; Work, "Negroes of Warsaw," 36; Murray, "In Behalf of the Negro Woman"; Thorn, "The Negroes of Litwalton," 1127, 1131; Fleming, "Servant Problem," 17.

35. Fleming, "Servant Problem," 3, 13; Woofter, "Negroes of Athens," 45. Another Athens mistress noted, "I think if the employers were as well organized as the employed, we would have more competent servants" (p. 62).

36. Rodgers, "Tradition, Modernity," 660–661. For a theoretical discussion of the clash between premodern and industrial work patterns (and values), see Thompson, "Time, Work-Discipline," 56–97.

37. Wiener, *Social Origins*, 137–221; see Woodward, *Origins of the New South*, 107–141. For studies of the iron and tobacco industries, see Kulik, "Black Workers and Technological Change" in Reed, Hough, and Fink, eds., *Southern Workers and Their Unions*, 22–42; Janiewski, "From Field to Factory."

38. U.S. Dept. of Commerce, *Negro Population, 1790–1915*, 521–522; U.S. Dept. of Labor, *Report on the Condition of Women and Children Vol. 1* (1913), 118; Rabinowitz, *Race Relations*, 66; Hall, et al., *Like a Family*. Wright discusses the relationship between the stunted pre-1880 textile industry and the unique southern labor market in "Cheap Labor." For evidence of the use of black workers as textile operatives in the antebellum period, see Starobin, *Industrial Slavery*, 12–14; Mitchell, *Rise of Cotton Mills*, 25, 41, 168, 209–212; Kohn, "The Cotton Mills of South Carolina," 24; Tindall, *South Carolina Negroes*, 130; Miller, "The Fabric of Control"; Jones, *American Work*, 222–232. For a general discussion of this topic, see Stokes, "Black and White Labor."

39. Several historians have cited the decline in cotton prices and the increase in tenancy among poor whites as an impetus to the creation of an all-white labor force in the postbellum textile industry. See, for example, Wright, "Cheap Labor," 678; Wiener, *Social Origins*, 192–194; Lemert, *Cotton Textile Industry*, 31–32; Mitchell, *Rise of Cotton Mills*, 174; Brewer, "Poor Whites and Negroes," 34; Stokes, "Black and White Labor." See also Carlton, *Mill and Town*, 115; Heardon, *Independence and Empire*.

40. White men quoted in Mitchell, *Rise of Cotton Mills*, 219.

41. Campbell, *White and Black*, 309, 347; Copeland, *Cotton Manufacturing*, 47–48; Dowd, "Negro Labor in Factories," 588–589. See also Greene and Woodson, *The Negro Wage-Earner*, 50.

42. U.S. Dept. of Commerce, *Negro Population, 1790–1915*, 521–522. Janiewski finds that "in 1890, the annual wages for male tobacco workers averaged $212, adult females earned $111 annually, and children received $66. Ten years later men's wages had fallen to $166 per year, women's and children's had risen to $140 for adults and $70 for children." Wages for North Carolina tobacco workers "did not even equal the notoriously low wages paid in textiles in the early years." "From Field to Factory," 117–118.

43. Tilley, *Bright Tobacco*; Shields, "A Half Century"; Abbott, "Cigar Making," in Meyer, ed., *Woman's Work in America*, 186–214.

44. U.S. Dept. of Labor, *Report on the Condition of Women and Children, Vol. 18* (1913), 86–101, 308–11, 317; Tilley, *Bright Tobacco*, 318, 515–17; Shields, "Tobacco Industry," 421–422; Janiewski, "From Field to Factory," 139, 150; Handy, "In a Tobacco Factory."

45. DuBois, ed., "The Negro Artisan," AUS 7, 92; Tilley, *Bright Tobacco*, 320–321. For wage data, see also U.S. Dept. of Labor, *Report on the Condition of Women and Children, Vol. 18*, 320–321; Women in Industry Committee "Conditions of Women's Labor in Louisiana," 28–50; Tindall, *South Carolina Negroes*, 93.

46. Jacobstein, *Tobacco Industry*, 142–143; employer quoted in Shields, "Tobacco Industry," 424; Janiewski, "From Field to Factory," 140.

47. Shields, "Tobacco Industry," 219–223. See also Tilley, *Bright Tobacco*, 318–320; Landon, "Tobacco Manufacturing"; Rhine, "Woman in Industry," in Meyer ed. *Woman's Work*, 308–309.

48. U.S. Dept. of Commerce, *Statistics of Women at Work (1916)*, 166, 174; government investigator quoted in Janiewski, "From Field to Factory," 149; U.S. Dept. of Labor, *Report on the Condition of Women and Children*, *Vol. 18*, 311–316. See also DuBois, ed., "Negro Artisan," AUS 7, 47; Women in Industry Committee, "Conditions of Women's Labor in Louisiana," 32.

49. Tilley, *Bright Tobacco*, 319–320; Shields, "Tobacco Industry," 419, 425; Landon, "Tobacco Manufacturing," 47.

50. Tilley, *Bright Tobacco*, 321–322; Shields, "Tobacco Industry," 425.

51. Song quoted in Shields, "Tobacco Industry," 420; visitors quoted in Tilley, *Bright Tobacco*, 318. Winston, North Carolina, stemmers sang this song in 1895:

Befo' I'd work for Simpkins, P.J.,

I'd walk all night an' sleep all day:

Walk all night tu keep f'om sleeping,

An' sleep all day tu keep f'om eatin'.

Quoted in Tilley, *Bright Tobacco*, 318. See also Campbell, *White and Black*, 285. French workers who visited northern factories in the late nineteenth century commented on the lack of singing in American industrial shops. Rodgers, *Work Ethic in Industrial America*, 161.

52. Magee quoted in Tilley, *Bright Tobacco*, 319.

53. Work, "The Negroes of Warsaw," 30–33; Engs, *Freedom's First Generation*, 168–171; Cooley, *Homes of the Freed*, 44; Kelsey, *The Negro Farmer*, 33; Williams, "Local Conditions Among Negroes."

54. Engs, *Freedom's First Generation*, 168–169; Work, "Negroes of Warsaw," 36.

55. Thorn, "Negroes of Litwalton," 1154.

56. On the black middle class in the urban South during this period, see, for example, Rabinowitz, *Race Relations*; Blassingame, *Black New Orleans*; Lamon, *Black Tennesseans*; Dittmer, *Black Georgia*.

57. Hunter, *To 'Joy My Freedom*, 111; U.S. Dept. of Commerce, *Statistics of Women at Work* (1916), 166, 174, lists the following categories of black "textile workers": dressmakers; hat and cap makers; milliners; seamstresses; shirt, collar, and cuff makers; tailoresses; and "other." DuBois, ed., "Negro Artisan," AUS 7, 90; Ransom and Sutch, *One Kind of Freedom*, 31–39.

58. On black education during slavery and the postwar period, see Woodson, *Education of the Negro*; Bullock, *History of Negro Education*. For more information on black women leaders, see White, *Too Heavy a Load*; Lerner, ed., *Black Women*; Loewenberg and Bogin, eds., *Black Women*; and Sterling, ed., *We Are Your Sisters*, 397–495.

59. U.S. Dept. of Commerce, *Statistics of Women at Work* (1916), 166, 174; DuBois, ed., "Morals and Manners Among Negro Americans," AUS 18, 72; DuBois, ed., "The Negro Common School," AUS 6, 15–17, 70–80; U.S. Dept. of Commerce, *Negro Population, 1790–1915*, 521–522.

60. Harlan, *Separate and Unequal*, 109, 168, 245, 257, 258, 260, 262–263. See also Christensen Jr., "The Negroes of Beaufort County," 483; Thom, "Negroes of Litwalton," 1119; DuBois, "Negro in the Black Belt," 407.

61. Rabinowitz, *Race Relations*, 152–181; Jones, *Soldiers of Light and Love*, 191–208. For overviews of the northern freedmen's aid societies' efforts in the area of black education during Reconstruction, see McPherson, *The Abolitionist Legacy*; Morris, *Reading, 'Riting, and Reconstruction*.

62. Dailey, *Before Jim Crow*; "none": quoted in Fairclough, *A Class of Their Own*, 128 (see also p. 225).

63. Rabinowitz, *Race Relations*, 164–181; U.S. Dept. of Commerce, *Negro Population, 1790–1915*, 388.

64. U.S. Dept. of Commerce, *Negro Population, 1790–1915*, 414, 434; Jones, ed., *Negro Education*; Rabinowitz, *Race Relations*, 178; DuBois, ed., "The College Bred Negro," AUS 5, and "The College-Bred Negro American," AUS 15; Fairclough, *A Class of Their Own*; Williams, *Self-Taught*.

65. Fields and Fields, *Lemon Swamp*, 187, 197. See also Wells-Barnett, *On Lynchings*; Dunster, ed., *Crusade for Justice*; Neverdon-Morton, "The Black Woman's Struggle" in Harley and Terborg-Penn, ed., *Afro-American Woman*, 28–42; Hamilton, "National Association of Colored Women"; Jones, "Mary Church Terrell"; Barrett, "Negro Women's Clubs," 33–34; Terrell, "Club Work of Colored Women"; Giddings, *When and Where I Enter*, 95–118; Scott, "Most Invisible of All."

66. "a defense": Lerner, "Community Work of Black Club Women," in Lerner, *The Majority Finds Its Past*, 86; Royster, *Lugenia Burns Hope*, 133; Walker, ed., *African American Business*, 602–603; Brown, "Womanist Consciousness"; Dabney, *Maggie L. Walker*.

67. "that": Burroughs quoted in Harvey, *Freedom's Coming*, 70–71; Higginbotham, *Righteous Discontents*, 135; Gilmore, *Gender and Jim Crow*.

68. Rabinowitz, *Race Relations*, 329–339. On the scope and means of black disfranchisement, see Kousser, *Shaping of Southern Politics*; Perman, *Struggle for Mastery*. On black protest and race riots, see Meier and Rudwick, "The Boycott Movement"; Crowe, "Racial Violence" and "Racial Massacre."

69. Rabinowitz, *Race Relations*, 70; Kann, "Knights of Labor"; Worthman and Green, "Black Workers in the New South," in Huggins, Kilson, and Fox, eds., *Key Issues*, 47–69; Meier and Elliott, "Attitudes of Negro Leaders," and Marshall, "The Negro in Southern Unions," in Jacobson, ed., *The Negro and the American Labor Movement*; Foner, *Organized Labor*, 66, 89, 90; Rachleff, *Black Labor*; Fink, *Workingmen's Democracy*; Jones, *American Work*, 303, 326–327, 338, 358–359.

70. Foner, *Organized Labor*, 89.

71. Stokes, "Black and White Labor," 206–208; Foner, *Women and the American Labor Movement: From Colonial Times*, 247; DuBois, ed., "Negro Artisan," AUS 7, 173, 175; Tilley, *Bright Tobacco*, 625.

72. *Atlanta Constitution* and washerwomen quoted in Rabinowitz, *Race Relations*, 74, 75. See also Sterling, *We Are Your Sisters*, 355–358. For accounts of other labor organizations involving southern black women workers, see Foner, *Women and the American Labor Movement*, 188; Tilley, *Bright Tobacco*, 320; Tindall, *South Carolina Negroes*, 137; Hunter, *To 'Joy My Freedom*.

73. Quoted in Clowes, *Black America*, 93. See also Meier and Rudwick, "Boycott Movement"; Barnes, *Journey from Jim Crow*, 1–19.

74. Smith, *Killers of the Dream*, 173. See, for example, Dollard, *Caste and Class*, 314–362.

75. Cooley, *Homes of the Freed*, 109; Negro Nurse, "More Slavery," 197–198; Washington-Williams, *Dear Senator*. See also Hobson and Hopkins, "Concerning the Colored Women," 6–7, 91.

76. DuBois, "Negroes of Farmville," 34; paper quoted in Clowes, *Black America*, 98; Rabinowitz, *Race Relations*, 329–339.

CHAPTER 5

1. Letter to "My Dear Pastor and Wife," Scott, comp., "Documents."

2. Harrison, ed., *Black Exodus*; Goodwin, *Black Migration*; Trotter, ed., *Great Migration*; Marks, *Farewell*; Henri, *Black Migration*, 64; Spear, *Black Chicago*, 137. See, for example, the following contemporary accounts based on interviews with migrants: Woofter Jr., *Negro Migration*, 117–121; U.S. Dept. of Labor, *Negro Migration in 1916–1917*; Scott, *Negro Migration During the War*. See also Higgs, "Boll Weevil"; Tuttle, *Race Riot*; Johnson, "How Much is the Migration a Flight," 272–274.

3. Lieberson, *A Piece of the Pie*. See also Work, "The Negro Migration"; Collins, "When the Tide Turned."

4. Jones, *The Dispossessed*; Gregory, *Southern Diaspora*.

5. For a case study, see Bodnar, Simon, and Weber, *Lives of their Own*. The debate over the respective histories of migrant blacks and immigrant whites is represented by the divergent positions of Sowell and Lieberson. In *Ethnic America*, Sowell suggests that the lack of a traditional work ethic in African American culture inhibited black occupational mobility during the twentieth century. In *Piece of the Pie*, Lieberson presents the much more convincing case that systemic discrimination was the chief obstacle to black economic success. (The analysis of black women's work in the urban North presented in this chapter confirms most of Lieberson's major points.) See also Themstrom, *The Other Bostonians*; like Lieberson, Thernstrom disputes the "blacks-as-the-last-of-the-immigrants" theory as an explanation for their lack of black mobility, and cites prejudice as the chief factor. Engerman sums up the main issues in this debate in "Three Recent Studies of Ethnicity." All of the major studies in this area fail to consider in any depth the economic significance of black women's work within ghetto communities. See also Greenwald, *Women, War, and Work*, 13–27.

6. Chicago Commission, *The Negro in Chicago*, 387; Tentler, *Wage-Earning Women*; Kennedy, *If All We Did Was to Weep at Home*, 91–156; Sharpless and Rury, "Political Economy of Women's Work"; Kessler-Harris, *Out to Work*, 142–214.

7. Greenberg, "Neighborhood Change." Lieberson, *Piece of the Pie*, 200–252.

8. Clark-Lewis, *Living In, Living Out*; Bunch-Lyons, *Contested Terrain*; White, "Women in the Great Migration."

9. Brown, *Manchild in the Promised Land*, 8.

10. Scott, comp., "Letters of Negro Migrants," 458.

11. Levine, *Black Culture and Black Consciousness*, 262.

12. "fired herself": Clark-Lewis, *Living In, Living Out*, 83; Bunch-Lyons, *Contested Terrain*, 3.

13. Lieberson, *Piece of the Pie*, 219–220; Johnson and Campbell, *Black Migration in America*, 56–70; Hill, "Recent Northward Migration"; Kiser, *Sea Island to City*, 99–100; Keller, "Assisted Emigration from the South," 11–14; Kruse, "Negro Women and Domestic Service"; Matthews, "Dangers Confronting Southern Girls."

14. Miller, "Surplus Negro Women"; Gutman, *Black Family*, 450, 521–530; Helen A. Tucker, "The Negroes of Pittsburgh," *Charities and the Commons* 21 (January 2, 1909): 599; Kusmer, *A Ghetto Takes Shape*, 39–40.

15. Hickel, "'Justice and the Highest Kind of Equality"; "Woman's Domestic": Arnesen, *Black Protest*, 140; "any woman": ibid., 141–143.

16. Johnson and Campbell, *Black Migration*, 71–89; Hill, "Recent Northward Migration," 100–105; Johnston, "The Migration and the Census." Between 1910 and 1920, the black population of Detroit increased by 611 percent, of Cleveland, by 308 percent, and of Chicago, by 150 percent.

17. See, for example, accounts of the migration provided by U.S. Dept. of Labor, *Negro Migration* (1919 and 1935); Scott, *Negro Migration During the War*; Baker, "The Negro Goes North"; Edens, "When Labor Is Cheap," 511; Epstein, *The Negro Migrant*, 7, 27.

18. Chicago Commission, *Negro in Chicago*, 386; Scott, comp., "Letters of Negro Migrants," 291, 296, 314, 412–413.

19. "When you," "go to": Kiser, *Sea Island to City*, 131, 133; "such a": Scott, comp., "Letters from Negro Migrants," 291, 296, 314, 412–413.

20. "for an unwise . . . live": Arnesen, ed., *Black Protest*, 125; Bunch-Lyons, *Contested Terrain*, 37, n. 20, 36–37; Clark-Lewis, *Living In, Living Out*, 29; Harrison, *Black Exodus*, 26–27.

21. Hine, "Black Migration to the Urban Midwest," in Trotter, ed., *Great Migration*, 127–146.

22. Gottlieb, *Making Their Own Way*, 27.

23. Ibid.; Hine, "Black Migration to the Urban Midwest," 131.

24. Gottlieb, *Making Their Own Way*, 12–38; Blocker, *A Little More Freedom*; Haynes, *Negro New-Comers*, 12; Kusmer, *A Ghetto Takes Shape*, 159–191; Chicago Commission, *Negro in Chicago*, 180.

25. Grant, "The Negro Comes to the City," 96–97; Scott, comp., "Letters of Negro Migrants," 456; Gottlieb, *Making Their Own Way*; Scott, *Negro Migration During the War*, 36.

26. Scott, *Negro Migration During the War*, 24, 48. On migration during the 1920s, see Kornweibel Jr., "An Economic Profile," 308; Kennedy, *The Negro Peasant Turns Cityward*, 35; Johnson, "The American Migrant"; Work, "The Negro Migration," 202–212.

27. On black employment patterns in nineteenth-century northern cities, see Pleck, *Black Migration and Poverty*, 23, 125; Katzrnan, *Before the Ghetto*, 217–222; Kusmer, *A Ghetto Takes Shape*, 20; Scheiner, *Negro Mecca*, 45–54; Harley, "Northern Black Female Workers," in Harley and Terborg-Penn, eds., *The Afro-American Woman*, 5–16.

28. Greene and Woodson, *The Negro Wage-Earner*, 228, 250; Wright Jr., "Economic Condition of Negroes" and "The Negro's Quest for Work," in Foner and Lewis, eds., *The Black Worker*, 38–39, 46–54. See also Warner, *New Haven Negroes*, 233–234; Kusmer, *A Ghetto Takes Shape*, 75.

29. Johnson, "American Migrant," 557; Herbst, *Negro in the Slaughtering and Meatpacking Industry*, xviii, xxii; Kornweibel, "Economic Profile of Black Life," 311; Harris, *The Harder We Run*, 51–76; Clark, "The Migrant in Pittsburgh," 305; Dutcher, *Negro in Modern Industrial Society*, 70–71, 95–98. U.S. Dept. of Commerce, *Negroes in the United States, 1920–1932*, 290; U.S. Dept. of Commerce, *Negro Population in the United States, 1790–1915*, 526. See also Bodnar, "The Impact of the 'New Immigration'"; Hershberg et al., "A Tale of Three Cities," in Hershberg, ed., *Philadelphia*, 473–476; Themstrom, *Other Bostonians*, 176–219.

30. "Negroes at Work in the United States," 216; U.S. Dept. of Commerce, *Negroes in the United States, 1920–1932*, 298–299; Hill, *Women in Gainful Occupations*, 275; Klaczynska, "Why Women Work."

31. Ovington, *Half a Man*, 138–140. See also Pleck, "A Mother's Wages" in Cott and Pleck, eds., *A Heritage of Her Own*, 367–392; Lieberson, *Piece of the Pie*, 177–179, 195; Engerman, "Black Fertility."

32. Ovington, *Half a Man*, 140–141.

33. Ibid., 142–143.

34. U.S. Dept. of Commerce, *Negroes in the United States, 1920–1932*, 273–274, 297; U.S. Dept. of Commerce, *Statistics of Women at Work* (1907), 133. See also Mossell, "Standard of Living."

35. Hill, *Women in Gainful Occupations*, 115; Kennedy, *Negro Peasant*, 90; Lieberson, *Piece of the Pie*, 320–322.

36. "had kicked": Chicago Commission, *Negro in Chicago*, 371. See Haynes, "Two Million Negro Women at Work"; Katzman, *Seven Days A Week*, 184–222.

37. On employers' preference for white servants, see Greene and Woodson, *Negro Wage-Earner*, 228; Berry, "The Negro in Cincinnati Industries," 363; Haynes, "Two Million Negro Women," 64. See also Strasser, *Never Done*, 1–144; Sutherland, *Americans and Their Servants*, 182–199.

38. Strasser, *Never Done*, 180–224; Haynes, "Negroes in Domestic Service"; "There Goes the China!" 571; Simpson, "A Note on Negro Industrial Problems,"182–183; Greene and Woodson, *Negro Wage-Earner*, 231.

39. "Employment of Colored Women," 24–25; Robinson, "Domestic Workers," 69–70; Katzman, *Seven Days a Week*, 198–199; Buckner, "Problems of Women Workers," 81.

40. U.S. Dept. of Commerce, *Statistics of Women at Work* (1907), 158; U.S. Dept. of Commerce, *Negroes in the United States, 1920–1932*, 290, 328–334.

41. Jones, *American Work*, 320; Arnesen, ed., *Black Protest*, 146.

42. U.S. Dept. of Labor, "Negro Women in Industry"; Haynes, "The Negro at Work"; U.S. Dept. of Labor, "Colored Women in Industry," 1046–1048; Irvin, "Conditions in Industry."

43. Woman quoted in Greenwald, *Women, War, and Work*, 27; Clark and McDougald, "A New Day for the Colored Woman."

44. Hill, *Women in Gainful Occupations*, 117; John P. Frey, "From Kitchen to Factory," *World Outlook* 5 (October 1919): 29; Kiser, *Sea Island to City*, 138.

45. "Complete Survey of Race Women," 1, 7; U.S. Dept. of Labor, "Colored Women in Industry," 1046; U.S. Dept. of Labor, "Negro Women in Industry," 34–35; U.S. Dept. of Labor, "Negro Women in Industry in Fifteen States."

46. "You are": quoted in Hine, "Black Migration to the Urban Midwest," 141; Klaczynska, "Why Women Work," 86; Chicago Commission, *Negro in Chicago*, 392–393; Greenwald, *Women, War, and Work*, 26–27; Haynes, *Negro New-Comers in Detroit*, 18; Johnson, "The Negro Population of Waterbury, Connecticut," 302–303. See also Henry, *Women and the Labor Movement*, 202–211.

47. Foner, *Women and the American Labor Movement*, 267–268, 313, 339–340; Chicago Commission, *Negro in Chicago*, 392–393; Greenwald, Women, *War, and Work*, 40–44; Harris, *The Harder We Run*, 77–94.

48. Herbst, *Negro in the Slaughtering and Meatpacking Industry*, 74, 76, 79–80.

49. Ibid., 70–71, 72–73, 75, 89.

50. Ibid., 73, 75; Best and Erickson, "A Survey of Laundries," 88; Hill, *Women in Gainful Occupations*, 113; Chicago Commission, *Negro in Chicago*, 385.

51. Best and Erickson, "Survey of Laundries," 56, 63–65, 77.

52. In *American Work*, I discuss "The Rise and Decline of the Racialized Machine," 301–394.

53. Mary Ryan, *Womanhood in America*, 15–182.

54. Hunter, "A Colored Working Girl," 32–34. See also "Employment of Colored Women in Chicago," 24–25.

55. Chicago Commission, *Negro in Chicago*, 381, 384.

56. Spear, *Black Chicago*, 154; U.S. Dept. of Commerce, *Negroes in the United States, 1920–1932*, 305–308; Osofsky, *Harlem*, 147–148; Berry and Blassingame, *Long Memory*, 351–352; Woofter, *Negro Problems in Cities*, 198.

57. Harmon, Lindsay, and Woodson, *The Negro as a Business Man*, 15; Spear, *Black Chicago*, 181–200.

58. Osofsky, *Harlem*, 137; Boyd, "The Great Migration to the North"; Walker, ed., *African American Business*, 581–585; Harmon, Lindsay, and Woodson, *Negro as a Business Man*, 29–34; Frazier, "Occupational Classes Among Negroes," 724; Davis, ed., *Contributions of Black Women to America*, 1: 339–344.

59. Chicago Commission, *Negro in Chicago*, 202–3; Frazier, "Chicago: A Cross-Section of Negro Life," 72; Haynes, *Negro New-Comers in Detroit*, 21; Scheiner, *Negro Mecca*, 114–115; Kusmer, *A Ghetto Takes Shape*, 48–49; Osofsky, *Harlem*, 151, 185.

60. Waterman, *Prostitution and Its Repression*, 51, 128. See also "Migration of Colored Girls from Virginia," 75–79; Chicago Commission, *Negro in Chicago*, 343. Secondary accounts of prostitution during this period include Connelly, *Response to Prostitution*; Rosen, *The Lost Sisterhood*.

61. Tentler, *Wage-Earning Women*, 8.

62. Comer, *Maggie's American Dream*, 142, 149, 150, 151.

63. Haynes, "Conditions Among Negroes in Cities," 108–109. Lieberson describes the process of increasing segregation among blacks in *Piece of the Pie*, 253–291. On the riots during the World War I era, see Tuttle, *Race Riot*; Rudwick, *Race Riot at East St. Louis*; Grimshaw, ed., *Racial Violence*, 60–115.

64. Hine, "Black Migration to the Urban Midwest," 133; White, "Women in the Great Migration," 435.

65. Kiser, *Sea Island to City*, 176; Kennedy, *Negro Peasant*, 139; Gutman, *Black Family*, 453; Reed, *Negro Illegitimacy*, 93.

66. Frazier, "Family Disorganization Among Negroes," 206; Chicago Commission, *Negro in Chicago*, 170–71. See also Newman, "The Housing of Negro Immigrants," 46–48; Jones, "The Negro in Community Life," 390–391, 394.

67. Epstein, *Negro Migrant*, 16, 65. See also Mossell, "Standard of Living," 197, 194; Woofter and Priest, "Negro Housing in Philadelphia," 12.

68. Ovington, "The Negro Home in New York," 26–27; Tentler, *Wage-Earning Women*, 169; Strasser, *Never Done*, 111–113; Martin, Our *Negro Population*, 117–118.

69. Phillips, "'But It Is a Fine Place to Make Money,'" 399; "I did," "Now the father": Clark-Lewis, *Living, In Living Out*, 79–80, 81.

70. Ovington, *Half a Man*, 56–59; Osofsky, *Harlem*, 147–148; Woofter, *Negro Problems in Cities*, 199; Tucker, "The Negroes of Pittsburgh," 607.

71. Washington woman quoted in Jones, *Recreation and Amusement*, 184; Chicago woman quoted in Chicago Commission, *Negro in Chicago*, 172.

72. Scott, comp., "Letters of Negro Migrants," 460; Frazier, "A Negro Industrial Group," 209, 211, 217–218, 230; Kennedy, *Negro Peasant*, 198–199; Kiser, *Sea Island to City*, 187; Epstein, *Negro Migrant in Pittsburgh*, 17; Chicago Commission, *Negro in Chicago*, 261.

73. Grant, "The Negro Comes to the City," 98.

74. Kusmer has compiled statistics from the Fifteenth Census (1930) related to "the percentage of families headed by women, by racial and ethnic group, for urban and rural areas" (Table 20) in *A Ghetto Takes Shape*, 226. See also Gutman, *Black Family*, 461–475, 521–530. The selective nature of the northward migration process probably helps to explain the relatively high percentage of widowed and divorced black women in the urban North during the first two or three decades of the twentieth century. See Lieberson's data in *Piece of the Pie*, 175.

75. Clark, "The Migrant in Pittsburgh," 306. See also Tucker, "Negroes of Pittsburgh," 608; Work, "Problems of Negro Urban Welfare."

76. Mosell, "Standard of Living," 173–218. See also Woofter, *Negro Problems in Cities*, 122–124; Kennedy, *Negro Peasant*, 161; R. R. Wright, "The Economic Condition of Negroes in the North: Tendencies Downward," *Southern Workman* 40 (December 1911): 707; Kiser, *Sea Island to City*, 32.

77. Kiser, *Sea Island to City*, 124; Wright, "Economic Condition," 707; Helen B. Pendleton, "Cotton Pickers in Northern Cities." *The Survey* 37 (February 17, 1917): 569.

78. Mary White Ovington, "The Negro Home in New York." *Charities* 15 (October 7, 1905): 25–28; Tucker, "Negroes of Pittsburgh," 601.

79. Graham, "Negro Family," 50.

80. Engerman, "Black Fertility," 125–131; Woofter, *Negro Problems in Cities*, 34; Osofsky, *Harlem*, 137–138; Gutman, *Black Family*, 454. In Chicago in 1920, 70 percent of all black households

contained a nuclear family plus either roomers, relatives, or another family; Graham, "Negro Family," 50.

81. U.S. Dept. of Commerce, *Negroes in the United States, 1920–1932*, 285; Modell and Hareven, "Urbanization and the Malleable Household" in Martin, ed., *The American Family*, 51–68; Bodnar, Weber, and Simon, "Migration, Kinship, and Urban Adjustment," 553–559, 562–563, 565. For discussions of the lodging system in specific cities, see Scheiner, *Negro Mecca*, 28; Clark, "Migrant in Pittsburgh," 303; Haynes, *Negro New-Comers in Detroit*, 22; Kennedy, *Negro Peasant*, 164–165.

82. Strasser, *Never Done*, 152–154; Klaczynska, "Why Women Work," 82; Chicago Commission, *Negro in Chicago*, 164.

83. White, *Too Heavy a Load*; Osofsky, *Harlem*, 66; Lerner, "Community Work of Black Club Women," in Lerner, *The Majority*, 83–93; Haynes, *Negro New-Comers in Detroit*, 18–19. See also Gottlieb, *Making Their Own Way*; Chicago Commission, *Negro in Chicago*, 193; Clark, "Migrant in Pittsburgh," 304–306; U.S. Dept. of Labor, *Negro Migration in 1916–1917*, 23; Strickland, *Chicago Urban League*, 25–103.

84. "The tinsel show": Clark-Lewis, *Living In, Living Out*, 91.

85. "My talking": ibid., 93; "Crowded": ibid., 75.

86. Scott, comp., "Letters of Negro Migrants," 457; Frazier, "Chicago," 73. See also Kiser, *Sea Island to City*, 51, 55, 206–207; Frazier, "A Negro Industrial Group," 227–230; Woofter, *Negro Problems in Cities*, 101–102; Chicago Commission, *Negro in Chicago*, 391.

87. Jones, *Recreation and Amusement Among Negroes*, 91; Thomas, "From Peasant to Proletarian," 56; Woofter, *Negro Problems in Cities*, 272–273. See also Kiser, *Sea Island to City*, 46, 51; Epstein, *Negro Migrant in Pittsburgh*, 46; Haynes, *Negro New-Comers in Detroit*, 24–25, 35; Mossell, "Standard of Living," 177; Kennedy, *Negro Peasant*, 188; Frazier, "A Negro Industrial Group," 227; Scheiner, *Negro Mecca*, 58.

88. Chicago Commission, *Negro in Chicago*, 387.

89. "We were living": Clark-Lewis, *Living In, Living Out*, 73; Nielson, *Black Ethos*, 190–191; Frazier, "A Negro Industrial Group," 215; Chicago Commission, *Negro in Chicago*, 172; Grant, "The Negro Comes to the City," 361. On the noninvolvement of churches in community welfare activities during this period, see Sampson, "The Diary of a Child Placing Agent," 10–11; George E. Haynes, "Negro Migration," 304.

90. Clark-Lewis, *Living In, Living Out*, 69, 73, 85–90.

91. Osofsky, *Harlem*, 144. See, for example, "The Star Centre and Its Co-Operative Coal Club," and Fannie Barrier Williams, "Social Bonds in the 'Black Belt' of Chicago," *Charities* 15 (October 7, 1905): 6, 40–44. The lack of professional medical services available to blacks in ghettos was all the more significant in light of their high rates of mortality and illness compared to immigrant and native-born groups. The black population suffered from tuberculosis to a much greater degree than did whites in general. For example, in New York, mortality rates attributed to TB among blacks were two and one-half times higher than the overall city rate. Moreover, between 1923 and 1927, twice as many Harlem mothers died in childbirth and almost twice as many black infants died relative to the same populations in the city's other neighborhoods. Osofsky, *Harlem*, 141–143.

92. White, *Too Heavy a Load*, 110–141; Seraile, "Henrietta Vinton Davis," 7–24. For an overview of Garvey and his career, see Martin, *Race First*.

93. U.S. Dept. of Commerce, *Negroes in the Untied States, 1920–1932*, 286. The percentages of black households that had radio sets in the largest northern and southern cities (in 1930) include:

New York, 40.1; Chicago, 42.6; Philadelphia, 23.3; Detroit, 29.6; Cleveland, 22.8; New Orleans, 21.0; Atlanta, 26.0.

94. U.S. Dept. of Commerce, Bureau of the Census, *Negroes in the United States, 1920–1932*, 210, 213, 233, 236; Lieberson, *Piece of the Pie*, 220–233; Baxter and Lansing, *Women and Politics*, 78.

95. White, *Too Heavy a Load*; Terborg-Penn, "Discrimination Against Afro-American Women" in Harley and Terborg-Penn, eds., *Afro-American Woman*; Terborg-Penn, "Discontented Black Feminists," in Scharf and Jensen, eds., *Decades of Discontent*.

96. Baker, "The Negro Goes North," 319.

CHAPTER 6

1. "No . . . business": Walker, *Style and Status*, 59; "As long": Smith, ed., *Encyclopedia of African American Business*, 2:821. See also Blackwelder, *Styling Jim Crow*.

2. Erickson, "Employment Conditions"; Jeffries, "The Decay of the Beauty Parlor," 49–52, 60; Gill, *Beauty Shop Politics*.

3. "We learned . . . said": Walker, *Style and Status*, 61–62; Gill, *Beauty Shop Politics*.

4. Sterner, *The Negro's Share*. This monograph is part of the Carnegie Study of the Negro in America, and includes a wealth of valuable statistical data, some of it from unpublished U.S. Census sources. See also Giddings, *When and Where I Enter*, 197–215, 220–230; "We have been": quoted in Weiss, *Farewell to the Party of Lincoln*, 143–144. See also Sitkoff, *A New Deal for Blacks*. On the role of Bethune in FDR's administration and in the larger black community, see Hanson, *Mary McLeod Bethune*; Ware, *Beyond Suffrage*, 12–13, 138; Weiss, *Farewell to the Party of Lincoln*, 137–148, 201, 255. For general overviews of the decade, see McElvaine, *The Great Depression*; Kirby, *Black Americans in the Roosevelt Era*; Harris, *The Harder We Run*, 95–113. Much useful information on blacks in the 1930s is provided by Myrdal in *An American Dilemma*.

5. Burroughs quoted in Hunter, "'Don't Buy From Where You Can't Work,'" 62; U.S. Dept. of Commerce, Sixteenth Census, vol. 3, *The Labor Force* pt. 1, U.S. Summary (1940), 25.

6. "The job is": Letter from W. H. Hyatt, Natchez, Mississippi, April 17, 1935, Box 119–1, "Urban Complaints," Works Progress Administration File (hereafter WPA File, Howard University). See Howard University for Note; "First things": quoted in McElvaine, *Great Depression*, 188–189; Weiss, *Farewell to the Party of Lincoln*. Long accustomed to the practices of exploitative white landowners and to falling cotton prices, rural black southerners only gradually realized that a nationwide depression had "seeped into [their] area slowly, like a thief with misgivings," in the words of Angelou, *I Know Why the Caged Bird Sings*, 41.

7. Wright, *12 Million Black Voices*, 144.

8. "You don't": Winegarten, "I am Annie Mae," 19; "I don't": quoted in Pidgeon, "The Employment of Women in Slaughtering and Meat Packing," 126. See also Drake and Cayton, *Black Metropolis*, 517–518.

9. "The devil": Nate Shaw (Ned Cobb), in Rosengarten, *All God's Dangers*, 282; Brehon, "Looking Back," in Cade, ed., *Black Woman*, 227.

10. Scharf, *To Work and To Wed*, 107–108; Sterner, *Negro's Share*, 360–361; U.S. Dept. of Commerce, *Negroes in the United States, 1920–1932*, 297; Ware, *Holding Their Own*, 21–54; "the breath": Cuthbert, "Problems Facing Negro Young Women." See also U.S. Dept. of Commerce, Sixteenth Census, vol. 3, *The Labor Force*, pt. 1, U.S. Summary (1940), 90; Pidgeon, "Employed Women Under N.R.A. Codes"; U.S. Dept. of Labor, "Women at Work"; Scharf, *To Work and To Wed*, 128; Sterner, *Negro's Share*, 214; Poole, *Segregated Origins of Social Security*, 75.

11. Kessler-Harris, *Out to Work*, 250–272; Milkman, "Women's Work and Economic Crisis"; Wandersee, *Women's Work and Family Values*, 84–102; U.S. Dept. of Commerce, Sixteenth Census, *The Labor Force*, pt. 1, U.S. Summary (1940), 90.

12. Kessler-Harris, *Out to Work*, 254. See also Oppenheimer, *Female Labor Force in the United States*, 44, 53; Scharf, *To Work and To Wed*, 43–65.

13. Johnson, *Shadow of the Plantation*, 41.

14. Holley, *The Second Great Emancipation*, 55–74; U.S. Dept. of Commerce, Sixteenth Census, *The Labor Force*, pt. 1, U.S. Summary (1940), 97. On the demise of the sharecropping system, see, for example, Kirby, "The Transformation of Southern Plantations"; Sterner, *Negro's Share*, 75; Johnson, Embree, and Alexander, *Collapse of Cotton Tenancy*; Raper, *Tenants of the Almighty*; Woofter, *Landlord and Tenant*.

15. Hoffsommer, "Landlord-Tenant Relations and Relief in Alabama," 7–10, 11 in Federal Emergency Relief Administration (FERA), Works Progress Administration Collection, Record Group 69 (hereafter WPA Collection, RG 69, National Archives). On the impact of AAA policies on black sharecroppers, see Wolters, *Negroes and the Great Depression*, 3–79; Conrad, *The Forgotten Farmers*.

16. Woman quoted in Brown, "The Negro Woman Worker," 7. For plantation owners' attitudes toward their black tenants, see, for example, "Landlord-Tenant Relations and Relief in Alabama," Federal Emergency Relief Administration Confidential Research Bulletin #2738 (July 10, 1934), 1, and A. R. Mangus, "The Rural Negro on Relief, February, 1935," Federal Emergency Relief Administration Research Bulletin #6950 (October 17, 1935), 3; WPA Collection, vols. 4–6, RG 69, National Archives.

17. Dollard, *Caste and Class*, 100. For descriptions of women field workers, see Janiewski, "From Field to Factory, 48; "No Stick-Leg," in Terrill and Hirsch, eds., *Such As Us*, 29–37; Ellis, "Women of the Cotton Fields," 333, 342; Virginia Federal Writers Project, *The Negro in Virginia*, 328; Jensen, ed., *With These Hands*, 248–277.

18. "she usually": Brown, "Negro Woman Worker," 7; Frazier, *The Negro Family in the United States*, 112; "no return": Allen, *The Labor of Women*, 200–201. In 1935 Mosel Brinson, a widow with seven children living in Millen, Georgia, wrote to officials at the Department of Agriculture and told how "these poor white people that lives around me wants the colored people to work for them for nothing." See letter in Lerner, ed., *Black Women*, 399–400.

19. Webb and Brown, "Migrant Families," Works Progress Administration Division of Social Research, Monograph 18(1938), 101; Brown, "Negro Woman Worker," 7–8; Sutherland, "The Migratory Labor Problem in Delaware," 15; Jones, *Dispossessed*, 167–204.

20. Conrad, *Forgotten Farmers*. For examples of FSA photographs, see Evans, *Walker Evans*; Dorothea Lange, *Dorothea Lange*; O'Neal and others, *A Vision Shared*; Caldwell, *You Have Seen Their Faces*; Stryker and Wood, *In This Proud Land*.

21. Grubbs, *Cry From the Cotton*; Harris, *Harder We Run*, 97–104; Kester, *Revolt Among the Sharecroppers*, ed. Lichtenstein; Conrad, *Forgotten Farmers*; Auerbach, "Southern Tenant Farmers"; Dyson, *Red Harvest*, 150–167. The work of Estelle Milner is described by Ellis in "Women of the Cotton Fields," 342. The quote is from Rosengarten, *All God's Dangers*, 315.

22. Interview with Stith and Williams in Wise and Thrasher, "The Southern Tenant Farmers' Union" in Miller, ed., *Working Lives*, 132, 125; Cantor, "Prologue to the Protest Movement." On the plight of "Bootheel" sharecroppers, see White and others, *Rich Land, Poor People*.

23. Grade Turner, "Tore Up and A-Movin'," in *These Are Our Lives*, Federal Writers' Project. 20, 25.

24. Gray, *Black Female Domestics*.

25. Baker and Cooke, "The Bronx Slave Market," 330, 340; Vivian Morris, "Bronx Slave Market," December 6, 1938, Federal Writers Project, Negro Folklore Division (New York), 1, Archive of Folk Song, Manuscript Division, Library of Congress, Washington, D.C. (hereafter FWP, Negro Folklore Division, Archive of Folk Song, LC, with the name of the author, date, and state). For other examples, see also Seeley, "Our Feudal Housewives"; Haley, "To Do Good and Do Well," 58; Rice, "It Takes A While to Realize," in Lerner, ed., *Black Women*, 275–276.

26. Byrne and Hillyer, "Unattached Women"; Carter, "The Negro Household Employee," 351; McElvaine, *Great Depression*, 187. See also Hansen, "'Try Being a Black Woman,'" in Taylor and Moore, eds., *African American Women Confront the West*, 207–227.

27. Dollard, *Caste and Class*, 107–108; Brown, "Negro Woman Worker," 3–4; Haley, "To Do Good and Do Well," 59. For other examples, see Anderson, "The Plight of Negro Domestic Labor"; Angelou, *I Know Why the Caged Bird Sings*, 88; Janiewski, "From Field to Factory," 197; Winegarten, "I am Annie Mae," 18; Powdermaker, *After Freedom*, 118–119.

28. "L-H-P": Gray, *Black Female Domestics*, 39; "as soon . . . situation": White, *Too Heavy a Load*, 144; Lett, "Work"; "Women Workers in Indianapolis"; Rawick, ed., *American Slave*, Series 1, *South Carolina Narratives*, pt. 4, 3:146; Powdermaker, *After Freedom*, 117–118.

29. "The Domestic Worker of Today," Radio Talk by Miss Mary Anderson, September 21, 1932, Station WJAY, sponsored by Cleveland Parent Teachers Association, Speeches no. 112 (Box 71), Women's Bureau Collection, Department of Labor Archives, Record Group 96, National Archives, Washington, D.C.; Dora Jones quoted in "The Domestic Workers' Union," in Lerner, ed., *Black Women*, 231–234. On the New York union, see Seeley, "Our Feudal Housewives," 614; on Baltimore, see article reprinted from *Baltimore Afro-American*, October 1936, in Foner and Lewis, eds., *The Black Worker*, 6:184–185; Ryon, "An Ambiguous Legacy," 29. For evidence of the Urban League's efforts in this area, see Program of Mass Meeting of General House Work Employees, September 21, 1933 (St. Louis) in Correspondence-Household (Domestic) File, General Correspondence Prior to 1934 (Box 926), Women's Bureau Collection, RG 86, National Archives.

30. Rawick, ed., *American Slave*, Series 1, *Alabama Narratives*, 6:251.

31. U.S. Dept. of Commerce, *Negroes in the United States, 1920–1932*, 328–331, and Sixteenth Census (1940), vol. 3, *The Labor Force*, pt. 1, U.S. Summary (1940), 90. For two excellent case studies of labor force segmentation within the female population, see the articles by Blackwelder, "Quiet Suffering" and "Women in the Work Force."

32. Wallace, *Black Women in the Labor Force*, 59; Sullivan and Blair, "Women in Texas Industries," 14; "Women in Florida Industries"; Manning, "Hours and Earnings," 11.

33. Janiewski, "From Field to Factory," 160, 236.

34. Interview with Evelyn Macon in Banks, ed., *First-Person America*, 126; Sullivan and Blair, "Women in Texas Industries," 69; Brown, "Negro Woman Worker," 10; Pidgeon, "Women in Slaughtering and Meatpacking," 20–21.

35. Janiewski, "From Field to Factory," 120–124, 159, 237, 277; Porter, "Negro Women."

36. Pidgeon, "Employed Women Under N.R.A. Codes"; U.S. Dept. of Labor, "Women at Work"; Scharf, *To Work and To Wed*, 128; Sterner, *Negro's Share*, 214; Manning, "Hours and Earnings in Tobacco Stemmeries," 1; Kessler-Harris, *Out to Work*, 262–263; Brown, "Negro Woman Worker," 4, 14.

37. Scharf, *To Work and To Wed*, 116; Pidgeon, "Employed Women Under N.R.A. Codes," 83; Wolters, *Negroes and the Great Depression*, 213–214; Janiewski, "From Field to Factory," 160.

38. For an overview, see Green, *The World of the Worker*, 133–209.

39. Janiewski, "From Field to Factory," 239–265.

40. Rosen, "The CIO Era, 1935–55," in Jacobson, ed., *The Negro and the American Labor Movement*, 188–208; Foner, *Women and the American Labor Movement*, 319–338; Foner, *Organized Labor*, 215–237.

41. Interview with Mary Sweet in Banks, ed., *First-Person America*, 133–135; "Negro Women in Industry," *Opportunity* 13 (September 1935): 286; Kine, "The Garment Union."

42. Interview with Evelyn Macon in Banks, ed., *First-Person America*, 127; Porter, "Negro Women," 23; Benham, "The Woman Wage Earner," 25; Brown, "Negro Woman Worker," 15; Martinez, "A Black Union Organizer," in Lerner, ed., *Black Women*, 263.

43. For evidence of black community support for CIO unions, see Martin, "Labor Relations in Transition"; Ryon, "An Ambiguous Legacy"; Meier and Rudwick, "Communist Unions"; Painter, *The Narrative of Hosea Hudson*. On women's auxiliaries, see Lewis, "Women of the Steel Towns," in Lemer, ed., *Black Women*, 261–262; Cayton and Mitchell, *Black Workers*, 188. The nutpickers' strike is recounted in Foner, *Women and the American Labor Movement*, 312.

44. Meier and Rudwick, "Communist Unions"; Naison, *Communists in Harlem*, 237, 262–263, 267–270; Cohen, *Making a New Deal*. Ryon uses the term "aracist" in "Ambiguous Legacy," 20. See also Jones, *American Work*, 337–368.

45. White, *Too Heavy a Load*, 152–157, 160–173; "We asked": quoted in Weisenfeld, *African American Women and Christian Activism*, 177.

46. Ottley and Weatherby, "The Depression in Harlem," in Stemsher, ed., *Hitting Home*, 113; Drake and Cayton, *Black Metropolis*, 2:478, 481, 493, 509; "The Negro in Retail Trade," U.S. Dept. of Labor. See also Frazier, *The Negro Family in Chicago*, 103.

47. Johnson, *Shadow of the Plantation*, 199; interview with Izzelly Haines in Banks, ed., *First-Person America*, 169. On the costs of a midwife's services, see Dollard, *Caste and Class*, 105; Allen, *Labor of Women in the Production of Cotton*, 178; interview with Susie W. Walker in Gordon, "Document: A Brief Look at Blacks in Depression Mississippi," 379.

48. Vivian Harris, "God Was Happy—Mother Horn" (November 23, 1938), FWP interview, Negro Folklore Division (New York), Archive of Folk Song, LC; Smith quoted in Drake and Cayton, *Black Metropolis*, 643–644.

49. Hine, *Black Women in White*, 153–154; Shaw, *What a Woman Ought to Be and to Do*.

50. Hunter, "'Don't Buy From Where You Can't Work,'" 284, 299.

51. Official quoted in Naison, *Communists in Harlem*, 281; Helen Cade Brehon, "Looking Back," in Bambara, ed., *Black Woman*, 227. Black women and men controlled the Party in the South to a much greater extent than in the North. See Hudson, *Black Worker in the Deep South*, 69, 72; Painter, *The Narrative of Hosea Hudson*. Ware includes a discussion of "Women on the Left" in *Holding Their Own*, 117–140.

52. Haley, "To Do Good and Do Well," 64; McElvaine, *Great Depression*, 193.

53. For general accounts of black participation in New Deal public works programs, see Wolters, *Negroes and the Great Depression*, 196–209; Kirby, *Black Americans*, 22–23, 32, 34, 127.

54. Alfred Edgar Smith, "1935 Summary: Negro Clients of Federal Unemployment Relief," 3–4, WPA Collection, RG 69, National Archives; Scharf, *To Work and To Wed*, 122–124; Wolters, *Negroes and the Great Depression*, 206; Mangus, "Rural Negro on Relief," 4, FERA Research Report (September 17, 1934), WPA Collection, RG 69, National Archives; Sterner, *Negro's Share*, 245.

55. Hemenway, *Zora Neale Hurston*, 251–252; Forrester B. Washington, "Accomplishment Report" (February 1, 1934–July 31, 1934), WPA Collection, RG 69, National Archives; Alfred Edgar

Smith, "An Annual Report on Work Relief Matters Affecting Negro Project Workers Peculiarly For the Year 1938" (January 1939), WPA Collection, RG 69, National Archives; Letter from Roy Wilkins to FERA, New York, New York. January 31, 1935, Box 119–1, "Rural Rehabilitation," WPA File, Howard University.

56. Scharf, *To Work and To Wed*, 124; Smith, "Negro Project Workers . . . For the Year 1938," 16, 33; Smith, "An Annual Report on Work Relief Matters Affecting Negro Project Workers Peculiarly For the Year 1937," 11, WPA Collection, RG 69, National Archives; "Women at Work," 64.

57. Dollard, *Caste and Class*, 125; Smith, "Negro Project Workers . . . For the Year 1938," 26, WPA Collection, RG 69, National Archives. See also Smith, "1935 Report-Summary: Negro Clients," WPA Collection, RG 69, National Archives; Sterner, *Negro's Share*, 245.

58. Smith, "Negro Project Workers . . . For the Year 1938," 25, 34; Smith, "Negro Project Workers . . . For the Year 1937," 50, WPA Collection, RG 69, National Archives; Letters from R. J. Wilson, M.D., Florence, S.C., February 26, 1936, and Thurgood Marshall, New York, New York, January 11, 1938, Box 119–2, "Women's Work," WPA File, Howard University; unsigned letter "To the Presandent" in Baxandall, Gordon, and Reverby, eds., *America's Working Women*, 249–250. See also Wolters, *Negroes and the Great Depression*, 208.

59. Letter from Mary Albright, Raleigh, North Carolina, October 12, 1937, Box 119–2, "Women's Work," WPA File, Howard University. Smith, "Negro Project Workers . . . For the Year 1937," 11; Smith, "Negro Project Workers . . . For the Year 1938," 24, 28; Pinkie Pelcher to President Roosevelt, in Lerner, ed., *Black Women*, 401.

60. Sitkoff, *New Deal for Blacks*, 71. See also Weiss, *Farewell to the Party of Lincoln*, 168–174, 285–286.

61. Wright, *12 Million Black Voices*, 128. Bessie Smith, "Washwoman's Blues," from *Empty Bed Blues*, Columbia Records, No. G30450. For revealing autobiographies of black female singers during the 1930s, see Waters, *His Eye is on the Sparrow*; Holiday and Duffy, *Lady Sings the Blues*; Anderson, *My Lord, What A Morning*; Jackson and Whylie, *Movin' On Up*. See also Levine, *Black Culture and Black Consciousness*, 190–297; Cripps, *Slow Fade to Black*; Arsenault, *Sounds of Freedom*.

62. Drake and Cayton, *Black Metropolis*, 2:609; Wright, *12 Million Black Voices*, 61. For discussions of white women who struggled to keep their families intact during the 1930s, see Westin, *Making Do*; Ware, *Holding Their Own*, 1–20; Wandersee, *Women's Work and Family Values*; Milkman, "Woman's Work and Economic Crisis"; Bird, *Invisible Scar*. By far the best treatment of both black and white women's survival strategies is Helmbold, "Making Choices, Making Do." See also the letters written to FDR by desperate women of both races in McElvaine, ed., *Down and Out in the Great Depression*, 156–172.

63. Engerman, "Black Fertility"; Cutright and Shorter, "Effects of Health"; Myrdal, *American Dilemma*, 1:157–181; Janiewski, "From Field to Factory," 37, 178; U.S. Dept. of Commerce, Sixteenth Census (1940), vol. 3, *Population: Differential Fertility 1940 and 1910; Women By Number of Children Ever Born* (Washington, D.C.: Government Printing Office, 1945), 209–11.

64. Powdermaker, *After Freedom*, 367; Drake and Cayton, *Black Metropolis*, 2:666; interview with Jim Jeffcoat in Terill and Hirsch, eds., *Such as Us*, 61. For a discussion of the ways domestic servants viewed their work in the context of improving the lives of their own children, see Dill, *Across the Barriers of Race and Class*.

65. Strasser, *Never Done*, 105; Mebane, *Mary*, 12, 88; Allen, *Labor of Women in the Production of Cotton*, 179; Janiewski, "From Field to Factory," 174, 192; Reverby, "From Aide to Organizer," in Berkin and Norton, eds., *Women of America*, 293; Walker, "Home Extension Work." Hagood pro-

vides an excellent description of the white tenant farm woman's resources for cooking and cleaning in *Mothers of the South*, 92–107.

66. Eason, "Attitudes of Negro Families on Relief," 367, 369; letters from Sarah Young and Pinkie Pelcher in Lemer, ed., *Black Women*, 401–403; Lett, "Work"; Bontemps and Conroy, *They Seek A City*, 183. For relief statistics, see Sterner, *Negro's Share*, 214; Drake and Cayton, *Black Metropolis*, 2:576, 578, 582; "Restriction in Employment," 361. FERA officials quoted: A. R. Mangus, "The Rural Negro on Relief," 4, and Harold C. Hoffsommer, "Rural Problem Areas Survey Report no. 2: Cotton Growing Region of the Old South, Dallas County, Alabama," FERA Research Report (September 17, 1934), 2, WPA Collection, RG 69, National Archives.

67. Byrne and Hillyer, "Unattached Women."

68. Sterner, *Negro's Share*, 282–285.

69. Frazier, "Some Effects of the Depression"; Drake and Cayton, *Black Metropolis*, 2:571. For the study, see Bryan, "Birth Rates and Death Rates."

70. Lett, "Work," 81. For another example, see Helmbold, "Making Choices," 160.

71. Sterner, *Negro's Share*, 50; Engerman, "Black Fertility," 117–138; Frazier, *Negro Family in the United States*, 103; U.S. Dept. of Commerce, Sixteenth Census (1940), vol. 4, *U.S. Summary: Characteristics by Age*, pt. 1, 29.

72. Eason, "Attitudes of Negro Families on Relief," 367, 369. See also Reid, "The Negro Woman Worker."

73. Raper, *Preface to Peasantry*, 74; Ellis, "Women of the Cotton Fields," 333, 342; Borchert, *Alley Life in Washington*, 89–93.

74. Harold C. Hoffsomer, "Landlord-Tenant Relations and Relief in Alabama," FERA Confidential Research Bulletin #2738 (July 10, 1934), WPA Collection, RG 69, National Archives; Allen, *Labor of Women in the Production of Cotton*, 240; Sterner, *Negro's Share*, 135. See also Helmbold, "Making Choices," 144, 147.

75. Angelou, *I Know Why the Caged Bird Sings*, 42, 144; Rosengarten, *All God's Dangers*, 258. See also Gordon, "Document: A Brief Look at Blacks in Depression Mississippi," 379; Drake and Cayton, *Black Metropolis*, 2:513, 579; Frazier, "Some Effects," 494; Sterner, *Negro's Share*, 93–115, 379; Helmbold, "Making Choices," 25; Mebane, *Mary*, 7, 11–12, 16, 18, 47; Woofter, *Black Yeomanry*, 128; Johnson, *Shadow of the Plantation*, 101.

76. Social worker quoted in Borchert, *Alley Life in Washington*, 69–70.

77. Reverby, "From Aide to Organizer," in Berkin and Norton, eds., *Women of America*, 292; Johnson, *Shadow of the Plantation*, 61. See also Janiewski, "From Field to Factory," 38, 40, 172; Allen, *Labor of Women in the Production of Cotton*, 206.

78. Edward J. Webster, "Survey of Cases Removed from Relief Rolls in Macon, Georgia, for Administrative Reasons in May, 1935," FERA Confidential Research Bulletin #6648 (September 24, 1935), 1, WPA Collection, RG 69, National Archives; Angelou, *I Know Why the Caged Bird Sings*, 146; Rawick, ed., *American Slave*, Series 1, *Georgia Narratives*, pt. 1, 12:250. See also Johnson, *Shadow of the Plantation*, 37; Frazier, *Negro Family in the United States*, 96; Allen, *Labor of Women in the Production of Cotton*, 186, 189. See Sterner, *Negro's Share*, 393, for survey data that indicate that in selected areas, higher percentages of blacks at the lowest income levels (compared to similarly situated whites) reported they had contributed to the financial support of relatives from 1935 to 1936.

79. Drake and Cayton, *Black Metropolis*, 2:572; Reverby, "Aide to Organizer," in Berkin and Norton, eds., *Women of America*, 295. On neighborhoods and mobility see, for example, Borchert, *Alley Life in Washington*, 123–127; Bodnar, Simon, and Weber, *Lives of Their Own*, 217; Johnson,

Shadow of the Plantation, 25. See also Mebane, *Mary*, 11–12, 18, 47; interview with Robin Langston in Terkel, *Hard Times*, 113; Helmbold, "Making Choices," 64–84.

80. Reverby, "From Aide to Organizer," in Berkin and Norton, eds., *Women of America*, 294; Westin, *Making Do*, 26; Frazier, "Some Effects of the Depression," 497; Dollard, *Caste and Class*, 72; Benham, "Woman Wage Earner," 21; Borchert, *Alley Life in Washington*, 131–132; Helmbold, "Making Choices," 180.

81. Mebane, *Mary*, 83; Angelou, *I Know Why the Caged Bird Sings*, 40, 116.

82. Mebane, *Mary*, 90; Marshall, "From the Poets in the Kitchen."

CHAPTER 7

1. "Members": Gilmore, *Defying Dixie*, 899; "guerilla-like": ibid., 348. See also ibid., 346–399.

2. "Your picture": ibid., 399; "a quieting": ibid., 400; "the rights": ibid., 441.

3. See Sugrue, *Sweet Land of Liberty*; Rupp, "The Survival of American Feminism," and Chafe, "The Civil Rights Revolution," both in Brember and Reichard, eds., *Reshaping America*, 33–66, 67–100.

4. "not aloud": quoted in Lerner, ed., *Black Women*, 405; Weaver, *Negro Labor*; Sitkoff, "Racial Militancy"; Meier and Rudwick, *CORE*; Marjorie McKenzie, "Against the Lean Years," *Aframerican Woman's Journal* 3 (Summer 1943): 7; Johnson, *To Stem This Tide*, 34; "you can never tell": Carolyn Chase in Gwaltney, *Drylongso*, 57; Chafe, "Civil Rights Revolution"; Sitkoff, "Racial Militancy"; Meier and Rudwick, *CORE*; Dalfiume, "The Forgotten Negro Revolution."

5. Newman and others, *Protest, Politics, and Prosperity*; "No one does": Margaret Wright quoted in Frank, Ziebarth, and Field, *The Life and Times of Rosie the Riveter*, 51; "We ought": woman quoted in Sitkoff, *A New Deal for Blacks*, 314; Herman, *The Politics of Civil Rights*; Alexander, *Holding the Line*; "thus we lived": Angelou, *Gather Together in My Name*, 5.

6. "do the job": propaganda poster quoted in Frank, Ziebarth, and Field, *Life and Times of Rosie the Riveter*, 100; Kessler-Harris, *Out to Work*, 273–299; Anderson, *Wartime Women*, 23–74; Tobias and Anderson, "What Really Happened to Rosie the Riveter?" in Kerber and DeHart, eds., *Women's America*, 354–373; Quick, "Rosie the Riveter."

7. Bedell, "Employment and Income of Negro Workers"; Blood, "Negro Women War Workers."

8. "the problem": Friedan, *The Feminine Mystique*, 11; "crammed on top": Petry, *The Street*, 130.

9. Ruth Shays in Gwaltney, *Drylongso*, 30.

10. "We brown": quoted in Sugrue, *Sweet Land of Liberty*, 80; Weaver, *Negro Labor*; Lichtenstein, *Labor's War at Home*; Glaberman, *Wartime Strikes*.

11. Williams, *Politics of Public Housing*; Sugrue, *Sweet Land of Liberty*, 67–68, 154–155; Johnson and Campbell, *Black Migration in America*, 101–113; Sitkoff, "Racial Militancy"; Reddick, ed., "Race Relations on the Pacific Coast"; Taylor, "The Great Migration"; Capeci, *The Harlem Riot of 1943*. On the status of black servicemen in the war, see Bell Jr., "The Negro Warrior's Home Front"; Berry and Blassingame, *Long Memory*, 320–329 and the book's bibliography.

12. Joyce Kornbluh, Oral History Interview with Lillian Hatcher, "The Twentieth Century Trade Union Woman: Vehicle For Social Change Oral History Project" (Ann Arbor, MI: Institute of Labor and Industrial Relations), 19 (hereafter Lillian Hatcher Interview); "wasn't going": Williams, *Politics of Public Housing*, 56; "utopia": Rice, "It Takes a While to Realize," in Lerner, ed., *Black Women*, 276.

13. Blood, "Negro Women War Workers," 1–19.

14. Rupp, *Mobilizing Women for War*; Honey, "Working-Class Woman and Recruitment"; "We think": Blood, "Negro Women War Workers," 8.

15. Pidgeon, "Women Workers and Recent Economic Change"; Frank, Ziebarth, and Field, *Life and Times of Rosie the Riveter*, 14; Hobbs, "The Whip Changes Hands"; Weaver, *Negro Labor*, 17, 38; Johnson, *To Stem This Tide*, 29; sociologist quoted in Charles Johnson, "The Present Status of Race Relations in the South," *Social Forces* 23 (October 1944): 29; Sugrue, *Sweet Land of Liberty*, 66.

16. Blood, "Negro Women War Workers," 20–22; Anderson, "Last Hired, First Fired"; Webster, "Employers, Unions, and Negro Workers"; Weaver, *Negro Labor*, 85; U.S. Dept. of Labor, "Women Workers in Some Expanding Wartime Industries."

17. Weaver, *Negro Labor*, 41–60, 114; personnel manager quoted in letter from Donna Rolland, August 24, 1943, Box 29, Local Union 50 folder, UAW War Policy Division Collection, Walter P. Reuther Library, Archives of Labor and Urban Affairs, Wayne State University, Detroit, MI (hereafter ALUA); DeMar, "Negro Women are American Workers, Too," 42; Foner, *Women and the American Labor Movement*, 348–349.

18. Anderson, "Last Hired, First Fired," 92–93; President's Committee on Civil Rights, *To Secure These Rights*; Straub, "United States Government Policy Toward Civilian Women"; Weaver, *Negro Labor*, 145–146. On efforts of local black workers to pressure the FEPC, see Harris, "Federal Intervention in Union Discrimination"; Walter, "Frank R. Crosswaith and Labor Unionization,"; Taylor, "Great Migration," 119–120.

19. Angelou, *I Know Why the Caged Bird Sings*, 224–229; Harris, *The Harder We Run*, 113–122.

20. Gabin, *Feminism in the Labor Movement*, 47–110; Clive, "Women Workers in World War II"; Anderson, "Last Hired, First Fired," 85; statistics compiled from Mary Ann Loeser, UAW Research Department, to Victor Reuther, Codirector of UAW War Policy Division, October 9, 1942, Box 6, Negro and Defense Industry, 1941–1942, and Oscar Noble to Victor Reuther, January 1943, Box 6, Negro and Defense Industry, 1943, UAW War Policy Division Collection, ALUA. The quote is from Boggs, "The Making of the Black Revolt in the USA," 15.

21. Meier and Rudwick, *Black Detroit and the Rise of the UAW*, 136–156; clipping from *Detroit News*, October 26, 1942 ("Women Seek Factory Jobs: Negro Rally Demands Share in War Work") in Box 14, Women Folder, UAW Public Relations Department—Frank Winn Collection, ALUA; UAW Research Department Memo, September 13, 1943, UAW Research Department Collection, Box 10, Folder 19, ALUA; Jones, *Dispossessed*, 233–265.

22. Milkman, "Redefining 'Women's Work'"; Denby, *Indignant Heart*, 88–93; Blood, "Negro Women War Workers," 5; Frank, Ziebarth, and Field, *Life and Times of Rosie the Riveter*, 63, 80; Anderson, "Last Hired, First Fired," 88; DeMar, "Negro Women are American Workers, Too," 77; Lillian Hatcher Interview, 17.

23. Foner, *Organized Labor*, 238–268; Weaver, *Negro Labor*, 28–40; Foner, *Women and the American Labor Movement*, 339–396; Green, *The World of the Worker*, 174–209; Taylor, "Great Migration," 111, 119.

24. Interview with Maida Springer Kemp, 18, Black Women Oral History Project, Schlesinger Library, Radcliffe College, Cambridge, MA (hereafter BWOHP), in cooperation with the 20th Century Trade Union Woman Project, Program on Women and Work, Institute of Labor and Industrial Relations, University of Michigan, Ann Arbor, MI; steward quoted in Lillian Hatcher Interview, 22. See also Meier and Rudwick, *Black Detroit*, 162; Gabin, *Feminism in the Labor Movement*, 11–87.

25. Lillian Hatcher Interview, 18, 45.

26. "Off guard," "Mr. Whitaker," "the black women": quoted in Korstad, "Those Who Were Not Afraid," in Miller, ed., *Working Lives*, 189, 195; "I want": Jones quoted in Korstad and Lichtenstein,

"Opportunities Found and Lost," in Arnesen, ed., *The Black Worker*, 26. Korstad (in "Those Who Were Not Afraid") writes, "The little steel formula was a labor/management/government agreement that allowed for moderate wage increases to offset wartime inflation" (p. 189). See also Foner, *Women and the American Labor Movement*, 385.

27. Quotes from Maida Springer Kemp, BWOHP, and Woods, "You Have to Fight for Freedom" in Lynd and Lynd, eds., *Rank and File*, 125–126. See also interview with Massie Eberhardt, BWOHP; Lillian Hatcher Interview, 21.

28. Green, *Race on the Line*, 202–208.

29. Anderson, "Last Hired, First Fired," 86, 89; Weaver, *Negro Labor*, 70, 128, 186–187; Oscar Noble Report attached to Victor Reuther to Lloyd Jones, President UAW Local 2, March 15, 1943, Box 29, Local Union 2 Folder, UAW Policy Division Collection, ALUA; Oscar Nobel, UAW International Representative, War Policy Division, to Montague Clark, District Director, WMC Detroit, February-March 1953, UAW War Policy Division Collection, ALUA; Winchester employer quoted in Schuster, "Negroes Working in Defense Industry."

30. Webb Anderson quoted in Jones and others, *Created Equal* (Third Edition), 738–739. Blood, "Negro Women War Workers," 1–2; Washington, "An Essay on Alice Walker," in Bell, Parker, and Guy-Sheftall, eds., *Sturdy Black Bridges*, 143; Anderson, "Negro Women on the Production Front"; Staupers, "The Negro Nurse," 333; Banner, "New York,"; Banner, "War and Post-War Trends," 1–3; Anderson, "Last Hired, First Fired," 89; Henderson, "Negroes in Government Employment," 118–121. On black women in the armed services, see Hampton, "Negro Women and the WAAC," 54–55, 93; Hartmann, *The Home Front and Beyond*, 40–45; Johnson, *Black Women in the Armed Forces*, 1; Macy, "Negro Women in the WAC," 14; Turner, "Alpha Kappa Alpha Sorority's Wartime Program," 22–23; Riddle and Nelson, "The Negro Nurse Looks Toward Tomorrow," 627–630.

31. Gates, *Colored People*, 85.

32. Drake, "The Negro in the North During Wartime," 266; Gregory Jr., "Wartime Guidance," 70–71, 90–91; Mebane, *Mary*, 119–120; Malcolm X, *Autobiography of Malcolm X*, 74. See also Angelou, *I Know Why the Caged Bird Sings*, 215. On the rise of female-headed households during the war, see U.S. Dept. of Labor, "Handbook of Facts on Women Workers," 24.

33. "It was": quoted in White, "'Eight Dollars a Day and Working in the Shade'" in Taylor and Moore, eds., *African American Women Confront the West*, 279; Faulkner and others, *When I Was Comin' Up*, 109; Mack, man, and wife quoted in Frank, Ziebarth, and Field, *Life and Times of Rosie the Riveter*, 55–56, 66, 68; Reagon, "World War II Reflected in Black Music," 181, 183.

34. "We the people . . . mixing": quoted in Williams, *The Politics of Public Housing*, 61.

35. "We do not": quoted in Cohen, *Consumer's Republic*, 92 (see also pp. 83–86); Lemke-Santangelo, *Abiding Courage*.

36. Hartmann, *Home Front and Beyond*, 84–85; Clive, "Women Workers in World War II," 58–66; Chafe, *The American Woman*, 159–172; Allen quoted in Frank, Ziebarth, and Field, *Life and Times of Rosie the Riveter*, 68. The Hackshaw essay is entitled "What My Job Means to Me," 52–53. See also interview with Massie Eberhardt, BWOHP, 2, 31.

37. Bullock, "An Analysis of Cases of Negro Working Mothers."

38. Interview with Frankie V. Adams, BWOHP, 11–12; Hartmann, "Women's Organizations During World War II" in Kelley, ed., *Woman's Being, Woman's Place*, 313–333; Neely, "Women of Philadelphia and Their Activities," 150–152; White, *Too Heavy a Load*, 56–60.

39. Baker, "Developing Community Leadership," in Lerner, ed., *Black Women*, 346.

40. Quotes from Marjorie McKenzie, "Against the Lean Years," *Aframerican Woman's Journal* 3 (Summer 1943):7, and Frank, Ziebarth, and Field, *Life and Times of Rosie the Riveter*, 95. See also

Kessler-Harris, *Out to Work*, 295–299; Tobias and Anderson, "What Really Happened to Rosie the Riveter?"; Anderson, "Last Hired, First Fired," 91, 95; U.S. Dept. of Labor, "Changes in Women's Occupations, 1940–1950"; Pidgeon, "Women Workers and Recent Economic Change."

41. "I like": Denby, *Indignant Heart*, 142–144; Shockley, *"We, Too, Are Americans,"* 149. See also ibid., 137–169.

42. Testimony of Josephine McCloudy, UAW Fair Practices Department Appeal, January 31, 1947, Box 11, Folder 9, and William Oliver, Director UAW Fair Practices Department to Ralph Urban, President Local 190, February 6, 1947, Box 11, Folder 9, Emil Mazey Collection, ALUA; Nancy Gabin to the author, January 24, 1983. For the government researcher's report, see Bedell, "Employment and Income of Negro Workers," 596. See also Harris, *Harder We Run*, 125, 130; Newman and others, *Protest, Politics, and Prosperity*, 32–70, 259; Johnson and Valien, "The Status of Negro Labor," in Wame and others, eds., *Labor in Postwar America*, 553–571; Shockley, *"We, Too, Are Americans,"* 149.

43. "I could": quoted in "Only 1 in 73 Former Maids Returning to New York Kitchens," *Christian Science Monitor*, Oct. 8, 1946; Goldstein, "The Changing Occupational Structure"; "I have always . . . alternative": *Post* clipping in Household Employment, Domestic Service—Postwar U.S.—1945, Box 1719, Women's Bureau Collection, Record Group 86, National Archives, Washington, D.C. (hereafter WB Collection).

44. U.S. Dept. of Labor, "1954 Handbook on Women Workers." The number of women in domestic service decreased by one-third from 1940 to 1950; see U.S. Dept. of Labor, "Changes in Women's Occupations, 1940–1950," 61.

45. Ackies quoted in Jacobson, "Ex-Domestics Prefer New Factory Jobs," typescript dated September 9, 1945, in Correspondence, Household (Domestic File), 1945, Box 923; Weaver, "Former Domestics Slow to Return to Kitchen Work," Baltimore *Afro-American*, September 8, 1945; "Domestic Service, Too, Has Its Labor Problem," Buffalo *Courier-Express*, October 14, 1945 in Correspondence, Household (Domestic File), 1945, Box 923; "New York Domestic Workers Average $35 Weekly in '46," Chicago *Defender* in Household Employment—Domestic Workers Folder: Household Employment Clippings, 1947, Box 1717, WB Collection.

46. Mary V. Robinson to Frieda S. Miller, December 23, 1944, WB Collection.

47. Household Employment Report, December 22, 1946, typescript, 5, 10, in Correspondence, Household (Domestic File) Folder: Correspondence 1947, Box 923, WB Collection. The *Family Circle* article is in Household Employment—Domestic Workers Folder: Domestic Service Postwar U.S. Magazine article, Box 1717. See other articles in this file, including "It's Getting to be a Maid's World!" New York *Daily News* (March 16, 1946).

48. "Better Trained Domestics Aim of 200 Negroes," AP story, December 26, 1945, in Household Employment Domestic Service Postwar U.S. 1945, Box 1719; U.S. Dept. of Labor, "Community Household Employment Programs."

49. Bea Rivers, Helen Satterwhite, Oneida Harris, and Jewell Prieleau quoted in Dill, "Across the Barriers of Race and Class," 69, 96, 104, 106, 149, 163. These are not the real names of the interviewees. See also the interviews of black domestics in Hamburger, *A Stranger in the House*.

50. Sugrue, *Origins of the Urban Crisis*; Cohen, *Consumer's Republic*, 158; Shockley, *"We, Too, Are Americans,"* 137–169; Williams, *Politics of Public Housing*; Jones, *American Work*, 355–360.

51. "I got": White, "'Eight Dollars a Day and Working in the Shade,'" in Taylor and Moore, eds., *African American Women Confront the West*, 281.

52. Johnson and Campbell, *Black Migration*, 114–151; White, "'Eight Dollars a Day and Working in the Shade,'" in Taylor and Moore, eds., *African American Women Confront the West*, 277.

53. Kirby, "The Transformation of Southern Plantations"; Melman, "An Industrial Revolution in the Cotton South"; U.S. Dept. of Labor, "1954 Handbook on Women Workers," 19.

54. "Going to Live Like My Father Lived," in Faulkner and others, *When I Was Camin' Up*, 135. See also Kirby, "Transformation of Southern Plantations," 272; Shofner, "The Legacy of Racial Slavery"; Daniel, *The Shadow of Slavery*, 170–192.

55. Price, *Changing Characteristics of the Negro Population*, 113. See also U.S. Dept. of Labor, "Handbook of Facts on Women Workers" (1948), 22. In 1946 the average year's earnings for white men amounted to $2,223; nonwhite men, $1,367; white women, $1,142; and nonwhite women, $497.

56. Berman, *Politics of Civil Rights*, 24–28, 32–37; Sitkoff, "Harry Truman and the Election of 1948." On the segmentation of workers by sex and race during the postwar period, see Gordon, Edwards, and Reich, *Segmented Work, Divided Workers*, 204–210.

57. Lieberson, *A Piece of the Pie*, 239–252; Wallace, *Black Women in the Labor Force*, 44; Oppenheimer, *The Female Labor Force*, 78–79.

58. Knupfer, *Chicago Renaissance*, 119; Women quoted in Hirsch, *Making the Second Ghetto*, 24–25.

59. Farley, *Growth of the Black Population*, 76–100; Cutright, "Components of Change in the Number of Female Family Heads."

60. Kunzel, "White Neurosis, Black Pathology," in Meyerowitz, ed., *Not June Cleaver*, 304–306; Mittelstadt, *From Welfare to Workfare*, 172; Patterson, "Poverty and Welfare in America," in Bremner and Reichard, eds., *Reshaping America*, 193–221; Bell, *Aid to Dependent Children*; Piven and Cloward, *Regulating the Poor*, 147–180, 189–198.

61. Caute, *The Great Fear*; Levenstein, *Communism, Anticommunism, and the CIO*.

62. Lichtenstein, *Labor's War at Home*; Foner, *Organized Labor*, 275–292; Marshall, *Labor in the South*, 246–269.

63. Flowers, "Why I Need a Pay Raise" (article in *FTA News*, January 15, 1947), and "Tobacco Workers Honor Fighting Union Leader" (article in *Union Voice*, June 3, 1951), in Lerner, ed., *Black Women*, 267, 273; Foner, *Organized Labor*, 282; Korstad and Lichtenstein, "Opportunities Found and Lost," in Arnesen, ed., *The Black Worker*.

64. Cooper, "A Rank and File Unionist Speaks" (article in *National Guardian*, September 26, 1949), in Lerner, ed., *Black Women*, 268. Foner, *Organized Labor*, 281–282.

65. Smith, "Black Workers and Unions" (from "Final Proceedings of the 9th Constitutional Convention of the CIO," October 15, 1947), in Lerner, ed., *Black Women*, 269–271.

66. Rice, "It Takes a While," in Lerner, ed., *Black Women*, 277, 279, 280, 281.

67. Ibid., 281; Svend Godfredsen, "Young Chicago Girl a CIO Union Leader," 104–105, 120.

68. "leftist": quoted in Sugrue, *Sweet Land of Liberty*, 109. This account is taken from Foner, *Organized Labor*, which contains the only published history of the NNLC (pp. 293–311). See also Hill, "The AFL-CIO and the Black Worker."

69. Chafe, "Civil Rights Revolution," 68, 72; Aptheker, "The Matriarchal Image" in *Woman's Legacy*, 148–149; Meier and Rudwick, CORE, 33–40.

70. Dittmer, *Local People*; Chafe, "Civil Rights Revolution," 96–97.

71. Dougherty, "'That's When We Were Marching for Jobs,'" 128; Carolyn Reed in Hamburger, *Stranger in the House*, 154.

72. Friedan, *Feminine Mystique*, 28, 45, 58.

73. Ibid., 60; Rupp, "Survival of American Feminism," in Bremner and Reichard, eds., *Reshaping America*. For a collection of documents related to antifeminist ideology during this period, see Lynn, ed., *Women's Liberation in the Twentieth Century*, 55–82. On the growing number of white wives and

mothers in the labor force in the postwar era, see Matthaei, *An Economic History of Women in America*, 235–255; Kennedy, *If All We Did Was to Weep*, 183–219; Harris, *Out to Work*, 300–315.

74. Cain, *Married Women in the Labor Force*; Ostlund, "Occupational Choice Patterns of Negro College Women."

75. Daniel, *Black Journals*, 159–183; Peterson, *Magazines in the Twentieth Century*, 65–66. Quoted articles *from Ebony*: "The NAACP," August 1946, 35; "Two Years after Roosevelt," April 1947, 36; "The Rise and Fall of Uncle Tom," December 1946, 34.

76. Quoted articles from *Ebony*: April 1946, 19; October 1946, 26; December 1953, 49; June 1947, 4.

77. For representative covers, see *Ebony*, July and November 1951. The article on women leaders is in July 1949, 17, 23.

78. *Ebony*, March 1947, 36.

79. *Ebony*, May 1953, 78. See, for example, "Lady Lifeguard," July 1948, 19; "Television Makeup Lady," February 1949, 27; "Lady Boxer," March 1949, 30; "Lady Cops," September 1954, 26; "Lady Lawyers," August 1947, 19; "Lady Cobbler," March 1953, 5; "Harlem's Lady Wholesaler," January 1955, 53. The last story, on Louise Varona, who managed a food distribution business that grossed $200,000 annually, noted that she had encountered several prospective white buyers but rejected their offers: "'I am of Harlem,' she says, 'and intend to stay here. . . . Negroes need to own their own businesses, and I for one intend to keep mine.'" See also "Labor Leaders," February 1947, 15, for mention of Louise Armstrong, an officer in her local of the United Steelworkers of America (CIO) in Chicago; the thirty-four-year-old mother had recently led a successful strike which won a union shop contract and a wage increase.

80. *Ebony*, January 1951, 71, 74; January 1954, 68–69. See also "Husband and Wife Teams: Couples Following Same Professions Find Happiness, Success," *Ebony*, January 1954, 68.

81. *Ebony*, November 1949, 52; April 1952, 64. One of the other maids featured was Margaret W. Ware, "Nursemaid to the [Fultz] Quadruplets," June 1948, 36.

82. "The Powells," *Ebony*, May 1946, 36; "At Home with Marian Anderson," February 1954, 52; "Lena Horne Begins a New Movie," March 1946, 20. According to Friedan, "When you wrote about an actress for a [white] woman's magazine, you wrote about her as a housewife. You never showed her doing or enjoying her work as an actress, unless she eventually paid for it by losing her husband or her child or otherwise admitting failure as a woman." *Feminine Mystique*, 47.

83. *Ebony*, March 1946, 20. See, for example, "Ruby Hill," May 1946, 15; "Ebony's Girls: Editors Pick Pinup Favorites from Issues of the Past Five Years," November 1950, 23; "New Beauties Versus Old," March 1954, 54 ("Lena Horne has become the criterion by which modem Negro beauties are judged").

84. "Mildred Pierce," *Ebony*, January 1946, 30; "Movie Maids," August 1948, 56; "The Member of the Wedding," December 1952, 35; "Hollywood Debut for Pearl Bailey," April 1947, 38; "Movie Maids: Eight New Hollywood Films . . . ," August 1948, 56; "Juanita Hall," July 1950, 29; "Joyce Bryant," March 1951, 61; "Josephine Baker Comes Home Again: She Finally Achieves Stardom That Long Eluded Her in Native Land," May 1951, 74. See also "Cass Timberlane: Movies Call Negro Maid 'Mrs.' For First Time," November 1947, 23.

85. "Is Jazz Going Highbrow?: Hot Pianist Dorothy Donegan is Newest Convert to the Classics," *Ebony*, July 1946, 19.

86. Bethune, "My Secret Talks With FDR," *Ebony*, April 1949, 43, and "My Last Will and Testament: Mary McLeod Bethune Dictated Legacy to Her People," August 1955, 69; "Women Leaders," July 1949, 21; "Edith Sampson Goes to Austria," October 1951, 82. On her visit to Austria, Sampson

told her hosts "that one of the bitter things about a lot of discrimination in America is that it often comes from the children of Europeans who immigrated to America to find the democracy and freedom which they in turn want to deny to others."

87. Hersh, *The Slavery of Sex*; Chafe, *Women and Equality*.

CHAPTER 8

1. Reagon, "My Black Mothers and Sisters."

2. Piven and Cloward, *Poor People's Movements*, 181–263; Oberschall, *Social Conflict and Social Movements*, 205–230; Sitkoff, *The Struggle for Black Equality*; "a very simple": Canterow and O'Malley, "Ella Baker: Organizing for Civil Rights," in Canterow, ed., *Moving the Mountain*, 82–83. For overviews, see Crawford, Rouse, and Woods., eds. *Women in the Civil Rights Movement*; Robnett, *How Long? How Long?*; Ling and Monteith, eds., *Gender and the Civil Rights Movement*; Collier-Thomas and Franklin, eds., *Sisters in the Struggle*.

3. Feldstein, "'I Wanted the Whole World to See," in Meyerowitz, ed., *Not June Cleaver*, 263–303; Wilson, *When Work Disappears*; Cohen, *A Consumer's Republic*, 372–383; Green, *Battling the Plantation Mentality*, 212.

4. Baxter and Lansing, *Women and Politics*, 78, 73–112. See also Prestage, "Political Behavior of American Black Women" in Rodgers-Rose, ed., *The Black Woman*, 233–245; Boyd, "Black Women's Gains Present Political Puzzle," *New York Times*, January 17, 1984.

5. McGuire, "'It Was Like all of Us Had Been Raped'"; McAdoo, "Patterns of Upward Mobility in Black Families," in McAdoo, ed., *Black Families*, 158; Freeman, *Black Elite*; Wilson, *When Work Disappears*; McLean, *Freedom Is Not Enough*.

6. These census data are conveniently summarized in Matney and Johnson, "America's Black Population"; "supersexist": Tillmon, "Welfare Is a Women's Issue," in Perrucci and Targ, eds., *Marriage and the Family*, 109.

7. Hall, "The Long Civil Rights Movement"; McLean, *Freedom is Not Enough*; Interviews with E. D. Nixon, Virginia Durr, and Johnny Carr conducted by Gardner; "Montgomery Bus Boycott," and interview with Rosa Parks by Stokes Brown; Gibson Robinson, *Montgomery Bus Boycott and the Women Who Started It*.

8. See, for example, the interviews with Montgomery black leaders in Raines, *My Soul Is Rested*, 37–74. See also King Jr., *Why We Can't Wait*, 99.

9. Hoose, *Claudette Colvin*. In her autobiography, Gibson Robinson recounts a similarly humiliating encounter with a white bus driver.

10. White, *Too Heavy a Load*, 193; Green, *Battling the Plantation Mentality*, 276. On SCLC, see Oates, *Let the Trumpet Sound*; on CORE, Meier and Rudwick, *CORE*; on SNCC, Carson, *In Struggle*, and Sellers, *The River of No Return*. See also Honey, *Going Down Jericho Road*, and *Southern Labor and Black Civil Rights*.

11. Green, *Battling the Plantation Mentality*, 210–213; Honey, *Southern Labor and Black Civil Rights*; Sokol, *There Goes My Everything*.

12. Maya Angelou, *Gather Together in My Name*, 78.

13. Charles Sherrod, quoted in Carson, *In Struggle*, 75.

14. Garland, "Builders of a New South"; Sutherland, ed., *Letters from Mississippi*, 61. See also Belfrage, *Freedom Summer*, 76; Sugarman, *Stranger at the Gates*, 54–55; Evans, *Personal Politics*, 51, 75, 76; Giddings, *When and Where I Enter*, 261–276.

15. Sugarman, *Stranger at the Gates*, 78; Webb and Nelson, *Selma*, 85. On demographic and migration patterns, see Johnson and Campbell, *Black Migration in America*, 101–151.

16. Belfrage, *Freedom Summer*, 52–53; Sugarman, *Stranger at the Gates*, 120; Webb and Nelson, *Selma*, 114, 142.

17. Sessions and Thrasher, "A New Day Begun," interview with John Lewis; Tracy, Thrasher, and Sessions, "To Be Prophetic," 42.

18. Reagon, "We Became Visible, Our Image Was Enlarged," 5; Pfister, "Twenty Years and Still Marching,"; Carson, *In Struggle*, 56–63; Cluster, "The Borning Struggle" (interviews with John Lewis, Jean Smith, and Bernice Reagon) in *They Should Have Served that Cup of Coffee*, 8–30; Webb and Nelson, *Selma*, 55; Garland, "Builders of a New South," 27.

19. Belfrage, *Freedom Summer*, 74; Wigginton and Thrasher, "To Make the World We Want," 27; Sessions and Thrasher, "A New Day Begun," 24; Sugarman, *Stranger at the Gates*, 78; interview with Rev. Joseph E. Lowery in Raines, *My Soul Is Rested*, 66–70. See also the introduction to Sugarman, *Stranger at the Gates*, by Fannie Lou Hamer.

20. Jones quoted in Mars, *Witness in Philadelphia*, 207; Oates, *Let the Trumpet Sound*.

21. Grant, "Black Women and the Church," in Hull, Scott, and Smith, eds., *All the Women Are White, All the Blacks Are Men*, 141–152; "as a woman": Baker, "Developing Community Leadership," in Lerner, ed., *Black Women*, 351; "Miss Baker tempered": Mary King quoted in Payne, *I've Got the Light of Freedom*, 97; Ransby, *Ella Baker and the Black Freedom Movement*; Bohannon, *Freedom Cannot Rest*; Dallard, *Ella Baker*. See also Cotton's discussion of "A Woman's Place" (in SCLC) in Raines, *My Soul Is Rested*, 432–434; Lewis and D'Orso, *Walking with the Wind*.

22. Evans, *Personal Politics*, 76–88, 233–240; Carson, *In Struggle*, 147–148; Cluster, "Borning Struggle" in *They Should Have Served that Cup of Coffee*.

23. Clark, *Echo in My Soul*; Bates, *Long Shadow of Little Rock*; Moody, *Coming of Age in Mississippi*; Cluster, "Borning Struggle" in *They Should Have Served that Cup of Coffee*; Patton, "Insurgent Memories."

24. Canterow and O'Malley, "Ella Baker," in Canterow, ed., *Moving the Mountain*, 53, 72; Kling, "Fannie Lou Hamer" in McAllister, ed., *Reweaving the Web of Life*, 106–112. The interview with Hamer is in Raines, *My Soul Is Rested*, 249–255. See also Garland, "Builders of a New South," 27–36; "Mississippi Freedom Democratic Party."

25. Raines, *My Soul Is Rested*, 253–254.

26. Bates, *Long Shadow of Little Rock*, 69–76; interview with Autherine Lucy Foster in Raines, *My Soul Is Rested*, 325–327; "Freedom Rides"; Forman, *The Making of Black Revolutionaries*, 247; Garland, "Builders of a New South," 36–37; Carson, *In Struggle*, 21. See also Chafe, *Civilities and Civil Rights*, 100–103.

27. Reagon, "My Black Mothers and Sisters," 91; Garland, "Builders of a New South," 5; Charity, Davis, and Kinoy, "The Danville Movement"; Sugarman, *Stranger at the Gates*, 58, 120–121, 188–189; Gladney, "If It Was Anything for Justice"; "Greensboro Sit-ins," 27.

28. Garland, "Builders of a New South," 27. See Clark, *Echo in My Soul*, 161–162; "Mississippi Movement," 40; Abubakari, "The Only Thing You Can Aspire To Is Nationhood," in Lerner, ed., *Black Women*, 553–558; Steele quoted in Fager, *Selma, 1965*, 151, 155.

29. Sutherland, ed., *Letters from Mississippi*, 43, 46–47, 63, 122.

30. Moody, *Coming of Age in Mississippi*, 24; Gladney, "If It Was Anything for Justice," 19–23; Forman, *Making of Black Revolutionaries*, 117–119; Garland, "Builders of a New South," 28. See also Canterow and O'Malley, "Ella Baker," in Canterow, ed., *Moving the Mountain*, 55.

31. Killens, "We Refuse to Look at Ourselves Through the Eyes of White America," in Meier and others, eds., *Black Protest Thought*, 424; Sugarman, *Stranger at the Gates*, 184; Sutherland, ed., *Letters from Mississippi*, 54, 208–209; Evans, *Personal Politics*, 51–53.

32. King, *Why We Can't Wait*, 99; interview with Yancey Martin in Raines, My *Soul Is Rested*, 61; "We Have No Government," in Grant, ed., *Black Protest*, 505; Lester, *Look Out Whitey*, 141; Sellers, *River of No Return*, 153; Stokely Carmichael, in Barbour, ed., *The Black Power Revolt*, 65.

33. Sugarman, *Stranger at the Gates*, 115; Moody, *Coming of Age in Mississippi*, 300; Mars, *Witness in Philadelphia*, 207.

34. Forman, *Making of Black Revolutionaries*, 126; Cobb and McLaurin, "The Economy of Ruleville, Mississippi," in Grant, ed., *Black Protest*, 473–474; Clark, *Echo in My Soul*, 112; Baker, "Freedom Village," 20.

35. King, *Why We Can't Wait*, 17; Belfrage, *Freedom Summer*, 114.

36. Interview with Franklin McCain in Raines, *My Soul Is Rested*, 77–78; Garland, "Builders of a New South," 1; Mississippi woman quoted in Sutherland, ed., *Letters from Mississippi*, 60. See also Moody, *Coming of Age in Mississippi*, 235, 246; Pfister, "Twenty Years Later and Still Marching," 30; Carson, *In Struggle*, 117.

37. Robinson quoted in Gill, *Beauty Shop Politics*, 111–112.

38. Interviews with Virginia Durr and Lucretia Collins, and Anne Braden, "A View from the Fringes," 15–19, 38, 68–74; Smith, *Killers of the Dream*; Webb and Nelson, *Selma*, 71; Forman, *Making of Black Revolutionaries*, 123–124; Belfrage, *Freedom Summer*, 77–78; Mars, *Witness in Philadelphia*, 87–89, 92–95, 97–111; Sokol, *There Goes My Everything*. For other examples of hostile female registrars, see *Hearings Before the United States Commission on Civil Rights* held in New Orleans, 59–62.

39. Interview with Virginia Durr, *Southern Exposure* 9 (Spring 1981):18; Raines, "The Birmingham Bombing," 12–13, 22–29.

40. Interview with Franklin McCain in Raines, *My Soul Is Rested*, 77; Moody, *Coming of Age in Mississippi*, 29. See also Morrison, "What the Black Woman Thinks About Women's Lib," 15.

41. Green, *Battling the Plantation Mentality*; Honey, *Going Down Jericho Road*; "The Charleston Hospital Strike," in Baxandall and others, eds., *America's Working Women*, 361; Foner, *Women and the American Labor Movement*, 416; Joan Griffin quoted in interview by Jupiter, "Without Fear," 66; Watriss, "It's Something Inside You," 81.

42. Dorothy Cotton interview in Raines, *My Soul Is Rested*, 434.

43. Green, "Discovering Hunger in America"; Duncan Lindsey, *The Welfare of Children*, 246; Milkis, *Great Society and the High Tide of Liberalism*.

44. Niemi Jr., "The Impact of Recent Civil Rights Laws"; Freeman, *Black Elite*; Matney and Johnson, "America's Black Population"; U.S. Dept. of Labor, "Perspectives on Working Women," 74.

45. Murray quoted in MacLean, *Freedom is Not Enough*, 121.

46. Anderson, "Equal Opportunity and Black Employment" in Wallace, ed., *Equal Employment Opportunity and the AT&T Case*, 170–200. See other articles in that volume, including Wallace, "Equal Employment Opportunity," 253–268, and Bergmann and King, "Diagnosing Discrimination," 49–110. See also Hacker, "Sex Stratification, Technology, and Organizational Change," in Kahn-Hut and others, eds., *Women and Work*, 248–266. On the relationship between education and mean income, see U.S. Dept. of Commerce "Money Income in 1976 of Families and Persons in the United States," 196, 201. Niemi, "Impact of Recent Civil Rights Laws," provides data on the dis-

crepancy between black men's economic and occupational progress relative to white men on the one hand, and black women's progress relative to white women on the other. An analysis of racial discrimination in the South is provided by Ray Marshall, "Black Employment in the South," in Wallace and LaMond, eds., *Women, Minorities, and Employment Discrimination*, 57–81.

47. Campbell, "Black Executives and Corporate Stress," 37; Allen, "Family Roles, Occupational Status, and Achievement," 672; Gurin and Gaylord, "Educational and Occupational Goals of Men and Women at Black Colleges"; Epstein, "Positive Effects of the Multiple Negative"; Fields, "Factors Contributing to Nontraditional Career Choices of Black Female College Graduates"; Freeman, *Black Elite*. On the tracking of black female vocational high school students into "the lowest paying, least desirable, and most marginal work" in New York City, see Baker, "Women in Blue Collar and Service Occupations," in Stromberg and Harkess, eds., *Women Working*, 339–376.

48. Lewis quoted in MacLean, *Freedom is Not Enough*, 81.

49. Sledge quoted in Conway, *Rise Gonna Rise*, 106–113. See also the description of the mill supervisor who was "rebish"—"Hateful to black people" (p. 104).

50. Apprentice quoted in Walshok, "Occupational Values and Family Roles," in Feinstein, ed., *Working Women and Families*, 79; Tucker quoted in Dill, "Across the Barriers of Race and Class," 130. See also Feldberg and Glenn, "Technology and Work Degradation," in *Machina Ex Dea*, 59–78. For histories of black women in blue collar jobs, see Walshok, *Blue Collar Women*, 128–132.

51. Joan Griffin quoted in Jupiter, "Without Fear," 64. On black women workers in the public sector, see Wallace, *Black Women in the Labor Force*, 53–55; Freeman, *Black Elite*, 151–173.

52. Educational figures: U.S. Dept. of Commerce, "The Social and Economic Status of the Black Population in the United States," 95; supportive families: Billingsley, *Black Families in White America*; McAdoo, "Patterns of Upward Mobility in Black Families" in *Black Families*; Anderson, "Equal Opportunity and Black Employment" in Wallace, ed., *Equal Employment Opportunity and the AT&T Case*, 195; Sledge quoted in Conway, *Rise Gonna Rise*, 109; Green, *Race on the Line*, 211–212.

53. Woody, *Black Women in the Workplace*, 71–91; Green, *Race on the Line*, 217; McLean, *Freedom is Not Enough*, 79–80; Fosu, "Occupational Mobility of Black Women"; Donahue III and Heckman, "Continuous Versus Episodic Change"; Frederickson, "Four Decades of Change," in Green, ed., *Workers' Struggles, Past and Present*, 74; Heckman and Payner, "Determining the Impact of Federal Antidiscrimination Policy on the Economic Status of Blacks"; Jones, *American Work*, 337–369; Minchin, *Hiring the Black Worker*.

54. "enough white": Green, *Race on the Line*, 213; Jones, *American Work*, 356–373; Brown quoted in Moore, *Women in the Mines*, 131.

55. "a bunch of": Mittelstadt, *From Welfare to Workfare*, 142; Orleck, *Storming Caesars Palace*; "Vegas Protest Draws 1,000," *Washington Post*, March 7, 1971.

56. "Because living": Orleck, "I Got to Dreamin': An Interview with Ruby Duncan," in Jetter, Orleck and Taylor, eds., *The Politics of Motherhood*, 124; Kotz and Kotz, *A Passion for Equality*.

57. Mittelstadt, From Welfare to Workfare, 69; Childers, "A Spontaneous Welfare Rights Protest by Politically Inactive Mothers," in Jetter, Orleck, and Taylor, eds., *Politics of Motherhood*, 100; Childers, *Welfare Brat*.

58. "Perspectives on Working Women," 66, 74; Matney and Johnson, "America's Black Population," 11–15; Bell, "Why Participation Rates"; Douglas, "Black Working Women." Landry and Jendrek, "The Employment of Wives in Middle-Class Black Families." See also Bell, "Participation Rates"; Aldridge, "Black Women in the Economic Marketplace"; Beckett, "Working Wives"; Wallace, *Black Women in the Labor Force*; Almquist and Wehrle-Einhorn, "The Doubly Disadvantaged,"

in Stromberg and Harkess, eds., *Women Working*, 63–88; Carroll, "Three's a Crowd," in Rossi and Calderwood, eds., *Academic Women On the Move*, 173–185; Lewis, "Response to Inequality."

59. On black women's attitudes toward wage labor and household work, see Gump, "A Comparative Analysis of Black and White Women's Sex-Role Attitudes"; Malson, "Black Women's Sex Role Integration and Behavior."

60. Matney and Johnson, "America's Black Population," 16–20; Click, "A Demographic Picture of Black Families," in McAdoo, ed., *Black Families*, 106–126; McEaddy, "Women Who Head Families"; Johnson, "Women Who Head Families." See also Nielsen and Endo, "Marital Status and Socioeconomic Status."

61. Matney and Johnson, "America's Black Population," 9, 20; Niemi, "Impact of Recent Civil Rights Laws"; Bernard, *Marriage and the Family Among Negroes*, 21; Jackson, "But Where are the Men?"; Guttentag and Secord, "Sex Roles and Family Among Black Americans," *Too Many Women?*, 199–230; Wallace, *Pathways to Work*.

62. "unifying . . . another": quoted in McLean, *Freedom Is Not Enough*, 150; Sugrue, *Sweet Land of Liberty*, 366; White, *Too Heavy a Load*, 232; Piven and Cloward, *Regulating the Poor*, 183–348, 350–366; Levitan, "Work and Welfare in the 1970s"; West, *National Welfare Rights Movement*, 231; Hertz, "The Politics of the Welfare Mothers Movement"; Kotz and Kotz, *A Passion for Equality*.

63. West, *National Welfare Rights Movement*, 257; Tillmon, "Welfare Is a Women's Issue," in Perrucci and Targ, eds., *Marriage and the Family*, 109, 111, 115; U.S. Commission on Civil Rights, "Women and Poverty," 19; Barbara Dugan quoted in Elman, *The Poorhouse State*, 119; Cohen, *Consumer's Republic*, 378–380. See also Valentine, "Women on Welfare," and Gilkes, "From Slavery to Social Welfare" in Swerdlow and Lessinger, eds., *Class, Race, and Sex*, 276–300; Carol Glassman, "Women and the Welfare System," in Morgan, ed., *Sisterhood is Powerful*, 102–115.

64. U.S. Commission on Civil Rights, "Women and Poverty," 26–33; Smith and others, "WIN, Work, and Welfare"; Pearce, "Women, Work, and Welfare," in Feinstein, ed., *Working Women and Families*, 103–124; Levitan, "Work and Welfare in the 1970s," 71–97.

65. Patricia Cayo Sexton, "Women and Work," United States Department of Labor R&D Monograph (1977), 51; Levitan, "Work and Welfare in the 1970s"; Mary Fish, "Income Inequality and Employment," United States Department of Labor R&D Monograph (1978). See also Molt, "Racial Differences in Female Labor Force Participation," in Feinstein, ed., *Working Women and Families*, 85–101.

66. U.S. Commission on Civil Rights, "Women and Poverty," 18; Elman, *Poorhouse State*, 18–19; Piven and Cloward, *Regulating the Poor*, 285–348; Newman and others, *Protest, Politics, and Prosperity*, 261–262.

67. Stack, *All Our Kin*, 32–44. See also Stack, "The Kindred of Viola Jackson," in Whitten and Szwed, eds., *Afro-American Anthropology*, 303–312; Manns, "Support Systems of Significant Others in Black Families," in McAdoo, ed., *Black Families*, 238–251; Hill, *The Strengths of Black Families*; Franklin, "Black Family Life-Styles," in Swerdlow and Lessinger, eds., *Class, Race, and Sex*, 189–199.

68. Interview with Charleszetta Waddles, BWOHP, 3, 10.

69. Gilkes, "Holding Back the Ocean With a Broom," in Rodgers-Rose, ed., *The Black Woman*, 217–232; Long and Hansen, "Trends in Return Migration to the South"; Sawers and Tabb, eds., *Sunbelt/Snowbelt*. According to Robert B. Hill, "These reverse migration patterns to the South strongly contradict the popular misconception that the primary reason blacks migrated to the North was to get welfare and not jobs." Hill, "The Economic Status of Black Families," 26; Kuttner, "The Declining Middle," 60.

70. Sugrue, *Sweet Land of Liberty*, 202, 395, 449–450, 493; "The social worker": ibid., 394.

71. Ibid., 395; Dougherty, "'That's When We Were Marching for Jobs,'" 121–141.

72. Boesal and Rossi, eds., *Cities Under Siege*; Geschwender, "Civil Rights Protest and Riots"; National Advisory Commission, *Report of the National Advisory Commission on Civil Disorders*; Oberschall, *Social Conflict and Social Movements*, 212; Jackson, *Soledad Brother*, 167.

73. "hastily": Current quoted in Trausch and Jordan, "The March: Assessing Gains Since '63," *The Boston Globe*, August 27, 1983; "Biologically": Wilkins quoted in McLean, *Freedom Is Not Enough*, 122–123; White, *Too Heavy a Load*, 221.

74. Combahee River Collective, "Black Feminist Statement," in Hull, Scott, and Smith, eds., *All the Women Are White, All the Blacks Are Men*, 19; Canaan, "Brownness," in Moraga and Anzaldúa, eds., *This Bridge Called My Back*, 236; Harris, "From the Kennedy Commission to the Combahee Collective," in Collier-Thomas and Franklin, eds., *Sisters in the Struggle*.

75. "with Fannie Lou Hamer": in Breitman, ed., *Malcolm X Speaks*, 117, 124. See also "'Ironies of the Saint': Malcolm X, Black Women, and the Price of Protection," in Collier-Thomas and Franklin, eds., *Sisters in the Struggle*.

76. Evans, *Personal Politics*, 81; Carson, *In Struggle*, 137, 163, 191, 198, 227; Newton, *Revolutionary Suicide*, 26; "Black Power Program," in Meier, Rudwick, and Broderick, eds., *Black Protest Thought*, 506; Brown, *Die Nigger Die!* 26–27, 42. See also Matthews, "'No One Ever Asks What a Man's Role in the Revolution Is,'" in Collier-Thomas and Franklin, eds., *Sisters in the Struggle*. For a concise statement defining the goals of the Black Power movement, see Carmichael and Hamilton, *Black Power*.

77. Moynihan, *The Negro Family*, 42–43, 45; Etzkowitz and Schaflander, *Ghetto Crisis*, 16; Rainwater and Yancey, *The Moynihan Report and the Politics of Controversy*, 423; Giddings, *When and Where I Enter*, 325–335.

78. Carmichael, "Notes and Comment" (1966 SNCC Position Paper) in Bracey Jr., Meier, and Rudwick, eds., *Black Nationalism in America*, 472. Black Muslims believed that black women, tainted by the lust of white men as well as by the "predatory sex ethos of the lower class [black] community," needed to be "elevated" and "purified," respected and protected within the all-encompassing fold of the Nation of Islam. See prescriptions for their "journey from shame" in "Minister Malcolm X . . . ," in Bracey, Meier, and Rudwick, eds., *Black Nationalism*, 415–416; Essien-Udom, *Black Nationalism*, 86–88. See, for example, the photos of women in the Essien-Udom volume. They are wearing ankle-length, white chador-like garments, and they remain strictly segregated from men during worship services. The male ghetto culture as it related to the Black Power movement is revealed in Newton, *Revolutionary Suicide*; Brown, *Die Nigger Die!*; Lester, *Look Out Whitey*; Seale, *Seize the Time*; Cleaver, *Soul on Ice*; Scheer, ed., *Eldridge Cleaver: Post-Prison Writings and Speeches*.

79. Reid, *"Together" Black Women*, 344; Scheer, ed., *Eldridge Cleaver*: xxxii; Seale, *Seize the Time*, 259. See Davis, *Angela Davis*, and Aptheker, *The Morning Breaks*.

80. See, for example, Joseph, *Waiting 'Til the Midnight Hour*.

81. Wigginton and Thrasher, "To Make the World We Want," 27; interview with Juanita Jewel Craft, BWOHP, 8–9.

82. Shakur, "Women in Prison: How We Are," 56; "Black Scholar Interview: Kathleen Cleaver," 56. On the role of women in the Party, including its "women's auxiliary," see Seale, *Seize the Time*, 62, 393–403; Cleaver, "The Courage to Kill," in Scheer, ed., *Eldridge Cleaver*, 26; Shakur, *Assata*.

83. Murray, "Jim Crow and Jane Crow," in Lerner, ed., *Black Women*, 594; Washington, "We Started From Different Ends of the Spectrum," reprinted in Evans, *Personal Politics*, 238–240; Rothschild, *A Case of Black and White*, 138; Beale, "Slave of a Slave No More," 16; "Black Scholar Inter-

view: Kathleen Cleaver," 147–148; Davis, *An Autobiography*, 181; Grant, "Black Women and the Church," in Hull, Scott, and Smith, eds., *All the Women Are White, All the Blacks Are Men*, 141; "considered": Brown quoted in White, *Too Heavy a Load*, 220; Brown, *A Taste of Power*; McLean, *Freedom Is Not Enough*, 219–220; Cleaver, "Woman, Power, and Revolution," in Cleaver and Katsiafiacas, eds., *Liberation, Imagination, and the Black Panther Party*, 123–127. See also Wallace, *Black Macho and the Myth of the Superwoman*, and "A Black Feminist's Search for Sisterhood," in Hull, Scott, and Smith, eds., *All the Women Are White, All the Blacks Are Men*, 5–12. Matthews, "'No One Ever Asks What a Man's Role in the Revolution Is,'" in Collier-Thomas and Franklin, eds., *Sisters in the Struggle*.

84. Morrison, "What the Black Woman Thinks About Women's Lib," 63; Walker, "In Search of Our Mothers' Gardens"; Smart-Grosvenor, "The Kitchen Crisis," in Bambara, ed., *The Black Woman*, 119–123; Gossett, "billie lives! billie lives!" in Moraga and Anzaldúa, eds., *This Bridge Called My Back*, 109–112.

85. Murray quoted in Rainwater and Yancey, *Moynihan Report*, 185; "Measley check": Reid, *"Together" Black Women*, 60; woman quoted in Ladner, *Tomorrow's Tomorrow*, 41, 46; Hare and Hare, "Black Women 1970," 66; "Our plainer gifts": Walker, "In Search of Our Mothers' Gardens," 62. See also Jackson, "But Where Are the Men?" 30–41; Scott, "Debunking Sapphire," in Hull, Scott, and Smith, eds., *All the Women Are White, All the Blacks Are Men*, 85–92; Nelson, "Myths About Black Women Workers in Modern America"; Sizemore, "Sexism and the Black Male."

86. Carroll, "Three's a Crowd," in Rossi and Calderwood, eds., *Academic Women On the Move*, 181; White interview in Gwaltney, *Drylongso*, 148; Linda M. LaRue, "Black Liberation and Women's Lib," *Trans-Action* 8 (November-December 1970):60. See also Giddings, *When and Where I Enter*, 299–324.

87. Domestic quoted in Gwaltney, *Drylongso*, 171; Lorde, "The Master's Tools Will Never Dismantle the Master's House," in Moraga and Anzaldúa, *This Bridge Called My Back*, 100; Lewis, "Response to Inequality," 346; Joseph and Lewis, *Common Differences*, 21. See also LaRue, "Black Liberation and Women's Lib," 61; Stokes, "Black Woman to Black Man," 17; Morrison, "What the Black Woman Thinks," 64. Furthermore, the notion that family life and the gendered division of household labor constituted the source of women's oppression found little support among black feminists regardless of their political views. As the locus of resistance against racism, the institution of the black family needed reinforcement, not dismantlement: "that's the mission" (Joseph and Lewis, *Common Differences*, 212).

88. Reagon, "My Black Mothers and Sisters," 96; Joseph and Lewis, *Common Differences*, 29; Smith, "Notes for Yet Another Paper on Black Feminism, Or Will the Real Enemy Please Stand Up?" 127; hooks, *Ain't I a Woman?*, 113. See also Sanders, "Dear Black Man," in Bambara, ed., *Black Woman*, 73–79.

89. Smith and Smith, "Across the Kitchen Table," in Moraga and Anzaldúa, eds., *This Bridge Called My Back*, 115; Stone, "The Limitation of Reformist Feminism," and Anderson and Mealy, "Who Originated the Crisis? A Historical Perspective," 27, 40–44; Higginbotham, "African-American Women's History and the Metalanguage of Race."

90. Guy-Sheftall, "Commitment: Toni Cade Bambara," in Bell, Parker, and Guy-Sheftall, eds., *Sturdy Black Bridges*, 235; Ladner, *Tomorrow's Tomorrow*; Hine, "To Be Gifted, Female, and Black"; Walker, "In Search of Our Mothers' Gardens," 62; Shakur, "Women in Prison," 55; Reagon, "My Black Mothers and Sisters," 85–86; Nancy White and May Anna Madison quoted in Gwaltney, *Drylongso*, 149, 174. See the material published by the National Project on Black Women's Health Issues (Atlanta, GA), including "Health Factsheet on Black Women" (Winter 1983) and also *Network News* (newsletter of the National Women's Health Network) (May–June 1983); Higgin-

botham, "Two Representative Issues in Contemporary Sociological Work on Black Women," and Smith, "Black Women's Health," in Hull, Scott, and Smith, eds., *All the Women Are White, All the Blacks Are Men*, 93–98, 103–114.

91. Golden, "Black Women's Liberation," 36–37, 75–76, 86; Beale, "Slave of a Slave No More," 22; Joseph and Lewis, *Common Differences*, 33–34; Lewis, "Response to Inequality," 339–347; West, *National Welfare Rights Movement*, 242–243; Eichelberger, "Voices of Black Feminism"; "Despite a sizable number": Wallace, "Black Feminist's Search," in Hull, Scott, and Smith, eds., *All the Women Are White, All the Blacks Are Men*, 12.

92. Troger, "The Coalition of Labor-Union Women," in Baxandall, Gordon, and Reverby, eds., *America's Working Women*, 390–399; Joseph and Lewis, *Common Differences*, 23, 33; Lewis, "Response to Inequality," 351, 353. See also Stimpson, "'Thy Neighbor's Wife, Thy Neighbor's Servants,'" in Gornick and Moran, eds., *Woman in Sexist Society*, 452–479.

93. See, for example, Angelou, *I Know Why the Caged Bird Sings*; "Each black male": Chisholm, "Race, Revolution and Women," 20; Chisholm, *Unbought and Unbossed*; Davis, *Autobiography*; Sherman, *Barbara Jordan*; King, *My Life With Martin Luther King, Jr.*; Morrison, *Song of Solomon*; Walker, *The Color Purple*.

94. Gossett, "who told you any body wants to hear from you? you ain't nothing but a black woman!" in Moraga and Anzaldúa, *This Bridge Called My Back*, 175–176.

CHAPTER 9

1. For the address, see http://www.timesonline.co.uk/tol/news/politics/article6025234.ece. See also http://topics.nytimes.com/topics/reference/timestopics/people/o/michelle_obama/index .html; Swarns, "A Human Bridge to the Have-Nots in Washington," *New York Times*, May 15, 2009.

2. Ibid.

3. Murray, "A Family Free Rooted in American Soil," *Washington Post*, Oct. 2, 2008; Kantor, "A Portrait of Change: Nation's Many Faces in Extended First Family," *New York Times*, Jan. 20, 2009.

4. "She has": Swarns, "An In-Law is Finding Work to Her Liking," *New York Times*, May 3, 2009; Helman, "Holding Down the Obama Family Fort: 'Grandma' Makes the Race Possible," *Boston Globe*, March 30, 2008.

5. Thompson, "The Ties that Align: Administration's Black Women Form a Strong Sisterhood," *Washington Post*, March 18, 2009.

6. Williams, "Mrs. Obama Meets Mrs. Windsor," 9; White, *Ar'n't I a Woman?*

7. http://www.gallup.com/poll/111817/Americans-See-Obama-Election-Race-Relations-Milestone.aspx; Saulny, "In Obama Era, Voices Reflect Rising Sense of Racial Optimism," *New York Times*, May 3, 2009.

8. Obama, *The Audacity of Hope*, 325–353.

9. Katz, Stern, and Fader, "New African American Inequality," 79–86; Self, *American Babylon*, 172–175.

10. Shull, *A Kinder, Gentler Racism?*; Carnoy, *Faded Dreams*; Hacker, *Two Nations*.

11. Johnson, "Women Who Head Families"; Nielsen and Endo, "Marital Status and Socioeconomic Status"; Hall, "The Long Civil Rights Movement"; Sugrue, *Sweet Land of Liberty*, 524.

12. Conyers, "Insensitive to Blacks' Health," *New York Times*, Dec. 28, 1983; Caldwell, "Baby Mortality Rate—The Gap Widens," *Boston Globe*, Jan. 8, 1984. The latter article summarizes a study conducted by the Food Research and Action Center in Washington, D.C.; Coalition on Women and the Budget, "Inequality of Sacrifice."

13. Sugrue, *Sweet Land of Liberty*, 518–530; Middletstadt, *From Welfare to Workfare*, 171–172.

14. Foner, *Women and the American Labor Movement*, 440–460; Cobble, *The Other Women's Movement*, 32, 201–206; 219; Canty quoted in Mosle, "Letter from Las Vegas: How the Maids Fought Back," 155; "collective bargaining": Donald Dotson quoted in Blau, *The Visible Poor*, 40–41.

15. Jones, *American Work*, 259–265; Katznelson, *When Affirmative Action Was White*.

16. Katz, Stern, and Fader, "The New African American Inequality," 89–106; Ward, ed., *Women Workers*; Abu-Lughod, *New York, Chicago, Los Angeles*; Cowie, *Capital Moves*.

17. Cowie, *Capital Moves*; "only Asians": McGraw, "Cheep Labor," 13; Hossfeld, "Hiring Immigrant Women: Silicon Valley's 'Simple Formula,'" in Zinn and Dill, eds., *Women of Color in United States Society*, 65, 75–76, 80–81; "lots . . . job": Holmes, "In Iowa Town, Strains of Diversity," *New York Times*, Feb. 17, 1996.

18. Hall, "I Feel What Women Feel" [Interview with Donna Bazemore]; Kotlowitz, *There Are No Children Here*, 140–141; Applebome, "Tourism Enriches an Island Resort, But Hilton Head Blacks Feel Left Out," *New York Times*, Sept. 2, 1994.

19. U.S. Dept. of Labor, "Facts on Working Women: Black Women in the Labor Force," 4; "universalizing . . . dark": Jackson quoted in Dudley, *The End of the Line*, 145–146; "still . . . culprit": Holmes, "A Rights Leader Minimizes Racism as a Poverty Factor," *New York Times*, July 24, 1994; Jones, *The Dispossessed*.

20. "as a cushion": Kilborn, "More Women Take Low-Wage Jobs So That Their Families Can Get By," *New York Times*, March 13, 1994.

21. Eisenstein, "The Sexual Politics of the New Right," and *Radical Future of Liberal Feminism*. See, for example, Clymer, "Poll Sees Gain Equaling Loss If Democrats Pick a Woman," *New York Times*, April 30, 1984, and the results of a *Woman's Day* poll (based on a sample of responses from 115,000 women) summarized in "A Women's Influence," *Woman's Day*, February 7, 1984, 65–70.

22. U.S. Equal Employment Opportunity Commission, *Job Patterns for Minorities and Women in Private Industry*; U.S. Dept. of Commerce, *Statistical Abstract of the United States* (1993), 400; U.S. Commission on Civil Rights, "Economic Status of Black Women (1990), 138; U. S. Dept of Commerce, "Poverty in the United States: 1991," 70–71; Schwarz and Volgy, *Thirty Million Working Poor*, 74; Badgett, "Rising Black Unemployment"; Osterman, "Gains from Growth?" in Jencks and Peterson, eds., *The Urban Underclass*, 122–134; Stein, "The Sobering Reality of America's Hiring Binge," *Boston Globe*, Sept. 4, 1994; Pear, "Poverty in U.S. Grew Faster Than Population Last Year," *New York Times*, October 5, 1993; U. S. Department of Labor, "Facts on Working Women: Earnings Differences Between Men and Women" (Dec. 1993).

23. Kirschenman and Neckerman, "'We'd Love to Hire Them, But . . . ,'" in Jencks and Peterson, eds., *The Urban Underclass*, 203–232.

24. Tienda and Stier, "Joblessness and Shiftlessness," in Jencks and Peterson, eds., *The Urban Underclass*, 135–154; Turner quoted in Rank, *Living on the Edge*, 122. On the condemnation of black women AFDC recipients in particular, see Kaus, *The End of Equality*.

25. Edin, "Single Mothers and Absent Fathers"; Amott, "Black Women and AFDC," in Gordon, ed., *Women, the State, and Welfare*, 280–298; DeParle, "The Clinton Welfare Bill Begins Trek in Congress," *New York Times*, July 15, 1994.

26. Massey and Denton, *American Apartheid*, 77; Children's Defense Fund, *The State of America's Children Yearbook, 1994*, 78; "persistence": West, *Race Matters*, 155; Wilson, *The Truly Disadvantaged*.

27. Reese, *Backlash Against Welfare Mothers*; Sugrue, *Sweet Land of Liberty*, 531–535.

28. See "Policy Basics: An Introduction to TANF," Center on Budget and Policy Priorities (revised March 19, 2009): http://www.cbpp.org/cms/index.cfm?fa=view&id=936; Hays, *Flat Broke with Children*.

29. Parrott and Sherman, "TANF at 10: Program Results are More Mixed than Often Understood," Center on Budget and Policy Priorities, http://www.centeronbudget.org/experts/index .cfm?fa=view&id=37; Hays, *Flat Broke with Children*.

30. "I mean": quoted in Hays, *Flat Broke with Children*, 201–202. See also Jencks, "What Happened to Welfare"; Blank and Hoskins, eds., *The New World of Welfare*.

31. Parrott and Sherman, "TANF at 10"; "Disappeared": DeParle, *American Dream*, 185.

32. DeParle, *American Dream*; "It's very": Reese, *Backlash Against Welfare*, 15–16; Alfred, "Welfare Reform and Black Women's Economic Development"; Blum and Deussen, "Negotiating Independent Motherhood."

33. Green-Brown quoted in Kozol, *Savage Inequalities*, 137–145; Cantor and Brenzel, "Urban Education and the 'Truly Disadvantaged,'" in Katz, ed., *The 'Underclass' Debate*, 366–402.

34. U.S. Dept. of Commerce, *Statistical Abstract of the United States* (1993), 115–116; U.S. Dept. of Health and Human Services, "Health United States" (1993), 49.

35. Abraham, *Mama Might Be Better Off Dead*, 2, 150–151.

36. Lillie-Blanton and others, "Latina and African-American Women"; Blendon and others, "Access to Medical Care for Black and White Americans"; Greenberg, "Urban/Rural Differences in Behavioral Risk Factors for Chronic Diseases"; Duelberg, "Preventive Health Behavior Among Black and White Women"; Quaye, "The Health Care Status of African Americans"; Jones, "American Others."

37. "kill . . . stepping": Bates, "The Kill Line," 23; Belgrave, "The Effects of Race Differences in Work History, Work Attitudes, Economic Resources, and Health on Women's Retirement." See also Cobb, *Most Southern Place on Earth*, 329–333; "Catfish Growers Worry They'll Go Belly Up With Current Supply," *Los Angeles Times*, Sept. 13, 1992; "Fish Farms Fall Prey to Excess: Economic Promise Ebbs with Market," *Washington Post*, Aug. 22, 1992.

38. Nelson, *Volunteer Slavery*, 18, 29, 54, 56, 62, 169–170.

39. Ibid., 63, 75, 240, 241.

40. Ibid., 77.

41. Obama, *Audacity of Hope*, 325–353.

42. "Strange name": quoted in White, *Too Heavy a Load*, 258; Guinier, *Tyranny of the Majority*; Bolick, "Clinton's Quota Queens," *Wall Street Journal*, April 30, 1993.

43. "Certainly": "Working and Coexisting," *Boston Globe*, May 24, 1995; "Have you": Collins, "Blacks on the Bubble," 442.

44. "With certain": quoted in Jones and Gooden, *Shifting*, 67 (see also appendix); Kelley, "Kickin Reality, Kickin Ballistics," *Race Rebels*, 183–228.

45. "race watch": Benjamin, *The Black Elite*, 104; Cose, *Rage of a Privileged Class*; "what": Evelyn Lewis quoted in Williams, "Notes from a Small World," 90.

46. "suddenly . . . magnetic": duCille, "The Occult of True Black Womanhood"; "daily": Edelman, *The Measure of Our Success*, 23; Carter, *Reflections of an Affirmative Action Baby*, 32–33; Lawrence-Lightfoot, *I've Known Rivers*; Gaiter, "The Revolt of the Black Bourgeoisie," *New York Times Magazine*, June 26, 1994; Johnson, "'All I'm Askin' is a Little Respect'"; Cose, *The Rage of a Privileged Class* (see pp. 56 and 167 for evidence of the "exhaustion" suffered by middle-class blacks on the job).

47. Gaillard and Walker quoted in "Work vs. Family, Complicated by Race," *New York Times*, Feb. 9, 2006.

48. Luckett quoted in ibid.; Parker, *I'm Every Woman*.

49. Fant quoted in Gill, *Beauty Shop Politics*, 129; Washington, *Medical Apartheid*.

50. Holmes, "In Fighting Racism, Is Sexism Ignored?" Week in Review, *New York Times*, Sept. 11, 1994; Benjamin, *The Black Elite*. For evidence of persistent discrimination against black professionals in a major U.S. industry, see Elliott, "A Lawyer's Call for a Greater Black Presence in Agencies," *New York Times*, Jan. 9, 2009.

51. Nelson, *Volunteer Slavery*, 180.

52. U.S. Equal Employment Opportunity Commission, *Job Patterns for Minorities and Women in Private Industry* (1991); U.S. Dept. of Commerce, *Statistical Abstract of the United States* (1993), 400; U.S. Commission on Civil Rights, "The Economic Status of Black Women" (Oct. 1990), 138; U.S. Department of Commerce, "Poverty in the United States: 1991."

53. Crenshaw, "Whose Story Is It, Anyway?" in Morrison, ed., *Race-ing Justice, En-Gendering Power*, 402.

54. Spencer, "Trends of Opposition to Multiculturalism," 3; Higginbotham, "African-American Women's History and the Metalanguage of Race," 274; Wright, "Annals of Politics." See also Fields, "Slavery, Race and Ideology in the United States of America"; Collins, "Setting Our Own Agenda."

55. Roediger, *Towards the Abolition of Whiteness*; Skocpol, "The New Urban Poverty and U.S. Social Policy"; hooks, *Yearning*, 27.

56. Walker, "Oprah Winfrey, the Tycoon," in Jalloh and Falola, eds., *Black Business and Economic Power*, 484–525.

57. Ibid.

58. "Immigrant Workers Find Support in a Growing Network of Assistance Centers," *New York Times*, April 23, 2006; "Blacks See Opening in AFL-CIO Leadership Fight," *New York Times*, July 15, 1995; Shipler, *The Working Poor*.

59. Gertner, "What Is a Living Wage?" *New York Times Magazine*, January 15, 2006; Clawson, *The Next Upsurge*; Shaw and Hill, "Raising the Minimum Wage," in King, ed., *Squaring Up*.

60. "Hotel Rooms Get Plusher, Adding to Maids' Injuries," *New York Times*, April 21, 2006.

61. Straus, "Making of the American School Crisis"; "Immigrants and the Economics of Hard Work," Week in Review, *New York Times*, April 3, 2006.

62. Carter-Lewis quoted in "Growing Unease for Some Blacks on Immigration," *New York Times*, May 4, 2006; "Immigrants Take to Streets in Show of Strength," *New York Times*, May 2, 2006.

63. Oliver and Shapiro, *Black Wealth/White Wealth*, 103.

64. See, for example, McGeehan and Warren, "Job Losses Show Wider Racial Gap in New York City: Blacks Hit Far Harder," *New York Times*, July 13, 2009; Herbert, "No Recovery in Sight," *New York Times*, June 27, 2009; Mahler, "GM, Detroit and the Fall of the Black Middle Class," *New York Times Magazine*, June 28, 2009; "Black and White Unemployment Over Time" (Jan. 2006), http://economistsview.typepad.com/economistsview/2006/01/black_and_white.html; "The Employment Situation: May 2009," Bureau of Labor Statistics News, June 5, 2009 (http://www.bls.gov/news.release/pdf/empsit.pdf).

65. Powell, "Suit Accuses Wells Fargo of Steering Blacks to Subprime Mortgages in Baltimore," *New York Times*, June 7, 2009; Powell and Roberts, "Minorities Hit Hardest as New York Foreclosures Rise," *New York Times*, May 16, 2009.

66. "I don't want . . . neighborhoods": Powell and Roberts, "Minorities Hit Hardest," *New York Times*, May 16, 2009.

67. "When you": Robinson quoted in Kantor, "A Portrait of Change" *New York Times*, Jan. 20, 2009; CNN poll May 2009: "Blacks in Survey Say Race Relations No Better With Obama," http://www.cnn.com/2009/POLITICS/06/25/obama.poll/?iref=hpmostpop.

68. Dyson, *Come Hell or High Water*; Bullard and Wright, eds., *Race, Place, and Environmental Justice After Hurricane Katrina*; Brinkley, *Great Deluge*.

BIBLIOGRAPHY

MANUSCRIPT COLLECTIONS

Howard University, Washington, D.C. Moorland-Spingarn Research Center. Works Progress Administration File. Archive Collection.

Library of Congress, Washington, D.C. Federal Writers Project, Negro Folklore Division, Archive of Folk Song. Manuscript Division.

National Archives, Washington, D.C. Southern Claims Commission Approved Claims, 1871–1880: Georgia. Records of the U.S. General Accounting Office. Record Group 217 (M1658).

National Archives, Washington, D.C. U.S. Bureau of Refugees, Freedmen, and Abandoned Lands. Record Group 105. (Portions available on microfilm.)

National Archives, Washington, D.C. U.S. Department of Commerce, Bureau of the Census. Manuscript Population Schedules for the Ninth, Tenth, and Twelfth Censuses (1870, 1880, and 1900). (Available on microfilm.)

National Archives, Washington, D.C. U.S. Department of Labor Archives, Women's Bureau Collection. Record Group 86.

National Archives, Washington, D.C. Works Progress Administration. Record Group 69.

Radcliffe College. Cambridge, MA. Schlesinger Library. Black Women Oral History Project.

University of Michigan. Ann Arbor, MI. Institute of Labor and Industrial Relations. Twentieth Century Trade Union Woman Project. Program on Women and Work.

Wayne State University. Detroit, MI. Walter P. Reuther Library, Archives of Labor and Urban Affairs. United Auto Workers Collection.

PRIMARY SOURCES

NEWSPAPERS AND MAGAZINES

Baltimore Afro-American
Boston Globe
Buffalo Courier-Express
Chicago Defender
Christian Science Monitor
Detroit News
Ebony
Los Angeles Times
New York Daily News

New York Times
Wall Street Journal
Washington Post

U.S. GOVERNMENT PUBLICATIONS

Benham, Elisabeth D. "The Woman Wage Earner: Her Situation Today." U.S. Department of Labor, Women's Bureau. Bulletin no. 172 (1939).

Blood, Kathryn. "Negro Women War Workers." U.S. Department of Labor, Women's Bureau. Bulletin no. 205 (1945).

Bradley, Frances, and M. A. Williamson. *Rural Children in Selected Counties of North Carolina*. U.S. Department of Labor, Children's Bureau. Rural Child Welfare Series no. 2 (Publication no. 33). Washington, D.C.: Government Printing Office, 1918.

Brown, Jean Collier. "The Negro Woman Worker." U.S. Department of Labor, Women's Bureau. Bulletin no. 165 (1938).

Byrne, Harriet A. "Child Labor in Representative Tobacco-Growing Areas." U.S. Department of Labor, Children's Bureau. Publication no. 155. Washington, D.C.: Government Printing Office, 1926.

Byrne, Harriet A., and Cecile Hillyer. "Unattached Women on Relief in Chicago, 1937." U.S. Department of Labor, Women's Bureau. Bulletin no. 158 (1938).

DuBois, W. E. B. "The Negroes of Farmville, Virginia: A Social Study." U.S. Department of Labor. Bulletin no. 14 (January 1898): 13.

———. "The Negro in the Black Belt: Some Social Sketches." U.S. Department of Labor. Bulletin no. 22 (May 1899): 401–417.

Erickson, Ethel. "Employment Conditions in Beauty Shops: A Study of Four Cities." U.S. Department of Labor, Women's Bureau. Bulletin no. 133 (1935).

Fish, Mary. "Income Inequality and Employment." U.S. Department of Labor R&D Monograph (1978).

Haynes, George E. *The Negro at Work During the World War and Reconstruction: Statistics, Problems, and Policies Related to the Greater Inclusion of Negro Wage Earners in American Industry and Agriculture*. U.S. Department of Labor, Division of Negro Economics. Washington, D.C.: Government Printing Office, 1921.

Hill, Joseph A. *Women in Gainful Occupations, 1870–1920*. U.S. Department of Commerce, Bureau of the Census Monograph. Washington, D.C.: Government Printing Office, 1929.

Laws, J. Bradford. "The Negroes of Cinclare Central Factory and Calumet Plantation, Louisiana." U.S. Bureau of Labor Statistics. Bulletin no. 37 (November 1901): 116–117.

Manning, Caroline. "Hours and Earnings in Tobacco Stemmeries." U.S. Department of Labor, Women's Bureau. Bulletin no. 127 (1934).

Matney, William C. and Dwight L. Johnson. "America's Black Population: 1970 to 1982: A Statistical View." U.S. Department of Commerce, Bureau of the Census Special Publication. P10/POP–83–1. Washington, D.C.: Government Printing Office, 1983.

Moynihan, Daniel Patrick. *The Negro Family: The Case for National Action*. Office of Policy Planning and Research, U.S. Department of Labor. Washington, D.C.: Government Printing Office, 1965.

National Advisory Commission on Civil Disorders. *Report of the National Advisory Commission on Civil Disorders*. New York: Bantam Books, 1968.

Official Records of the Union and Confederate Navies in the War of the Rebellion. 30 vols. Washington D.C.: Government Printing Office, 1894–1922.

Pidgeon, Mary Elizabeth. "The Employment of Women in Slaughtering and Meat Packing." U.S. Department of Labor, Women's Bureau. Bulletin no. 88 (1932).

———. "Employed Women Under N.R.A. Codes." U.S. Department of Labor, Women's Bureau. Bulletin no. 130 (1935).

President's Committee on Civil Rights. *To Secure These Rights: The Report of the President's Committee on Civil Rights.* Washington, D.C.: Government Printing Office, 1947.

Price, Daniel O. *Changing Characteristics of the Negro Population.* U.S. Bureau of the Census, 1960 Census Monograph. Washington, D.C.: Government Printing Office, 1969.

Robinson, Mary V. "Domestic Workers and their Employment Relations." U.S. Department of Labor, Women's Bureau. Bulletin no. 39 (1924).

Sexton, Patricia Cayo. "Women and Work." U.S. Department of Labor R&D Monograph (1977).

Sullivan, Mary Loretta, and Bertha Blair. "Women in Texas Industries: Hours, Wages, Working Conditions, and Home Work." U.S. Department of Labor, Women's Bureau. Bulletin no. 126 (1936).

Sutherland, Arthur T. "The Migratory Labor Problem in Delaware." U.S. Department of Labor, Women's Bureau. Bulletin no. 185 (1941).

Testimony Taken by the Joint Select Committee to Inquire into the Condition of Affairs in the Late Insurrectionary States: South Carolina. Vol. 3. Washington, D.C.: Government Printing Office, 1872.

Thorn, William Taylor. "The Negroes of Litwalton, Virginia: A Social Study of the 'Oyster Negro.'" U.S. Department of Labor, Bureau of Labor Statistics. Bulletin no. 37 (November 1901): 115–170.

U.S. Commission on Civil Rights. "Women and Poverty." Staff Report. Washington, D.C.: Government Printing Office, 1974.

U.S. Commission on Civil Rights. "The Economic Status of Black Women: An Explanatory Investigation." Washington, D.C.: Government Printing Office, 1990.

U.S. Congress. 42nd Congress, 1st sess. *Testimony Before the Joint Select Committee to Inquire into the Affairs in the Late Insurrectionary States* (KKK Hearings). 13 vols. Washington, D.C.: Government Printing Office, 1871–72.

U.S. Congress. *Hearings Before the United States Commission on Civil Rights* held in New Orleans (1960 and 1961). Washington, D.C.: Government Printing Office, 1961.

U.S. Department of Commerce. Bureau of the Census. *Statistics of Women at Work.* Washington, D.C.: Government Printing Office, 1907.

U.S. Department of Commerce. Bureau of the Census. *Plantation Farming in the United States.* Washington, D.C.: Government Printing Office, 1916.

U.S. Department of Commerce. Bureau of the Census. *Statistics of Women at Work.* Washington, D.C.: Government Printing Office, 1916.

U.S. Department of Commerce. Bureau of the Census. *Negro Population, 1790–1915.* Washington, D.C.: Government Printing Office, 1918.

U.S. Department of Commerce. Bureau of the Census. *Negroes in the United States, 1920–1932.* Washington, D.C.: Government Printing Office, 1935.

U.S. Department of Commerce. Bureau of the Census. Sixteenth Census (1940), vol. 3, *The Labor Force.* Washington, D.C.: Government Printing Office, 1945.

U.S. Department of Commerce. Bureau of the Census. Sixteenth Census (1940), vol. 3, *Population: Differential Fertility 1940 and 1910; Women By Number of Children Ever Born.* Washington, D.C.: Government Printing Office, 1945.

U.S. Department of Commerce. Bureau of the Census. "Money Income in 1976 of Families and Persons in the United States." Series P-60, no. 114 (July 1978).

U.S. Department of Commerce. Bureau of the Census. "The Social and Economic Status of the Black Population in the United States: An Overview." Current Population Series P–23, no. 80 (1979).

U.S. Department of Commerce. Current Population Reports on Consumer Income. "Poverty in the United States: 1991." Series P-60, no. 181 (1992).

U.S. Department of Commerce. Bureau of the Census. *Statistical Abstract of the United States, 1993.* Washington, D.C.: Government Printing Office, 1993.

U.S. Department of Health and Human Services. "Health United States: 1993." Washington, D.C.: Government Printing Office, 1993.

U.S. Department of Labor. *Report on the Condition of Women and Children Wage Earners in the United States, Vol. 1: Cotton Textile Industry.* Washington, D.C.: Government Printing Office, 1913.

U.S. Department of Labor. *Report on the Condition of Women and Children Wage Earners in the United States, Vol. 18: Employment of Women and Children in Selected Industries.* Washington, D.C.: Government Printing Office, 1913.

U.S. Department of Labor. "Facts on Working Women: Earnings Differences Between Men and Women." no. 93–5 (Dec. 1993).

U.S. Department of Labor. Bureau of Labor Statistics. "Colored Women in Industry in Philadelphia." *Monthly Labor Review* 12 (May 8, 1921): 1046–1048.

U.S. Department of Labor. Bureau of Labor Statistics. "The Negro in Retail Trade." *Monthly Labor Review* 45 (Nov. 1937): 1136–1139.

U.S. Department of Labor. Bureau of Labor Statistics. "Perspectives on Working Women: A Databook." Bulletin no. 2080 (October 1980).

U.S. Department of Labor. Division of Negro Economics. *Negro Migration in 1916–1917.* Washington, D.C.: Government Printing Office, 1919.

U.S. Department of Labor. Women's Bureau. "Negro Women in Industry." Bulletin no. 20 (1922).

U.S. Department of Labor. Women's Bureau. "Negro Women in Industry in Fifteen States." Bulletin no. 70 (1929).

U.S. Department of Labor. Women's Bureau. "Women in Florida Industries." Bulletin no. 80 (1930).

U.S. Department of Labor. Women's Bureau. "Women at Work: A Century of Industrial Change." Bulletin no. 161 (1939).

U.S. Department of Labor. Women's Bureau. "Women Workers in Some Expanding Wartime Industries." Bulletin no. 197 (1943).

U.S. Department of Labor. Women's Bureau. "Community Household Employment Programs." Bulletin no. 221 (1948).

U.S. Department of Labor. Women's Bureau. "Handbook of Facts on Women Workers." Bulletin no. 225 (1948).

U.S. Department of Labor. Women's Bureau. "Handbook of Facts on Women Workers." Bulletin no. 242 (1952).

U.S. Department of Labor. Women's Bureau. "Changes in Women's Occupations, 1940–1950." Bulletin no. 253 (1954).

U.S. Department of Labor. Women's Bureau. "1954 Handbook on Women Workers." Bulletin no. 255 (1954).

U.S. Department of Labor. Women's Bureau. "Facts on Working Women: Black Women in the Labor Force." Bulletin no. 90–4 (June 1991).

U.S. Equal Employment Opportunity Commission. *Job Patterns for Minorities and Women in Private Industry.* Washington, D.C.: Office of Program Operations, 1991.

Woofter, Thomas Jackson, Jr. *Landlord and Tenant on the Cotton Plantation.* Works Progress Administration, Division of Social Research, Monograph V. Washington, D.C.: Government Printing Office, 1936.

BOOKS

Adams, Nehemiah. *South-Side View of Slavery: Three Months at the South, in 1854.* New York: Negro Universities Press, 1969. First published 1854.

Allen, Ruth Alice. *The Labor of Women in the Production of Cotton.* New York: Amo Press, 1975. First published 1931.

Allison, Robert J., ed. *The Interesting Narrative of the Life of Olaudah Equiano, Written by Himself.* Boston: Bedford Books, 1995.

Ames, Mary. *From a New England Woman's Diary in Dixie in 1865.* New York: Negro Universities Press, 1969. First published 1906.

Anderson, Marian. *My Lord, What a Morning: An Autobiography.* New York: Viking Press, 1956.

Andrews, Eliza F. *The War-Time Journal of a Georgia Girl, 1864–1865.* New York: D. Appleton and Co., 1908.

Andrews, Sidney. *The South Since the War: As Shown by Fourteen Weeks of Travel and Observation in Georgia and the Carolinas.* Boston: Ticknor and Fields, 1866.

Angelou, Maya. *Just Give Me A Cool Drink of Water 'Fore I Diiie.* New York: Random House, 1971.

———. *I Know Why the Caged Bird Sings.* New York: Bantam Books, 1971.

———. *Gather Together in My Name.* New York: Random House, 1974.

Baker, Ray Stannard. *Following the Color Line: An Account of Negro Citizenship in the American Democracy.* New York: Doubleday, Page, and Co., 1908.

Banks, Ann, ed. *First-Person America.* New York: Knopf, 1980.

Barbour, Floyd B., ed. *The Black Power Revolt: A Collection of Essays.* Boston: Extending Horizons, 1968.

Bates, Daisy. *The Long Shadow of Little Rock: A Memoir.* New York: David McKay, 1962.

Baxandall, Rosalyn, Linda Gordon, and Susan Reverby, eds. *America's Working Women: A Documentary History, 1600 to the Present.* New York: Random House, 1976.

Belfrage, Sally. *Freedom Summer.* New York: Viking Press, 1965.

Berlin, Ira, Joseph P. Reidy, and Leslie S. Rowland, eds. *A Documentary History of Emancipation, 1861–1867. Series II: The Black Military Experience.* New York: Cambridge University Press, 1982.

Blassingame, John W., ed. *Slave Testimony: Two Centuries of Letters, Speeches, and Autobiographies.* Baton Rouge: Louisiana State University Press, 1977.

Bontemps, Arna, and Jack Conroy. *They Seek A City.* New York: Doubleday, Doran and Co., 1945.

Botume, Elizabeth Hyde. *First Days Amongst the Contrabands.* New York: Arno Press, 1968. First published 1893.

Brady, Mathew. *Illustrated History of the Civil War*. New York: Fairfax Press, n.d. First published 1912.

Breitman, George, ed. *Malcolm X Speaks: Selected Speeches and Statements*. New York: Ballantine Books, 1965.

Brent, Linda, ed. *Incidents in the Life of a Slave Girl, Written by Herself*. Boston: Lydia Maria Child, 1861.

Brooks, Robert Preston. *The Agrarian Revolution in Georgia*. Madison, WI: University of Wisconsin Press, 1914.

Brown, Claude. *Manchild in the Promised Land*. New York: Macmillan, 1965.

Brown, Elaine. *A Taste of Power: A Black Women's Story*. New York: Pantheon Books, 1992.

Brown, H. Rap. *Die Nigger Die!* New York: Dial Press, 1969.

Brown, William Wells. *My Southern Home: Or, The South and Its People*. Boston: A. G. Brown, 1882.

Caldwell, Erskine. *You Have Seen Their Faces*. New York: Arno Press, 1975. First published 1937.

Campbell, George. *White and Black: The Outcome of a Visit to the United States*. London: Chatto and Windus, 1879.

Campbell, Helen. *Prisoners of Poverty*. Boston: Little, Brown, 1900.

Carmichael, Stokely, and Charles V. Hamilton. *Black Power: The Politics of Liberation in America*. New York: Random House, 1967.

Carter, Stephen L. *Reflections of an Affirmative Action Baby*. New York: Basic Books, 1991.

Cayton, Horace R., and George S. Mitchell. *Black Workers and the New Unions*. Chapel Hill: University of North Carolina Press, 1939.

Chicago Commission on Race Relations. *The Negro in Chicago: A Study of Race Relations and a Race Riot*. Chicago: University of Chicago Press, 1922.

Childers, Mary. *Welfare Brat: A Memoir*. New York: Bloomsbury Publishing, 2005.

Children's Defense Fund. *The State of America's Children Yearbook, 1994*. Washington, D.C.: Children's Defense Fund, 1994.

Clark, Septima Poinsette. *Echo in My Soul*. New York: E. P. Dutton, 1962.

Cleaver, Eldridge. *Soul on Ice*. New York: McGraw-Hill, 1968.

Clinton, Catherine, ed. *Reminiscences of My Life in Camp: An African American Woman's Civil War Memoir by Susie King Taylor*. Athens: University of Georgia Press, 2006. First published 1902.

Clowes, William Laird. *Black America: A Study of the Ex-Slave and His Late Master*. Westport, CT: Negro Universities Press, 1971. First published 1891.

Cluster, Dick, ed. *They Should Have Served that Cup of Coffee: Seven Radicals Remember the '60s*. Boston: South End Press, 1979.

Cooley, Rossa B. *Homes of the Freed*. New York: New Republic, 1926.

Cooper, Anna. *A Voice from the South, By a Black Woman of the South*. Xenia, OH: Aldine Printing House, 1892.

Copeland, Melvin Thomas. *The Cotton Manufacturing Industry of the United States*. Cambridge, MA: Harvard University Press, 1912.

Dabbs, Edith M. *Face of an Island: Leigh Richmond Miner's Photographs of St. Helena's Island*. New York: Grossman Publishers, 1971.

Dabney, Wendell P. *Maggie L. Walker and the Independent Order of Saint Luke: The Woman and Her Work*. Cincinnati: Dabney, 1927.

Davis, Angela. *Angela Davis: An Autobiography*. New York: Random House, 1974.

De Forest, John W. *A Union Officer in the Reconstruction.* New Haven, CT: Yale University Press, 1948.

Dennett, John Richard. *The South As It Is: 1865–1866.* Edited by Henry M. Christman. New York: Viking Press, 1965.

Dollard, John. *Caste and Class in a Southern Town.* New Haven, CT: Yale University Press, 1937.

Douglass, Frederick. *Life and Times of Frederick Douglass, Written by Himself.* Hartford, CT: Park Publishing Company, 1881.

———. *Narrative of the Life of Frederick Douglass, An American Slave, Written by Himself.* Edited by David W. Blight. Boston: Bedford Books, 1993.

Drake, St. Clair, and Horace R. Cayton. *Black Metropolis: A Study of Negro Life in a Northern City.* Vol. 2. New York: Harcourt, Brace and World, 1970. First published 1945.

DuBois, W. E. B. *The Souls of Black Folk: Essays and Sketches.* Chicago: A. C. McClurg, 1904.

Dutcher, Dean. *The Negro in Modern Industrial Society: An Analysis of Changes in the Occupations of Negro Workers, 1910–1920.* Lancaster, PA: Science Press, 1930.

Earle, Alice Morse. *Home Life in Colonial Days.* New York: Macmillan, 1935.

Epstein, Abraham. *The Negro Migrant in Pittsburgh.* New York: Amo Press, 1969. First published 1918.

Evans, Walker. *Walker Evans at Work.* New York: Harper & Row, 1982.

Faulkner, Audrey Olsen, Marcel A. Heisel, Wendell Holbrook, and Shirley Geismer. *When I Was Comin' Up: An Oral History of Aged Blacks.* Hamden, CT: Archon Books, 1982.

Federal Writers' Project. *These Are Our Lives: As Told by the People and Written by Members of the Federal Writers' Project of the Works Progress Administration in North Carolina, Tennessee, and Georgia.* New York: W. W. Norton, 1975. First published 1939.

Fields, Mamie Garvin, with Karen Fields. *Lemon Swamp and Other Places: A Carolina Memoir.* New York: Free Press, 1983.

Foner, Philip S., and Ronald L. Lewis, eds. *The Black Worker: A Documentary History from Colonial Times to the Present.* Vol. 5, *The Black Worker from 1900 to 1919.* Philadelphia: Temple University Press, 1980.

Frazier, Edward Franklin. *The Negro Family in the United States.* Rev. and abr. ed. Chicago: University of Chicago Press, 1969. First published 1939.

Gates, Henry Louis. *Colored People: A Memoir.* New York: Knopf, 1994.

Grandy, Moses. *Narrative of the Life of Moses Grandy, Late a Slave in the United States of America.* Boston: Oliver Johnson, 1844.

Gray, Lewis Cecil. *History of Agriculture in the Southern United States to 1860.* Vol. 1. Washington, D.C.: Carnegie Institution, 1933.

Greene, Lorenzo J., and Carter G. Woodson. *The Negro Wage Earner.* Washington, D.C.: Association for the Study of Negro Life and History, 1930.

Gwaltney, John Langston. *Drylongso: A Self-Portrait of Black America.* New York: Random House, 1980.

Hagood, Margaret. *Mothers of the South: Portraiture of the White Tenant Farm Woman.* New York: W. W. Norton, 1977. First published 1939.

Hammond, M. B. *The Cotton Industry: An Essay in American Economic History.* New York: Johnson Reprint Co., 1966. First published 1897.

Hancock, Cornelia. *South After Gettysburg: Letters of Cornelia Hancock From the Army of the Potomac, 1863–1865.* Edited by Henrietta S. Jaquette. New York: T. Y. Crowell, 1956.

Harmon, John Henry, Arnett Lindsay, and Carter G. Woodson. *The Negro as a Business Man.* College Park, MD: McGrath Publishing Co., 1929.

Haviland, Laura S. *A Woman's Life-Work: Labors and Experiences of Laura S. Haviland.* Chicago: C. V. Waite and Co., 1887.

Hayes, John D., ed. *Samuel Francis DuPont: A Selection from His Civil War Letters.* 3 vols. Ithaca, NY: Cornell University Press, 1969.

Haynes, George E. *Negro New-Comers in Detroit, Michigan.* New York: Arno Press, 1969. First published in 1918.

Henry, Alice. *Women and the Labor Movement.* New York: G. H. Doran, 1923.

Herbst, Alma. *The Negro in the Slaughtering and Meatpacking Industry in Chicago.* Boston: Houghton Mifflin, 1932.

Herskovits, Melville J. *The Myth of the Negro Past.* New York: Harper and Brothers, 1941.

Higginson, Thomas Wentworth. *Army Life in a Black Regiment.* Boston: Fields, Osgood and Co., 1870.

Hine, Darlene Clark, ed., *Black Women in Nursing: An Anthology of Historical Sources.* New York: Garland Publishing, 1984.

Holiday, Billie, and William Duffy. *Lady Sings the Blues.* New York: Doubleday, 1956.

Hoose, Philip. *Claudette Colvin: Twice Toward Justice.* New York: Farrar, Straus, and Giroux, 2009.

Howard, Oliver Otis. *Autobiography of Oliver Otis Howard, Major General, United States Army.* Vol. 2. New York: Baker and Taylor, 1908.

Hudson, Hosea. *Black Worker in the Deep South.* New York: International Publishers, 1972.

Hughes, Langston, and Arna Bontemps, eds. *The Poetry of the Negro, 1746–1970.* New York: Doubleday, 1970.

Hurston, Zora Neale. *Their Eyes Were Watching God.* London: J. M. Dent and Sons, 1938.

———. *I Love Myself When I am Laughing . . . And Then Again When I Am Looking Mean and Impressive.* Edited by Alice Walker. Old Westbury, NY: Feminist Press, 1979.

Jackson, George. *Soledad Brother: The Prison Letters of George Jackson.* New York: Coward McCann, 1970.

Jackson, Mahalia, and Evan McLeod Whylie. *Movin' On Up.* New York: Hawthorne Books, 1966.

Jacobstein, Meyer. *The Tobacco Industry in the United States.* New York: Columbia University Press, 1907.

Jetter, Alexis, Annelise Orleck, and Deana Taylor, eds. *The Politics of Motherhood: Activist Voices from Left to Right.* Hanover, NH: University Press of New England, 1997.

Johnson, Charles S. *Shadow of the Plantation.* Chicago: University of Chicago Press, 1934.

———. *To Stem This Tide: A Survey of Racial Tension Areas in The United States.* Boston: Pilgrim Press, 1943.

Johnson, Charles S., Edwin R. Embree, and W. W. Alexander. *The Collapse of Cotton Tenancy: Summary of Field Studies and Statistical Surveys, 1933–35.* Chapel Hill: University of North Carolina Press, 1935.

Jones, Charles C., Jr. *Gullah Folktales from the Georgia Coast.* Athens: University of Georgia Press, 2000. First published 1888.

Jones, Thomas Jesse. *Negro Education: A Study of the Private and Higher Schools for Colored People in the United States.* New York: Arno Press, 1969. First published 1917.

Jones, William H. *Recreation and Amusement Among Negroes in Washington, D.C.: A Sociological Analysis of the Negro in an Urban Environment.* Westport, CT: Negro Universities Press 1970. First published 1927.

Kelsey, Carl. *The Negro Farmer*. Chicago: Jennings and Pye, 1903.

Kemble, Frances A. *Journal of a Residence on a Georgian Plantation in 1838–1839*. London: Longman, Green, 1863.

Kennedy, Louise V. *The Negro Peasant Turns Cityward: Effects of Recent Migrations to Northern Centers*. New York: Columbia University Press, 1930.

Kester, Howard. *Revolt Among the Sharecroppers*. Edited by Alex Lichtenstein. Knoxville: University of Tennessee Press, 1997.

King, Coretta Scott. *My Life with Martin Luther King, Jr*. New York: Holt, Rinehart, and Winston, 1969.

King, Edward. *The Great South: A Record of Journeys in Louisiana, Texas, the Indian Territory . . .* Hartford, CT: American Publishing Co., 1875.

King, Martin Luther, Jr. *Why We Can't Wait*. New York: Harper & Row, 1964.

Kiser, Clyde Vernon. *Sea Island to City: A Study of St. Helena Islanders in Harlem and Other Urban Centers*. New York: Columbia University Press, 1932.

Knox, Thomas W. *Camp-Fire and Cotton-Field: Southern Adventure in Time of War; Life with the Union Armies and Residence on a Louisiana Plantation*. New York: Blelock and Co., 1865.

Ladner, Joyce A. *Tomorrow's Tomorrow: The Black Woman*. New York: Doubleday, 1971.

Lange, Dorothea. *Dorothea Lange: Photographs of a Lifetime*. Millerton, NY: Aperture, 1982.

Leigh, Frances Butler. *Ten Years on a Georgia Plantation Since the War*. London: R. Bentley and Sons, 1883.

Lemert, Benjamin Franklin. *The Cotton Textile Industry of the Southern Appalachian Piedmont*. Chapel Hill: University of North Carolina Press, 1933.

Lerner, Gerda, ed. *Black Women in White America: A Documentary History*. New York: Random House, 1972.

Lester, Julius. *Look Out Whitey! Black Power's Gon' Get Your Mama!* New York: Dial Press, 1968.

Loewenberg, Bert J., and Ruth Bogin, eds. *Black Women in Nineteenth-Century American Life: Their Words, Their Thought, Their Feelings*. University Park: Pennsylvania State University Press, 1976.

Loring, Francis W., and C. F. Atkinson. *Cotton Culture and the South Considered With Reference to Emigration*. Boston: A. Williams, 1869.

Lynd, Alice, and Staughton Lynd, eds. *Rank and File: Personal Histories by Working-Class Organizers*. Princeton, NJ: Princeton University Press, 1981. First published 1973.

Mars, Florence. *Witness in Philadelphia*. Baton Rouge: Louisiana State University Press, 1977.

Martin, Asa E. *Our Negro Population: A Sociological Study of the Negroes of Kansas City, Missouri*. New York: Negro Universities Press, 1969. First published 1913.

McElvaine, Robert S., ed., *Down and Out in the Great Depression: Letters from the "Forgotten Man."* Chapel Hill: University of North Carolina Press, 1983.

Mebane, Mary. *Mary*. New York: Viking Press, 1981.

Meyer, Annie Nathan, ed. *Woman's Work in America*. New York: Henry Holt, 1891.

Mitchell, Broadus. *The Rise of Cotton Mills in the South, 1877–1900*. Baltimore: Johns Hopkins University Press, 1921.

Moody, Anne. *Coming of Age in Mississippi*. New York: Dial Press, 1968.

Moore, Marat. *Women in the Mines: Stories of Life and Work*. New York: Twayne Publishers, 1996.

Moraga, Cherrie, and Gloria Anzaldúa, eds. *This Bridge Called My Back: Writings By Radical Women of Color*. Watertown, MA: Persephone Press, 1981.

Morrison, Toni. *Song of Solomon*. New York: Knopf, 1977.

Myers, Robert M., ed. *The Children of Pride: A True Story of Georgia and the Civil War*. New Haven, CT: Yale University Press, 1972.

Myrdal, Gunnar. *An American Dilemma: The Negro Problem and Modern Democracy*. 2 vols. New York: Harper & Row, 1944.

Newton, Huey P. *Revolutionary Suicide*. New York: Harcourt Brace Jovanovich, 1973.

Nordhoff, Charles. *The Cotton States in the Spring and Summer of 1875*. New York: D. Appleton and Co., 1876.

Obama, Barack. *The Audacity of Hope: Thoughts on Reclaiming the American Dream*. New York: Crown, 2006.

Olmsted, Frederick L. *A Journey in the Seaboard Slave States*. New York: Dix and Edwards, 1856.

———. *A Journey in the Back Country in the Winter of 1853–1854*. New York: Mason Brothers, 1860.

Ovington, Mary White. *Half a Man: The Status of the Negro in New York*. New York: Longmans, Green, and Co., 1911.

Painter, Nell Irvin. *The Narrative of Hosea Hudson: His Life as a Negro Communist in the South*. Cambridge, MA: Harvard University Press, 1979.

Pearson, Elizabeth W., ed. *Letters from Port Royal, 1862–1868*. New York: Arno Press, 1969. First published 1906.

Perdue, Charles L., Jr., Thomas E. Barden, and Robert K. Phillips, eds. *Weevils in the Wheat: Interviews with Virginia Ex-Slaves*. Charlottesville: University Press of Virginia, 1976.

Petry, Ann. *The Street*. New York: Pyramid Books, 1946.

Pickens, William. *Bursting Bonds*. Boston: Jordan and More, 1923.

Powdermaker, Hortense. *After Freedom: A Cultural Study in the Deep South*. New York: Atheneum, 1968. First published 1939.

Raines, Howell. *My Soul Is Rested: Movement Days in the Deep South Remembered*. New York: G. P. Putnam's Sons, 1977.

Raper, Arthur F. *Preface to Peasantry: A Tale of Two Black Belt Counties*. Chapel Hill: University of North Carolina Press, 1936.

———. *Tenants of the Almighty*. New York: Macmillan, 1943.

Rawick, George P., ed. *The American Slave: A Composite Autobiography*. 41 vols., Series 1, Supplement Series 1 and 2. Westport, CT: Greenwood Press, 1972, 1978, 1979.

Reed, Ruth. *Negro Illegitimacy in New York City*. New York: Columbia University Press, 1926.

Reid, Inez Smith. *"Together" Black Women*. New York: Third Press, 1972.

Robinson, Jo Ann Gibson. *The Montgomery Bus Boycott and the Women Who Started It: The Memoir of Jo Ann Gibson Robinson*. Knoxville: University of Tennessee Press, 1987.

Rosengarten, Theodore, comp. *All God's Dangers: The Life of Nate Shaw*. New York: Knopf, 1974.

Scheer, Robert, ed. *Eldridge Cleaver Post-Prison Writings and Speeches*. New York: Random House, 1969.

Scott, Emmett J. *Negro Migration During the War*. New York: Oxford University Press, 1969. First published 1920.

Seale, Bobby. *Seize the Time: The Story of the Black Panther Party and Huey P. Newton*. New York: Random House, 1968.

Sellers, Cleveland. *The River of No Return: The Autobiography of a Black Militant and the Life and Death of SNCC*. New York: William Morrow, 1973.

Shakur, Assata. *Assata: An Autobiography*. Chicago: Lawrence Hall Books, 2001.

Smith, Lillian. *Killers of the Dream*. New York: W. W. Norton, 1961.

Social Science Institute, Fisk University. *Unwritten History of Slavery: Autobiographical Accounts of Negro Ex-Slaves*. Nashville, TN: Social Science Institute, 1945.

Somers, Robert. *The Southern States Since the War, 1870–1871*. London: Macmillan, 1871.

Stack, Carol. *All Our Kin: Strategies for Survival in a Black Community*. New York: Harper & Row, 1974.

Starobin, Robert S., ed. *Blacks in Bondage: Letters of American Slaves*. New York: New Viewpoints, 1974.

Stearns, Charles. *The Black Man of the South, and the Rebels: or, The Characteristics of the Former, and the Recent Outrages of the Latter*. New York: American News Co., 1872.

Sterner, Richard. *The Negro's Share: A Study of Income, Consumption, Housing and Public Assistance*. New York: Harper and Brothers, 1943.

Stone, Alfred Holt. *Studies in the American Race Problem*. New York, 1908.

Stryker, Roy Emerson, and Nancy Wood. *In This Proud Land: America 1935–1943; As Seen in the FSA Photographs*. New York: Galahad Books, 1973.

Sugarman, Tracy. *Stranger at the Gates: A Summer in Mississippi*. New York: Hill and Wang, 1966.

Sutherland, Elizabeth, ed. *Letters from Mississippi*. New York: McGraw-Hill, 1965.

Swint, Henry L., ed. *Dear Ones at Home: Letters from Contraband Camps*. Nashville, TN: Vanderbilt University Press, 1966.

Sydnor, Charles S. *Slavery in Mississippi*. Gloucester, MA: P. Smith, 1933.

Taylor, Susie King. *Reminiscences of My Life in Camp With the 33rd United States Colored Troops Late 1st S.C. Volunteers*. Boston: Published by the author, 1902.

Terkel, Studs. *Hard Times: An Oral History of the Great Depression*. New York: Avon Books, 1970.

Terrill, Tom E., and Jerrold Hirsch, eds. *Such As Us: Southern Voices of the Thirties*. New York: W. W. Norton, 1978.

Tilley, Nannie May. *The Bright Tobacco Industry, 1860–1929*. Chapel Hill: University of North Carolina Press, 1948.

Towne, Laura M. *Letters and Diary of Laura M. Towne; Written from the Sea Islands of South Carolina, 1862–1884*. Edited by Rupert Sargent Holland. Cambridge, MA: Riverside Press, 1912.

Trowbridge, John Townsend. *The South: A Tour of Its Battlefields and Ruined Cities; A Journey Through the Desolated States, and Talks with the People*. Hartford, CT: L. Stebbins, 1866.

Turner, Lorenzo Dow. *Africanisms in the Gullah Dialect*. Chicago: University of Chicago Press, 1949.

Virginia Federal Writers' Project. *The Negro in Virginia*. New York: Hastings House, 1940.

Walker, Alice. *The Color Purple*. New York: Harcourt Brace Jovanovich, 1982.

Wame, Colston E., and others, eds. *Labor in Postwar America*. Brooklyn, NY: Remsen Press, 1949.

Warner, Robert Austin. *New Haven Negroes: A Social History*. New Haven, CT: Yale University Press, 1940.

Washington, Mary Helen, ed. *Black-Eyed Susans: Classic Stories By and About Black Women*. New York: Anchor Press, 1975.

Washington-Williams, Essie Mae. *Dear Senator: A Memoir by the Daughter of Strom Thurmond*. New York: Harper, 2005.

Waterman, Willoughby Cyrus. *Prostitution and Its Repression in New York City, 1900–1931.* New York: Columbia University Press, 1932.

Waters, Ethel. *His Eye Is on the Sparrow: An Autobiography.* New York: Doubleday, 1951.

Weaver, Robert C. *Negro Labor: A National Problem.* New York: Harcourt, Brace, 1946.

Webb, Sheyann, and Rachel West Nelson. *Selma, Lord, Selma: Girlhood Memories of the Civil Rights Days.* New York: William Morrow, 1980.

Wells-Barnett, Ida B. *On Lynchings: Southern Horrors: A Red Record. Mob Rule in New Orleans.* New York: Amo Press, 1969. First published 1892.

White, Max R., Douglas Ensminger, and Cecil L. Gregory. *Rich Land, Poor People.* FSA Research Report No. 1. Indianapolis, January 1938.

Willets, Gilson. *Workers of the Nation.* Vol. 2. New York: P. F. Collier and Son, 1903.

Wilson, Emily Herring. *Hope and Dignity: Older Black Women of the South.* Philadelphia: Temple University Press, 1983.

Woodson, Carter G. *Education of the Negro Prior to 1861.* New York: Arno Press, 1968. First published 1919.

Woodward, C. Vann, ed. *Mary Chesnut's Civil War.* New Haven, CT: Yale University Press, 1981.

Woofter, Thomas Jackson, Jr. *Negro Migration: Changes in Rural Organization and Population of the Cotton Belt.* New York: AMS Press, 1971. First published 1920.

———. *Negro Problems in Cities.* New York: Harper & Row, 1969. First published 1928.

———. *Black Yeomanry: Life on St. Helena Island.* New York: H. Holt, 1930.

Wright, Richard. *12 Million Black Voices: A Folk History of the Negro in the United States.* New York: Viking Press, 1941.

X, Malcolm. *Autobiography of Malcolm X.* New York: Grove Press, 1964.

ARTICLES AND PAMPHLETS

Aframerican Woman's Journal. National Council of Negro Women. Vols. 1–8 (1940–1950).

Anderson, Mary. "The Plight of Negro Domestic Labor." *Journal of Negro Education* 5 (January 1936): 66–72.

———. "Negro Women on the Production Front." *Opportunity* 21 (April 1943): 37–38.

Baker, Ella, and Marvel Cooke. "The Bronx Slave Market." *Crisis* 42 (November 1935): 330–331, 342.

Baker, Ray Stannard. "The Negro Goes North: The Great Southern Migration to the Mirage-Land of War-Boom High Wages, and Some Saddening As Well As Hopeful Sidelights on the Problems Thus Created." *World's Work* 34 (July 1917): 314–319.

Banner, Warren M. "New York." *Journal of Educational Sociology* 17 (January 1944): 272–279.

———. "War and Post-War Trends in Employment of Negroes." *Monthly Labor Review* 60 (January 1945): 1–3.

Barrett, Mrs. Harris. "Negro Women's Clubs and the Community." *Southern Workman* 39 (January 1910): 33–34.

Barrow, David C. "A Georgia Plantation." *Scribner's Monthly* 21 (April 1888): 830–836.

Barry, Richard. "Slavery in the South To-Day." *Cosmopolitan Magazine* 45 (March 1907): 488.

Baumann, Hermann. "The Division of Work According to Sex in African Hoe Culture." *Africa* 1 (July 1928): 289–319.

Bedell, Mary S. "Employment and Income of Negro Workers: 1940–52." *Monthly Labor Review* 76 (June 1953): 596–601.

Bell, W. Y., Jr., "The Negro Warrior's Home Front." *Phylon* 5 (1944): 271–278.

Berry, Theodore M. "The Negro in Cincinnati Industries." *Opportunity* 8 (December 1930): 361–364.

Best, Ethel L., and Ethel Erickson. "A Survey of Laundries and their Women Workers in Twenty-three Cities." U.S. Department of Labor, Women's Bureau. Bulletin no.78 (1930).

Brewer, W. M. "Poor Whites and Negroes Since the Civil War." *Journal of Negro History* 15 (January 1930): 26–37.

Buckner, Jenny C. "Problems of Women Workers." *Chronicle* 3 (April 1930): 81–82.

Burrell, W. P. "Report of the Committee on Business and Labor Conditions in Richmond, Va." *Proceedings of the Hampton Negro Conference* 6 (July 1902).

Cade, John B. "Out of the Mouths of Ex-Slaves." *Journal of Negro History* 20 (July 1935): 294–337.

Carter, Elmer Anderson. "The Negro Household Employee." *Woman's Press* 28 (July–August 1934).

Christensen, Niels, Jr. "The Negroes of Beaufort County, South Carolina." *Southern Workman* 32 (October 1903).

Clark, Jessie, and Elise Johnson McDougald. "A New Day for the Colored Woman Worker: A Study of Colored Women in Industry in New York City." (New York, 1919).

Clark, John T. "The Migrant in Pittsburgh." *Opportunity* 1 (October 1923).

Coalition on Women and the Budget. "Inequality of Sacrifice: The Impact of the Reagan Budget on Women." Washington, D.C.: Coalition on Women and the Budget, 1983.

"Complete Survey of Race Women in Local Industries." *New York Age* 32 (March 22, 1919).

Cooper, Anna J. "Colored Women as Wage-Earners." *Southern Workman* 28 (August 1899): 295–298.

Cuthbert, Marion. "Problems Facing Negro Young Women." *Opportunity* 14 (February 1936): 47–49.

DeMar, George E. "Negro Women are American Workers, Too." *Opportunity* 21 (April 1943): 41–44.

Dillingham, Pitt. "Black Belt Settlement Work. Part II: The Community." *Southern Workman* 31 (August 1902): 437–444.

Dowd, Jerome. "Negro Labor in Factories." *Southern Workman* 31 (November 1902).

Drake, J. G. St. Clair. "The Negro in the North During Wartime: Chicago." *Journal of Educational Sociology* 17 (January 1944): 261–271.

DuBois, W. E. B., ed. "Mortality Among Negroes in Cities." Atlanta University Study No. 1. Atlanta, GA: Atlanta University Press, 1896.

———. "Social and Physical Conditions of Negroes in Cities." Atlanta University Study No. 2. Atlanta, GA: Atlanta University Press, 1897.

———. "Some Efforts of American Negroes for their Own Social Betterment." Atlanta University Study No. 3. Atlanta, GA: Atlanta University Press, 1898.

———. "The College Bred Negro." Atlanta University Study No. 5 Atlanta, GA: Atlanta University Press, 1900.

———. "The Negro Common School." Atlanta University Study No. 6. Atlanta, GA: Atlanta University Press, 1901.

———. "The Problem of Housing the Negro. Pt. III: The Home of the Country Freeman." *Southern Workman* 30 (October 1901): 535–542.

———. "The Negro Artisan." Atlanta University Study No. 7. Atlanta, GA: Atlanta University Press, 1902.

———. "The Negro Church." Atlanta University Study No. 8. Atlanta, GA: Atlanta University Press, 1903.

———. "Economic Cooperation Among Negro Americans." Atlanta University Study No. 12. Atlanta, GA: Atlanta University Press, 1907.

———. "The Negro American Family." Atlanta University Study No. 13. Atlanta, GA: Atlanta University Press, 1908.

———. "Efforts for Social Betterment Among Negro Americans." Atlanta University Study No. 14. Atlanta, GA: Atlanta University Press, 1910.

———. "The College-Bred Negro American." Atlanta University Study No. 15. Atlanta, GA: Atlanta University Press, 1910.

———. "Morals and Manners Among Negro Americans." Atlanta University Study No. 18. Atlanta, GA: Atlanta University Press, 1914.

Eason, Newell D. "Attitudes of Negro Families on Relief Toward Work, Toward Home, Toward Life." *Opportunity* 12 (December 1935): 367–379.

Edens, Boyce M. "When Labor Is Cheap." *The Survey* 38 (September 8, 1917).

Edwards, Thomas J. "Negro Farmers of Alabama. Pt. I: Wage Earners." *Southern Workman* 40 (August 1911): 459–462.

Ellis, Elaine. "Women of the Cotton Fields." *Crisis* 45 (October 1938): 333–342.

"Employment of Colored Women in Chicago." *Crisis* 1 (January 1911): 24–25.

Fleming, Walter L. "The Servant Problem in a Black Belt Village." *The Sewanee Review* 13 (January 1905).

Frazier, E. Franklin. "A Negro Industrial Group." *Howard Review* 1 (June 1924): 196–211.

———. "Chicago: A Cross-Section of Negro Life." *Opportunity* 7 (March 1929): 70–73.

———. "Occupational Classes Among Negroes in Cities." *American Journal of Sociology* 35 (March 1930): 718–738.

———. "Family Disorganization Among Negroes." *Opportunity* 9 (July 1931): 204–207.

———. "Some Effects of the Depression on the Negro in Northern Cities." *Science and Society* 2 (Fall 1938): 495–496.

Garland, Phyl. "Builders of a New South: Negro Heroines of Dixie Play Major Role in Challenging Racist Traditions." *Ebony* 21 (August 1966): 27–37.

Godfredsen, Svend. "Young Chicago Girl a CIO Union Leader." *Opportunity* 25 (Spring 1947): 104–106.

Goldstein, Harold. "The Changing Occupational Structure." *Monthly Labor Review* 65 (December 1947): 654–665.

Gordon, Lawrence. "Document: A Brief Look at Blacks in Depression Mississippi, 1929–1934: Eyewitness Accounts." *Journal of Negro History* 46 (Fall 1979): 377–390.

Graham, Irene. "The Negro Family in a Northern City." *Opportunity* 8 (February 1930): 48–51.

Gregory, George, Jr. "Wartime Guidance for Tomorrow's Citizens." *Opportunity* 21 (April 1943): 70–72.

Hackshaw, Leotha. "What My Job Means to Me." *Opportunity* 21 (April 1943): 50–53.

Hall, Bob. "I Feel What Women Feel." Interview with Donna Bazemore, *Southern Exposure* 17 (Summer 1989): 30–33.

Hampton, Elizabeth. "Negro Women and the WAC." *Opportunity* 21 (April 1943): 54–56.

Handy, M. P. "In a Tobacco Factory." *Harper's New Monthly Magazine* 47 (October 1873): 713–719.

Harper, Frances. "Coloured Women of America." *Englishwoman's Review* 9 (January 1878): 10–15.

Haynes, Elizabeth Ross. "Two Million Negro Women at Work." *Southern Workman* 51 (February 1922): 64–72.

———. "Negroes in Domestic Service in the United States." *Journal of Negro History* 8 (October 1923): 384–442.

Haynes, George E. "Conditions Among Negroes in Cities." American Academy of Political and Social Science *Annals* 49 (September 1913): 108–109.

———. "Negro Migration: Its Effects on Family and Community Life in the North." *Opportunity* 2 (October 1924): 303–306

Heard, George Alexander. "St. Simons Island During the War Between the States." *Georgia Historical Quarterly* 22, no. 3 (September 1938): 249–272.

Henderson, Elmer W. "Negroes in Government Employment." *Opportunity* 21 (July 1943): 118–121.

Hill, Joseph A. "The Recent Northward Migration of the Negro." *Opportunity* 2 (April 1924): 100–105.

Hobbs, Clark S. "The Whip Changes Hands." *Baltimore Evening Sun*, May 16, 1941, reprinted in *Aframerican Woman's Journal* 2 (1941): 29–30.

Hobson, Elizabeth C., and Charlotte Everet Hopkins. "A Report Concerning the Colored Women of the South." John F. Slater Occasional Paper No. 9. Baltimore: Slater Trustees, 1896.

Hoffsommer, Harold C. "Landlord-Tenant Relations and Relief in Alabama." Confidential Research Bulletin #2738 (July 10, 1934).

Holmes, George K. "The Peons of the South," American Academy of Political and Social Science *Annals* 4 (September 1893): 65–74.

Holtzclaw, W. H. "A Negro's Life Story." *World's Work* 12 (September 1906): 79–89.

Hunter, Addie W. "A Colored Working Girl and Race Prejudice." *Crisis* 6 (April 1916): 32–34.

Irvin, Helen Brooks. "Conditions in Industry as They Affect Negro Women." National Conference of Social Work *Proceedings*, 46th Annual Meeting (1919): 521–531.

Jefferson, Olive Ruth. "The Southern Negro Women." *Chautauquan* 18 (1888): 91–94.

Jeffries, LeRoy W. "The Decay of the Beauty Parlor Industry in Harlem." *Opportunity* 16 (February 193S): 49–60.

Johnson, Beverly L. "Women Who Head Families, 1970–1977: Their Numbers Rose, Income Lagged." *Monthly Labor Review* 101 (February 1978): 32–37.

Johnson, Charles S. "How Much *is* the Migration a Flight from Persecution?" *Opportunity* 1 (September 1923): 272–274.

———. "The Negro Population of Waterbury, Connecticut." *Opportunity* 1 (October 1923): 302–303.

———. "The American Migrant: The Negro." National Conference of Social Work *Proceedings*, 54th Annual Meeting (1927): 554–558.

Johnston, V. D. "The Migration and the Census of 1920." *Opportunity* 1 (August 1923): 235–238.

Jones, Eugene Kinckie. "The Negro in Community Life." National Conference of Social Work *Proceedings*, 56th Annual Meeting (1929).

Jones, Thomas Jesse. "Social Studies in the Hampton Curriculum. Pt. V: United States Census and Actual Conditions." *Southern Workman* 35 (May 1906): 317–318.

———. "The Negroes of the Southern States and the U.S. Census of 1910." *Southern Workman* 41 (August 1912): 459–472.

Keller, Frances A. "Assisted Emigration from the South: The Women." *Charities* 15 (October 7, 1905): 11–14.

Kine, Edith. "The Garment Union Comes to the Negro Worker." *Opportunity* 12 (April 1934): 107–110.

Kohn, August. "The Cotton Mills of South Carolina, 1907: Letters Written to the *News and Courier*." Charleston, SC: Press of the Daggett Printing Company, 1907.

Kruse, Edwina B. "Negro Women and Domestic Service." Hampton Negro Conference *Proceedings* no. 8 (July 1904): 39–51.

Landon, Charles E. "Tobacco Manufacturing in the South." American Academy of Political and Social Science *Annals* 153 (January 1931): 43–53.

Laycock, James Z., Jr., "Infantile Mortality." Report of the Negro Conference, 1906, *Hampton Bulletin* 2 (September 1906): 78–81.

Lett, Harold. "Work: Negro Unemployed in Pittsburgh." *Opportunity* 9 (March 1931): 79–81.

Lorde, Audre, and Adrienne Rich. "An Interview with Audre Lorde." *Signs* 6 (Summer 1981): 713–736.

Macy, J. Noel. "Negro Women in the WAC." *Opportunity* 23 (Winter 1945): 14–15.

Marshall, Paule. "From the Poets in the Kitchen." *New York Times Book Review*, January 9, 1983, 3.

Matthews, Mrs. V. E. "Some of the Dangers Confronting Southern Girls in the North." Hampton Negro Conference *Proceedings* no. 2 (July 1898): 62–69.

McEaddy, Beverly Johnson. "Women Who Head Families: A Socio-economic Analysis." *Monthly Labor Review* 99 (June 1976): 3–9.

Melman, Seymour. "An Industrial Revolution in the Cotton South." *Economic History Review* 2 (1949): 59–72.

"Migration of Colored Girls from Virginia." Hampton Negro Conference *Bulletin* 1 (September 1905): 75–79.

Miller, Kelly. "Surplus Negro Women." *Southern Workman* 34 (October 1905): 522–528.

Morrison, Toni. "What the Black Woman Thinks About Women's Lib." *New York Times Magazine*, August 22, 1971, 14.

Mossell, Sadie T. "The Standard of Living Among One Hundred Migrant Families in Philadelphia." American Academy of Political and Social Science *Annals* 98 (November 1921): 71–218.

Murray, Anna E. "In Behalf of the Negro Woman," *Southern Workman* 33 (April 1904): 232–234.

Negro Nurse. "More Slavery at the South." *Independent* 72 (January 25, 1912): 196–200.

"Negroes at Work in the United States." *Opportunity* 1 (July 1923): 216.

Newman, Bernard J. "The Housing of Negro Immigrants in Pennsylvania." *Opportunity* 2 (February 1924): 46–48.

Ostlund, Leonard A. "Occupational Choice Patterns of Negro College Women." *Journal of Negro Education* 26 (Winter 1957): 86–91.

Ovington, Mary White. "The Negro Home in New York." *Charities* 15 (October 7, 1905): 25–31.

Pidgeon, Mary Elizabeth. "Women Workers and Recent Economic Change." *Monthly Labor Review* 65 (December 1947): 666–671.

Porter, Ruth P. "Negro Women in the Clothing, Cigar, and Laundry Industries of Philadelphia, 1940." *Journal of Negro Education* 12 (Winter 1943): 21–23.

Reddick, L. D., ed. "Race Relations on the Pacific Coast." *Journal of Educational Sociology* 19 (November 1945): 129–145.

Reid, Ira DeA. "The Negro Woman Worker," *Woman's Press* 26 (April 1932): 205–206.

Riddle, Estelle M., and Josephine Nelson. "The Negro Nurse Looks Toward Tomorrow." *American Journal of Nursing* 45 (August 1945): 627–630.

Rowe, George C. "The Negroes of the Sea Islands." *Southern Workman* 29 (December 1900): 709.

Sampson, Edith. "The Diary of a Child Placing Agent." *Opportunity* 1 (February 1923): 10–11.

Schuster, Louis H. "Negroes Working in Defense Industry." *Opportunity* 19 (September 1941): 267–268.

Scott, Emmett J., comp. "Documents: Letters of Negro Migrants of 1916–1918." *Journal of Negro History* 4 (July–October 1919): 290–340, 412–65.

Seeley, Evelyn. "Our Feudal Housewives." *Nation* 46 (May 28, 1938): 613–615.

Sessions, Jim, and Sue Thrasher. "A New Day Begun." *Southern Exposure* 4 (Winter 1977): 14–24.

Shields, Emma L. "A Half Century in the Tobacco Industry." *Southern Workman* 51 (September 1922): 419–425.

Simpson, Gordon H. "A Note on Negro Industrial Problems." *Opportunity* 2 (June 1924): 182–183.

South Carolinian. "South Carolina Society." *The Atlantic Monthly* 39 (June 1877): 677.

Southern Colored Woman, "The Race Problem: An Autobiography." *Independent* 56 (March 17, 1904).

Staupers, Mabel Keaton. "The Negro Nurse." *Opportunity* 20 (November 1942): 332–334

Terrell, Mary C. "Club Work of Colored Women." *Southern Workman* 30 (August 1901): 435–438.

"There Goes the China!" *The Survey* 42 (July 12, 1919).

Tillman, Katherine Davis. "Afro-American Women and Their Work." *AME Church Review* 11 (1895): 477–499.

Tracy, Bill, Sue Thrasher, and Jim Sessions. "To Be Prophetic: Black Ministers Speak Out on the Church." *Southern Exposure* 4 (Winter 1977): 38–46.

"Truck Farming in Tidewater Virginia." *Southern Workman* 30 (July 1901): 396–401.

Turner, Zatella R. "Alpha Kappa Alpha Sorority's Wartime Program." *Aframerican Woman's Journal* 3 (Summer 1943): 22–23.

"War and Post-War Trends in Employment of Negroes." *Monthly Labor Review* 60 (January 1945): 1–5.

Washington, Georgia. "Condition of the Women in the Rural Districts of Alabama." *Proceedings of the Hampton Negro Conference* 6 (July 1902).

Webb, John N. and Malcolm Brown. "Migrant Families." Works Progress Administration Division of Social Research, Monograph 18 (1938).

Webster, Thomas A. "Employers, Unions, and Negro Workers." *Opportunity* 19 (October 1941): 295–297.

Williams, Fannie Barrier. "The Problem of Employment for Negro Women." *Southern Workman* 32 (September 1903): 432–437.

———. "Social Bonds in the 'Black Belt' of Chicago." *Charities* 15 (October 7, 1905).

Williams, W. T. B. "Local Conditions Among Negroes. Pt. I: Gloucester County, Virginia." *Southern Workman* 35 (February 1906): 103–106.

Women in Industry Committee, "Conditions of Women's Labor in Louisiana: New Orleans and Louisiana Industrial Survey." New Orleans: Louisiana Commission of Labor, 1919.

"Women Workers in Indianapolis," *Crisis* 37 (June 1930): 189–191.

Woofter, Thomas J. "The Negroes of Athens, Georgia." Phelps-Stokes Fellowship Studies No. 1, *Bulletin of the University of Georgia* 14 (December 1913).

Woofter, Thomas J., Jr., and Madge Hadley Priest. "Negro Housing in Philadelphia." Philadelphia: Friends' Committee on Interests of the Colored Race, 1927.

Work, Monroe N. "The Negroes of Warsaw, Georgia." *Southern Workman* 37 (January 1908): 29–40.

———. "Problems of Negro Urban Welfare." *Southern Workman* 51 (January 1922): 10–16.

———. "The Negro Migration." *Southern Workman* 53 (May 1924): 202–212.

SECONDARY SOURCES

BOOKS

Abraham, Laurie Kaye. *Mama Might Be Better Off Dead: The Failure of Health Care in Urban America*. Chicago: University of Chicago Press, 1993.

Abu-Lughod, Janet L. *New York, Chicago, Los Angeles: America's Global Cities*. Minneapolis: University of Minnesota Press, 1999.

Alexander, Charles C. *Holding the Line: The Eisenhower Era, 1952–1961*. Bloomington: Indiana University Press, 1975.

Anderson, Karen. *Wartime Women: Sex Roles, Family Relations and the Status of Women During World War II*. Westport, CT: Greenwood Press, 1981.

Aptheker, Bettina. *Woman's Legacy: Essays on Race, Sex, and Class in American History*. Amherst: University of Massachusetts Press, 1982.

———. *The Morning Breaks: The Trial of Angela Davis*. Ithaca, NY: Cornell University Press, 1999.

Arnesen, Eric. *Black Protest and the Great Migration: A Brief History with Documents*. Boston: Bedford/St. Martin's, 2003.

———. *The Black Worker: Race, Labor, and Civil Rights Since Emancipation*. Urbana: University of Illinois Press, 2007.

Arsenault, Raymond. *The Sounds of Freedom: Marian Anderson, the Lincoln Memorial, and the Concert That Awakened America*. New York: Bloomsbury Press, 2009.

Ayers, Edward. *The Promise of the New South: Life After Reconstruction*. New York: Oxford University Press, 1992.

Bambara, Toni Cade. *The Black Woman: An Anthology*. New York: New American Library, 1970.

Barnes, Catherine A. *Journey from Jim Crow: The Desegregation of Southern Transit*. New York: Columbia University Press, 1983.

Baxter, Sandra, and Marjorie Lansing. *Women and Politics: The Visible Majority*. 2nd ed. Ann Arbor: University of Michigan Press, 1983.

Bell, Roseann P., Bettye J. Parker, and Beverly Guy-Sheftall, eds. *Sturdy Black Bridges: Visions of Black Women in Literature*. New York: Anchor Books, 1979.

Bell, Winifred. *Aid to Dependent Children*. New York: Columbia University Press, 1965.

Benjamin, Lois. *The Black Elite: Facing the Color Line in the Twilight of the Twentieth Century*. Chicago: Nelson-Hall Publishers, 1991.

Berkin, Carol, and Mary Beth Norton, eds. *Women of America: A History*. Boston: Houghton Mifflin, 1979.

Berlin, Ira. *Slaves Without Masters: The Free Negro in the Antebellum South*. New York: Random House, 1974.

———. *Many Thousands Gone: The First Two Centuries of Slavery in North America*. Cambridge, MA: Harvard University Press, 1998.

Berlin, Ira, and Philip Morgan, eds. *The Slaves' Economy: Independent Production by Slaves in the Americas*. London: Frank Cass and Co., 1991.

———. *Cultivation and Culture: Labor and the Shaping of Slave Life in the Americas*. Charlottesville: University Press of Virginia, 1993.

Berlin, Ira, and Leslie S. Rowland, eds. *Families and Freedom: A Documentary History of African-American Kinship in the Civil War Era*. New York: New Press, 1997.

Berlin, Ira, Joseph P. Reidy, and Leslie S. Rowland, eds. *Freedom: A Documentary History of Emancipation, 1861–1867, Series 2: The Black Military Experience*. New York: Cambridge University Press, 1982.

———. *Freedom's Soldiers: The Black Military Experience in the Civil War*. New York: Cambridge University Press, 1998.

Berman, William. *The Politics of Civil Rights in the Truman Administration*. Columbus: Ohio State University Press, 1970.

Bernard, Jessie. *Marriage and the Family Among Negroes*. Englewood Cliffs, NJ: Prentice Hall, 1966.

Berry, Daina Ramey. *Swing the Sickle for the Harvest is Ripe: Gender and Slavery in Antebellum Georgia*. Urbana: University of Illinois Press, 2007.

Berry, Mary Frances, and John W. Blassinigame. *Long Memory: The Black Experience in America*. New York: Oxford University Press, 1982.

Billingsley, Andrew. *Black Families in White America*. Englewood Cliffs, NJ: Prentice Hall, 1968.

Bird, Caroline. *The Invisible Scar*. New York: David McKay Co., 1966.

Blackwelder, Julia Kirk. *Styling Jim Crow: African American Beauty Training During Segregation*. College Station: Texas A&M University Press, 2003.

Blank, Rebecca M., and Ron Hoskins, eds. *The New World of Welfare*. Washington, D.C.: Brookings Institution, 2001.

Blassingame, John W. *The Slave Community: Plantation Life in the Antebellum South*. New York: Oxford University Press, 1972.

———. *Black New Orleans, 1860–1880*. Chicago: University of Chicago Press, 1973.

Blau, Joel. *The Visible Poor: Homelessness in the United States*. New York: Oxford University Press, 1992.

Blocker, Jack S. *A Little More Freedom: African Americans Enter the Urban Midwest, 1860–1930*. Columbus: Ohio State University Press, 2008.

Bodnar, John, Roger Simon, and Michael P. Weber. *Lives of their Own: Blacks, Italians, and Poles in Pittsburgh, 1900–1960*. Urbana: University of Illinois Press, 1982.

Boesal, David, and Peter H. Rossi, eds. *Cities Under Siege: An Anatomy of the Ghetto Riots, 1964–1968*. New York: Basic Books, 1971.

Boggs, James. *Racism and the Class Struggle*. New York: Monthly Review Press, 1970

Bohannon, Lisa Fredericksen. *Freedom Cannot Rest: Ella Baker and the Civil Rights Movement*. Greensboro, NC: Morgan Reynolds Publishing, 2005.

Borchert, James. *Alley Life in Washington: Family, Community, Religion, and Folklife in the City, 1850–1970*. Urbana: University of Illinois Press, 1980.

Boserup, Ester. *Woman's Role in Economic Development*. New York: St. Martin's Press, 1974.

Bracey, John H., Jr., August Meier, and Elliott Rudwick, eds. *Black Nationalism in America*. Indianapolis: Bobbs Merrill, 1970.

Bremner, Robert H., and Gary W. Reichard, eds. *Reshaping America: Society and Institutions, 1945–1960*. Columbus: Ohio State University Press, 1982.

Brewer, James H. *The Confederate Negro: Virginia's Craftsmen and Military Laborers, 1861–1865*. Durham, NC: Duke University Press, 1969.

Brinkley, Douglas. *The Great Deluge: Hurricane Katrina, New Orleans, and the Mississippi Gulf Coast*. New York: William Morrow, 2006.

Bruchey, Stuart, ed. *Cotton and the Growth of the American Economy; 1790–1860*. New York: Harcourt, Brace, 1967.

Bullard, Robert D., and Beverly Wright, eds. *Race, Place, and Environmental Justice After Hurricane Katrina: Struggles to Reclaim, Rebuild, and Revitalize New Orleans and the Gulf Coast*. Boulder, CO: Westview Press, 2009.

Bullock, Henry Allen. *A History of Negro Education in the South: From 1619 to the Present*. Cambridge, MA: Harvard University Press, 1967.

Bunch-Lyons, Beverly A. *Contested Terrain: African American Women Migrate from the South to Cincinnati, Ohio, 1900–1950*. New York: Routledge, 2002.

Cain, Glen G. *Married Women in the Labor Force: An Economic Analysis*. Chicago: University of Chicago Press, 1966.

Camp, Stephanie M. H. *Closer to Freedom: Enslaved Women and Everyday Resistance in the Plantation South*. Chapel Hill: University of North Carolina Press, 2004.

Canterow, Ellen, ed. *Moving the Mountain: Women Working for Social Change*. Old Westbury, NY: Feminist Press, 1980.

Capeci, Dominic J. *The Harlem Riot of 1943*. Philadelphia: Temple University Press, 1977.

Carlton, David L. *Mill and Town in South Carolina, 1880–1920*. Baton Rouge: Louisiana State University Press, 1982.

Carnoy, Martin. *Faded Dreams: The Politics and Economics of Race in America*. New York: Cambridge University Press, 1994.

Carson, Clayborne. *In Struggle: SNCC and the Black Awakening of the 1960s*. Cambridge, MA: Harvard University Press, 1981.

Caute, David. *The Great Fear: The Anti-Communist Purge Under Truman and Eisenhower*. New York: Simon and Schuster, 1978.

Chafe, William H. *Women and Equality: Changing Patterns in American Culture*. New York: Oxford University Press, 1977.

———. *Civilities and Civil Rights: Greensboro, North Carolina, and the Black Struggle for Freedom*. New York: Oxford University Press, 1980.

Chisholm, Shirley. *Unbought and Unbossed*. Boston: Houghton Mifflin, 1970.

Cimbala, Paul A. *Under the Guardianship of the Nation: The Freedmen's Bureau and the Reconstruction of Georgia, 1865–1870*. Athens: University of Georgia Press, 1997.

Clark-Lewis, Elizabeth. *Living in, Living Out: African American Domestics in Washington, D.C., 1910–1940*. Washington D.C.: Smithsonian Institute Press, 1994.

Clawson, Dan. *The Next Upsurge: Labor and the New Social Movements*. Ithaca, NY: ILR Press, 2003.

Cleaver, Kathleen Neal, and George Katsiaficas, eds. *Liberation, Imagination, and the Black Panther Party: A New Look at the Panthers and their Legacy*. New York: Routledge, 2001.

Clifton, James M. ed. *Life and Labor on Argyle Island: Letters and Documents of a Savannah River Plantation, 1835–1867*. Savannah, GA: Beehive Press, 1978.

Clinton, Catherine. *The Plantation Mistress: Women's World in the Old South.* New York: Pantheon, 1982.

———, ed. *Half Sisters of History: Southern Women and the American Past.* Durham, NC: Duke University Press, 1994.

———. *Southern Families at War: Loyalty and Conflict in the Civil War South.* New York: Oxford University Press, 2000.

———. *Harriet Tubman: The Road to Freedom.* New York: Little, Brown, 2004.

Cobb, James C. *The Most Southern Place on Earth: The Mississippi Delta and the Roots of Regional Identity.* New York: Oxford University Press, 1992.

Cobble, Dorothy Sue. *The Other Women's Movement: Workplace Justice and Social Rights in Modern America.* Princeton, NJ: Princeton University Press, 2004.

Cohen, Lizabeth. *Making a New Deal: Industrial Workers in Chicago, 1919–1939.* New York: Cambridge University Press, 1990.

Cohen, William. *At Freedom's Edge: Black Mobility and the Southern White Quest for Racial Control, 1861–1915.* Baton Rouge: Louisiana State University Press, 1991.

Collier-Thomas, Bettye, and V. P. Franklin. *Sisters in the Struggle: African-American Women in the Civil Rights-Black Power Movement.* New York: New York University Press, 2001.

Comer, James P. *Maggie's American Dream: The Life and Times of a Black Family.* New York: NAL Books, 1988.

Connelly, Mark Thomas. *The Response to Prostitution in the Progressive Era.* Chapel Hill: University of North Carolina Press, 1980.

Conrad, David Eugene. *The Forgotten Farmers: The Story of Sharecroppers in the New Deal.* Urbana: University of Illinois Press, 1965.

Conway, Mimi. *Rise Gonna Rise: A Portrait of Southern Textile Workers.* New York: Anchor Press, 1979.

Cose, Ellis. *Rage of a Privileged Class.* New York: HarperCollins, 1993.

Cott, Nancy F. *The Bonds of Womanhood: "Woman's Sphere" in New England, 1780–1835.* New Haven, CT: Yale University Press, 1977.

Cott, Nancy F., and Elizabeth Pleck, eds. *A Heritage of Her Own: Toward a New Social History of American Women.* New York: Simon and Schuster, 1979.

Cowie, Jefferson. *Capital Moves: RCA's Seventy-Year Quest for Cheap Labor.* Ithaca, NY: Cornell University Press, 1999.

Crawford, Vicki L., Jacqueline A. Rouse, and Barbara Woods, eds. *Women in the Civil Rights Movement: Trailblazers and Torchbearers, 1941–1965.* Brooklyn, NY: Carlson Pub., 1990.

Creel, Margaret. *"A Peculiar People": Slave Religion and Community Culture Among the Gullahs.* New York: New York University Press, 1988.

Cripps, Thomas. *Slow Fade to Black: The Negro in American Film, 1900–42.* New York: Oxford University Press, 1977.

Crow, Jeffrey, and Flora J. Hatley, eds. *Black Americans in North Carolina and the South.* Chapel Hill: University of North Carolina Press, 1984.

Curtin, Philip D., ed. *Africa Remembered: Narratives by West Africans from the Era of the Slave Trade.* Madison: University of Wisconsin Press, 1967.

Dailey, Jane. *Before Jim Crow: The Politics of Race in Postemancipation Virginia.* Chapel Hill: University of North Carolina Press, 2000.

Dallard, Shrylee. *Ella Baker: A Leader Behind the Scenes.* Englewood Cliffs, NJ: Silver Burdett Press, 1990.

Daniel, Pete. *The Shadow of Slavery: Peonage in the South, 1901–1969.* New York: Oxford University Press, 1972.

Daniel, Walter C. *Black Journals of the United States.* Westport, CT: Greenwood Press, 1982.

David, Paul A., Herbert Gutman, Richard Sutch, Peter Temin, and Gavin Wright. *Reckoning With Slavery: A Critical Study in the Quantitative History of American Negro Slavery.* New York: Oxford University Press, 1976.

Davis, Angela V. *Women, Race, and Class.* New York: Random House, 1981.

Davis, Marianna W., ed. *Contributions of Black Women to America.* Vols. 1 and 2. Columbia, SC: Kenday Press, 1982.

Davis, Ronald L. F. *Good and Faithful Labor: From Slavery to Sharecropping in the Natchez District, 1860–1890.* Westport, CT: Greenwood Press, 1982.

Denby, Charles. *Indignant Heart: Testimony of a Black American Worker.* London: Pluto Press, 1979.

DeParle, Jason. *American Dream: Three Women, Ten Kids, and a Nation's Drive to End Welfare.* New York: Viking, 2004.

Dew, Charles B. *Bond of Iron: Master and Slave at Buffalo Forge.* New York: W. W. Norton, 1994.

Dill, Bonnie Thornton. *Across the Barriers of Race and Class: An Exploration of Work and Family Among Black Female Domestic Servants.* New York: Routledge, 1993.

Diouf, Sylviane. *Servants of Allah: African Muslims Enslaved in the Americas.* New York: New York University Press, 1998.

Dittmer, John. *Black Georgia in the Progressive Era, 1900–1920.* Urbana: University of Illinois Press, 1980.

———. *Local People: The Struggle for Civil Rights in Mississippi.* Urbana: University of Illinois Press, 1995.

Dorsey, Allison. *To Build Our Lives Together: Community Formation in Black Atlanta, 1875–1906.* Athens: University of Georgia Press, 2004.

Dray, Philip. *Capitol Men: The Epic Story of Reconstruction through the Lives of the First Black Congressmen.* New York: Harcourt Brace, 2008.

Dudley, Kathryn Marie. *The End of the Line: Lost Jobs, New Lives in Postindustrial America.* Chicago: University of Chicago Press, 1994.

Dunaway, Wilma A. *The African-American Family in Slavery and Emancipation.* New York: Cambridge University Press, 2003.

Dunster, Alfreda, ed., *Crusade for Justice: The Autobiography of Ida B. Wells.* Chicago: University of Chicago Press, 1970.

Durden, Robert F. *The Gray and the Black: The Confederate Debate on Emancipation.* Baton Rouge: Louisiana State University Press, 1972.

Dusinberre, William. *Them Dark Days: Slavery in the American Rice Swamps.* Athens: University of Georgia Press, 2000.

Dyson, Lowell K. *Red Harvest: The Communist Party and American Farmers.* Lincoln: University of Nebraska Press, 1982.

Dyson, Michael Eric. *Come Hell or High Water: Hurricane Katrina and the Color of Disaster.* New York: Basic Civitas, 2007.

Edelman, Marian Wright. *The Measure of Our Success: A Letter to My Children and Yours.* Boston: Beacon Press, 1992.

Edwards, Laura F. *Scarlet Doesn't Live Here Anymore: Southern Women in the Civil War Era.* Urbana: University of Illinois Press, 2000.

Eisenstein, Zillah R., ed. *Capitalist Patriarchy and the Case for Socialist Feminism.* New York: Monthly Review Press, 1979.

————. *The Radical Future of Liberal Feminism.* New York: Longman, 1981.

Elman, Richard. *The Poorhouse State: The American Way of Life on Public Assistance.* New York: Pantheon, 1966.

Engerman, Stanley L., and Eugene D. Genovese, eds. *Race and Slavery in the Western Hemisphere: Quantitative Studies.* Princeton, NJ: Princeton University Press, 1975.

Engs, Robert F. *Freedom's First Generation: Black Hampton, Virginia, 1861–1890.* Philadelphia: University of Pennsylvania Press, 1979.

Escott, Paul D. *Slavery Remembered: A Record of Twentieth-Century Slave Narratives.* Chapel Hill: University of North Carolina Press, 1979.

Essien-Udom, E. U. *Black Nationalism: A Search for an Identity in America.* Chicago: University of Chicago Press, 1962.

Etzkowitz, Henry, and Gerald M. Schaflander. *Ghetto Crisis: Riots or Reconciliation?* Boston: Little, Brown, 1969.

Evans, Sara. *Personal Politics: The Roots of Women's Liberation in the Civil Rights Movement and the New Left.* New York: Knopf, 1979.

Fager, Charles E. *Selma, 1965.* New York: Charles Scribner's Sons, 1974.

Fairclough, Adam. *A Class of Their Own: Black Teachers in the Segregated South.* Cambridge, MA: Harvard University Press, 2000.

Faragher, John Mack. *Women and Men on the Overland Trail.* New Haven, CT: Yale University Press, 1979.

Farley, Reynolds. *Growth of the Black Population: A Study of Demographic Trends.* Chicago: Markham Publishing Co., 1970.

Feinstein, Karen Wolk, ed. *Working Women and Families.* Beverly Hills, CA: Sage, 1979.

Feldstein, Ruth. *Motherhood in Black and White: Race and Sex in American Liberalism, 1930–1965.* Ithaca, NY: Cornell University Press, 2000.

Fett, Sharla. *Working Cures: Healing, Health, and Power on Southern Slave Plantations.* Chapel Hill: University of North Carolina Press, 2002.

Fink, Leon. *Workingmen's Democracy: The Knights of Labor and American Politics.* Urbana: University of Illinois Press, 1983.

Fitzgerald, Michael W. *Urban Emancipation: Popular Politics in Reconstruction Mobile, 1860–1890.* Baton Rouge: Louisiana State University Press, 2002.

Flynn, Charles L., Jr. *White Land, Black Labor Caste and Class in Late Nineteenth-Century Georgia.* Baton Rouge: Louisiana State University Press, 1983.

Fogel, Robert William, and Stanley L. Engerman. *Time on the Cross: The Economics of American Negro Slavery.* Boston: Little, Brown, 1974.

Foner, Eric. *Free Soil, Free Labor, Free Men: The Ideology of the Republican Party Before the Civil War.* New York: Oxford University Press, 1970.

————. *Politics and Ideology in the Age of the Civil War.* New York: Oxford University Press, 1980.

————. *Nothing But Freedom: Emancipation and Its Legacy.* Baton Rouge: Louisiana State University Press, 1983.

Foner, Philip S. *Organized Labor and the Black Worker, 1619–1973.* New York: Praeger, 1974.

————. *Women and the American Labor Movement: From Colonial Times to the Eve of World War I.* New York: Free Press, 1979.

———. *Women and the American Labor Movement: From the First Trade Unions to the Present.* New York: Free Press, 1982.

Forman, James. *The Making of Black Revolutionaries: A Personal Account.* New York: Macmillan, 1972.

Fox-Genovese, Elizabeth. *Within the Plantation Household: Black and White Women of the Old South.* Chapel Hill: University of North Carolina Press, 1988.

Frank, Miriam, Marilyn Ziebarth, and Connie Field. *The Life and Times of Rosie the Riveter: The Story of Three Million Working Women During World War II.* Emeryville, CA: Clarity Educational Productions, 1982.

Frankel, Noralee. *Freedom's Women: Black Women and Families in Civil War Era Mississippi.* Bloomington: Indiana University Press, 1999.

Freeman, Richard B. *Black Elite: The New Market for Highly Educated Black Americans.* New York: McGraw-Hill, 1976.

Friedan, Betty. *The Feminine Mystique.* New York: Dell, 1974. First published 1963.

Gabin, Nancy F. *Feminism in the Labor Movement: Women and the United Auto Workers, 1935–1975.* Ithaca, NY: Cornell University Press, 1990.

Galenson, David. *White Servitude in America: An Economic Analysis.* New York: Cambridge University Press, 1981.

Gallay, Alan. *The Indian Slave Trade: The Rise of the English Empire in the American South, 1670–1717.* New Haven: Yale University Press, 2002.

Garraty, John A. *Unemployment in History: Economic Thought and Public Policy.* New York: Harper & Row, 1978.

Gaspar, David Barry, and Darlene Clark Hine. *More Than Chattel: Black Women and Slavery in the Americas.* Bloomington: Indiana University Press, 1996.

Gaston, Paul M. *The New South Creed: A Study in Southern Mythmaking.* New York: Knopf, 1970.

Genovese, Eugene D. *Roll, Jordan, Roll: The World the Slaves Made.* New York: Random House, 1974.

Gerteis, Louis S. *From Contraband to Freedman: Federal Policy toward Southern Blacks, 1861–1865.* Westport, CT: Greenwood Press, 1973.

Giddings, Paula. *When and Where I Enter: The Impact of Black Women on Race and Sex in America.* New York: William Morrow, 1984.

Gill, Tiffany. *Beauty Shop Politics: African American Women's Activism in the Beauty Industry.* Urbana: University of Illinois Press, 2010.

Gilmore, Glenda. *Gender and Jim Crow: Women and the Politics of White Supremacy in North Carolina, 1896–1920.* Chapel Hill: University of North Carolina Press, 1996.

———. *Defying Dixie: The Radical Roots of Civil Rights: 1919–1950.* New York: W. W. Norton, 2008.

Glaberman, Martin. *Wartime Strikes: The Struggle Against the No-Strike Pledge in the HAW During World War II.* Detroit, MI: Bewick Press, 1980.

Goldfield, David R. *Cotton Fields and Skyscrapers: Southern City and Region, 1607–1980.* Baton Rouge: Louisiana State University Press, 1982.

Goldin, Claudia Dale. *Urban Slavery in the American South, 1820–1860: A Quantitative History.* Chicago: University of Chicago Press, 1976.

Gomez, Michael A. *Exchanging Our Country Marks: The Transformation of African Identities in the Colonial and Antebellum South.* Chapel Hill: University of North Carolina Press, 1998.

Goodwin, E. Marvin. *Black Migration from 1915 to 1960: An Uneasy Exodus*. Lewiston, ME: E. Mellen Press, 1990.

Goodwyn, Lawrence. *Democratic Promise: The Populist Movement in America*. New York: Oxford University Press, 1976.

Gordon, David M., Richard Edwards, and Michael Reich. *Segmented Work, Divided Workers: The Historical Transformation of Labor in the United States*. New York: Cambridge University Press, 1982.

Gordon, Linda, ed. *Women, the State, and Welfare*. Madison: University of Wisconsin Press, 1990.

Gordon, Michael, ed. *The American Family in Socio-Historical Perspective*. 2nd ed. New York: St. Martin's Press, 1978.

Gordon-Reed, Annette. *The Hemmingses of Monticello: An American Family*. New York: W. W. Norton, 2008.

Gornick, Vivian, and Barbara K. Moran, eds. *Woman in Sexist Society: Studies in Power and Powerlessness*. New York: Basic Books, 1971.

Gottlieb, Peter. *Making Their Own Way: Southern Blacks' Migration to Pittsburgh, 1916–1930*. Urbana: University of Illinois Press, 1987.

Grant, Joanne, ed. *Black Protest: History, Documents, and Analyses, 1619 to the Present*. Greenwich, CT: Fawcett, 1974.

Gray, Brenda Clegg. *Black Female Domestics During the Depression in New York City, 1930–1940*. New York: Garland Press, 1993.

Green, James R. *The World of the Worker: Labor in Twentieth-Century America*. New York: Hill and Wang, 1980.

———. *Workers' Struggles, Past and Present: A 'Radical America' Reader*. Philadelphia: Temple University Press, 1983.

Green, Laurie B. *Battling the Plantation Mentality: Memphis and the Black Freedom Struggle*. Chapel Hill: University of North Carolina, 2007.

Green, Venus. *Race on the Line: Gender, Labor, and Technology in the Bell System, 1880–1980*. Durham: Duke University Press, 2001.

Greene, Lorenzo J., and Carter G. Woodson. *The Negro Wage Earner*. Washington, D.C.: Association for the Study of Negro Life and History, 1930.

Greenwald, Maurine Wiener. *Women, War, and Work: The Impact of World War I on Women Workers in the United States*. Westport, CT: Greenwood Press, 1980.

Gregory, James N. *The Southern Diaspora: How the Great Migrations of Black and White Southerners Transformed America*. Chapel Hill: University of North Carolina Press, 2005.

Grimshaw, Allen D., ed. *Racial Violence in the United States*. Chicago: Aldine Publishing Co., 1969.

Grubbs, Donald H. *Cry From the Cotton: The Southern Tenant Farmers' Union and the New Deal*. Chapel Hill: University of North Carolina Press, 1971.

Guinier, Lani. *The Tyranny of the Majority: Fundamental Fairness in Representative Democracy*. New York: Free Press, 1995.

Gutman, Herbert G. *The Black Family in Slavery and Freedom, 1750–1925*. New York: Pantheon, 1976.

Guttentag, Marcia, and Paul Secord. *Too Many Women? The Sex Ratio Question*. Beverly Hills, CA: Sage, 1983.

Hacker, Andrew. *Two Nations: Black and White, Separate, Hostile, Unequal*. New York: Macmillan International, 1992.

Hafkin, Nancy J., and Edna G. Bay, eds. *Women in Africa: Studies in Social and Economic Change.* Stanford, CA: Stanford University Press, 1976.

Hahn, Steven. *The Roots of Southern Populism: Yeoman Farmers and the Transformation of the Georgia Upcountry, 1850–1890.* New York: Oxford University Press, 1983.

———. *A Nation Under Our Feet: Black Political Struggles in the Rural South; From Slavery to the Great Migration.* Cambridge, MA: Harvard University Press, 2003.

Hall, Jacquelyn Dowd, James Leloudis, Robert Korstad, Mary Murphy, Lu Ann Jones, and Christopher B. Daly. *Like a Family: The Making of a Southern Cotton Mill World.* Chapel Hill: University of North Carolina Press, 1987.

Hamburger, Robert. *A Stranger in the House.* New York: Collier Books, 1978.

Hanson, Joyce Ann. *Mary McLeod Bethune and Black Women's Political Activism.* Columbia: University of Missouri Press, 2003.

Harding, Vincent. *There Is a River: The Black Struggle for Freedom in America.* New York: Harcourt Brace Jovanovich, 1981.

Harlan, Louis R. *Separate and Unequal: Public School Campaigns and Racism in the Southern Seaboard States, 1901–1915.* New York: Atheneum, 1968.

Harley, Sharon, and Rosalyn Terborg-Penn, eds. *The Afro-American Woman: Struggles and Images.* Port Washington, NY: Kennikat Press, 1978.

Harris, William H. *The Harder We Run: Black Workers Since the Civil War.* New York: Oxford University Press, 1982.

Harrison, Alferdteen, ed. *Black Exodus: The Great Migration from the American South.* Jackson: University Press of Mississippi, 1991.

Hartmann, Susan M. *The Home Front and Beyond: American Women in the 1940s.* Boston: Twayne, 1982.

Harvey, Paul. *Freedom's Coming: Religious Culture and the Shaping of the South from the Civil War through the Civil Rights Era.* Chapel Hill: University of North Carolina Press, 2005.

Hays, Sharon. *Flat Broke with Children: Women in the Age of Welfare Reform.* New York: Oxford University Press, 2003.

Heardon, Patrick J. *Independence and Empire: The New South's Cotton Mill Campaign, 1865–1901.* DeKalb: Northern Illinois University Press, 1982.

Hemenway, Robert F. *Zora Neale Hurston: A Literary Biography.* Urbana, IL: University of Illinois Press, 1980.

Henri, Florette. *Black Migration: Movement North, 1900–1920. The Road from Myth to Man.* New York: Anchor Press, 1975.

Hersh, Blanche Glassman. *The Slavery of Sex: Feminist-Abolitionists in America.* Urbana: University of Illinois Press, 1978.

Hershberg, Theodore, ed. *Philadelphia: Work, Space, Family, and Group Experience in the Nineteenth Century.* New York: Oxford University Press, 1981.

Higginbotham, Evelyn Brooks. *Righteous Discontent: The Women's Movement in the Black Baptist Church, 1880–1920.* Cambridge, MA: Harvard University Press, 1993.

Higgs, Robert. *Competition and Coercion: Blacks in the American Economy, 1865–1914.* New York: Cambridge University Press, 1977.

Hill, Robert. *The Strengths of Black Families.* New York: National Urban League, 1972.

Hiller, Dana V., and Robin Ann Sheets, eds. *Women and Men: The Consequences of Power.* Cincinnati, OH: Office of Women's Studies, University of Cincinnati, 1977.

Hine, Darlene Clark. *When the Truth Is Told: A History of Black Women's Culture and Community in Indiana, 1875–1950.* Indianapolis, IN: National Council of Negro Women, 1981.

————. *Black Women in White: Racial Conflict and Cooperation in the Nursing Profession, 1890–1950.* Bloomington: Indiana University Press, 1989.

Hirsch, Arnold R. *Making the Second Ghetto: Race and Housing in Chicago, 1940–1960.* New York: Cambridge University Press, 1983.

Holley, Donald. *The Second Great Emancipation: The Mechanical Cotton Picker, Black Migration, and How They Shaped the Modern South.* Fayetteville: University of Arkansas Press, 2000.

Holt, Sharon Ann. *Making Freedom Pay: North Carolina Freedpeople Working for Themselves, 1865–1900.* Athens: University of Georgia Press, 2000.

Honey, Michael. *Southern Labor and Black Civil Rights: Organizing Memphis Workers.* Urbana: University of Illinois Press, 1993.

————. *Going Down Jericho Road: The Memphis Strike, Martin Luther King's Last Campaign.* New York: W. W. Norton, 2007.

hooks, bell. *Ain't I a Woman: Black Women and Feminism.* Boston: South End Press, 1981.

————. *Yearning: Race, Gender, and Cultural Politics.* Boston: South End Press, 1990.

Huggins, Nathan I., Martin Kilson, and Daniel M. Fox, eds. *Key Issues in the Afro-American Experience,* Vol. 2. New York: Harcourt Brace Jovanovich, 1971.

Hull, Gloria T., Patricia Bell Scott, and Barbara Smith, eds. *All the Women Are White, All the Blacks Are Men, But Some of Us Are Brave: Black Women's Studies.* Old Westbury, NY: Feminist Press, 1982.

Humez, Jean McMahon. *Harriet Tubman: The Life and the Life Stories.* Madison: University of Wisconsin Press, 2003.

Hunter, Tera W. *To 'Joy My Freedom: Southern Black Women's Lives and Labors after the Civil War.* Cambridge, MA: Harvard University Press, 1997.

Jackson, Kenneth T., and Stanley K. Schultz, eds. *Cities in American History.* New York: Knopf, 1972.

Jacobs, Donald M. *Index to the American Slave.* Westport, CT: Greenwood Press, 1981.

Jacobson, Julius, ed. *The Negro and the American Labor Movement.* New York: Anchor Books, 1968.

Jalloh, Alusine, and Toyin Falola, eds., *Black Business and Economic Power Black Business and Economic Power.* Rochester: University of Rochester Press, 2002.

Jencks, Christopher, and Paul E. Peterson, eds. *The Urban Underclass.* Washington, D.C.: Brookings Institution, 1991.

Jensen, Joan M., ed. *With These Hands: Women Working on the Land.* Old Westbury, NY: Feminist Press, 1981.

Johnson, Daniel M., and Rex Campbell. *Black Migration in America: A Social Demographic History.* Durham, NC: Duke University Press, 1981.

Johnson, Jesse J. *Black Women in the Armed Forces, 1942–1974.* Hampton, VA: published by the author, 1974.

Johnson, Michael P., and James Roark. *Black Masters: A Free Family of Color in the Old South.* New York: W. W. Norton, 1981.

Johnson, Walter. *Soul by Soul: Life Inside the Antebellum Slave Market.* Cambridge, MA: Harvard University Press, 1999.

Johnston, James Hugo. *Race Relations in Virginia and Miscegenation in the South, 1776–1860.* Amherst: University of Massachusetts Press, 1970.

Jones, Charisse, and Kumea Shorter Gooden. *Shifting: The Double Lives of Black Women in America*. New York: HarperCollins, 2003.

Jones, Jacqueline. *Soldiers of Light and Love: Northern Teachers and Georgia Blacks, 1865–1873*. Chapel Hill: University of North Carolina Press, 1980.

———. *The Dispossessed: America's Underclasses from the Civil War to the Present*. New York: Basic Books, 1992.

———. *American Work: Four Centuries of Black and White Labor*. New York: W. W. Norton, 1998.

———. *Saving Savannah: The City and the Civil War*. New York: Knopf, 2008.

Jones, Jacqueline, Peter H. Wood, Thomas Borstelmann, Elaine Tyler May, and Vicki L. Ruiz. *Created Equal: A Social and Political History of the United States*. 3rd ed. New York: Longman, 2002.

Joseph, Gloria I., and Jill Lewis. *Common Differences: Conflicts in Black and White Feminist Perspectives*. New York: Anchor Books, 1981.

Joseph, Peniel. *Waiting 'Til the Midnight Hour: A Narrative History of Black Power in America*. New York: Henry Holt, 2007.

Kahn-Hut, Rachel, Arlene Kaplan Daniels, and Richard Clovard, eds. *Women and Work: Problems and Perspectives*. New York: Oxford University Press, 1982.

Katz, Michael B., ed. *The 'Underclass' Debate: Views from History*. Princeton, NJ: Princeton University Press, 1993.

Katzman, David M. *Before the Ghetto: Black Detroit in the Nineteenth Century*. Urbana: University of Illinois Press, 1973.

———. *Seven Days a Week: Women and Domestic Service in Industrializing America*. New York: Oxford University Press, 1978.

Katznelson, Ira. *When Affirmative Action Was White: An Untold History of Racial Inequality in Twentieth-Century America*. New York: W. W. Norton, 2005.

Kaus, Mickey. *The End of Equality*. New York: Basic Books, 1992.

Kaye, Anthony E. *Joining Places: Slave Neighborhoods in the Old South*. Chapel Hill: University of North Carolina Press, 2007.

Kelley, Mary, ed. *Woman's Being, Woman's Place: Female Identity and Vocation in American History*. Boston: G. K. Hall, 1979.

Kelley, Robin D. G. *Race Rebels: Culture, Politics, and the Black Working Class*. New York: Maxwell Macmillan International, 1994.

Kennedy, Susan Estabrook. *If All We Did Was to Weep at Home: A History of White Working-Class Women in America*. Bloomington: Indiana University Press, 1979.

Kerber, Linda K., and Jane DeHart Mathews, eds. *Women's America: Refocusing the Past*. New York: Oxford University Press, 1982.

Kessler-Harris, Alice. *Out to Work: A History of Wage-Earning Women in the United States*. New York: Oxford University Press, 1982.

King, Mary C., ed. *Squaring Up: Policy Strategies to Raise Women's Incomes in the United States*. Ann Arbor: University of Michigan Press, 2001.

King, Wilma. *Stolen Childhood: Slave Youth in Nineteenth-Century America*. Bloomington: Indiana University Press, 1995.

Kirby, John B. *Black Americans in the Roosevelt Era: Liberalism and Race*. Knoxville: University of Tennessee Press, 1980.

Knupfer, Anne Meis. *The Chicago Renaissance and Women's Activism*. Urbana: University of Illinois Press, 2006.

Koger, Larry. *Black Slaveowners: Free Black Slave Masters in South Carolina, 1790–1860.* Columbia: University of South Carolina Press, 1995.

Kolchin, Peter. *First Freedom: The Responses of Alabama's Blacks to Emancipation and Reconstruction.* Westport, CT: Greenwood Press, 1972.

Kotlowitz, Alex. *There Are No Children Here: The Story of Two Boys Growing Up in the Other America.* New York: Doubleday, 1991.

Kotz, Nick, and Mary Lynn Kotz. *A Passion for Equality: George A. Wiley and the Movement.* New York: W. W. Norton, 1977.

Kousser, J. Morgan. *The Shaping of Southern Politics: Suffrage Restriction and the Establishment of the One-Party South, 1880–1910.* New Haven, CT: Yale University Press, 1974.

Kousser, J. Morgan, and James M. McPherson, eds. *Region, Race, and Reconstruction: Essays in Honor of C. Vann Woodward.* New York: Oxford University Press, 1982.

Kozol, Jonathan. *Savage Inequalities: Children in America's Schools.* New York: Crown Publishers, 1991.

Kuhn, Annette, and Annmarie Wolpe, eds. *Feminism and Materialism: Women and Modes of Production.* London: Routledge and Kegan Paul, 1978.

Kusmer, Kenneth L. *A Ghetto Takes Shape: Black Cleveland, 1870–1930.* Urbana: University of Illinois Press, 1976.

Ladner, Joyce. *Tomorrow's Tomorrow: The Black Woman.* New York: Doubleday, 1972.

Lamon, Lester C. *Black Tennesseans, 1900–1930.* Knoxville: University of Tennessee Press, 1977.

Larson, Kate Clifford. *Bound for the Promised Land: Harriet Tubman, Portrait of an American Hero.* New York: Ballantine, 2004.

Lawrence-Lightfoot, Sarah. *I've Known Rivers: Lives of Loss and Liberation.* Reading, MA: Addison-Wesley, 1994.

Lawson, Bill E., and Frank M. Kirkland, eds. *Frederick Douglass: A Critical Reader.* Hoboken, NJ: Wiley-Blackwell, 1999.

Lebsock, Suzanne. *The Free Women of Petersburg: Status and Culture in a Southern Town, 1784–1860.* New York: W. W. Norton, 1984.

Leith–Ross, Sylvia. *African Women: A Study of the Ibo of Nigeria.* New York: Frederick A. Praeger, 1965.

Lemke-Santangelo, Gretchen. *Abiding Courage: African American Migrant Women in the East Bay Community.* Chapel Hill: University of North Carolina Press, 1996.

Lerner, Gerda. *The Majority Finds Its Past: Placing Women in History.* New York: Oxford University Press, 1979.

Levenstein, Harvey. *Communism, Anticommunism, and the CIO.* Westport, CT: Greenwood Press, 1981.

Levine, Lawrence. *Black Culture and Black Consciousness: Afro-American Folk Thought from Slavery to Freedom.* New York: Oxford University Press, 1977.

Lewis, John, and Michael D'Orso. *Walking with the Wind: A Memoir of the Movement.* New York: Houghton Mifflin Harcourt, 1999.

Lichtenstein, Nelson. *Labor's War at Home: The CIO in World War II.* New York: Cambridge University Press, 1982.

Lieberson, Stanley. *A Piece of the Pie: Blacks and White Immigrants Since 1880.* Berkeley: University of California Press, 1980.

Lindsey, Duncan. *The Welfare of Children.* New York: Oxford University Press, 1994.

Ling, Peter J., and Sharon Monteith, eds. *Gender and the Civil Rights Movement*. New Brunswick, NJ: Rutgers University Press, 2004.

Litwack, Leon. *Been in the Storm So Long: The Aftermath of Slavery*. New York: Knopf, 1979.

Logan, Frenise A. *The Negro in North Carolina, 1876–1894*. Chapel Hill: University of North Carolina Press, 1964.

Logan, Rayford. *The Betrayal of the Negro: From Rutherford B. Hayes to Woodrow Wilson*. New York: Collier Books, 1970. First published 1954.

Lynn, Mary C., ed. *Women's Liberation in the Twentieth Century*. New York: John Wiley and Sons, 1975.

Mack, Kibibi Voloria C. *Parlor Ladies and Ebony Drudges: African American Women, Class, and Work in a South Carolina Community*. Knoxville: University of Tennessee Press, 1999.

MacLean, Nancy. *Freedom Is Not Enough: The Opening of the American Workplace*. New York: Russell Sage Foundation; Cambridge, MA: Harvard University Press, 2006.

Magdol, Edward. *A Right to the Land: Essays on the Freedmen's Community*. Westport, CT: Greenwood Press, 1977.

Magdol, Edward, and Jon L. Wakelyn. *The Southern Common People: Studies in Nineteenth Century Social History*. Westport, CT: Greenwood Press, 1980.

Malone, Ann Patton. *Sweet Chariot: Slave Family and Household Structure in Nineteenth Century Louisiana*. Chapel Hill: University of North Carolina Press, 1992.

Mandle, Jay R. *The Roots of Black Poverty: The Southern Plantation Economy After the Civil War*. Durham, NC: Duke University Press, 1978.

Marks, Carole. *Farewell: We're Good and Gone: The Great Migration*. Bloomington: Indiana University Press, 1989.

Marshall, F. Ray. *Labor in the South*. Cambridge, MA: Harvard University Press, 1967.

Martin, Tony. *Race First: The Ideological and Organizational Struggles of Marcus Garvey and the Universal Negro Improvement Association*. Westport, CT: Greenwood Press, 1977.

Massey, Douglas S., and Nancy A. Denton. *American Apartheid: Segregation and the Making of the Underclass*. Cambridge, MA: Harvard University Press, 1993.

Matthaei, Julie A. *An Economic History of Women in America: Women's Work, the Sexual Division of Labor, and the Development of Capitalism*. New York: Schocken Books, 1982.

McAdoo, Harriette Pipes, ed. *Black Families*. Beverly Hills, CA: Sage, 1981.

McAllister, Pam, ed. *Reweaving the Web of Life: Feminism and Nonviolence*. Philadelphia: New Society, 1982.

McElvaine, Robert S. *The Great Depression: America, 1929–1941*. New York: Three Rivers Press, 1993.

McFeely, William S. *Yankee Stepfather: General O. O. Howard and the Freedmen*. New Haven, CT: Yale University Press, 1968.

McPherson, James M. *The Abolitionist Legacy: From Reconstruction to the NAACP*. Princeton, NJ: Princeton University Press, 1975.

Meier, August, and Elliott Rudwick. *CORE: A Study in the Civil Rights Movement, 1942–1968*. New York: Oxford University Press, 1973.

———. *Black Detroit and the Rise of the UAW*. New York: Oxford University Press, 1979.

Meier, August, Elliot Rudwick, and Francis Broderick, eds. *Black Protest Thought in the Twentieth Century*. 2nd ed. Indianapolis, IN: Bobbs-Merrill, 1971.

Melish, Joanne Pope. *Disowning Slavery: Gradual Emancipation and Race in New England, 1780–1860*. Ithaca: Cornell University Press, 2000.

Meyerowitz, Joanne, ed. *Not June Cleaver: Women and Gender in Postwar America, 1945–1960*. Philadelphia: Temple University Press, 1994.

Milkis, Sidney. *The Great Society and the High Tide of Liberalism*. Amherst: University of Massachusetts Press, 2005.

Miller, Marc S., ed. *Working Lives: The Southern Exposure History of Labor in the South*. New York: Pantheon, 1980.

Minchin, Timothy J. *Hiring the Black Worker: The Racial Integration of the Southern Textile Industry, 1960–1980*. Chapel Hill: University of North Carolina Press, 1999.

Mittelstadt, Jennifer. *From Welfare to Workfare: The Unintended Consequences of Liberal Reform, 1945–1965*. Chapel Hill: University of North Carolina Press, 2005.

Mohr, Clarence. *On the Threshold of Freedom: Masters and Slaves in Civil War Georgia*. Athens: University of Georgia Press, 1986.

Morgan, Edmund S. *American Slavery, American Freedom: The Ordeal of Colonial Virginia*. New York: W. W. Norton, 1975.

Morgan, Philip D. *Slave Counterpoint: Black Culture in the Eighteenth-Century Chesapeake and Lowcountry*. Chapel Hill: University of North Carolina press, 1998.

Morgan, Robin, ed. *Sisterhood is Powerful: An Anthology of Writings from the Women's Liberation Movement*. New York: Random House, 1970.

Morris, Robert C. *Reading, 'Riting, and Reconstruction: The Education of Freedmen in the South, 1861–1870*. Chicago: University of Chicago Press, 1981.

Morrison, Toni, ed. *Race-ing Justice, En-Gendering Power: Essays on Anita Hill, Clarence Thomas, and the Construction of Social Reality*. New York: Pantheon, 1992.

Morton, Patricia, ed. *Discovering the Women in Slavery: Emancipating Perspectives on the American Past*. Athens: University of Georgia Press, 1996.

Naison, Mark. *Communists in Harlem During the Depression*. Urbana: University of Illinois Press, 1983.

Nelson, Jill. *Volunteer Slavery: My Authentic Negro Experience*. New York: Penguin, 1994.

Newman, Dorothy K., Barbara L. Carter, and Nancy J. Amidei. *Protest, Politics, and Prosperity: Black Americans and White Institutions, 1940–1975*. New York: Pantheon, 1978.

Newton, James E., and Ronald L. Lewis, eds. *The Other Slaves: Mechanics, Artisans, and Craftsmen*. Boston: G. K. Hall, 1978.

Nielson, David Gordon. *Black Ethos: Northern Urban Negro Life and Thought, 1890–1930*. Westport, CT: Greenwood Press, 1977.

Noble, Jeanne. *Beautiful, Also, Are the Souls of My Black Sisters: A History of the Black Woman in America*. Englewood Cliffs, NJ: Prentice-Hall, 1978.

Oakes, James. *The Ruling Race: A History of American Slaveholders*. New York: Knopf, 1982.

Oates, Stephen B. *Let the Trumpet Sound: The Life of Martin Luther King, Jr.* New York: Harper & Row, 1982.

Oberschall, Anthony. *Social Conflict and Social Movements*. Englewood Cliffs, NJ: Prentice Hall, 1973.

O'Donovan, Susan. *Becoming Free in the Cotton South*. Cambridge, MA: Harvard University Press, 2007.

Oliver, Melvin L., and Thomas M. Shapiro. *Black Wealth/White Wealth: A New Perspective on Racial Inequality*. 2nd ed. Hoboken, NJ: Routledge, 2006.

O'Neal, Hank, and others. *A Vision Shared: A Classic Portrait of America and Its People, 1935–1943*. New York: St. Martin's Press, 1976.

Oppenheimer, Valerie Kincaide. *The Female Labor Force in the United States: Demographic and Economic Factors Governing Its Growth and Changing Composition.* Westport, CT: Greenwood Press, 1970.

Orleck, Annelise. *Storming Caesar's Palace: How Black Mothers Fought Their Own War on Poverty.* Boston: Beacon Press, 2005.

Osofsky, Gilbert. *Harlem: The Making of a Ghetto; Negro New York, 1890–1930.* New York: Harper & Row, 1966.

Owens, Harry P., ed. *Perspectives and Irony in American Slavery.* Jackson: University Press of Mississippi, 1976.

Owens, Leslie Howard. *This Species of Property: Slave Life and Culture in the Old South.* New York: Oxford University Press, 1976.

Painter, Nell I. *Exodusters: Black Migration to Kansas after Reconstruction.* New York: Knopf, 1977.

———. *Sojourner Truth: A Life, A Symbol.* New York: W. W. Norton, 1996.

Parker, Lonnae O'Neal. *I'm Every Woman: Remixed Stories of Marriage, Motherhood, and Work.* New York: Amistad, 2005.

Paulme, Denise, ed. *Women of Tropical Africa.* Berkeley: University of California Press, 1963.

Payne, Charles. *I've Got the Light of Freedom: The Organizing Tradition and the Mississippi Freedom Struggle.* Berkeley: University of California Press, 1995.

Penningroth, Dylan C. *The Claims of Kinfolk: African American Property and Community in the Nineteenth-Century South.* Chapel Hill: University of North Carolina Press, 2003.

Perman, Michael. *Struggle for Mastery: Disfranchisement in the South, 1888–1908.* Chapel Hill: University of North Carolina Press, 2000.

Perrucci, Carolyn C., and Dena B. Targ, eds. *Marriage and the Family: A Critical Analysis and Proposals for Change.* New York: D. McKay, 1974.

Peterson, Theodore. *Magazines in the Twentieth Century.* 2nd ed. Urbana: University of Illinois Press, 1964.

Piven, Frances Fox, and Richard A. Cloward. *Regulating the Poor: The Functions of Public Welfare.* New York: Vintage Books, 1971.

———. *Poor People's Movements: Why They Succeed, How They Fail.* New York: Vintage Books, 1977.

Pleck, Elizabeth. *Black Migration and Poverty, Boston, 1865–1900.* New York: Academic Press, 1979.

Pollitzer, William S. *The Gullah People and their African Heritage.* Athens: University of Georgia Press, 1999.

Poole, Mary. *The Segregated Origins of Social Security: African Americans and the Welfare State.* Chapel Hill: University of North Carolina Press, 2006.

Postel, Charles. *The Populist Vision.* New York: Oxford University Press, 2007.

Powell, Lawrence N. *New Masters: Northern Planters During the Civil War and Reconstruction.* New Haven, CT: Yale University Press, 1980.

Rabinowitz, Howard N. *Race Relations in the Urban South: 1865–1890.* New York: Oxford University Press, 1978.

———, ed. *Southern Black Leaders of the Reconstruction Era.* Urbana: University of Illinois Press, 1982.

Raboteau, Albert. *Slave Religion: The 'Invisible Institution' in the Antebellum South.* New York: Oxford University Press, 1978.

Rachleff, Peter. *Black Labor in Richmond, 1865–1890.* Urbana: University of Illinois Press, 1989.

Rainwater, Lee, and William L. Yancey. *The Moynihan Report and the Politics of Controversy.* Cambridge, MA: MIT Press, 1967.

Rank, Mark Robert. *Living on the Edge: The Realities of Welfare in America.* New York: Columbia University Press, 1994.

Ransby, Barbara. *Ella Baker and the Black Freedom Movement: A Radical Democratic Vision.* Chapel Hill: University of North Carolina Press, 2003

Ransom, Roger L., and Richard Sutch. *One Kind of Freedom: The Economic Consequences of Emancipation.* New York: Cambridge University Press, 1977.

Reed, Merle E., Leslie S. Hough, and Gary M. Fink, eds. *Southern Workers and Their Unions, 1880–1975: Selected Papers, The Second Southern Labor History Conference, 1978.* Westport, CT: Greenwood Press, 1978.

Reese, Ellen. *Backlash Against Welfare Mothers: Past and Present.* Berkeley: University of California Press, 2005.

Regosin, Elizabeth Ann. *Freedom's Promise: Ex-slave Families and Citizenship in the Age of Emancipation.* Charlottesville: University Press of Virginia, 2002.

Reid, Inez Smith. *"Together" Black Women.* New York: Third Press, 1972.

Renoff, Gregory. *The Traveling Circus in Georgia, 1820–1930.* Athens: University of Georgia Press, 2008.

Richardson, Joe M. *The Negro in the Reconstruction of Florida, 1865–1877.* Tallahassee: Florida State University Press, 1965.

Ripley, C. Peter. *Slaves and Freedmen in Civil War Louisiana.* Baton Rouge: Louisiana State University Press, 1976.

Roark, James. *Masters Without Slaves: Southern Planters in the Civil War and Reconstruction.* New York: W. W. Norton, 1977.

Robinson, Armstead L. *Bitter Fruits of Bondage: The Demise of Slavery and the Collapse of the Confederacy, 1861–1865.* Charlottesville: University Press of Virginia, 2004.

Robnett, Belinda. *How Long? How Long? African-American Women in the Struggle for Civil Rights.* New York: Oxford University Press, 1997.

Rodgers, Daniel T. *The Work Ethic in Industrial America, 1850–1920.* Chicago: University of Chicago Press, 1978.

Rodgers-Rose, La Frances, ed. *The Black Woman.* Beverly Hills, CA: Sage, 1980.

Rodrigue, John C. *Reconstruction in the Cane Fields: From Slavery to Free Labor in Louisiana's Sugar Parishes, 1862–1880.* Baton Rouge: Louisiana State University Press, 2001.

Roediger, David. *Towards the Abolition of Whiteness.* London: Verso Press, 1994.

Rose, Willie Lee. *Rehearsal for Reconstruction: The Port Royal Experiment.* Indianapolis, IN: Bobbs-Merrill, 1964.

Rosen, Hannah. *Terror in the Heart of Freedom: Citizenship, Sexual Violence, and the Making of Race in the Postemancipation South.* Chapel Hill: University of North Carolina Press, 2008.

Rosen, Ruth. *The Lost Sisterhood: Prostitution in America, 1900–1918.* Baltimore: Johns Hopkins University Press, 1982.

Rossi, Alice S., and Ann Calderwood, eds. *Academic Women On the Move.* New York: Russell Sage, 1973.

Rothschild, Joan, ed. *Machina Ex Dea: Feminist Perspectives on Technology.* New York: Pergamon Press, 1983.

Rothschild, Mary A. *A Case of Black and White: Northern Volunteers and the Southern Freedom Summers, 1964–1965.* Westport, CT: Greenwood Press, 1982.

Royster, Jacqueline Jones. *Lugenia Burns Hope: Black Southern Reformer*. Athens: University of Georgia Press, 1989.

Rudwick, Elliott M. *Race Riot at East St. Louis, July 2, 1917*. Carbondale: Southern Illinois University Press, 1964.

Rupp, Leila J. *Mobilizing Women for War: German and American Propaganda, 1939–1945*. Princeton, NJ: Princeton University Press, 1978.

Ryan, Mary. *Womanhood in America: From Colonial Times to the Present*. 2nd ed. New York: New Viewpoints, 1979.

Sawers, Larry, and William K. Tabb, eds. *Sunbelt/Snowbelt: Urban Development and Regional Restructuring*. New York: Oxford University Press, 1984.

Scharf, Lois. *To Work and To Wed: Female Employment, Feminism, and the Great Depression*. Westport, CT: Greenwood Press, 1980.

Scharf, Lois, and Joan M. Jensen, eds. *Decades of Discontent: The Women's Movement, 1920–1940*. Westport, CT: Greenwood Press, 1983.

Scheiner, Seth M. *Negro Mecca: A History of the Negro in New York City, 1865–1920*. New York: New York University Press, 1965.

Schnore, Leo F., ed. *The New Urban History: Quantitative Explorations by American Historians*. Princeton, NJ: Princeton University Press, 1975.

Schultz, Janet E. *Women at the Front: Hospital Workers in Civil War America*. Chapel Hill: University of North Carolina Press, 2004.

Schwalm, Leslie. *A Hard Fight for We: Women's Transition from Slavery to Freedom in South Carolina*. Urbana: University of Illinois Press, 1997.

Schwartz, Marie Jenkins. *Born in Bondage: Growing Up Enslaved in the Antebellum South*. Cambridge, MA: Harvard University Press, 2000.

————. *Birthing a Slave: Motherhood and Medicine in the Antebellum South*. Cambridge, MA: Harvard University Press, 2006.

Schwartz, Michael. *Radical Protest and Social Structure: The Southern Farmers' Alliance and Cotton Tenancy, 1880–1890*. New York: Academic Press, 1976.

Schwarz, John E., and Thomas J. Volgy. *Thirty Million Working Poor in the Land of Opportunity*. New York: W. W. Norton, 1992.

Scott, Anne Firor. *The Southern Lady: From Pedestal to Politics, 1830–1930*. Chicago: University of Chicago Press, 1970.

Sekora, John, and Darwin T. Turner, eds. *The Art of Slave Narrative: Original Essays in Criticism and Theory*. Macomb: W. Illinois University, 1982.

Self, Robert O. *American Babylon: Race and the Struggle for Postwar Oakland*. Princeton, NJ: Princeton University Press, 2003.

Sernett, Milton C. *Harriet Tubman: Myth, Memory, and History*. Durham: Duke University Press, 2007.

Shaffer, Donald R. *After the Glory: The Struggles of Black Civil War Veterans*. Lawrence: University Press of Kansas, 2004.

Shaw, Stephanie J. *What a Woman Ought to Be and to Do: Black Professional Women Workers During the Jim Crow Era*. Chicago: University of Chicago Press, 1996.

Sherman, Max. *Barbara Jordan: Speaking the Truth with Eloquent Thunder*. Austin: University of Texas Press, 2007.

Shipler, David K. *The Working Poor: Invisible in America*. New York: Knopf, 2004.

Shockley, Megan Taylor. *"We, Too, Are Americans": African American Women in Detroit and Richmond, 1940 to 1954.* Urbana: University of Illinois Press, 2004.

Shull, Steven A. *A Kinder, Gentler Racism? The Reagan-Bush Civil Rights Legacy.* Armonk, NY: M. E. Sharpe, 1993.

Sidbury, James. *Becoming African in America: Race and Nation in the Early Black Atlantic.* New York: Oxford University Press, 2007.

Sitkoff, Harvard. *A New Deal for Blacks: The Emergence of Civil Rights as a National Issue.* New York: Oxford University Press, 1978.

————. *The Struggle for Black Equality, 1954–1980.* New York: Hill and Wang, 1981.

Sitterson, J. Carlyle. *Sugar Country: The Cane Sugar Industry in the South, 1753–1950.* Louisville: University Press of Kentucky, 1953.

Smallwood, Stephanie. *Saltwater Slavery: A Middle Passage from Africa to American Diaspora.* Cambridge, MA: Harvard University Press, 2007.

Smith, Jessie Carney, ed. *Encyclopedia of African American Business.* Vol. 2. Westport, CT: Greenwood Press, 2006.

Smith, Mark M. *Mastered by the Clock: Time, Slavery, and Freedom in the American South.* Chapel Hill: University of North Carolina Press, 1997.

Sokol, Jason. *There Goes My Everything: White Southerners in the Age of Civil Rights, 1945–1975.* New York: Vintage Books, 2007.

Sowell, Thomas. *Ethnic America: A History.* New York: Basic Books, 1981.

Spear, Allan H. *Black Chicago: The Making of a Negro Ghetto, 1890–1920.* Chicago: University of Chicago Press, 1967.

Starobin, Robert S. *Industrial Slavery in the Old South.* New York: Oxford University Press, 1970.

Steady, Filomina Chioma, ed. *The Black Woman Cross-Culturally.* Cambridge, MA: Schenkman, 1981.

Stemsher, Bernard, ed. *Hitting Home: The Great Depression in Town and Country.* Chicago: Quadrangle Books, 1970.

Sterling, Dorothy, ed. *We Are Your Sisters: Black Women in the Nineteenth Century.* New York: W. W. Norton, 1984.

Stevenson, Brenda E. *Life in Black and White: Family and Community in the Slave South.* New York: Oxford University Press, 1996.

Stewart, Mart. *'What Nature Suffers to Groe': Life, Labor and Landscape on the Georgia Coast, 1680–1920.* Athens: University of Georgia Press, 1996.

Strasser, Susan. *Never Done: A History of American Housework.* New York: Pantheon, 1982.

Strickland, Arvah E. *History of the Chicago Urban League.* Urbana: University of Illinois Press, 1966.

Stromberg, Ann H., and Shirley Harkess, eds. *Women Working: Theories and Facts in Perspective.* Palo Alto, CA: Mayfield Publishing Company, 1978.

Sugrue, Thomas. *Origins of Urban Crisis: Race and Inequality in Postwar Detroit.* Princeton, NJ: Princeton University Press, 1996.

————. *Sweet Land of Liberty: The Forgotten Struggle for Civil Rights in the North.* New York: Random House, 2008.

Sutherland, Daniel E. *Americans and Their Servants: Domestic Service in the United States from 1800 to 1920.* Baton Rouge: Louisiana State University Press, 1981.

Swerdlow, Amy, and Hanna Lessinger, eds. *Class, Race, and Sex: The Dynamics of Control*. Boston: G. K. Hall, 1983.

Taylor, Alrutheus A. *The Negro in South Carolina During the Reconstruction*. New York: Russell and Russell, 1969. First published 1924.

———. *The Negro in the Reconstruction of Virginia*. Washington, D.C.: Association for the Study of Negro Life and History, 1926.

Taylor, Joel Gray. *Louisiana Reconstructed, 1863–1877*. Baton Rouge: Louisiana State University, Press, 1974.

Taylor, Quintard, and Shirley Ann Wilson Moore, eds. *African American Women Confront the West: 1600–2000*. Norman: University of Oklahoma Press, 2003.

Tentler, Leslie Woodcock. *Wage-Earning Women: Industrial Work and Family Life in the United States, 1900–1930*. New York: Oxford University Press, 1979.

Thernstrom, Stephan. *The Other Bostonians: Poverty and Progress in the American Metropolis, 1880–1970*. Cambridge, MA: Harvard University Press, 1973.

Tilley, Nannie May. *The Bright-Tobacco Industry, 1860–1929*. Chapel Hill: University of North Carolina Press, 1948.

Tindall, George Brown. *South Carolina Negroes, 1877–1900*. Columbia: University of South Carolina Press, 1952.

Trelease, Allen W. *White Terror: The Ku Klux Klan Conspiracy and Southern Reconstruction*. New York: Harper & Row, 1971.

Trotter, Joe William, ed. *The Great Migration in Historical Perspective: New Dimensions of Race, Class, and Gender*. Bloomington: Indiana University Press, 1991.

Tuttle, William M., Jr. *Race Riot: Chicago in the Red Summer of 1919*. New York: Atheneum, 1970.

Wade, Richard C. *Slavery in the Cities: The South, 1820–1860*. New York: Oxford University Press, 1964.

Walker, Alice. *In Search of Our Mothers' Gardens: Womanist Prose*. San Diego, CA: Harcourt Brace Jovanovich, 1983.

Walker, Juliet E. K., ed. *Encyclopedia of African American Business History*. Westport, CT: Greenwood Press, 1999.

Walker, Susannah. *Style and Status: Selling Beauty to African American Women, 1920–1975*. Louisville: University Press of Kentucky, 2007.

Wallace, Michele. *Black Macho and the Myth of the Superwoman*. New York: Dial Press, 1979.

Wallace, Phyllis A. *Pathways to Work: Unemployment Among Black Teenage Females*. Lexington, MA: Lexington Books, 1974.

———, ed. *Equal Employment Opportunity and the AT&T Case*. Cambridge, MA: MIT Press 1976.

———. *Black Women in the Labor Force*. Cambridge, MA: MIT Press, 1980.

Wallace, Phyllis A., and Annette M. LaMond, eds. *Women, Minorities, and Employment Discrimination*. Lexington, MA: Lexington Books, 1977.

Walshok, Mary Lindenstein. *Blue Collar Women: Pioneers on the Male Frontier*. New York: Anchor Books, 1981.

Wandersee, Winifred D. *Women's Work and Family Values, 1920–1940*. Cambridge, MA: Harvard University Press, 1981.

Ward, Kathryn, ed. *Women Workers and Global Restructuring*. Ithaca, NY: ILR Press, School of Industrial and Labor Relations, Cornell University, 1990.

Ware, Susan. *Beyond Suffrage: Women in the New Deal*. Cambridge, MA: Harvard University Press, 1981.

———. *Holding Their Own: American Women in the 1930s*. Boston: Twayne Publishers, 1982.

Wayne, Michael. *The Reshaping of Plantation Society: The Natchez District, 1860–1880*. Baton Rouge: Louisiana State University Press, 1983.

Webber, Thomas L. *Deep Like the Rivers: Education in the Slave Quarter Community, 1831–1865*. New York: W. W. Norton, 1978.

Weisenfeld, Judith. *African American Women and Christian Activism: New York's Black YWCA, 1905–1945*. Cambridge, MA: Harvard University Press, 1997.

Weiss, Nancy J. *Farewell to the Party of Lincoln: Black Politics in the Age of FDR*. Princeton, NJ: Princeton University Press, 1983.

West, Cornel. *Race Matters*. New York: Vintage Books, 1994.

West, Guida. *The National Welfare Rights Movement: The Social Protest of Poor Women*. New York: Praeger, 1981.

Westin, Jeane. *Making Do: How Women Survived the '30s*. Chicago: Follette, 1976.

White, Deborah Gray. *Ar'n't I a Woman? Female Slaves in the Plantation South*. New York: W. W. Norton, 1985.

———. *Too Heavy a Load: Black Women in Defense of Themselves, 1894–1994*. New York: W. W. Norton, 1999.

White, Shane. *Somewhat More Independent: The End of Slavery in New York City, 1780–1810*. Athens: University of Georgia Press, 1991.

Whitten, Norman E., and John F. Szwed, eds. *Afro-American Anthropology: Contemporary Perspectives*. New York: Free Press, 1970.

Wiener, Jonathan M. *Social Origins of the New South: Alabama, 1860–1885*. Baton Rouge: Louisiana State University Press, 1978.

Wiener, Marli. *Mistresses and Slaves: Plantation Women in South Carolina, 1830–1880*. Urbana: University of Illinois Press, 1997.

Wilkison, Kyle G. *Yeomen, Sharecroppers, and Socialists: Plain Folk Protest in Texas, 1870–1914*. College Station: Texas A&M Press, 2008.

Williams, Heather Andrea. *Self-Taught: African-American Education in Slavery and Freedom*. Chapel Hill: University of North Carolina Press, 2007.

Williams, Thonda Y. *The Politics of Public Housing: Black Women's Struggles Against Urban Inequality*. New York: Oxford University Press, 2004.

Williamson, Joel. *New People: Miscegenation and Mulattoes in the United States*. New York: Free Press, 1980.

Wilson, William J. *The Truly Disadvantaged: The Inner-City, The Underclass, and Public Policy*. Chicago: University of Chicago Press, 1987.

———. *When Work Disappears: The World of the New Urban Poor*. New York: Knopf, 1996.

Wolcott, Victoria W. *Remaking Respectability: African American Women in Interwar Detroit*. Chapel Hill: University of North Carolina Press, 2001.

Wolters, Raymond. *Negroes and the Great Depression*. Westport, CT: Greenwood Press, 1970.

Wood, Betty. *Women's Work, Men's Work: The Informal Slave Economies of Lowcountry Georgia*. Athens: University of Georgia Press, 1995.

Wood, Peter. *Black Majority: Negroes in Colonial South Carolina from 1670 Through the Stono Rebellion*. New York: Knopf, 1974.

Woodruff, Nan Elizabeth. *American Congo: The African American Freedom Struggle in the Delta.* Cambridge, MA: Harvard University Press, 2003.

Woodward, C. Vann. *Origins of the New South, 1877–1913.* Baton Rouge: Louisiana State University Press, 1951.

Woody, Bette. *Black Women in the Workplace: Impacts of Structural Change in the Economy.* New York: Greenwood Press, 1992.

Wyatt-Brown, Bertram. *Southern Honor: Ethics and Behavior in the Old South.* New York: Oxford University Press, 1982.

Yee, Shirley. *Black Women Abolitionists: A Study in Activism, 1828–1860.* Knoxville: University of Tennessee Press, 1992.

Yellin, Jean Fagan. *Harriet Jacobs: A Life.* New York: Basic Civitas Books, 2004.

Young, Jeffrey Robert. *Domesticating Slavery: The Master Class in Georgia and South Carolina, 1670–1837.* Chapel Hill: University of North Carolina Press, 1999.

Zinn, Maxine Baca, and Bonnie Thornton Dill, eds. *Women of Color in United States Society.* Philadelphia: Temple University Press, 1993.

Articles

Aldridge, Delores. "Black Women in the Economic Marketplace: A Battle Unfinished." *Journal of Social and Behavioral Sciences* 21 (Winter 1975): 48–62.

Alfred, Mary V. "Welfare Reform and Black Women's Economic Development." *Adult Education Quarterly* 57 (2007): 293–311.

Allen, Walter. "Family Roles, Occupational Status, and Achievement Orientation Among Black Women in the United States." *Signs* 4 (Summer 1979): 670–686.

Anderson, Karen Tucker. "Last Hired, First Fired: Black Women Workers During World War II." *Journal of American History* 69 (June 1982): 82–97.

Anderson, S. E., and Rosemari Mealy. "Who Originated the Crisis? A Historical Perspective." *Black Scholar* 10 (May–June 1979): 40–44.

Armstrong, Thomas F. "From Task Labor to Free Labor: The Transition Along Georgia's Rice Coast, 1820–1880." *Georgia Historical Quarterly* 64 (Winter 1980): 432–447.

Auerbach, Jerold. "Southern Tenant Farmers: Socialist Critics of the New Deal." *Labor History* 7 (Winter 1966): 3–18.

Badgett, M. V. Lee. "Rising Black Unemployment: Changes in Job Stability or in Employ-ability?" *Review of Black Political Economy* 22 (Winter 1994): 55–75.

Bailey, David T. "A Divided Prism: Two Sources of Black Testimony on Slavery." *Journal of Southern History* 46 (August 1980): 381–404.

Baker, Ella. "Freedom Village." *Southern Exposure* 9 (Fall 1981): 20.

Barr, Alwyn. "Black Urban Churches on the Southern Frontier, 1865–1900." *Journal of Negro History* 82 (1997): 368–383.

Bates, Eric. "The Kill Line." *Southern Exposure* 19 (Fall 1991): 23.

Beale, Frances. "Slave of a Slave No More: Black Women in Struggle." *Black Scholar* 12 (November–December 1981): 16–24.

Beckert, Sven. "Emancipation and Empire: Reconstructing the Worldwide Web of Cotton Production in the Age of the American Civil War." *American Historical Review* 109 (December 2004): 1405–1438.

Beckett, Joyce A. "Working Wives: A Racial Comparison." *Social Work* 21 (November 1976): 463–471.

Belgrave, Linda Liska. "The Effects of Race Differences in Work History, Work Attitudes, Economic Resources, and Health on Women's Retirement." *Research on Aging* 10 (September 1988): 383–398.

Bell, Duran. "Why Participation Rates of Black and White Wives Differ." *Journal of Human Resources* 9 (Fall 1974): 465–479.

Berlin, Ira. "Time, Space, and the Evolution of Afro-American Society on British Mainland North America." *American Historical Review* 85 (February 1980): 44–78.

Biggert, M. Langley. "Legacy of Resistance: Uncovering the History of Collective Action by Black Agricultural Workers in Central East Arkansas from the 1860s to the 1930s." *Journal of Social History* 32 (Autumn 1998): 73–100.

"Black Scholar Interview: Kathleen Cleaver." *Black Scholar* 3 (December 1971): 54–59.

Blackwelder, Julia Kirk. "Quiet Suffering: Atlanta Women in the 1930's." *Georgia Historical Quarterly* 61 (1977): 112–124.

———. "Women in the Work Force: Atlanta, New Orleans, and San Antonio, 1930 to 1940." *Journal of Urban History* 4 (May 1978): 331–358.

Blassingame, John W. "Before the Ghetto: The Making of the Black Community in Savannah, Georgia, 1865–1880." *Journal of Social History* 6 (Summer 1973): 463–487.

Blendon, Robert J., Linda H. Aiken, Howard E. Freeman, and Christopher R. Corey. "Access to Medical Care for Black and White Americans." *Journal of the American Medical Association* 261 (January 13, 1989): 278–281.

Blum, Linda M., and Theresa Deussen. "Negotiating Independent Motherhood: Working-Class African American Women Talk About Marriage and Motherhood." *Gender and Society* 10 (1996): 199–211.

Bock, E. Wilbur. "Farmer's Daughter Effect: The Case of the Negro Female Professionals." *Phylon* 30 (Spring 1969): 18–19.

Bodnar, John. "The Impact of the 'New Immigration' on the Black Worker: Steelton, Pennsylvania, 1880–1920." *Labor History* 17 (Spring 1976): 214–29.

Bodnar, John, Michael Weber, and Roger Simon. "Migration, Kinship, and Urban Adjustment: Blacks and Poles in Pittsburgh, 1900–1930." *Journal of American History* 66 (December 1979): 548–565.

Boyd, Robert L. "The Great Migration to the North and the Rise of Ethnic Niches for African American Women in Beauty Culture and Hair-Dressing, 1910–1920." *Sociological Focus* 29 (February 1996): 33–45.

Braden, Anne. "A View from the Fringes." *Southern Exposure* 9 (Spring 1981): 68–74.

Brown, Cynthia Stokes, and Tom Gardner. "Montgomery Bus Boycott." *Southern Exposure* 9 (Spring 1981): 12–21.

Brown, Elsa Barkley. "Womanist Consciousness: Maggie Lena Walker and the Independent Order of Saint Luke." *Signs* 14 (Spring 1989): 610–633.

Brown, Judith K. "A Note on the Division of Labor by Sex." *American Anthropologist* 72 (October 1970): 1073–1078.

Brown, Steven E. "Sexuality and the Slave Community." *Phylon* 42 (Spring 1981): 1–10.

Butchart, Ronald. "'We Can Best Instruct Our Own People': New York African Americans in the Freedmen's Schools, 1861–1875." *Afro-Americans in New York Life and History* 12 (January 1988): 27–49.

———. "Perspectives on Gender, Race, Calling, and Commitment in 19th-Century America: A Collective Biography of the Teachers of the Freedpeople, 1862–1875." *Vitae Scholasticae* 13 (Spring 1994): 15–32.

Campbell, Bebe Moore. "Black Executives and Corporate Stress." *New York Times Magazine*, December 12, 1982, 39.

Campbell, Randolph B., and Donald K. Pickens. "Document: 'My Dear Husband': A Texas Slave's Love Letter, 1862." *Journal of Negro History* 65 (Fall 1980): 361–364.

Cantor, Louis. "A Prologue to the Protest Movement: The Missouri Sharecropper Roadside Demonstration of 1939." *Journal of American History* 55 (March 1969): 804–822.

Charity, Ruth Harvey, Christina Davis, and Arthur Kinoy. "The Danville Movement: The People's Law Takes Hold." *Southern Exposure* 10 (July 1982): 35–39.

Chisholm, Shirley. "Race, Revolution and Women." *Black Scholar* 3 (December 1971): 17–21.

Cimprich, John. "Slave Behavior During the Federal Occupation of Tennessee, 1862–1865." *Historian* 44 (May 1982): 335–346.

Clive, Alan. "Women Workers in World War II: Michigan as a Test Case." *Labor History* 20 (Winter 1979): 44–69.

Cody, Cheryll A. "Naming, Kinship, and Estate Dispersal: Notes on Slave Family Life on a South Carolina Plantation, 1786 to 1833." *William and Mary Quarterly* 39 (January 1982): 192–211.

Collins, Patricia Hill. "Setting Our Own Agenda." *Black Scholar* 23 (Summer/Fall 1993): 52–55.

Collins, Sharon. "Blacks on the Bubble: The Vulnerability of Black Executives in White Corporations." *Sociological Quarterly* 34 (1993): 429–447

Collins, William J. "When the Tide Turned: Immigration and the Delay of the Great Black Migration." *The Journal of Economic History* 57 (September 1997): 607–632.

Crouch, Barry A. "The 'Chords of Love': Legalizing Black Marital and Family Rights in Postwar Texas." *Journal of Negro History* 79 (1994): 334–351.

Crowe, Charles. "Racial Violence and Social Reform-Origins of the Atlanta Riot of 1906." *Journal of Negro History* 53 (July 1968): 234–256.

————. "Racial Massacre in Atlanta, September 22, 1906." *Journal of Negro History* 54 (April 1969): 150–173.

Cutright, Phillip. "Components of Change in the Number of Female Family Heads Aged 15–44; United States, 1940–1970." *Journal of Marriage and the Family* 36 (November 1974): 714–722.

Cutright, Phillip, and Edward Shorter. "The Effects of Health on the Completed Fertility of Nonwhite and White United States Women Born Between 1865 and 1935." *Journal of Social History* 13 (Winter 1979): 191–218.

Dalfiume, Richard. "The Forgotten Negro Revolution." *Journal of American History* 55 (June 1968): 90–106.

Davis, Angela. "Reflections on the Black Woman's Role in the Community of Slaves." *Black Scholar* 3 (December 1971): 2–15.

Donahue, John J., III, and James Heckman. "Continuous Versus Episodic Change: The Impact of Civil Rights Policy on the Economic Status of Blacks." *Journal of Economic Literature* 29 (December 1991): 1603–1643.

Dougherty, Jack. "'That's When We Were Marching for Jobs': Black Teachers and the Early Civil Rights Movement in Milwaukee." *History of Education Quarterly* 38 (Summer 1998): 121–141.

Drago, Edmund L. "Militancy and Black Women in Reconstruction Georgia." *Journal of American Culture* 1 (Winter 1978): 838–844.

————. "Sources at the National Archives for Genealogical and Local History Research: The Black Family in Dougherty County, Georgia, 1870–1900." *Prologue* 14 (Summer 1982): 81–88.

duCille, Ann. "The Occult of True Black Womanhood: Critical Demeanor and Black Feminist Studies." *Signs* 19 (Spring 1994): 591–630.

Duelberg, Sonia I. "Preventive Health Behavior Among Black and White Women in Urban and Rural Areas." *Social Science Medicine* 34 (1992): 191–198.

Eblen, Jack E. "New Estimates of the Vital Rates of the United States Black Population During the Nineteenth Century." *Demography* 2 (May 1974): 301–319.

Eichelberger, Brenda. "Voices of Black Feminism." *Quest* 3 (Spring 1977): 16–28.

Eisenstein, Zillah. "The Sexual Politics of the New Right: Understanding the 'Crisis of Liberalism' for the 1980s." *Signs* 7 (Spring 1982): 567–588.

Engerman, Stanley L. "Black Fertility and Family Structure in the U.S., 1880–1940." *Journal of Family History* 2 (June 1977): 117–138.

———. "Three Recent Studies of Ethnicity and Relative Economic Achievement: A Review Essay." *Historical Methods* 16 (Winter 1983): 30–35.

English, Beth. "I Have . . . a Lot of Work to Do: Cotton Mill Work and Women's Culture in Matoaca, VA, 1888–1895." *Virginia Magazine of History and Biography* 114 (2006): 356–383.

Epstein, Cynthia Fuchs. "Positive Effects of the Multiple Negative: Explaining the Success of Black Professional Women." *American Journal of Sociology* 78 (January 1973): 912–935.

Faust, Drew Gilpin. "Culture, Conflict and Community: The Meaning of Power on an Antebellum Plantation." *Journal of Social History* 14 (Fall 1980): 83–97.

Fields, Barbara Jeanne. "Slavery, Race and Ideology in the United States of America." *New Left Review* (May 1990): 95–118.

Follett, Richard. "Heat, Sex, and Sugar: Pregnancy and Childbearing in the Slave Quarters." *Journal of Family History* 28 (October 2003): 236–250.

Forman, James. "Freedom Rides." *Southern Exposure* 9 (Spring 1981): 34–39.

Fosu, Augustin Kwasi. "Occupational Mobility of Black Women, 1958–1981: The Impact of Post-1964 Anti-Discrimination Measures." *Industrial and Labor Relations Review* 45 (January 1992): 281–286.

Gabin, Nancy. "Women Workers and the UAW in the Post-World War Period, 1945–54." *Labor History* 21 (Winter 1980): 5–30.

———. "'They Have Placed a Penalty on Womanhood': The Protest Action of Women Auto Workers in Detroit-Area UAW Locals, 1945–1947." *Feminist Studies* 8 (Summer 1982): 373–398.

Geschwender, James A. "Civil Rights Protest and Riots: A Disappearing Distinction." *Social Science Quarterly* 49 (December 1968): 474–484.

Gladney, Margaret Rose. "If It Was Anything for Justice: Interview with Sallie Mae Hadnott." *Southern Exposure* 4 (Winter 1977): 19–23.

Glave, Dianne D. "'A Garden So Brilliant with Colors, So Original in Its Design': Rural African American Women, Gardening, Progressive Reform, and the Foundation of an African American Environmental Perspective." *Environmental History* 8 (July 2003): 395–411.

Golden, Bernette. "Black Women's Liberation." *Essence* 4 (February 1974): 35.

Goldin, Claudia D. "Female Labor Force Participation: The Origin of Black and White Differences, 1870–1880." *Journal of Economic History* 16 (Summer 1983): 39–48.

Goody, Jack, and Joan Buckley. "Inheritance and Women's Labour in Africa," *Africa* 63 (April 1973): 108–121.

Greenberg, M. "Urban/Rural Differences in Behavioral Risk Factors for Chronic Diseases." *Urban Geography* 8 (1987): 146–151.

Greenberg, Stephanie W. "Neighborhood Change, Racial Transition, and Work Location: A Case Study of an Industrial City, 1880–1930." *Journal of Urban History* 7 (May 1981): 267–314.

Griffin, Jean T. "West African and Black Working Women: Historical and Contemporary Comparisons." *Journal of Black Psychology* 8 (February 1982): 55–74.

Gump, Janice. "A Comparative Analysis of Black and White Women's Sex-Role Attitudes." *Journal of Consulting and Clinical Psychology* 43 (1975): 858–863.

Gurin, Patricia and Carolyn Gaylord. "Educational and Occupational Goals of Men and Women at Black Colleges." *Monthly Labor Review* 99 (June 1976): 10–16.

Hall, Jacquelyn Dowd. "The Long Civil Rights Movement and the Political Uses of the Past." *Journal of American History* 91, no. 4 (March 2005): 1233–1263.

Hare, Nathan, and Julia Hare. "Black Women 1970." *Trans-Action* 8 (November–December 1970): 65–90.

Hareven, Tamara K. "The Family Process: The Historical Study of the Family Cycle," *Journal of Social History* 7 (Spring 1974): 322–329.

———. "Modernization and Family History: Perspectives on Social Change," *Signs* 2 (Autumn 1976): 190–206.

Harris, William H. "Work and the Family in Black Atlanta, 1880." *Journal of Social History* 9 (Spring 1976): 319–330.

———. "Federal Intervention in Union Discrimination: FEPC and West Coast Shipyards During World War II." *Labor History* 22 (Summer 1981): 325–247.

Heckman, James J., and Brook S. Payner. "Determining the Impact of Federal Antidiscrimination Policy on the Economic Status of Blacks: A Study of South Carolina." *American Economic Review* 79 (March 1989): 138–177.

Hertz, Susan M. "The Politics of the Welfare Mothers Movement: A Case Study." *Signs* 2 (Spring 1977): 600–611.

Hickel, K. Walter. "'Justice and the Highest Kind of Equality Require Discrimination': Citizenship, Dependency, and Conscription in the South, 1917–1919." *Journal of Southern History* 66 (November 2000): 749–780.

Higginbotham, Evelyn Brooks. "African-American Women's History and the Metalanguage of Race." *Signs* 17, no. 2 (Winter 1992): 251–274.

Higgs, Robert. "The Boll Weevil, the Cotton Economy, and Black Migration, 1910–1930." *Agricultural History* 50 (April 1976): 335–350.

Hill, Herbert. "The AFL-CIO and the Black Worker: Twenty-five Years After the Merger." *Journal of Intergroup Relations* 10 (Spring 1982): 5–79.

Hill, Robert B. "The Economic Status of Black Families." In *The State of Black America: 1979*. National Urban League, 1979.

Hine, Darlene Clark. "To Be Gifted, Female, and Black." *Southwest Review* 67 (Autumn 1982): 357–369.

Holmes, William F. "The Demise of the Colored Farmers' Alliance." *Journal of Southern History* 41 (May 1975): 187–200.

Honey, Maureen. "The Working-Class Woman and Recruitment Propaganda During World War II: Class Differences in the Portrayal of War Work." *Signs* 8 (Summer 1983): 672–687.

Howard, Victor B. "The Civil War in Kentucky: The Slave Claims His Freedom." *Journal of Negro History* 67 (Fall 1982): 245–256.

Howe, Daniel Walker. "American Victorianism as a Culture." *American Quarterly* 27 (December 1975): 507–532.

Jackson, Jacquelyne J. "But Where are the Men?" *Black Scholar* 3 (December 1971): 30–41.

Jencks, Christopher. "What Happened to Welfare?" *New York Review of Books*, December 15, 2005, 76.

Johnson, Beverly L. "Women Who Head Families, 1970–1977: Their Numbers Rose, Income Lagged." *Monthly Labor Review* 101 (February 1978): 32–37.

Johnson, Chalis. "'All I'm Askin' is a Little Respect': Black Women in the Academy: A Conference Report from MIT." *Black Scholar* 24 (Winter 1994): 2–4.

Johnson, Michael P. "Smothered Slave Infants: Were Slave Mothers at Fault?" *Journal of Southern History* 47 (November 1981): 439–520.

Johnson, Whittington B. "Free Blacks in Antebellum Savannah: An Economic Profile." *Georgia Historical Quarterly* 64 (Winter 1980): 418–431.

———. "Free African American Women in Savannah, 1800–1860: Affluence and Autonomy Amid Adversity." *Georgia Historical Quarterly* 76 (Summer 1992): 260–283.

Jones, Beverly W. "Mary Church Terrell and the NACW, 1896–1901." *Journal of Negro History* 47 (Spring 1982): 20–33.

Jones, Jacqueline. "Encounters, Likely and Unlikely, Between Black and Poor White Women in the Rural South, 1865–1940." *Georgia Historical Quarterly* 76 (Summer 1992): 333–353.

———. "American Others." *In These Times* 18 (February 7, 1994): 14–17.

Jupiter, Clare. "Without Fear." *Southern Exposure* 9 (Winter 1981): 63–66.

Kann, Kenneth. "The Knights of Labor and the Southern Black Worker." *Labor History* 18 (Winter 1977): 49–70.

Katz, Michael, Mark Stern, and Jamie Fader. "The New African American Inequality." *Journal of American History* 92 (June 2005): 75–108.

Kelly, Brian. "Black Laborers, the Republican Party, and the Crisis of Reconstruction in Lowcountry South Carolina." *International Review of Social History* 51 (2006): 375–414.

Kelly, Joan. "The Doubled Vision of Feminist Theory: A Postscript to the 'Women and Power' Conference." *Feminist Studies* 5 (Spring 1979): 216–227.

Kiple, Kenneth F., and Virginia H. Kiple. "Slave Child Mortality: Some Nutritional Answers to a Perennial Puzzle." *Journal of Social History* 10 (March 1977): 284–309.

Kirby, Jack Temple. "The Transformation of Southern Plantations, c. 1920–1960." *Agricultural History* 57 (July 1983): 257–276.

Klaczynska, Barbara. "Why Women Work: A Comparison of Various Groups; Philadelphia, 1910–1930." *Labor History* 17 (Winter 1976): 73–87.

Kornweibel, Theodore, Jr. "An Economic Profile of Black Life in the Twenties." *Journal of Black Studies* 6 (June 1976): 307–320.

Krech, Shepard, III. "Black Family Organization in the Nineteenth Century: An Ethnological Perspective." *Journal of Interdisciplinary History* 12 (Winter 1982): 429–452.

Kremm, Thomas W., and Diane Neal. "Challenges to Subordination: Organized Black Agricultural Protest in South Carolina, 1886–1895." *South Atlantic Quarterly* 77 (Winter 1978): 98–112.

Kuttner, Bob. "The Declining Middle." *The Atlantic* 252 (July 1983): 60–72.

Landry, Bart, and Margaret Platt Jendrek. "The Employment of Wives in Middle-Class Black Families." *Journal of Marriage and the Family* 40 (November 1978): 787–798.

Lantz, Herman, and Lewellyn Hendrix. "Black Fertility and the Black Family in the Nineteenth Century: A Re-Examination of the Past." *Journal of Family History* 3 (Fall 1978): 251–261.

Legan, Marshall Scott. "Disease and the Freedmen in Mississippi During Reconstruction." *Journal of the History of Medicine and Allied Sciences* 28 (July 1973): 257–267.

Levitan, Sara A. "Work and Welfare in the 1970s." Welfare Policy Project Institute of Policy Studies and Public Affairs, Duke University (Spring 1977).

Lewis, Diane K. "Response to Inequality: Black Women, Racism, and Sexism." *Signs* 3 (Winter 1977): 339–361.

Lightner, David L., and Alexander M. Ragan. "Were African American Slaveholders Benevolent or Exploitative? A Quantitative Approach." *Journal of Southern History* 21 (August 2005): 535–558.

Lillie-Blanton, Marsha, Rose Marie Martinez, Andrea Kidd Taylor, and Betty Garman. "Latina and African-American Women: Continuing Disparities in Health." *International Journal of Health Services* 23 (1993): 573–574.

Long, Larry H., and Kristin A. Hansen. "Trends in Return Migration to the South." *Demography* 12 (November 1975): 601–614.

Marshall, Paule. "From the Poets in the Kitchen." *New York Times Book Review*, January 9, 1983, 3.

Martin, Charles H. "Labor Relations in Transition: Gadsden, Alabama, 1930–1943." *Journal of Southern History* 47 (November 1981): 545–568.

McDonald, Forrest, and Grady McWhiney. "The South from Self-Sufficiency to Peonage: An Interpretation." *American Historical Review* 85 (December 1980): 1095–1118.

McEaddy, Beverly Johnson. "Women Who Head Families: A Socio-economic Analysis." *Monthly Labor Review* 99 (June 1976): 3–10.

McFalls, Joseph A., Jr., and George S. Masnick. "Birth Control and the Fertility of the Black Population, 1880 to 1980." *Journal of Family History* 6 (Spring 1981): 89–106.

McGraw, Mike. "Cheep Labor: Programs Place Americans Low in Pecking Order." *Mother Jones* 21 (January–February 1996): 13.

McGuire, Danielle. "'It Was Like All of Us Had Been Raped': Sexual Violence, Community Mobilization, and the African American Freedom Struggle." *Journal of American History* 91 (December 2004): 906–931.

McLaughlin, Virginia Yans. "Patterns of Work and Family Organization: Buffalo's Italians." *Journal of Interdisciplinary History* 2 (Autumn 1971): 297–314.

Meeker, Edward. "Mortality Trends of Southern Blacks, 1850–1910: Some Preliminary Findings." *Explorations in Economic History* 13 (January 1976): 13–42.

Meier, August, and Elliott Rudwick. "The Boycott Movement Against Jim Crow Streetcars in the South, 1900–1906." *Journal of American History* 55 (March 1969): 756–775.

———. "Communist Unions and the Black Community: The Case of the Transport Workers Union, 1934–1944." *Labor History* 23 (Spring 1982): 165–197.

Milkman, Ruth. "Women's Work and Economic Crisis: Some Lessons of the Great Depression." *Review of Radical Political Economics* 8 (Spring 1976): 73–97.

———. "Redefining 'Women's Work': The Sexual Division of Labor in the Auto Industry During World War II." *Feminist Studies* 8 (Summer 1982): 337–372.

Miller, Randall M. "The Fabric of Control: Slavery in Antebellum Southern Textile Mills." *Business History Review* 55 (Winter 1981): 471–490.

"Mississippi Freedom Democratic Party." *Southern Exposure* 9 (Spring 1981): 45–48.

"Mississippi Movement." *Southern Exposure* 9 (Spring 1981): 40.

Mohr, Clarence L. "Before Sherman: Georgia Blacks and the Union War Effort, 1861–1864." *Journal of Southern History* 45 (August 1979): 331–352.

Morgan, Philip D. "Work and Culture: The Task System and the World of Lowcountry Blacks, 1700 to 1880." *William and Mary Quarterly* 39 (October 1982): 563–599.

Morrison, Toni. "What the Black Woman Thinks About Women's Lib." *New York Times Magazine*, August 22, 1971, 14.

Mosle, Sara. "Letter from Las Vegas: How the Maids Fought Back." *New Yorker*, February 26 and March 4, 1996, 155.

Neely, Sara. "Women of Philadelphia and Their Activities." *Crisis* 51 (May 1944): 150–159.

Nelson, Charmeynne D. "Myths About Black Women Workers in Modern America." *Black Scholar* 6 (March 1975): 11–15.

Nielsen, Joyce McCarl, and Russell Endo. "Marital Status and Socioeconomic Status: The Case of Female-Headed Families." *International Journal of Women's Studies* 6 (March–April 1983): 130–147.

Niemi, Albert W., Jr. "The Impact of Recent Civil Rights Laws: Relative Improvement in Occupational Structure, Earnings and Income by Non-Whites, 1960–70." *American Journal of Economics and Sociology* 33 (April 1974): 137–144.

Notman, Malkah T., and Carol C. Nadelson. "The Rape Victim: Psychodynamic Considerations." *American Journal of Psychiatry* 133 (April 1976): 408–413.

Patton, Gwendolyn M. "Insurgent Memories." *Southern Exposure* 9 (Spring 1981): 58–63.

Perrin, Liese M. "Resisting Reproduction: Reconsidering Slave Contraception in the Old South." *Journal of American Studies* 35 (2001): 255–274.

Pfaff, Eugene. "Greensboro Sit-ins." *Southern Exposure* 9 (Spring 1981): 23–28.

Pfister, Joe. "Twenty Years and Still Marching." *Southern Exposure* 10 (January–February 1982): 20–27.

Phillips, Kimberley L. "'But It Is a Fine Place to Make Money': Migration and African-American Families in Cleveland, 1915–1929." *Journal of Social History* (1996): 393–413.

Piker, Joshua. "Indians and Race in Early America: A Review Essay." *History Compass* 3 (January 2005): 1–17.

Pollard, Leslie J. "Aging and Slavery: A Gerontological Perspective." *Journal of Negro History* 66 (Fall 1981): 228–234.

Quaye, Randolph. "The Health Care Status of African Americans." *Black Scholar* 24 (Spring 1994): 12–18.

Quick, Paddy. "Rosie the Riveter: Myths and Realities." *Radical America* 9 (July–August 1975): 15–32.

Raines, Howell. "The Birmingham Bombing." *New York Times Magazine*, July 24, 1983, 12.

Ransom, Roger L., and Richard Sutch. "Growth and Welfare in the American South of the Nineteenth Century." *Explorations in Economic History* 16 (April 1979): 142–152.

Raphael, Alan. "Health and Social Welfare of Kentucky Black People, 1865–1870." *Societas* 2 (Spring 1972): 143–157.

Reagon, Bernice Johnson. "World War II Reflected in Black Music: 'Uncle Sam Called Me.'" *Southern Exposure* 1 (Winter 1974): 170–184.

———. "We Became Visible, Our Image Was Enlarged." *Southern Exposure* 9 (Spring 1981): 5.

———. "My Black Mothers and Sisters, or On Beginning a Cultural Autobiography." *Feminist Studies* 8 (Spring 1982): 81–96.

Reid, Joseph D., Jr. "White Land, Black Labor, and Agricultural Stagnation: The Causes and Effects of Sharecropping in the Post-Bellum South." *Explorations in Economic History* 16 (January 1979): 31–55.

Reiff, Janice L., Michel R. Dahlin, and Daniel Scott Smith. "Rural Push and Urban Pull: Work and Family Experiences of Older Black Women in Southern Cities, 1880–1900." *Journal of Social History* 16 (Summer 1983): 39–48.

Rivers, Larry. "'Dignity and Importance': Slavery in Jefferson County, Florida—1827 to 1860." *Florida Historical Quarterly* 61 (April 1983): 422–423.

Robinson, Armstead L. "In the Shadow of Old John Brown: Insurrection Anxiety and Confederate Mobilization, 1861–1863." *Journal of Negro History* 65 (Fall 1980): 279–297.

———. "Beyond the Realm of Social Consensus: New Meanings of Reconstruction for American History." *Journal of American History* 68 (September 1981): 276–297.

Rodgers, Daniel T. "Tradition, Modernity, and the American Industrial Worker: Reflections and Critique." *Journal of Interdisciplinary History* 7 (Spring 1977): 655–681.

Ryon, Roderick N. "An Ambiguous Legacy: Baltimore Blacks and the CIO, 1936–1941." *Journal of Negro History* 65 (Winter 1980): 18–33.

Scott, Anne Firor. "Most Invisible of All: Black Women's Voluntary Associations." *Journal of Southern History* 56 (February 1990): 3–22.

Seraile, William. "Henrietta Vinton Davis and the Garvey Movement." *Afro-Americans in New York Life and History* 7 (July 1983): 7–24.

Shakur, Assata. "Women in Prison: How We Are." *Black Scholar* 12 (November–December 1981; first published 1978): 50–57.

Sharpless, John, and John Rury. "The Political Economy of Women's Work: 1900–1920." *Social Science History* 4 (Summer 1980): 317–346.

Shifflett, Crandall A. "The Household Composition of Rural Black Families: Louisa County, Virginia, 1880." *Journal of Interdisciplinary History* 6 (Autumn 1975}: 235–260.

Shlomowitz, Ralph. "The Origins of Southern Sharecropping." *Agricultural History* 53 (July 1979): 557–575.

Shofner, Jerrell H. "The Legacy of Racial Slavery: Free Enterprise and Forced Labor in Florida in the 1940s." *Journal of Southern History* 47 (August 1981): 411–426.

Silver, Timothy. "Learning to Live with Nature: Colonial Historians and the Southern Environment." *Journal of Southern History* 73 (August 2007): 539–552.

Sitkoff, Harvard. "Harry Truman and the Election of 1948: The Coming of Age of Civil Rights in American Politics." *Journal of Southern History* 37 (November 1971): 597–616.

———. "Racial Militancy and Interracial Violence in the Second World War." *Journal of American History* 58 (December 1971): 661–681.

Sizemore, Barbara A. "Sexism and the Black Male." *Black Scholar* 4 (March–April 1973): 2–11.

Skocpol, Theda. "The New Urban Poverty and U. S. Social Policy." *Michigan Quarterly Review* 33 (Spring 1994): 274–281.

Smallwood, James M. "Emancipation and the Black Family: A Case Study in Texas." *Social Science Quarterly* 57 (March 1977): 849–857.

Smith, Audrey D., Anne E. Fortune, and William J. Reid. "WIN, Work, and Welfare." *Social Service Review* 49 (September 1975): 396–405.

Smith, Barbara. "Notes for Yet Another Paper on Black Feminism, Or Will the Real Enemy Please Stand Up?" *Conditions Five: The Black Women's Issue* 2 (Autumn 1979): 123–132.

Spear, Jennifer M. "Race Matters in the Colonial South." *Journal of Southern History* 73 (August 2007): 579–588.

Spencer, Jon Michael. "Trends of Opposition to Multiculturalism." *Black Scholar* 23 (Winter/Spring 1993): 2–5.

Steckel, Richard. "Slave Mortality: Analysis of Evidence From Plantation Records." *Social Science History* 3 (October 1979): 86–114.

———. "Miscegenation and the American Slave Schedules." *Journal of Interdisciplinary History* 2 (Autumn 1980): 251–263.

Stokes, Gail. "Black Woman to Black Man." *Liberator* 1 (December 1968): 17.

Stone, Pauline Terrelonge. "The Limitation of Reformist Feminism." *Black Scholar* 10 (May–June 1979): 24–27.

Straub, Eleanor F. "United States Government Policy Toward Civilian Women During World War II." *Prologue* 5 (Winter 1973): 240–255.

Tadman, Michael. "Demographic Cost of Sugar: Debates on Slave Societies and Natural Increase in the Americas." *American Historical Review* 105 (December 2000): 1535–1575.

Taylor, Quintard. "The Great Migration: The Afro-American Communities of Seattle and Portland During the 1940s." *Arizona and the West* 23 (Summer 1981): 109–126.

Temin, Peter. "Patterns of Cotton Agriculture in Post-Bellum Georgia." *Journal of Economic History* 43 (September 1983): 661–674.

Thompson, E. P. "Time, Work-Discipline and Industrial Capitalism." *Past and Present* 38 (December 1967): 56–97.

Trussell, James, and Richard Steckel. "The Age of Slaves at Menarche and Their First Birth." *Journal of Interdisciplinary History* 8 (Winter 1978): 477–505.

Walker, Alice. "In Search of Our Mothers' Gardens." *Southern Exposure* 4 (Winter 1977): 60–64.

Walker, Melissa. "Home Extension Work Among African American Farm Women in East Tennessee, 1920–1939." *Agricultural History* (1996): 487–502.

Walter, John C. "Frank R. Crosswaith and Labor Unionization in Harlem, 1939–45." *Afro-Americans in New York Life and History* 7 (July 1983): 47–58.

Watriss, Wendy. "It's Something Inside You." *Southern Exposure* 4 (Winter 1977): 76–81.

Wetherell, Charles. "Slave Kinship: A Case Study of the South Carolina Good Hope Plantation, 1835–1856." *Journal of Family History* 6 (Fall 1981): 294–308.

White, Katherine J. Gurtis. "Women in the Great Migration: Economic Activity of Black and White Southern-Born Female Migrants in 1920, 1940, and 1970." *Social Science History* 29 (2005): 413–455.

Wiener, Jonathan M. "Class Structure and Economic Development in the American South, 1865–1955." *American Historical Review* 84 (October 1979): 970–992.

Wiggins, David K. "The Play of Slave Children in the Plantation Communities of the Old South, 1820–1860." *Journal of Sport History* 7 (Summer 1980): 21–39.

Wigginton, Eliot and Sue Thrasher. "To Make the World We Want." *Southern Exposure* 10 (September–October 1982): 25–31.

Williams, Patricia J. "Notes from a Small World." *New Yorker*, April 29 and May 6, 1996, 87.

———. "Mrs. Obama Meets Mrs. Windsor." *Nation* (April 27, 2009): 9.

Winegarten, Ruthe. "I Am Annie Mae: The Personal Story of a Texas Black Woman." *Chrysalis* 4 (Spring 1980): 15.

Wood, Kristen E. "Broken Reeds and Competent Farmers: Slaveholding Widows in the Southeastern United States, 1783–1861." *Journal of Women's History* 13 (2001): 34–57.

Woodman, Harold D. "Comment" [On Goldin, "Female Labor Force Participation"]. *Journal of Economic History* 37 (March 1977): 109–112.

———. "Sequel to Slavery: The New History Views the Postbellum South." *Journal of Southern History* 43 (November 1977): 523–554.

———. "Comment." *American Historical Review* 84 (October 1979): 997–1001.

———. "Postbellum Social Change and Its Effects on Marketing the South's Cotton Crop." *Agricultural History* 56 (January 1982): 215–231.

Woodward, C. Vann. "History from Slave Sources." *American Historical Review* 79 (April 1974): 470–481.

Wright, Gavin. "Cheap Labor and Southern Textiles Before 1880." *Journal of Economic History* 39 (September 1979): 655–680.

Wright, Lawrence. "Annals of Politics: One Drop of Blood." *New Yorker*, July 25, 1994, 46.

Wynne, Lewis N. "The Role of Freedmen in the Post Bellum Cotton Economy." *Phylon* 42 (December 1981): 309–321.

UNPUBLISHED DISSERTATIONS, WORKING PAPERS, AND TYPESCRIPTS

Brooks, Evelyn. "The Women's Movement in the Black Baptist Church, 1880–1920." PhD diss., University of Rochester, 1984.

Bryan, Herbert L. "Birth Rates and Death Rates in Relation to Dependency in Selected Health Areas in Harlem." Master's thesis, Columbia University, 1936.

Bullock, Dorothy Josephine. "An Analysis of Cases of Negro Working Mothers Known to the Family Welfare Society, Atlanta, Georgia; 1940–1942." Master's thesis, Atlanta University, 1943.

Burton, Orville V. "Ungrateful Servants: Edgefield's Black Reconstruction: Part I of the Total History of Edgefield County, South Carolina." PhD diss., Princeton University, 1976.

Darling, Marsha J. "The Growth and Decline of the Afro-American Family Farm." PhD diss., Duke University, 1982.

Dill, Bonnie Thornton. "Across the Barriers of Race and Class: An Exploration of the Relationship Between Work and Family Among Black Female Domestic Servants." PhD diss., New York University, 1979.

Douglass, Priscilla Harriet. "Black Working Women: Factors Affecting Labor Market Experience." Working paper no. 39, Wellesley College Center for Research on Women, Wellesley, MA, 1980.

Edin, Kathryn. "Single Mothers and Absent Fathers: The Possibilities and Limits of Child Support Policy." Working paper, Center for Urban Policy Research, Rutgers University, December, 1993.

Fields, Jacqueline P. "Factors Contributing to Nontraditional Career Choices of Black Female College Graduates." Working paper no. 83, Wellesley College Center for Research on Women, Wellesley, MA, 1981.

Goodson, Martia Graham. "An Introductory Essay and Subject Index to Selected Interviews from the Slave Narrative Collection." PhD diss., Union Graduate School, 1977.

Gottlieb, Peter. "Making Their Own Way: Southern Blacks' Migration to Pittsburgh, 1916–1930." PhD diss., University of Pittsburgh, 1977.

Grant, Robert Bruce. "The Negro Comes to the City: A Documentary History from the Great Migration to the Great Depression." EdD diss., Columbia University, 1970.

Green, Laurie B. "Discovering Hunger in America: The Politics of Race, Poverty, and Malnutrition after the Fall of Jim Crow." Paper presented at the Institute for Historical Studies, Department of History, University of Texas at Austin, April 3, 2009.

Haley, Charles T. "To Do Good and Do Well: Middle-Class Blacks and the Depression, Philadelphia, 1929–1941." PhD diss., State University of New York at Binghamton, 1980.

Hamilton, Tullia B. "The National Association of Colored Women, 1896–1920." PhD diss., Emory University, 1978.

Helmbold, Lois Rita. "Making Choices, Making Do: Black and White Working Class Women's Lives and Work During the Great Depression." PhD diss., Stanford University, 1983.

Hunter, Gary Jerome. "'Don't Buy From Where You Can't Work': Black Urban Boycott Movements During the Depression, 1929–1941." PhD diss., University of Michigan, 1977.

Janiewski, Dolores E. "From Field to Factory: Race, Class, Sex, and the Woman Worker in Durham, 1880–1940." PhD diss., Duke University, 1979.

Malson, Michelene Ridley. "Black Women's Sex Role Integration and Behavior: Report on Research in Progress." Working paper no. 87, Wellesley College Center for Research on Women, Wellesley, MA, 1981.

Mohr, Clarence. "Georgia Blacks during Secession and Civil War, 1859–1865." PhD diss., University of Georgia, 1975.

Pruneau, Leigh Anne. "All the Time is Work Time: Gender and the Task System on Antebellum Lowcountry Rice Plantations." PhD diss., University of Arizona, 1997.

Stokes, Allen H., Jr. "Black and White Labor and the Development of the Southern Textile Industry, 1800–1920." PhD diss., University of South Carolina, 1977.

Straus, Emily. "The Making of the American School Crisis: Compton, California and the Death of the Suburban Dream." PhD diss., Brandeis University, 2007.

Thomas, Richard Walter. "From Peasant to Proletarian: The Formation and Organization of the Black Industrial Working Class in Detroit, 1915–1945." PhD diss., University of Michigan, 1976.

White, Deborah G. "Ain't I a Woman? Female Slaves in the Antebellum South." PhD diss., University of Illinois–Chicago Circle, 1979.

———. "Female Slaves: Sex Roles and Status in the Antebellum Plantation." Unpublished.

Woody, Betty, and Michelene Malson. "In Crisis: Low Income Black Employed Women in the U.S. Workplace." Working paper no. 131, Wellesley College Center for Research on Women, Wellesley, MA, 1984.

INDEX